The Cause
of Ireland

In memory of my grandmother,
Nona Jean

The Cause
of Ireland

From the United Irishmen
to Partition

by
Liz Curtis

First published in 1994
by
Beyond the Pale Publications
PO Box 337
Belfast BT9 7BT
Tel: +44 232 645930

British Library Cataloguing-in-Publication Data.
A catalogue record for this book is available from the British Library.

ISBN 0 9514229 6 0

Typeset in 10 on 13pt Times
Printed by
Colour Books Ltd, Dublin

The publishers would like to thank Mary and Katherine for assistance with the production of this book.

Cover photograph:
Countess Markievicz arriving in Dublin from Aylesbury Prison, June 1917.

C o n t e n t s

Acknowledgements

This book has taken the best part of eight years to research and write. The process has been fascinating and often exciting, but the practical side has been a bit of a struggle. (OK... I hear the cries from Belfast of 'Dry your eyes'!) The love, help, support and encouragement – not to mention information and ideas – given by many people have been vital to seeing the project through.

First, for generously giving their time to read and comment on the text, and all sorts of other help, warm thanks to Peter Berresford Ellis, Tim Binding, Declan Kiberd, Brian MacDonald, Bríghid Mhic Sheáin, Tim O'Grady, Ruth Taillon and Margaret Ward. For commenting on parts of the text, many thanks to the late Flann Campbell, Tommy Graham, Seán Hutton, Cormac · Gráda and Kevin Whelan.

For being friendly and helpful in the face of endless requests, thanks (once again) to the staff of Hammersmith Reference Library. Thanks, too, for their courteous help to the staff of the British Library at the British Museum and at the Newspaper Library at Colindale. Also to Kensington Library, whose special collection of biographies was invaluable. Thanks to Robert Bell and the staff of the Linen Hall Library in Belfast for unearthing some obscure texts, and to the National Library of Ireland in Dublin, where I would like to have spent more time. Thanks also to the Public Record Office at Kew, the House of Commons Public Information Office, the Library of the Society of Friends, London, and the Local History Department of Finsbury Public Library. And once again thanks to my friends at Bush Books in Shepherds Bush precinct.

For assorted information and help, thanks to Dipak Basu, Geoff Bell, Tony Birtill, Val Cardwell, Dodie Carter, Tony Coughlan, Virginia Crossman, Sarah Grimes, Jonathan Hardy, Mary Hickman, Ted Howell, Nina Hutchison, Ian Jack, Mitchel McLaughlin, Gerry Mac Lochlainn, Francis McNamee, Joe McVeigh, Michael G.P. Maguire, Joy Melville, David Miller, Don Mullan and AFrI, Pat O'Hare, Elizabeth Platt, Seán

Prendiville, and Denis Smyth. A mention, too, for the compiler of the 'On This Day' column in the Irish News – often a useful pointer to good stories!

On the personal side, I must first thank my long-time friend Susan Schonfield, who has repeatedly stepped in to the rescue. Secondly, Aly Renwick, who lived alongside the book for several years (which wasn't easy!) and gave a lot of help.

For being there, in various ways at various times, love and thanks to Billy Armstrong, Hilary Arnott, Dorothy Berresford Ellis, Bairbre de Brún, Frances Mary Blake, Mary Campbell, Anne Clarke, Craig (of the Cuts), Maggie Cronin, Oliver Donohue, Faith Evans, Joëlle Gartner, Ronald Grant, Josephine Hadley, Maggie Hay, Margaret Henry, Annie Janowitz, Pat Kahn, Claire Keatinge, John Lloyd, Colin Lyons, Kirsty Malcolm, Alex McDonnell, Joanne O'Brien, Frank O'Neill, Joyce Pratt, Colin Robertson, Liz Rodgers, Bill Rolston, Victor Schonfield, Duncan Smith, Mike Tomlinson, Rita Wall and Jane Winter. Fond appreciation, too, to the late Miriam James, who lent me some wonderful books when I was starting the project.

I promised a mention to my friends at Circle 33 in Tottenham, who made a temping stint so pleasurable: Angela, Aniekan, Cornelius, Debbie, Deji, Evadney, Fiona, Gaynor, Jen, Margaret, Maureen, Mervyn, Oseni, Proscovia, Sharon, Sherron, Vicky and Zafar. Love ya all!

Finally, warm thanks to my publishers for taking the book on so enthusiastically and having faith that it would one day be finished.

The mistakes, as it is customary to say, are all mine.

Sin é!

Liz Curtis
October 1994

Introduction

This book, though it ends in 1921, aims above all to provide a background to events in the North of Ireland today.

At its core is the long struggle, both constitutional and through force, of Irish people for independence from Britain. Interwoven with this are developments among Irish Protestants, from their brief revolutionary flowering in the 1790s, to the emergence of a pro-British bloc in the northeast.

Britain's colonisation of Ireland, and desire at all costs to hang onto it, is shown as part of a much wider process – Britain's acquisition of an overseas empire.

The great progressive movements of labour and women are also part of the story, as are the efforts of the many in Britain, North America and elsewhere who 'did their bit' for the Irish cause.

As well as sketching in the broad pattern of events, the book aims to bring the past alive by introducing individual people – both famous and 'ordinary' – and by evoking the atmosphere of the day. To this end, there are many quotes throughout the book from people who lived through those times.

Hopefully this book will make a small contribution towards informed discussion of the political situation in Ireland. As the black American poet Langston Hughes wrote:

The past has been a mint
Of blood and sorrow.
That must not be
True of tomorrow.

1
Conquest and Resistance

From 1169 onwards, when Norman feudal lords invaded Ireland, England's ruling classes battled to control Ireland. Their reasons were both economic and strategic. They wanted to enrich themselves through land ownership and taxation, and they wanted to prevent Ireland becoming a base from which rival European powers or contenders for the English throne could attack England. The Irish, later joined by descendants of the early invaders who had been absorbed into Gaelic society, put up a fierce resistance. But the pitiless wars waged by the English Elizabethans in the 16th century, followed by the ferocity of Cromwell's forces in the 17th, eventually brought Ireland under English rule.

The English rulers maintained control as they had won it, by force. They also established a settler population as a garrison. Lowland Scots farmers colonised parts of the north of Ireland, and Cromwell's soldiers were rewarded with grants of land throughout the country. By 1685, the settlers had expropriated nearly 80 per cent of the land. In the process, the Gaelic social system was destroyed, with the native upper class suffering particularly severely. Some Irish landowners remained: some were 'Old English' descendants of early colonists, while others were Gaelic chieftains who, often as a reward for siding with the English, had become the private owners of land that had previously belonged to a wider kin group. But most of the Irish were pushed onto the poorer land or were reduced to tenant status.

The settlers' position was secured by the victory of William of Orange over King James in 1691. Their war was mainly over who should rule England, and the people of Ireland were little more than pawns in the game. In his attempt to retain the throne, James was backed by the English aristocracy, by France and by the Irish Catholic aristocracy. William, who was James's son-in-law and king of Holland, was backed by the English merchant class, by the Pope, by Spain and Germany, and by Protestant settlers in Ireland. When William landed in England in 1688, James fled to

France, then Ireland. William followed him there and defeated him in a series of battles beginning with the battle of the Boyne in July 1690. Many of the Irish feudal lords and their soldiers departed for France, and more land confiscations followed, soon bringing the amount in Catholic hands down to some 14 per cent.

The Protestant ascendancy

Because the Reformation had taken place in England and Scotland before the bulk of the colonisers arrived, the settlers were Protestants while the native Irish and the descendants of the early colonisers were Catholics. Thus the new rulers were distinguished by religion – as well as national origin, class, language and culture – from the people they had dispossessed.

The wealthiest settlers – great landlords and their relations – became a governing caste, known as the Protestant ascendancy, thinly spread across the whole of Ireland. Adherents of the Church of Ireland, they owned most of the land and monopolised political power. Less privileged settlers – traders, artisans and peasants, many of them Scots Presbyterians – clustered in the northeast. A few Catholic landowners survived, shut out from public affairs, and a small Catholic middle class of traders and professionals developed in the cities and towns. But the majority of Catholics were at the bottom of the social pile: dispossessed Irish-speaking peasants who formed three-quarters of the population, which probably stood at less than two million in 1700 and three million in the 1770s.

The Irish Houses of Parliament, like their English counterparts, consisted mainly of big landowners and their nominees. In 1692 Catholics were excluded, as they already were in England. The tiny Protestant landowning class then used the Irish parliament – which could only make laws if they were approved by the English parliament in advance – to entrench their position. Between about 1695 and 1727 the Irish parliament enacted the notorious 'penal laws', which were mainly aimed at stripping the Catholic elite of their remaining land, wealth and power, and depriving them of any means of fighting back.

The penal laws severely restricted the ability of Catholics to buy, lease or inherit land. This accelerated the transfer of land ownership, and by 1775 Catholics owned only five per cent of the land in Ireland. These laws also barred Catholics from bearing arms, from enlisting in the army or navy, from voting or sitting in parliament, from any government job, and from jury service, or becoming a lawyer or judge. Intermarriage between Catholics and Protestants carried heavy penalties. Catholics were also hindered from freely practising their religion and from access to education.

The penal laws also limited the rights of Presbyterians, though not as drastically. They were not allowed to teach in schools, had to pay taxes to the established church, and were barred from seeking government jobs. Many emigrated to America, where they were to the forefront of the colonists' campaign for independence from Britain.

The ascendancy landlords and absentee landlords living in England amassed enormous wealth from the rents they imposed on the Irish peasantry. They built great houses and lived in luxury while many peasants and poor townspeople lived in hovels and suffered recurrent famines. Smaller landlords and middlemen, too, squeezed as much profit as they could from the peasants. The landlords' rule was harsh. The eminent English agriculturalist Arthur Young, who investigated conditions in Ireland in the 1770s, wrote:

> A landlord in Ireland can scarcely invent an order which a servant, labourer or cottar dares to refuse to execute. Nothing satisfies him but an unlimited submission. Disrespect or anything tending towards sauciness he may punish with his cane or his horsewhip with the most perfect security, a poor man would have his bones broke if he offered to lift a hand in his own defence... Landlords of consequence have assured me, that many of their cottars would think themselves honoured by having their wives or daughters sent for to the bed of their master; a mark of slavery that proves the oppression under which such people must live.[1]

The peasants responded militantly, using sabotage to resist evictions, the enclosure of land for grazing, and the payment of tithes. Tithes were a tax levied for the upkeep of the established Anglican church and its ministers, which meant that Catholics and Presbyterians were forced to pay for the upkeep of an alien church. From the 1760s, they formed numerous secret societies, both Catholic and Presbyterian. In midnight raids, bands of peasants tore down new enclosures on what had been common land and hamstrung cattle belonging to rich graziers.

A contemporary observer described how in early 1762, in the counties of Tipperary, Waterford and Cork, men 'calling themselves Whiteboys, wearing white cockades and white linen frocks', moved in large groups:

> In February there were five or six parties of them, 200 to 300 men in each, who moved up and down chiefly in the night...levelled a few fences, dug up some grounds, and hamstrung some cattle, perhaps fifty or sixty in all. One body of them came into Clogheen, of about 500 foot and 200 horse. They moved as exactly as regular troops, and appeared to be thoroughly disciplined.[2]

In 1786, in their fight against tithes, Munster Whiteboys held a mass meeting and issued a manifesto listing the maximum tithes they were prepared to pay, and resolving:

> That we will continue to oppose our oppressors by the most justifiable means in our power, either until they are glutted with our blood or until humanity raises her angry voice in the councils of the nation to protect the toiling peasant and lighten his burden.[3]

The Volunteer movement

Rule by England and the landlords also caused problems for merchants and manufacturers, and retarded Ireland's overall economic development. English parliaments banned the colonies from trading directly with countries other than England, and imposed heavy duties on goods, such as woollen cloth, entering England if they competed with English products. By these means England helped to suppress Irish industry, except linen which had no serious English rivals. The country remained underdeveloped, a kind of colonial farmyard supplying beef, butter, grain and cheap labour to England. Large sums paid in rent left Ireland for England, where many of the landlords lived, so that Ireland's resources were drained while England's development was strengthened.

As the 18th century progressed, the Irish middle class, especially the Presbyterian manufacturers of Belfast, increasingly chafed against the restrictions imposed on them. They identified with the American colonists who declared their independence from Britain in 1776, and many of whom were themselves Presbyterian emigrants from Ireland.

While England's forces were deployed against the American colonists, Ireland was left undefended against a possible French invasion. So companies of Volunteers were spontaneously raised all over Ireland, mostly Protestant and totalling some 40,000 men by the end of 1779 and 100,000 two years later. Protestants of all classes joined up – country gentry and their tenants, merchants, and artisans – and Belfast Presbyterians were among the keenest organisers. But the parliamentary leaders of the movement were aristocrats, including Lord Charlemont, Henry Flood and Henry Grattan.

The English regime in Ireland was now very vulnerable, and the Volunteers used their new-found strength to press for concessions. At the end of 1779 they paraded in Dublin with cannons which bore placards reading 'Free Trade or this'. The British parliament gave in before the threat of rebellion, and lifted restrictions on Irish exports and on trade with the colonies. The Volunteers then launched a campaign for the Irish parliament to be able to make laws without interference from the British parliament. Again they implicitly threatened force by organising spectacular military displays involving thousands of armed men and watched by tens of thousands of spectators.

Then on 15 February 1782, delegates from the Ulster Volunteer regiments – which numbered some 30,000 men organised in 143 corps – assembled, uniformed and armed, in the church at Dungannon. Here they debated the current state of affairs and passed a series of resolutions. They decided unanimously:

> That a claim of any body of men, other than the King, Lords, and Commons of Ireland, to make laws to bind this kingdom, is unconstitutional, illegal, and a grievance.[4]

A bill aiming to end the drastic restrictions on Catholic rights was being introduced in the Irish parliament, and the Dungannon convention declared its approval, stating, with two dissenting voices:

> That, as men and as Irishmen, as Christians and as Protestants, we rejoice in the relaxation of the penal laws against our Roman Catholic fellow-subjects...[5]

Volunteers throughout Ireland followed the Dungannon example, meeting to adopt the same resolutions. English rule was becoming increasingly shaky. On 16 April 1782 the Irish parliament unanimously passed a motion, moved by Grattan, asserting its independence of the English parliament, though protesting loyalty to the crown, and the English authorities swiftly conceded.

Though the Irish parliament was now nominally independent, power still remained in the hands of the Protestant ascendancy class and the English government. The Irish House of Commons still consisted mainly of people controlled by big landowners or by the English government. As in England and everywhere else in Europe prior to the French revolution, the parliamentary system was blatantly unrepresentative and corrupt. Few could vote, there was no secret ballot and elections were rare. While only a few wealthy Protestants could vote or sit in parliament, none of the more than three million Catholics had these rights. Seats in parliament were openly bought and sold, and many members sold their vote to the highest bidder, which was often the English government. Further, the administration was still run by England, through the lord lieutenant.

The Irish aristocrats and lawyers who led the Volunteers were willing to abolish most of the penal laws, but wanted to maintain the Protestant ascendancy. They baulked at the idea of radically extending voting rights and thus putting the upper classes at risk. One camp, led in parliament by Henry Flood, thought the vote should be given to virtually all male Protestants, but to no Catholics at all. Another camp, led by Henry Grattan, thought that all property-owners, Catholic and Protestant, should get the vote, but no poor people of either persuasion.

Many Volunteers lost their enthusiasm for Catholic rights, though impatiently demanding wider voting rights for Protestants. The newly independent parliament, however, rejected a bill in 1784 to extend the Protestant franchise and end the system by which most parliamentary seats were bought and sold. The new parliament remained as corrupt and manipulable as the old. Unwilling to exert pressure on the government through the use of force, or through aligning themselves with the Catholic masses, the Volunteers were left without influence, frustrated and directionless, and in many areas their organisation decayed. Having failed to achieve any meaningful reform, the Volunteer leadership then helped to disarm the Volunteers.

Belfast's Volunteers in particular were angered and disappointed by these events. They were passionately in favour of reform, and the behaviour of the leadership confirmed their view that the ascendancy aristocrats were not to be trusted and that, for reasons of both practicality and principle, an alliance with the Catholics was necessary for future progress.

The United Irishmen

The French revolution against the aristocracy in 1789 inspired revolutionaries throughout Europe and gave a new impetus to Irish demands for reform. Belfast Presbyterians – factory owners, merchants and shop-keepers – were especially enthusiastic. They wanted a state in which the business and professional classes could operate freely, unhindered by the English government or ascendancy landowners. The Catholic middle classes shared their aim, but Catholic landowners and bishops were less keen: they preferred to keep on good terms with the government at Dublin Castle and indeed did not even press for an end to the penal laws.

In July 1791 the townspeople of Belfast celebrated the second anniversary of the fall of the Bastille with a procession through the town and a review of the local Volunteers, followed by a meeting of some 6,000 people. The procession included a 'triumphal car' drawn by four horses, which bore an eight foot by six foot banner depicting the release of the prisoners from the Bastille.

The following year, the Belfast democrats organised a harp festival to coincide with the Bastille celebrations, bringing ten harpers to Belfast for the first great revival of Irish traditional music. Tom Paine's *Rights of Man* – a spirited defence of the French revolution, which argued that governments should be chosen by the people, not imposed on them by a hereditary aristocracy – was rapturously received in Belfast. When Louis XVI was guillotined in 1793, Belfast people celebrated with a grand illumination. The cropped hair worn by French Jacobins became the fashion, and Irish republicans were soon dubbed 'croppies'.

In October 1791 Belfast democrats formed the first Society of United Irishmen. They wanted a strong Irish government and called for parliamentary reform with equal representation for all Irish males, regardless of religion. Their badge showed the harp without the crown, with the motto, 'It is new strung and shall be heard.' They launched a newspaper, the *Northern Star*.

Among the founders of the United Irishmen was Theobald Wolfe Tone, a young and talented Dubliner from a Protestant middle-class background. Tone was a clear-headed analyst of power relations in Ireland. He believed that for the commercial and professional classes, many of whom were Presbyterians, to win freedom to organise society as they wished, they must overthrow the ascendancy aristocrats, who were able to hold power only because they were propped up by British force. At an early age Tone arrived at his fundamental belief

> that the influence of England was the radical vice of our Government, and consequently that Ireland would never be either free, prosperous, or happy, until she was independent; and, that independence was unattainable, whilst the connexion with England existed.[6]

Tone recognised that on their own the Presbyterians – also known as Dissenters – were too weak to overturn the combined power of the ascendancy and Britain. Therefore the Presbyterians must ally themselves with the Catholics and espouse their rights. In a famous passage in his autobiographical notes, Tone summed up the theory on which he had 'unvaryingly acted':

> To subvert the tyranny of our execrable Government, to break the connection with England, the never-failing source of all our political evils, and to assert the independence of my country – these were my objects. To unite the whole people of Ireland, to abolish the memory of all past dissensions, and to substitute the common name of Irishman in place of the denominations of Protestant, Catholic and Dissenter – these were my means.[7]

Tone had no sympathy with organised Catholicism, scorning the 'Papal tyranny' with its opposition to the French revolution, and the 'priestcraft and superstition' of the clergy.[8] But he passionately advocated political rights for Catholics, and as a result he was invited to become secretary of the General Committee of the Catholics of Ireland, a campaigning body formed by Catholic bishops, gentry and merchants.

Tone believed it was necessary to enlist the support of the peasant organisations as well as the middle class, and that in the last resort, if the 'men of property' did not rally to the cause, the revolutionaries would have to rely on the 'men of no property'. But he was, in essence, a classic middle-class revolutionary of his era, and did not aim for the redistribution of property or land.

Some of the United leaders wanted extensive social change, among them the only working class leader, James Hope, a linen weaver. Hope was a Presbyterian from Templepatrick in County Antrim, whose grandfather, a Scottish Covenanter, had fled to Ireland to escape the persecution directed against his sect. Hope later recorded:

> It was my settled opinion that the condition of the labouring class was the fundamental question at issue between the rulers and the people, and there could be no solid foundation for liberty, till measures were adopted that went to the root of the evil, and were specially directed to the restoration of the natural right of the people, the right of deriving a subsistance from the soil on which their labour was expended.[9]

The prospect of collaboration between Presbyterians and Catholics worried the British authorities. The foreign minister, Lord Grenville, wrote to the lord lieutenant of Ireland, Lord Westmorland, in 1791:

> I cannot help feeling a very great anxiety that such measures may be taken as may effectually counteract the union between the Catholics and Dissenters, at which the latter are evidently aiming. I may be a false prophet, but there is no evil that I would not prophesy if that union takes place in the present moment...[10]

Westmorland wrote to Pitt, the British prime minister:

> The present frame of Irish government... is particularly well calculated for our purpose. That frame is a Protestant garrison... in possession of the land, magistracy and power of the country; holding that property under the tenure of British power and supremacy, and ready at every instant to crush the rising of the conquered.[11]

By February 1793 Britain and France were at war, and the government rapidly moved to disarm the Volunteers, first in Dublin and then in Belfast. Troops rampaged through Belfast, wrecking taverns which displayed the portraits of French heroes. The United Irish Societies went underground, meeting in secret. They organised a huge network of armed militants, mobilising Presbyterians who had trained in the Volunteers and also the Catholic peasant bodies, the Defenders. Women as well as men became sworn members of the secret organisation.

The authorities used various means to undermine Catholic support for the United cause. Alarmed by the energetic campaigning of the Catholic Committee, with Wolfe Tone now its secretary, and hoping to placate its well-to-do Catholic supporters, the English government forced the Dublin parliament to pass the Catholic Relief Acts of 1792 and 1793. These gave Catholics voting rights on the same terms as Protestants, provided they swore allegiance to the crown. The poorest people now able to vote were some 30,000 Catholic smallholders, the '40-shilling freeholders', who rented land which yielded that sum each year. The Relief Acts also lifted several of the remaining penal laws, but Catholics were still barred from sitting in parliament and from holding important government posts.

Wanting to stop Catholic priests seeking education in Europe where they might be influenced by revolutionary ideas, the government for the first time allowed the Catholic church to establish a college for training priests at Maynooth near Dublin in 1795. The government gave the Maynooth seminary an annual grant of £9,000, and in return its staff and students pledged loyalty to the British crown. They swore an oath which included the words:

> I will do my utmost endeavour to disclose and make known to his Majesty, and his heirs, all treasons and traitorous conspiracies, which may be formed against him or them...[12]

The authorities also encouraged the divisions between Anglicans, Presbyterians and Catholics in the Ulster countryside, where competition for land was fierce. Armed Protestant bands, the Peep O'Day Boys, terrorised Catholics, who formed their own force, the Defenders, in response. In September 1795 rival groups clashed in County Armagh at a crossroads near Loughgall known as the Diamond. The Catholics were routed and the victorious Protestants went on to form the Orange Order, which linked existing groups and aimed to defend Protestant privilege. The Orangemen unleashed a ruthless persecution of Catholics in order to drive them from their holdings, and thousands of Catholics became refugees. On 28 December 1795 the British governor of Armagh, Lord Gosford, told a meeting of magistrates:

> It is no secret that a persecution, accompanied with all the circumstances of ferocious cruelty which have in all ages distinguished that dreadful calamity, is now raging in this country... The only crime which the wretched objects of this ruthless persecution are charged with, is a crime of easy proof. It is simply a profession of the Roman Catholic faith. A lawless banditti have constituted themselves judges of this species of delinquency, and the sentence they pronounced is equally concise and terrible; it is nothing less than a confiscation of all property, and immediate banishment.[13]

Many Catholics joined the United Irishmen, while others joined the new government militia.

The gentry recognised the potential of the Orange movement and took over its leadership. A Dungannon magistrate wrote:

> As for the Orangemen, we have rather a difficult card to play; they must not be entirely discountenanced – on the contrary, we must in a certain degree uphold them, for with all their licentiousness, on them must we rely for the preservation of our lives and properties should critical times occur.[14]

Bantry Bay

In 1795 Wolfe Tone and several other leading United Irishmen climbed Cave Hill on the outskirts of Belfast where, Tone recorded, they

> took a solemn obligation, which, I think, I may say, I have, on my part, endeavoured to fulfil – never to desist in our efforts until we had subverted the authority of England over our country, and asserted her independence.[15]

Tone then left with his family to travel via America to France, where he sought the help of the French government. He presented the French with a concise analysis of the situation, and asked them to send a substantial force of 20,000 soldiers. He argued that such a force would act as a rallying point: the middle classes, seeing the prospect of victory, would desert the ascendancy, the Catholic masses would mobilise, and British rule would be rapidly toppled, possibly without any fighting. If the French sent only 5,000 soldiers, 'we should have to fight hard for our liberties'. To send any less would be to risk defeat and 'bringing Ireland, even more than she is at present, under the yoke of British tyranny'.[16]

England was the most dangerous enemy of revolutionary France, and its major rival for overseas trade and colonies. The French saw that they could attack England by supporting the Irish revolutionaries. They raised a force of 14,000 under General Hoche, and in December 1796 they embarked in 43 ships, with Tone on board, for Ireland. They planned to land off Bantry Bay in the southwest, but an easterly gale blew relentlessly, scattering the fleet and making it impossible to land. Tone expressed his frustration in his diary:

> I could tear my flesh with rage and vexation, but that advances nothing, and so I hold my tongue in general, and devour my melancholy as I can.[17]

After a week, they had to turn back. Tone wrote:

> England has not had such an escape since the Spanish Armada, and that expedition, like ours, was defeated by the weather; the elements fight against us, and courage here is of no avail.[18]

After their narrow escape, the English authorities moved to suppress the revolutionary north. In March 1797 General Lake, then northern commander and later commander-in-chief for the whole of Ireland, began a reign of terror in Belfast which reduced the population to 'a sort of stupor hardly distinguishable from fear', as an observer put it.[19] In April he wrote to the chief secretary, Pelham, urging that martial law be introduced to disarm the province, and saying, 'Belfast ought to be proclaimed and punished most severely, as it is plain every act of sedition originates in this town'.[20] In May he wrote to Pelham, 'Nothing but terror will keep them in order.'[21]

The British generals took advantage of the divisions between the Orangemen and the United Irishmen. General Knox, commander of the British army at Dungannon, wrote to General Lake, commander in Ulster:

> I have arranged a plan to scour a district full of unregistered arms, or said to be so... And this I do, not so much with a hope to succeed to any extent, as to increase the animosity between the Orangemen and the United Irishmen... Upon that animosity depends the safety of the centre counties of the North.[22]

In July 1797 a Dutch invasion fleet, with 13,500 troops on board, and Wolfe Tone with them, was ready to sail for Ireland. But again the wind was unfavourable, and after waiting for six weeks in harbour, the expedition was called off. In Ulster the repression continued. Thirty-four leading suspects were held on a prison ship, the hulk *Postlethwaite*, and a young United leader, William Orr, a Presbyterian farmer, was hanged and was soon revered as a martyr. The English engraver George Cumberland, a friend of the poet William Blake, summed up Britain's activities internationally:

> No news, save that *Great Britain* is hanging the Irish, hunting the Maroons [escaped slaves], feeding the Vendée [a counter-revolutionary district of France], and establishing the human flesh trade.[23]

The French revolution prompted a ferment of radical activity throughout Britain in the 1790s, including many mass demonstrations and two major naval mutinies. But the revolutionary impetus never reached the same level as elsewhere in Europe, mainly because the upper classes put up a united front against it. In other European countries businessmen and professionals opposed the aristocracy, but in Britain they were already privileged, and sided with the aristocracy against the mass of the people.

The United Irishmen found little support among England's upper classes. But there was widespread sympathy among working class people, especially among radical artisans and Irish immigrants. An underground sister organisation, the United Englishmen, had numerous branches in several major cities. In Scotland, the Friends of the People and the United Scotsmen, both of which aimed to end the union with England, had close links with the United Irishmen. But such groups were themselves soon crushed by government repression.

Radicals in England easily identified with the Irish republican struggle, as they did with the campaign against slavery, because they shared a common enemy. The Protestant ascendancy in Ireland, like the West Indian slave-owners, were a wealthy and influential section of the landowning class that ruled England. In January 1798 the radical London Corresponding Society published an *Address to the Irish Nation*, which read in part:

GENEROUS, GALLANT NATION

> May the present Address convince you how truly we sympathize in all your sufferings... May Nations... learn... that when a People once permits Government to violate the genuine Principles of Liberty, Encroachment will be grafted upon Encroachment; Evil will grow upon Evil; Violation will follow Violation, and Power will engender Power, till the Liberties of ALL will be held at despotic command...[24]

The address included an appeal to English soldiers in Ireland to refuse to act as 'Agents of enslaving Ireland'. Soon, however, the London Corresponding Society was suppressed, its leaders jailed or in exile.

In March 1798 the British authorities extended the repression southwards to the province of Leinster. They first arrested the United leaders, then unleashed a systematic terror against the peasantry, burning houses and farms, aiming to terrify them into giving up their weapons. Unable to wait any longer for the French to arrive, and facing a choice of rebellion or being destroyed, some 100,000 people rose in revolt in May and early June 1798.

They rose first in the midlands and southeast, and were followed by the Presbyterians of Antrim and Down. In some places it was as if the whole countryside was on the move.

The Catholic bishops, followed by the big Catholic landowners, immediately denounced the rising, calling on Catholics to defend 'our constitution, the social order and the Christian religion'.[25]

The rebels took over large areas of the country, and in Wexford town they established a short-lived republic, proclaiming ideals based directly on the French revolutionary model. A Wexford catechism stated: 'I believe in a revolution founded on the rights of man, in the natural and imprescriptible right of *all* Irish citizens to the land.'[26]

They aimed to abolish the privileged orders

> who consider the people as an inferior and degraded mass, only made for their amusement or convenience, to dig, plow or enlist whatever the tyrant's amusement...[27]

But within weeks the rebellion began to collapse, overcome by the lack of central organisation, the failure of the French to arrive, and the superior military force of the opposition. At the end of August 1,000 French troops led by General Humbert – the first instalment of a new invasion force – landed in Killala, County Mayo. They won some initial victories, including the famous 'races of Castlebar' when the defending troops fled ignominiously at their arrival, but they were too few and too late. The peasantry in much of the country were already crushed.

Then on 12 October the English intercepted a second French fleet: among those captured was Wolfe Tone. He was brought in irons to Dublin where he died on 19 November, having reportedly cut his own throat to avoid the indignity of being publicly hanged – though whether in fact he was murdered by the authorities will never be known.

By now the rebellion was over. At least 30,000 people had died. Some 12 towns and countless villages had been partly or completely destroyed. The authorities mopped up the last vestiges of resistance, forcing hundreds to join the British army or navy, and transporting at least 775 to the brutal convict settlements established a decade earlier in Australia, so that by 1802 Irish people made up a quarter of the convict population of New South Wales.

The British authorities now moved to restructure the relationship between Britain and Ireland in order, they hoped, to prevent any repeat of the tumultuous events which had so nearly seen a major enemy power take control of England's most strategically important colony.

2
The Act of Union

The British upper classes saw control of Ireland as essential to their survival. Not only was Ireland the 'back door' into Britain, but it stood on the sea routes vital for trade and for access to regions which they controlled or coveted: the West Indies and the Americas, Africa, India, the Far East and the South Pacific. An enemy power in control of the Irish ports could cut the life-line of British commerce.

The upheavals of the 1790s had shown that the Protestant ascendancy class, which controlled the Irish parliament, was an inefficient instrument for maintaining British rule. The ascendancy had proved highly reluctant to compromise with the middle classes, especially the Catholics, and had treated the peasantry with unrestrained cruelty. Such behaviour had been counter-productive, stimulating rather than discouraging revolt. The British establishment also saw the existence of the Irish parliament as a potential threat, since it might one day – in the event of parliamentary reform and Catholic emancipation – decide to take an independent line in foreign policy, or even to break the link with Britain altogether. Prime Minister William Pitt told parliament on 31 January 1799:

> Suppose, for instance, that the present war [against France], which the Parliament of Great Britain considers to be just and necessary, had been voted by the Irish Parliament to be unjust, unnecessary, extravagant, and hostile to the principle of humanity and freedom. Would that Parliament have been bound by this country? If not, what security have we, at a moment the most important to our common interest and common salvation, that the two kingdoms should have but one friend and one foe?[1]

Pitt and other establishment figures had thought for some years that the best way to keep Ireland firmly under British control was to abolish the 500-year-old Irish parliament altogether and absorb Ireland into the British political system, just as Wales had been absorbed in 1536 and Scotland in 1707. If the Irish sent members of parliament to Westminster, they would be in a permanent minority. Under-secretary Cooke wrote to Pitt in 1799:

> By giving the Irish a hundred members in an Assembly of six hundred
> and fifty they will be impotent to operate upon that Assembly, but it will
> be invested with Irish assent to its authority.[2]

The Irish parliament contained 300 MPs. With only 100 MPs at
Westminster, Ireland would have less than a sixth of the total, though its
people would be a third of the population of the proposed 'United Kingdom'.

Many ascendancy landowners, along with lawyers, bankers and merchants,
were strongly opposed to the idea of a Union. They feared that their power,
privileges and freedom to manoeuvre would be undermined. But some
ascendancy leaders supported the plan. The Irish lord chancellor, Lord Clare,
who had mercilessly pursued the United Irishmen, argued that the ascendancy
could not exist without British backing. He said:

> The whole power and property has been conferred by successive monarchs
> of England upon an English colony composed of three sorts of English
> adventurers who poured into this country at the termination of three
> successive rebellions. Confiscation is their common title and from their
> first settlement they have been hemmed in on every side by the old
> inhabitants of this island, brooding over their discontents in sullen
> indignation. What was the security of the English settlers for their physical
> existence? And what is the security of their descendants at this day? The
> powerful and commanding position of Great Britain. If, by any fatality, it
> fails, you are at the mercy of the old inhabitants of this island...[3]

The Presbyterians of the northeast put up no serious opposition. They had
been frightened by the violence of the recent rising, and now the government
cajoled them with promises of subsidies for Presbyterian ministers, an end
to tithes, and advantages for the linen trade.

The British government similarly undermined Catholic opposition by
dishonestly promising that the Union would be followed by Catholic
emancipation, which would allow Catholics to sit in parliament and to hold
senior legal and government posts, and promising subsidies for the Catholic
clergy and an end to tithes. The government refused, however, to include
these pledges in the terms of the Union, because this would make it impossible
to persuade the ascendancy class to agree to the Union.

The Catholic upper classes, though they shared an allegiance to the existing
social order and an abhorrence of revolutionary change, split on the Union
issue. The archbishops and many bishops were easily persuaded to endorse
the Union plan, as did some Catholic peers. Further, in return for the
government's vague promises, the archbishops agreed to give the
government the right of veto over appointments of all Irish bishops. But
others, including Daniel O'Connell, a young lawyer from a Catholic landowning family, strongly opposed the Union. They saw their chances as
better with a separate Irish parliament, even one that was for the time being
exclusively Protestant.

To the mass of the Catholic peasantry, the issue apparently meant little: whatever the outcome, they would remain unrepresented, and the landlords' stranglehold over their lives would continue.

To achieve the Union, the English leaders needed to persuade the Irish parliament to vote for its own abolition. But when the proposal for a Union was first put to the Irish House of Commons in January 1799, it was defeated by 111 votes to 106. Dublin's citizens reacted with delight, lighting up their houses – a customary form of celebration at the time – and breaking the windows of those, such as Lord Clare, who refused to do so.

Having failed to win the Union through persuasion, Pitt and his associates turned to other methods. They intimidated the general populace by sending extra troops to Ireland, increasing the army to a huge 137,000 soldiers for a population of some five million, and they banned public meetings and protests against the Union plan. They also offered money, jobs and peerages to many members of parliament, and paid out more than one-and-a-quarter million pounds – a vast sum for the time – to owners of boroughs which would no longer send MPs to parliament, to compensate them for their loss of influence. Lord Cornwallis, the lord lieutenant, who 'managed' the affair, wrote to a friend:

> My occupation is now of the most unpleasant nature, bargaining and jobbing with the most corrupt people under Heaven. I despise and hate myself every hour for engaging in such dirty work, and am supported only by the reflection that without an Union the British Empire must be dissolved.[4]

His efforts were successful. When the Irish parliament voted again on the question in February 1800, the result was 158 in favour and 115 against.

Ireland was now to send 100 MPs to Westminster, though the administration remained with the lord lieutenant and his officials in Dublin. The new unit was named the 'United Kingdom of Great Britain and Ireland', and Ireland's absorption was symbolised by the addition of the cross of St Patrick to the Union Jack. Protestantism – the religion of the minority – remained the state religion, and the established Church of Ireland was united with the Church of England.

Following the Union, Prime Minister Pitt was unable to deliver on his promises to the Catholics. Irish MPs – for whom emancipation would mean an end to their careers – intrigued with British MPs and with the notoriously bigoted king, George III, to block the measure. George III refused to sign such a bill on the grounds that it would contravene his coronation oath: he subsequently blamed Pitt and the Catholics for a bout of insanity that he suffered in 1801. Pitt resigned; he later returned to power pledged never again to raise the Catholic question in the lifetime of the king.

In 1803 came the last flicker of the United Irish rebellion, when a 25-year-old Protestant, Robert Emmet, poet, orator and reluctant businessman,

led a short-lived insurrection. Emmet had been expelled from Trinity College
for his links with the United Irish societies and had travelled to France on
their behalf. Like the United Irish societies, Emmet aimed to establish an
Irish republic and saw himself as part of an international movement for
'liberty, equality and fraternity'. His associates included veterans of the
United Irishmen, among them Thomas Russell, who had been a close friend
of Wolfe Tone; Michael Dwyer, who had held out with a guerrilla band in
the Wicklow mountains since the 1798 rising; and James Hope, the linen
weaver from County Antrim.

The middle classes were by now wary of revolution, so the new movement
relied more closely on the working people than its predecessors – and,
perhaps as a result, was much more successful in keeping its plans secret
from the authorities. Among those closest to Emmet was Anne Devlin, a
cousin of Michael Dwyer and daughter of a tenant farmer. Anne Devlin
subsequently became famous for her heroic refusal to inform on her fellow
revolutionaries despite torture and years of imprisonment.

The movement's programme declared that church property would be
nationalised and forbade the transfer of landed property and financial
holdings until a national government, elected by universal suffrage, should
decide what should be done with it.

But plans for the rising went badly wrong. An explosion in the rebels'
gunpowder factory prompted them to rise prematurely, on 23 July 1803.
The Dublin leaders failed to link up with Michael Dwyer in Wicklow and
Thomas Russell in Ulster. Only a hundred or so Dublin workers took up
arms and they were quickly crushed. Emmet was publicly hanged and
beheaded and his words from the dock are remembered still: 'When my
country takes her place among the nations of the earth, then, and not till
then, let my epitaph be written.'[5]

Industrial revolution

The first decades of the 19th century saw England and Scotland undergoing
a traumatic upheaval as they were transformed from agricultural into
industrial societies. As manufacturing industry developed, so did the
capitalist class, who owned it, and the new working class, who sold their
labour to make it function.

In the English countryside, landowners took over the lands that had
formerly been held in common, consolidating large estates and building
grandiose 'stately homes'. Many peasants, reduced to casual labouring,
faced the choice between stark poverty on the land or the agonising disruption
of moving to the towns. Here they joined the men, women and children who
worked themselves to the bone all hours in factories and mines in return for
barely enough money to keep themselves alive, while the burgeoning

business class grew wealthy from their labours. Many craft-workers, too, such as those who lived by spinning or weaving at home, faced the same fate, as the new power-driven machines, vastly more productive than their spinning-wheels and handlooms, undercut their prices and forced them out of business.

In Scotland, thousands of highlanders were evicted from their homes by aristocratic landowners in the infamous 'clearances' and were forced to move to the industrial towns or take ship for North America.

Many artisans and peasants violently resisted the dislocation of their lives. They rioted, attacked and burnt factories and the houses of their owners, smashed machines, and planned insurrections, making the first thirty years of the 19th century some of the most violent in British history. At the same time, many workers petitioned for minimum wages. Their petitions were inevitably rejected by a parliament dominated by big landowners, so workers and peasants began to demand the vote and gave increasing support to the campaign led by the business class to end the aristocrats' stranglehold on parliament.

The government responded viciously to both violent and non-violent protests. Radicals were arrested, imprisoned and sentenced to death or transported to Australia. To the fore in organising the repression was the hated foreign secretary, Lord Castlereagh, an Anglo-Irish aristocrat who previously, as chief secretary for Ireland, had overseen the ruthless suppression of the 1798 rebellion. Byron wrote of him in 1818:

> Cold-blooded, smooth-faced, placid miscreant!
> Dabbling its sleek young hands in Erin's gore,
> And thus for wider carnage taught to pant,
> Transferred to gorge upon a sister shore...[6]

The poet Percy Bysshe Shelley, too, attacked Castlereagh. After the 'Peterloo massacre' of 1819 when troops on horseback charged a pro-reform demonstration of more than 80,000 people in Manchester, leaving 11 dead and hundreds injured, Shelley wrote:

> I met Murder on the way -
> He had a mask like Castlereagh –
> Very smooth he looked, yet grim;
> Seven blood-hounds followed him...
> He tossed them human hearts to chew
> Which from his wide cloak he drew.[7]

When Castlereagh committed suicide in 1822 Byron penned an epigram:

> So He has cut his throat at last! – He! Who?
> The man who cut his country's long ago.

Colonial expansion

The industrial revolution propelled British manufacturers and traders into worldwide expansion and into drastically altering the economies of the countries which Britain influenced or controlled. In the old colonial system, merchants from the major European powers, dealing mainly in luxury goods and slaves, had established their dominance of world trade, while additional luxuries, such as sugar and tobacco, had been produced by slave labour in the plantation colonies. That system was now superseded: the manufacturers and financiers who owned and ran the factories had different needs. The factory system demanded ever greater quantities of raw materials, such as cotton and vegetable oils, and cheap food to feed the growing working class. At the same time it needed ever-larger markets where the mass-produced goods could be sold.

So from the late 18th century the British capitalists, assisted by their government, increasingly forced the non-industrialised countries to service their needs. They flooded them with imports, destroyed their native industries, and made them produce crops that suited Britain's need for raw materials rather than crops to feed themselves.

In India, for example, the British East India Company annexed the rich and fertile province of Bengal in 1757, soon ruining the economy and contributing to a cataclysmic famine in 1769-70 in which some ten million people died. Before the depredations of British businessmen, India was a prosperous country, more economically advanced than any European country of the time. Its society was based on village communities which were largely self-sufficient. But Britain destroyed the Indian cotton industry, and India, like Ireland, became a purely agricultural colony, supplying Britain with food and raw materials. The towns decayed and the formerly self-sufficient communities disintegrated. The Indian peasants got poorer and poorer, and famine became endemic. Spurred by poverty, hundreds of thousands crossed the seas to work as semi-slave indentured labourers in the West Indies and other parts of the British empire.

Though the workers and peasants in Britain faced bitter hardships in the first half of the 19th century, conditions for the mass of the people in the colonies, such as Ireland and India, were even worse.

Life for Irish peasants was already harsh at the time of the Union in 1800, but it grew even worse as the century progressed. During England's wars with France, grain was in heavy demand and prices rose. The Irish landlord class – which numbered only some 10,000 people, a third of whom were absentees, out of a population of more than five million – pushed up rents in order to make bigger profits. But when the Napoleonic wars ended in 1815 and the price of grain dropped, the landlords did not lower the rents. Instead, wanting to clear the land for cattle-raising or to auction it to the highest bidder, they often evicted those who could not pay. The Westminster parliament, dominated by landlords, passed laws to make it easy to evict tenants and to seize crops in lieu of unpaid rent. A prominent Irish Tory said in 1825:

> The landlords of Ireland are at length deeply convinced that, though a stock of cattle or sheep will afford profit, a stock of mere human creatures, unemployed, will afford none.[8]

While agricultural exports rose and the landlords grew wealthier, the peasants' hold on existence became increasingly fragile. Many landlords sublet their land to middlemen, who in turn sublet to other middlemen, while at the bottom millions of near-destitute peasants struggled to retain a foothold on the land. The life-or-death competition for land forced up rents yet further.

One-third of the Irish population depended solely on the potato for survival

Many peasants survived by selling their labour and their small crop to pay the rent and tithes, and raising a pig which could be sold when times were hard, while they themselves ate only potatoes, which were nutritious and used little land. Others eked out a bare living by casual labouring. Many became indebted to the local 'gombeen man', the dealer and moneylender. In the months when the old potato crop had run out and before the new crop appeared, vast multitudes of peasants took to migratory begging – visitors to Ireland often commented on the crowds of beggars who importuned them – while those who could raise the fare travelled to England and Scotland to seek work doing heavy manual labour on the growing network of roads and canals.

The migrant population was further swollen by unemployed workers who had lost their livelihoods as Irish industries and home-based crafts succumbed to the competition from mass-produced English goods. Spinners and weavers previously employed in the silk, woollen and cotton industries joined the struggle for land or sought work in England and Scotland, where many came to the fore in the working class resistance.

The peasants' increasing dependence on potatoes made them extremely vulnerable, for, as was well known, the potato crop was very unreliable. It had failed repeatedly and on a large scale since the 1720s when its cultivation began, with major failures recorded in 1728, 1739, 1740, 1770, 1800 and 1807. Then in 1821 and 1822 there were severe crop failures in Connacht and Munster, resulting in widespread famine and disease. Throughout the 1830s there were serious crop failures virtually every year.

Many peasants responded to their oppressive conditions by becoming active in the secret societies which took violent action against landlords, tithe collectors and anyone who assisted them. In effect, these societies were like secret agricultural trades unions, the only means by which the peasants could protect themselves from evictions and exorbitant demands for rent. Much of the countryside was in an almost continual state of actual or potential insurrection, which intensified in periods of particular hardship, such as during the famine of 1821-2.

The British authorities reacted to the tumult on the one hand by setting up numerous commissions of enquiry while at the same time increasing the direct repression of the peasantry. Between 1810 and 1833 the Westminster parliament appointed no less than 114 commissions and 60 select committees to investigate Irish affairs. These enquiries accumulated a massive amount of information about the appalling conditions of the peasantry, and prophesied disaster unless reforms were made.

But successive governments, dominated by landlords, ignored the recommendations for reform. They espoused a non-interventionist laissez-faire economic doctrine, whose underlying principle was freedom for property owners to pursue their own interests regardless of the consequences for others. While they refused to change the law to benefit the poor, arguing that this would be an unwarranted interference with 'natural' economic laws, they repeatedly changed the law to benefit the landlords.

Instead of making reforms, they tried to subdue the people by force. They enforced a battery of old and new repressive laws, collectively known as Coercion Acts, and suspended the Habeas Corpus Act. The large professional army, numbering around 25,000 troops, was in almost continuous operation.

In 1814 Robert Peel, dubbed 'Orange Peel' by the nationalist leader Daniel O'Connell because of his pronounced political sympathies, founded a new kind of police force, known as the 'Peelers', which was controlled by central government. This force was at first organised on a piecemeal basis in rebellious districts, but in 1836 it was amalgamated with the constabulary to become a centralised national force, the Irish Constabulary, run directly from Dublin Castle. Numbering some 8,500 in 1840, the police were housed in 1,400 newly built posts, known as 'barracks', mostly placed in towns and villages. Always armed, they resembled more an army of occupation with police functions than a conventional police force, such as that introduced soon afterwards in Britain where the working people were less rebellious.

Hopes for the future

A very few members of the Anglo-Irish landowning class broke away from their origins and radically reappraised the crisis in the Irish countryside and its wider context.

At this period early socialist thinkers in several European countries were responding to the development of industrial capitalism not by wanting to retreat to an idealised peasant past, but by looking for new forms of social organisation in which workers could enjoy better conditions while at the same time becoming more productive. Such thinkers became known as 'Utopian socialists', because they believed the ruling classes could be persuaded to voluntarily renounce their privileges and initiate the new order. They experimented with 'co-operative communities', such as the famous cotton-spinning community at New Lanark in Scotland, which was owned by a business partnership and managed by Robert Owen with a mixture of philanthropy, innovative educational ideas, strict discipline and commercial sense.

One of the most outstanding of the early socialists was William Thompson, who was born in Cork in 1775, son of a wealthy merchant who was part of the Protestant ascendancy class. Thompson, the principal socialist thinker of his day, was an uncompromising critic of capitalism, a fervent advocate of women's equality, and a supporter of Catholic emancipation in Ireland. He promoted the idea of co-operative communities, but unlike Robert Owen he believed that the workers must depend on their own efforts. A fore-runner of Karl Marx, he recognised that the wealth and power of the ruling class was based on their appropriation of the wealth produced by working people. In a book published in 1824 he argued:

> The tendency of the existing arrangement of things as to wealth, is to enrich a few at the expense of the mass of producers; to make the poverty of the poor more hopeless, to throw back the middling classes upon the poor, that a few may be enabled, not only to accumulate in perniciously large masses the real national, which is only the aggregate of individual, capital, but also, by means of such accumulations, to command the products of the yearly labor of the community.[9]

One of his closest friends was Anna Wheeler, who had also rebelled against her Anglo-Irish ascendancy background. Born in 1785, she married in her teens a dissolute member of a wealthy landowning family who – as her daughter Rosina put it – had been 'titled fools' at the conquest, and had 'continued uninterrupted so without the plebeian taint of brains having come between them and their nobility.'[10] While her husband rode and drank, Anna

Wheeler gave birth to six children – only two of whom survived infancy – and studied social and political philosophy. She read voluminously, obtaining from London the works of the foremost European democratic thinkers, including Mary Wollstonecraft's pioneering *Vindication of the Rights of Woman*. In 1812 she fled from her husband, taking her two surviving children and her sister, and travelled first to Guernsey, and later to France and England. She settled in London where she became a well-known thinker and lecturer in the co-operative, feminist and socialist movements. She also became a close friend and collaborator of William Thompson.

Anna Wheeler

Anna Wheeler's advocacy of women's emancipation inspired William Thompson to write, in collaboration with her, his *Appeal of one-half of the human race, women, against the pretensions of the other half, men, to retain them in political, and thence in civil and domestic, slavery*. The *Appeal* was published in 1825 and bore Anna Wheeler's picture as a frontispiece. Dedicating the book to her, Thompson explained that he was merely 'your interpreter and the scribe of your sentiments', and had only written the book because she had not had the 'leisure and resolution' to do so.[11] The *Appeal* argued for complete equality for women in voting rights and in all other spheres of human activity, and called on them to

> assert everywhere your right as human beings to equal individual liberty, to equal laws, political, civil, and criminal, to equal morals, to equal education, – and, as the result of the whole, to equal chances... of acquiring the means of happiness, with men.[12]

But Thompson and Wheeler recognised that there could be no genuine equality until capitalism was abolished and replaced by a new type of society in which women and children were not financially dependent on men. In his dedication to her, Thompson wrote:

> You look forward, as I do, to a state of society very different from that which now exists, in which the effort of all is to outwit, supplant, and

snatch from each other; where interest is systematically opposed to duty; where the system of morals is little more than a mass of hypocrisy preached by knaves, unpractised by them, to keep their slaves, male as well as female, in blind uninquiring obedience; and where the whole motley fabric is kept together by fear and blood. You look forward to a better aspect of society, where the principle of benevolence shall supersede that of fear; where restless and anxious individual competition shall give place to mutual co-operation and joint possession; where individuals in large numbers, male and female, forming voluntary associations, shall become a mutual guarantee to each other for the supply of all useful wants... where perfect freedom of opinion and perfect equality will reign amongst the co-operators; and where the children of all will be equally educated and provided for by the whole...[13]

Thompson and Wheeler also saw that women did not want merely to be the same as men currently were. Thompson continued:

Really enlightened women... would find it difficult to meet with associates worthy of them in men as now formed, full of ignorance and vanity, priding themselves on a sexual superiority, entirely independent of any merit... claiming respect from the strength of their arm and the lordly faculty of producing beards attached by nature to their chins![14]

Thompson transformed the lives of the tenants on his own estate, providing them with secure leases, slate-roofed cottages and tools. His cherished scheme to set up a co-operative community on his estate was still at an early stage when he died in 1833. In his will, he left an annuity to Anna Wheeler, the rest of his estate to the co-operative movement and his body to medical science. But his relatives contested the will on the grounds that he was insane, and after more than 25 years of wrangling, the main beneficiaries were the lawyers. Anna Wheeler died in London's Camden Town in May 1848.

Catholic emancipation

Most members of the landowning, business and professional classes were not interested in changing the social order in favour of the peasantry or urban poor. Rather, they wanted to maintain or improve their own position within the existing system.

The Irish middle class was small and weak. The collapse of Irish industry in most of the country in the first decades of the 19th century meant that a strong commercial class – such as existed in England – failed to develop. The exception was the northeast, where the Presbyterian-owned cotton industry prospered – though with fluctuations – till the 1830s, after which it was replaced with linen manufacturing based on new steam-powered machinery.

Elsewhere the middle class was predominantly Catholic, and consisted of priests, dealers, and better-off tenant farmers in the countryside, and traders, lawyers and lower-grade officials in the towns. They were frustrated by the British government's failure to concede Catholic emancipation, which meant that their chances of promotion to high levels in government, the law, the army and the university were blocked, and that they could not sit in parliament. The Catholic church, too, was aggrieved by the government's breach of promise on emancipation, and by the continuing dominance of the established Protestant church, whose upkeep was paid by tithes extracted from an overwhelmingly Catholic population.

Soon after the Union a new campaign for emancipation got underway, and by 1808 the lawyer Daniel O'Connell had become a prominent figure in it. Many middle-class Protestants and Presbyterians supported the campaign, because they saw it as a way of cutting back the power of the ascendancy landowners.

The government attempted to stifle the emancipation agitation by invoking the Convention Act of 1793: this forbade people forming assemblies which could appear representative of the Irish nation and thus threaten the hegemony of parliament. But O'Connell used his legal expertise to get round the law: banned organisations simply reappeared under new names with altered constitutions. The emancipation campaign was supported by a large majority of Irish MPs but still had a difficult time in parliament. The Irish were a minority in the Commons, which repeatedly threw out bills for emancipation.

English radicals, too, supported Catholic emancipation. Among them was the as yet unknown poet Percy Bysshe Shelley, who in February 1812 at the age of 19 travelled to Dublin with his equally enthusiastic 16-year-old wife Harriet to spread his ideas. They spent two months in Dublin, seeing their visit as the first step in a general campaign against oppression.

In Dublin Shelley published two pamphlets calling for emancipation and the repeal of the Act of Union. In the first, *An Address to the Irish People,* drafted before he left England, Shelley criticised the historical record of the Protestant and Catholic religions – neither of which he believed in – and affirmed his belief in complete religious freedom. He went on to argue that Irish people should bring about change not through violence but through 'peace, philanthropy, wisdom.'[15] He also urged people to stand up for freedom of the press: this was non-existent under the government of the day and an Irish journalist, Peter Finnerty, was then in prison for criticising Lord Castlereagh.

The Address was printed cheaply and was distributed in the streets by the Shelleys and their servant Daniel Healey (or Hill). As well as handing them to passers-by in the street, Shelley and Harriet would stand on the balcony of their lodgings in Sackville Street and throw copies to likely looking people.

Shelley was shocked and distressed by the poverty and injustice he saw in Dublin: 'I had no conception of the depth of human misery until now,' he wrote.[16] He intervened with practical help where he could: for example, he dissuaded a constable from arresting a woman for stealing a loaf.

In his second pamphlet, written in Dublin and proposing the formation of a campaigning organisation, Shelley pointed to the limitations of the emancipation demand:

> It is my opinion that the claims of the Catholic inhabitants of Ireland, if gained tomorrow, would in a very small degree aggrandize their liberty and happiness. The disqualifications principally affect the higher orders of the Catholic persuasion, these would principally be benefited by their removal.[17]

Shelley thought that the repeal of the Union would be much more beneficial than emancipation. He wrote:

> The latter affects few, the former affects thousands. The one disqualifies the rich from power, the other impoverishes the peasant, adds beggary to the city, famine to the country, multiplies abjectedness, whilst misery and crime play into each other's hands under its withering auspices... The aristocracy of Ireland suck the veins of its inhabitants and consume the blood in England.[18]

Not surprisingly, Shelley and the Catholic nobility did not see eye-to-eye: he disliked them, and they avoided him.

When the dissolute and much-despised King George IV visited Ireland in 1821, the Catholic bishops and upper classes laid on a lavish and fawning welcome, aimed in part at softening the king's attitude to emancipation. Daniel O'Connell was prominent in the proceedings, presenting the king with a laurel crown and pledging to donate money towards building a palace for him in Ireland. This sycophancy led to widespread criticism from Irish and English radicals, among them Lord Byron, who composed a long poem on the subject, *The Irish Avatar*. Referring to Lord Fingal's acceptance of an honour from the king, Byron wrote:

> Will thy yard of blue riband, poor Fingal, recall
> The fetters from millions of Catholic limbs?
> Or, has it not bound thee the fastest of all
> The slaves, who now hail the betrayer with hymns?

> Let thy tables be loaded with feasts till they groan!
> Till they *groan* like thy people, through ages of woe!
> Let their wine flow around the old Bacchanal's throne,
> Like their blood which has flow'd, and which yet has to flow.[19]

The Catholic leaders' hopes proved misplaced: the king did not help their cause. And when the Commons did eventually pass a Catholic Relief Bill in 1821, it was hedged with conditions and was anyway thrown out by the Lords.

Daniel O'Connell

More than 20 years after the Union, the middle class campaigners had got nowhere with their polite pleading. Soon Daniel O'Connell and his colleagues realised that if they were to have any impact, they must harness the dynamism of the peasants, who could put real pressure on the government through the threat of a mass uprising. So O'Connell set about constructing a new type of mass organisation through which the middle class could channel the peasant unrest – which was widespread in the wake of the 1821-2 famine – to its own ends, by fashioning it into a weapon to extract concessions from the government.

The new Catholic Association, formed in 1823, was a two-tier body. At the centre was a club – so designed in order to evade the Convention Act – which met weekly and whose members, drawn from both Protestant and Catholic upper and middle classes, paid a guinea a year. At its base, within two years of its formation, were hundreds of thousands of peasants, each paying a penny a month 'Catholic rent', organised in local associations under the presidency of Catholic priests. The Catholic church, the only nationwide organisation with which the peasantry identified, provided the mechanism linking the middle class to the masses.

The ambitions of the Catholic prelates were limited and conservative, as Bishop Doyle stressed when he appeared before a parliamentary committee in 1825:

> I am convinced in my soul ... that if we were freed from the disabilities under which we labour, we have no mind, and no thought, and no will, but that which would lead us to incorporate ourselves most fully and essentially with this great kingdom; for it would be our greatest pride, to share in the glories and riches of England.[20]

Daniel O'Connell, at the centre of the organisation, was an astute organiser and a public speaker of extraordinary magnetism. He came from a Catholic landowning family in County Kerry and, until he took up full-time politics, he was one of the most successful and best-paid lawyers in Ireland, though as a Catholic he was prevented from becoming a senior barrister. O'Connell was a fluent Irish speaker, but had no brief for the language: he remarked in 1833 that

> the superior utility of the English tongue, as the medium of all modern communication, is so great, that I can witness without a sigh the gradual disuse of the Irish...[21]

O'Connell's views on political and social issues were a shifting mixture of conservatism and liberalism, which made for volatile relationships with Irish and English radicals. He strongly opposed the principles of the French revolution and its Irish admirers, such as Wolfe Tone, and joined the lawyers' yeomanry corps to help put down Robert Emmet's rebellion. He denounced the use of violence – although he had no scruples about threatening it – against people or property. He was a royalist – later referring to Victoria as 'the darling queen' – and saw loyalty to the throne as a corrective to dangerous revolutionary tendencies. He nevertheless supported parliamentary reform and religious liberty for all – he espoused, for example, the cause of Jewish emancipation – and vehemently opposed slavery, even though this cost him support in America.

O'Connell objected to the worst manifestations of English landlordism in Ireland, in particular absenteeism and the enforced payment of tithes. But he supported the existing system of property ownership, and strongly opposed agrarian reform. He also became increasingly anti-trade union, denouncing the activities of Irish trade unionists and, after he became a member of parliament, voting against measures designed to improve the desperate conditions of workers in British factories.

In 1826 the Catholic Association took advantage of a general election to step up the pressure. Its leaders toured the country urging the 40-shilling freeholders – tenant farmers who had gained the vote in 1793 – to defy their landlords and vote for the Association's candidates. The freeholders responded and, risking eviction and other reprisals, ousted the landlords' candidates in four constituencies: Louth, Monaghan, Westmeath and Waterford. But still they did not win emancipation.

Then in 1828 Daniel O'Connell stood as a candidate in a by-election in Clare, backed by all the resources of the now-formidable Catholic Association. The contest brought feelings throughout Ireland to fever pitch, and after O'Connell's victory it was clear to all that the country was on the verge of an uprising.

Alarmed by this prospect, the government yielded – but not unconditionally. In 1829 it passed the Emancipation Act: this allowed Catholics to be admitted to almost all posts, but it also raised the franchise qualification to £10, and so took away the voting rights of the 40-shilling freeholders, the very people who had risked their livelihoods to vote for O'Connell and win the Act. Ironically, though the Act theoretically emancipated wealthy Catholics, in practice they gained little in the short term, because with the disenfranchisement of their peasant base they lost their means of threatening the landowners. The ascendancy class still held power, and was reluctant to dispense key posts to Catholics.

When the French sociologist Alexis de Tocqueville visited Ireland in 1835, he was told by a Dublin Protestant barrister that the administration was still entirely Protestant and that there was almost no social mixing across class lines. 'Believe me,' said the barrister, 'I have only *once* in my life dined in the house of a Catholic and that was by accident.'[22]

For the mass of the peasantry, Catholic emancipation was a huge disillusionment. With the loss of their voting rights, small tenants were even more vulnerable. Previously landowners had often divided up their land into as many small plots as possible to increase the number of people voting in their interest. But voteless tenants were worthless, and landlords now rapidly evicted them in order to create larger farms. The number of 40-shilling freeholders fell from 191,000 in 1828 to 14,200 in 1830.

The pressure of evictions, added to heavy demands for rent and tithes, drove many peasants to desperate measures. The early 1830s saw an upsurge in the violent activities of the secret peasant societies: Whitefeet, Ribbonmen and others. A widespread campaign of refusal to pay tithes, backed by Daniel O'Connell and Catholic bishops, added to the tension: attempts to collect tithes by force led to many bloody battles between peasants and police or yeomanry. In early 1832 the lord lieutenant, Lord Anglesey, a distinguished general, described the situation:

> The country is at this moment all but in a state of rebellion... I tremble at every day's post. I cannot cover the whole country, and can only subdue two or three counties at a time and then fall upon others.[23]

The leader of a band of Whitefeet explained their reasons to a priest who had reproached them:

> The law does nothing for us. We must save ourselves. We have a little land which we need for ourselves and our families to live on, and they drive us out of it. To whom should we address ourselves? We ask for work at eight pence a day and we are refused. To whom should we address ourselves? Emancipation has done nothing for us. Mr. O'Connell and the rich Catholics go to Parliament. We die of starvation just the same.[24]

The Bishop of Carlow recalled visiting a prison in 1833 to see a man who had killed the agent of a rich landowner:

> This agent wanted to change the method of cultivation and to this end he evicted the small farmers and destroyed their houses. One of them had a sick wife and asked for a respite. The agent had the sick woman brought out into the open air and destroyed her house before her very eyes. A few days later he was murdered by the man who was speaking to me, and who was not in any way personally interested in the action of which I told you, but did it in vengeance for that deed.[25]

Though often gruesome, the actions of the secret societies were effective. George Poulett Scrope, an English MP, explained in 1834, appealing for a poor law rather than coercion:

> The peasantry of Ireland do more or less obtain from the Whitefoot associations that essential protection to their existence which the established law of the country refuses to afford. The Whitefoot system is the practical and effective check upon the Ejectment system. It cannot be denied that but for the salutary terror inspired by the Whitefeet, the

clearance of estates… would proceed with a rapidity and to an extent that must occasion the most horrible sufferings to hundreds and thousands of the ejected tenantry.[26]

The government responded to the disturbances with the Coercion Bill of 1833, the most repressive piece of legislation since the Union. The bill, introduced by Lord Althorp, was passed by 363 votes to 84. It allowed the proclamation of martial law – involving the suspension of jury trials, curfews, and drastic powers of search, arrest and transportation – and also the suppression of all kinds of political activity. As O'Connell and his supporters noted bitterly, it was the first Irish bill promoted by their supposed allies, the Whigs, in the first reformed parliament that assembled after the Reform Act of 1832 which O'Connell had contributed to carrying. The Coercion Bill shocked and alarmed radicals in Britain, not only because they were sympathetic to the Irish cause, but because they feared the bill's provisions would be extended to them. Nottingham radicals, reflecting widespread fears, sent a resolution to the House of Commons, stating:

> Should your petitioners witness these acts of injustice done to Ireland, the most fearful apprehensions will be excited in their minds, that the same odious tyranny will be perpetrated towards themselves.[27]

The reformed parliament also produced widespread disillusionment among English working people. They dubbed the Reform Act the 'Great Betrayal' because, by extending the franchise to £10 freeholders, it gave the employers and middle classes access to the parliamentary system alongside the landowners, but excluded the workers. The reformed parliament proceeded to set up the punitive workhouse system and to prosecute the 'Tolpuddle martyrs', the six Dorset farmworkers who were transported to Australia in 1834 because they joined a trade union.

Disillusionment with the reformed parliament led to the setting up of the Chartist movement in the 1830s. Based on a 'people's charter' which included demands for universal male suffrage, secret ballots, and the abolition of property qualifications for MPs, Chartism rapidly became a mass working-class movement.

Ireland, too, was a key issue for the Chartists, not least because many were themselves Irish. In 1842 they presented a petition to parliament, signed by over three million people, which included in its long list of demands:

> That your petitioners complain of the many grievances borne by the people of Ireland, and contend that they are fully entitled to a repeal of the legislative union.[28]

The Ralahine commune

One Irish landlord, John Scott Vandeleur, an admirer of Robert Owen's ideas, was prompted by an outbreak of violence on his estate at Ralahine in

County Clare into setting up a commune. The results were spectacular, and during its two years' flowering the commune became a Mecca for social reformers.

The 'Ralahine Agricultural and Manufacturing Co-operative Association' was established in November 1831, under the guidance of a leading Manchester co-operator, Edward Thomas Craig. While Vandeleur still owned the estate and demanded a substantial rent, the workers ran it themselves through a committee elected by all adult male and female members. The workers were paid according to hours worked by a 'labour note', which they could exchange for goods in the commune store. Prices for food, rent and fuel were fixed and cheap, and the children's food and education were provided for out of a common fund. An insurance scheme was established for the care of the sick. Freedom of religious belief and practice was guaranteed, and no religion was taught in the schools. Disputes were settled by a general meeting from which lawyers were excluded.

Ralahine rapidly fulfilled its organisers' ambitions. Secure and free from want, the peasants had no need to resort to violence. They even introduced the first reaping machine used in Ireland.

Tragically the commune soon came to an end, foundering on the fact that the workers did not own the land outright and on hostile land laws which did not recognise the community's right to hold a lease. In 1833 Vandeleur lost all his money while gambling in Dublin and fled the country. The people who took over the estate treated the community as labourers with no rights, and seized the buildings and grounds. Soon the area returned to its previous distressed and violent state.

Cobbett in Ireland

In 1834 William Cobbett, the outstanding English radical journalist, visited Ireland at the age of 71 in order to observe conditions there. Cobbett was a long-standing advocate of Catholic rights and had strongly opposed the disenfranchisement of the small tenants. He wrote: 'I do not wish to see rich Catholics let into power, while poor Catholics are deprived even of the rights that they now enjoy'.[29]

He was also an outspoken critic of English misrule and believed that the Union should be repealed: though this, he thought, would not much help the working people unless the law was changed to guarantee them 'the due share of what they laboured for'.[30]

Cobbett travelled widely for two-and-a-half months in the southern half of Ireland and was everywhere welcomed with tremendous enthusiasm. He described what he saw in a series of articles published in his paper, the *Political Register*, and written in the form of letters to a labourer on his Surrey farm. Himself of peasant stock, and a lifelong champion of country workers, Cobbett had a keen and angry sympathy for the plight of the Irish peasants. He described a visit to the 'mendicity' in Dublin, a building, formerly an aristocrat's mansion, where thousands of beggars were fed. In one place, he wrote,

> I saw a great crowd of women sitting and doing nothing, each with *a baby* in her arms… Some of them were young and naturally handsome; but made ugly by starvation, rags, and dirt. It was one mass of rags; and, not what *you* call rags… far worse than any that you ever saw tied round a stake to frighten the birds from our wheat and our peas…
>
> In another place I saw the most painful sight of all: *women*, with heavy hammers, *cracking stones* into very small pieces, to *make walks in gentlemen's gardens*![31]

Cobbett described how the peasants – 'poor half-naked creatures' – lived in indescribable poverty, eating the worst sort of potatoes, 'lumpers', while they worked to produce copious amounts of meat, flour and butter that were exported to England and America. Near Waterford Cobbett came upon a fair:

> There might be 4,000 people; there were about 7 acres of ground covered with cattle (mostly fat), and all over the streets of the town there were about THREE THOUSAND BEAUTIFUL FAT HOGS, lying all over the road and the streets; and our chaise was *actually stopped and blocked up by fat hogs*… Ah! but there arose out of this fine sight reflections that made my blood boil; that the far greater part of those who had bred and fatted these hogs were never to taste one morsel of them, no not even the offal, and had lived *worse* than the hogs, not daring to taste any part of the *meal* used in fattening of the hogs! the hogs are to be killed, dried or tubbed, and sent out of the country to be sold for money to be *paid to the landowners*, who spend it in London, Bath, Paris, Rome, or some other place of pleasure, while these poor people are raising all this food from the land, and are starving themselves.[32]

Cobbett went to visit an estate owned by one such landlord, Lord Midleton, who lived in England a few miles from Cobbett's farm. According to Cobbett, Midleton drew £25,000 to £30,000 each year – a huge sum for the time – from his Irish estate. Though Midleton was considered one of the better landlords, his tenants lived in wretched conditions. Cobbett described a hamlet of 40 or 50 hovels:

> They all consisted of mud-walls, with a covering of rafters and straw. None of them so good as the place where you keep your little horse. I took a particular account of the first that I went into. It was 21 feet long and 9 feet wide. The floor, the bare ground. No fire-place, no chimney, the fire (made of potato-haulm) made on one side against the wall, and the smoke going out of a hole in the roof. No table, no chair… There was one window, 9 inches by 5, and the glass broken half out… No bed: no mattress; some large flat stones, to keep the bodies from the damp ground; some dirty

straw and a bundle of rags were all the bedding. The man's name was Owen Gumbleton. *Five small children*; the mother, about thirty, naturally handsome, but worn into half-ugliness by hunger and filth; she had no shoes or stockings, no shift, a mere rag over her body and down to her knees... Gumbleton's hog was lying in the room... There is a nasty dunghill (no privy) to each hovel. The dung that the hog makes *in the hovel* is carefully put into a heap by itself, as being the most precious. This dung and the pig are the main things to raise the rent and to get fuel with...[33]

Official statistics gave grim confirmation of the peasants' plight. In 1836 a government inquiry stated:

we cannot estimate the number of persons in Ireland out of work and in distress during thirty weeks of the year at less than 585,000, nor the number of persons dependent upon them at less than 1,800,000, making in the whole 2,385,000.[34]

At this period the total value of Irish agricultural produce was £36 million. Of this £10 million went in rent, and £20 million in taxes, tithes and the payment of middlemen and merchants. The actual producers, the smallholders and labourers, received less than £6 million, which was only some 16 per cent of the total.

A kind of West Britons

Between 1835 and 1841 Daniel O'Connell's group of MPs held the balance of power in parliament. Both Tories and Whigs were adamantly opposed to repeal of the Union: when a pro-repeal motion was put to the Commons in 1834, only one English MP, the member for Tiverton, voted in favour. But many Whigs were willing to make concessions to Ireland, so O'Connell made a pact with them. He agreed to keep them in power on the basis of a deal: O'Connell would stop agitating for repeal and in return the Whigs would resolve various Irish grievances. O'Connell aimed to win a share of power for the Catholic middle class, within the British system if possible. He said in a speech:

The people of Ireland are ready to become a portion of the Empire, provided they be made so in reality and not in name alone; they are ready to become a kind of West Britons if made so in benefits and in justice; but if not, we are Irishmen again.[35]

He also became a hardened opponent of social reform, and voted with the Whigs against attempts to limit the working hours of women and children, and to prevent the employment of children under nine years old.

For most Irish people, these six years produced no substantial change. In 1838 a bill was passed which modified and disguised the tithe system but did not abolish it: tithe payments were reduced by 25 per cent and made payable by the landlord, who could then pass the cost on to the tenants by raising the rent. A change for the worse came with the introduction of the hated workhouse system to Ireland: this meant that in order to obtain food, destitute people had to give up what little land they had and go and live in the workhouses, which were run like prisons.

Wealthy Catholics, however, benefited from O'Connell's pact with the Whigs, since the government began to reform the Irish administration and promote them to prestigious posts. They became judges, privy councillors, sheriffs and magistrates, while Orangemen were removed from such posts and their processions were prohibited.

One of O'Connell's angriest critics was Feargus O'Connor, who was MP for County Cork from 1832 until, after being re-elected in 1835, he was removed from his seat on the grounds that he did not have the correct property qualification. O'Connor, a Protestant and nephew of one of the leaders of the 1798 rising, objected strongly both to O'Connell's weakness on the repeal issue and to his anti-working-class stance. A dynamic organiser and charismatic speaker, who believed in the need for working people to form their own organisations, O'Connor went on to become a key figure in the Chartist movement in Britain.

Most middle-class Catholics, though disappointed at the slow pace of change, were mollified by the flow of jobs and perks that came their way. But as the Whigs lost seats to the Tories and their hold on power weakened, O'Connell came under increasing pressure from his supporters to break the pact and raise the stakes. As a result, he restarted the agitation for repeal of the Union and in 1840 he formed the Loyal National Repeal Association. O'Connell aimed to organise the repeal campaign on the same lines as the earlier campaign for Catholic emancipation. But while he once again won support from the Catholic church and the peasantry, this time both the English Whigs and the middle-class Presbyterians of Belfast withheld their backing.

Changes in Belfast

Before 1800, Belfast's Presbyterian business community had been the mainstay of the United Irish societies. Successful capitalists, they had resented the restrictions imposed by the landowning ascendancy elite and the British government. Then, frightened by the blood-letting of 1798, they abandoned thoughts of revolution. The Act of Union, they found, at least had the merit of getting rid of the Dublin parliament, the seat of ascendancy power. Further, it did not hinder Belfast's continuing development into a successful commercial and manufacturing centre: by 1835 Belfast had overtaken Dublin to become the first port in Ireland in terms of the value of its trade.

Belfast experienced a boom in cotton manufacturing in the years after 1800. The industry concentrated in Belfast because the raw cotton imports arrived there first. Workers flooded into Belfast from the surrounding countryside, attracted by the prospect of work and driven by hunger. The population grew from 19,000 in 1801 to 53,287 in 1831, with the proportion of Catholics rising from around 16 per cent to 32 per cent. With continuing industrial growth, the population went on increasing till the end of the century. With a huge pool of unemployed people to draw on, employers were able to keep wages low and to shift the burden of depressions onto the workers. The cotton was spun in factories but woven by home-based handloom weavers, who were paid piece-rates and were particularly vulnerable. James Hope, a former United Irish leader, was for a while employed as a handloom weaver by John McCracken of the prominent radical family. In 1808 Hope wrote to Mary Ann McCracken, John's sister:

> I was obliged to tell Mr John that I must Leave his Employment for want of wages, not being able Longer to support my family out of my small salary...[36]

During the depression years after 1815, the weavers mobilised to try to prevent wage cuts, using violence and strikes. Though their actions did force employers to modify wage reductions, weavers' conditions remained grim. Many were unemployed, while others worked from 4 a.m. to midnight, seven days a week, for starvation wages.

Ireland's cotton industry was exposed to serious competition from British cottons, which were factory-woven and often of finer quality. The pressure increased when in 1824 the British government lifted all duties on goods passing between Ireland and Britain. But Belfast's manufacturers avoided disaster by shifting from cotton into linen-manufacturing. Linen was a traditional Irish industry, and Belfast's manufacturers revived it on a new basis, taking advantage of a new process developed in England in 1825, which for the first time allowed high-quality linen to be spun by machine. This 'wet-spinning' process involved soaking the flax in cold water for six hours before feeding it into the machines.

Belfast's pioneer was a cotton-mill owner, Thomas Mulholland. When his mill in York Street burned down in 1828, he decided that in view of the competition from English and Scottish cotton manufacturers, and Ireland's tradition of linen-making, it would be advisable to rebuild the mill to spin linen instead of cotton. The new mill began working in 1830 and by 1856 was probably the biggest of its kind in the world. Other manufacturers soon followed suit. In 1832 there were 19 cotton mills and one flax mill in Belfast. In 1837 there were six cotton mills and 15 flax mills. By 1861 there were just two cotton mills and 32 flax mills.

More than two-thirds of the spinners in the linen mills were women and children. Their pay was low and conditions were very poor. The air was thick with flax dust and life expectancy for hacklers, who dressed the flax, was only 45 years. Living conditions in Belfast's working-class districts were squalid. Over-crowding and lack of sanitation together with low incomes contributed to the spread of disease and high mortality rates: in 1841 Belfast had the worst death rate in Ireland and possibly also in the United Kingdom.

From the mill-owners' point of view, however, business was booming. The upswing in trade made it essential to improve the port: the shallowness of the water meant that larger ships had to anchor three miles away from the quays. Major alterations eventually began in 1839. Belfast's role as a trading port also encouraged the development of a ship-building industry, though Cork was the main Irish ship-building centre in the first half of the 19th century. The port alterations allowed bigger ships to be built, and by 1900 Belfast was to have the biggest ship-building output in the world.

Though leading Belfast Presbyterians were still willing to support Catholic emancipation and campaigned for reform of the Westminster parliament, they became less keen on full separation from Britain. Some, notably the radical landowner William Sharman Crawford, who became an O'Connellite MP in 1835, advocated a federal union between Britain and Ireland. In this early 'home rule' scheme Ireland would still be represented at Westminster, where decisions regarding British imperial interests would be made, but there would also be a parliament in Ireland to deal with exclusively Irish matters.

But by the late 1820s many Presbyterians were moving towards outright support for the Union, a trend which was reflected in a controversy within the Presbyterian church. Henry Cooke, a leading minister and a theological traditionalist, led a strongly anti-Catholic and pro-Tory faction, opposing both Catholic emancipation and repeal of the Union. Cooke aimed to ally Presbyterians with the Church of Ireland in a single Protestant anti-Catholic bloc. The rival faction was led by a liberal minister, Henry Montgomery, who supported Catholic emancipation and parliamentary reform. As Montgomery was proud to say, his two elder brothers had fought with the United Irish rebels in 1798.

At the Synod of Ulster in 1829 the dispute came to a head over theological issues, such as whether the Pope was anti-Christ, a view which Cooke supported but Montgomery abhorred. Cooke's faction won the debate and Montgomery's group departed.

Cooke formed an alliance with the landlords, the Orange Order and the leaders of the Church of Ireland. In 1834, speaking at a rally at Hillsborough organised by the Orange gentry, he announced, 'Between the divided churches I publish the banns of a sacred marriage'.[37] The same year, the Orange Order opened its doors to all non-Catholics, and Presbyterians joined in large numbers.

The shift in Presbyterians' political attitudes emerged sharply in the 1832 general election. This was the first election held since passing of the Reform Act, which had extended voting rights to the middle class. Many in Belfast had campaigned hard for reform, and had high hopes of a Whig victory. They were horrified when the Tories won. The two Tory candidates had 1,585 votes between them, while the Whigs had 1,210. Only about 200 Presbyterians had voted for the Whigs: the rest of their support had come from Catholics. Most Presbyterians, along with Episcopalians and Methodists, had voted for the Tories.

Belfast Orangemen had assisted the Tories in their election campaign, and their supporters celebrated their victory by attacking a Catholic street and provoking fierce and prolonged fighting, in which the police shot four people dead. There had been occasional clashes between Catholics and Protestants in Belfast in the past, such as after Orange parades in 1813 and 1825, but this was the most serious episode in the town to date. The *Northern Whig* described how a prominent Orangeman had harangued the crowd from the window of the Tories' committee-room:

> Mr Boyce... flourished a staff exultingly, and told them, that the Protestants had gained this victory, and that they would continue to maintain their ascendancy: they had trodden down their enemies, and they would keep them down...[38]

Up to now the Orange Order had been weak in Belfast, though elsewhere in the northeast it was strong. A government inquiry into the Orange lodges in 1835 found that there were 220,000 Orangemen in Ireland, and that 75,000 members of the Antrim and Down lodges paraded each year on 12 July to Hillsborough. Such marches, which commemorated King William of Orange's victory at the battle of the Boyne in 1690, often provoked violence. A justice of the peace said:

> It is the outward manifestation that destroys the people. The Orange flags and arches, the drums, the tunes and then a report goes round the country and they are a very inflammable people. The Catholics imagine there is a large body of Orangemen coming into the town armed and both parties turn out armed although there was no original intention of anything and then comes a conflict.[39]

As the 1835 select committee's report showed, the Orange Order was by now a formidable organisation. Operating in Britain as well as Ireland, its leadership included powerful Tory aristocrats including the Dukes of York and Cumberland, and senior clergy of the Churches of England and Ireland. In Ireland, the Order had become an important mechanism for upholding landlord power and British rule. Orangemen controlled the Irish yeomanry and had lodges in the army. The upper-class leaders of the movement were embarrassed by the rank-and-file Orangemen, with their crude and aggressive activities, but they also found them useful. So when Orangemen broke the law, magistrates dealt with them leniently.

From 1832, Orange violence became a regular feature of Belfast life, accompanying Tory election campaigns and the 12 July marches. Tory campaigning, for both local and national elections, was also marked by anti-Catholic propaganda and by electoral malpractices, including manipulating the register and impersonation of deceased voters. In 1835, for instance, the Tories ensured that 80 Liberals – as the Whigs were now known – were disqualified from voting because they had described their premises as 'house and shop' instead of 'house, shop'.

In early 1841, hoping to attract Presbyterian support for the repeal cause, Daniel O'Connell announced that he would visit Belfast. The Presbyterian minister Henry Cooke immediately challenged him to a public debate calling him 'a great bad man engaged in a great bad cause'. O'Connell declined, contemptuously ridiculing 'Bully Cooke'. Their public exchanges brought feelings in Belfast to such a pitch that O'Connell travelled there incognito. When he tried to address an open-air meeting he was drowned out by hooting and groaning. Then, while he was attending an evening reception, crowds rampaged through the streets breaking windows, stoning the homes of repealers and attacking a chapel. 'To hell with the Pope!', they roared. 'Down with rebellious repeal!'

As O'Connell, protected by a police escort, left Belfast, Henry Cooke addressed a huge anti-repeal demonstration. He contended that repeal was a threat to the economic and religious interests of Belfast Protestants. Belfast, he said, had till recently been 'merely a village', but was now 'a glorious sight':

> Turn in what direction we will, our eyes meet new streets and public buildings – numbers of new manufactories rise up on every side – look where we may, we see signs of increasing prosperity...
>
> And to what cause is all this prosperity owing? Is it not to the free intercourse which the Union enables us to enjoy with England and Scotland – to that extension of our general commerce which we derive through that channel? I can fancy I see the genius of industry seated upon the hills which look down upon our lovely town... while, accompanied by the genius of Protestantism, her influence is shed, from that point, over the length and breadth of Ulster. (Hear, hear and loud cheers)... [40]

'Monster meetings'

The Tories came to power towards the end of 1841 and O'Connell continued to build the repeal campaign, hoping to pressurise them into making concessions to the Irish middle class as he had successfully done with the campaign for Catholic emancipation. On the repeal issue, however, the Whigs and Tories were united against him and offered no splits which he could exploit. Although O'Connell pledged that Ireland would continue to be ruled by the British crown even after the setting up of a separate parliament, the British establishment saw repeal as a threat to their strategic and economic interests.

In Ireland, O'Connell played for the support of both the middle-class and the increasingly destitute and militant peasantry. He combined a weak programme, bare of proposals to improve the peasants' lot, with a messianic open-air speech-making campaign. Between March and October 1843 the Repeal Association held nearly 30 'monster meetings', attended by hundreds of thousands of people, who arrived from many miles around in disciplined processions. At these meetings O'Connell stirred his huge audiences with images of Ireland's beauty and future glory, and made scarcely veiled threats of mass revolt if the British government did not concede.

By May 1843 Lord de Grey, the British viceroy, was warning: 'Matters are looking so serious that delay or temporising will be ruin.'[41] The Catholic hierarchy, the corporations and America all supported repeal, he wrote.

The prime minister, Sir Robert Peel, responded to the agitation in uncompromising terms. On 9 May 1843 he told parliament:

> there is no influence, no power, no authority, which the prerogatives of the Crown and the existing law give to the Government, which shall not be exercised for the purpose of maintaining the Union – the dissolution of which would involve, not merely the repeal of an act of Parliament, but the dismemberment of this great empire... deprecating as I do all war, but, above all, civil war, yet there is no alternative which I do not think preferable to the dismemberment of this empire.[42]

Extra troops were sent to Ireland, barracks were fortified, and warships assembled in Ireland's harbours. The Arms Act, which permitted house-searches and other measures, was renewed against bitter opposition in parliament from Repealers and Radicals.

O'Connell responded with increasingly defiant speeches, saying the Irish would resist if attacked by Britain and boasting of the physical force at his disposal. The Repeal Association began to resemble an alternative administration, run by the Irish middle class. The Repealers set up their own police and arbitration courts, designed to defuse agrarian disturbances. Libraries were established where literature such as the new paper, the *Nation*, was eagerly read. A new meeting hall, which could hold 5,000, was built in Dublin.

In June the 22-year-old revolutionary Frederick Engels commented on O'Connell's campaign with intense frustration:

> How much could be achieved if a sensible man possessed O'Connell's popularity, or if O'Connell had a little more sense and a little less egoism and vanity! Two hundred thousand men, and what kind of men! Men who have nothing to lose, two-thirds of them not having a shirt to their backs,

they are real proletarians and sans-culottes, and moreover Irishmen – wild, headstrong, fanatical Gaels. If one has not seen the Irish, one does not know them. Give me two hundred thousand Irishmen and I could overthrow the entire British monarchy…

But what does O'Connell do with all his power and with his millions of militant and desperate Irishmen? He is unable to attain even the wretched Repeal of the Union. Of course, solely because he does not really mean to achieve it, since he uses the impoverished, oppressed Irish people to embarrass the Tory ministers and to help his middle-class friends to get back into office… If the people were set free even for a moment, Daniel O'Connell and his moneyed aristocrats would soon find themselves in the wilderness, where O'Connell himself would like to drive the Tories. This is the reason for O'Connell's close association with the Catholic clergy; that is why he exhorts the Irish to be on their guard against the dangerous socialists; that is why he rejects the assistance offered by the Chartists…[43]

O'Connell was, indeed, threatening an uprising that he did not want to deliver, and in October Peel finally called his bluff. The climax of the repeal campaign was to be a 'monster meeting' on Sunday 8 October at Clontarf near Dublin, scene of the Irish king Brian Boru's victory over Viking invaders in 1014. On the Saturday, the government banned the meeting. Troops moved into strategic positions, heavy guns were turned towards the meeting place and warships entered Dublin Bay. O'Connell immediately gave in, ordering his supporters to obey the government's ban. His capitulation disappointed many of his supporters and his prestige never fully recovered.

The British authorities swiftly pressed home their advantage. They prosecuted O'Connell and several other Repeal leaders for sedition and then moved to split the nationalist camp by giving concessions to the Catholic church and the middle classes. In 1845 a bill was passed which substantially increased the grant to the Catholic seminary at Maynooth, while another bill provided for three new colleges to be established in Belfast, Cork and Galway, to give full access to university education to Catholics and Presbyterians. While the Catholic bishops, followed by Daniel O'Connell, fought the proposal for non-denominational education, extra money for Maynooth was another matter. Richard Lalor Shiel, the Catholic orator who had been prominent in the emancipation campaign, congratulated the government on the Maynooth grant with the words:

You are taking a step in the right direction. You must not take the Catholic clergy into your pay, but you can take the Catholic clergy under your care… Are not lectures at Maynooth cheaper than State prosecutions? Are not professors less costly than Crown solicitors? Is not a large standing army, and a great constabulary force more expensive than the moral police with which by the priesthood of Ireland you can be thriftily and efficaciously supplied?[44]

3
The Famine

Meanwhile conditions for the peasantry continued to deteriorate, moving remorselessly towards disaster. After a series of calamitous harvests, emigration swelled. Nearly a quarter of a million people left for the United States and British North America between 1840 and 1844, and many thousands more went to the industrial towns of Britain.

In February 1845 the Devon Commission, yet another in a long line of government inquiries, published a voluminous report. Despite the fact that the commission's members were all landowners, the report highlighted the bad relations between landlords and tenants as the main cause of Irish distress. The commissioners noted the extreme poverty of labourers and their families:

> It would be impossible adequately to describe the privations which they and their families habitually and patiently endure.
> It will be seen in the Evidence, that in many districts their only food is the potato, their only beverage water, that their cabins are seldom a protection against the weather, that a bed or a blanket is a rare luxury, and that nearly in all, their pig and manure heap constitute their only property.[1]

The commission recommended some minor improvements in the legal position of tenants, but the proposals aroused such protests from the House of Lords that the government could not implement them.

Then in the autumn of 1845 the potato crop, sole food of some three million peasants, was struck by a new disease, a 'blight' that had recently crossed the Atlantic from North America. The catastrophe known as an gorta mór – the great hunger – had begun.

The blight, which still afflicts potato crops today, is caused by a fungus which was not properly understood in the 1840s. The fungus, phytophthora infestans, multiplies with lightning speed when the weather is damp and muggy. It invades and destroys the potato plant: the leaves wither and turn black, and the potatoes decompose into a rotten, stinking, inedible mess. The stench of decay hangs over the fields.

In October 1845 blight appeared in places all over Ireland: Antrim, Armagh, Bantry, Bandon, Kildare, Wicklow, Monaghan, Tyrone. Alarmed Dublin citizens sent a delegation of prominent people to appeal to the lord lieutenant to take immediate measures to avert disaster. The measures, drawn up by Daniel O'Connell, included the immediate stoppage of exports of grain and provisions, the opening of the ports to the free import of food, the setting up of food stores and the provision of employment on works of public utility. The lord lieutenant responded coldly that the proposals would have to be 'maturely weighed'. The *Freeman's Journal* raged the next day: '*They may starve!* Such in spirit, if not in words, was the reply given yesterday by the English Viceroy'. [2]

For the British government, commercial considerations came first: nothing must be done which would interfere with private enterprise. Advocates of this laissez-faire economic theory held that if market forces were given free rein, everything would work out all right. The 'great hunger' was to testify how grotesquely wrong they were. While some merchants, traders and speculators benefited from laissez-faire, the poor people of rural Ireland paid an unimaginable price.

Throughout the worst years of famine, Ireland continued to export food. Between 10 October 1845 and 5 January 1846 alone, over 30,000 oxen, bulls and cows, over 30,000 sheep and lambs, and over 100,000 pigs left Ireland for England, as well as large quantities of wheat, barley and oats. The peasants who produced this abundance were unable to eat it: they had to turn it over to the landlords in payment of rent, to avoid eviction. The government refused to stop exports, or to buy up and distribute the food. From 1847, imports of maize swelled, so that grain imports began to exceed exports considerably, but very little was given away and the peasants had no money to buy it. Further, in much of Ireland there was no network of shops or traders to offer food for sale.

As the reports of blight came in, a prominent Irish doctor, Dominic Corrigan, wrote a pamphlet forecasting famine and epidemic fever. He pointed out that the poor

> *starve* in the midst of plenty, as literally as if dungeon bars separated them from a granary. When distress has been at its height, and our poor have been dying of starvation in our streets, our corn has been going to a foreign market. It is, to our own poor, a forbidden fruit.[3]

He analysed past epidemics in Ireland, and concluded that one condition was common to all of them: famine. The remedy, therefore, was to be found

> not in medicine, but in employment, not in the lancet, but in *food*, not in raising lazarettos for the reception of the sick, but in establishing manufactories for the employment of the healthy.[4]

The impending crisis in Ireland prompted Tory prime minister Sir Robert Peel to take a step he had been considering for several years: the repeal of the corn laws. These laws imposed duties on corn imported into the United Kingdom, pushing up its price: this protected landowners from competition and allowed them to keep their prices high. The repeal of the corn laws was a cause espoused by British industrialists, who wanted an ample supply of cheap food for the growing workforce in factories and mines, so that wages could be kept low. The corn laws were repealed some months later amid prolonged and bitter wrangling that cost Peel his political career. The move was of little use to Ireland, for while it lowered the price of imported food, it also cut the price of Irish corn exported to Britain.

Peel also planned a number of relief measures, all to be taken within the confines of the laissez-faire policy. In November 1845 he ordered that £100,000 of Indian corn – maize – be bought in the United States and shipped to Ireland. This was not to be distributed freely to the hungry: rather, it was to be used as a lever to prevent prices rising. Peel's plan was to store the corn and offer it for sale when prices rose. The government planned that the main burden of organising relief would be carried by a network of voluntary local committees, made up of landlords, clergy and other middle-class people, and supervised by a relief commission comprised of government officials. The committees were to collect donations to buy food, which would be sold or, in extreme cases, given away. The government would make financial contributions according to the amount collected. But many committees found it difficult to raise money, because many landlords were unable or unwilling to contribute.

Riots and Starvation

In many parts of the country peasants reacted to the loss of the potato crop by trying to keep their other produce. They refused to pay rent, stole arms, and threatened landlords who refused to help their tenants. In one week in November 1845, notices were posted outside churches in Clare, Limerick, Louth and Cavan telling the people to pay no rent and thrash no corn.

By March 1846, with about three-quarters of the potato crop lost through blight, many people were starving. Lord Monteagle, one of the few enlightened landlords, said that in Clare people were eating food from which 'so putrid and offensive an effluvia issued that in consuming it they were obliged to leave the doors and windows of their cabins open'.[5] By now, too, dysentery and fever had broken out in many places.

Since destitute tenants were unable to pay their rents, many landlords proceeded to evict them and turn the land over to grazing. Troops and police evicted the families and demolished their houses, and the homeless people often took shelter in holes dug in the ground and roofed with sticks and turf.

In March 1846 the government launched a scheme for public works, such as roadbuilding, to be undertaken, so that destitute people could earn money to buy food. This was a traditional method of famine relief. The works were to be funded by government grants and by loans repayable from the rates. But the Board of Works was overwhelmed with proposals, and there were interminable delays before projects were put in motion. Most of the works undertaken were useless. The law stipulated that no works could be financed that would profit individual property-owners, so much-needed agricultural improvements such as drainage projects were not permitted. Instead, many thousands of labourers were set to work breaking stones and building unnecessary roads.

In April there were increasing reports that starving men, women and children were raiding for food, attacking ships, carts and flour mills. The authorities responded by assigning heavy military escorts to food convoys. An official wrote from Waterford on 24 April:

> The barges leave Clonmel once a week for this place, with the export supplies under convoy which, last Tuesday, consisted of 2 guns, 50 cavalry and 80 infantry escorting them on the banks of the Suir as far as Carrick.[6]

In charge of the purse-strings for the entire relief operation was Charles Trevelyan, the top civil servant at the Treasury in London. Trevelyan was the key British official throughout the famine years. Then in his late thirties, he was totally dedicated to laissez-faire principles and also despised the Irish.

In May, as the mood of the destitute labourers became increasingly threatening, Trevelyan decided to open the government depots for the sale of Indian corn. This, he planned, would be a one-off operation: as soon as supplies ran out, the depots would be closed. The depots were besieged by starving people, and by the end of June the supplies were almost exhausted. By now many people in remote districts were nearing death from starvation.

At the end of June, Peel's government fell and was replaced by the Whigs under Lord John Russell. The Whigs were allied in parliament to Daniel O'Connell, but their handling of the famine was to prove callous in the extreme. The new chancellor of the exchequer, Sir Charles Wood, firmly believed, like Trevelyan, that the government should not interfere with private enterprise. Despite pleas from relief committees and government officials in Ireland, the new government pushed ahead with closing down the relief operations. On 8 July Trevelyan turned back a cargo of Indian corn brought by the ship *Sorcière*, saying it was 'not wanted'.

When Trevelyan heard that the new potato crop showed signs of disease, this seemed to him all the more reason for hurrying ahead with closing the food depots. Otherwise, he considered, when people became aware of the crop failure they would demand to be fed. On 17 July he wrote to Sir Randolph Routh, chairman of the Relief Commission:

> The only way to prevent the people from becoming habitually dependent on Government is to bring the operations to a close. The uncertainty about the new crop only makes it more necessary.[7]

At the start of August came total disaster. Almost overnight the entire potato crop, across the whole country, was lost. Father Mathew, a priest well-known as the leader of the temperance movement, wrote to Trevelyan imploring him to take action to feed the people. Father Mathew described how on 27 July: 'I passed from Cork to Dublin and this doomed plant bloomed in all the luxuriance of an abundant harvest.' But when he returned on 3 August:

> I beheld with sorrow one wide waste of putrefying vegetation. In many places the wretched people were sitting on the fences of their decaying gardens, wringing their hands and wailing bitterly the destruction that had left them foodless.[8]

But the government still adamantly refused to import or supply food, causing consternation on all sides in Ireland. Sir Randolph Routh, chairman of the Relief Commission, wrote sharply to Trevelyan on 4 August: 'You cannot answer the cry of want by a quotation from political economy.'[9]

For millions of people, the public works schemes were the only hope of survival. The government had reorganised the schemes, ending all outright grants and making local rate-payers responsible for the full cost. But long-term treasury loans were available, so a deluge of applications came in. Once again there were endless bureaucratic obstacles. Those who did get taken on were paid below the prevailing rate so as not to upset private enterprise. Often workers went unpaid for weeks, labouring on in a starved and exhausted condition.

By the end of September many people were starving and even prosperous eastern districts were running out of food. Prices rose to exorbitant heights. Furious crowds attacked ships laden with food for export, threatened merchants and plundered shops. In response the government formed a mobile force of 2,000 soldiers to quell food riots, and assigned military guards to ships, food depots, and harvest fields. Trevelyan now reluctantly agreed that Indian corn could be purchased in the United States. But it was too late: winter was closing in on the Atlantic seaways, and no imports could reach Ireland till the following spring. By mid-October many thousands of people had nothing to eat but blackberries, cabbage leaves, or nettles, and with the onset of winter even these pathetic supplies would disappear.

Officials all over Ireland pleaded with the government to open the food depots – though in truth they were almost empty. Instead, the government sent more troops to distressed districts. 'Would to God the government would send us food instead of soldiers', a starving inhabitant of a Mayo town was heard to say as a contingent of Hussars arrived.[10] Soon, hundreds were dying. The parish priest of Hollymount, County Mayo, wrote:

> Deaths, I regret to say, innumerable from starvation are occurring every day; the bonds of society are almost dissolved... The pampered officials... removed as they are from these scenes of heart-rending distress, can have no idea of them and don't appear to give themselves much trouble about them – I ask them in the name of humanity, is this state of society to continue and who are responsible for these monstrous evils?[11]

The poet 'Speranza' – Jane Francesca Elgee, later Lady Wilde – wrote:

> Weary men, what reap ye? – Golden corn for the stranger.
> What sow ye? – Human corses that wait for the avenger.
> Fainting forms, hunger-stricken, what see you in the offing?
> Stately ships to bear our food away, amid the stranger's scoffing.
> There's a proud array of soldiers – what do they round your door?
> They guard our masters' granaries from the thin hands of the poor.
> Pale mothers, wherefore weeping? Would to God that we were dead -
> Our children swoon before us, and we cannot give them bread.[12]

Desperate for food, farmers ate their seed corn and seed oats, but the government refused all petitions to supply seed to provide for the next year's crop.

A famine funeral

Then in early November a winter of appalling severity set in. Snow, hail and sleet, driven by icy winds, swept the land,making roads impassable. Labourers on the public works, drenched and frozen, died in increasing numbers of starvation and exposure. Bewildered and panic-stricken country people descended in their thousands on the towns and besieged the public works schemes. By Christmas there were 400,000 on the public works, but they were only a fraction of the destitute. Their wages were hopelessly insufficient to meet the rocketing prices. In Wicklow there were 25,000 paupers and no food. Five thousand beggars roamed the streets of Cork and were dying at the rate of 100 a week. In Belfast, the *News-Letter* reported that 'starving wretches hourly swarm into the streets from the country'.[13]

A government official based in South Armagh reported:

> There are no farming operations going forward in the mountainous district I have visited, and the misery and destitution of the people is extreme...[14]

Meanwhile speculators made fortunes from Indian corn, and the landowning class continued with their social whirl of hunting and parties. Trevelyan wrote on 2 December that 'the great evil with which we have to contend' was 'not the physical evil of the famine, but the moral evil of the selfish, perverse and turbulent character of the people.'[15]

Skibbereen in County Cork was a particularly gruesome scene. While the market was amply supplied with meat, bread and fish, and local landowners creamed off many thousands of pounds in rent, the people had no money to buy food. A prominent Cork magistrate, Nicholas Cummins, visited the district on 15 December 1846 and wrote a horrified letter to the Duke of Wellington:

> I entered some of the hovels... and the scenes which presented themselves were such as no tongue or pen can convey the slightest idea of. In the first, six famished and ghastly skeletons, to all appearance dead, were huddled in a corner on some filthy straw, their sole covering what seemed a ragged horsecloth, their wretched legs hanging about, naked above the knees. I approached with horror, and found by a low moaning they were alive – they were in fever, four children, a woman, and what had once been a man... in a few minutes I was surrounded by at least 200 of such phantoms, such frightful spectres as no words can describe.[16]

Government officials confirmed that people were dying daily in Skibbereen, their corpses often eaten by rats. But still Trevelyan refused all entreaties to send emergency aid, saying that funds must first be raised through local committees. But, as Trevelyan knew, no relief committee was operating in Skibbereen.

On 24 December a Board of Works official, Captain Wynne, visited Clare Abbey, where the works had been closed down after an attack on the principal overseer. Pleading for the re-opening of the works, Wynne wrote:

> altho' a man not easily moved, I confess myself unmanned by the intensity and extent of the suffering I witnessed more especially among the women and little children, crowds of whom were to be seen scattered over the turnip fields like a flock of famishing crows, devouring the raw turnips, mothers half naked, shivering in the snow and sleet, uttering exclamations of despair while their children were screaming with hunger.[17]

At the end of December, Trevelyan at last agreed that food depots in the west, the worst-hit region, could be opened. But he insisted that the food must be sold at the market price plus five per cent. He refused all pleas to lower the price, and the people, penniless, continued dying.

Government officials later summed up that during the famine years:

> the actually starving people lived upon the carcasses of diseased cattle, upon dogs, and dead horses, but principally on the herbs of the field, nettle tops, wild mustard, and watercresses, and even in some places dead bodies were found with grass in their mouths.[18]

Fever and Emigration

Hard on the heels of starvation came, as always, disease: the killer fevers, typhus and relapsing fever; bacillary dysentery, known as the 'bloody flux' and often fatal; hunger oedema, which grotesquely swells the body; and scurvy, from vitamin C deficiency, which causes teeth to fall out and blood-vessels to burst. Most terrifying of all was typhus. The sufferer's face swells and becomes almost unrecognisable, the temperature rises sharply and delirium sets in, accompanied by incontinence, a rash, agonising sores and sometimes gangrene. The sufferer has fearful nightmares, the tongue trembles and the limbs twitch. The body gives off a very unpleasant smell, characteristic of the disease.

Both typhus and relapsing fever – which is characterised by repeated bouts of high fever and vomiting – are spread by lice, but this was not understood until many years later. Today, both diseases can be cured with antibiotics. These fevers were an ordinary feature of life for the Irish poor in the last century, and in time of famine they spread like wildfire. The destitute people were often filthy, unable to change their clothes or heat water for washing, and the wandering homeless carried the fevers to every district. People who were not themselves louse-ridden were easily infected with typhus, since a tiny deposit of excrement from a stricken louse was enough to spread the disease, and many middle-class people who aided famine victims themselves caught typhus and died.

By early 1847 the fever epidemic was raging throughout the country and government health inspectors reported on 'appalling, awful, heart-sickening' scenes in hopelessly inadequate hospitals. Fever spread rapidly in workhouses, reaching a peak in April when in just one week 2,613 inmates were officially reported to have died. Dublin and Belfast were severely hit and in both cities the epidemic continued well into the following year. In Belfast 13,678 fever victims were admitted to hospital in 1847. The *News-Letter* reported on 20 July:

> It is really melancholy to witness the frequency of funerals passing through the streets, and conveyances from the hospitals, each laden with from three to six coffins, daily wending their way towards the burying-grounds... It is now a thing of daily occurrence to see haggard, sallow,

and emaciated beings, stricken down by fever, or debility from actual want, stretched prostrate upon the footways of our streets and bridges...[19]

Panic-stricken by the spectre of famine and fever, tens of thousands rushed to emigrate. Some landlords took advantage of their tenants' desperation to clear them off the land, offering them a few shillings for their passage-money. Others frightened their tenants into leaving by threatening them with court action for non-payment of rent, so that thousands fled rather than risk imprisonment.

Liverpool, the nearest English port, was deluged with emigrants, while many others went to Glasgow or South Wales. In Liverpool in December 1846 more than 13,000 Irish paupers were receiving relief, compared to less than 1,000 the year before, and by February 1847 the number was over 23,000, of whom nearly 15,000 were children. By June, 300,000 destitute Irish had arrived in Liverpool in five months, more than doubling the population. But misery accompanied them. Crammed into damp and dirty cellars and lodging-houses, 60,000 people developed typhus, of whom many died, while 2,500 died of dysentery and diarrhoea.

Most emigrants wanted to go to the United States, and all who could muster the fare headed across the Atlantic. But the US government, aiming to stem the flow of paupers, imposed strict controls on the number of passengers ships could carry, so that fares were high. Instead, most trans-Atlantic emigrants went to British North America (later Canada), hoping later to cross the border into the US.

For most, emigration proved no escape from their nightmare. Frantic to leave their doomed country, they embarked in 'coffin ships', which were grossly overcrowded, lacking adequate water and provisions, without toilet facilities and often old and unseaworthy. To make matters worse, the fever went with them. Stephen de Vere, who took a steerage passage to Quebec in order to witness the conditions, described what he saw:

> Hundreds of poor people, men, women and children, of all ages from the drivelling idiot of 90 to the babe just born, huddled together, without light, without air, wallowing in filth, and breathing a foetid atmosphere, sick in body, dispirited in heart... the fevered patients lying between the sound... by their agonised ravings disturbing those around them...[20]

The authorities in Quebec required all arriving passenger ships to put in at Grosse Isle, a beautiful island 30 miles down the St Lawrence river, where there was a small quarantine station. The first ship to reach the St Lawrence after the ice cleared was the *Syria*, which arrived on 17 May. Of the *Syria*'s 241 passengers, 84 had fever, and nine had died on the voyage.

Ship after ship arrived, all carrying fever victims. On 26 May, 30 ships, with 10,000 emigrants on board, were waiting at Grosse Isle. Five days later there were 40 ships waiting in a line two miles down the St Lawrence;

over 1,000 fever victims were on Grosse Isle and the same number were on the ships, waiting to be taken off. Conditions on the ships grew worse as they waited. A medical officer on Grosse Isle recorded visiting such ships, 'I have seen a stream of foul air issuing from the hatches as dense and as palpable as seen on a foggy day from a dung heap.'[21]

Conditions in the sheds and tents on Grosse Isle were appalling. Altogether in 1847 at least 5,300 people died there, while many more went on upriver only to die in Quebec, Montreal, Kingston and Toronto. Of the more than 100,000 emigrants who took ship from Irish and British ports for British North America in 1847, more than a third died: 17,000 died on the voyage, mostly of typhus, while another 21,000 died soon after they arrived.

On 8 February 1847 Daniel O'Connell, old and sick, made a last, barely audible plea to the House of Commons:

> Ireland is in your hands, she is in your power. If you don't save her, she can't save herself; and I solemnly call upon you to recollect that I predict, with the sincerest conviction, that one-fourth of her population will perish unless you come to her relief.[22]

Benjamin Disraeli later recalled him as 'a feeble old man muttering at a table.'[23] O'Connell's all-too-accurate warning was disregarded and he died three months later.

The government had by now decided to shift the entire burden of famine relief onto Irish ratepayers. The plan was drastic: instead of earning wages through the public works, with which they could buy food, the destitute would have to go into workhouses, and the additional expense would have to be met from the rates. This was, as many warned, an impossible requirement in a country ravaged by famine where rates were very difficult to collect at the best of times.

During the spring and early summer of 1847 the government closed down the public works schemes and – following the example of the Quakers and other charities – opened soup kitchens as an interim measure. But in many places the works closed down before the soup kitchens were ready. The soup was humiliating to collect and often of poor quality, but it staved off starvation and by July over three million people were receiving rations. But their respite was short-lived. In June the Irish Poor Law Extension Act became law, enabling the government to transfer the destitute to the new system. In August the food depots were closed down, followed by the soup kitchens.

The government refused to heed the warnings of impending disaster. Though the new potato crop was not blighted, only a fraction of the normal crop had been planted because of the shortage of seed potatoes. Grain was abundant, but once again the farmers dared not eat it. A senior official told Trevelyan on 4 September, 'The face of the country is covered with ripe corn while the people dread starvation. The grain will go out of the country, sold to pay rent'.[24] But the government refused to alter its course. Trevelyan wrote:

> It is my opinion that too much has been done for the people. Under such treatment the people have grown worse instead of better, and we must now try what independent exertion can do...[25]

The impoverished Choctaw Indians of Oklahoma showed much more compassion. Seventeen years earlier, 14,000 of them had died on their way across swamps after being cheated out of their ancestral lands by US president Andrew Jackson. Now prospering, in March 1847 they contributed 170 dollars to a fund for the starving poor in Ireland.[26]

To deter applicants, Trevelyan made the new relief scheme as unattractive as possible. The able-bodied could obtain relief only if they lived in the workhouse, so the aged, infirm and children were turned out to make way for them, and were given 'outdoor relief' in the form of cooked food only. Only those with less than a quarter of an acre qualified for relief, so many gave up their land in order to gain entry to the workhouses, and the new law was nicknamed the 'eviction-made-easy' act.

The utter inadequacy of the new system was soon clear. The workhouses were administered by 130 poor law unions, most of which were responsible for vast areas. By August, 122 of the unions were already in debt. Many workhouses were unable to provide for existing inmates, let alone take in new ones. Yet now many thousands more were to demand entry. But the government still insisted that the funds to run the workhouses must be raised from the rates. In vain Lord Clarendon, the new lord lieutenant, protested on 20 September:

> There are whole districts in Mayo and Donegal and parts of Kerry where people swarm and are even now starving and where there is no landed proprietor to levy on... What is to be done with these hordes? Improve them off the face of the earth, you will say, let them die... but there is *a certain amount of responsibility* attaching to it.[27]

But the government remained unbending and rate collection went ahead ruthlessly, with collectors seizing even the clothes and tools of paupers and workhouse inmates. On 23 October Clarendon begged the prime minister, Lord John Russell:

> whatever may be the anger of people or parliament in England, whatever may be the state of trade or credit, Ireland *cannot be left to her own resources*, they are manifestly insufficient, we are not to let the people die of starvation, we must not believe that rebellion is impossible.[28]

But Russell refused to change course, replying:

> The state of Ireland for the next few months must be one of great suffering. Unhappily the agitation for repeal has contrived to destroy nearly all sympathy in this country.[29]

Some bankrupt workhouses were closed down and the inmates expelled, to live in holes in the hillside. But still the government insisted that the money must come from the rates, which must be collected by any cost. The chancellor of the exchequer, Charles Wood, wrote to Clarendon on 22 November:

> Arrest, remand, do anything you can, send horse, foot and dragoons, all the world will applaud you, and I should not be at all squeamish as to what I did, to the verge of the law, and a little beyond.[30]

By mid-December, tens of thousands were besieging the workhouses, and soon 150,000 were packed into temporary shelters, many of them disused warehouses without sanitation, heating or water. Dead bodies lay by the roadsides and in bankrupt workhouses people starved.

Since landlords were liable for the rate on the smallest holdings, valued at £4 and under, they rushed to evict the tenants. A woman evicted from an estate in County Mayo described in a formal statement how the landlord with two 'drivers' – men employed to drive away cattle seized for rent or rates and to evict tenants – came a few days before Christmas:

> The people were all turned out of doors and the roofs of their houses pulled down. That night they made a bit of a tent, or shelter, of wood and straw; that however the drivers threw down and drove them from the place... It would have 'pitied the sun' to look at them as they had to go head foremost under hail and storm. It was a night of high wind and storm and their wailing could be heard at a great distance. They implored the drivers to allow them to remain a short time as it was so near the time of festival but they would not...[31]

Other landlords achieved the same result by shipping off their unwanted tenants to British North America. This made it virtually impossible for them to return, and was much cheaper than maintaining them in the workhouse. Most notorious of these landlords was Lord Palmerston, then foreign secretary and later prime minister. Half of his income came from his Irish estates. Palmerston's view was that the changes needed in Irish agriculture required 'a long and continued and systematic ejectment of smallholders and of squatting cottiers'.[32] Palmerston's agents emigrated over 2,000 people from his Sligo estates in 1847, many of them old, sick, or widows with children. Few were in a fit state to work and many arrived nearly naked and had to be clothed by charity before they could leave the ships. The citizens of Quebec and of St John, New Brunswick, where the ships docked, protested furiously to the British government about Palmerston's action.

Towards the end of 1847, six landlords were killed and another horribly injured. Fearing a rising, Clarendon, the lord lieutenant, pressed the government into passing the Crime and Outrage (Ireland) Act: this allowed emergency measures to be taken in disturbed districts, and became law in December 1847.

In parliament, only 18 members voted outright against the bill. The opposition was led not by the Repeal MPs – some of whom even voted in favour of the bill – but by Feargus O'Connor, who was by now the Chartist MP for Nottingham.

An extra 15,000 troops were sent to Ireland, and a number of landlords left the country. A government official reported: ' The personal insecurity of all property owners is so hideous that the impression is of being *in an enemy country*'.[33] Another official stated: 'Not one of the proprietors or their agents dare go out alone, even in daylight, and everyone is armed to the teeth.'[34] But as events of the next few months were to prove, the peasants had neither the leadership, nor the organisation, nor the physical strength to mount a full-scale insurrection against British rule.

The Young Irelanders

After the débâcle at Clontarf in 1843, the Repeal Association had fallen into disarray. Daniel O'Connell was a broken man and his son John, a sly and ambitious person of bigoted religious views, became a powerful figure.

Within the Repeal Association, the opposition to the O'Connells was led by a group of enthusiastic young intellectuals around the *Nation* paper. They were dubbed the 'Young Irelanders' because their nationalist vision was similar to that of the revolutionary movements then sweeping Europe: Young Italy, Young Switzerland, Young France and Young Germany.

The Young Irelanders' world-view was most potently expressed by Thomas Davis, who was the chief writer of the *Nation* until his premature death, aged 31, in September 1845. Davis, a Protestant barrister, presented an inspiring image of a future Ireland which would combine the heritages of all its people, Gaels and settlers, Catholics and Protestants, in a vibrant, bilingual and prosperous culture. Many of his ballads – such as 'A Nation Once Again' – are still sung. Also important in spreading the new patriotic sentiment were many women poets who contributed to the Nation, including 'Speranza' and Mary Kelly, known as 'Eva', daughter of a Galway country gentleman.

The 'tone' of the *Nation*, as a current witticism neatly put it, was 'Wolfe Tone'. The Young Irelanders shared with the United Irishmen a cosmopolitan outlook, and the belief that Ireland must become completely independent of England, by force if necessary. They were also vehemently non-sectarian, and ran into a storm of outrage from the Catholic hierarchy – backed by Daniel O'Connell, who had done an about-turn on the issue – when they supported Peel's proposal for non-denominational colleges: a plan which the bishops condemned as a 'Satanic scheme'.

The Young Irelanders were strongly opposed to the Repealers' pact with the Whigs, and after the Whigs returned to power in July 1846, the O'Connells tried to bring them under control. After an acrimonious dispute, the Young Irelanders seceded from the Repeal Association. In January 1847 they set up a rival organisation, the Irish Confederation, with William Smith O'Brien, a Protestant landlord and MP, at its head.

The Young Irelanders were full of revolutionary rhetoric but they were isolated from the mass of the people: they had no aid from the Catholic church's network, except from a few sympathetic priests, and on the land question they did not wish to side outright with the peasants. They wanted to win the landlords to their side, regarding them as the natural leaders of the people, and they refused any link with the Chartists in England or Ireland.

A lone radical voice was that of James Fintan Lalor, whose father was a prosperous Catholic farmer and leader of the anti-tithe movement in the 1830s. Lalor was frail and hunchbacked, but tenacious in spirit and with a powerful and humane intelligence. He recognised that the Young Ireland leaders were fatally hampered by their pro-landlord stance. He had no time for the repeal movement – 'a leaky collier-smack, with a craven crew to man her'.[35] He believed independence meant nothing unless the people of Ireland regained control of the land, and wrote: 'My object is to repeal the Conquest – not any part or portion, but the whole and entire conquest of seven hundred years'.[36]

The land was what the peasants would fight for, and force was justified while England continued to use it. Lalor declared:

> Let England pledge not to argue the question by the prison, the convict-ship or the halter; and I will readily pledge not to argue it in any form of physical logic. But dogs tied and stones loose is no bargain. Let the stones be given up; or unmuzzle the wolf-dog.[37]

As for property rights, his view was clear:

> I acknowledge no right of property in eight thousand persons, be they noble or ignoble, which takes away all rights of property, security, independence, and existence itself, from a population of eight millions, and stands in bar to all the political rights of the island, and all the social rights of its inhabitants. I acknowledge no right of property which takes the food of millions and gives them a famine – which denies to the peasant the right of a home, and concedes, in exchange, the right of a workhouse... Against them I assert the true and indefeasible right of property – the right of our people to live in this land, and possess it, – to live in it in comfort, security, and independence, and to live in it by their own labour, on their own land, as God and nature meant them to do.[38]

Lalor believed that the people of Ireland must become the collective owners of the land, ousting the English conquerors. He declared:

> The principle I state, and mean to stand upon, is this, that the entire ownership of Ireland, moral and material, up to the sun and down to the centre, is vested of right in the people of Ireland; that they, and none but they are the land-owners and law-makers of this island; that all laws are null and void not made by them, and all titles to land invalid not conferred or confirmed by them; and that this full right of ownership may and ought to be asserted and enforced by any and all means which God has put in the power of man.[39]

Lalor urged that as a first step the tenants should refuse to pay rents and should resist eviction. He argued that they should pay no rents until, through a national convention, the people had decided what rents should be paid and whom they should be paid to. In his view, they should decide 'that those rents shall be paid *to themselves*, the people, for public purposes, and for behoof and benefit of them, the entire general people.'[40] Lalor thought that the existing social system should be replaced, and that Ireland should have

> a new Constitution, under which the natural capacity of this country would be put into effective action; the resources of its land, labour, and capital developed and made available; its slumbering and decaying energies of mind and muscle excited, directed, and employed...[41]

Lalor wrote repeatedly to the Young Irelanders in 1847 but, with the exception of John Mitchel and a few of his supporters, they would not listen. Lalor wrote later:

> They wanted an alliance with the landowners. They chose to consider them as Irishmen, and imagined they could induce them to hoist the green flag. They wished to preserve an Aristocracy. They desired, not a *democratic*, but a merely *national* revolution.[42]

Mitchel, a passionate and impetuous Ulster Protestant, adopted Lalor's ideas and tried to convince the Confederation of the need for the people to unite to stop food leaving the country. When he failed, he left the Confederation in early February 1848 and founded a paper, the *United Irishman*, through which he preached open rebellion. Mitchell began and ended his political life as a conservative, but was impelled during the famine years into a fiery radicalism. Later he recalled:

> a kind of sacred wrath took possession of a few Irishmen at this period. They could endure the horrible scene no longer, and resolved to cross the British car of conquest, though it should crush them to atoms.[43]

But his anger was rhetorical rather than practical: he failed to take account of the famine-stricken state of the people or to make any serious preparations for revolution, preferring to trust in improvisation and spontaneity.

Then on 24 February 1848 came an event that shook Europe, when a popular rising in Paris overthrew the French monarchy. Risings followed in nearly every major European city, and crowned heads fled. In Ireland people celebrated with bonfires and illuminations, and the Confederation's leaders were instantly converted to the need for rebellion.

The British government was seriously alarmed, fearing a rising not only in Ireland but also in Britain, where the Chartists were once more buoyant. They were secretly plotting insurrection, as well as planning a mass petition to parliament to be presented by a 'monster procession' on 10 April. The Irish 'confederates' now openly aligned themselves with the Chartists, promising to march in the procession 'under the green flag of Erin', and on St Patrick's Day, 17 March, Thomas Meagher spoke alongside Feargus O'Connor at a public meeting in Manchester. In nervous anticipation, the authorities poured 10,000 troops into Dublin and filled London with 7,000 soldiers and some 85,000 special constables to augment the 4,000 police. They rushed through parliament a new law, known as the Treason Felony Act, which made it an offence punishable by transportation to say anything that threatened the crown or parliament. They banned the Chartists' monster procession, and the Chartists, faced with streets full of police, soldiers and cannons, called it off.

In May, John Mitchel was tried and convicted under the Treason Felony Act. Sentenced on 27 May to 14 years' transportation, he was immediately bundled onto a warship waiting in Dublin Bay. After nearly two years in transit on convict ships, Mitchel arrived in Van Diemen's Land in April 1850, and escaped three years later to the United States.

Ten days later the English Chartist Ernest Jones was arrested for a speech he had made on 4 June in London's Tower Hamlets district. Jones had exhorted his audience to organise, and had pictured a political upheaval which would result in John Mitchel and the transported Chartist John Frost being brought back from their political exile, and the home secretary and prime minister being transported in their place. He said: 'Only preparation – only organisation is wanted, and the Green Flag shall float over Downing Street, and St. Stephen's.'[44] Jones, along with five other Chartists, was sentenced to two years' imprisonment for seditious speech.

Among the first English victims of the Treason Felony Act was another prominent London Chartist, William Cuffay, a black tailor whose African grandfather had been sold into slavery in the West Indies. Cuffay was arrested in August 1848 and he too was transported to Van Diemen's Land. In his speech from the dock he said: 'I feel no disgrace at being called a felon... I am almost one of the first victims after glorious Mitchel to fall under that Act.'[45]

Both Mitchel and the British authorities expected that his conviction would prompt an attempt to rescue him, which in turn would spark a rising. But the Young Ireland leaders dampened their followers' ardour, arguing that insufficient preparations had been made.

In early July, three of the leaders, Charles Gavan Duffy, Michael Doheny and Thomas Meagher, were arrested in different places. In each case, crowds of people attempted to rescue them. But, unable to respond to the popular momentum, they insisted on behaving according to the law and refused to be rescued. As a result, they demoralised their supporters.

Finally the Young Irelanders were pushed willy-nilly into rebellion when, on 22 July, the government suspended Habeas Corpus and ordered the arrest of all the leaders. In these circumstances, they considered, honour demanded that they rebel. William Smith O'Brien went to Kilkenny and Tipperary to rally support, and at first thousands of peasants turned out to follow him. But no arrangements had been made to feed them – a necessity in time of famine – and many deserted. Smith O'Brien was also shackled by his pro-landlord sympathies: he refused to allow his followers to seize carts of grain, and forbade them to cut down trees for barricades without first asking permission from the trees' owners.

In the pages of the *Nation* – edited since Gavan Duffy's arrest by his sister-in-law Margaret Callan – Speranza rallied Irishmen to fight:

> Oh! for a hundred thousands muskets glittering brightly in the light of Heaven, and the monumental barricades stretching across each of our noble streets, made desolate by England… The Castle is the key-stone of English power; take it, destroy it, burn it…[46]

That issue was the last: the police raided the offices and the printers were jailed. The authorities later used Speranza's editorial as evidence against Gavan Duffy in his trial.

The enterprise ended in fiasco on 30 July in a skirmish at Ballingarry between police and the insurgents. The rebels fled, and William Smith O'Brien was later captured and deported to Van Diemen's Land, along with Thomas Meagher, Patrick O'Donohoe and Terence Bellew McManus. But the embers of revolt were not dead. Fintan Lalor was released early from prison because of his wretched health, and soon he and a group of young veterans of 1848 began planning another rising. Among them were John O'Leary and Thomas Clarke Luby, who were later to lead the next generation of revolutionaries.

Most of Lalor's supporters were from the artisan class. On 11 September 1849 a few scattered groups rose, but without success. Lalor, never a healthy person, died on 27 December. The *Times* said of him:

> Mr Lalor was undoubtedly one of the (if not the) ablest, as well as most dangerous, of those men who perverted abilities of a high order to the very worst of purposes.[47]

Chilling calculation

Meanwhile the relentless misery of the famine continued. In July 1848, as the Young Irelanders tried to plan rebellion, blight reappeared in the potato fields. By October, the crop failure proved total, with potatoes everywhere once again reduced to a stinking, rotten mess. The people, already ruined, faced their worst winter yet.

Landlords continued evicting their destitute tenants, who wandered half-naked in their tens of thousands in the winter weather, starving and diseased, sheltering in rough lean-tos or pouring into towns. A new wave of emigration began, but this time it was only the more prosperous who could afford to go. Huge tracts of land lay deserted and in the towns many shops were shuttered up, abandoned by their departing owners.

A deserted village

The government remained unmoved, refusing to restart food aid and ending grants to distressed poor law unions. They even refused to continue to feed 200,000 destitute children, formerly cared for by the British Association, a charity whose funds had now run out. Trevelyan and others in the British establishment assessed the effects of the famine with the cold logic of the rising business class. They saw emigration as an economic bonus. Trevelyan wrote:

> I do not know how farms are to be consolidated if small farmers do not emigrate, and by acting for the purpose of keeping them at home, we should be defeating our own object. We must not complain of what we really want to obtain. If small farmers go, and then landlords are induced to sell portions of their estates to persons who will invest capital, we shall at last arrive at something like a satisfactory settlement of the country.[48]

Trevelyan considered that Ireland should be left to 'the operation of natural causes'. In vain did Lord Clarendon, the lord lieutenant, protest that this meant 'wholesale deaths from starvation and disease'.[49] In private, influential members of the establishment regarded even deaths by starvation with chilling calculation. Benjamin Jowett, master of Balliol College, Oxford, was referring to one of the government's economic advisers, Nassau Senior, when he said:

I have always felt a certain horror of political economists since I heard
one of them say that he feared the famine of 1848 in Ireland would not kill
more than a million people, and that would scarcely be enough to do
much good.[50]

Senior British officials on the ground in Ireland, however, were appalled
by the government's policy. In March 1849 Mr Twisleton, the Dublin-
based chief Poor Law commissioner, resigned because, Clarendon told the
prime minister, he was placed in a position 'which no man of honour and
humanity can endure'. Clarendon wrote:

he thinks that the destitution here is so horrible, and the indifference of
the House of Commons to it is so manifest, that he is an unfit agent of a
policy which must be one of extermination...[51]

Even when an epidemic of Asiatic cholera swept Ireland, the government
refused to advance funds. On 26 April Clarendon made yet another desperate
plea to the prime minister, Lord John Russell:

I don't think there is another legislature in Europe that would disregard
such suffering as now exists in the west of Ireland, or coldly persist in a
policy of extermination.[52]

But his appeals had no effect.

The same week in April, in the workhouse in the small town of Ballinasloe,
County Galway, 226 people died. The following week, 490 died there. An
eye-witness wrote from Ballinrobe, County Mayo:

The streets are daily thronged with moving skeletons. The fields are strewn
with dead... The curse of Russell, more terrible than the curse of Cromwell,
is upon us...[53]

During and after the famine, a frightening silence and melancholy fell
upon the country, a mark of the profound trauma inflicted on the people.
The census for 1851 noted:

the once proverbial gaiety and light-heartedness of the peasant people
seemed to have vanished completely, and village merriment or marriage
festival was no longer heard or seen throughout the regions desolated by
the intensity and extent of the famine...[54]

George Petrie, who collected traditional music, wrote in the 1850s:

'The land of song' was no longer tuneful; or, if a human sound met the
traveller's ear, it was only that of the feeble and despairing wail for the
dead. This awful, unwonted silence, which, during the famine and
subsequent years, almost everywhere prevailed, struck more fearfully
upon their imaginations, as many Irish gentlemen informed me, and gave
them a deeper feeling of the desolation with which the country had been
visited than any other circumstance which had forced itself upon their
attention...[55]

It is impossible to say precisely how many died because many deaths went unrecorded. The 1851 census estimated that between 1841 and 1851, Ireland's population dropped by two and a half million people. In the worst famine years, from 1845 to 1849, about a million people died of starvation and disease, with the highest death toll among children under ten. Between 1845 and 1855 almost two million people emigrated to North America and Australia, but many of them also died during or soon after their voyage. Some 750,000 more went to Britain. Those who died or fled were overwhelmingly the rural poor. The 1851 census noted that all the counties except Dublin had decreased in population, and that Connacht had the highest loss. Many of those affected were Irish-speakers, and the famine proved a devastating blow to the language.

Before the 'great hunger', Ireland's people made up one-third of the population of the 'British Isles'. By 1851, with six-and-a-half million, they made up just under a quarter. In the next fifty years, the population of Britain almost doubled, reaching 37 million in 1901. But the population of Ireland continued to shrink, falling to four-and-a-half million in 1901, a figure which was scarcely to change in the next eighty years.

Charles Trevelyan was knighted in 1848 for his work in the famine in Ireland. He went on to reorganise the British civil service, creating a bastion against encroaching democracy, and later applied the same thinking to the reorganisation of the imperial administration in India. Sir Charles Wood, too, went on to serve in India, where he became secretary of state.

Although by 1850 the worst of the famine was over, many thousands were still destitute, and hunger and poverty continued. The authorities had done nothing to extend the range of crops available to the peasants, nor to protect tenants in their relations with landlords. While rejecting bills that would have improved the tenants' lot, the government put through in 1849 the Encumbered Estates Act, which made it much easier to sell bankrupt estates. In ten years, more than 3,000 such estates changed hands, many of them bought at rock-bottom prices by members of the Irish middle class – land agents, solicitors and large shopkeepers – whose main interest was in making high profits.

They were, if anything, even more unscrupulous than the landlords they replaced. They had no sense of feudal responsibility for the tenants and were not interested in improving the land. They did not hesitate to rack-rent or evict, and in the years after the famine, a wave of evictions, often at their behest, swept the countryside. In the 'great clearances' of 1849-53, some 47,000 families – more than 239,000 people – lost their homes.

4
The Fenians

The terrible experience of the famine left many Irish people – both those still in Ireland and those now scattered across the world – with a bitter determination never to allow the same circumstances to arise again. John Denvir, who joined the Irish revolutionary movement in Britain, recalled his boyhood in Liverpool:

> Young as I was, I shall never forget the days of the famine, for Liverpool, more than any other place outside of Ireland itself, felt its appalling effects. It was the main artery through which the flying people poured to escape from what seemed a doomed land. Many thousands could get no further, and the condition of the already overcrowded parts of the town in which our people lived became terrible, for the wretched people brought with them the dreaded famine fever, and Liverpool became a plague-stricken city... Our own family were nearly left orphans, for both father and mother were stricken down by the fever, but happily recovered.
>
> It will not be wondered at that one who saw these things, even though he was only a boy, should feel it a duty stronger than life itself to reverse the system of misgovernment which was responsible.[1]

For the mass of the people in Ireland, the most urgent issue was land tenure: how to get protection against eviction and rack-renting. In 1850 tenants' defence societies sprang up in various parts of the country, including Ulster. In Ulster, landlords trying to attract tenants had in the past offered them greater security than elsewhere, and they were regarded as owning the improvements they made to the land. But now this 'Ulster custom' was threatened and tenants wanted it to be protected by law.

In August 1850 a national campaign, the Irish Tenant League, was launched at a 'tenant right' conference in Dublin. This was a remarkable gathering, spanning north and south, Presbyterian and Catholic. The moving spirit behind it was the former Young Ireland leader Charles Gavan Duffy of the *Nation*; others prominent at the meeting included Frederick Lucas, founder of the Catholic *Tablet*, and the Presbyterian Dr James McKnight, proprietor of the *Banner of Ulster*. Also present were tenants, a few liberal landlords,

Catholic priests and Presbyterian ministers. The meeting called for the 'three Fs': fixity of tenure, fair rents and freedom of sale – the right of tenants to sell their interest in the property. They also decided to press all parliamentary candidates to pledge themselves to 'independent opposition': this meant remaining independent of all British parties and opposing any party which rejected the tenants' demands.

But the momentum of the Tenants' League was soon undermined, sabotaged by the unscrupulous ambition of a small group of Irish MPs. The leaders of this group were John Sadleir, a very wealthy self-made financier, and William Keogh, a lawyer-turned-demagogue.

In 1850 the Vatican decided to restore the organisation of the Catholic church in England after a lapse of two-and-a-half centuries. This involved Catholic archbishops and bishops taking the titles of English places, and created for instance an archbishop of Westminster. This provoked a wave of anti-Catholic bigotry in England, and an Ecclesiastical Titles Bill was put forward to outlaw the Pope's move.

Tenant-right supporters thought the issue should be ignored, since it was likely to promote sectarian division. But Sadleir and Keogh led a vociferous fight against the bill, earning a spurious reputation for patriotism in Ireland, where they were dubbed the 'Irish brigade', while in England they were derisively known as the 'Pope's brass band'. As the focus of agitation in Ireland changed from land to religion, many Protestants left the Tenant League. The Ecclesiastical Titles Bill was passed but was never enforced.

In the 1852 general election Sadleir and Keogh, after initial reluctance, pledged support to 'tenant right' and 'independent opposition'. Altogether 40 MPs who supported this policy were elected, but they did not stay united for long. At the end of 1852 the Irish group joined the opposition in a vote which helped to bring down the Tory government. When the list of the minor appointments in the new government was published, there was widespread dismay in Ireland. Keogh was Irish solicitor-general and Sadleir was a lord of the treasury, and two of their associates had also received offices. They had abandoned the policy of independent opposition and had not even obtained any promise of benefits for Ireland in return.

The Tenant League began to dissolve, its end hastened by the hostility of the powerful archbishop of Dublin, Paul Cullen, who ordered all priests to leave the movement. The fraudulent dealings of the 'Pope's brass band' were soon publicly exposed. In 1856 Sadleir committed suicide, having ruined thousands of Munster farmers who had invested in his bank. Two others were exposed for forgery and fraud. William Keogh, however, became Irish attorney-general and a judge, a ferocious scourge of nationalists: he took to drink and in 1878 he too committed suicide.

By 1856, two-thirds of the MPs elected to support tenant right and independent opposition had gone over to the government. Charles Gavan Duffy, disillusioned, emigrated to Australia: he became governor of Victoria and was, ironically, knighted by Queen Victoria in 1873.

The names of Sadleir and Keogh remained notorious in Ireland for generations. Their corruption and careerism spawned disgust with parliamentary politics and helped rekindle the flames of revolution. John Denvir wrote:

> Their infamous betrayal of the Irish tenantry dashed the hopes and destroyed the union of North and South from which so much was expected, besides creating a distrust in constitutional agitation which lasted for nearly a generation.[2]

Resistance reawakens

In May 1856 the revolutionary Frederick Engels toured Ireland with his companion Mary Burns: she was born in Keady, County Armagh and became a factory worker in Manchester. In a letter to Karl Marx he graphically described what they saw:

> 'Strong measures' are visible in every corner of the country, the government meddles with everything... one can already notice here that the so-called liberty of English citizens is based on the oppression of the colonies. I have never seen so many gendarmes in any country...
>
> The whole of the west, especially in the neighbourhood of Galway, is covered with ruined peasant houses, most of which have only been deserted since 1846. I never thought that famine could have such tangible reality. Whole villages are devastated, and there among them lie the splendid parks of the lesser landlords, who are almost the only people still living there, mostly lawyers. Famine, emigration and clearances together have accomplished this.[3]

By now the first tentative steps towards a new revolutionary organisation were being taken. Exiles from the 1848 rising living in France and America took the initiative. In 1856 James Stephens, a former civil engineer in his early thirties, returned to Ireland from Paris, where he had mixed with revolutionaries and fought at the barricades in 1851. Stephens, a charismatic figure with a self-confidence bordering on arrogance, began touring the country on foot to assess people's opinions and the prospects for another uprising. He earned the name an seabhac siúlach, 'the wandering hawk'. At the suggestion of exiles in America, Stephens and Thomas Clarke Luby founded a new secret organisation on St Patrick's Day, 17 March 1858, in Dublin. The new body, later known as the Irish Republican Brotherhood, aimed to make Ireland an independent republic through force of arms.

Next day Stephens and Luby took to the road and began recruiting. They organised the IRB on the model favoured by continental revolutionaries, a cell-type system of 'circles' commanded by 'centres', with Stephens as the 'head centre'. They rapidly absorbed existing republican groups, such as Jeremiah O'Donovan Rossa's Phoenix Society in West Cork: soon afterwards the Phoenix Society was verbally attacked by the Catholic church and physically suppressed by the authorities. At the same time a similar organisation was set up in New York, the Fenian Brotherhood. It was headed by another 1848 exile, John O'Mahony, whose interest in Irish history inspired him to name the movement after the Fianna, the warriors of ancient Ireland. The name 'Fenians' came to be used for all Irish revolutionaries of the day, including those in Ireland and Britain.

The first impetus to the movement came from the National Petition Movement, which began in about 1859 in response to statements from British political leaders advocating the right of every people to choose their own rulers: a right which of course they did not intend to apply to Ireland. Over 500,000 signatures were collected and presented to parliament, and several of the local committees became part of the Irish Republican Brotherhood.

The reawakening of nationalist feeling was potently demonstrated in 1861 by the funeral of Terence Bellew MacManus. Born in Monaghan, MacManus had become an import-export agent in Liverpool before returning to Ireland to join the 1848 rising. He was transported to Van Diemen's Land and escaped to America, where he died in poverty in San Francisco. His body was returned to Ireland for burial and its journey across the United States was like one long demonstration, as Irish people turned out in their thousands along the route. In New York his remains were placed before the high altar of St Patrick's Cathedral and the archbishop celebrated a requiem mass. The remains were shipped to Cork and thence to Dublin, met by large crowds at every stage. In Dublin a committee dominated by Fenians, but with some opposition from constitutional nationalists, made the arrangements for the funeral procession, aiming to make the event an inspiration for a new generation of nationalists.

The archbishop of Dublin, Dr Paul Cullen, refused to allow the body to lie in state at the cathedral: he explained later that since the funeral 'was intended as a declaration in favour of the rebellion of 1848', to allow the body into the cathedral would have been 'giving sanction to revolutionary principles which are destroying religion everywhere they prevail'.[4] John Denvir wrote that Cullen's action

> deeply stung many whose orthodoxy was beyond question. To them it seemed that the Irish people and their cause were as nothing in his eyes, compared to the temporal advantages the church might gain from the British government. The action... was, undoubtedly, instrumental in making more Fenians than the efforts of all the 'centres', from James Stephens downwards, for they held that here was the fact plainly brought before Irishmen, that they were slaves in their own land.[5]

The remains were taken instead to the Mechanics' Institute, where vast crowds, including many priests, paid their respects. Then on 10 November tens of thousands from city and country followed the hearse through bleak, wet streets to Glasnevin cemetery.

A flow of recruits

The enthusiasm created by the MacManus funeral brought a flow of recruits into the Irish Republican Brotherhood. John Devoy, a peasant's son who was to be an indefatigable Fenian organiser for more than half a century, recalled that he had read about the funeral in a tent in Algeria, where he was serving in the French Foreign Legion in order to get military experience. He wrote:

> when I returned to Dublin in 1862... I was amazed at the extraordinary change which had taken place in the spirit of the country. It marked a turning point in the history of the movement, and Fenianism made rapid progress thereafter.[6]

Although several of its leaders came from middle-class backgrounds, the movement's overwhelming appeal was to workers in the towns and labourers and small farmers in the countryside. The well-to-do, fearing its militancy, stayed away, and the Catholic hierarchy remained vociferously hostile.

The movement was strongest in the towns, and its formation coincided with an upsurge in labour agitation, in particular a vehement two-year struggle among bakers in many towns to limit Sunday work and night work, particularly for under-18s. In Dublin, where more than 8,000 members were soon signed up, the chief recruiting grounds were the trade unions and the big drapery establishments: in the absence of an industrial working class, shop assistants were the most radical element in the towns. In the northeast the movement had a strong organisation in both Belfast and County Down. John Devoy observed that in Newtownards the tradition of the United Irishmen seemed to be still alive: the Fenian 'centre' was a Presbyterian linen manufacturer, while the membership was 'about evenly divided between Catholics, Presbyterians and Episcopalians'.[7]

The IRB also recruited extensively in England and Scotland, where Irish artisans were the backbone of the organisation. The main channel for recruitment was the Brotherhood of St Patrick, which had branches in many provincial towns. This body's single aim was 'to compass the union of Irishmen for the achievement of Irish independence', while the sole qualification for membership was 'honest devotion to Irish nationality, based on the conviction that no foreign power has any right to make laws for Ireland.'[8]

By 1865, according to James Stephens' estimates, there were 80,000 IRB members in Ireland, England, Scotland and Wales, plus a further 15,000 in the British army. These trained soldiers were critical to the success of a rising. Many had considerable experience and had served in far-flung parts of the British empire, including China, Africa and India. Some 8,000 of the soldier Fenians were serving in Ireland itself, making nearly a third of the 25,000 troops stationed there.

The first Fenian organiser in the British army was 'Pagan' O'Laoghari, who swore in thousands of soldiers. Pagan was dedicated, somewhat eccentric, and warmly regarded by his colleagues. He described himself as a 'hereditary rebel and Milesian pagan', and considered the pre-Christian Gaelic ways much preferable to Roman Catholicism. He dropped his given name, Patrick, because of his objections to St Patrick, who, he contended, had demoralised the Gaels and laid them open to foreign conquest. O'Laoghari was born in Cork and then studied for the priesthood in America. In 1846, aged about 20, he scaled the walls of the college to enlist in a regiment going to serve in the Mexican war. During a battle he was hit on the head by a spent ball: an incident which his more orthodox friends invoked to account for his unusual views about religion.

Many other Fenians questioned the church's political stance, if not its theology. The hierarchy and the Fenians were constantly at loggerheads. As soon as the new movement got underway in the early 1860s, the church, along with the papers run by constitutional nationalists, attacked it. Confessional boxes were shut to Fenians; priests denounced readers and sellers of the organisation's paper, the *Irish People*, engineered the dismissal of Fenian schoolteachers, and encouraged people to turn informer. The Fenians responded by, in John O'Leary's words, waging 'a steady war against what came to be called "Priests in Politics."' The *Irish People*, usually through the pen of Charles Kickham, an orthodox Catholic, repeatedly repudiated the church's interference. In what turned out to be the paper's last issue, Kickham wrote:

> We have over and over declared it was our wish that people should respect and be guided by their clergy in spiritual matters. But when priests turn the altar into a platform; when it is pronounced a "mortal sin" to read the *Irish People*, a "mortal sin" even to *wish* that Ireland should be free; when priests actually call upon the people to turn informers... when, in a word, bishops and priests are doing the work of the enemy, we believe it is our duty to tell the people that the bishops and priests may be bad politicians and worse Irishmen.[9]

O'Leary, the paper's editor, stopped going to mass and described himself as belonging to the 'broad church'. He remained strongly opposed to 'priests in politics' to the end of his life.

Recruits in America

By 1861 the famine emigration had brought the Irish-born population of America to nearly one million. During the civil war of 1861 to 1865, some 200,000 Irish-Americans fought in both armies, though mainly in the Union army of the North. Many of them enlisted with the idea of getting military training which they could later use to fight for Ireland's freedom. The Fenians organised openly in the Union army with the blessing of the generals. The Union side had no love for England, most of whose landowners and capitalists stood solidly behind the Southern slave-owners.

With the end of the civil war in May 1865, many thousands of Irish-American soldiers were released from service, clamouring for action in Ireland. That year, the Fenian Brotherhood sent some 150 commissioned officers to Ireland. All over Ireland, Fenians were confidently preparing for a rising: their leader, James Stephens, had repeatedly declared that 1865 would be the 'year of action'. But now he procrastinated, worried by the failure of arms and money to arrive from America.

The delay was fatal. The British government, realising that a formidable movement was burgeoning beneath their noses, moved to crush it. On 15 September 1865 a strong force of police raided the offices of the *Irish People* in Dublin, seized the paper and arrested everyone on the premises. These included the editor, John O'Leary, Thomas Clarke Luby and Jeremiah O'Donovan Rossa. O'Leary and Luby were later sentenced to 20 years each for treason, while Rossa was sentenced to life. Stephens was eventually arrested on 11 November, along with three others including the writer Charles Kickham, who was virtually blind and deaf as a result of a childhood accident with gunpowder and was to suffer greatly in prison.

A fortnight later, on 24 November, Stephens was dramatically rescued from Dublin's Richmond prison in an operation carried out by the prison hospital steward and a nightwatchman, and organised on the outside by the Irish-American Colonel Kelly. Stephens was spirited out of his cell, over the prison wall and into the house of a staunch supporter, Mrs Boland, who had agreed to shelter him. The successful rescue brought jubilation. Devoy recalled:

> The people were wild with delight. Men who had till then looked with open hostility or cold indifference on Fenianism were seized with a sudden enthusiasm. They shook hands with their Fenian acquaintances in the streets and congratulated them on the victory. It was the one proud day of the Fenian movement. The Government had been beaten in their own stronghold, and not a man ever suffered the loss of a hair.[10]

Devoy considered that the time was ripe for insurrection: 'Had Stephens been ready to give the word then he could have got five followers for the one that would have answered his call at any previous time.'[11] But Stephens once again hesitated, unnerved by a split in the American organisation and the consequent failure to send military aid. Morale deteriorated and soon the authorities again moved against the organisation. The American officers in Ireland urged a rising regardless, but Stephens overrode them. His position of supreme authority was, in Devoy's view, the 'chief defect' of the organisation.

In January 1866 the extent of Fenian subversion in the army finally dawned on the British authorities. On 17 February the Habeas Corpus Act was suspended – the suspension was rushed through both Houses of Parliament and signed by Queen Victoria all in one day. Within 24 hours, several hundred people were arrested, and in a few weeks the jails were overflowing with 3,000 prisoners. The chance of success was lost. Devoy wrote:

> I do not say that an insurrection in 1865, or during the first weeks of 1866, would surely have been successful... But a fight at that time would have found Ireland in better condition from a military point of view than she had been in for several hundred years previously and England at a great disadvantage. England had underestimated Fenianism and she was very badly prepared for such an emergency... Under the military leadership which we then had and with the promise of some of the ablest generals in America to join us if we made a good showing, there certainly would have been a war that would have taxed England's resources to the utmost.[12]

That summer, the authorities held a series of courts-martial and many soldier Fenians were convicted. They were sent along with civilian Fenians to serve their sentences in jails in England, where conditions were extremely harsh. One of those sentenced was Colour Sergeant Charles McCarthy: he had been sent to India where he was so angered by the ruthlessness with which the British authorities suppressed the rebellion of 1857 that he joined the Fenians. The brutality of the prison system broke his health and he died 12 days after his release in 1878.

In 1867, 15 of the convicted soldier Fenians, along with 48 other Fenian prisoners and 320 ordinary prisoners, were transported to Western Australia in the *Houguemont*, the last shipment of convicts to be sent there. The authorities finally succeeded in shattering Fenianism within the army by moving the disaffected regiments out of Ireland.

The invasion of British North America

The dwindling prospects of a rising in Ireland spurred Fenians in America to push ahead with a plan which had been in the air for some months: an invasion of British North America. The idea was that an army made up of veterans of the US civil war would cross the border and wrest the territory from the British. Then they would set up an Irish republic-in-exile which would be a base from which to launch a future struggle for Irish freedom.

The project seemed realistic enough at the time, and indeed a group of influential Americans made a similar plan. The provinces of British North America were unstable, with French-Canadians hostile to British rule and many people opposed to Britain's plan to unite the provinces into a single Dominion of Canada under the crown. The Fenians also believed that the US president, Andrew Johnson, would turn a benevolent blind eye to their enterprise: by invading British North America they would violate the USA's neutrality agreement.

The American Fenians were weakened by a now-unbridgeable split in their ranks. John O'Mahony, who had all along opposed the idea of invading British North America, did a sudden about-turn in an attempt to regain lost prestige, and sent his own expedition northwards in April 1866. The aim was to capture a British-held island called Campobello, but the British moved 5,000 troops and two warships to the border, and the 1,000-strong Fenian force was unable to cross. The other section of the Fenian Brotherhood, led by William Roberts, planned to send a 25,000-strong army across the border at three different points. The attack began on the night of 31 May, when some 800 Fenians under Colonel John O'Neill crossed the Niagara river from Buffalo to Fort Erie. On 2 June they defeated a force of British militia at the battle of Ridgeway: this was the first conventional battle between Irish and British forces since 1798.

But their efforts were undermined by the US president, Andrew Johnson, who was in effect using the Fenians as a bargaining counter in his efforts to obtain reparations from the British for damage caused during the civil war. When the British let it be understood that they would negotiate on the issue, Johnson gave the go-ahead for US troops to prevent the Fenians moving further. The Fenian soldiers who had crossed into British North America from Buffalo and Vermont were forced to withdraw. At the end of June, the Buffalo *Commercial Advertiser* commented:

> There is no longer any reasonable doubt from the demonstration of Fenian strength and preparation... that, but for the prompt interference of our government, the Canadian provinces would today have been utterly and irretrievably vanquished and subjugated by the Fenian hordes... There is no doubt but that we should now be witnessing a mighty exodus of Irishmen from all over this country to join in a consolidated and harmonious movement upon the island Mecca of the *Fianna*... Ireland.[13]

Colonel O'Neill, the victor of Ridgeway, clung to the Canadian project. In 1870 he again, on two occasions, led armies across the border, but without success.

Fenian women

Back in Ireland, the wholesale arrests of 1866 badly damaged the organisation and dislocated its communications. But as John Devoy, himself a victim of the round-up, explained:

> Connections were soon partially restored... by a small band of devoted women, mostly the wives and sisters of the leading male members, and they were efficiently aided by the women friends of the men throughout the country.[14]

Although the Fenian organisations focused on recruiting men, women were often keen to get involved, becoming couriers, organisers and propagandists. John Devoy recorded:

> In America there was a Fenian Sisterhood... In Ireland there was no regular organisation of Fenian women, but a large number of them worked as well as if they had been organised. They took no pledge, but were trusted by the men without one, were the keepers of important secrets, travelled from point to point bearing important messages, and were the chief agents in keeping the organisation alive in Ireland from the time that Stephens left for America early in 1866 until the Rising of March 5, 1867. And not one woman betrayed a secret, proved false to the trust reposed in her, or by carelessness or indiscretion was responsible for any injury to the cause. It was a fine record for Irish womanhood.[15]

Fenian women formed their own organisation, the Ladies Committee, which, wrote Devoy, 'collected funds to provide counsel for the prisoners on trial, fed those who were sick and did other work of a benevolent character.'[16] Among the leading spirits were wives and sisters of prominent Fenians, among them Mrs Luby, Mrs Mary O'Donovan Rossa, and Ellen O'Leary, poet and sister of John O'Leary. Women without such connections also participated.

The American-born Delia Parnell, whose son Charles was later to be famous, supported the movement with money and helped Fenians who were 'on the run'. Her daughter Fanny while still in her mid-teens followed a strong female tradition by writing passionate patriotic poems, which she contributed to the Fenian paper, the *Irish People*, under the pen-name Aleria.

Another of the many keen women supporters was a fashionable dressmaker called Mrs Butler, a widow whose only daughter, Sarah Jane, had contributed verse to the *Nation*. They had no male Fenian relatives. Mrs Butler, 'a stout, grey-haired lady, with a cheerful, smiling face', lived opposite the loyalist headquarters in Dublin. She hosted top-level Fenian meetings in her house and offered to keep the lord lieutenant prisoner if the Fenians could capture him. Later the story that she had sheltered Stephens leaked out, and she was deserted by her loyalist customers and died in poverty.

Better to fight and lose

With the organisation in the British army broken and many Fenian leaders arrested, as well as a chronic shortage of arms, there could be little hope of a successful rising. But the Irish-Americans who had crossed the Atlantic decided that, as Devoy said, it 'was better to have fought and lost, than never to have fought at all'.[17]

A number of Irish-American officers lived in London as they awaited the rising. They endured considerable discomfort, contrary to British propaganda which had them living in luxury on money supplied by 'the Irish servant girls of New York'.[18] One of the Irish-Americans described visiting some fellow officers in a decrepit lodging-house in Holborn. The doorbell was broken so they rapped on the door:

> Presently a shrill female voice sounds through the house and a man, whose name is John, emerges from a subterranean passage. The female has irritated him. He blasts, blows, and damns his own sanguinary eyes... We are requested to state 'what the 'ell we want?' We ask if Mr Webb is at home. John doesn't know, but if we go up to the top landing, turn to the right, and knock at the door, we may find him... There is no light, the stairs are in the last stage of consumption, and keen blasts of air striking us in the face tell of broken windows... At last we are at the door which is opened wide by General Thomas F. Burke. A word or two in whispers (walls have ears), a fraternal grasp of the hand all round, and we seat ourselves on an empty coal scuttle, kindly kicked over for our accommodation. There is no fire, though the night is cold, and a small piece of candle stuck in the bedpost gives all the light there is. The bed is occupied by Colonel – from Missouri, who is suffering from fever and ague.[19]

James Stephens, now in America, still wanted to delay the rising. He was deposed as head of the IRB and replaced by Colonel Thomas J. Kelly, a Galway-born Irish-American who had been chief of staff. Kelly travelled from America to London in early 1867 and drew up plans for a rising, working with, among others, General Cluseret, a Frenchman who later became commander-in-chief of the revolutionary forces in the Paris commune of 1871. They issued a proclamation from the 'provisional government', stating:

> We have suffered centuries of outrage, enforced poverty, and bitter misery. Our rights and liberties have been trampled on by an alien aristocracy, who, treating us as foes, usurped our lands, and drew away from our unfortunate country all material riches... To-day, having no honourable alternative left, we again appeal to force as our last resource... unable longer to endure the curse of Monarchical Government, we aim at founding a Republic based on universal suffrage, which shall secure to all the intrinsic value of their labour.
>
> The soil of Ireland, at present in the possession of an oligarchy, belongs to us, the Irish people, and to us it must be restored.

> We declare, also, in favour of absolute liberty of conscience, and the
> complete separation of Church and State... we intend no war against the
> people of England – our war is against the aristocratic locusts, whether
> English or Irish, who have eaten the verdure of our fields...[20]

The new plan was for a rising in Ireland on 11 February 1867, with a
simultaneous raid on Chester Castle on the border between England and
Wales, where a considerable store of arms was guarded by a small garrison.
But the plan was betrayed to the authorities, so the leaders postponed the
rising to 5 March. The news of the change of plan did not reach the Fenians
in Britain or in Kerry.

Altogether some 2,000 Irish people living in Britain were mobilised to
take part in the Chester raid. On the night of Sunday 10 February, and the
next morning, groups of Irishmen set off by train from Liverpool,
Manchester, Leeds, and other towns in Lancashire and Yorkshire, and
perhaps a thousand arrived in Chester. But on the Sunday night the spy John
Joseph Corydon betrayed the plan to the head constable of Liverpool. Troops
and police were rushed to Chester, the Fenians there quietly departed –
many going straight to Ireland where they were promptly arrested at the
ports – while those still on their way to Chester were intercepted and turned
back.

Fenians in Kerry, likewise unaware of the postponement of the rising,
went ahead as planned. A group under Colonel O'Connor was supplied
with arms by the children of the head constable of Cahirciveen: the daughter
smuggled all the rifles out of the police barrack under her cloak and gave
them to her brothers, who passed them on to the Fenians. On their way to
Killarney, O'Connor's group captured a policeman and found on him a
Fenian order changing the date of the rising. O'Connor ordered his men to
disperse, but some of them took up a position on a mountain. Here they
were surrounded by troops from a Scottish regiment: these included Fenians
and Irish-speakers, who allowed the rebels to slip through their lines under
cover of night.

These events created panic among the local gentry, who fled to Killarney
and took refuge in a hotel behind sandbagged windows. Their pleas for aid
made the authorities think the rising was much larger than it was, and they
sent trainloads of soldiers.

Preaching in Killarney Cathedral on 17 February 1867, Dr Moriarty, bishop
of Kerry, delivered his still-notorious condemnation of the Fenian leaders,
calling down on them 'God's heaviest curse, His withering, blasting,
blighting curse', and continuing:

> when we look down into the fathomless depth of this infamy of the heads
> of the Fenian conspiracy, we must acknowledge that eternity is not long
> enough, nor hell hot enough to punish such miscreants.[21]

The night of 5 March was bitterly cold with blizzards of sleet and snow. Several thousand Fenians rose nonetheless in many areas. But they were poorly armed – in Cork, for instance, 4,000 men had less than 50 rifles – and could not hope to succeed. They did, however, capture a few police barracks and coastguard stations. Altogether only about 12 people were killed on both sides. The rising was soon over, the jails once again filled to overflowing, and press and pulpit rang with denunciations. Large numbers of prisoners were tried and convicted – often with the help of the spy Corydon and a captured officer, Godfrey Massey, who had turned informer. Many were sent to serve their sentences in England. The police, as a reward for defending their barracks, were restyled the 'Royal' Irish Constabulary.

The arms that the Fenians had so badly needed arrived more than two months later. On 20 May the *Erin's Hope* arrived in Sligo Bay bearing 8,000 rifles and 40 Irish-American officers. They were much too late, and the ship headed home for the United States.

The Manchester Martyrs

The failure in March was soon followed by a series of events that galvanised interest in the Fenians as never before. On 11 September 1867 Colonel Thomas J. Kelly, the head of the IRB, and another Irish-American officer, Captain Timothy Deasy, were arrested in Manchester. The Fenians immediately began planning to rescue their leader.

On 19 September Kelly and Deasy were taken from Bellevue jail to the courthouse, where they were again remanded in custody. On their return journey, the horse-drawn prison van in which they were travelling was ambushed by a party of Fenians as it passed under a railway bridge. The rescuers tried to batter their way into the van through the roof and through the door. One of them tried to force the lock by firing into it: the shot fatally wounded a policeman, Sergeant Brett, who was inside the van and had put his eye to the keyhole to see what was going on. A woman prisoner then took the keys from him and handed them out. The rescuers freed Kelly and Deasy and spirited them away. A few of the rescue party were arrested on the spot. Then, as John Denvir recorded:

> There was a reign of terror that night for the Irish in Manchester. Raids were made on the quarters where they lived, and about sixty Irishmen were dragged from their homes and flung into jail.[22]

On 28 October 26 prisoners were put on trial before a 'Special Commission', with the attorney-general prosecuting. The five 'principal offenders', all of them Irish-born, were William Philip Allen, a 19-year-old carpenter; Michael Larkin, a tailor and the only married man of the group, with four children; Michael O'Brien, a 30-year-old shop assistant from County Cork who had served in the Union army in the American civil war;

Edward O'Meagher Condon, 32 years old and also a Cork-born Irish-American officer; and Thomas Maguire, who had served ten years in the Royal Marines and had just come home on leave. The defence barristers included the English Chartist leader, Ernest Jones. The trial took place in a climate of anti-Irish hysteria. The radical weekly *Reynolds's Newspaper*, lambasting the trial as 'a deep and everlasting disgrace to the English government', declared:

> This special trial is the shameful product of an ignoble panic. Because, in an isolated attempt at the rescue of two men suspected of Fenianism, a policeman happened to be killed, a violent trembling seized the governing classes, and a yell of vengeance issued from every organ of the aristocratic plunderers of the English working classes. Wholesale and indiscriminate arrests were made. Before a particle of evidence had been formally obtained against the prisoners, their guilt was assumed, and their execution demanded.[23]

The prosecution produced several witnesses who identified the men in the dock and testified that the Marine, Thomas Maguire, was in the forefront of the attack.

On 1 November the jury announced they had found the five men guilty of murder – a crime for which the only penalty was death. Each of the five then spoke from the dock – Edward O'Meagher Condon ending his speech with the words 'God save Ireland!' which soon became the rallying cry of Irish people worldwide, and the refrain of a famous song:

> 'God save Ireland' said the heroes;
> 'God save Ireland' said they all;
> Whether on the scaffold high
> Or the battle-field we die,
> Oh, what matter, when for Erin dear we fall.

The judge then pronounced the death sentence.

Irish and radical opinion was appalled. There was a great wave of protest against the impending executions. In the case of the Marine, Thomas Maguire, the evidence was so transparently false that thirty or more English reporters who had been present at the trial sent an appeal to the home secretary to pardon him. The doubts about Maguire's conviction were so widespread that the government yielded to the pressure and he was granted a 'free pardon'. Many now believed that the other four would not now be hanged, since they had been convicted on the evidence of the same witnesses who had blatantly perjured themselves in the case of Maguire. But as the day set for the executions approached, the Home Office remained inflexible, and the pleas and petitions grew intense.

Leading radicals such as John Bright and Charles Bradlaugh, and the famous philosopher John Stuart Mill, appealed for clemency, while eminent lawyers tried to halt the executions through legal means. Working class people gathered in large numbers to sponsor their own petitions: meetings at London's Clerkenwell Green drew thousands of people. The general council of the International Working Men's Association sent an appeal to the home secretary, with Karl Marx among the signatories. Others expressed their support in practical ways. An old lady turned up at Salford jail with a pint of beer – 'a little luxury' – for William Allen, while the Marchioness of Queensberry sent £100 for Michael Larkin's family.

On 22 November, the day before the executions were due, Edward O'Meagher Condon was reprieved. He was an American citizen and the US government had twice demanded that his execution be stopped. His sentence was subsequently commuted to life imprisonment.

While politically aware English workers protested against the executions, the depressed and deprived urban poor were easily moved by anti-Irish sentiment: a 'no-popery' demagogue named Murphy had that year already stirred up mob attacks on the Irish in Birmingham and other towns.

The night before the executions, large crowds gathered below the massive walls of Salford jail, where the gallows had been erected on a platform some 30 feet above the ground. Father Gadd, the priest who comforted the condemned men, recorded how

> A crowd of inhuman ghouls… had been gathered for hours in the streets abutting on the gaol and had made the night and early morning hideous with the raucous bacchanalian strains of 'Champagne Charlie', 'John Brown' and 'Rule Britannia'.

The Irish had stayed away:

> Throughout Manchester and Salford, silent congregations with tear-stained faces and hearts throbbing with a thousand emotions assembled in the various churches for a celebration of early Mass for the eternal welfare of the young Irishmen doomed to die a dreadful death that morning.[24]

Thousands of troops and police also assembled round the prison.

In their last hours, the three remaining condemned men, William Allen, Michael Larkin and Michael O'Brien, drew up their final statements. The 19-year-old Allen wrote:

> In a few hours more I will be going before my God. I state in the presence of that great God that I am not the man who shot Sergeant Brett…
>
> I state this to put juries on their guard for the future, and to have them inquire into the character of witnesses before they take away the lives of innocent men…
>
> In reference to the attack on the van, I confess I aided in the rescue of the gallant Colonel Kelly and Captain Deasy. It is well known to the whole world what my poor country has to suffer, and how her sons are exiles the world over; then, tell me where is the Irishman who could look on unmoved, and see his countrymen taken prisoners, and treated like murderers and robbers in British dungeons?…

May the Lord have mercy on our souls, and deliver Ireland from her sufferings. God save Ireland.[25]

Just after eight in the morning on 23 November, amid a murky fog, the three men were led to the gallows. Thousands looked on as their bodies dropped into the pit. Allen died instantly, but Larkin was finished off below by the hangman, while O'Brien, protected by the priest, took three-quarters of an hour to die.

As so often in imperial history, this act of retribution had the opposite effect to that intended. The Liverpool Irishman John Denvir wrote:

> Their DEATH, which was intended to strike terror into the heart of Ireland, was in truth the LIFE of Irish freedom, for even the coldest hearts now flowed with that spirit of patriotism which has never yet been subdued in our country and NEVER WILL...[26]

As the French paper *Paris Temps* reported, the names of Allen, Larkin and O'Brien, 'obscure names belonging to oblivion', had become names which 'Ireland will remember eternally thanks to yesterday's executions'.[27]

The execution of the Manchester Martyrs

Funeral processions were held all over Ireland, and in London's Hyde Park a vast crowd gathered to kneel and pray. Among the millions who mourned were Karl Marx's 23-year-old daughter, Jenny – who, Marx wrote on 28 November, 'goes in black since the Manchester executions'[28] – and Frederick Engels' Irish companion, Lizzie Burns, sister of Mary who had died in 1863. The day after the executions Engels assessed their effect in a letter to Marx:

> So yesterday morning the Tories, by the hand of Mr Calcraft [the public hangman], accomplished the final act of separation between England and Ireland. The *only thing* that the Fenians still lacked were martyrs.[29]

The Clerkenwell explosion

Within weeks there was another cataclysm, but this time very damaging to Fenian support. On 27 November Ricard O'Sullivan Burke, a leading Fenian arms purchaser and organiser of the Manchester rescue, was arrested in London. He and his assistant Joseph Casey were remanded to the Clerkenwell House of Detention, in the heart of a working-class area where many Irish and Italian immigrants lived, and where many protests had been held against the Manchester executions. Communicating through his lawyer and his sister, Burke suggested an escape plan to the Fenians outside: they should place a gunpowder charge against the prison wall in a cutting which workmen had made while laying pipes. The charge should be exploded while the prisoners were in the exercise yard on the other side of the wall.

But the plan went badly wrong. On 12 December the would-be rescuers made their first attempt, wheeling a cask full of gunpowder to the prison wall on a barrow, but the fuse failed to light properly and they called off the venture. Next day, Friday 13 December, the authorities had got wind of the rescue plan and changed the prisoners' exercise time. Soon after 3.30 the rescue party again planted the cask by the wall, though not in the cutting which had by now been filled in. They lit the fuse and this time the barrel exploded. The blast was heard all over London. It blew a huge hole in the wall – the prisoners were not in the yard to avail of it – but, disastrously, too much gunpowder had been used and the main force of the blast went outwards, destroying a row of working-class homes and damaging many more. Three people – a seven-year-old girl, a 36-year-old woman and a 47-year-old man – were killed immediately, and a 65-year-old woman died next day. Some 40 more were injured, about 11 of them fatally.

Sympathy for the Fenians evaporated overnight. Karl Marx wrote next day to Engels that the exploit 'was a very stupid thing.' He continued:

> The London masses, who have shown great sympathy for Ireland, will be made wild by it and driven into the arms of the government party. One cannot expect the London proletarians to allow themselves to be blown up in honour of the Fenian emissaries.[30]

On 20 April 1868 five men and a woman were put on trial for murder at the Old Bailey. The woman, Ann Justice, had visited Casey in prison and had evidently relayed messages about the escape plans. Her husband was also involved with the Fenians. A fellow Fenian, who turned informer to escape a death sentence, told the police:

> Justice went to Ireland for the rising. He took a lot of ammunition, so did Mrs Ann Justice. She carried a sword under her crinoline as well as ammunition. Justice is a tailor... Colonel Kelly gave him £15 to buy arms and he went and bought a sewing machine.[31]

Ann Justice's barrister, Montagu Williams, wrote that she 'appeared to be from 40 to 45 years of age,' and 'was poorly dressed and plain-looking.'[32] Montagu Williams was only 32 years old: the Fenians were too poor to afford any but very junior members of the bar, while the prosecution team was led by the attorney-general and solicitor-general. The defence nevertheless succeeded in getting the case against Ann Justice withdrawn, and 'not guilty' verdicts for all but one of the prisoners.

The jury found one prisoner, Michael Barrett, guilty of murder. Barrett had been arrested in Glasgow and brought to London, and produced several witnesses to testify that he had been in Glasgow at the time of the explosion. Montagu Williams described him:

> On looking at the dock, one's attention was principally attracted by the appearance of Barrett, for whom I must confess I subsequently felt great commiseration. He was a square-built fellow, scarcely five feet eight in height, and dressed something like a well-to-do farmer. The resemblance was certainly increased by the frank, open expression of his face. A less murderous countenance than Barrett's, indeed, I do not remember to have seen. Good-humour was latent in every feature. He took the greatest interest in the proceedings.[33]

Before he was sentenced, Barrett spoke from the dock. Next morning the *Daily Telegraph*, while agreeing with the death sentence, reported that Barrett had

> delivered a most remarkable speech, criticising with great acuteness the evidence against him, protesting that he had been condemned on insufficient grounds, and eloquently asserting his innocence.[34]

Barrett also stressed his love for his native land, saying:

> If I could in any way remove the miseries or redress the grievances of that land by the sacrifice of my own life I would willingly, nay, gladly, do so.[35]

Montagu Williams recalled that during the speech 'there was not a dry eye in the court.'

The judge then sentenced Barrett to death. Many people pressed for clemency, from leading radical MPs to Barrett's mother, who trudged six miles through heavy snow in Fermanagh to see the local MP, a Unionist, who predictably rejected her plea. But powerful people supported the execution, not least Queen Victoria herself, who wrote to the home secretary on 1 May that she was grieved that the evidence against the other five prisoners had failed:

> it seems dreadful for these people to escape... one begins to wish that these Fenians should be lynch-lawed and on the spot. What is to be done about Barrett?[36]

On 26 May 1868 Michael Barrett was hanged outside Newgate prison with thousands of people looking on, in England's last public execution. *Reynolds's Newspaper* commented:

> millions... will continue to doubt that the guilty man has been hanged at all; and the future historian of the Fenian panic may declare that Michael Barrett was sacrificed to the exigencies of the police, and the vindication of the good old Tory principle, that there is nothing like blood.

The sympathies of the watching crowd, the paper observed, were with Barrett:

> The impression was prevalent that Barrett was innocent; that the police and the Government had made a dreadful mistake; that here was another frightful miscarriage of justice, exemplified in the judicial murder of an innocent man.

The editorial concluded:

> It has a strong smack of political vindictiveness about it, and foreign nations will be apt to say that, unless Michael Barrett had been an Irishman and a suspected Fenian, no English jury would have credited the witnesses on whose evidence he was found guilty.[37]

The government scared

The events in Manchester and Clerkenwell had one major positive result: they concentrated British minds on Ireland to an unprecedented degree. The Fenian organiser John Devoy later offered this assessment:

> While the deaths among the English civilians was regrettable, and though the immediate purpose of this dynamite operation failed of accomplishment, the Clerkenwell incident, coming so soon after the daring rescue at Manchester, scared the government and people of England and had good results later.[38]

Within days of the Clerkenwell explosion, the Liberal leader William Ewart Gladstone, then in opposition, had said in a speech that the Irish had grievances and it was the duty of British people to remove them. When this had been done, then

> instead of hearing in every corner of Europe the most painful commentaries on the policy of England towards Ireland we may be able to look our fellow Europeans in the face.[39]

Aiming to stabilise Britain's control of Ireland, Gladstone began to formulate a policy based on the advice of the Catholic hierarchy and Irish middle-class MPs. In doing so, he shifted away from the traditional British reliance on the Protestant ascendancy class. He planned reforms which were aimed at undermining support for the Fenians by redressing various grievances, in particular the Protestant Church of Ireland's privileged position and the land-holding system.

In late 1868 Gladstone fought and won an election on his pledge to disestablish the Church of Ireland, ending its link with the state. He chose to fight on the issue because it united all sections of his party as well as being popular in Ireland. 'My mission is to pacify Ireland,' he said on receiving the summons from the queen to form a new government. On becoming prime minister for the first time, Gladstone immediately brought forward a bill for disestablishment. During the debates on the bill he told the House of Commons that Fenianism had had 'an important influence with respect to Irish policy':

> The influence of Fenianism was this – that when the Habeas Corpus Act was suspended, when all the consequent proceedings occurred, when the overflow of the mischief came into England itself, when the tranquillity of the great city of Manchester was disturbed, when the metropolis itself was shocked and horrified by an inhuman outrage, when a sense of insecurity went abroad far and wide... then it was that these phenomena came home to the popular mind and produced that attitude of attention and preparedness on the part of the whole population of this country which qualified them to embrace, in a manner foreign to their habits in other times, the vast importance of the Irish controversy.[40]

Despite bitter Conservative opposition, the Irish Church Act became law in mid-1869. Under the act, the union between the English and Irish churches was dissolved, and the Church of Ireland became a voluntary body and much of its property was confiscated. The grants to the Catholic Maynooth seminary and to the Irish Presbyterian church were also ended. The act, though popular, had little practical effect on people's lives.

Gladstone next brought in the Land Act of 1870. This legalised the 'Ulster custom' – which allowed tenants to benefit from improvements they made to the land they rented – and extended it to the rest of Ireland. The act also provided for tenants to be compensated for eviction in certain circumstances, and for loans to be made to tenants wishing to buy their holdings, but it did not provide security of tenure at a fair rent. The Land Act was an unprecedented attack on the interests of landowners, but it made almost no impact on the lives of the peasantry. Those wishing to avail of its provisions faced the prospect of long and expensive lawsuits, and evictions went ahead as before, since most of those evicted for non-payment of rent still had no protection under the law.

Gladstone's other project, to give the Irish a sentimental interest in the link with Britain by installing the Prince of Wales in a court in Ireland in place of the viceroy, foundered on the opposition of Queen Victoria.

The amnesty movement

Sympathy for Fenianism remained widespread, and within a year of the Clerkenwell explosion it came to the surface in a mass movement in support of the Fenian prisoners. During 1868 there was extensive lobbying on their behalf, with Mary O'Donovan Rossa and Mrs Clarke Luby, both wives of prominent prisoners, in the forefront. One of those reached was the poet laureate Alfred Tennyson, who wrote to Gladstone that he had received a pamphlet about the treatment of Irish prisoners in Dartmoor:

> I don't much believe in the accuracy of the Irish generally but I wish you who enlightened us formerly on the Neapolitan prisons to consider whether here too there be not a grievous wrong to be righted.[41]

At the end of 1868 an Amnesty Association was set up in Dublin, and support grew rapidly. John Nolan, a Dublin shop assistant and member of the IRB, was its hard-working secretary, while the Irish MP Isaac Butt subsequently became its president.

In March 1869 Gladstone responded to the pressure by releasing 49 selected prisoners while keeping the leaders incarcerated. But he refused to concede to the demand, pressed in parliament by George Henry Moore, for an enquiry into the treatment of Fenian prisoners. Gladstone differed over how to respond to the amnesty movement from Earl Spencer, the lord lieutenant of Ireland. Spencer was against releasing the Fenians, believing they would once again resume their subversive activities, and thought that popular concern could best be defused by treating them as political prisoners. He told Gladstone that it was 'mere prudery to say that we cannot admit of the distinction between political and ordinary crime'.[42]

During 1869 there were huge demonstrations in support of the imprisoned Fenians: 30,000 marched in Limerick, 200,000 marched in Dublin, and on 24 October 200,000 marched in London. The London demonstration, which demanded 'Justice for Ireland', was backed by a wide range of organisations from the Irish community, the labour and reform movements, and the French and Italian communities. The marchers assembled in many different parts of London and converged on Trafalgar Square where they joined the 'great procession of ladies' under the control of the Ladies National Committee.[43] Led by horsemen bearing flags, the procession moved off to Hyde Park for a mass meeting.

Karl Marx, his wife Jenny, and daughters Jenny and Eleanor were among those in the park. Jenny afterwards described the vast crowds, the bright banners and the defiant placards: 'Disobedience to Tyrants is a Duty to God', and 'Keep your Powder Dry'. Two days later Marx commented that the press had 'ignored the main feature of the demonstration', which was 'that at least a part of the English working class had lost their prejudice against the Irish.'[44] Engels, too, castigated the press, writing to Marx that the demonstration was

> merely another proof of what the official publicity of the press is worth. A couple of hundred thousand people assemble and stage the most imposing demonstration London has seen for years, and as the interest of respectability requires it, the entire London press without exception can describe it as a shabby failure.[45]

A month later the movement received a sensational boost when on 25 November Jeremiah O'Donovan Rossa, then serving a life sentence in Chatham, was elected MP for Tipperary. He was the first Irish felon ever to stand for election. Marx wrote delightedly that 'the Irish have played a capital joke on the English government'.[46] In Engels' view the election was an event which roused the Fenians

> from their tedious conspiracies and small outrages on to a road of action which, although legal in appearance, was nevertheless much more revolutionary than anything they had undertaken since the failure of their insurrection...[47]

In the spring of 1870, while Engels worked on an ambitious history of Ireland which he was never to complete, the Marx family threw themselves passionately into the campaign to end the cruel treatment of the Fenian prisoners. In an article published at the end of February in the Brussels paper *L'Internationale*, Marx itemised the accusations:

> *Mulcahy*, sub-editor of the newspaper the *Irish People* ... was harnessed to a cart loaded with stones with a metal band round his neck at Dartmoor.
> *O'Donovan Rossa*... was shut up for 35 days in a pitch-black dungeon with his hands tied behind his back day and night. They were not even untied to allow him to eat the miserable slops which were left for him on the earthen floor.
> *Kickham* ... although he was unable to use his right arm because of an abscess, was forced to sit with his fellow prisoners in the November cold and fog and break up stones and bricks with his right hand...
> *O'Leary*... was put on bread and water for three weeks because he would not renounce *paganism*...
> *Martin H. Carey* is incarcerated in a lunatic asylum at Millbank...[48]

Marx reported that Colonel Ricard Burke, too, was said to have lost his reason.

Marx's 25-year-old daughter Jenny took up the campaign in a series of articles published in *La Marseillaise*, a widely read French daily paper, between 1 March and 24 April, under the pseudonym J. Williams. She concluded her first article with the words:

> Suffice it to say that since 1866, when there was a raid on the *Irish People*'s offices, *20 Fenians have died or gone mad* in the prisons of humanitarian England.[49]

Marx explained his reasons for campaigning:

> You understand at once that I am not only acted upon by feelings of humanity. There is something besides. To accelerate the social development in Europe, you must push on the catastrophe of official England. To do so, you must attack her in Ireland. That's her weakest point. Ireland lost, the British 'Empire' is gone, and the class war in England, till now somnolent and chronic, will assume acute forms.[50]

Expanding on the same theme soon afterwards, he made the famous observation: 'Any nation that oppresses another forges its own chains.'[51]

Both Marx and Engels saw their support for the Fenians in the much wider context of the struggle for the emancipation of the working class worldwide. Their view of how Irish freedom would be accomplished changed over time. Twenty years earlier, in the heyday of the Chartist movement, they had envisaged that the working class would come to power in England and would then accomplish the liberation of Ireland. Now, however, after the collapse of Chartism and the rise of Fenianism, they saw the process in reverse: a successful rebellion in Ireland, leading to either a free confederation with England or complete separation, could bring about a workers' revolution in England. This in turn – because England was the most advanced capitalist country – could lead to revolution internationally.

Later, when the prospects of a successful rising in Ireland receded, Marx and Engels supported the demand for 'home rule' – an Irish parliament subservient to the British parliament – as a step on the way to full independence.

Jenny Marx's second letter to the *Marseillaise*, published on 9 March 1870, had a major impact. In it she included extracts from a long letter from O'Donovan Rossa which had been smuggled out of prison:

> I have already told you about the hypocrisy of these English masters who, after placing me in a position which forced me to get down on my knees and elbows to eat, are now depriving me of food and light and giving me chains and a Bible. I am not complaining of the penalties which my masters inflict on me – it is my job to suffer – but I insist that I have the right to inform the world of the treatment to which I am subjected, and that it is illegal to hold back my letters describing this treatment. The minute precautions taken by the prison authorities to prevent me writing letters are as disgusting as they are absurd. The most insulting method was to strip me once a day for several months and then examine my arms, legs and all other parts of my body. This took place at *Millbank* daily from February to May 1867. One day I refused, whereupon five prison officers arrived, beat me mercilessly and tore off my clothes.

He described how two prisoners had died as a result of the very harsh conditions, then went on to castigate 'the lies of our English oppressors' and question their distribution of bibles:

Many a time the circumstances have reminded me of Machiavelli's words: 'that tyrants have a special interest in circulating the Bible so that the people understand its precepts and offer no resistance to being robbed by brigands'.

So long as an enslaved people follows the sermons on morality and obedience preached to them by the priests, the tyrants have nothing to fear.[52]

Rossa's allegations were then taken up by the English papers, which were in the main scathingly dismissive, and by papers in the United States and Europe, which gave him a more sympathetic hearing. On 17 March George Henry Moore, the MP for County Mayo, pressed in parliament for a 'full, free and public enquiry' into the treatment of the Fenian prisoners. Jenny Marx indignantly reported that as Moore spoke, 'he was constantly interrupted by hoots of bestial laughter.'[53]

Gladstone had refused a similar request from Moore the previous year, but now, embarrassed by the international publicity, he conceded an enquiry which subsequently confirmed Rossa's allegations. The same evening, however, in response to continuing anti-landlord violence, Gladstone introduced a new coercion bill, returning Ireland to its virtually permanent condition under British rule, a 'state of emergency'.

Finally in December 1870 Gladstone agreed to release 33 of the remaining Fenian prisoners, but only on condition that they left the United Kingdom. Many went into exile in the United States, where they gave new life to the Irish movement. Among them, in a group known as the 'Cuba Five' after the ship which carried them, were Jeremiah O'Donovan Rossa and the formidable activist John Devoy, who was to be the mainstay of the Irish Republican Brotherhood's American wing, Clan-na-Gael, for the next fifty years.

Agitation for amnesty continued unabated, since some Fenians were still imprisoned. These included those convicted of the Manchester rescue, as well as the young organiser and arms-buyer Michael Davitt, and also the Fenians who had been soldiers in the British army. A group of these soldier Fenians was imprisoned in Fremantle, in the remote penal colony of Western Australia. These abandoned prisoners sent repeated messages to their freed comrades, pleading to be rescued, as a result of which several rescue plans were made. The most elaborate plan, set in motion by John Devoy, involved financing, buying, equipping and crewing a whaling-ship and despatching it to Western Australia. The whaler, the *Catalpa*, was captained by an American who was not of Irish descent and crewed by a normal whaling crew of Malays, Africans and Sandwich Islanders. The *Catalpa* arrived in Western Australia after an 11-month voyage at the end of March 1876, and three weeks later, amid dramatic adventures, successfully rescued six soldier Fenians, a feat which prompted triumphant Irish celebrations worldwide.[54]

5

'Home Rule' and the Land League

In May 1870, at a meeting in Dublin organised by Isaac Butt at which well-to-do Protestants were strongly represented, the Home Government Association was formed. The meeting agreed to Butt's proposal that 'the true remedy for the evils of Ireland is the establishment of an Irish Parliament, with full control over our domestic affairs.'[1] This policy of federal home rule fell far short of the demand for repeal of the Union. Rather, the idea was that a Dublin parliament, attended by the Irish MPs, would deal only with Ireland's internal affairs, while the Westminster parliament would continue to control all imperial matters. Irish MPs would be able to intervene in the imperial debates but not in internal English questions.

Isaac Butt, then president of the Amnesty Association, was a Donegal-born Protestant and lifelong conservative who had opposed the disestablishment of the Church of Ireland. Originally a unionist, he had come to support federal home rule for fundamentally conservative reasons, seeing it as a means of staving off progressive social change. In the wake of the 1867 Reform Act which gave the vote to every adult male householder, democracy appeared to be sweeping England, making it an unreliable ally for the Irish upper classes. A separate Irish parliament, Butt felt, could be a bulwark against democracy, allowing the Irish landlords, gentry and professionals to continue to hold the reins of power. He explained:

> There is no people on earth less disposed to democracy than the Irish. The real danger of democratic or revolutionary violence is far more with the English people. The time may not be far distant when a separate Irish Parliament might be, in the best sense of the word, the Conservative element in the British Confederation.[2]

As a barrister Butt had defended leading Irish rebels, first Young Irelanders and then Fenians, and had come to respect their reasons for revolt. He concluded that home rule was the best way to defuse such militancy, arguing that once misgovernment by England was ended, the essential conservatism of the Irish would assert itself.

Like-minded Protestant landlords gave their support to the home rule campaign at the start, while the Catholic hierarchy, fearing a Protestant Tory government in Dublin, opposed it. Soon, however, the character of the campaign changed. The landlords' enthusiasm soon waned when home rule candidates in a series of by-elections sought to win votes by identifying themselves with popular causes such as land reform and denominational education. By 1873 most of the movement's conservative supporters had withdrawn their backing, and the Catholic middle classes became dominant. When Gladstone in 1873 proposed a major reform of the Irish universities, refusing to offer state aid to the Catholic university while leaving aid to the Protestant-orientated colleges untouched, the Catholic bishops swung round to supporting home rule. Irish Liberal MPs, mindful of the next election, followed suit.

Fenian support

Some leading Fenians gave their support to the new movement, though others were doubtful. Fenians in England soon became involved, helping to set up home rule associations in various towns. In January 1873, on the initiative of John Barry, secretary of the Manchester Home Rule Association, these came together to form the Home Rule Confederation of Great Britain. The Confederation's main practical task was to register and organise the Irish vote.

Barry, a linoleum manufacturer, was a member of the supreme council – the 11-member ruling body – of the Irish Republican Brotherhood, and had been involved in smuggling arms for the organisation. With great persistence, he managed to secure Isaac Butt's presence at the inaugural meeting of the Confederation, and Butt, who was by now an MP, was elected president.

The Fenian journalist John Denvir became the Confederation's first general secretary. He later explained why he joined the home rule movement, writing that it appealed to him

> precisely on the same grounds as Fenianism, namely, first, that it was based on justice; and, secondly, that it was practicable...
>
> My principles have never altered, and I can see nothing inconsistent in my adapting myself to changed conditions. I and those who thought like me were driven into Fenianism because it seemed likely to achieve success, and what was called 'constitutional agitation' seemed hopeless. Now the position was reversed. On the one hand Fenianism had collapsed, and on the other there seemed a prospect, partly owing to the change wrought by Fenianism, that a constitutional movement might succeed.[3]

But Denvir drew the line at standing for parliament himself. He explained:

> With me it was a matter of conscience; I could not take an oath of allegiance to any but an Irish Government. At the same time, I have always been practical, and willing to fight Ireland's battles with the weapons that come

readiest to my hand. I, therefore, always gave what support I could to the Irish Parliamentary Party...[4]

In March 1873 the IRB adopted a revised constitution, which was to remain virtually unchanged until after 1916. The third clause paved the way for involvement in the home rule movement:

> The I.R.B. shall await the decision of the Irish nation as expressed by a majority of the Irish people as to the fit hour of inaugurating a war against England, and shall, pending such an emergency, lend its support to every movement calculated to advance the cause of Irish independence consistently with the preservation of its own integrity.[5]

In November, at a great conference in Dublin, the Home Government Association was transformed into the Home Rule League, again with IRB support. Though in theory the League was a single-issue organisation, in practice its leaders, as a conservative journal put it, advocated 'denominational education, land without rent, and home rule', in that order.[6]

A general election was held in February 1874, and the Home Rulers were remarkably successful, winning 60 of the 103 Irish seats. But virtually all the Home Rule MPs – 47 of whom were Catholics – were landowners, businessmen and lawyers, and two-thirds of them were in fact Liberals who had donned a new hat in order to win popular support. Their insincerity and self-interest meant that once elected they had little desire to press either the home rule issue or the land question. Once in the House of Commons, the Home Rulers found themselves treated with contempt. The Conservatives had won with an absolute majority and could afford to ignore them, while the Liberals could gain nothing from an alliance. When Isaac Butt asked the Commons on 30 June to consider his proposals for home rule, they rejected his motion by 458 votes to 51. This rebuff was repeated many times: Butt, however, remained wedded to the view that peaceful persuasion would in the end prevail.

A handful of the Irish MPs, however, were less sanguine. Joseph Ronayne, a veteran Young Irelander, proposed that they should interfere more in English and imperial questions, especially those affecting the working class. This would win English sympathy for Ireland, hamper reactionary legislation, and turn the weapon of obstruction back upon the English MPs who had so often thwarted Irish measures.

Ronayne's ideas were disregarded except by Joseph Gillis Biggar, MP for Cavan. Biggar, the son of a wealthy Belfast businessman, was a Presbyterian who later turned Catholic – a move which some Fenians regretted because they felt he would be more useful as a Protestant. Devoy recalled telling him:

> Now... when young Protestants in Ulster showed a tendency towards Nationality their mothers would say to them: 'The next thing we'll know is that you've turned Papish like Joe Biggar.'

'And what about my soul?' asked Biggar.
'Oh, I'd be willing to see you damned for the sake of Ireland,' I said jocularly.[7]

After his election Biggar joined the IRB and later became a member of the supreme council. Biggar was courageous and honest and fiercely determined to get results for Ireland. Hunchbacked, completely lacking in oratorical ability, and with a Belfast accent that was impenetrable to the English, he ignored his disadvantages and stubbornly set out to delay legislation and aggravate the Commons by talking as long as possible. When a coercion bill was under discussion in 1875, he talked continuously for four hours. He did not deliver a reasoned speech, but related anything that came to hand, including newspaper reports and extracts from official enquiries. When the speaker complained he could not hear, Biggar calmly moved to another place and said everything again. He used these tactics repeatedly over the next year, and on one occasion caused consternation by declaring 'I spy a stranger' on seeing the Prince of Wales in the gallery, and thus forcing him to leave.

Biggar was helped in his efforts by another member of the IRB's supreme council, John O'Connor Power MP, a one-time journeyman painter and long-standing Fenian, who had been brought up in Ballinasloe workhouse. O'Connor Power led the parliamentary agitation for an amnesty for the remaining Fenian prisoners. The two of them conducted their IRB correspondence on House of Commons notepaper. But the MPs' failure to shift government policy on Ireland exacerbated the differences within the IRB over the question of involvement with the home rule movement. Broadly speaking, intellectual idealists such as Charles Kickham and John O'Leary distrusted any involvement in parliamentary politics and believed that all efforts should go into preparing for an eventual insurrection, while pragmatists such as Biggar and the Manchester-based John Barry believed that during the period when no rising was feasible they should inject militancy into the constitutional movement and use it to hasten their ends. In August 1876 the idealists on the supreme council won majority support for a resolution stating that:

> the countenance which we have hitherto shown to the Home Rule movement be from this date, and is hereby, withdrawn, as three years' experience of the working of the movement has proved to us that the revolutionary principles which we profess can be better served by our organisation existing on its own basis pure and simple, and we hereby request that all members of our organisation who may have any connection with the Home Rule movement will definitely withdraw from it their active co-operation within six months from this date.[8]

But the supreme council remained deeply divided, and in March 1877 four of its members, Biggar, O'Connor Power, John Barry and Patrick Egan, were expelled or forced to resign.

By now Biggar and O'Connor Power had acquired an effective ally: the young MP for Meath, Charles Stewart Parnell. Parnell was an Anglo-Irish Protestant country squire who owned an estate, Avondale, in County Wicklow. His American mother and two of his sisters, Fanny and Anna, were passionate nationalists, but Charles's nationalism seems to have been dormant till the execution of the Manchester martyrs in 1867. Parnell was elected to Westminster in 1875 on a home rule platform, and during his campaign he declared his support for denominational education, the release of political prisoners, and fair rents and fixity of tenure.

Parnell raised the amnesty question in parliament, but made no serious impression on the Fenians till 30 June 1876, when he scandalised the House of Commons by protesting when a government spokesman referred to the 'Manchester murderers'. Parnell asserted: 'I wish to say as publicly and directly as I can that I do not believe, and never shall believe, that any murder was committed at Manchester.'[9]

Parnell allied himself with the handful of Fenian obstructionists, and in 1877 they began a systematic campaign of wrecking government legislation. They succeeded in destroying several bills by talking them out and by moving amendments – some of which were genuine improvements – and adjournments. The English MPs were infuriated and the Home Rule leader Isaac Butt became distraught, fearing the obstructionists would frustrate his efforts to win over the English. Parnell defended himself succinctly in a letter published in the *Freeman's Journal* on 17 April 1877:

> The instinct of snobbery, which seems to compel some Irishmen to worship at the shrine of English prejudice, and to bow down before the voice and censure of the English Press, will never gain anything for Ireland, and will only secure for such panderers the secret contempt of Englishmen.
>
> England respects nothing but power, and it is certain that the Irish party, comprising, as it does, so many men of talent and ability, might have that power, which attention to business, method and energy always give, if it would only exhibit these qualities.[10]

He expressed himself even more vigorously at a meeting in Liverpool on 21 July, clearly bidding for Fenian support:

> What did they ever get in the past by trying to conciliate them? Did they get the abolition of tithes by the conciliation of their English taskmasters? No; it was because they adopted different measures. Did O'Connell gain Emancipation for Ireland by conciliation?... Catholic Emancipation was gained because an English king and his ministers feared revolution. Why was the English church in Ireland disestablished and disendowed? Why was some measure of protection given to the Irish tenant? It was because there was an explosion at Clerkenwell and because a lock was shot off a prison van in Manchester [great applause]. They would never gain anything

from England unless they trod upon her toes – they would never gain a single sixpennyworth from her by conciliation.[11]

A few days later Parnell and six other Irish MPs brought their campaign of obstruction to a climax in the final stages of the South Africa Bill, when, holding out against 300 British members, they forced the House of Commons to sit continuously for 45 hours, a sitting unparalleled in parliamentary history. Their notoriety in the Commons was matched by their growing popularity among Irish people. This was recognised on 28 August at the annual convention of the Home Rule Confederation of Great Britain. The Confederation, which had a mainly working class and Fenian membership and was consequently more militant than its Irish equivalent, deposed Isaac Butt from the presidency and elected Parnell in his place.

The 'new departure'

In Ireland, 1877 saw the start of a series of disastrous harvests which brought to an end a decade of relative security. Peasants in the impoverished western counties were especially threatened. Their plight was made worse by an economic depression in Britain, which meant that demand for Irish migrant labour was reduced, cutting off a vital source of income.

The worsening tensions were highlighted by the assassination of one of Ireland's biggest landowners, Lord Leitrim, who was ambushed on 2 April 1878 as he set out from his residence in Donegal for the quarter sessions carrying eviction orders against a number of tenants. His 19-year-old driver and his clerk were killed by gunfire, while Lord Leitrim himself was wounded by gunshot and then battered to death. There were bizarre scenes at the funeral in Dublin as the poor vented their hatred. The *Freeman's Journal* reported next day, 11 April:

> The crowd closed around the hearse as it approached the graveyard, groaning, cheering, and hissing. The occupants of the mourning coaches on descending from their carriages were jostled about and scattered. The police in vain sought to clear a passage for the coffin… Over a quarter of an hour elapsed before the coffin could be finally removed. In the meantime the mob hooted and groaned, and voices came from the worst of them saying, "Out with the old b-", "Lug him out," "Dance on him.".… The last prayers being over, the coffin was borne through the southern door, towards the vaults… Immediately that the bareheaded mourners were sighted by the mob outside the railings, a new howl of execration went up, and amid hisses, cheers, and indecent jests, the coffin of the unfortunate nobleman was hurried to its last resting-place.[12]

Tenant farmers in the west had already begun to organise, with local Fenians to the fore, holding mass meetings in 1876 and 1877 to protest against rack-renting and evicting landlords and against large graziers, and to demand the 'three Fs'. The protests intensified as tenants unable to pay their rents were faced with eviction and starvation. The Fenian organisers not only involved themselves in the land struggle, but also joined forces in pursuit of tenant rights with non-Fenians such as James Daly, editor of the *Connaught Telegraph*, and the MPs O'Connor Power and Parnell.

Meanwhile in the United States the Clan-na-Gael leader John Devoy was abandoning the orthodox Fenian view that Fenians should remain aloof from constitutional struggle and put all their efforts into preparing for eventual insurrection. In 1878 he began to work out a programme which would allow both forms of struggle to proceed. Influenced by Patrick Ford, the proprietor of the *Irish World* and messianic anti-capitalist who held that the landlords were robbers who should be expropriated, Devoy placed the land issue high on the agenda. He called for peasant ownership, an idea very different from the traditional demand for fair rents and fixity of tenure.

The 'Irish new departure', as Devoy termed it, was essentially a plan to create an alliance between Fenians and parliamentarians on the basis of a programme which would commit the MPs to a radical stance dramatically different from the conservatism and imperialism of Isaac Butt. In October 1878 Devoy drafted a cable to Parnell, which was published in papers in New York and Dublin:

> Nationalists here will support you on the following conditions:
> (1) abandonment of the federal demand and substitution of a general declaration in favour of self-government;
> (2) vigorous agitation of the land question on the basis of a peasant proprietary, while accepting concessions tending to abolish arbitrary eviction;
> (3) exclusion of all sectarian issues from the platform;
> (4) Irish members to vote together on all imperial and home questions, adopt an aggressive policy and energetically resist coercive legislation;
> (5) advocacy of all struggling nationalities in the British Empire or elsewhere.[13]

Soon afterwards Devoy described how he saw the 'new departure' taking shape:

> The change… will take the shape of a combination between the advocates of physical force and those who believe in constitutional agitation, such as will leave the former free to prepare for active work while, in the meantime, giving a reasonable support to a dignified and manly demand for self-government on the part of the constitutionalists.[14]

Devoy hoped that when the time for insurrection arrived, the parliamentarians would secede from Westminster and form an Irish parliament in Dublin. This idea of collective withdrawal had first been formulated by the Young Irelander Charles Gavan Duffy in 1848.

In working out the 'new departure' policy, Devoy worked closely with Michael Davitt, who had been released from prison in December 1877 and went to America on a speaking tour from July to December 1878. Perhaps the best-loved Irish revolutionary of his day, Davitt personified in his own life the experience of many Irish peasants and industrial workers. He was born in 1846, at the height of the great famine, in Straide, County Mayo, the poorest part of Ireland. His parents were peasants, and survived the famine only because Davitt's father obtained work as an overseer of roads on a relief scheme. But they fell into rent arrears, and in 1850, when Michael was four-and-a-half, they were evicted. He later recalled:

> I have a distinct remembrance (doubtless strengthened by the frequent narration of the event by my parents in after years) of that morning's scene: the remnant of our household furniture flung about the road; the roof of the house falling in and the thatch taking fire; my mother and father looking on with four young children, the youngest only two months old, adding their cries to the other pangs which must have agitated their souls at the sight of their burning homestead.[15]

The family then emigrated to Lancashire, where more than a third of Britain's Irish community lived, and settled in Haslingden, a small textile town near Manchester. At the age of nine, Michael went to work in a cotton mill, working a 60-hour week. In May 1857, when he was 11, his right arm was mangled in a machine and had to be amputated just below the shoulder. He then went to school, and in 1861 began work in a printing business.

In 1865, aged 19, like many other idealistic Irish youths Michael joined the Irish Republican Brotherhood, and became the 'centre' of the local 'circle' of some 50 members. In February 1867 he took part in the unsuccessful arms raid on Chester Castle, reputedly carrying a store of cartridges in a bag made from a handkerchief. Three years later he became a full-time organiser and arms-buyer for the IRB. Davitt operated an effective smuggling system, buying large numbers of weapons in Birmingham and despatching them to Ireland. But on 14 May 1870 he was arrested at Paddington station as he waited for an arms supplier, who was also arrested. Davitt was held initially at Paddington Green police station, then remanded to the Clerkenwell House of Detention, and subsequently tried at the Central Criminal Court at the Old Bailey, where he was convicted of treason-felony and sentenced to 15 years.

Davitt spent seven-and-a-half years in prison, all but one of them in Dartmoor, where conditions for all prisoners were extremely harsh. They were locked in corrugated-iron cells with no daylight or access to open air. Ventilation was very poor and the stench was foul. The food was filthy and the work, such as stone-breaking and bone-breaking, very strenuous. Prisoners were also searched four times a day and were liable to be strip-searched, which meant their whole bodies were minutely examined.

Outside the prisons, supporters waged an unremitting campaign for amnesty for the Fenian prisoners, and on 19 December 1877 Davitt was released on 'ticket of leave', which meant his freedom was conditional on good behaviour. He left prison just as Parnell was bringing a new vigour to the constitutional movement and as the land issue was entering a critical phase. Within two years he was to be a national leader.

Devoy and Davitt failed to win over the old guard of the IRB to the 'new departure' idea. Charles Kickham, in an unsigned editorial in the *Irishman* in November 1878, stated:

> a Nationalist must of necessity cease to be a Nationalist when he enters the House of Commons... we hold to the conviction, which has stood the test of lengthened experiment, and has never been controverted, that the English Parliament is no place for an Irish patriot...[16]

John O'Leary shared Kickham's view, writing that the 'most manly and effective' course would be 'that we should imitate the Hungarians in refusing altogether to elect members to any Parliament save our own... The next best course... would be that men should be elected *not* to go there.' The 'very worst' course was the obstructionist policy, O'Leary contended.[17]

Support for the 'new departure' came from the veteran Mayo Fenian Matthew Harris, who had been involved both in importing arms and in organising tenant agitation. He argued strongly that, while 'peaceable means *alone*' would not free any country, it was foolish to ignore those 'two powerful agents of public opinion', the press and the platform. As for parliament, 'is it not better to utilise it than leave it as it is at present, a powerful weapon in the hands of our enemies?' He reprimanded the purists:

> while our devotion to principle, especially the principle of national independence, is in many ways our strength, our fondness for making every mode of procedure a matter of principle is our greatest weakness... Let any man of thought reflect... that even at the present day the pulpit, the press, the platform, every means – even the very sacraments of religion – are pressed into the service of England, and then ask himself whether he is justified in shutting out his countrymen from every means of achieving their liberty except by means of whatever crochet may have got into his own head, be it physical force, or moral force, or any other single force to which we fancy to give the name of principle.[18]

On 19 January 1879 the IRB's supreme council gathered in Paris for a week-long meeting which was mainly concerned with routine business such as the procurement of arms. Of its 11 members, only two, Davitt and Harris, supported the 'new departure'. The supreme council refused to endorse an alliance between the IRB and constitutional nationalists. It opposed Fenians taking part in parliamentary agitation except where they were putting up a candidate as a demonstration against Britain, as had been done with O'Donovan Rossa and others. Nor would the council commit the IRB to involvement in the land agitation. Kickham, who sympathised with the peasants, felt they had more to gain from the indirect effects of Fenianism, such as the 1870 Land Act. Harris, by contrast, argued that agrarian agitation could be a powerful weapon to aid political revolution.

Devoy and Davitt, undeterred, continued to try to implement the 'new departure' policy. They held meetings with Parnell, who was friendly and implied that he would favour a working arrangement, although he rejected a formal alliance. At the same time they continued to be concerned with military preparations, and Devoy worked hard to reactivate the flow of arms to Ireland. At the same time Clan-na-Gael continued to sponsor the development, begun two years earlier, of a submarine torpedo boat designed by John Holland, a Fenian who had emigrated to the USA from County Clare. The idea was that the submarine, nicknamed the 'Fenian Ram', would wreak havoc on Britain's navy and merchant shipping. Though the early versions were not viable, a later Holland was purchased by the US navy and was the prototype of a generation of submarines.

The Clan was also considering one of its periodic schemes to assist other nationalist movements fighting Britain. James J. O'Kelly wrote to Davitt from New York in March 1879 about a plan to help the Zulus, led by Cetshwayo. In January the Zulus had inflicted a devastating defeat on the British at Isandhlwana, leaving 1,500 British dead, as well as over 2,000 of their own. O'Kelly wrote that 'one million cartridges placed in the hands of the Zulus would help the Irish cause more than the equivalent amount of arms landed in Ireland'.[19]

But not all American Fenians were happy with Clan-na-Gael's policy of backing the 'new departure' while pursuing long-term plans for insurrection. In particular, the passionate and erratic Jeremiah O'Donovan Rossa advocated a policy of 'skirmishing', based on the military practice of sending out small advance parties of select troops to launch surprise attacks. Rossa and others were to put this idea into action with a series of bomb attacks in English cities between 1881 and 1885.

Irishtown

Meanwhile in the west of Ireland the peasants faced disaster. The collapse of prices for agricultural products, together with two successive bad harvests, had left them unable to pay their rents to the landlords or their debts to the shopkeepers. As a result, many were threatened with eviction. Dreading a repeat of the mass dispossession of the 'great hunger', the tenant farmers responded militantly, organising to resist rack-renting and eviction. As the land agitation gathered momentum, it swept the advocates of the 'new departure' policy along with it.

Michael Davitt visited his native Mayo in February 1879 and witnessed the mounting distress. He threw himself into the land movement, bringing to it the 'new departure' ideas about the need for Fenians to co-operate with constitutionalists and for the land question to be fused with the cause of independence. In Mayo local activists, with Fenians prominent among them, were planning a mass meeting to demand a reduction of rents and to highlight the conditions of tenants generally. Davitt joined the organisers, helping to book speakers and draft the resolutions. The gathering was to be held on 20 April at Irishtown, a hamlet near the meeting-point of Counties Mayo, Galway and Roscommon. The locally produced posters announced:

THE WEST AWAKE!!
GREAT TENANT RIGHT MEETING IN IRISHTOWN

From the China towers of Pekin to the round towers of Ireland, from the cabins of Connemara to the kraals of Kaffirland, from the wattled homes of the isles of Polynesia to the wigwams of North America the cry is: 'Down with invaders! Down with tyrants!' Every man to have his own land – every man to have his own home.[20]

Several thousand people arrived for the meeting. From the platform, James Daly called for 'the land of Ireland for the people of Ireland', and declared that 'those who take the land of the evicted are the enemies of the country, and are as culpable as the landlords'.[21]

The meeting passed three resolutions, the first two written by Davitt. The first stated the nationalist case, noting that 'the social condition of the Irish people' had been 'reduced through their subjection to England and its coercive legislation to a state below that of any civilised country in the world', and asserting 'our unceasing determination to resort to every lawful means whereby our inalienable rights – political and social – can be regained from our enemies.'

The second resolution set out the moral case against landlordism:

That as the land of Ireland, like that of every other country, was intended by a just and all-providing God for the use and sustenance of those of His people to whom He gave inclination and energies to cultivate and improve it, any system which sanctions its monopoly by a privileged class or assigns its ownership and control to a landlord caste, to be used as an instrument of usurious or political self-seeking, demands from every aggrieved Irishman an undying hostility, being flagrantly opposed to the first principle of their humanity – self-preservation.[22]

The third resolution addressed the pressing practical issue, demanding an immediate reduction of unjust rents pending a settlement of the land question.

The meeting was an enthusiastic success and produced unprecedented results. Landlords in Mayo and Galway quickly allowed rent reductions, prompting tenants elsewhere to follow the example of Irishtown.

As the distress continued to increase in many parts of the country, the Fenian MP John O'Connor Power warned parliament on 27 May 1879 that if parliament did nothing to relieve the depression in agriculture scenes would arise in Ireland that would be far more dangerous to the rights of property and to the order and tranquillity which should prevail in that country than any that Ireland had been afflicted with in her long struggle with the ignorance, if not the incompetence, of the English Parliament.[23]

But the government remained unmoved.

On 8 June a mass meeting was held at Westport, County Mayo. Several thousand attended despite dire admonitions from the Catholic hierarchy. Parnell reluctantly agreed to speak, his presence gaining the movement its first widespread publicity. He told his audience:

> You must show the landlords that you intend to keep a firm grip of your homesteads and lands. You must not allow yourselves to be dispossessed as you were dispossessed in 1847.[24]

Devoy returned to the USA in July, while Davitt pressed ahead with the land campaign in Ireland. More mass meetings were held, making the same demands as Irishtown and Westport: reduction of rents, peasant proprietorship and national self-government. On 16 August, together with local leaders, Davitt organised a delegate convention of tenant farmers at Castlebar, County Mayo. This meeting set up a new body, the National Land League of Mayo, to control and direct the land movement. The league's manifesto, drafted by Davitt, stated that its aim was to abolish the present land laws and replace them with peasant proprietorship. The League also declared its opposition to people who rented land or farms from which people had been evicted.

The League pointed out that Ireland would be able to support 12 to 20 million people were it not for restrictive land laws, and that the artificial famine and continuing impoverishment had reduced the population from eight million before 1847 to little over five million today. Less than 300 people owned more than six million acres, while five million people owned nothing. To protect the rights of a few thousand landlords, a standing army of semi-military police was maintained, paid for by the landless millions. The landlord class extracted £20 million a year from the soil of Ireland without returning any benefits to the land or the farmers. The solution, the manifesto stated, was for the land to be divided up between the cultivators and for the landlords to be compensated for their losses.[25]

The National League

The agitation now began to spread all over Ireland, with mass meetings in many places. These gatherings often had a festive air, with bands and banners and people wearing green ribbons in their buttonholes or bay leaves in their hats. Faced with a unified and militant tenantry, many landlords agreed to reduce rents.

After a year of incessant rain, the 1879 harvest was the worst since the 'great hunger', and the failure of the potato crop threatened a winter of starvation. Evictions continued to rise, going from 406 in 1877 to 834 in 1878 to 1,098 in 1879. The distress affected not just the poor but also sections of the middle class, such as large tenant farmers, banks, shopkeepers, traders and moneylenders. As the peasants' plight worsened and the agitation mounted, and the British government continued to do nothing, Parnell finally agreed to become the formal leader of the land movement. For several months Devoy and then Davitt had been pressing him to do this, but he had resisted, fearing that in a nationwide movement it would be impossible to control the more militant people in the branches. But as the situation deteriorated, he found it politically necessary to take the risk.

Parnell agreed to convene a meeting in Dublin on 21 October 1879 to form a new organisation, the Irish National Land League. The League's aims were twofold: to reduce rack-rents and to facilitate peasant ownership. Like the Mayo League, it advocated that the tenants organise themselves and defend those threatened with eviction. Parnell became its president, while Davitt was one of its three secretaries and three other Fenians, including Joseph Biggar MP, also held positions. The church was now less uniformly hostile, and a number of priests joined the committee.

A month later, on 19 November, Davitt and two other Land Leaguers were arrested and charged with using seditious language. This provoked a wave of indignation and helped publicise the Land League. Protest meetings were held in England and Scotland as well as in Ireland. On Sunday 30 November a mass meeting was held in London's Hyde Park, attended by representatives of many radical and working-class organisations, to protest against the arrests and express sympathy to the people of Ireland in their present distress. The same day Parnell addressed an immense meeting of 50,000 in Liverpool, while Davitt spoke to a meeting of Tyneside Irish at Gateshead.

Soon Land League branches were set up in England, and the Home Rule Confederation of Great Britain, in keeping with the mood of the times, changed its name to the Irish National Land League of Great Britain. The first English branch was set up in Poplar in London's East End by Jim Connell, a former Fenian from County Meath. A few years later, in 1889, inspired by the dock strike of that year as well as by the struggles in Ireland, Russia and America, Connell was to write the words of the 'Red Flag', which became the anthem of the British Labour Party. He set it to the tune 'The White Cockade', much livelier than its present 'Tannenbaum'.

In the west, some peasant meetings began to take the form of mass mobilisations to try to prevent evictions. At Balla, County Mayo, on 22 November 1879, some 8,000 demonstrators, with Parnell at their head, confronted 100 armed police at the cottage of a small farmer threatened with eviction. Then in early January 1880, in a wild and remote place on the Galway coast, the people of Carraroe prevented a process-server escorted by 60 armed police from delivering an eviction notice. This sensational act of resistance became known as the 'battle of Carraroe'. Davitt described what happened:

> On Fenton [the process-server] attempting to approach the house he was set upon by the women and the process snatched from his hand and torn to pieces...
>
> The force next marched to Mrs Mackle's and received such a warm reception that bayonets were freely used by the police in efforts to protect Fenton. Mrs Mackle succeeded in throwing a shovelful of burning turf upon Sub-Inspector Gibbons, and thereby driving him from the house. A fierce fight now commenced, in which the constabulary used their bayonets, but not in any savage manner.
>
> This attack upon the women roused the men to action, and in a second the police were surrounded and attacked with stout blackthorns and stones and compelled to retire from the front of the house.
>
> They re-formed again on the road and fired a volley over the heads of the people, but this, instead of having the desired effect, only excited those the more who were thought to be intimidated, and they rushed upon the constabulary and drove them completely before them, pursuing the flying peelers and Fenton to the doors of the barracks.[26]

At the same time, incidents of violence and intimidation rose rapidly in the west: 233 incidents were logged by police in Connacht in the last three months of 1879, compared with 90 in the previous quarter. Landlords and unionists blamed the violence on the Land League and saw themselves as victims of a monstrous conspiracy which attacked their property rights, social status and loyalty to the union.

Mass starvation was successfully averted by the efforts of voluntary relief agencies, who supplied food, clothing and seed potatoes. The Land League, too, became deeply involved in relief work, and expanded its activities to include support for the families of people imprisoned for fighting eviction cases, and providing grants to help people pursue such cases in the courts.

In January 1880 Parnell travelled to the USA to raise money for the League. Before he left in March, he set up an American Land League as a means of channelling funds independently of Clan-na-Gael. Later that year, Fanny Parnell and Ellen Ford set up a Ladies' Land League in New York.

Captain Boycott

In March 1880 the Tory prime minister, Benjamin Disraeli, unexpectedly called a general election. Ireland was not an issue in the campaign: the overriding concerns were the domestic recession and the Tories' record of costly bungling in imperial affairs further afield. Though Britain had eventually won the Zulu war of the previous year, the price had been enormous: £5 million spent and 2,400 soldiers dead. In Afghanistan, Britain had been humiliated by the murder of the members of a British mission to Kabul, and had replied with invasion and wholesale hangings.

The election was held in April, and the Liberals under Gladstone won a resounding victory, with 347 seats to the Tories' 240. The Liberal majority was so large that they were independent of the 63 Irish Home Rulers.

The Home Rulers were split between 'moderates', led by William Shaw and identified with the landowning interest, and Parnellites, who represented the business and professional middle class. The two camps fought each other at the polls, and the result was a substantial increase in the number of landless MPs, supporters of Parnell, at the expense of the landowners who had previously been dominant. In line with this shift, Parnell was soon elected party leader in place of Shaw.

On 3 August the House of Lords by a huge majority threw out a bill which would have allowed tenants to claim compensation if evicted for non-payment of rent. Evictions rose sharply, provoking riots and assaults. On 11 August a party of Fenians raided a British gunboat in Queenstown harbour and carried off 40 cases of rifles and ammunition.

The harvest was better than in previous years, prompting landlords to try to recover arrears of rent. But many tenants, encouraged by Davitt and the Land League, were determined to 'hold the harvest', retaining enough to cover their needs and paying only the rent they could afford. Fanny Parnell wrote a ballad titled 'Hold the harvest' which Davitt dubbed the Marseillaise of the Irish peasants. It evoked the memory of the 'great hunger':

> Three hundred years your crops have sprung, by murdered corpses fed;
> Your butchered sires, your famished sires, for ghastly compost spread;
> Their bones have fertilised your fields, their blood has fallen like rain;
> They died that you might eat and live. God! have they died in vain?[27]

The League grew rapidly, attracting relatively prosperous tenant farmers as well as impoverished ones. While continuing to fight evictions by legal means, its branches increasingly used the method that became known as the 'boycott'. This weapon was supplemented by the use of intimidation and violence, though without the League's official approval. When, for instance, a County Leitrim landlord, Thomas Corscadden, evicted seven families in August for rent arrears, his tenants responded with months of defiance. They refused to herd his cattle, 150 of his sheep disappeared, his hay was scattered, and his estate stables were burned. Wherever he went he was jeered and ridiculed. Corscadden was given police protection.

Parnell gave national publicity to this method of social ostracism in a speech at a big Land League demonstration in Ennis on 19 September. He asked his audience: 'Now, what are you to do to a tenant who bids for a farm from which another tenant has been evicted?' Several voices responded, 'Shoot him!', whereupon Parnell offered 'a very much better way':

> When a man takes a farm from which another has been evicted you must shun him on the roadside when you meet him – you must shun him in the streets of the town – you must shun him in the shop – you must shun him in the fair-green and in the market place, and even in the place of worship, by leaving him alone, by putting him into a moral Coventry, by isolating him from the rest of his country as if he were the leper of old...[28]

Within days came the start of the events that gave the tactic its name, when tenants on Lord Erne's estate beside Lough Mask in County Mayo retaliated against the land agent, an English farmer named Captain Charles Boycott. The tenants had demanded a rent reduction which Lord Erne refused, and they had then refused to pay any rent. On 22 September a process-server, escorted by 17 policemen, attempted to deliver eviction notices, and was driven off. In a letter published in the *Times* on 18 October 1880, Boycott gave his account of what happened next:

> On the ensuing day, September 23, the people collected in crowds upon my farm, and some hundred or so came up to my house and ordered off, under threats of ulterior consequences, all my farm labourers, workmen, and stable men, commanding them never to work for me again. My herd has been also frightened by them into giving up his employment... The shopkeepers have been warned to stop all supplies to my house... My crops are trampled upon, carried away in quantities, and destroyed wholesale... I say nothing about the danger to my own life, which is apparent to anybody that knows the country.

The danger was real: on 25 September a few miles away Lord Mountmorres had been shot and killed as he drove home.

The peasants' obduracy was doubtless strengthened by their dislike of Boycott, whom they accused of being harsh and domineering. He used to fine his labourers for the slightest misdemeanour: for instance, he fined them one penny for every hen that trespassed on his grass farm.

As the disorder grew, the chief secretary, William Forster, poured police and troops into the disturbed areas. Forster had come to office full of good intentions. He had an impressive record of service with Quaker famine relief during the 'great hunger', and hoped to do good in Ireland. But the pressures of his position soon compromised him. When he announced that the police would be issued with buckshot instead of the more dangerous ball cartridge, the Irish derisively nicknamed him 'Buckshot' Forster. But the English papers and Tory MPs denounced him for not doing enough to combat illegality and murder, and gradually he was driven towards repression. Forster pressed for the suspension of Habeas Corpus, to allow internment without trial. Gladstone hesitated, but allowed the ordinary law to be used in an attempt to silence the League's leaders. On 2 November

Parnell and 13 other leading figures were charged with conspiracy to incite activities such as non-payment of rents and boycotting in order to impoverish the landlords and frustrate the administration of justice.

The League responded defiantly: many new branches were formed, including ladies' branches, and a defence fund was quickly raised to cover the legal expenses. Contributors included two archbishops and three bishops – an indication of growing support among the Catholic upper middle class. Eventually, after a 20-day trial in January 1881 – the greatest state trial since that of O'Connell in 1844 – the jury failed to agree, and the prosecution failed.

Protestant farmers, too, joined the organisation, and on 9 November Parnell appeared at a land meeting in Belleek, County Fermanagh, to launch a campaign in the north. He declared:

> Men of Ulster, – We open today the land campaign in the North of Ireland (hear, hear), and this meeting has been convened to declare that the land movement is not a sectarian movement, and that upon this platform of the land for the people all creeds and classes of Irishmen may unite. (Cheers.) I, as a Protestant (cheers)... feel proud that the Protestant North has opened her arms to this movement. (Cheers.)[29]

He was followed by John Dillon, a Catholic Home Rule MP, who told the audience that he was ashamed to say that they had as bad Catholic landlords in the south as any Protestant that ever was born. The League, he said, supported Protestant as well as Catholic farmers. He went on:

> Do not let, then, the Protestant farmers of Ulster listen to men calling themselves ministers of the Christian religion who entered on the un-Christian task of sowing religious animosity among the inhabitants of this country...[30]

By the end of November 1880, every Ulster county had a Land League branch, and meetings were subsequently held in Orange heartlands such as Saintfield, County Down, and Loughgall in County Armagh. The Loughgall meeting, in January, was held with the master of an Orange Lodge in the chair, and Davitt told the crowd:

> the landlords of Ireland are all of one religion – their God is mammon and rack-rents, and evictions their only morality, while the toilers of the fields, whether Orangemen, Catholics, Presbyterians or Methodists are the victims...[31]

But the Ulster landowners were mobilising too, trying to retain the allegiance of their tenants by appealing to their sectarian prejudices. In early November 1880 the Grand Orange Lodge of Ireland launched a manifesto, with Lord Enniskillen one of the signatories, which denounced the League as a monstrous conspiracy against property rights, with the ulterior object of subverting Protestantism, civil and religious liberty, and the British constitution. The landowners went on to set up special organisations to combat the League.

The plight of Captain Boycott in the autumn of 1880 gave the landowners' campaign a focus. Boycott's cause was championed by the Dublin *Daily Express*, a pro-landlord paper. Through its columns a Dublin gentleman named William Manning raised a fund to organise an expedition to harvest Boycott's crops. Ulster Orangemen, too, pledged support for their 'loyal brethren' in the 'disturbed counties', and there were plenty of volunteers for Manning's expedition. The chief secretary for Ireland, William Forster, set a limit of 50 men – fearing that more would provoke a clash – and promised to protect them. He despatched three trains, each with more than 25 wagons, carrying cavalry, infantry and ambulances, to Ballinrobe. This brought the number of soldiers in the town to 900, while 7,000 stood ready throughout the west.

'The Boycott expedition is the most exciting topic of the day,' began the *Times*' report from Ireland on 10 November. 'It has... filled the minds of the public with mingled curiosity, irritation, and fear.' Several newspaper correspondents accompanied the expedition, and their reports were redolent of other imperial expeditions such as Lord Roberts' march to Kandahar in Afghanistan three months earlier.

The contingent of Orangemen, raised in Cavan and Monaghan, travelled by train under police escort to Claremorris, arriving on 11 November. The *Times* reported:

> The whole road from Ballinrobe to Claremorris, a distance of 13 miles, was patrolled by police, and a force of military was in readiness at Claremorris sufficient to make any attempt to attack the strangers hopeless. Two squadrons of the 10th Hussars and one of the 1st Dragoon Guards left Ballinrobe this morning for Claremorris. Two guns of the Royal Artillery were telegraphed for to Athlone, and the escort from Claremorris to Holymount consisted of 150 infantry, two field-pieces, and 150 men of the Royal Irish Constabulary. All the forces which could be spared from the garrisons in the West were concentrated upon the line of march, and the whole district presented a strange and stirring spectacle. A stranger who did not know the circumstances might have supposed he was in a campaign country on the eve of an expected battle.[32]

Next day the column moved on to Boycott's home, Lough Mask House. The *Times* reported that 'a crowd of women and boys followed behind, and indulged in abusive language at the expense of Captain Boycott and the Orangemen.'[33]

The Orange labourers, guarded by some 160 soldiers and 50 police, spent a fortnight successfully harvesting Boycott's crops. But from the authorities' point of view, the expedition was a fiasco, helping only to publicise and strengthen the Land League. Davitt claimed it had cost £3,500 to harvest a crop worth £350. The Ulstermen left on 26 November, and the next day

Captain Boycott and his family left too, and did not return until many months later when the land agitation had abated.

The Land League gained confidence. In many parts of rural Ireland it was becoming the effective government, setting up courts to try those who offended against its rules. Many land meetings were held, and tension was high as incidents of intimidation, assault and arson increased. Of the extraordinary total of 2,590 'outrages' recorded in 1880, no less than 1,696 occurred in the last three months. Landlords learnt their lesson: evictions dropped dramatically, with 152 families evicted in the last three months of 1880 compared with 629 the preceding quarter.

The Coercion Bill

Forster continued to press for a coercion bill, arguing that a few arrests would at once check outrages, since the main perpetrators and planners were known to the police. Joseph Chamberlain protested that this 'would be like firing with a rifle at a swarm of gnats'.[34]

The cabinet eventually agreed to a coercion bill provided that it was combined with a measure to reform landlord-tenant relations. At the opening of parliament on 6 January 1881 the queen's speech announced that the government would present both a coercion bill and a land bill.

The Parnellite MPs fought back fiercely against the coercion proposal, using obstructionist tactics to drag out the debate on the queen's speech for two weeks. The bill, titled the Protection of Person and Property Bill, was introduced by Forster on 24 January, but the obstructionists, who now numbered about 30, managed to delay the vote on the first reading till 2 February. The obstructionists were only stopped when the speaker, after a marathon 41-hour sitting, declared the debate closed. New parliamentary rules were subsequently drawn up to make it easier to halt the obstructionists.

The bill allowed the arrest and imprisonment without trial of anyone suspected of treasonable practices and agrarian offences. Anticipating its effects, the Land League's executive announced on 26 January that a 'provisional central committee' of ladies would be formed, which could keep the League's work going if the men were imprisoned. Davitt suggested the idea, which was based on the precedent of the Ladies' Land League set up in New York the previous October. Parnell strongly opposed the plan, but was over-ruled. His sister Anna, then 29 years old, agreed to take charge of the Dublin office of the new organisation, which was named the Ladies' National Land League. A committee was formed, and a call was immediately issued to women to form branches and aid people who were being evicted:

> Women of Ireland, you must do your duty whilst our countrymen do theirs... Be ready at least to help the evicted sufferers in every part of

Ireland. You cannot prevent the evictions, but you can and must prevent them from becoming massacres.[35]

The writer Katharine Tynan, a youthful and enthusiastic member, warmly recalled Anna Parnell:

> She had a delightful laugh, clear, ringing, soft, as she had a voice delicate and distinguished, like her brother's. A gentle, shy-looking little lady, with a delicately pretty face and an air of extreme quietness, she had the heart of a Joan of Arc.[36]

Another member of the Ladies' Land League, Jennie Wyse-Power, remembered Anna Parnell's 'strong personality and iron will', and wrote:

> She rarely left our office in O'Connell Street [then Sackville Street] before midnight, frequently crossing the city alone to where she lived in Hume Street, only to rise early next day to another round of unbroken work.[37]

Katharine Tynan also remembered asking at one of the first meetings, 'Why not Women's Land League?' and being told she was too democratic.

On 3 February Davitt was arrested in Dublin and brought to London amid heavy security – for part of the journey his train was preceded by a pilot engine, a measure normally only used for Queen Victoria. The police were especially vigilant in the wake of a gunpowder attack by O'Donovan Rossa's men on 14 January: the first of their 'skirmishing' attempts, it killed a seven-year-old boy and injured three other people.

Davitt's ticket-of-leave was revoked and he was incarcerated in Portland prison on the Dorset coast. His arrest had been instigated by Lord Randolph Churchill, who had drawn parliament's attention to his recent fiery speeches. Davitt's imprisonment was greeted with approval by the *Daily Telegraph* and the *Times*, but the Irish nationalist papers warned that it was a political blunder which would only perpetuate Irish antipathy to foreign rule.

The vigorous campaign against the Coercion Bill continued inside and outside parliament, and included a huge demonstration in London's Hyde Park on 13 February. Finally after 22 stormy sittings the Coercion Act became law on 2 March, and three weeks later it was followed by an Arms Act, banning the possession of arms in proclaimed districts.

The Ladies' Land League now came to the fore. It grew rapidly, with branches springing up all over the country and women assembling in their thousands for public meetings. In Keadue, County Roscommon, for instance, 3,000 gathered on 6 March to listen to a platform of women speakers including Anna Parnell. She told them that the duty of the Ladies' Land League was

> to ensure that when a landlord comes down with all the powers of the law on any of his tenants, that this tenant should not suffer and that no one who could help it should be idle...[38]

Three weeks later 1,500 women assembled in nearby Drumkeerin, County Leitrim, to establish a branch. By mid-May in North Leitrim alone there were eight Ladies' Committees.

The women took on the day-to-day running of the League, aiding evicted and imprisoned tenants and also doing general work including public speaking. They soon found themselves the focus of contention, with the right-wing Archbishop McCabe of Dublin issuing a stern public warning in March against such immodest behaviour, while Archbishop Croke of Cashel and other 'moderate' nationalists sprang to the women's defence. The women carried on with their work undeterred either by the controversy or by the danger of arrest.

Women in England and Scotland, many of them Irish by birth or descent, also set up branches of the Ladies' Land League. A prominent organiser in London was the labour movement activist and feminist Helen Taylor, who set up branches, raised money to aid the tenants, and spoke alongside Anna Parnell and others at crowded public meetings.

The Land Bill

While the Coercion Bill was going through parliament, the government was preparing its other, conciliatory response to the Land League, a land bill. This was intended to undercut the League, and, according to the Irish attorney-general, it went through no less than 22 drafts: 'as lawlessness and outrage increased in Ireland, the Bill was broadened until it reached its final dimensions.'[39]

The Land Bill was introduced on 7 April 1881 and, after 58 sittings and much argument in the Lords, it became law on 22 August. It conceded the 'three Fs' – fixity of tenure, freedom of sale and fair rents – and thus made tenants more secure, but it fell far short of the Land League's demand for peasant ownership. The bill's most significant provision was for the setting up of land courts to fix fair rents between landlords and tenants. This could only benefit the better-off tenant farmers, since it could not help those whose holdings were so small that they could afford no rent at all. The bill thus promised to split the better-off tenants – including those in Ulster – from the poorest, by offering those who could pay the chance to resolve their grievance through the courts, and so forestalling collective action against rack-renting landlords.

The Land League was divided over how to respond to the new legislation. Davitt and the radicals wanted an uncompromising response, whereas many of the MPs and other middle-class nationalists hesitated, fearing to unleash uncontrollable forces. Davitt and his Fenian colleagues saw the land movement as an immensely positive and potentially revolutionary force. In a letter to Devoy in December 1880, Davitt had written candidly that the outlook for the land movement was 'splendid'. The people were realising their collective power and learning to use it for their own benefit, and if the movement could carry on without government interference for another year, 'we could do almost anything we pleased... The courage of the people is magnificent. All classes are purchasing arms openly.'[40]

In January 1881 Davitt proposed that on the day the Coercion Act became law, the Irish parliamentary party should withdraw from Westminster and return to Ireland to head a 'no rent' campaign – a general strike in which the peasants would withhold all rents. The time was ripe for such a move, the radicals felt, because Britain was in difficulties with the Boer rebellion in the Transvaal. But influential Parnellite MPs would not back the idea, and it came to nothing.

On 21 and 22 April – by which time Davitt was in prison – the League held a national convention in Dublin to consider the Land Bill. The radicals demanded that it should be completely rejected. Thomas Brennan, secretary of the League and a close associate of Davitt's, denounced the bill for not helping the poor. The *Irish Times'* report of his speech continued:

> The bill which was wanted was such a measure as would benefit not only the people in the country, but also the people in the cities and towns as well – a bill that would replace poverty by plenty, and secure to the many the fruits which were yielded by the earth. He believed that such a result could only be obtained under the fostering care of a National Government, and the time was fast coming when they would be forced to take a step beyond this mere social question. (Applause.) The country was organised as it had never been before.[41]

The League, however, while condemning the bill as wrong in principle, adopted a proposal put by Parnell to make the best of the bill by securing amendments to it.

When the act was passed, it was welcomed by the right wing of the land movement, including the bishops and many of the Home Rule MPs. But the radicals, including many Irish-Americans, denounced the act and demanded a 'no rent' campaign.

Anna Parnell, who like Davitt saw the Land League as pursuing a course that would lead to Irish independence, later described the Land Act as 'the ridiculous mouse resulting from the upheaval of the whole island,' and added: 'Perhaps it would be more proper to liken it to a centipede than a mouse, on account of its great length and complexity.'[42]

Her brother trod a typically careful path. He rejected the 'no rent' plan, proposing instead that the League should take test cases to the land courts to see how the act would operate. But at the same time, in order to retain grassroots support and the flow of funds from America, he made a series of uncompromising public speeches suggesting that the test cases would demonstrate the 'hollowness' of the act.

Gladstone, however, took Parnell's speeches at face value and believed he was trying to destroy the Land Act. On 12 October 1881 the cabinet decided to arrest Parnell, and early next morning two policemen came to his Dublin hotel and took him to Kilmainham prison, where he was soon joined by five other Land League leaders. Another Home Rule MP, T.M. Healy, wrote caustically of the government's misjudgement of Parnell, saying:

> the enemies of the alleged agrarian Jacquerie in Ireland little supposed that at its head was a moderate, almost a conservative, leader, averse, except when driven to it by the 'stokers' of the movement, to lend his approval to extreme demands...[43]

The arrests were greeted with rapture in England, except by radicals, and with widespread anger in Ireland. Parnell himself privately thought his arrest convenient, as he revealed in a letter to his mistress Katharine O'Shea:

> Politically it is a fortunate thing for me that I have been arrested, as the movement is breaking fast, and all will be quiet in a few months, when I shall be released.[44]

The imprisoned leaders struck back at the government by issuing a manifesto, written in impassioned style by William O'Brien, editor of the League's paper *United Ireland*, calling on the tenant farmers

> to pay no rent under any circumstances to their landlords until the government relinquishes the existing system of terrorism and restores the constitutional rights of the people...[45]

It is doubtful whether any of the signatories had any confidence in the manifesto's protestations. Even John Dillon, who had earlier strongly advocated a 'no rent campaign', now felt that such a campaign had little chance: he thought it might lead to violence and that neither the League nor the tenants were adequately organised to meet government coercion.

The manifesto immediately split the League's supporters. It was denounced by 'moderates', even the usually sympathetic Archbishop Croke, while the Fenian-orientated 'advanced' nationalists acclaimed it.

Chief secretary Forster informed Gladstone that the manifesto was an 'excellent excuse' for banning the League. He moved quickly, issuing a proclamation on 20 October declaring the League to be 'an unlawful and criminal association'.

A period of uncontrolled coercion began, and the land war became more inflamed than ever. Forster deployed police, military and magistrates to arrest League leaders, disperse League meetings, raid the League's offices and confiscate its property. The staff and printers of its paper, *United Ireland*, were imprisoned, and its sellers were harassed, so that although it was not formally banned, the paper was driven underground.

In the countryside, special magistrates were appointed in December with extraordinary powers. Suspected activists were batoned, arrested and imprisoned. The jails filled with hundreds of detainees.

An eviction, 1880

On 20 October the land courts started to operate. Many tenants resorted to them – 20,000 applied by 10 November – with some obtaining substantial rent reductions. At the same time, tenants in arrears were evicted in their thousands. In a letter to the central committee of the Ladies' Land League in November, Miss Marion Hawkes of the Kiltyclogher branch in County Leitrim described the evictions on the estate of Arthur Loftus Tottenham, a

Conservative MP, including the case of a woman whose husband had gone to America some months earlier to earn money to pay the rent:

> She had seven children, four of them under six years of age. Her troubles had been too much for her reason; she was lightheaded and when turned out of her dwelling she had no possible place of shelter. The nearest house was a quarter of a mile distant and there was no pathway – a steep hillside, ditches and marshy ground all the way. Something had to be done, so two little girls and myself persuaded her to go with us, taking the four smallest children and leaving the others to watch the throwing out of their effects. The girls carried the two babies on their backs. The mother was so worn out in mind and body that I often despaired of getting her over the ground into which we were sinking ankle-deep and often deeper...[46]

Such evictions soon reached unprecedented heights, with 4,338 families evicted in the first nine months of 1882, more than 20,000 people. The evictions and attempts by poorer tenants to enforce the 'no rent' policy led to an increase in violence and intimidation: 1,619 incidents were recorded in the last quarter of 1881 and 1,417 in the first quarter of 1882.

The Ladies' Land League

The Ladies' Land League worked with energy and dedication. They kept *United Ireland* in circulation. William O'Brien contrived to continue editing it from his prison cell, while the women contributed articles, kept the accounts, and helped arrange for it to be printed clandestinely in London, Liverpool and Paris and smuggled into Ireland. Katharine Tynan recalled:

> Hannah Lynch carried over the type to Paris, and the paper was issued from there. I remember going in and out of the offices in Lower Abbey Street, where the women, girls rather, were in command both in the editorial rooms and the counting house.[47]

Anna Parnell regretted that they did not have printing among their accomplishments, and advised all Irish people who wished to benefit Ireland 'to learn the art of printing if they can'.[48]

In the countryside, the women continued to help evicted families, providing them with money and with prefabricated wooden huts which they ordered from a builder in Dublin. They also supplied food to those in prison: the women wanted to give each prisoner a weekly allowance for food, but the Land League men insisted that catering be organised, which was much more expensive and complicated. The women also did their best to encourage tenants to carry out the 'no rent' policy.

On 16 December 1881 the Ladies' Land League was banned. The women responded defiantly, with thousands turning out for protest meetings on New Year's Day. Many were subsequently imprisoned. The first victim was Hanna Reynolds, who was jailed for a month for inciting a tenant not to pay rent. The prison regime was rigorous: they were only allowed out of their cells for two hours a day, when they walked round the yard in silence.

The radical campaigner Annie Besant, in a pamphlet denouncing coercion, described the case of Miss O'Connor, the 20-year-old sister of T.P. O'Connor MP, imprisoned at Mullingar and suffering from weakness of the lungs. Annie Besant asked:

> Surely this poor young delicate girl, so young, moved by the misery around her to protest, and trying to restrain the starving from desperate deeds, ought not to be left in jail. What sort of Government is it in Ireland that needs such acts as these to be done in its support?[49]

The women were deeply disillusioned when they realised that the Land League was not genuinely committed to the rent resistance. They found themselves hampered by the hostility of the men of the League, who were annoyed, as Anna Parnell put it, by 'the discovery that we were taking the Land League seriously, and thought that not paying rent was intended to mean not paying it.'[50] She wrote later to a friend: 'When I joined the Ladies' Land League I did not know the Land League was not a bona fide affair or I never would have had anything to do with it.'[51]

Anna Parnell subsequently wrote a scathing critique of the League titled *The Tale of a Great Sham*, which failed to find a publisher till the 1980s. Here she expressed her opinion that a genuine all-out 'no rent' campaign should have been launched much earlier, and could have been successful. She contested the view that 'no one who could pay would refrain from doing it', saying that: 'the only conclusion we could come to was that the Land League had discovered no such places simply because they had not tried to.'[52]

Gladstone's strategy

But though Anna Parnell, with the eyes of an insider and a radical, saw the Land League as a 'fiasco', the British government saw it very differently. The endemic tension and disorder led them urgently to question their Irish policy. As Davitt wrote later:

> it began to dawn on some of the official minds that the imprisonment of the male leaders had only rendered confusion worse confounded for Dublin Castle, and made the country infinitely more ungovernable under the sway of their lady successors.[53]

Not only did the coercion policy, especially the detention of three MPs, lead to embarrassing criticism on moral grounds, but also it did not work: by early 1882 more than a thousand people had been detained but the 'outrages' continued.

While the chief secretary for Ireland, William Forster, backed by Dublin Castle officials, argued for the continuation of coercion, Gladstone was thinking in more ambitious terms. In February 1882 he expressed the view that Ireland should be given autonomy in local affairs, provided that the British parliament remained supreme and the unity of the empire was not threatened. Queen Victoria and other conservative elements were much alarmed by this. The queen wrote an agitated note to Gladstone, who replied on 13 February with a letter that revealed that his aim was to make concessions in order to split the Irish MPs and thus head off any united move for a serious measure of independence for Ireland. He said in his letter:

> There is a very real danger which may come above the horizon, and which Mr Gladstone humbly desires to avert. That danger will have arisen, should a decisive majority of the representatives of Ireland unitedly demand on behalf of their country the adoption of some scheme of Home Rule, which Parliament should be compelled to refuse. To prevent the formation of such an Irish majority is, in Mr Gladstone's view, a great object of Imperial policy... Mr Gladstone can for himself only follow the course which will, as he believes, prevent its consolidation upon any basis dangerous to the Empire or the Throne.[54]

The continuing turbulence, together with rent reductions made by the land court, were by now persuading landowners that their best option was to get the state to advance the money to the tenants to buy them out. This perception, soon adopted by a succession of governments, marked the beginning of the end of the landlords as the dominant class within Ireland. It also started the process of changing the peasantry from radical tenants to conservative owners.

Gladstone coupled the issues of local self-government and land purchase, and drafted a plan for elected provincial councils which would handle the transfer of land from landlords to tenants. On 12 April he wrote to Forster:

> until we have seriously responsible bodies to deal with us in Ireland, every plan we frame comes to Irishmen... as an English plan...
>
> For the Ireland of today the first question is the rectification of the relations between landlord and tenant, which happily is going on; the next is to relieve Great Britain from the enormous weight of the government of Ireland unaided by the people...[55]

Gladstone argued that 'local institutions of self-government should be set up.' In essence, this meant making the Irish middle class into Britain's junior partners in governing Ireland, and in the process displacing the landowners from their role as Britain's garrison.

Parnell, too, was anxious to break the stalemate. He wanted to bring the agrarian unrest to an end before it turned into the full-scale revolution that its Fenian founders and his sister Anna hoped for. While on parole in April 1882 for his nephew's funeral, Parnell approached Gladstone through an intermediary, William O'Shea, husband of his mistress Katharine. Parnell's offer was summarised by Joseph Chamberlain in a memorandum on 22 April:

> If the Government announce a satisfactory plan of dealing with arrears, Mr Parnell will advise all tenants to pay rents and will denounce outrages, resistance to law and all processes of intimidation whether by Boycotting or in any other way.[56]

Gladstone soon concluded that Parnell's offer was genuine and that he and the other two MPs, John Dillon and James O'Kelly, should be released. The government announced the releases on 2 May; the same day Forster, unhappy with the government's direction, resigned his post as chief secretary for Ireland. Two days later Lord Frederick Cavendish, who was married to Gladstone's niece, was appointed in Forster's place.

Events then went dramatically out of control. On 5 May, people all over Ireland celebrated Parnell's victory, sometimes by stoning the police. In Ballina, County Mayo, police fired on a boisterous crowd, fatally wounding a youth and injuring several others, an event which soon became known as the 'Ballina massacre'. Next morning, 6 May, Cavendish arrived in Dublin, accompanying the new lord lieutenant, Earl Spencer, in his ceremonial entry into the capital. That evening at about quarter past seven, as Cavendish walked through Phoenix Park towards the Viceregal Lodge with the under secretary, T.H. Burke, they were attacked and stabbed to death by assassins armed with long surgical knives of a type designed for major amputations.

The attackers belonged to the Invincibles, a secret organisation recently set up for the purpose of killing the top people in the British regime in Ireland. Leading Land League Fenians were probably behind the organisation, including Patrick Egan, who was living in Paris to avoid arrest, and Frank Byrne, Liverpool-based secretary of the Land League of Great Britain, whose pregnant wife brought the knives used in the assassinations to Ireland concealed in her skirts. Their recruits in Dublin were mostly tradesmen and craftsmen, with a few labourers: those executed a year later for the Phoenix Park killings were a stone cutter, a carpenter, a coachbuilder, a blacksmith and a labourer.

The conspirators had made several unsuccessful attempts to ambush the former chief secretary, William Forster – even searching for him at the station on the day of his departure – and then they transferred their attention to the hated Burke. Many people believed at the time – though the evidence is inconclusive – that Burke was their main target that night, while the newcomer Cavendish was, in Anna Parnell's words, 'sacrificed to the accident of his being in Burke's company'.[57]

The Phoenix Park assassinations caused a huge sensation, appalling the British establishment and prompting mob attacks on the homes of Irish people in Britain. Assassinations of political figures were unheard of in Britain or Ireland at the time. They were regarded as outlandish acts which might happen in America or Russia but were inconceivable at home. The victims of killings in the land war – 22 in 1881 – had been mainly landlords, agents, bailiffs and land grabbers.

On 11 May the government introduced a draconian measure, the Prevention of Crimes (Ireland) Bill, which suspended jury trials for certain cases and increased the powers of magistrates and police. This bill had been proposed in outline by Lord Spencer before the Phoenix Park assassinations, but the altered political climate meant that the bill met no opposition from English liberals.

The Irish MPs were horrified by the killings. Parnell, Dillon and Davitt – who had likewise just been released – issued a manifesto appealing to the Irish people

> to show by every manner of expression possible, that amidst the universal feeling of horror which the assassination has excited, no people are so intense in their detestation of this atrocity, or entertain so deep a sympathy for those whose hearts must be seared by it...[58]

The killings were also condemned by leaders of the Irish Republican Brotherhood, including Charles Kickham and John O'Leary.

Anna Parnell bravely wrote to the *Times* referring to the Ballina massacre:

> Mr Forster butchered men and women; for Lord Spencer has been reserved the distinction of butchering children... This is conciliation. If there are any who are surprised that the assassin's arm is not idle because of it they must forget that there is such a thing as human nature among Irishmen.[59]

She later wrote angrily of the 'cringing attitudes' of the Irish MPs, and attacked their manifesto in terms which echoed the feelings of other Land League radicals:

> To accept responsibility on behalf of a people for the crime in their country, when that people does not govern that country, is in itself inconsistent with the claim of that country to nationality. It is quite natural that the English should want to go shares with the Irish in governing Ireland on the principle of their having the power and the Irish the responsibility. But why should the Irish want to sanction the arrangement? While England holds Ireland, any responsibility there may be on a people as a whole for anything wrong in the country rests on the English people and not on the Irish...[60]

End of the Ladies' Land League

Despite the Phoenix Park murders, the government and Parnell went ahead with the moves agreed in the 'Kilmainham treaty'. Immediately after the Coercion Bill, the government moved an arrears bill which empowered the Land Commission to cancel part of the arrears of rent owed by small tenants. For his part, Parnell damped down the land agitation. Paradoxically, the Phoenix Park murders assisted him in carrying this through against the wishes of the left wing of the land movement. The killings had discredited the revolutionaries in the eyes of many, and also Parnell's opposition to the coercion bill maintained his reputation as an opponent of the government.

Parnell had emerged from Kilmainham extremely anxious to suppress the Ladies' Land League. Davitt later recalled a conversation with him on 6 May, after Parnell had collected him from Portland prison:

> I never saw him so wild and angry; the Ladies' Land League had... taken the country out of his hands and should be suppressed. I defended the ladies, saying that, after all, they had kept the ball rolling while he was in jail. 'I am out now,' said he, 'and I don't want them to keep the ball rolling any more. The league must be suppressed, or I will leave public life.'[61]

Initially, however, the women were left to continue their day-to-day work of providing support to victims of evictions and to prisoners, but they were given no encouragement to restart the resistance to rent. According to Anna Parnell's account, the women were by now anxious to be released from their thankless task – only to find that the men's plan was for the Ladies'

Land League to dissolve but for the women to continue to do the most difficult task: assessing grant applications and recommending which ones should be met. The men said they would pay off the Ladies' Land League's debts if the women agreed to their plan. Anna Parnell considered that the men wanted the women to be 'a perpetual petticoat screen behind which they could shelter, not from the government, but from the people.'[62] Eventually a compromise was reached, and in August 1882 the women dissolved the Ladies' Land League.

Anna Parnell's experiences left her bitter and deeply sceptical about the character of Irish male political leaders: she never spoke to her brother again. She doubted the capacity of the men – women at this time were excluded from public affairs – to lead an Irish independence movement. She wrote later:

> We know... that the character of Irishmen is at present incompatible with any great change for the better in Ireland... I say 'Irishmen', because, whatever the relative values of men and women may be, it is certain that the former cannot be done without, when it is a question of altering the status of a country. If the men of that country have made up their minds it shall not be done, the women cannot bring it about.[63]

Anna Parnell left Ireland to live as a near-penniless recluse in England, but she kept up her contacts with Ireland and continued to support the independence movement. In 1911 she drowned while swimming in heavy seas near Ilfracombe in Devon.

Like Anna Parnell, Davitt and other Land League radicals, including those in America, regarded Parnell's Kilmainham 'treaty' with Gladstone as a sell-out. They felt he had surrendered on terms far short of the League's basic demands, and had stopped the agitation too soon, when it was on the verge of victory.

While Parnell with his conservative outlook was sympathetic to the tenants' desire to become the owners of their farms, the radicals wanted the complete abolition of landlordism. Davitt, who had given the issue much thought while in prison, saw the goal as national ownership of the land, with the tenants in effect holding freeholds from the state. They would be able to enjoy the full fruits of their work, in return for paying a basic tax and observing certain conditions. This in turn was part of his vision of a regeneration of the Irish economy and society that would benefit all the working people of Ireland.

Davitt incorporated his ideas in a plan for a new organisation to be called 'The National Land and Industrial Union of Ireland', which would 'improve the social and political condition of the Irish people'. This would not only aim for the abolition of landlordism, but would aim to better the conditions of agricultural labourers and improve housing; it would develop industry, fishing and agriculture; it would improve educational standards among artisans and workers, and encourage the national literature and the Irish language; and it would aim for the repeal of the Act of Union and for national self-government.

Parnell, who shared neither Davitt's enthusiasm for land nationalisation nor his sympathy for the working class, refused to discuss these proposals. But he eventually agreed to set up a new organisation, the Irish National League, which had a more limited programme. The new body, set up in October 1882, was designed mainly to be an electoral machine for the Irish parliamentary party. Its organising committee was dominated by MPs and chaired by Parnell. It excluded women from membership. Davitt later described the founding of the National League as:

> the complete eclipse, by a purely parliamentary substitute, of what had been a semi-revolutionary organisation... the overthrow of a movement and the enthronement of a man...[64]

Despite his reservations about the National League, Davitt supported it and joined its organising committee because of his overriding anxiety not to split the national forces. But from now on his main role was as an independent activist: through his speeches and writings he promoted Irish nationalism and independence movements elsewhere, and agitated for the interests of workers, agricultural labourers and small farmers. He spent much time and energy in Britain supporting the rising movement for independent working class representation in parliament, and worked to link this with the Irish cause.

The dynamite campaign

The land movement in its heyday had been a mass movement encompassing politicians and clergy, tenant activists and agrarian secret societies, and Fenians in Ireland, Britain and America. Methods used by the movement had ranged from parliamentary pressure to local mobilisations to intimidation and violence.

Old-style Fenians such as Charles Kickham and John O'Leary, disapproving both of parliamentary activity and the land agitation, had remained aloof and virtually inactive pending the dreamed-of day of a general rising. Some Fenians in America, however, including opponents of the Land League such as Jeremiah O'Donovan Rossa, and supporters of the League such as the newspaper editor Patrick Ford, advocated a policy of 'skirmishing', or surprise attacks on Britain. As Ford had explained in December 1875, skirmishing was an alternative to insurrection, which was not then feasible:

> A few active, intrepid and intelligent men can do so much to annoy and hurt England. The Irish cause requires Skirmishers. It requires a little

band of heroes who will initiate and keep up without intermission a guerrilla warfare – men who will fly over land and sea like invisible beings – now striking the enemy in Ireland, now in India, now in England itself, as occasion may present.[65]

The outcome was several overlapping conspiracies to bomb Britain. Organised by O'Donovan Rossa, Dr Thomas Gallagher and Captain William Mackey Lomasney, these campaigns aimed not at assassination – as did the short-lived Invincible conspiracy – nor at causing large-scale destruction, but simply at frightening the British government. Their targets were barracks, public utilities and symbolic public buildings.

O'Donovan Rossa, exuberant, disorganised and impetuous, was first into the field. Frustrated by Clan-na-Gael's support for the Land League and its failure to carry out any explosions, he set up his own paper, the *United Irishman*, in June 1880, and set about raising funds. His 'skirmishers' soon went into action, carrying out four attacks in England between January and June 1881. The land movement was still very much alive, and these attacks merely added an extra element to the already high tension. Using gunpowder – a method made old-fashioned by the recent invention of dynamite by the Swedish chemist Alfred Nobel – and with little technical competence, Rossa's men began by placing a bomb behind a ventilation grid in the wall of Salford Barracks near Manchester on 14 January. The bomb killed a seven-year-old boy and injured three other people, and destroyed a butcher's shed. The bombing was widely interpreted as O'Donovan Rossa's challenge to the threatened Coercion Bill. Troops and police were put on alert and police were deployed to protect army barracks and London's major buildings.

William Mackey Lomasney, who was planning a separate bombing campaign sponsored by Clan-na-Gael, watched O'Donovan Rossa's efforts with alarm and scorn, writing to Devoy in March 1881:

> they are such stupid blundering fools that they make our cause appear imbecile and farcical... what will the world think but that Irish revolutionists are a lot of fools and ignoramuses, men who do not understand the first principles of the art of war, the elements of chemistry or even the amount of explosive material necessary to remove or destroy an ordinary brick or stone wall.[66]

The Clan and the Irish Republican Brotherhood tried and failed to stop O'Donovan Rossa's men. On 16 March, on a foggy night, they placed a bomb on a ledge outside the Mansion House, residence of the mayor of the city of London. The mayor's banquet had been due that night, but had been cancelled because of the assassination of Tsar Alexander II three days earlier. A patrolling constable discovered the smouldering parcel and carried it off before it could explode.

Another two months elapsed before the next attempt, this time in Liverpool. On the night of 16 May 1881 James McGrath, a 27-year-old Glasgow-born ship's steward, and James McKevitt, a 32-year-old Liverpool dock labourer born in County Down, left a bomb outside the accommodation block of Liverpool police station. It exploded, damaging the door and windows.

Then on 10 June they were seen lighting the fuse of a bomb – this time made of dynamite imported from America – outside Liverpool Town Hall. The bomb exploded and the two men were captured soon afterwards, later receiving long prison sentences. Customs surveillance at Liverpool was increased, and several bombs were intercepted arriving on ships from the USA.

There were no more such incidents till nearly a year later, when on 12 May 1882, six days after the Phoenix Park killings, a bomb containing blasting powder was left on a windowsill at London's Mansion House. The rag fuse failed to stay alight, and the press suggested it was a hoax. The home secretary, William Harcourt, wrote on 14 May to the lord lieutenant in Dublin that the attempted explosion

> was a Fenian scare of the old clumsy kind. I made it a reason for having all the Irish quarters in Lond. beat up last night. My police report very little Fenianism in London but of course it may be imported any day either from America or Ireland...[67]

But Harcourt's assurance was not shared by Queen Victoria, who was reportedly 'in a great state of fuss'.[68]

By 1883 the British Liberal government, through the viceroy, Lord Spencer, was operating a rigorously repressive regime in Ireland. Not only were those suspected of agrarian violence rounded up and jailed, but meetings were banned and newspapers suppressed. Michael Davitt and the Irish MP T.M. Healy were jailed for making seditious speeches.

By this time, since the evaporation of the mass movement in the wake of the Kilmainham agreement, only two kinds of Irish nationalist resistance remained: Parnell's parliamentary campaign and its conservative supporters on the one hand, and the America-based dynamiters on the other.

The dynamiters redoubled their efforts, and were encouraged by the new leadership of Clan-na-Gael under Alexander Sullivan, who was extremely impatient with the Irish Republican Brotherhood's inactivity. Rossa's men came back with a vengeance on the night of 20 January 1883 in Glasgow, using dynamite to blow up a gasometer in a massive explosion that injured 11 people, and blowing up a disused railway coaling shed. They also narrowly failed to blow up an aqueduct carrying a canal over a main road.

Then on 15 March they attacked in London. They left one bomb on the window sill of the *Times'* offices near Blackfriars Bridge which failed to detonate properly, and another on a window ledge of a new block of government office buildings between Downing Street and the House of Commons. The Parliament Street bomb went off at 9 p.m. with a huge explosion said to have been heard 46 miles away, which destroyed most of the window panes in the building.

The government responded by deploying 355 police to guard public buildings, ministers and their residences, and members of parliament moving to and from their houses. London was effectively in a state of siege.

The previous year, after the Phoenix Park killings, a Secret Service had been created in Ireland to collect intelligence by infiltrating Irish organisations and by employing informers. Its efforts extended to Britain, France and America. Now, after the Whitehall bomb, plans were put rapidly in motion to create a Special Irish Branch within the Criminal Investigation Division of the Metropolitan Police. This was apparently the idea of the home secretary, Sir William Harcourt, under whose control it would come. The purpose was to co-ordinate and improve intelligence-gathering activities – surveillance, the use of informants and the pooling of information – which had previously been run on an ad hoc basis. The word 'Irish' was dropped from its title in 1888 when it had become clear that the Branch's interests extended more widely. A handful of officers, including four from the Royal Irish Constabulary, were allocated to the Special Irish Branch, which was given offices in a building in Great Scotland Yard. These were – disastrously as it proved – situated above a public lavatory, much used by the frequenters of the Rising Sun public house opposite.

The police soon made a number of arrests. The conspirators' weak point was that they were manufacturing the explosives themselves, so they could be identified when they bought the relevant chemicals. Through keeping a watch on chemical suppliers, the Irish Secret Service tracked down a group of Rossa's men in Cork at the end of March, who were subsequently arrested and imprisoned.

Almost simultaneously the police had another major coup. This time the storeman at a chemical supplier in Birmingham became suspicious when a customer, purporting to be a paint and paper retailer, ordered a large amount of pure glycerine. The storeman told the police, who put the man, calling himself Albert Whitehead, under surveillance. Whitehead was part of a team organised by Dr Thomas Gallagher, an Irish-American who was funded by Clan-na-Gael but had a secret arrangement with O'Donovan Rossa. Gallagher was a very intelligent and assiduous man. Born in Glasgow in 1851, he had worked as a child in a foundry. When he was in his teens, his widowed mother had emigrated to the USA taking her eight children. Here Gallagher had again worked in a foundry, but studied medicine in his spare time and became a doctor, setting up a practice in the Irish community. His knowledge of chemistry enabled him to manufacture dynamite and teach the skill to others. One of his pupils was Tom Clarke, born in 1857 and the son of an Irishman serving in the British army, who had recently emigrated from Dungannon to the USA. Gallagher recruited Clarke and three others and they prepared to plant bombs in London in the spring of 1883.

After several days' surveillance of visitors to Whitehead's shop, the Birmingham police and the Special Irish Branch between them arrested all five members of Gallagher's team on 5 April after one of them had transported over 400 pounds of nitroglycerine to London. This instantly persuaded the home secretary of the need to tighten up the law on explosives – at that time private individuals were allowed to possess large quantities of dynamite or gunpowder. On 9 April the Explosive Substances Bill, which made it a serious crime to make or possess explosives for illegal purposes, was rushed through both Houses of Parliament and became law the next day.

Two months later, four of the bomb team were sentenced to life imprisonment and one, who turned Queen's evidence but gave away little of significance, was deported. Conditions in Chatham prison were extremely harsh, and two of the prisoners, Gallagher and Whitehead, were driven insane. Tom Clarke, who later chronicled their experiences, was eventually released in 1898, and became a key figure in a new phase of the nationalist struggle.

The last and most determined series of attacks were again sponsored by Clan-na-Gael, but organised this time by William Mackey Lomasney, a veteran Fenian known as 'the little Captain'. These attacks, using dynamite, ran from October 1883 to January 1885, and were all in London.

Lomasney was born in Cincinnati, Ohio, in 1841. His family came from Cork and had a long revolutionary tradition: his great grandfather had been killed in the rising of 1798. Lomasney returned to Ireland and joined the 1867 rising, winning fame for his part in the capture of Ballyknockane police barracks near Cork, and for his daring raids on gunshops and coastguard stations. He was arrested in early 1868 and sentenced to 12 years, but was released in the 1871 amnesty. While in Millbank prison in London, Lomasney met John Devoy, who wrote later that they became 'fast friends'.[69] Devoy wrote of him:

> William Mackey Lomasney was one of the most remarkable men of the Fenian movement. A small man of slender build, who spoke with a lisp, modest and retiring in manner, one who did not know him well would never take him for a desperate man, but no man in the Fenian movement ever did more desperate things.[70]

Before embarking on the dynamite campaign in 1883, Lomasney discussed the policy with John Devoy, who recalled:

> He wanted simply to strike terror into the Government and the governing class and would not hurt the hair of an Englishman's head except in fair fight... I told him the most he could expect through Terrorism was to wring some small concessions from the English which could be taken

back at any time when the Government's counter-policy of Terrorism achieved some success. Lomasney admitted this, but contended that the counter-Terrorism would not succeed; that the Irish were a fighting race who had through the long centuries never submitted to coercion; that their fighting spirit would be aroused by the struggle... and that in the end Ireland would win her full Freedom.[71]

London under siege

Lomasney's team began with two attacks on the London underground railways on 30 October 1883. At about 8 p.m. a bomb was dropped from the middle of a moving Metropolitan line train which had just left Praed Street station (now Paddington) going westwards. The three third-class coaches at the back were wrecked and 72 passengers were taken to hospital with injuries and shock. A large gas main in the tunnel was also shattered. A few minutes later another bomb was dropped from the back of a westbound District Line train just after it left Charing Cross station: this caused limited damage and no injuries.

The authorities were very concerned. The home secretary arranged for a second pilot engine to travel in front of Queen Victoria's train, and a round-the-clock guard was put on the Albert Memorial, which had been constructed a decade earlier at great expense to commemorate the Queen's husband.

Clan bombers attacked again on 26 February 1884, planting bombs in four London railway stations. Only one of these, in the luggage room in Victoria station, exploded.

The government repeated its efforts – but without success – to try to persuade the American government to clamp down on newspapers which raised funds for the dynamiters. A special port protection scheme was set up, with 79 police drawn from Scotland Yard and the Royal Irish Constabulary assigned to watch some 36 ports, and plainclothes police were sent to ports on the continent.

John Sweeney, a Kerry-born detective stationed at Hull, a busy transit point for European emigrants travelling to America via Liverpool, later recalled:

> We seemed to spend night and day in boarding vessels and hunting keenly about for doubtful characters; we had to guard against an excess of zeal which might lead us into interfering with perfectly respectable and harmless travellers, or into making ourselves into a laughing-stock by over-eagerness in following up some false scent...[72]

In April, police and Secret Service surveillance in the Midlands resulted in several arrests.

On the night of 30 May there were three more explosions, the most serious of which was in the public lavatory underneath the Special Irish Branch's offices in Great Scotland Yard. The bomb badly damaged the building and destroyed a significant part of the Branch's records on Fenian affairs. The worried authorities searched out other strategically placed public toilets, closing one near Windsor Castle, and were alarmed to discover that the entire sanitation of the Houses of Parliament was being overhauled by Irish workmen.

The next incident came several months later on 13 December. William Mackey Lomasney, with his brother and another Fenian named John Fleming – whom Devoy described as 'a splendid man' – hired a boat and rowed to London Bridge, where they attached a bomb to one of the arches. The bomb exploded prematurely just after 6 p.m., killing the three men. Their bodies were never recovered. The bomb caused only slight damage to the bridge: this, Devoy considered, was all that Lomasney intended. Devoy wrote:

> He was, in my opinion, carrying out his policy of frightening the English Government and England's Ruling Class. And that it did frighten them, as all the other dynamite operations did, there can be no reason to doubt.[73]

A final spate of bombings soon followed, co-ordinated by a 30-year-old Irish-American cabinet maker named Harry Burton who had been involved in earlier incidents. On 2 January 1885, 23-year-old James Cunningham left a bomb in a westbound Metropolitan Line train which exploded as it approached Gower Street (now Euston Square). It severely damaged the train but caused few injuries.

Two weeks later, on Saturday 24 January, Cunningham placed a bomb in the Tower of London, in the banqueting room of the White Tower. He put it behind a gun carriage which took most of the blast, but two young women and two boys were seriously injured. Cunningham was arrested at the gates on his way out.

That same afternoon, two other bombers, one of them probably an Irish-American named Luke Dillon, went to the House of Commons, mingling with the many sightseers. They put a small diversionary bomb in the crypt: this was spotted by a constable and exploded as he carried it away, leaving him with four broken ribs. Hearing the explosion, the constable in the Chamber of the House left his post, as intended, whereupon the second bomber – possibly disguised as a woman – dropped a bomb into the Chamber. It exploded almost immediately, causing extensive damage. The two bombers escaped in the confusion.

Consternation ensued, and the home secretary ordered that plainclothes officers be placed on major public buildings, while special precautions were taken throughout London. Harry Burton was arrested, and he and Cunningham were put on trial in May and sentenced to life imprisonment. It was the end of the first – but by no means the last – Irish republican bombing campaign in Britain.

The Irish-Americans continued to collect money for a bombing campaign, but failed to renew it, probably because of internal disputes within Clan-na-Gael and also the changing political environment across the Atlantic. Clan-na-Gael was riven with dissension over the leadership of Alexander Sullivan. A Chicago lawyer, Sullivan had appealed to Clan militants by promoting the dynamite policy, while at the same time playing for the support of the new middle class of Irish-Americans by calling on the US government to curtail pauper immigration from Ireland. An opposing faction, centred on John Devoy, attacked Sullivan for using the Clan as a machine for American electioneering, for breaking the link with the Irish Republican Brotherhood and for their lavish expenditure. Clan-na-Gael was to remain split until 1900, when it reunited behind Devoy's leadership.

Meanwhile in Ireland the Irish Republican Brotherhood was expanding its support by working through open organisations. In 1884 IRB members helped to set up the Gaelic Athletic Association, which rapidly attracted thousands of members. The GAA's founders aimed to stem the 'denationalising' influence of English-run games such as rugby and cricket, reviving instead traditional Irish sports such as hurling. They also wanted to extend sport to the working class: the GAA's first president, Maurice Davin, believed there was a need for games 'especially for the humble and hard-working who seem now to be born into no other inheritance than an everlasting round of labour'.[74] The IRB, for its part, not only saw the GAA as a means of inspiring nationalist feeling, but also saw its nationwide network of disciplined athletes as the nucleus of an army.

At the same time, the IRB set up the Young Ireland Society, with its headquarters in Dublin and branches elsewhere, which organised lectures on Irish history and literature as well as mobilising for events such as the return from exile of the veteran Fenian John O'Leary in 1884. O'Leary, now in his fifties, became the focus of attraction for a bevy of young intellectuals. These included the 20-year-old poet William Butler Yeats and the Gaelic scholar Douglas Hyde, both from Protestant upper-middle-classily. With his honourable ideals and vague and elitist politics – he disapproved of action whether by dynamiters or parliamentarians, and preferred monarchy to republicanism – O'Leary seemed a romantic figure. Yeats later recalled him as

> the handsomest old man I had ever seen... He had the moral genius that moves all young people and moves them the more if they are repelled by those who have strict opinions and yet have lived commonplace lives.[75]

6
Parnellites and Loyalists

M eanwhile developments at Westminster in 1885 seemed to promise gains through political action. In the early 1880s Parnell and the Irish Party in parliament established good relations with a small group of dissident Tories led by Lord Randolph Churchill. Together they attacked the coercion policy of the Liberal government.

Churchill, then in his thirties, was born into the English and Anglo-Irish aristocracy: his father was the Duke of Marlborough and his mother was a daughter of the Marquess of Londonderry. Churchill became member of parliament for the 'family seat' of Woodstock in 1874 – though he then had little interest in politics – and in late 1876 he went to Ireland as private secretary to his father, who had been appointed lord lieutenant. Here Churchill stayed till 1880, and – as well as indulging in many sporting pursuits – made friends with Dublin Unionists and gained the knowledge of Ireland which was to be the mainspring of his short political career. Churchill was clever but inconsistent, and by turns charming and vitriolic. His instability was heightened by his syphilis, a then incurable venereal disease which attacks the nervous system. By 1885 Churchill was periodically confined to bed and his moods became more intense: bouts of feverish activity alternated with apathetic despair and violent rage.

As with most of his contemporaries, the guiding principle of his political actions was opportunism. His aim was at all costs to divide or embarrass the Liberal government, and he did this by exploiting the differences in the party between the Radical manufacturers and the aristocratic landowning Whigs, and by highlighting the contradiction between the Liberals' professed philosophy and the coercion they needed to employ to keep the empire under control. His son Winston later wrote:

> To split the Government majority by raising some issue on which conscientious Radicals would be forced to vote against their leaders, or, failing that, by some question on which the Minister concerned would be likely to utter illiberal sentiments, and bound to justify a policy or a system

which the Liberal party detested, was his perpetual and almost instinctive endeavour.[1]

From 1877, when the Tories were still in power, Churchill had called for reform of the Irish educational system on denominational lines so that the Catholic church would control Catholic schools, and advocated conciliation rather than repression as the way to defuse the Irish Party obstructionists. The Parnellites' appreciation of him grew when in 1884 he supported their calls for a public inquiry into the possibility that an innocent man, Myles Joyce, had been hanged for the notorious 'Maamtrasna murders', in which a family had been killed in County Mayo two years earlier. Churchill stated his position frankly in a letter to a friend:

> It is the Bishops entirely to whom I look in the future to turn, to mitigate or to postpone the Home Rule onslaught. Let us only be enabled to occupy a year with the Education Question. By that time, I am certain, Parnell's party will have become seriously disintegrated. Personal jealousies, Government influences, Davitt and Fenian intrigues will all be at work on the devoted band of eighty: and the Bishops, who in their hearts hate Parnell and don't care a scrap for Home Rule, having safely acquired control of Irish education, will, according to my calculation, complete the rout.[2]

Parnellites and Tories

Beguiled by Churchill's assurances that the Tories would oppose coercion, the Parnellites routinely voted with them against the Liberal government, apparently regardless of the issue in question. In early 1885, for instance, they threw their vote behind the Tories in a motion of censure against the government's handling of Egypt and the Sudan, where the popular hero General Gordon, after disobeying orders to evacuate Khartoum, had been speared to death by nationalist followers of the Mahdi. The Irish nationalist view, expressed in parliament by William Redmond, was that Egypt and the Sudan should have self-government: nine-tenths of the Irish, said Redmond, desired to see the Mahdi successful. Redmond also noted that the Conservatives were even more hardline than the Liberals, and would have liked a more prolonged and bloody war resulting in complete occupation. But despite this, the Parnellites backed the Tories on the motion of censure, which was lost by only 14 votes. But while engaging in this and other parliamentary manoeuvres, Parnell was careful to reassure his followers in Ireland of his long-term aims. He told a packed public meeting in Cork in January 1885, to repeated cheers:

> We cannot under the British constitution ask for more than the restitution of Grattan's Parliament, but no man has the right to fix the boundary to

the march of a nation. No man has a right to say to his country, "Thus far shalt thou go and no further," and we have never attempted to fix the *ne plus ultra* to the progress of Ireland's nationhood, and we never shall.[3]

In May Gladstone announced that the government would partially renew the Crimes Act, which was soon due to expire. Churchill promptly announced that a Tory government would not renew the act. On 8 June the Parnellites backed the Tories on a carefully contrived amendment to the budget, and, aided by dissident and absent Liberals, succeeded in outvoting the government. Gladstone resigned and the Tories took office with Lord Salisbury as prime minister. Churchill was rewarded for his efforts by being elevated to the coveted post of secretary of state for India.

Meanwhile outside parliament Michael Davitt, who deeply disagreed with Parnell's alliance with the Tories, was pursuing a very different strategy, pouring his energy into encouraging the British working-class movement, which he saw as the true ally of the Irish people. He told a mass rally in Hyde Park on 28 June:

> The industrial classes in these countries can, if they combine at the polls, hurl the party of wars and waste, of land monopoly and the plunder of labour... from the helm of the state, and substitute government of the people and by the people...
> This, then, ought to be your programme at the coming election. Demand universal adult suffrage... the nationalisation of agricultural and pasture land... the municipalisation of land on which centres of population stand... the state ownership of mines and the payment out of the revenues thereof of an insurance upon the lives of all who labour in coal pits. Demand eight hours per day as the regulation time of employment, and, of course, demand the abolition of the hereditary chamber of obstruction, the House of Lords... And finally demand that atonement be made to Ireland for the crimes which your statesmen have been guilty of... by restoring to her the right to manage her own affairs in a national assembly in Dublin.[4]

Having come into office on the back of the Irish MPs, the Tories strove to keep them happy in order both to stay in power and to have their support in the general election that was due at the end of the year. A home rule supporter, Lord Carnarvon, was appointed lord-lieutenant, and the coercion policy was dropped. Despite opposition from orthodox Tories and Ulster MPs, Carnarvon agreed to investigate the Maamtrasna affair: this satisfied the Irish MPs, despite the fact that in the event he upheld the original verdicts. An Irish Educational Endowments Bill, which had had its first reading during Gladstone's administration, was redrafted and pushed through with Randolph Churchill's aid: this gratified the Catholic hierarchy by bringing substantial funds to Catholic schools and colleges.

The Tory government's most significant measure was a land act, known as the 'Ashbourne Act', after Lord Ashbourne who introduced it. This act made it much easier for tenants to buy their land, enabling them to borrow the full price from the state, instead of three-quarters as before. It also allowed them to repay the loan over a longer period, 49 years, at four per cent interest. Over the next three years, more than 25,000 tenants, many of them in Ulster, purchased between them nearly a million acres. The act, which was improved on by a succession of later acts, was an important step in the dissolution of the Anglo-Irish landlords as a class, and the creation in their place of a class of small proprietors.

But it was probably the secret meetings between Parnell and government ministers that clinched the Irish Party's support for the Tories in the next election. On 1 August 1885 Parnell met Lord Carnarvon, the lord lieutenant, in an unoccupied house in London's fashionable Mayfair district. There were no witnesses present and each man later gave a different version of what was said. Parnell, who made the episode public the following year, said Carnarvon had agreed with him on the need for a home rule settlement with arrangements to protect Irish industries from English and foreign competition, and that he assumed Carnarvon would impress this view upon the cabinet. Carnarvon, however, said that he was acting solely on his own behalf, and that the conversation was merely an exchange of opinions.

Also that summer Parnell visited Randolph Churchill's house several times. Parnell never spoke of these meetings, but Churchill said later that they had 'arranged a great many things' in connection with the general election, with 'the most perfect confidence existing between us'.[5] Churchill certainly gave the impression when it suited him that he was, in the words of Wilfrid Scawen Blunt, 'friendly to Ireland's hopes' and a supporter of home rule. As a result Blunt, an English explorer, poet, and passionate advocate of independence for Egypt, Ireland and India, stood in the 1885 general election – albeit unsuccessfully – as 'a Tory Home Ruler... and as a supporter of Lord Randolph Churchill.'[6]

The Tories had an additional attraction in the Parnellites' eyes: if they brought in a home rule bill, they would be much more likely to have the support of the House of Lords than the Liberals would. The Irish MP T.M. Healy wrote privately in October:

> We have to make the best fight we can for a small country, and clearly, if we could put the Tories in and hold them dependent on us, that is our game. With the House of Lords behind them and our help, they could play ducks and drakes with the Union, were they so minded.[7]

Parnell, for his part, was enmeshed in behind-the-scenes manoeuvres with both parties. He was simultaneously trying to play off the Tories against the Liberals, Randolph Churchill against the Tory leadership, and, within the Liberal Party, Gladstone against Chamberlain.

Parnell and his followers decided that Gladstone was likely to be more use than Chamberlain. As a result, when Chamberlain made overtures, proposing to visit Ireland and saying that Ireland should be given 'the right to govern itself in the matter of its purely domestic business', they contemptuously snubbed him.[8] Faced with a complete lack of co-operation, Chamberlain was forced to call off the visit, and nurtured a resentment that may have exacerbated his later, very damaging, antipathy to home rule. Both through public speeches and through private letters – using his lover Katharine O'Shea as the ostensible author – Parnell pressed Gladstone to see how much he was willing to give. Gladstone appeared to be willing to concede a limited form of self-government, provided it did not jeopardise the unity of the empire. But he refused to make any definite promises before the election.

The Parnellites weighed the odds, and on 21 November 1885, two days before voting was due to start, they issued a blistering manifesto calling on the Irish in Britain to vote for Tory candidates. Couched in highly charged language, the manifesto called on them to vote against the Liberals, whom it described as

> the men who coerced Ireland, deluged Egypt with blood, menaced religious liberty in the school, the freedom of speech in parliament, and promise to the country generally a repetition of the crimes and follies of the last administration.[9]

John Denvir, who was the secretary for the Irish election campaign in Liverpool, later wrote:

> The Irish in the country had, as a rule, hitherto voted for the Liberal party, and, therefore, it can readily be imagined how much it now went against their grain to support the Tories...[10]

The revolutionary Frederick Engels admired this tactical use of the Irish vote, writing: 'They have thus shown the Liberals the extent to which they can decide the issue even in England. The 80 to 85 Home Rulers... can wreck any government.'[11] But Michael Davitt, who had been campaigning on behalf of Scottish land-nationalisation candidates and who believed that working-class constituencies should elect working class MPs, was horrified by the 'vote Tory' manifesto. He wrote to a friend:

> Parnell and his crowd are going in for a new form of toryism. They fear the democracy. Priests, parsons, Parnellites and peers appear to be on the one platform now, and the programme is: keep the democracy out of Westminster.[12]

But what most upset Denvir and his fellow Liverpool Irish was when Parnell – inexplicably, it seemed at the time – at the last minute withdrew his candidature from Liverpool's Exchange division and called on the voters to support not the Tories but the Liberal candidate, Captain William O'Shea, who was reviled as a renegade Irishman. There was little regret among the Irish when O'Shea lost – and much jubilation at the victory in another

Liverpool division of T.P. O'Connor, the first and only member of the Irish Home Rule Party to be elected for a British constituency. Two months later, again as the price of O'Shea's silence about his wife's relationship, Parnell imposed him as a Home Rule candidate in a by-election in Galway, where he was elected.

The overall result of the 1885 election became clear in early December. The Liberals had won 335 seats, and the Tories and Parnellites together had also won 335 seats. The Irish Party, with its 86 MPs, held the balance of power. Estimates suggested that in Britain the transfer of the Irish vote had cost the Liberals between 20 and 40 seats: enough to damage the Liberals but not to give the Tories a majority.

Within Ireland, the Parnellites benefited from the 1884 electoral reforms which trebled the number of Irish males eligible to vote, winning 24 seats more than they had five years earlier. They now held an overwhelming majority of the Irish seats – 85 out of 103. The Irish Home Rule MPs were almost all drawn from the middle class: 31 came from the professions, 22 were farmers and shopkeepers, and only five were landed. All but 11 were Catholics. Twenty-two of them had been imprisoned under the Liberal regime.

In most of Ireland, English parties had been eliminated. The Irish Liberals, lacking any popular base, had been wiped out and the Tories held only 18 seats, all but two of them in Ulster. But even in Ulster the Parnellites were in a majority, with 17 of the 33 seats, a result which delighted them. The *Nation* commented, with an optimism that would prove tragically misplaced:

> Ulster is Ireland's at last. This, perhaps, is the most gratifying result of the whole election. Nevermore will a West-British faction or a bitter Orange clique be able to rise in the House of Commons and deny that a united Ireland demands the restoration of a native Parliament.[13]

After the election, events moved rapidly as each party – Tories, Liberals and Irish Home Rulers – assessed the new situation and switched allegiance. Although such crass considerations were not publicly admitted, the arithmetic was clear. If the Liberals could gain the Parnellites' support, they would have a substantial parliamentary majority. A leading Radical told Randolph Churchill, 'we shall have to cut you out with the Irish'.[14] On the other hand, the benefits of the Tory-Parnellite alliance were less obvious: the Parnellites had not brought the Tories either an overall majority or sufficient numbers to carry conciliatory policies on Ireland against the wishes of the Orange element in the party.

The Tories, with Randolph Churchill in the lead, swiftly jettisoned the Parnellites. Wilfrid Scawen Blunt recorded in his diary on 8 December 1885: 'When I mentioned Ireland to Churchill the other day, an odd mischievous look came over his face. I fear he won't stick to his flag.'[15] On

14 December the Tory cabinet decided not to touch home rule, and the lord-lieutenant, Carnarvon, threatened resignation.

Parnell had already concluded that the Liberals were the best prospect, and was pressurising Gladstone – through Mrs O'Shea – to find out his intentions. Gladstone however rebuffed him. Then on 17 December the press revealed that Gladstone was about to come out in favour of home rule. This leak – dubbed the 'Hawarden kite' after the Gladstone family home – came from Gladstone's son Herbert, and may have been premature. But many at the time believed Gladstone had deliberately inspired it. At the same time Gladstone was making overtures to the Tories, hoping they would put forward a home rule proposal. He explained in a letter to Lord Hartington on 17 December:

> I consider that Ireland has now spoken; and that an effort ought to be made *by the Government* without delay to meet her demands for the management by an Irish legislative body of Irish as distinct from Imperial affairs.[16]

On 20 December he wrote to Arthur Balfour, nephew of the Tory leader Lord Salisbury: 'I think it will be a public calamity if this great subject should fall within the lines of party conflict.'[17]

Gladstone decided that if the government would not produce a settlement that he and the Irish Nationalists could support, he would turn them out and, on taking office, would put forward a plan for 'duly guarded Home Rule'.[18] The Tories rejected his appeals, dismissing him as a hypocrite, and an opportunity which could have changed the course of history was lost.

Signs of rebellion against Gladstone began rumbling among landowning Liberals. On 30 December Blunt described in his diary a dinner with three such dissenters:

> They are all for blood and iron in Ireland, and are going to support Lord Salisbury if he goes in for martial law. They are for disfranchising the whole country, suspending *habeas corpus*, and dragooning the people... [They are] Whigs of the old school, who are a bloody race; and they are maddened with the thought of losing property in Ireland.[19]

In early January 1886 Lord Salisbury, the prime minister, decided to bring in a coercion policy, and the lord-lieutenant, Lord Carnarvon, resigned.

The queen's speech for the opening of parliament, drafted by the government and read out by the lord chancellor on 21 January, reaffirmed the government's commitment to the Union in a passage modelled on her speech 52 years earlier in 1834 in the face of Daniel O'Connell's agitation for repeal. The speech also forecast the introduction of coercive legislation.

The Liberals and Parnellites had already prepared the means of bringing down the government. As a formality, the government would answer the queen's speech with an 'address', on which a vote would be taken. A Radical

MP, Jesse Collings, put down an amendment to the address regretting that no measures had been announced to improve the lot of agricultural labourers.

On 26 January the government announced that a bill would be introduced in two days' time 'for the purpose of suppressing the National League and other dangerous associations'.[20] The same day the debate on the Jesse Collings amendment began, and at 1 o'clock the next morning the vote was taken: 329 in favour and 250 – including 18 Liberals, led by Lord Hartington – against. Defeated by 79 votes, Lord Salisbury's administration resigned. Gladstone, now aged 76, became prime minister once again, and began drafting a home rule bill.

The Orange card

Randolph Churchill had already spotted the potential for using the home rule issue as a means of damaging the Liberals by undermining their support at home. The way to do this was by stirring up feeling in the northeast of Ireland. In December he had told a leading Radical:

> that, even if the Government went out and Gladstone introduced a Home Rule Bill, I should not hesitate, if other circumstances were favourable, to agitate Ulster even to resistance beyond constitutional limits; that Lancashire would follow Ulster, and would lead England...[21]

His attitude to Ulster unionists was frankly opportunist: he had no love for them and had described them not long before as 'foul Ulster Tories'.

Churchill shelved his plans for more educational concessions to the Catholic hierarchy, and threw himself into 'agitating Ulster' and into building a coalition of Tories and dissident Liberals against home rule. In a series of demagogic speeches, he raised the spectre of Irish Protestants resorting to civil war rather than accept a Dublin parliament. After the first speech, in London on 13 February 1886, Wilfrid Blunt wrote disgustedly in his diary: 'Randolph has made a speech at Paddington in the most violent Orange Protestant sense, an absurd speech. I wash my hands of him and the Tory Party.'[22]

On 16 February Churchill, about to visit Belfast, wrote to his friend Lord Justice Fitzgibbon, a Dublin unionist:

> I decided some time ago that if the G.O.M. [Gladstone, the 'grand old man'] went for Home Rule, the Orange card would be the one to play. Please God it may turn out the ace of trumps and not the two.[23]

Orangeism brought together Protestants from various social classes and was concentrated in the northeast of the country, where most of the Protestants lived. Protestants made up 1.2 million of Ireland's 5.1 million people in 1881, but nearly a million of them lived in Ulster. Outside Ulster, Episcopalian Protestants formed a thin layer of landowners and professionals at the top of the social pyramid. In the northeast, however, where colonists of all classes had settled, there were Protestants at all levels of the social scale: landowners, tenant farmers and labourers in the countryside, and business people, professionals, and skilled and unskilled workers in the towns. More than half of them were Presbyterians. The Protestants did not, however, form a self-contained society, but were mixed in with the Catholic population.

Ulster's Protestants were unevenly spread across the nine counties. Over half of them – more than 500,000 – were concentrated in the easternmost counties of Antrim and Down, where they made up 73 per cent of the population. In three counties – Cavan, Donegal and Monaghan – Catholics greatly outnumbered Protestants, while in the remaining four counties numbers were relatively balanced.

Most Protestants supported the union with Britain, but until home rule became a serious threat they did not organise as a body, but were divided on party lines, fighting elections as Conservatives, Liberals and Orangemen. Now, however, they began to marshal themselves into a distinctive, though by no means united, movement.

In May 1885 a group of southern landowners, including Lords Longford, Castletown and de Vesci, along with some academics, founded the Irish Loyal and Patriotic Union to co-ordinate the electoral campaign against Parnell. Soon afterwards, landowners in the north formed the short-lived Loyal Irish Union, which aimed to offer 'a strenuous resistance' to all attempts to sever the union, and to organise 'a strenuous opposition to revolutionary and socialistic agitation in Ireland.'[24]

In Belfast, Protestant businessmen, associated with the Tory Party in the town, provided the backbone of the anti-home rule movement. From December 1885 they held frequent meetings of the Chamber of Commerce and manufacturers' associations, and in January 1886 Belfast Conservatives and Orangemen formed a committee to organise the campaign. The committee, which later became the Ulster Loyalist Anti-Repeal Union, included James Henderson, the editor of the *Belfast News-Letter*, the Rev. R.R. Kane, the Grand Master of the Belfast Orangemen, and the Rev. Hugh 'Roaring' Hanna, a demagogic Presbyterian preacher. The committee planned a series of 31 meetings in Ulster, culminating in Lord Randolph Churchill's visit in February, and more in England and Scotland.

Belfast had by now become Ireland's largest and most prosperous town, and the third most important port in the United Kingdom, after London and Liverpool. Its wealth was based on the linen industry, with its huge mills dotted around the town, and on its shipbuilding and engineering, which had grown spectacularly in the years since 1850. The shipbuilding industry had been stimulated by the Harbour Commissioners' initiative in excavating and organising the channels and docks, and by the expertise of a Yorkshire engineer, Edward Harland, and a German businessman, Gustav Wolff. Harland and Wolff teamed up to produce the most advanced trans-Atlantic liners, and created the most successful shipbuilding yard in the world. Harland became mayor of Belfast in 1885 and subsequently Tory MP for North Belfast.

The industrialists in Belfast and Dublin opposed home rule because it would break their vital link with Britain and the empire, which supplied their fuel and raw materials, as well as markets for their manufactured goods. They feared home rule would bring a parliament dominated by small farmers which would tax them heavily and impose customs duties on imports, and would provoke a collapse in business confidence. The Belfast Chamber of Commerce passed a resolution recording its belief

> that the commercial prosperity which has blessed the peaceable parts of this country will receive a sudden shock and lasting injury from any legislation which would have any tendency to imperil the connection between this country and Great Britain...[25]

The Dublin Chamber of Commerce similarly felt that:

> Any measure calculated to weaken the Union... would be productive of consequences most disastrous to the trading and commercial interests of both countries.[26]

On 19 January 1886 deputations representing Irish trade and commerce from Belfast, Cork and Dublin visited the prime minister, Lord Salisbury, to protest against any measure that would separate Ireland from the rest of the United Kingdom.

The Tory businessmen had an uneasy relationship with the more militant Orange Order, which they saw as useful but also rather wild and disreputable, with its drunken festivities and working class membership. The Order was strongly prejudiced against Catholics and frankly sectarian in its aim of defending Protestant privilege. 'Marrying a Papist' was the most frequent cause of expulsion from its ranks.

The Order had its roots in the countryside, where it embraced Protestant landowners and tenant farmers alike, despite their differences over land, in a common front against nationalists. The Order declined in the mid-nineteenth century, but the agitation of the early 1880s prompted a revival: landlords found it useful for mobilising Protestant counter-demonstrations against nationalist meetings. One such landlord was Major Edward Saunderson, from Cavan, a ruthless and energetic man, who joined the Order in 1882 and became deputy grand master for Ireland two years later. Saunderson joined, he said, 'because the Orange Society is alone capable of dealing with the conditions of anarchy and rebellion which prevail in Ireland'.[27] In 1885 he became Tory MP for North Armagh and later became the leader of the Unionist MPs. He advocated armed resistance to home rule and helped organise Lord Randolph Churchill's trip to Belfast.

There were also Orange lodges in the towns. Protestant country people moving to the towns took the organisation with them, and used it alongside their trade associations to control entry to employment, and in particular to exclude Catholics. Employers, such as mill-owners in Sandy Row – the main Protestant working class area in the first half of the century – found the Order a useful channel for dispensing favours and gifts in return for political support, and businessmen gradually developed their own lodges.

By 1851 there were 35 lodges in Belfast with 1,335 members. Numbers grew rapidly, and by 1878 there were more than a hundred lodges with some 4,000 members, organised in six districts. There were very large numbers of Orangemen in the shipyards, and in 1871 a seventh district was set up just to cater for the workers on Queen's Island, base of Harland and Wolff.

Bitter divisions

Belfast's business elite – overwhelmingly Protestant – was visibly prosperous: grandiose banks, offices and public buildings rose in the town centre, while spacious villas were built on the roads leading out of the town, away from the damp and smoke. Paschal Grousset, a French journalist and home rule supporter who visited Belfast in 1887, wrote admiringly of 'the most flourishing town of Ireland':

> The public walks are vast and carefully kept, the houses well built, the shops substantial and elegant, the educational establishments important and richly endowed. The town has a thoroughly Anglo-Saxon aspect. London fashions are scrupulously followed there... If you follow the road up to Cave Hill, one of the heights on the western side of Belfast, you embrace a vast landscape, where the flying steamers on the Lagan, the smoking factory-chimneys, the innumerable and opulent villas round its shores, all speak of wealth and prosperity.[28]

But behind the aura of wealth lay bitter divisions and extensive poverty. The working class population, densely clustered around the mills, foundries and engineering works, was deeply split along sectarian lines. Protestants and Catholics lived separately and worked separately. Protestants monopolised the skilled jobs, so that Catholics – 29 per cent of the town's 208,000 people in 1881 – suffered disproportionately from poverty.

Catholic and Protestant workers had settled in separate, though adjoining, areas. An official report published in 1887 noted:

> The extremity to which party and religious feeling has grown in Belfast is shown strikingly by the fact that the people of the artisan and labouring class, disregarding the ordinary considerations of convenience, dwell to a large extent in separate quarters, each of which is almost entirely given

up to persons of one particular faith, and the boundaries of which are sharply defined. In the district of West Belfast, the great thoroughfare of Shankhill-road, with the network of streets running into it… is an almost purely Protestant district… The great Catholic quarter is due south of the Shankhill district, and consists of the thoroughfare known as the Falls-road, and the streets running south of it… The great points of danger to the peace of the town are open spaces in the border land between the two quarters…[29]

Any intermingling was swiftly undone in the outbreaks of sectarian rioting which had repeatedly convulsed West Belfast at times of heightened political tension from as far back as 1812. The *Times* described the aftermath of one such outbreak in August 1872:

It was pitiable to see the families leaving their homes as though going into captivity or exile, and to hear the lamentations of women and children… Protestants living in Roman Catholic districts, and Catholics living in Protestant districts, have found it necessary to change their quarters and go to their respective friends for protection.[30]

By mid-century, Protestants already monopolised the skilled jobs in the engineering and building industries, and the few in the mills. They were the fitters, boilermakers, carpenters and bricklayers: the artisan élite of the town. As shipbuilding developed, they took most of the skilled jobs there too. A third or more of Protestant male workers made up this 'labour aristocracy'. Their wages were on a par with those of skilled workers in Britain – but were three times the wages of Belfast mill-workers. Shipyard workers were particularly well paid. Most lived in the Shankill – built in the 1870s and regarded then as the town's healthiest working class area – or, increasingly, across the river in Ballymacarrett. Few shipyard workers were Catholics: Sir Edward Harland said in 1887 that only 225 of his 3,000 operatives were Catholics.

Skilled Protestants maintained their relatively privileged position by using their craft unions and Orange lodges to control access to jobs, with the acquiescence or even encouragement of employers. In 1864 Bernard Hughes, a Catholic who owned a bakery which employed many Catholics, told an official inquiry:

There are few Catholic employers in the town and the others will not take Catholic apprentices, for the workers will not work with them as either apprentices or journeymen. Every trade has an Orange Lodge and their people know each other, for they have signs and passwords, so that the Catholic population has no chance at all.[31]

The many Protestants employed in unskilled jobs, such as the women mill-workers of Sandy Row, had much lower wages. But even the worst-off Protestants were usually marginally better off than the poorest Catholics: the 1901 census revealed that 13 per cent of Protestant families lived in the lowest-rated housing, compared to 32 per cent of Catholic families. Protestants tended to get the best of the unskilled jobs: in the mills, they were weavers rather than spinners, and in the docks they worked on the cross-channel quays where employment was regular, while Catholics worked as casual labourers in the deep-sea docks.

Catholics worked overwhelmingly in the worst unskilled jobs. The Catholic middle class was small, comprising mainly shopkeepers, publicans, lawyers, clergy and civil servants, and there were few Catholic artisans. Most Catholics worked in low-paid jobs in the linen mills, in domestic service or in construction: Belfast's docks, mills and railways were built by Catholic navvies. Belfast's unskilled workers were paid even less than their equivalents in Britain. As elsewhere in Ireland, wages were low because of the infinite supply of cheap labour from the countryside, where agricultural workers, too, were paid much less than their English or Scottish counterparts.

The largest sector of employment was the mills, which employed some 62,000 workers in the 1880s. Most were women and children: 70 per cent of the workers were women or girls, while more than 30 per cent were aged between 10 and 17. Wages were extremely low and hours were very long: from 6.30 in the morning till 6 at night, plus six hours on Saturdays. The workers existed mainly on a diet of tea and bread. Women worked until they were nearly due to give birth, and returned to work within days. Working conditions were horrific. Dangerous machinery caused mutilations and death. The air was thick with flax dust, which penetrated the lungs, causing chronic illness and early death. A medical officer's report in 1877 described how one 40-year-old woman suffered from half-hour-long attacks of coughing and difficulty with breathing:

> when they come on, she has to lie across one of the cans in order to get relief, and the paroxysm does not cease till she throws off the content of her stomach and sometimes blood. Has to get up at five o'clock in the morning in order to be dressed in time for the mill at six, as she is often obliged to stop on account of the paroxysm coming on.[32]

Workers in the spinning-room, which was hot, soaking wet and full of steam, suffered from numerous illnesses.

The mill-workers lived in tiny, badly constructed houses, often built by the mill-owners. The houses were invariably sub-let, often with two families of six or more members in each. Some streets near the docks were periodically flooded at high tide. In these conditions, sickness and disease flourished. Some 30 per cent of the factory class died under the age of two-and-a-half. Typhoid and tuberculosis were endemic, causing more deaths than anywhere else in Britain or Ireland.

Protestant workers knew that their marginal privileges over Catholics were dependent on the maintenance of British rule and of Protestant ascendancy within the island. The rioting which had periodically shaken Belfast had generally been triggered by upsurges in nationalist militancy which threatened the status quo.

The home rule crisis of 1886 coincided with a period of severe unemployment and wage cuts in Belfast: conditions which made Protestant workers all the more determined to hold on to what they had. Conservative leaders campaigning against home rule stressed the benefits of Protestant control of the labour market. In January 1886 the Reverend Hugh 'Roaring' Hanna, who had spent a lifetime stirring up sectarian strife, exploited Protestant fears with a vision of a topsy-turvy Ireland after home rule:

> there is a ragged little urchin selling newspapers, and crying every morning the *Morning News*. That ragged urchin under the new code is to be Marquis of Donegal. There is a Nationalist riveter on Queen's Island, and he is to be successor to W.J. Pirrie [head of Harland and Wolff], and Mr Pirrie, for some service he has shown to the Nationalists, is to be relegated to the superintendence of a little smithy in Connemara; and Paddy O'Rafferty, a ragman, resident in the slums of Smithfield, is to succeed Sir Edward Harland as the next mayor of Belfast...[33]

In other towns, too, Protestants feared the effects of home rule. Wilfrid Scawen Blunt, visiting Derry, was shown the city walls and told of the famous siege of 1689. He wrote in his diary:

> It is not difficult to understand, with these memories kept alive as they are, that the local Protestants should be fighting hard against Home Rule. It will mean for them the end of the Protestant ascendancy. At present they monopolize all public offices from Town Councillor to Town Crier, although the Catholics are half the population of the town; also there are none but Protestant J.P.s in the county, and this holds good even in the adjoining districts of Donegal, where the proportion of Catholics to Protestants is four or even six to one.[34]

Early on the morning of 22 February 1886 Churchill sailed into Larne to a hero's welcome from loyalist crowds. Thousands more turned out to meet him when the train stopped at Carrickfergus, and again at Belfast. That night a huge meeting in the Ulster Hall, organised by leaders of the Orange Order and local Conservatives, cheered him to the echo before listening to his barely concealed call to insurrection:

> I believe that this storm will blow over and that the vessel of the Union will emerge with her Loyalist crew stronger than before; but... if the struggle should continue... then I am of the opinion that the struggle is not likely to remain within the lines of what we are accustomed to look upon as constitutional action... if it should turn out that the Parliament of the United Kingdom was so recreant from all its high duties... as to hand over the Loyalists of Ireland to the domination of an Assembly in Dublin which must be to them a foreign and an alien assembly... in that dark hour there will not be wanting to you those of position and influence in England who would be willing to cast in their lot with you...

A roar of applause greeted the verse he offered in conclusion:

> The combat deepens; on, ye brave,
> Who rush to glory or the grave.
> Wave, Ulster – all thy banners wave,
> And charge with all thy chivalry.[35]

Churchill's intervention brought the Orange case from obscurity to the front of the political agenda. It also raised the temperature to fever pitch. In the impoverished working-class districts of Belfast, clashes began between loyalists and nationalists – Protestants and Catholics – that would develop into the most serious sectarian disturbances the town had yet experienced.

Churchill at the Ulster Hall, Belfast 1886

The home rule debate

The Ulster unionists were, however, only a noisy sideshow in the larger game. With only 16 MPs they could exert no serious pressure, although their grievances provided a useful propaganda tool for English politicians with quite different motives for opposing home rule. Much more threatening to Gladstone's plans was the dissent within the Liberal ranks. This came from two sources: a group of aristocrats led by Lord Hartington, and manufacturers and businessmen led by Joseph Chamberlain. For both groups, the threat that home rule posed to the maintenance of the empire was the main concern.

Gladstone introduced his Home Rule Bill amid much excitement on 8 April 1886 to an overflowing House of Commons with vast crowds assembled outside. Officially titled the Government of Ireland Bill, it provided for Ireland to have a parliament with two tiers, one wholly elected and one a mixture of wealthy people elected on a restricted franchise and peers. This parliament would have control of the civil service, the judiciary, the post office, income tax and eventually the police. But it would not have control of areas involving the security or economic interests of the British empire: foreign and colonial relations, trade and navigation, the armed forces, and customs and excise. Nor would it be able to establish or endow any religion. These areas would remain under the control of the Westminster parliament. In addition, Ireland would have to contribute one-fifteenth of the cost of running the empire.

For three-and-a-half hours Gladstone explained the details of the bill, arguing that home rule was the best way of bringing order to Ireland and ensuring its loyalty to the empire. Repressive legislation had become 'not exceptional, but habitual,' he said. He pointed out that since the Reform Act of 1832, while 'free institutions' were being extended in Britain, there had been 'but two years which were entirely free from the action of this special legislation for Ireland.'[36] Law was 'discredited in Ireland,' he said, especially because it came 'in a foreign garb.' This state of law was not conducive to 'the real unity of this great, noble, and world-wide Empire.'

Gladstone touched on the question of the 'Protestant minority', especially those living in Ulster, and said:

> I cannot conceal the conviction that the voice of Ireland, as a whole, is at this moment clearly and Constitutionally spoken. I cannot say it is otherwise when five-sixths of its lawfully-chosen Representatives are of one mind in this matter... Certainly, Sir, I cannot allow it to be said that a Protestant minority in Ulster, or elsewhere, is to rule the question at large for Ireland. I am aware of no Constitutional doctrine tolerable on which such a conclusion could be adopted or justified.[37]

Gladstone said that the wishes of the Protestant minority should nevertheless be considered, and noted the various schemes that had been suggested: the exclusion of 'Ulster itself, or, with more appearance of reason, a portion of Ulster' from the bill; the provision of autonomy for all or part of Ulster; or the placing of certain issues, such as education, under the control of provincial councils. But he considered that none of these schemes merited inclusion in the bill as yet.

Ulster Loyalist MPs rose to make their protests. Colonel Waring, MP for North Down, declared, as *Hansard* reported:

> They were now part and parcel of one of the greatest Empires of the world that the sun ever shone upon, and were utterly determined that they would not be changed into Colonials, and made a Dependency... which would be at the mercy of those from whom they differed politically.

Gladstone's course would, he went on, 'turn over those who had been England's faithful garrison in Ireland, bound hand and foot, to the tender mercies of their bitterest enemies.'[38]

Mr O'Neill, MP for Mid-Antrim, feared that an Irish government would be unable to borrow money because 'he did not think that a prudent person, with a proper idea of financial security, would be foolish enough to lend money to a financially independent Ireland.' Without the help of the British treasury, no more railways, harbours, roads or other public works would be constructed. Further, the new Irish parliament would agitate until it achieved the establishment of an Irish Republic, 'which would be the focus of foreign intrigue in time of peace, and would be a source of imminent danger in England in time of war.'[39]

Major Saunderson, MP for North Armagh, vehemently rejected the idea that Ulster be treated differently from the rest of Ireland:

> On the part of Ulster and every loyal man in that Province I repudiate that suggestion. We are prepared and determined to stand and fall, for weal or woe, with every loyal man who lives in Ireland.[40]

The Irish nationalists, for their part, accepted the bill, though with reservations. Parnell praised Gladstone for devoting 'his great mind, his extraordinary energy, to the unravelling of this question,' but went on to criticise the financial aspects of the bill – Britain's control of customs and the Irish contribution to the imperial expenditure – as well as the 'unsatisfactory' arrangements for control of the police, and the blocking powers given to the upper tier of the parliament. If these defects were remedied, the bill would be 'cheerfully accepted by the Irish people and by their Representatives,' said Parnell.[41]

But with the Liberals split on the issue, and the Tories united in opposition, virtually the entire British establishment was ranged against Gladstone, and the issue that united them was the empire.

Joseph Chamberlain, who had written that 'Mr. G's Irish scheme is death and damnation,'[42] resigned from the cabinet in protest against the bill. A successful Birmingham businessman and pioneer of municipal social reform, Chamberlain was prominent in the Radical wing of the Liberal Party. The Radicals in essence represented an alliance between middle-class and working-class interests, and their adherents in parliament ranged from wealthy capitalists such as Chamberlain to the freethinker, republican and anti-imperialist, Charles Bradlaugh, who supported Gladstone in the home rule battle.

On 9 April Chamberlain rose in the House of Commons to explain his resignation. He said that despite calling himself a Radical, he had always given 'great consideration to Imperial interests.' He continued:

> I have cared for the honour and the influence and the integrity of the Empire, and it is because I believe these things are now in danger that I have felt myself called upon to make the greatest sacrifice that any public man can be expected to make.[43]

Chamberlain said that like Gladstone he was willing 'to give to Ireland the largest possible extension of local government consistent with the integrity of the Empire and the supremacy of Parliament'.[44] He felt, however, that Gladstone's plan went beyond these limitations, and conceded too much power to an Irish parliament. It was, he said, 'a thinly veiled scheme of separation,' and would be burdensome for the British taxpayer. Instead he proposed 'some form of federation,' which would both 'maintain the Imperial unity' and conciliate the Irish desire 'for a national local government'.[45]

The first reading of the Home Rule Bill came to an end on 13 April 1886. As the second reading neared, unionist activity became increasingly feverish. The Anti-Repeal Committee, formed in January, organised about 100 meetings in Britain, hoping to kill home rule by encouraging the defeat of the Liberal Party: some speakers found their audiences regrettably favourable to the nationalists. Belfast Liberals condemned home rule and split from Liberals in west Ulster, most of whom wanted an alliance with the nationalists.

Newspaper editorials stirred Protestant feelings with flagrantly sectarian and racist comments. The *Fermanagh Times* said it was 'shameless effrontery' to consider entrusting the government of Ireland to 'illiterates', 'criminals', 'murderers' and 'untrained nobodies'.[46] The *Londonderry Sentinel* complained that Gladstone favoured the 'five-sixths of disloyal, bigoted... and largely incapable inhabitants' who supported the Nationalists, against 'the numerical minority who contribute five-sixths of the entire taxation of the country'.[47] The Home Rule Bill had inspired 600 prominent Indians in Bengal to set up a National League, and on 11 May the *Sentinel* expressed the fear that the bill 'would stir up natives in every country over which the British flag waves'.[48]

The Orange Order held demonstrations throughout the north, while Unionist leaders began planning to raise a 100,000-strong army to resist home rule by force. Major Saunderson told a meeting in Belfast that 'rather than submit to such a Romish and Rebel despotism, the minority would take the field and defend their rights at the point of the sword'.[49] At a banquet in Belfast on 6 May, William Johnston, an MP and prominent Orangeman, spelled out their plans and said that Lord Wolseley and 1,000 British officers would support them. Wolseley was a Dublin-born Protestant general and famous veteran of ferocious imperial wars against the Indians, the Chinese, the Ashanti, the Zulus and the Egyptians. In 1885 he had led the controversial relief expedition to Khartoum which failed to arrive in time to rescue General Gordon.

The news of the threatened rebellion, reported in the *Pall Mall Gazette*, caused a sensation in London. It was rumoured that the queen had suggested Wolseley should head the Orangemen in her name. Lord Randolph Churchill added his encouragement with an open letter which carried the rallying cry that would resound across the next century:

> If political parties and political leaders... should... hand over coldly... the lives and liberties of the Loyalists of Ireland to their hereditary and most bitter foes, make no doubt on this point – Ulster will not be a consenting party; Ulster at the proper moment will resort to the supreme arbitrament of force; Ulster will fight, Ulster will be right...[50]

But in the event, the home rule crisis passed so rapidly that only one group, the Orangemen of Richhill, County Armagh, actually began drilling, although without guns.

The second reading of the Home Rule Bill began on 10 May 1886, with the outcome a foregone conclusion. On 15 May the Tory leader Lord Salisbury caused a sensation with an arrogant and racist speech against home rule at St James's Hall. 'You would not confide free representative institutions to the Hottentots, for instance,' he said, going on to cite the people of India, Russia and Greece as being similarly unsuited to self-government. He concluded:

> When you come to narrow it down you will find that this – which is called self-government but is really government by the majority – works admirably when it is confided to people who are of Teutonic race, but that it does not work so well when people of other races are called upon to join in it.[51]

On the last night of the debate, 7 June, the House of Commons was packed. Wilfrid Scawen Blunt travelled specially to London, but recorded in his diary:

> I got down before four to the House and found the central hall already crowded. But Flower got me through into the lobby, and there I stayed till eight unable to get any further, for every place in the galleries was crammed, and there was even a *queue* of people with tickets outside…[52]

Parnell argued against the proposal, made by Chamberlain, for a separate legislature for Ulster, detailing the arithmetic of the situation:

> there are outside the Province of Ulster over 400,000 Protestants who would still be without any protection… you would not even protect the Protestants in Ulster, because the Protestants, according to the last Census, were in the proportion of 52 to 48 Catholics; and we have every reason to believe that now the Protestants and Catholics in Ulster are about equal in number… the Nationalists have succeeded in returning the majority of Ulster members… the very first thing that the Ulster Legislature would do would be to unite itself with the Dublin Parliament.

He went on:

> Well, being driven away from the fiction of Protestant Ulster and the great majority of Protestants which until recently was alleged to exist in Ulster, the opponents of this Bill have been compelled to seek refuge in the north-east corner of Ulster, consisting of three counties.

But this, he pointed out, meant that a majority of Protestants in Ireland would be abandoned to a Dublin parliament because seven-twelfths of them lived outside those three counties. Parnell – himself a Protestant – declared:

> No, Sir; we cannot give up a single Irishman. We want the energy, the patriotism, the talents, and the work of every Irishman to insure that this great experiment shall be a successful one… The class of Protestants will

form a most valuable element in the Irish Legislature of the future, constituting as they will a strong minority, and exercising... a moderating influence in making the laws.

Parnell went on to predict that if the bill were not passed, it would mean a return to the coercion measures of the last five years:

you have had during those five years the suspension of the Habeas Corpus Act; you have had a thousand of your Irish fellow-subjects held in prison without specific charge, many of them for long periods of time... you have had the Arms Acts; you have had the suspension of trial by jury... You have authorized your police to enter the domicile of a citizen... at any hour of the day or night, and to search every part of this domicile, even the beds of the women, without warrant... you have gagged the Press and seized and suppressed newspapers; you have manufactured new crimes and offences, and applied fresh penalties unknown to your laws for these crimes and offences. All this you have done for five years, and all this and much more you will have to do again.[53]

Gladstone wound up the debate with an eloquent appeal:

Ireland stands at your bar expectant, hopeful, almost suppliant. Her words are the words of truth and soberness. She asks a blessed oblivion of the past, and in that oblivion our interest is deeper than even hers... Go into the length and breadth of the world, ransack the literature of all countries, find, if you can, a single voice, a single book... in which the conduct of England towards Ireland is anywhere treated except with profound and bitter condemnation... Think, I beseech you, think well, think wisely, think, not for the moment, but for the years that are to come, before you reject this Bill.[54]

The vote was taken at one o'clock in the morning: 311 voted in favour of the bill, 341 against. Ninety-three Liberals had defected, and the bill was lost.

The Belfast riots

In Belfast, tension was already high. A dispute between a Catholic overseer and a Protestant labourer at the Alexandra Dock construction site was the spark for a horrific incident. The Protestant had been sacked, and a rumour went round that the Catholic had told him that after home rule none of his kind would be able to earn a crust of bread.

Next day, 4 June, hundreds of Protestant shipyard workers from the Harland and Wolff yard at Queen's Island rushed to the Alexandra Dock in their lunch hour armed with iron bars, hammers and other weapons. Most of the Catholics fled, jumping into the river Lagan, and the remainder were beaten up or hurled into the river and then pelted with missiles. An 18-year-old from the neighbouring Short Strand district, James Curran, was unable to swim and died in full view of the assailants. He was from a poverty-stricken family, and the post mortem revealed he had severe tuberculosis.

Ten other Catholics were so badly beaten that they had to be taken to hospital. Two days later, thousands of Catholics joined Curran's funeral procession to Milltown cemetery, an event that was sporadically jeered and stoned by Protestants. There was more rioting the following day.

On 8 June, following the defeat of the Home Rule Bill, people in the Catholic Falls district set their chimneys on fire to mourn its failure, while the Protestants lit bonfires and burned tar barrels in celebration, and paraded the streets with bands playing Orange tunes. Soon their festivities degenerated into looting and wrecking: the police intervened, came under attack and fired buckshot in response.

On 9 June vicious fighting developed, with the police laying into Protestant foundrymen with their batons. An enraged 200-strong crowd besieged a police station: the police opened fire indiscriminately, killing seven people – only two of whom had been rioting – and wounding many more.

Rioting began again after the Protestant 12 July celebrations, when crowds from the Falls and Shankill fought and the police again became involved. Four people – two rioters, a soldier and a policeman – died on the night of 13-14 July. More rioting at the end of July brought 13 deaths. A few days later almost all Catholics were driven from the shipyards. Catholics were forced out of many other workplaces too, including some mills and the huge ropeworks.

By mid-September 1886, when the rioting stopped with the onset of bad weather, some 50 people had been killed, 371 police had been injured, 190 Catholics had been driven from the shipyards, 31 pubs had been looted and a considerable amount of property had been damaged. It had been probably the worst outbreak of violence in Ireland that century, causing more bloodshed than any of the rebellions or the land war.

Gladstone insisted on placing the home rule issue before the electorate. Parliament was dissolved at the end of June and in the resulting bitterly fought election – home rulers were even ostracised by the upper classes and denied invitations to country-houses and dinner parties – the home rulers were routed. The Gladstonian Liberals won 191 seats and the Irish nationalists 85 – a total of 276. On the other side, the Tories won 316 seats and the dissenting Liberals 78 – a total of 394. The home rule crisis shattered the uneasy coalition of interests that had made up the Liberal Party, and its businessmen and aristocrats deserted *en masse* to the Tories.

The crisis had propelled the question of the empire to the forefront of British politics. The Tory leader Lord Salisbury later commented that Gladstone had 'awakened the slumbering genius of imperialism.'[55] The election result ushered in a period of Tory rule that lasted almost unbroken for the next 20 years. This coincided with the most aggressive and self-conscious period of British imperial expansion, as Britain, previously unchallenged in overseas trade, found itself frantically competing with other European nations to carve up Africa and acquire large chunks of the rest of the world's surface in pursuit of new markets.

Lord Hartington and Joseph Chamberlain, leaders of the dissenting Liberal factions, came together to form the Liberal Unionists, and allied themselves with the Tories. Chamberlain became a leading imperialist, seeing the empire as the lifeline of the British economy. In 1888 he said:

> If tomorrow it were possible, as some people apparently desire, to reduce by a stroke of the pen the British Empire to the dimensions of the United Kingdom, half at least of our population would be starved.[56]

In 1895 Chamberlain became secretary of state for the colonies, spearheading the drive to extend the empire and increase its economic yield to Britain.

Randolph Churchill, for his part, was rewarded for his anti-home rule campaign by being made chancellor of the exchequer in the new Tory government in 1886. But after a dispute with Lord Salisbury, the prime minister, Churchill resigned that December, effectively bringing his political career to an end. Though increasingly disabled by syphilis, he continued to attend the House of Commons, where his speeches became unintelligible and terrible to observe. 'He died by inches in public,' wrote his friend Lord Rosebery of one such occasion in 1894.[587]Churchill's actual death came a year later, at the age of 45.

Evictions and 'moonlighting'

After the collapse of the home rule bill, Irish politics returned to its familiar pattern of grassroots militancy followed by government repression.

The land question had been festering while the bill was in progress. Prices of crops and livestock had dropped steeply, so that many tenants, even those whose rents had been fixed by the land courts, had no money to pay their rent. Evictions rose sharply, from 698 families in the first quarter of 1886 to 1,309 families in the second. 'Moonlighting' – arms raids, cattle-maiming, and attacks on bailiffs and land agents – was rife, and boycotting dramatically increased. The English anti-imperialist Wilfrid Blunt, visiting tenants in Kerry in May 1886, noted in his diary:

> the fall of prices has ruined them. Butter from £4 and even £5 a firkin [cask] has dropped to 35s. and 30s. Calves from £6 to 20s., hay from £4 a ton to less than 20s. Yet never a reduction in rent, and this has bled them slowly to death.[58]

In April Blunt had seen his first eviction, in County Roscommon, writing with horror:

> It was a brutal and an absurd spectacle, 250 armed men, soldiers in all but name, storming the cottages one after the other of half starved tenants,

and faced by less than half their number of women and boys. Tatlow, the agent, was there, howled and jeered at by the crowd, with his bailiff and his emergency men, a disgraceful sight. The houses were ransacked, the furniture thrown out, the fires quenched, and a bit of thatch was taken possession of as a token in each case that the landlord had re-entered on his rights. Then the inhabitants were turned adrift upon the world.[59]

On a later occasion, after a day of evictions in Kerry, he admired the spirited response of the tenants:

We got into a house where the evicting party had been by mistake, and it was amusing to hear the women especially making fun of the sheriffs whom they had helped to mislead. The house was full of neighbours, men and women, and one got some idea of how they are able to combine against the Government and outwit and survive their conquerors. The power of wit is great...[60]

A particularly notorious landlord was Lord Clanricarde, popularly known as Lord 'Clanrackrent', who owned extensive estates in County Galway with thousands of tenants. Since his father died 12 years earlier, according to the *Pall Mall Gazette*:

no tenant on all the Clanricarde estates has seen his landlord or has ocular or aural proof of his existence... It was as if they addressed their petitions to the ghost of a marquess...[61]

Clanricarde, a former diplomat, was extremely wealthy and lived in London at the Albany, an exclusive establishment in Piccadilly occupied mainly by rich bachelors. While other landlords in the area agreed to reductions in rent in view of the drop in agricultural prices, Clanricarde's agent, Frank Joyce, refused. Some 300 tenants on the Clanricarde estate at Woodford appealed to Clanricarde but heard nothing. Joyce took the tenants to court and then targeted four families for eviction.

The evictions, in August, became a major battle. The bailiffs' escort of 100 'emergency men' armed with pickaxes and crowbars, backed up by 500 constables with rifles and revolvers and 200 cavalry, confronted huge crowds of locals and the besieged tenants, who threw everything from scalding water to hives of bees at the attackers. Altogether it took eight days' fighting to accomplish the four evictions.

The more militant of the Irish MPs, including John Dillon and the ebullient journalist William O'Brien, had already decided that if the government refused to improve the tenants' lot they would renew the land campaign.

In September Parnell presented to parliament a Tenants' Relief Bill which would allow the land courts to suspend evictions and reduce rents. Predictably, the bill was heavily defeated, and soon afterwards, at a meeting on the Clanricarde estate at Woodford, Dillon and O'Brien launched the Plan of Campaign. The Plan involved tenants on estates getting together to decide how much rent they were able to pay and then negotiating collectively with the landlord. Where the landlord refused to reduce the rent, the tenants would pay the agreed rent into a fund which would be used to support their fight, and to provide for people who had been evicted. The boycott tactic was to be used against evicting landlords.

The Plan was soon put into effect and spread rapidly through the south and west of Ireland, till by the end of 1886 it was operating on 116 estates and involving some 20,000 tenants. Parnell, who was worried that this militancy would endanger his alliance with the Liberals, then persuaded the organisers not to allow the Plan to spread further. As resistance mounted, the government tried to halt the campaign by bringing Dillon and O'Brien to trial on conspiracy charges, but the trial collapsed in February 1887. The health of the chief secretary for Ireland, Sir Michael Hicks-Beach, broke under the strain of his post, and Lord Salisbury brought in Arthur Balfour to replace him.

Balfour, a very rich aristocrat, was Salisbury's nephew and had been chiefly known as a languid dilettante and member of Randolph Churchill's parliamentary clique. He was now, however, proving tough and ruthless. Appointed secretary for Scotland for a few months, he sent a military expedition to crush a revolt by crofters in the Highlands: inspired by the Irish Land League, the poverty-stricken crofters had for several years been putting up a fierce resistance to landlords who charged high rents and appropriated the land for grazing or sport. His methods as chief secretary for Ireland soon earned him a new nickname: previously known as 'Pretty Fanny', he was now dubbed 'Bloody Balfour'. When police launched a bayonet charge on a crowd in Youghal in March, killing a fisherman named O'Hanlon, Balfour defended the magistrate who had instructed them: 'Deal very summarily if any organized resistance to lawful authority. If necessary, do not hesitate to shoot them.'[62]

Then on 28 March Balfour introduced a new coercion bill, the eighty-seventh such bill, and even more draconian than its predecessors. As well as allowing the banning of organisations and meetings, the Crimes Bill curtailed suspects' access to trial before Irish juries: the government believed such juries to be nationalist in sympathy and prone to being intimidated, and therefore not able to produce a 'fair verdict'.[63] The bill abolished jury trial for offences such as criminal conspiracy and boycotting, giving magistrates the power to impose sentences of up to six months with hard labour. It also provided for people charged with serious offences such as murder or arson to be transferred to England for trial: Irish judges had objected to the idea of dropping jury trial altogether for such cases. Further, this act was to be permanent, not temporary.

The Crimes Bill was hotly contested in parliament, and many protest meetings were held in Britain as well as Ireland. On Easter Monday, 11

April, there was a huge demonstration in Hyde Park against the bill, reportedly the largest political gathering in London for thirty years. Estimates of the attendance ranged from 50,000 to 150,000 people, many of whom were Irish. There were 15 platforms, and speakers included Gladstone, Bernard Shaw, Michael Davitt, Wilfrid Blunt, and Eleanor Marx, who came dressed in green. The *Daily Telegraph* reported on Eleanor Marx's speech, commenting on her 'excellent fluency and clear intonation', and continued:

> The lady has a winning and rather pretty way of putting forth revolutionary and Socialistic ideas as though they were quite the gentlest thoughts on earth. Her speech was chiefly confined to impressing on her Socialist friends the necessity for helping poor Ireland, as in so doing they would be helping their own poor selves and the cause to which they were attached. She was enthusiastically applauded for a speech delivered with perfect self-possession.[64]

The *Times*, meanwhile, had begun a smear campaign against Parnell with a series of three articles, published on 7, 10, and 14 March, titled 'Parnellism and Crime'. The series, aimed at aiding the passage of the crimes bill, purported to give a history of the Land League, proving that 'it is essentially a foreign conspiracy' and demonstrating 'that its chief authors have been, and are, in intimate, notorious, and continuous relations with avowed murderers.'[65] The *Times* claimed to show

> how Mr. Parnell's "constitutional organization" was planned by Fenian brains, founded on a Fenian loan, and reared by Fenian hands; how the infernal fabric "rose like an exhalation" to the sound of murderous oratory; how assassins guarded it about, and enforced the high decrees of the secret conclave within by the bullet and the knife.[66]

On 18 April the *Times* published a full-size facsimile of the first and last pages of a letter purporting to have been signed by Parnell a week after the Phoenix Park murders of May 1882. The *Times* admitted:

> It is requisite to point out that the body of the manuscript is apparently not in Mr Parnell's handwriting, but the signature and the 'Yours very truly' unquestionably are so...[67]

The letter implied that Parnell's denunciation of the murders had not been genuine:

> Dear Sir,
>   I am not surprised at your friend's anger but he and you should know that to denounce the murders was the only course open to us. To do that promptly was plainly our best policy.
>   But you can tell him and all others concerned that though I regret the accident of Lord Cavendish's death I cannot refuse to admit that Burke got no more than his deserts.[68]

In parliament at one o'clock the following morning – Balfour had refused to allow him to speak earlier in the debate -Parnell declared the letter 'a villainous and barefaced forgery'.[69] But it was not till two years later that the truth was revealed. The letter had been produced by Richard Pigott, a disreputable Irish journalist. Pigott had been paid by the secretary of the Irish Loyal and Patriotic Union, Edward Houston, a former *Times* reporter, to find material that would incriminate Parnell. Pigott forged letters ostensibly written by Parnell and Land League leader Patrick Egan, and sold them to Houston, who in turn sold them to the *Times*. Finally exposed in 1889, Pigott fled to Madrid and, when the police arrived to arrest him, shot himself.

The *Times* subsequently paid Parnell £5,000 in libel damages. Altogether the case cost the paper more than £200,000, and irretrievably damaged its reputation.

'Evictoria'

On 21 June 1887, as the Crimes Bill neared its final reading, came the celebrations of Queen Victoria's golden jubilee, marking 50 years on the throne. In contrast to previous royal occasions in the nineteenth century, which were ineptly managed and sparse on ceremonial, the jubilee was carefully organised and replete with pomp and pageantry – though the queen herself participated very reluctantly, and refused to wear ceremonial clothing.

In Westminster Abbey there was a ceremony attended by, as the Guardian put it, a 'vast crowd of all that is great and illustrious in this England of ours', as well as a brilliant array of Indian maharajahs, Eastern princes and European royalty.[70]

The general populace, too, were brought into the festivities. Beacons were lit the length of the country, and the *Daily Telegraph* laid on a 'treat' – a party – for some 27,000 London schoolchildren in Hyde Park. Businesses cashed in on the popularity of the event, selling commemorative mugs and plates: these carried pictures such as flags of the colonised countries, and portraits of Queen Victoria or Britannia, and mottoes such as 'The Empire on which the Sun never Sets'.

The glorification of monarchy was a response by the upper classes to major changes within British society and in Britain's place in the world. At home, democracy was encroaching, with most adult males now having the vote, while abroad Britain's economic and political dominance was increasingly threatened by other European powers and by America, and a frantic competition for colonies had begun. The new image of monarchy transformed the queen from the unpopular head of an outmoded aristocracy to a symbol of the nation and the empire, uniting all classes in Britain and the subject nations in a feudal-style entity, whose grandeur asserted Britain's superiority. The *Times* wrote of the jubilee: 'Not London alone, but all England transformed itself for the time into a huge Court at which the nation and empire rendered fealty to its Sovereign.'[71]

Most Irish people stood apart from the celebrations. While the aristocratic Marchioness of Londonderry presented the queen with a casket carved from Irish bog oak containing signatures of loyal Irishwomen, Michael Davitt's Irish-American wife Mary Yore, with pointed humour, displayed a flag over the door of their cottage with the word 'Evictoria' sewn onto it. A group of Fenians hoped to disrupt the jubilee with dynamite explosions, but their plans were inefficient and resulted only in two Clan-na-Gael members being arrested and receiving 15-year jail sentences for their part in the plot.

The Crimes Bill was passed on 8 July 1887 by 349 votes to 262 and quickly became law. On 9 August William O'Brien flouted the new act by calling on tenants on the Countess of Kingston's estate near Mitchelstown, County Cork, who were faced with eviction, to resist the evictors by force. His words, according to the government shorthand writer, were:

> There is nobody to oppose except a parcel of broken-down landlord robbers and the base blood-suckers and hirelings that cling to them. Fight out with those ruffians like men to the last act.[72]

As a result, the evicting party left Mitchelstown next morning, but O'Brien and a local leader, John Mandeville, were ordered to appear before the town's magistrates on 9 September.

Meanwhile on 19 August Balfour invoked the Crimes Act to 'proclaim' the Irish National League a dangerous association, a move which led to 141 of its 1,200 branches being suppressed.

O'Brien and Mandeville refused to appear in court at Mitchelstown: the hearing went ahead without them and warrants were issued for their arrest. The National League held a meeting in the town the same day. The authorities drafted in extra police and soldiers. Several thousand people marched into the town square, with banners waving and bands playing popular and patriotic airs. An array of prominent people arrived in carriages, including many English sympathisers, among them the Liberal MP Henry Labouchere, a staunch friend of Ireland, with 'a party of ladies', as the *Times* described them.[73] Also present was the Press Association's young reporter Frederick Higginbottom, whose account of the afternoon's events was to circulate worldwide.

Trouble began when police tried to escort a government shorthand writer through to the wagonette being used by the speakers as a platform. The police drew their batons against a line of horsemen at the back of the crowd: the horsemen raised their whips and a fight started. The crowd drove the police across the square and into the barrack, whereupon the police opened fire from the barrack windows killing three people, one outright, and wounding others. 'A great cry, partly of anger, partly of fear, rose from the people round,' wrote Higginbottom later.[74]

Thomas Casey, a 17-year-old, was hit in the forehead and shoulder and died five days later. John Shinnick, an old army pensioner and veteran of the terrible trenches of the Crimea, was hit in the forehead: after lying in a yard for 24 hours, he was taken to the workhouse hospital where he died. An old man named Michael Lonergan, who had been watching from a distance leaning on his stick, was hit in the left eye and died immediately.

While Balfour told parliament that the conduct of the police had been 'absolutely in self-defence' and 'absolutely justifiable',[75] the National League organised impressive funerals for the victims, and Liberals taunted Tories with the cry, 'Remember Mitchelstown!'

Prison protests

William O'Brien and John Mandeville were sentenced to three months and two months respectively for using seditious language. The crown prosecutor was Edward Carson, later to become famous as a unionist leader. O'Brien described him in his memoirs as a 'liverish young man, with the complexion of one fed on vinegar, and with features as inexpressive as a jagged hatchet', who behaved with 'cold insolence'.[76]

These were the first prosecutions under the new act. Balfour's view – which O'Brien described as 'the hallucination which has haunted every successive English ruler for ages'[77] – was that the nationalist agitation would collapse if its leaders were imprisoned. But over the next three years more than 1,600 people, including numerous MPs, among them the lord mayor of Dublin, were to be jailed.

Balfour reversed the previous prison policy, in which those convicted under emergency legislation had been in effect treated as political prisoners and had received privileged treatment. Now, those convicted under the new Crimes Act were to be treated as ordinary prisoners and subjected to a harsh regime of hard labour and plank beds. Wilfrid Blunt, while staying in the same English country house as Balfour in early September, noted in his diary:

> Balfour is clever and light in hand, but with a certain hardness and cynicism which are not altogether pleasant. 'I am sorry for Dillon,' he said at dinner, 'as if he gets into prison it is likely to kill him. He will have hard labour, and it will be quite a different thing from Forster's ridiculous imprisonments at Kilmainham.'[78]

O'Brien and Mandeville decided they would refuse to be branded as criminals, and would therefore refuse to wear prison clothes, do menial prison work or take exercise with criminals. O'Brien explained in his memoirs:

> The mere hardships attending imprisonment – unpalatable food, the plank bed and so on – were fairly part of the *régime*, and would be cheerfully

accepted... We warred only against Mr. Balfour's wilful determination
to degrade his prisoners into criminals, and that not even through motives
of personal susceptibility but because the question whether he was right
in his contention involved the question of the justice or guilt of our cause
and must consequently decide the entire issue between the two countries.[79]

In the vain hope of reducing the publicity surrounding O'Brien, the
authorities transferred the two prisoners to Tullamore jail in County Offaly
on 2 November, away from the nationalist ferment of Cork.

In London, the Irish National League called for a meeting in Trafalgar
Square on Sunday 13 November 1887 at 4 p.m. to protest against William
O'Brien's imprisonment. But on 8 November the commissioner of police,
Sir Charles Warren, a former special commissioner of Bechuanaland and
governor of Sudan, issued an order banning demonstrations in the square.
He did this because the square had become the venue for daily demonstrations
by the unemployed, and a resting place for hundreds of homeless people by
night. These gatherings were causing anger and alarm among the well-to-
do, who feared that 'the mob' would attack their property and would deter
customers from visiting shops and hotels in the area.

But the organisers of the 13 November demonstration decided to go ahead,
and were now joined by the Metropolitan Radical Federation and other
organisations who were outraged by the ban on the square and wished to
assert the rights of freedom of speech and assembly.

Sir Charles Warren amassed 4,000 constables, 300 mounted police, 300
foot soldiers and 350 cavalry to guard Trafalgar Square. Some 20,000
demonstrators moved off in contingents from many parts of London –
Clerkenwell Green, Bermondsey, Deptford, Battersea, Notting Hill,
Paddington – only to be ambushed by the police in the streets surrounding
the square. Fierce battles ensued as demonstrators tried to force their way
through. Mounted police cleared the square with baton charges, and by 6
p.m. all resistance was over. Some 200 demonstrators were taken to hospital,
and two later died, while 112 police were injured. The day became known
as 'Bloody Sunday' and was commemorated for years afterwards.

Many well-known socialists were present, including William Morris,
George Bernard Shaw, Annie Besant and Eleanor Marx, who wrote that she
had 'never seen anything like the brutality of the police'. She continued:

> I got pretty roughly used myself. My cloak and hat... are torn to shreds;
> I have a bad blow across the arm from a policeman's baton, and a blow on
> the head knocked me down – but for a sturdy Irishman (a perfect stranger
> to me), whose face was streaming with blood, I must have been trampled
> on by the mounted police. But this is nothing to what I saw done to others.[80]

A week later the radicals held a meeting in Hyde Park to protest once
more against William O'Brien's imprisonment and also to condemn the
ban on Trafalgar Square and the police brutality of the previous Sunday. On

the same day, a large crowd gathered around Trafalgar Square and was baton-charged by the police. An onlooker named Alfred Linnell, a poor widower whose three children were in the workhouse, was trampled by a police horse and died on 2 December. His funeral cortège, an immense procession of more than 100,000 people, travelled from Soho to Tower Hamlets behind the hearse from which flew the red flag of the socialists, the green flag of the Irish, and the red, yellow and green flag of the radicals. The authorities refused to allow the procession to enter Trafalgar Square.

In prison in Ireland, William O'Brien and John Mandeville continued their battle of wills with the authorities. O'Brien was transferred to the prison hospital in the hope that he would agree to wear the hospital outfit. He refused. One night a warder stole O'Brien's civilian clothes from his bedside and replaced them with a hospital suit. O'Brien then refused to leave his bed until his clothes were returned. Friends then smuggled in a new outfit and eventually, six weeks after his imprisonment, the authorities conceded defeat.

John Mandeville's experience was less happy. Unlike O'Brien, who was attended by streams of visitors and was the focus of constant press interest, Mandeville was outside the protective glare of publicity. When he refused to wear prison clothes, five warders forcibly stripped him and he spent a day wearing only a blanket before submitting to the indignity of a uniform. He still refused to do prison work or associate with criminals: in return he was put in solitary confinement in a punishment cell, with a plank bed and a diet of bread and water.

Mandeville was released on Christmas Eve in poor health and died seven months later, in July 1888, of a throat infection. The inquest jury unanimously decided that this resulted from his 'brutal and unjustifiable' treatment in jail. Soon after the inquest opened, the prison doctor, Ridley, who had reluctantly pronounced Mandeville physically fit to bear the punishment regime, committed suicide. While the authorities maintained that financial problems and an impending throat operation had driven Ridley to take his life, the inquest jury concluded that he had been 'labouring under temporary insanity produced by the apprehension of disclosures at the Mitchelstown inquest'.[81]

Among the hundreds arrested towards the end of 1887 was Wilfrid Blunt. On 23 October he spoke at an illegal meeting on Lord Clanricarde's estate at Woodford in County Galway, where evictions were again taking place. Those on the platform, it had been decided, would all be English. Accordingly Blunt mounted the platform along with his wife Anne, an MP named Rowlands and his wife – who was, Blunt wrote, 'a valiant little lady' and of 'a more heroic temper' than her husband – and a former parson from Norfolk, the Rev. Fagan.[82] When Blunt, as chairman, began to speak, the police rushed the platform. Blunt was charged with resisting arrest and, after an unsuccessful appeal at the start of 1888, was sentenced to two months' imprisonment.

Blunt found prison life gruelling. Incarcerated in Galway jail alongside non-political prisoners, he suffered the same hardships and indignities: coarse clothes, a plank bed – 'a real instrument of torture'[83] – picking oakum, with no books save the bible nor writing materials, communicating through letters scribbled on fragments of tissue paper and smuggled out.

Blunt spent the last four weeks of his sentence in Kilmainham jail in Dublin, which he found deeply depressing with its 'thieves and pickpockets, and its stony-visaged warders... and the solitude, blank and unbroken, of my cell'.[84]

He was discharged on 6 March 1888 by the governor, Mr Beer, who informed him:

> Last night my wife was safely delivered of a son, and in memory of your visit to Kilmainham, Mrs. Beer and I have decided to christen him after you by your name, Wilfrid Blunt.[85]

Blunt duly expressed his appreciation, shook hands, and departed.

After John Mandeville's death, Balfour continued the punitive prison regime for those convicted under the Crimes Act. But he was fully aware that the death of a leading figure would be politically catastrophic, so he ordered that a close eye be kept on the health of the more prominent prisoners such as John Dillon, who was sentenced to six months with hard labour in 1888 and was consumptive. In August that year Balfour complained to his under secretary, Ridgeway:

> It is a singular piece of ill-luck that so many of these so-called Irish patriots have such very bad constitutions. Possibly there may be some physiological connection between criminal agitation and weak lungs...[86]

Continued public concern over the ill-treatment of prisoners led to a relaxation of the rules, with some prisoners being classified as first-class misdemeanants and gaining privileges of dress and prison routine, a move that chiefly benefited priests and members of parliament.

Charles Conybeare MP

In 1889 a second prominent Englishman went to jail under the Crimes Act, this time Charles Conybeare, the 36-year-old Liberal MP for Camborne Division of Cornwall. He became the first English MP to be imprisoned in Ireland.

The Plan of Campaign activists encouraged English visitors to come to Ireland to witness evictions, and on 14 April 1889 Conybeare arrived in Falcarragh, in a remote part of Donegal, on an estate owned by Wybrants Olphert, an elderly landlord of Dutch extraction. The land was so poor that it did not produce enough to eat let alone pay the rent, and the younger people travelled regularly to England and Scotland as seasonal labourers. In January Olphert had begun evicting large numbers of tenants, but the 'emergency men' had met a determined resistance from the people and their redoubtable local priest, Father MacFadden, a prominent land agitator.

Also in Falcarragh when Conybeare arrived were Henry Harrison, an undergraduate and nephew of an Irish judge, and a Mr Benson, both from Balliol College, Oxford. Evicted tenants had returned to their homes and barricaded themselves in, and Conybeare, Harrison and Benson went to their houses and lowered food to them through the chimneys. Harrison was arrested while delivering bread on 17 April, and Conybeare was arrested on 22 April. Both were charged with taking part in a criminal conspiracy – the Plan of Campaign – and were tried by two resident magistrates.

The large attendance in the court included Irish MPs and priests, and visitors from England, women and men. Harrison was acquitted but Conybeare was found guilty: the clinching evidence was that when Harrison was arrested, Conybeare had called for 'three cheers for the Plan of Campaign'. Conybeare appealed, but on 5 July the county court judge upheld the conviction and sent him to Derry jail for three months. Before leaving the court, Conybeare handed over to a Campaign supporter, Father Boyle, two cheques – one from himself and one from a collection made at a radical demonstration in London – and a letter, in which he asserted:

> how little I care for the sentence just passed upon me, how determined I am in every way to thwart, defy and resist the Coercion Act on the ground of its unconstitutional character, and my resolve whenever I come out, if opportunity offers, to repeat my offences, which, as the judge has emphatically insisted on, are the giving of bread to the starving poor and cheering the Plan of Campaign, neither of which is an offence under English law or in any civilised country, except Ireland.[87]

Nor was it only sympathetic members of the English middle classes who visited Ireland. In 1889 George Lansbury, a working-class Liberal Party activist in the East End of London, suggested that Radical working-men should send a delegation of twelve to go to Ireland and see for themselves what crimes were being committed in their name.[88]

Lansbury's family had moved to Whitechapel in the East End when he was a schoolboy. He remembered:

> Here we lived among what may be described as mixed populations – Irish, Jews, and foreigners of all nationalities... The Irish boys at our school were all 'Fenians'; consequently, when the wall of Clerkenwell Prison was blown down and three Irish martyrs executed in Manchester because a police officer was accidentally killed, very great excitement prevailed in our classes and playground. The teachers tried to make us understand how wicked the Irishmen had been on both occasions, but my Irish friends would have none of it, and when a few months later T.D.

Sullivan's song *God Save Ireland* came out, we boys were shouting it at the tops of our voices every playtime.[89]

The Radical Clubs took up Lansbury's idea and sent a twelve-man delegation to Ireland. They travelled first to Dublin, where Lansbury noted 'the foul housing conditions': he was concerned that the Nationalists appeared uninterested in the towns and industrial problems.[90] The group then split into three parties, going north, south and west. Lansbury's group went north; they made public speeches and visited the holdings and cabins of country people. They also visited Belfast, where, he recalled,

> we tried to get into touch with Protestants as well as Catholics. We found this almost impossible. We were able to hold one monster meeting in St. Mary's Hall – a meeting which for red-hot enthusiasm, fine speaking, and good singing would be hard to beat.[91]

His visit to Ireland helped Lansbury to decide to change his allegiance from the Liberals to the growing socialist movement, and he spent the rest of his long life crusading, both outside and inside parliament, on behalf of the poor, women's suffragists, and Irish, Indian and Egyptian nationalists.

As well as using repression, the British government tried to undermine the Plan of Campaign by enlisting the help of the Vatican. The Catholic church in Ireland was divided over the Plan, with bishops both for and against it, while many priests took the tenants' side.

In response to British diplomatic pressure, and to complaints from two Irish bishops, the Vatican despatched an envoy, Monsignor Persico, to Ireland in 1887 to report on the situation. Persico was personally sympathetic to the Irish nationalists, but the Vatican was also influenced by other sources, including a deputation led by the leading English Catholic, the Duke of Norfolk. The wider interests of the Vatican proved paramount, and in April 1888 the Pope issued a statement condemning the Plan of Campaign and the practice of boycotting. This, however, succeeded only in making many nationalists, priests included, very angry with the Vatican. John Dillon, in a speech at Drogheda on 7 May, complained that English Catholics – 'a miserable crew' – had prevailed at the Vatican over the Irish bishops. He asked:

> Are we to be free men in Ireland or are we to conduct our public affairs at the bidding of any man who lives outside Ireland? We owe it to ourselves, we owe it to our friends in England, we owe it to the ancient traditions of our country, we owe it to our Protestant fellow-countrymen, who expect they are about to share with us a free Ireland, that it will not be an Ireland that will conduct its affairs at the bidding of any body of cardinals...[92]

In the end, it was largely lack of funds that brought the land agitation to an end. In 1890, in an attempt to rescue tenants and shopkeepers evicted from Tipperary town, the Plan's leaders sank a large sum into building a substitute town, New Tipperary. But within a few years the project failed, and the land reverted to the landlord, who levelled the town.

The Plan petered out over the next three years, but it had had considerable success, both symbolic – in demonstrating the willingness of nationalists to defy the British government no matter how harsh the penalty – and practical. In 1891 Balfour brought in a major Land Act, which greatly increased the amount of government money available to provide loans to tenants to buy their land. By 1893 the Plan had resulted in settlements on 84 estates, including the Countess of Kingston's at Mitchelstown, which was regarded as a special triumph. On 15 estates the tenants had returned on the landlords' terms, and on 18 others no settlement had been reached.

The fall of Parnell

Meanwhile the Irish Party in the Commons had plunged into crisis. The year 1890 had begun well but ended in calamity. After the *Times* series on 'Parnellism and Crime' in 1887, the government had set up a special commission to investigate – and, they hoped, prove – Parnell's alleged involvement in illegal activities. The commission's hearings began in October 1888, and in February 1889 the forger Richard Pigott was exposed under cross-examination, making Parnell the hero of the hour. In February 1890 the Commission's report was published, largely exonerating Parnell.

But already the seeds of disaster had been sown. On 24 December 1889 William O'Shea, husband of Parnell's mistress Katharine, had filed for divorce, naming Parnell as co-respondent. O'Shea may have been encouraged to make this move by Parnell's opponents in England, including Chamberlain, but his main motive was almost certainly financial. Katharine had by now borne Parnell three children, one of whom died in infancy, and their relationship had settled into domesticity. William had tolerated the situation, not wishing to jeopardise the source of his income: the O'Sheas had been living off money supplied by a rich aunt of Katharine's, known as Aunt Ben. But in May 1889 Aunt Ben died, leaving her fortune to Katharine.

Even before her death, Willie and Katharine's sisters and brothers had contested the will, trying to get Aunt Ben declared insane. Now Willie may have hoped that a divorce would discredit Katharine, and result in part of the inheritance being diverted to him; or he may have hoped that Katharine and Parnell would pay him off.

Parnell stilled the anxieties of his colleagues and the Liberals by assuring them everything would be all right. In February 1890 he told Michael Davitt that he would emerge from the case 'without a stain on his name or reputation'.[93] But when the case came to court on 15 November 1890 Parnell did not contest it, because he wanted to marry Katharine. Consequently Willie's version of events went unchallenged, and a series of humiliating details unfolded, among them Parnell's use of disguises and false names, and his alleged recourse to a fire-escape when O'Shea arrived one day unexpectedly. On 18 November O'Shea was given a divorce.

The response in Ireland was initially supportive to Parnell, though confused. At first Michael Davitt, furious at the way Parnell had deceived him, was the only major Irish figure to speak out against him, calling for him to retire temporarily. The Irish Catholic hierarchy made no move, not wanting to be seen to interfere openly in the political arena.

In England, the reaction was different. Parnell's relationship was widely known in political circles, and, by the standards of the Victorian upper classes, his behaviour had been quite restrained: his crime was to have been found out. The Tories revelled in his disgrace, but it was the nonconformists, the backbone of the Liberal Party, whose chorus of outrage set events on course for disaster. An eminent Baptist, Dr Clifford, declared in a letter published on 19 November:

> If the members of the Irish parliamentary party do not wish to alienate the sympathy of the radicals of England and Wales... they must insist on Mr Parnell's immediate retirement. *He must go...* The conscience of the nation is aroused. Men legally convicted of immorality will not be permitted to lead in the legislation of the kingdom.[94]

A leading Methodist, Hugh Price Hughes, told his audience:

> it would be an infamous thing for any Englishman to compel his chaste and virtuous Queen to receive as the first Irish prime minister an adulterer of this type...[95]

The view among secular Liberals, too, was that Parnell should withdraw, because his reputation was tainted. For him to remain leader of the Irish Party which was formally allied with the Liberals, would, they felt, have a disastrous effect on the Liberal vote.

Gladstone, hitherto cautious, now sent messages to Parnell through intermediaries implying that he should stand down. He wrote to his colleague John Morley that for Parnell to continue in the leadership

> would be productive of consequences disastrous in the highest degree to the cause of Ireland... [and] would render my retention of the leadership of the Liberal party, based as it has been mainly upon the prosecution of the Irish cause, almost a nullity.[96]

On 25 November the Irish MPs re-elected Parnell as chairman for the coming session. They did not at that stage know Gladstone's views, and many apparently thought that if they re-elected Parnell he would then be able to resign with dignity – but he did not.

Gladstone then stepped up the pressure by publicising his letter to Morley. This caused consternation among the Irish MPs. It placed them in a very awkward position: to back Parnell would mean the end of the Liberal alliance and home rule, but to oust Parnell at Gladstone's behest would be interpreted as yielding to British dictation.

Important members of the Irish Party began to turn against Parnell, and Irish Catholic bishops began publicly urging him to retire from the leadership.

Parnell, faced with the choice of sacrificing either the Liberal alliance, which he had nurtured, or his position, chose to jettison the alliance. He issued a manifesto attacking Gladstone and asserting that his proposals for home rule were seriously limited.

From 1 to 6 December, 73 of the 86 Irish MPs assembled in Committee Room 15 of the House of Commons to debate the issue. In the end, when Parnell ruled out of order a proposal to terminate his chairmanship, 45 of the MPs walked out of the meeting. The rift in the party would not be healed for another ten years.

Over succeeding weeks, several Irish MPs, with William O'Brien and John Dillon to the fore, tried through complex negotiations to persuade Parnell to retire from the leadership, but in vain.

Parnell took the argument to Ireland, where he forcibly took over the paper *United Ireland* and addressed mass meetings first in Dublin – where he had considerable support – then further afield. Weekend after weekend he made the long journey by train and boat from Brighton via London to Ireland. Such behaviour was completely at odds with his previous aloofness. The substance of his speeches, too, was changed. Abandoned by the Liberals, he in turn rejected the Liberal alliance, advocating instead the necessity of 'independent opposition'. He hinted that if constitutional methods failed, other steps would follow: as a result, Fenians round the country rallied to his support.

Senior members of the Irish Republican Brotherhood formed Parnell Leadership Committees in Dublin, Belfast, and other towns. The old guard, James Stephens and John O'Leary, gave their backing, as did John Devoy and O'Donovan Rossa in the USA. The Gaelic Athletic Association, controlled by the IRB, strongly supported Parnell.

Repudiated by Irish businessmen and lawyers, Parnell turned to the working class in London and Dublin, manifesting a sudden conversion to causes such as shorter working hours. But the combined opposition of the well-to-do and the Catholic hierarchy – though priests in some areas supported him – plus widespread concern about his political judgement, undermined his support, and his candidates lost three successive by-elections.

Despite fatigue and ill-health, Parnell persisted with his incessant campaign of travelling and speech-making, taking just one day off in June to marry Katharine. But the strain proved too much, and on 6 October 1891 he died in Brighton, aged 45, with Katharine at his side. He was buried in Dublin on

11 October. Some 200,000 people attended his funeral, which was organised by the IRB and led by 2,000 members of the Gaelic Athletic Association.

The 1893 Home Rule Bill

A general election was due in 1892, and Gladstone once more promised a Home Rule Bill if the Liberals came to power.

In Belfast, the Ulster Loyalist Anti-Repeal Union set about mobilising unionist opinion. They organised an 'Ulster Unionist Convention', which was held on 17 June 1892 in Belfast's Botanic Gardens. A pavilion was specially built which covered an acre and held 11,000 men – women were excluded. Many thousands more people listened to speakers in the gardens outside. The Convention marked a new stage in unionist organisation. It not only brought together Liberals and Conservatives, but it was also carefully staged to demonstrate that the unionist cause united Protestants of all classes. Although the majority of delegates were professionals, farmers and businessmen, there were also nearly 2,000 artisans and over 600 labourers present.

The Duke of Abercorn told the meeting, in words that would echo across succeeding decades: 'You are fighting for Home, for Liberty, for everything that makes life dear to you... Men of the North, once more I say, we will not have Home Rule.'[97]

Thomas Johnston, a well known trade unionist from the linen industry, implied that the interests of Protestant workers and their employers were the same:

> A good many Roman Catholics... seemed to think that if Home Rule were granted all they would have to do would be to seize upon their neighbours' property. But the Unionists of Ulster had had to work for what they had, and they intended to stick to it... If Home Rule were granted, the machinery in their mills and factories would be idle, and their shipbuilding would leave the country, for there would be no security for capital under such a Government.[98]

The election, held in July, brought the Liberals back into power – but only because of the vote in Ireland. In Britain, 277 Liberals were elected to 290 Unionists, while in Ireland 81 Home Rulers were elected to 23 Unionists. In Ireland the election had a particularly bitter dimension because Parnellites fought Anti-Parnellites: only nine of the former won seats, to 72 of the latter. In a new development, two of the Anti-Parnellites were labour-nationalists, who had been nominated by Michael Davitt.

On 13 February 1893 Gladstone, now 83 years old, introduced the second Home Rule Bill. The bill was in its essentials similar to its predecessor: it provided for an Irish parliament which would deal with most internal affairs, while the Westminster parliament would retain control of areas such as defence and external trade.

The unionists continued to agitate, mainly in Ulster. Elsewhere, except in Dublin and Cork where there were significant numbers of Anglo-Irish, unionists were reluctant to get involved: they were scattered and isolated, and either feared reprisals or saw resistance as pointless.

A procession of English politicians travelled to Belfast to add their weight, among them Arthur Balfour, Lord Salisbury and Joseph Chamberlain. In early April 1893, Balfour was on the grandstand as 100,000 Belfast loyalists took four hours to march past. He told a packed and cheering meeting in the Ulster Hall:

> Home Rule means for you that you are to be put under the heel of a majority which, if greater than you in numbers, is most undoubtedly inferior to you in political knowledge and experience... You, the wealthy, the orderly, the industrious, and the enterprising portion of Ireland, are to supply the money for that part of Ireland [which] is less orderly, less industrious, less enterprising and less law-abiding.[99]

Balfour went on to Dublin where he said that if the Home Rule Bill were passed, 'Ulster can at all events fight: the last refuge of brave men fighting for their freedom cannot be denied them.'[100]

On the bill's second reading, Gladstone pointed out that a change had taken place since the extension of the vote in Britain:

> During all the previous long, weary, deplorable centuries the question was, in the main, between a governing class on one side of the Channel and a nation on the other side. Sir, it is not so now. It is now a question between a nation and a nation... and not only between a nation and a nation, but between a great nation and a small nation, between a strong nation and a weak nation, between a wealthy nation and a poor nation. There can be no more melancholy and... degrading spectacle upon earth than the spectacle of oppression... inflicted by the deliberate act of a nation upon another nation, especially by the deliberate act of such a country as Great Britain upon such a country as Ireland.[101]

The second reading was carried on 21 April 1893 by 347 votes to 304, and the third reading was carried on 1 September, by 301 to 267. But then, predictably, the House of Lords killed the bill: every possible hostile peer was brought up to London, regardless of health or age, and they voted the bill down on 8 September after only four days' debate by 419 votes to 41.

Six months later, in March 1894, Gladstone resigned. In his place Lord Rosebery, a committed imperialist who was less than enthusiastic about Irish home rule, became prime minister.

At a general election in July 1895 the Liberals were routed. The Unionists – as the alliance of Conservatives and Liberal Unionists was described – won with a huge majority of 152. The 82 Irish MPs, no longer holding the balance of power, were now irrelevant, and their weakness was compounded by their disunity. As an issue in the House of Commons, home rule was dead.

7
The Irish Revival

The desire of Irish people for home rule had been overwhelmingly registered in the general elections of 1885, 1886 and 1892, with more than 80 Home Rule MPs elected in each case, only to be frustrated by the Commons in 1886, then accepted by the Commons in 1893 but promptly squashed by the Lords. The nationalist momentum was now unstoppable, and there was a new confidence in the air. But the failure of parliamentary politics to achieve results, coupled with disillusionment with the now-divided Irish Party, led many people to seek other channels for expressing their views. So the 1890s saw a burgeoning of cultural as well as political extra-parliamentary movements, whose members often overlapped.

There was a literary revival, which ranged from attempts – with W.B. Yeats to the fore – to create a new élite culture for Ireland, to the writing of straightforwardly patriotic verse, stories, and history. A new organisation aiming to revive the Irish language, the Gaelic League, was formed in 1893 and soon flourished. The proliferating literary and language societies attracted young intellectuals – writers, scholars and teachers – from both Protestant and Catholic backgrounds, and they set about creating cultural forms which they thought would be appropriate for an independent Irish nation.

Middle-class women were keen to participate in these developments, reflecting the increasing assertiveness of women generally, at a time when womens' property rights and access to education were improving, and when the suffrage movement was gathering pace. But they were barred from joining the literary societies, as they were from the National League, the support organisation for the Irish parliamentary party. The Gaelic League became the first association to admit women and men on equal terms.

Meanwhile the Irish Republican Brotherhood revitalised the amnesty movement, launching a vigorous, and ultimately successful, campaign for the release of prisoners jailed in Britain for the bombings of the 1880s.

The 1890s also saw the founding of Ireland's first explicitly socialist party, the Irish Socialist Republican Party, in 1896. It was formed by James Connolly, the son of unskilled Irish emigrants in Scotland. Connolly was influenced by the 'new unionism' – the organisation of unskilled workers into trade unions – then sweeping the industrialised countries, as well as by Marx and Engels, and by Irish republicanism. Combining these elements, he campaigned for an Ireland not only politically free but also socially transformed.

The literary revival

The Irish literary revival had its roots in the 1880s when young Irish middle-class intellectuals, mostly from Protestant backgrounds, had gathered round the veteran Fenian and book-lover John O'Leary in Dublin. Among them were the poet William Butler Yeats, the romantic poet Katharine Tynan, who was Catholic, the Irish language enthusiast Douglas Hyde, and the mystic George Russell – known as AE from an early pseudonym, Aeon.

The young writers began to choose Irish themes for their work, such as stories from Celtic mythology: these had recently been popularised by the writer – and dedicated unionist – Standish O'Grady. They coloured these tales with the romantic medievalism then fashionable in Britain, where writers and artists were looking to the past in search of an ideal world, free from the exploitation and drudgery of the industrial present. The earthy vigour of the original Celtic stories was transmuted into the wan beauties, posing in rich attire, favoured by the pre-Raphaelite painters. In Katharine Tynan's second book of poems, which she dedicated to the poet Christina Rosetti and her brother William, she described a Celtic mythic figure thus:

> There in the midst was Grainne, the King's daughter.
> Like a clear pearl her pure and pallid face;
> Her dreaming eyes were deep as moonlit water;
> The proud head poised itself with staglike grace.[1]

Yeats wrote to Tynan in 1887: 'I feel more and more that we shall have a school of Irish poetry – founded on Irish myth and history – a neo-romantic movement.'[2] He embarked on a long poem on a Celtic theme titled 'The Wanderings of Oisin'. This too was in the pre-Raphaelite style, but was also replete with private symbols: an early manifestation of Yeats's lifelong preoccupation with the occult, which involved him in tireless attempts to discover mystical systems which might govern the universe.

Oscar Wilde, already a celebrity, admired 'The Wanderings of Oisin', finding in it 'nobility of treatment and nobility of subject matter, delicacy of poetic instinct, and richness of imaginative resource.'[3] Wilde's parents

were deeply interested in the Irish past – consequently naming him Oscar
Fingal O'Flahertie – and his mother was the passionate nationalist poet
'Speranza'. Although Wilde transformed himself into a London wit and
aesthete, he retained a profound sympathy for Ireland and its struggle
against British rule.

Another Irish writer resident in London was George Bernard Shaw.
While he dedicated most of his political energy to the English labour
movement and his literary energy to the London stage, Shaw remained
interested in Irish affairs and wrote with acid wit in favour of home rule.

Yeats had spent much of his childhood in London, and returned there in
1887, aged 21, with his family: his father was a painter, the atheist son of
a Protestant rector. In London Yeats got to know the designer William
Morris, whom he greatly admired although he did not adopt Morris's
socialist politics. Yeats' elder sister Lilly went to work as an assistant
embroiderer with May Morris, William's daughter, and developed the
skills she would later bring to Celtic-style embroidery in Ireland.

Yeats was also a frequent visitor to the Russian occultist Madame
Blavatsky, who had developed a philosophy-cum-religion known as
theosophy, which won many adherents among people seeking a system of
beliefs in a world where science had discredited Christianity. Yeats joined
the Esoteric Section of the Theosophical Society, and then, in 1890, the
Hermetic Students of the Golden Dawn, which included prominent
scientists and writers among its members.

Yeats also went to meetings of the Southwark Irish Literary Club,
which had been founded in 1883 and sponsored lectures, dances and other
cultural activities. The club developed out of the Southwark Junior Irish
Literary Club, which aimed to teach London Irish children their history
and culture. At the heart of both societies was Francis Fahy, a Galway-
born songwriter and civil servant, described by a fellow activist, W.P.
Ryan, as 'an enthusiast and tireless worker'.[4] Ryan also described Yeats
on his first visit to the club:

> he was tall, slight and mystic of the mystical. His face was not so much
> dreamy as haunting: a little weird even... He spoke in a hushed, musical,
> eerie tone...[5]

In December 1891 Yeats founded the Irish Literary Society of London,
which absorbed the Southwark Literary Club, and then in May 1892 he
helped form the National Literary Society in Dublin. As an organised
movement, the literary revival had begun. At the same time Yeats worked
hard writing articles, editing anthologies of poems and folk-tales, and
collecting tales in Sligo: a volume of these that he published in 1893, *The
Celtic Twilight*, gave its name to the style of the literary revival. He also
wrote poems, including 'The Lake Isle of Innisfree', which prefigured the

incantatory rhythms typical of his later poems:

> I will arise and go now, and go to Innisfree,
> And a small cabin build there, of clay and wattles made...

He also wrote a play, *The Countess Cathleen*, set in 'old times' in Ireland, in which starving peasants and the countess – an idealised feudal ruler, full of concern for her tenants – sell their souls to two merchants, emissaries of the devil, in return for gold with which to buy food.

Yeats was beginning to conceive of constructing a high culture for Ireland, and its elements were beginning to take shape. It would combine English élite literary styles with the artist's own vision and Irish themes. These Irish themes were narrow in scope, encompassing Celtic mythology and an idealised rural aristocracy and peasantry. Absent were the realities of contemporary Ireland: exploitative landlords, the business class, manufacturing industry, the working class, urban life in general, the unionists of the northeast, and Catholic culture. It was an ideal Ireland as imagined by a member of the Protestant ascendancy caste, influenced by Victorian romanticism.

Yeats' ideas soon brought him into conflict with other Celtic revivalists. He clashed with Sir Charles Gavan Duffy over what sort of books the literary societies should produce. Gavan Duffy, a veteran of the 1848 rising who had returned to Europe after an illustrious career in Australia, wished to promote the straightforward patriotic verse of the Young Irelanders of his day. Yeats, by contrast, increasingly disapproved of conventional patriotic sentiment and imagery, complaining later that among the National Literary Society's 'persons of authority' and their friends:

> there were many who at that time found it hard to refuse if anybody offered for sale a pepper-pot shaped to suggest a round tower with a wolf-dog at its foot, who would have felt it inappropriate to publish an Irish book that had not harp and shamrock and green cover...[6]

The Gaelic League

The Gaelic scholar Douglas Hyde became president of the Irish National Literary Society in Dublin, and gave an inaugural address in November 1892 titled 'The Necessity for De-Anglicising Ireland'.[7] Hyde contended that Irish people should rediscover their Gaelic names, their literature, their history, their music and their games: the Gaelic Athletic Association had, he said, 'done more for Ireland than all the speeches of politicians for the last five years.' He emphasised above all that

> every Irish-feeling Irishman, who hates the reproach of West-Britonism, should set himself to encourage the efforts which are being made to keep alive our once great national tongue. The losing of it is our greatest blow, and the sorest stroke that the rapid Anglicisation of Ireland has inflicted upon us.

The lecture inspired an upsurge of efforts to preserve the language, and in July 1893 Douglas Hyde, along with Eoin MacNeill and Father Eugene O'Growney, who were also Irish language specialists, founded Conradh na Gaeilge, the Gaelic League.

Hyde, then in his early thirties, became the League's first president, and his great energy and charm contributed to its immediate success. He was the son of a Church of Ireland rector from Roscommon, and, unusually for one of his class, had learnt Irish as a child by making friends with local people. From them he also learnt about their terrible experiences during the famine years, and became for a time a fervent supporter of the Fenians. But he did his best to keep overt politics out of the Gaelic League, fearing its divisive effects. Many years later, in 1938, he became the first president of Ireland.

Within a few years the League became a mass movement, with many hundreds of branches, including several in Belfast. It attracted Protestants as well as Catholics, and clergy as well as radicals. It had many middle-class members, with teachers and civil servants forming the backbone of its network of branches: prevented by their terms of employment from joining political organisations, the League provided an outlet for their nationalist views.

The League organised feiseanna – competitions – to encourage singing, dancing and Irish music. An annual cultural festival, an tOireachtas, was established. Language classes were held, and travelling teachers visited remote areas. People wrote and staged plays in Irish. Activists campaigned successfully for the right to address letters and parcels in Irish. Though ostensibly non-political, by encouraging pride in Ireland the League had an immensely politicising influence, and many of those who joined would become the revolutionaries of the next century. Among them were Padraic Pearse, son of an English-born Dublin stone-carver and his Irish wife, who joined at the age of 16 in 1896, and later became editor of the League's paper, *An Claideamh Soluis*. Looking back in 1914, Pearse wrote that the League 'will be recognised in history as the most revolutionary influence that has ever come into Ireland.'[8]

Agricultural co-operation

In the economic sphere, the new mood of self-reliance was reflected in a movement for agricultural co-operatives. Such organisations enabled farmers to club together to buy machinery, manure and seeds, and to market their produce, thus enabling them to cut out the middle-men and save money. The movement began in 1890 in County Limerick, and spread through the dairy-farming regions of the south and east. In 1894 a co-ordinating body, the Irish Agricultural Organisation Society, was founded, and the movement spread to every county in Ireland.

The movement's best-known leader was Sir Horace Plunkett, a Unionist MP. Plunkett had been born in England and educated at Eton and Oxford: he then spent ten years in Wyoming as a rancher, before returning to Ireland in 1888 to manage the family estate in County Meath. He became a member of the Congested Districts Board, whose task was to improve conditions for peasants in the poverty stricken west. The board's policies, though well-meaning, achieved little, and Plunkett moved on to advocate self-help and co-operation. Although himself a capitalist – he owned coal-mines, ranches, estates and a shipping-line – Plunkett was sympathetic to socialist ideas, and was a lifelong friend of members of the Fabian Society including George Bernard Shaw and Beatrice and Sydney Webb.

In 1895 the *Irish Homestead*, the journal of the co-operative movement, was launched, with financial backing from Plunkett. Its editor was George Russell, otherwise known as AE, the poet, painter and mystic. Russell attracted other leading writers of the revival, such as his friend Yeats, to contribute to the paper. Through his writings on economic matters, Russell gained an international reputation as an agronomist.

Plunkett organised a committee made up of MPs, industrialists and clergy, from both unionist and nationalist camps, to pressurise the government to create a department to aid Irish agriculture. They were successful, and in 1899 an act was passed to establish a Department of Agriculture and Technical Instruction. The new department, with Plunkett as vice-president, set up an educational network to provide classes in practical subjects, and deployed agricultural inspectors and instructors to raise standards in the countryside.

Several years later Plunkett changed his political allegiance, becoming a supporter of home rule.

The amnesty campaign

Members of the clandestine Irish Republican Brotherhood were active in the literary and language societies, and also, in March 1892, launched a new amnesty campaign for Fenian prisoners in British jails, this time for those convicted for the bombing campaigns of the early 1880s. Nineteen such prisoners were held in Chatham prison in Kent, and in Portland jail on a bleak promontory off the Dorset coast. As 'treason-felony' prisoners they were put under a 'special' regime of such cruelty that several died in prison while others went insane. They were subjected to the notorious 'silent system', under which they were forbidden to talk to either prisoners or warders; for years they were woken hourly at night by the banging of the iron spyhole on their doors; they were made to do hard labour; they were put on punishment regimes of bread-and-water in freezing cells; and they were subjected to humiliating 'rub-down' searches – at least four a day – and the even more degrading 'special search' about twice a month. Tom Clarke, who was held for nearly 16 years, later described the 'special search':

> On these occasions we would be stripped stark naked and subjected to the most minute examination of our person – so minute that oftentimes the bull's eye lamp was used. Had this search stopped short at a minute examination of the hands and between the fingers, of the soles of the feet and between the toes, of the mouth and inside the jaws and under the tongue, it would be disagreeable enough; but it went further, and to such a disgustingly indecent extent that I must not here do more than imply the nature of it.[9]

Nevertheless, as Clarke recounted, some of the prisoners managed to retain their spirits and their sanity, communicating with each other through smuggled notes written with pencils secretly manufactured in the prison workshops.

A leading figure in the amnesty campaign was Ireland's best-known woman activist, Maud Gonne. Then in her twenties, Maud Gonne was an inspirational figure, courageous, beautiful and unconventional. The daughter of English parents – though her father, an army officer, was of Irish descent – both of whom died young, Gonne became an ardent and life-long revolutionary, moving between Ireland, France and Britain, and sustained by a private income. When the Irish National League refused to enrol her because she was a woman, she threw herself into campaigning against evictions in Donegal. She also became involved in the literary movement, and was misleadingly immortalised as the object of the poet Yeats' unrequited passion: her independent achievements were far greater. She and Yeats were close friends and lifelong correspondents – and, it seems, briefly lovers – but they differed politically. Gonne's concern for the poor contrasted sharply with Yeats's élitism.

Like many independent women, then and since, Gonne had difficulty making happy relationships with men. During the 1890s, unbeknownst to Yeats, she had a relationship with a French political activist, Lucien Millevoye, who was married. She had two children with him, one of whom died in infancy. Millevoye left her for a singer, and Gonne later had a brief and disastrous marriage to an Irish hero of the Boer war, John MacBride, father of her son Seán, who became a famous statesman. The marriage to MacBride swiftly disintegrated under the impact of his drunkenness and allegations that he had made sexual advances to several members of her household, including her 10-year-old daughter.

Over the years, Gonne was to work in many different campaigns, with a great variety of people. Her philosophy, as she later expressed it, was: 'Everyone must work according to his temperament.' She went on:

> I never willingly discouraged either a Dynamiter or a constitutionalist, a realist or a lyrical writer. My chief preoccupation was how their work could help forward the Irish Separatist movement.[10]

When Gonne heard of the conditions in Portland jail, and that most of the Irish prisoners never got visits – 'distance and the poverty of the families prevented'[11] – she wrote to the home secretary in the guise of a concerned lady who had met some of the prisoners' families, and requested a visit. She obtained permission for two visitors to see eight prisoners in Portland, and took an English journalist along with her. In her autobiography she recalled:

> We arrived at the prison at two o'clock. On the way up the hill from the station we saw gangs of convicts harnessed like horses to great carts of stones; they were all dressed in hideous yellow clothes decorated with broad arrows in black. Uniformed warders stood by each gang directing operations.[12]

The visitors were taken into a cage with iron bars, faced by another such cage into which the prisoners were brought one by one. They were forbidden to see one of the prisoners on their list, and later discovered he had gone insane. Another of the prisoners, Gonne wrote,

> looked apathetic and had great difficulty in articulating. He was almost unintelligible, as if he had forgotten how to speak, – the silent system has this effect on some.[13]

The last prisoner they saw, named O'Callaghan, told them he was going blind: the warders immediately took him away, stopping the visit. Maud Gonne's subsequent efforts to publicise conditions in Portland led to O'Callaghan being taken to hospital and released from prison within a few months.

The amnesty campaign, with separate organisations in Britain and Ireland, gathered momentum. It enrolled, Maud Gonne estimated, at least 200,000 people in England and Scotland. Their weight achieved the defeat of two Liberal cabinet ministers in elections, in a protest vote against the failure to release the prisoners. Gonne toured the USA to raise funds, and also raised money in France, where she gained extensive press coverage of the prison issue. One of the prisoners, John Daly, attracted considerable attention when he was elected MP for his native city, Limerick: he was promptly disqualified by a vote in the House of Commons. The campaign was successful: the prisoners were gradually released, with Tom Clarke, the last, leaving Portland in 1898. But two of the freed prisoners, Dr Thomas Gallagher and Albert Whitehead, had gone insane as a result of their experiences.

Alice Milligan and Ethna Carbery

The cultural revival flourished even in unionist-dominated Belfast, where the Gaelic League attracted enthusiastic support from Protestants as well as Catholics. Two of its keenest activists were the writers Alice Milligan and Anna Johnston, who became a very popular poet under her pen-name Ethna Carbery.

Milligan was born in Omagh, County Tyrone, in 1866, into a Methodist family. Her father, a wealthy businessman, was interested in Irish antiquities and she had a great-uncle who spoke Irish. She studied at the elite Methodist College in Belfast, then at Magee College in Derry, and King's College, London.

Ethna Carbery was born in 1864 in Ballymena. Her father, Robert Johnston, a Catholic, was a carpenter who became a successful Belfast timber merchant. He was for many years the leading IRB organiser in the city, and a member of the IRB's supreme council.

In early 1895 a literary society named after the local 1798 hero Henry Joy McCracken was formed in Belfast. In October, the society launched a paper, the *Northern Patriot*, with Alice Milligan as editor and Ethna Carbery working with her. The paper was produced to a high professional standard, and included poems, short stories, historical articles about heroes and heroines of past rebellions, and reports of meetings and other activities.

The second issue of the *Northern Patriot* was devoted to the Fenians. It included an article by Maud Gonne about the prisoners in Portland. She had recently visited the paper's office to enlist support, and in an editorial Alice Milligan took her side against John O'Leary, who, she wrote, 'could never endure to hear the dynamite prisoners spoken of in the same breath as men who had suffered for Ireland in a stainless cause.' Milligan went on:

> Generously and eloquently, by voice and by pen, Miss Gonne pleads their cause. She appeals for far more than freedom for them; she asks that we shall admit them to Ireland's roll of hero-martyrs. She tells us, and we know it well, that those who are proven guilty of this offence have no selfish aim; they thought only of Ireland...[14]

But Milligan's militant Fenianism and support for the amnesty cause led to her being ousted from the editorship of the *Northern Patriot* after the third issue, and she and Ethna Carbery then founded their own journal, the *Shan Van Vocht* – the poor old woman, from the poem of that title. Milligan was once again the editor, and Carbery became the secretary. The paper, which came out monthly and was a fully professional production, carried similar material to its predecessor and became an important outlet for the literary revival. Maud Gonne described the two women:

They were so different but worked so well together, – Anna, tall and romantic with her long face and dreamy eyes, – Alice small, aggressive and full of observant curiosity.[15]

Seumas MacManus, who married Ethna Carbery in 1901, recalled:

For three and a half years these two girls edited the magazine, and managed it. They themselves wrote almost all of the magazine... They read the proofs. They kept the books. They sent the bills. They wrote the letters. With their own hands they folded and addressed every copy that was to go out, and licked every stamp...[16]

Alice Milligan continued to write, lecture and campaign for the next two decades, but her close friend Ethna Carbery died of gastritis in 1902 aged only 37. She was very widely mourned in Ireland, and her popularity continued after her death; her ballad 'Rody McCorley', about a hero of 1798, is still sung:

Up the narrow street he stepped,
Smiling and proud and young;
About the hemp-rope on his neck
The golden ringlets clung.
There's never a tear in the blue, blue eyes,
Both glad and bright are they
As Rody McCorley goes to die
On the Bridge of Toome today.[17]

James Connolly

One of the *Shan Van Vocht*'s occasional contributors was James Connolly, a 28-year-old socialist who had recently arrived in Dublin. Connolly argued vigorously not only for national independence but also for social revolution in Ireland, bringing a new dimension to the nationalist struggle. The cultural revival was predominantly a middle-class affair, and, although some of its activists sympathised with the socialists, they generally ignored social questions. The Fenians, by contrast, mainly came from working-class backgrounds, but, with a few exceptions such as Michael Davitt, they did not have a class-based critique of Irish society, nor articulate a desire for a radically changed social system. Instead, their concerns tended to be with tactical questions such as the merits and demerits of bombing campaigns or participation in parliamentary politics.

Connolly was born in Edinburgh, the son of unskilled Irish Catholic immigrants. His father worked as a manure carter, removing dung from the streets at night, and his mother was a domestic servant, who suffered from chronic bronchitis and died young. The family lived in extreme poverty in the district known as Little Ireland. James started work at 10 or 11 years old, and in 1882 at the age of 14 he followed his brother into the British army. He spent nearly seven years in the army, all of it in Ireland,

and met his wife, Lillie, a domestic servant from a Protestant background, in Dublin. Back in Scotland, Connolly found work as a carter like his father and brother. He immediately became whole-heartedly involved in the socialist movement and in the 'new unionism': the movement to organise unskilled workers into unions that was sweeping the industrial towns, with workers from Irish backgrounds – such as Ben Tillett, who led the great dock strike of 1889 – in the vanguard.

Connolly was greatly influenced by another Edinburgh Irishman, John Leslie, a Marxist who lectured regularly on socialist ideas and admired the radical strands in Irish nationalism, including Fintan Lalor and the Land League. Leslie developed the view that the Irish working class needed their own party, independent of the upper-class nationalists of the Irish parliamentary party. He wrote:

> I speak as an Irish wage-worker... who does not believe that the Alpha and the Omega of the Irish Question consists in the hoisting of the green and gold banner above the old Parliament House in Dublin. Neither do I believe that the interests of the Irish working-class are any more likely to be advanced by the men who constitute the overwhelming bulk of the present Irish party than the interests of the British working-class are to be advanced by the men who compose either of the great British parties.

He wrote that he understood the passion of the Irish for their history, but their national sentiment and poetic instincts would be exploited by politicians

> until the lesson is learned that the Ireland of the past is gone forever; that it would not be very desirable, even if it were possible, to have it back again; and that the Ireland of the present is no beautiful abstraction, the fiction of the poet's mind; but that Ireland means all the people enclosed within its four seas, the Irish People one and indivisible – only that and nothing more.

He argued that

> the cause of Irish misery is not to be found in the incorporation of the Irish Parliament in that of England (although such incorporation undoubtedly tends to aggravate the evil), but it is to be found in the fact that the means by which the Irish people must live are in possession of a class, which class will not allow the people to use these means unless by so doing a profit will accrue to this class.[18]

Leslie's work provided the starting-point for Connolly's thinking. In 1896, on the edge of destitution, Connolly accepted an offer from the Dublin Socialist Club to become its paid organiser. He arrived in Dublin in May, and moved into a one-room tenement with his wife and three daughters. Soon he persuaded seven other socialists to join him in forming the Irish Socialist Republican Party, which held its first meeting on 29 May. In his first public statement on behalf of the ISRP Connolly wrote:

The struggle for Irish freedom has two aspects; it is national and it is social. The national ideal can never be realised until Ireland stands forth before the world as a nation, free and independent. It is social and economic because no matter what the form of government may be, as long as one class owns as private property the land and instruments of labour from which mankind derive their substance, that class will always have it in their power to plunder and enslave the remainder of their fellow creatures.[19]

The new party's manifesto called for the

Establishment of an Irish Socialist Republic based upon the public ownership by the Irish people of the land and instruments of production, distribution and exchange.

Except in its opposition to colonialism and commitment to Irish independence, the manifesto echoed the demands being made by British socialists. It called for the nationalisation of railways and canals, the abolition of private banks, the renting of advanced agricultural machinery by the state, a graduated income tax, a 48-hour week and a minimum wage, free maintenance for all children, control of schools by elected boards, free education at all levels, and universal suffrage.

Despite energetic campaigning, the party remained tiny: the trade union movement was dominated by the old craft unions, which were not sympathetic to the new ideas. Nor were they encouraged by the fact that the ISRP's members were very young and somewhat bohemian in appearance.

The cultural nationalists were more welcoming. Connolly submitted articles to the *Shan Van Vocht*, which printed them in a column titled 'Other People's Opinions'. The editors declared they were 'in full sympathy with Mr. Connolly's views on labour and social questions,' but disagreed with his proposal for 'an Irish Republican party in the British Parliament.' No conscientious republican could take the oath of allegiance, they said.[20]

In the January 1897 issue, Connolly gave his perspective on the cultural revival, arguing that while the literary and language societies were 'undoubtedly doing a work of lasting benefit to this country', there was a danger they might neglect 'vital living issues'. The national movement, he contended,

must demonstrate to the people of Ireland and the world at large that Irish Nationality is not merely a morbid idealising of the past, but is also capable of formulating a distinct and definite answer to the problems of the present, and a political and economic creed capable of adjustment to the wants of the future.

The goal should be a socialist republic, he wrote, for true freedom for the people of Ireland could only come through the ending of the 'property system founded upon spoliation, fraud, and murder' which English conquerors had forced upon Ireland. He asserted:

> If you could remove the English army tomorrow and hoist the green flag
> over Dublin Castle, unless you set about the organisation of the Socialist
> Republic, your efforts would be in vain. England would still rule you;
> she would rule you through her capitalists, through her landlords, through
> her financiers, through her usurers, through the whole array of commercial
> and individualist institutions she has planted in this country and watered
> with the tears of our mothers and the blood of our martyrs, England
> would rule you to your ruin even while your lips offered hypocritical
> homage at the shrine of that Freedom whose cause you had betrayed.[21]

Alice Milligan was so impressed by Connolly's articles that she sent her
18-year-old brother Ernest, a student, to find out more about the ISRP. He
visited the Connolly family in their one-room lodgings, then soon joined
the ISRP himself and organised a branch in Belfast.

The British empire in 1897

As Ireland became more confidently nationalist, a frenzy of imperialism
was sweeping Britain: a clash of outlooks which was vividly demonstrated
during the celebrations of Queen Victoria's jubilee in 1897.

Driven by the quest for raw materials – rubber, palm oil, cotton,
minerals – to supply the multiplying factories, and for markets for the
goods they manufactured, Britain had extended its tentacles to the furthest
reaches of the world. Its empire had swelled fivefold during the 60 years
of Victoria's reign, and now covered a quarter of the earth's land mass and
a fifth of its population.

Earlier in the century, Britain's dominance of world trade had been
unchallenged, and informal control of overseas territories had sufficed.
Now, however, Britain's hegemony was threatened by other powers,
especially Germany and the USA, and a fierce race was on to formally
colonise every corner of the globe. 'I would annex the planets if I could,'
said the gold and diamond magnate Cecil Rhodes, the most aggressive
imperialist in Africa.[22] Africa was the main focus of contention: the
European powers were frantically carving up the continent between them,
meting out slaughter and destruction on a horrendous scale as they forced
their rule on unwilling peoples.

The empire not only brought wealth and employment to Britain's
business and professional classes, but was now the main source of national
pride, generating a frenetic jingoism and racism which extended even to
the numerous poor. The *Daily Mail*, founded in 1896 and the vanguard of
mass journalism, trumpeted tales of imperialist derring-do to the middle
classes. Its founder, Alfred Harmsworth, described the paper as 'the
embodiment and mouthpiece of the imperial idea'.[23] On Jubilee Day, 22
June, the *Daily Mail* burbled ecstatically,

The jubilonged-for day is upon us at last. Before these lines are read six million people will have started out to jubiline the streets by day and jubilluminate them by night.[24]

Vast crowds thronged the capital to applaud the queen as she travelled through gaudily decorated streets to St Paul's Cathedral in a procession that included troops from every corner of the globe. The Irish sounded the only discordant note, with many nationalist MPs refusing to accept seats on the stands provided for MPs to view the cavalcade. Next day the *Mail* brought out alongside its normal edition a special souvenir number printed throughout in gold. The paper marvelled at the implications of 'the great pageant':

Until we saw it all passing through the streets of our city we never quite realised what the Empire meant... It makes life newly worth living, worth living better and more strenuously, to feel that one is a part of this enormous, this wondrous machine, the greatest organisation the world ever saw. How many millions of years has the sun stood in heaven? But the sun never looked down until yesterday on the embodiment of so much energy and power.[25]

The *Mail* described every detail of the procession, writing of the colonial troops:

white men, yellow men, brown men, black men, every colour, every continent, every race, every speech – and all in arms for the British Empire and the British Queen. Up they came, more and more, new types, new realms, at every couple of yards, an anthropological museum – a living gazetteer of the British Empire. With them came their English officers, whom they obey and follow like children. And you began to understand, as never before, what the Empire amounts to... that all these people are working, not simply under us, but with us – that we send out a boy here and a boy there, and the boy takes hold of the savages of the part he comes to, and teaches them to march and shoot as he tells them, to obey him and believe in him and die for him and the Queen. A plain, stupid, uninspired people, they call us, and yet we are doing this with every kind of savage man there is. And each one of us – you and I and that man in his shirt-sleeves at the corner – is a working part of this world-shaping force.[26]

Across the Irish Sea there was little sympathy for the jubilee. The Belfast-based *Irish News* observed:

In Ireland, metaphorically within earshot of the cannonades of rejoicing, the 'Jubilee' demonstrations took the shape of funeral processions, and black flags floated from pinnacles where the loyal authorities thought the Royal Standard should have waved. There was no rejoicing – beyond the pale of the English garrison, and even within that pale the jubilations were of a most perfunctory and apathetic sort.[27]

Belfast's main streets, in the words of the *Irish News*, 'groaned under a tremendous weight of tawdry bunting,' and bands of disorderly loyalists paraded through the town. But an attempt to light a great bonfire at McArt's Fort, the historic site of the United Irishmen's pledge on Cave Hill, proved a miserable failure. 'Evidently the ground didn't like the auspices under which the fire was made,' the paper commented.[28]

In Dublin, James Connolly and Maud Gonne were the leading spirits in the anti-jubilee protests. Gonne returned specially from Paris, where she had recently launched a campaigning paper, *L'Irlande Libre*. Later she recalled the Dublin protests:

> All the shops which relied on Unionist custom had decorations and electric lamps for night-display. James Connolly and other friends arranged our Jubilee display also. I had obtained a window in the National Club in Parnell Square from which, on a huge screen, Pat O'Brien's photos of the Eviction scenes could be shown and the photos of the men who, during Victoria's reign, had been executed or who had died in prison.
>   With the help of the Corporation workmen, we had arranged for the cutting of wires to prevent the display by the Unionist shops of their electric decorations and I had been busy making black flags with suitable inscriptions in white, showing the numbers who had died of famine during Victoria's reign, the number of houses destroyed and the number of men jailed, etc.[29]

One of these flags was on display at an outdoor ISRP meeting the night before the jubilee, addressed by Maud Gonne. The *Daily Mail* described disapprovingly how

> a large crowd assembled carrying a black flag bearing a statement in silver-coloured letters to the effect that during the Record Reign over 1,500,000 people have been starved in Ireland, over 300,000 were alleged to have been evicted, and more than 4,000,000 compelled to emigrate.[30]

The meeting was attacked by unionist students from Trinity College.

Next day, James Connolly and his fellow ISRP members organised a jubilee procession featuring a big black coffin with the words 'British Empire' on it, which was mounted on a rickety handcart draped to resemble a hearse. There was also a workers' band which played a dead march on instruments which Gonne described as 'so old and battered that if they were broken by the police it would be no great loss.'[31] The police attacked the procession, and furious fighting ensued. Connolly called for the coffin to be thrown in the river Liffey, whereupon, as Gonne related, the whole crowd shouted, 'Here goes the coffin of the British Empire. To hell with the British Empire!' Connolly was arrested and spent the night in prison. Gonne remembered:

> People began to notice the city was in darkness; none of the Jubilee illuminations were visible. Everywhere could be seen excited crowds being dispersed by the police. Willie Yeats and I proceeded up O'Connell

Street to see how my magic lantern show in honour of Victoria was faring.[32]

Later the police baton-charged the crowd watching the magic lantern display, fatally injuring a 75-year-old woman, Mrs Anna Maria Fitzsimons. As the news spread, people went on a rampage of revenge, smashing the windows of shops with jubilee decorations.

In Skibbereen, nationalists held a funeral procession to the graveyard where Fenians were buried, while Limerick was decorated with black flags. In Dundalk, quay labourers refused to unload two steam colliers until their jubilee bunting had been hauled down. In several towns, attempts two weeks later to distribute free Australian 'jubilee mutton' to the poor were met with protests or boycotted by the Catholic clergy who were supposed to organise the handouts.

There were rumblings of dissent in many parts of the empire. In India, a nationalist movement was taking shape, fuelled by widespread resentment among the middle classes of Britain's despotic system of government and colonial exploitation of the economy. Much of the country was being ravaged by a terrible famine, accompanied by epidemics, which killed more than five million people.

In Bombay, thousands were dying in India's first outbreak of bubonic plague. The British responded ruthlessly, deploying troops who removed suspected victims and contacts to special plague camps, and destroyed property suspected of contamination. In the process, they looted, raped and damaged religious shrines, and outraged all sections of the community. On jubilee night, the civil servant in charge of the plague operations in Poona, Walter Rand, was shot and fatally wounded as he left a celebration dinner at Government House.

Commemorating 1798

In Ireland, the nationalist momentum continued. In the months before the jubilee, activists with IRB links – including John O'Leary, Alice Milligan and W.B. Yeats – had begun setting up commemoration committees to organise activities to mark the following year's centenary of the 1798 rising. Their plans included organising demonstrations and erecting monuments to the heroes of '98. A large part of their work was educational: Maud Gonne, Alice Milligan, Anna Johnston and others travelled the country lecturing on the United Irishmen, and publicising their ideal of an independent Irish republic uniting all its people regardless of their religion.

On new year's eve, the last night of 1897, torchlight processions were held in Dublin, Cork, Belfast and Limerick to inaugurate the centenary. In Dublin some 5,000 people marched with bands. There were many more demonstrations during the year, including a large one at Castlebar to commemorate the French general Humbert's famous battle. The *Shan Van Vocht* and, in Paris, Maud Gonne's *L'Irlande Libre*, gave extensive coverage to the activities. The commemoration movement gained so much support that the constitutional nationalists, fearing the growing influence of the separatist IRB, moved into the main committee in Dublin and, to the anger of Gonne, Connolly and the other republicans, took it over. Right-wing Catholics, including William Martin Murphy, Dublin's biggest capitalist and an avowed royalist, publicly supported the new-look organisation.

The climax of the commemorations was a huge demonstration of some 100,000 people in Dublin on 15 August 1898 to mark the laying of the foundation stone for a Wolfe Tone monument. A French deputation arrived to an enthusiastic welcome. In the event, the monument was never completed, though several local '98 memorials were erected, including one in Ballina commemorating General Humbert, which was unveiled by Maud Gonne.

James Connolly had the first issue of the ISRP paper, the *Workers' Republic*, on the streets for the demonstration. Its masthead carried Connolly's favourite saying, in Irish: 'Is dóigh linn gur mór iad na daoine móra mar ataimid féin ar ár nglúnaibh – eirimís.' 'The great appear great to us because we are on our knees – let us rise.' Vividly agitational in style, the paper led off with a polemic against the praise then being lavished on Irishmen fighting in the American army against Spain:

> When the Boer has to be robbed of his freedom, the Egyptian has to be hurled back under the heel of his taskmaster, the Zulu to be dynamited in his caves, the Matabele slaughtered beside the ruins of his smoking village, or Afridi to be hunted from his desolated homestead, wheresoever in short the bloody standard of the oppressors of Ireland is to be found over some unusually atrocious piece of scoundrelism, look then for the sons of our Emerald Isle, and under the red coats of the hired assassin army you will find them.
>
> Yes, we are a fighting race. In Africa, India or America, wherever blood is to be spilt there you will find Irishmen, eager and anxious for a fight, under any flag, in anybody's quarrel, in any cause – except their own...

The editorial ended by stating the ISRP's credo:

> We are Socialists because we see in Socialism not only the modern application of the social principle which underlay the Brehon Laws of our ancestors, but because we recognise in it the only principle by means of which the working class can in their turn emerge into the dignity of freemen, with a right to live as men and not as mere profit-making machines for the service of another.
>
> We are Republicans because we are Socialists, and therefore enemies to all privileges; and because we would have the Irish people complete

masters of their own destinies, nationally and internationally, fully competent to work out their own salvation.[33]

The Boer war

The outbreak of war in southern Africa in October 1899 between Britain and the Boers – a people of Dutch descent – provided yet another spur to nationalist dissent. While jingoism swept Britain, taking many liberals and socialists along with it, most Irish people, like the rest of Europe, instantly sided with the Boers, whom they saw as a doughty race of less than 250,000 people up against the might of the British empire. Irish separatists saw the Boer struggle as directly paralleling their own: the loyalists of northeast Ulster likewise saw the similarity, and vehemently supported Britain.

Like most in Europe who took sides in the war, the Irish tended to ignore the situation of the native Africans. Irish attitudes in international affairs were dictated largely by whether people were for or against Britain, and they supported Britain's enemies regardless of race or creed. But the Africans' plight was obscured by the titanic struggle between Britain and the Boers. British propaganda played on the Boers' cruelty to the Africans and intolerance of Catholics: the Irish responded by persuading themselves that such accusations were hypocritical calumnies, and pointed instead to Britain's sorry record in such affairs, such as the recent slaughter inflicted on the Matabele, and the continuing exclusion of Catholics from high offices in Britain.

But Irish nationalists were undoubtedly afflicted by the racism endemic in the white Christian nations of Europe, and even the radical Michael Davitt habitually referred to the Africans as 'savages'.[34] Anti-semitism, too, was rife, with the pro-Boer camp hurling crude insults at Jewish capitalists on the British side.

The Boer war was the latest phase of a long struggle by the British to wrest southern Africa from earlier colonists, mainly of Dutch descent, known as Afrikaners or Boers – the Dutch word for farmers, reflecting their way of life. By the 19th century, the British controlled two colonies, Cape Colony and Natal, while the Boers held two republics, the Transvaal and the Orange Free State. Both British and Boers dealt ruthlessly with the indigenous African peoples, fighting repeated wars to take over their land, and harshly exploiting their labour, whether on Boer farms or British-owned mines.

The discovery of first diamonds in 1867 and then gold in 1886 added a powerful economic motive to British designs. The great mining millionaires, such as Cecil Rhodes, wanted an end to the Boer regime in the Transvaal because it was not geared to the needs of the big capitalist enterprises, and in particular did not assist them in recruiting and controlling the unskilled African labour they needed. Rhodes, like imperialist politicians back in Britain, also dreamed of dramatically extending British rule in Africa. By August 1899, it was clear that Britain was likely to go to war. In time-honoured fashion, Connolly saw the impending war as a case of 'England's difficulty is Ireland's opportunity', writing:

> if the working class of Ireland were only united and understood their power sufficiently well, and had shaken off their backs the Home Rule-Unionist twin brethren – keeping us apart that their class may rob us – they would see in this complication a chance for making a long step forward towards better conditions of life – and, seeing it, act upon it in a manner that would ensure the absence from the Transvaal of a considerable portion of the British army.[35]

On 27 August the ISRP, by now a political force despite having less than 100 members, held the first public protest against English policy in southern Africa. The *United Irishman* reported:

> The abnormally large gathering was characterised by the greatest and most unbounded enthusiasm, and frequent cries of 'Long Live the Boers,' and 'Down with the British Empire,' were heard...[36]

The campaign gathered momentum, and on 1 October several thousand people attended a protest meeting in Dublin. They passed resolutions supporting the Boers and condemning the enlistment of Irishmen in the English army. The platform included John O'Leary, Michael Davitt, who was now a member of parliament, and Maud Gonne, who told the cheering crowd that it was 'a terrible humiliation to think that regiments with Irish names had gone out to fight the Transvaal'.[37] She said she hoped the Irish soldiers would change sides, and called on the Irish people to put a stop to recruiting.

A few days later Maud Gonne, Anna Johnston (the poet Ethna Carbery) and others formed an Irish Transvaal Committee. The committee's main drive was against recruitment, and it issued a statement headed, 'Enlisting in the English Army is Treason to Ireland', which declared:

> In the past Irishmen have too often won battles for England, and saved her from defeat, and thus have riveted the chains upon their motherland! Let them do so no more.[38]

One of the committee's founder-members was Arthur Griffith, a young printer and journalist who had just spent two years in the Transvaal. On his return to Dublin, he and another enthusiastic nationalist, William Rooney, had founded a new nationalist weekly paper, the *United Irishman*, named after John Mitchel's paper of 1847. The new paper was launched in March 1899 and was partly funded by Maud Gonne. Griffith was a passionate separatist and dismissive of parliamentarians, but he was also conservative in his social outlook, lacking any socialist perspective.

In the Transvaal, too, the Irish were making preparations. There were numerous Irish workers among the *uitlander*, the foreigners who had crowded into the country in the gold rush. The previous year, Irish nationalists in Johannesburg – including Arthur Griffith, John MacBride, who also worked for a mining company, and a decorator named Robert Noonan, later famous as Robert Tressell, author of *The Ragged Trousered Philanthropists* – had organised celebrations for the 1798 centenary. Now MacBride set about organising an Irish Brigade to fight on the Boer side. A former officer in the US army, John Blake, was chosen to lead the brigade, while MacBride became second-in-command.

In January 1900 a second Irish Brigade was formed, led by an Irish-Australian journalist named Arthur Lynch. An able linguist, Lynch recruited 'Irishmen' of various European nationalities, including one Englishman. Altogether more than 2,000 European volunteers, and a contingent of 40 Irish-Americans from Chicago, were to fight on the Boer side.

In mid-October 1899 Britain finally provoked the two Boer republics into war, but the Boers proved a much tougher enemy than expected. They besieged three British-held towns, Ladysmith, Mafeking and Kimberley, and Britain immediately sent out some 50,000 imperial troops, including brigades from Ireland and Scotland, to try to break the sieges. But the British soldiers were mostly infantry, marching in regular columns, and the mounted Boer sharpshooters inflicted a succession of humiliating defeats involving heavy casualties.

Irish protests continued. Michael Davitt resigned his parliamentary seat, making what he later called 'a personal and political protest against a war which I believed to be the greatest infamy of the nineteenth century'.[39] Soon afterwards Davitt went to the Transvaal where he spent several months compiling information, and later published a book titled *The Boer Fight for Freedom*.

On 17 December there were dramatic scenes in Dublin when the Transvaal Committee attempted to hold a meeting in protest against a visit by Joseph Chamberlain, now a leading unionist, who was to receive an honorary degree from Trinity College. The meeting was banned and a large force of police occupied Beresford Place, the intended venue. Nevertheless just after one o'clock a brake carrying Maud Gonne, James Connolly, Arthur Griffith and two others drove into the square, where a large crowd, 'cheering enthusiastically for the Boers', rushed towards it.[40] The police charged in, dragged the driver from his seat, and tried to lead the horses away. But Connolly – doubtless using his experience as a carter – climbed into the driver's seat, whipped up the horses, and drove through the police, amidst, as the *United Irishman* reported, 'the enthusiastic cheers of the people who immediately fell in behind the brake and formed an impromptu procession.'[41] The brake then led a spirited demonstration round Dublin. The *United Irishman* recounted:

> Viewed from the brake as it crossed the bridge the scene was magnificent. Half the length of O'Connell Street was black with people, marching slowly after the 'suppressed' members of the Transvaal Committee in the brake. Passing Trinity College the storm of hissing and hooting was terrific.[42]

The Jingo spirit

Pouring more troops into southern Africa, Britain began to make inroads against the Boers in early 1900, relieving the sieges and capturing important towns. From then on, the Boers turned to guerrilla war, and the British retaliated by burning their farmhouses and crops.

In the northeast of Ireland, loyalists and nationalists passionately aligned themselves with the opposing sides. The redoubtable Orangeman and MP William Johnston complained in the House of Commons in February 1900 about a nationalist band

> who, whenever any check to the British arms in South Africa is announced, are in the habit of parading the streets of Downpatrick chanting for the Boers and cursing the Queen...[43]

The relief of Ladysmith on 28 February was deliriously celebrated by loyalists, who paraded with bands, and attacked Catholic workers and buildings in several towns. In Belfast, the Millfield Foundry workers triumphantly waved union jacks at nationalist workers leaving Smithfield Mill, provoking a riot which spread to the Falls Road area. In the Broadway Spinning Mill a Catholic worker named Mary Maclean was attacked by some 50 of her Protestant colleagues, and when she retaliated in self-defence she was issued with a summons for assault. The magistrate dismissed the case and the next day she reported for work, but the Protestants stayed outside, refusing to work with 'Fenians'. The manager then dismissed her. The incident was reported in the *United Irishman* in a regular column, 'Northern Notes', contributed by Alice Milligan and Ethna Carbery under the name of their former paper, 'an tsean bhan bhocht'. They commented:

> The obvious intolerance of the manager's action proves that no Catholic need look for justice or peace to pursue their daily work in these establishments so long as the Jingo spirit is in the ascendancy.[44]

In Canada, a group of Fenians tried to obstruct the British effort in the Boer war by blowing up a lock on the Welland Ship Canal near Niagara. They had hoped to destroy a mile-long tier of locks, but the explosion did little damage. Three men were arrested and given life sentences, among them Luke Dillon, a former soldier in the American army, who had been involved in the London bombings of 1884 and 1885. After his release 14 years later, Dillon recalled:

> The object of the dynamiting was not so much to inflict injury to lives or property, but to create a condition by which the Canadian Government would be compelled to keep its troops at home to protect the country, rather than send them abroad to help the English fight the Boers.[45]

Children's treats

The anti-recruitment campaign in Ireland proved very effective, and in an attempt to counteract it Queen Victoria was despatched there for a three-week tour. To encourage enlistment, the Queen decreed that the shamrock – previously forbidden – must now be worn by Irishmen in the army and navy on St Patrick's Day.

There were lively impromptu demonstrations when the queen arrived in Dublin on 4 April, and two days later 'G men' – members of G Division, the intelligence-gathering section of the Dublin police force – went to the office of the *United Irishman* and seized all copies of the paper, which carried an article by Maud Gonne protesting against the 'famine queen'. The police also took stocks of the paper from newsagents, and intercepted parcels of them at railway stations throughout the country.

One of the events held to celebrate the queen's visit was a free party, or 'treat', attended by some 5,000 children in Phoenix Park. In response, Maud Gonne and other women formed a ladies' committee to organise an excursion for as many as they could reach of the 30,000 schoolchildren who had stayed away from the queen's treat. Soon the committee's weekly meeting was attracting some 60 women, and promises of donations – 1,000 oranges, 100 dozen minerals, hams, biscuits and confectionery – were pouring in from businesses and individuals. Bands of pipers offered their services, and plans were made to buy 30,000 buns and put food into paper bags for each child. On the day of the Patriotic Children's Treat, Sunday 1 July 1900, some 30,000 children marched to Clonturk Park in a procession two miles long. The *United Irishman* reported:

> Over 60 schools were represented, and the little ones carried French, Irish, Boer, and American flags, while as they marched along they sang lustily "God Save Ireland," "The Memory of the Dead," "The Green Flag," "O'Donnell Abu," and various amusing and significant parodies on well-known songs *apropos* of the war in South Africa...[46]

The children spent the afternoon playing games and running races, and then returned home singing national songs and, according to the *United Irishman*, cheering vociferously for President Kruger, Major MacBride and Miss Maud Gonne.

Many members of the Ladies' Committee were relatives of members of the Celtic Literary Society, which excluded women. They were delighted to find a role through organising the children's treat, and decided to form a permanent organisation. This they named Inghinidhe na hÉireann – Daughters of Ireland. The Inghinidhe (pronounced 'inyeenee') attracted mainly young working women who had been attending Irish classes. They started evening classes to teach children the Irish language, Irish history and singing, and planned a Christmas entertainment for them. The Inghinidhe were also deeply involved in the Irish Literary Theatre, and several Inghinidhe members became famous actresses.

The Conservatives took advantage of British successes against the Boers to call a general election in October 1900. The 'khaki election', as it was known, swept the Tories back to power with 402 seats, an increase of four, giving them a huge majority of 134. On the other side, the Liberals, deeply split over the war, won 186 seats, while the Irish Nationalists held their previous 82 seats.

In December 1900 Lord Kitchener, a callous imperialist veteran, assumed overall command against the Boers. In 1898 he had overseen the massacre of 11,000 Sudanese nationalists at Omdurman, together with the desecration of their leader the Mahdi's tomb and the removal of his skull and fingernails by British officers for souvenirs. As the year ended, Wilfrid Blunt wrote in his diary:

> The old century is very nearly out, and leaves the world in a pretty pass, and the British Empire is playing the devil in it as never an empire before on so large a scale. We may live to see its fall. All the nations of Europe are making the same hell upon earth in China, massacring and pillaging and raping in the captured cities as outrageously as in the Middle Ages. The Emperor of Germany gives the word for slaughter and the Pope looks on and approves. In South Africa our troops are burning farms under Kitchener's command, and the Queen and the two Houses of Parliament, and the bench of bishops thank God publicly and vote money for the work. The Americans are spending fifty millions a year on slaughtering the Filipinos; the King of the Belgians has invested his whole fortune on the Congo, where he is brutalizing the negroes to fill his pockets... The whole white race is revelling openly in violence, as though it had never pretended to be Christian. God's equal curse be on them all![47]

In March 1901 Kitchener devised a systematic plan for dealing with the Boers: his troops would sweep the country in 'drives' organised like a sporting shoot, destroying the guerrillas' sustenance by burning farms, killing animals, and 'concentrating' women and children in fortified camps with minimal facilities, which became known as 'concentration camps'. Then Kitchener added a new ploy: his forces would divide up the countryside with a grid of barbed wire and blockhouses – concrete forts –

to create a net into which they would drive the enemy.

Altogether the war was to last two-and-a-half years, costing over £200 million and a huge number of lives. Of the 400,000 soldiers on Britain's side, who came from all over the empire, 22,000 died. Some 7,000 Boer fighters were killed, while between 18,000 and 28,000 Boer civilians, the majority of them children, died in the disease-ridden concentration camps. Such gruesome realities eroded the glamour of imperialism, even in Britain.

The people who lost the most were the native Africans. Some 107,000 Africans – Boers' farm servants and their families – were imprisoned in separate concentration camps, of whom 12,000 or more died. Some 50,000 Africans worked for the British in the mistaken belief that Britain would liberate them from the Boers, and an uncounted number of them perished. Far from liberating the Africans, the victorious British enforced the passbook system, while the mine-owners drastically lowered African wages. The British helped Boer farmers to re-establish control of farms which Africans had taken over, and allowed many Boers to keep their guns while disarming the Africans. Then when Britain handed back power to the Boers in the Transvaal and Orange Free State, it allowed them to retain whites-only franchises; and when the Union of South Africa was created in 1910, its constitution, approved by the British parliament, stipulated that only whites could be elected to the Union parliament.

The British authorities responded to the pro-Boer protests in Ireland with coercion, and in 1901 and 1902 more than 40 prominent people, including 11 MPs and the woman owner of the *Waterford Star*, were imprisoned for political offences.

In other respects, however, Britain was pursuing a conciliatory policy known as 'killing home rule with kindness'. In 1898 a bill was passed democratising local government. Previously county affairs had been managed by non-elected bodies known as 'grand juries', which were made up of landlords and were notoriously corrupt. These were now replaced by elected councils and for the first time the voters included women, albeit subject to a property qualification. The landlords' power was removed, and in the towns labour candidates won significant victories; but appointments to local government posts were still made by patronage rather than through competition, so corruption flourished as before.

Then in 1903 a land act was passed, known as the Wyndham Act, after the Tory chief secretary for Ireland, George Wyndham, who introduced it. Wyndham was a cousin of Wilfrid Blunt, the veteran anti-imperialist and poet, who acted as a go-between for him with John Redmond, leader of the Irish MPs. The Wyndham Act's provisions were largely inspired by suggestions made by landlords. Its main innovation was to give a cash incentive to landlords to sell their entire estates, by offering them a 12 per cent bonus on top of the agreed price. It also provided for tenants to be lent the full price of the land at three-and-a-half per cent interest repayable over 68-and-a-half years.

Taken together, the reform of local government and the Wyndham Act hastened the process of undermining the political and economic power of the old Protestant ascendancy, and strengthening local businessmen and small farmers, most of whom were anti-British in both political and economic matters. As the landlords' holdings declined, the main groups with a continuing economic interest in the union with Britain were the farmers with big cattle ranches in Munster and the large capitalists who, save for a few in Dublin and Cork, were mainly based in the northeast.

At the same time, the British establishment's economic interest in Ireland weakened. Once a rich source of revenue through rents and taxes, Ireland became a drain on the exchequer, as 'killing home rule with kindness' brought lower rents and increased public spending. The security of the empire was now the chief motive for maintaining the union.

Britain's stranglehold on Irish political life continued, administered through Dublin Castle and deeply resented by all classes save the ascendancy and Protestants in the northeast. A contemporary historian, the Rev. E.A. D'Alton, wrote:

> Not in Europe is there a system of Government like that controlled and directed by Dublin Castle. A number of unrepresentative Boards, usually inefficient, and manned by chiefs who care nothing for Ireland – this is Irish administration. The Chief Secretary controls everything – police, magistrates, law officers, prisons, lunatics, land, education, local government. He is head of all these Boards... Usually the Chief Secretary is an Englishman and knows nothing of Ireland. The Under-Secretary, who does, is a permanent official, and has enormous power.[48]

John Redmond

Nationalist Ireland entered the new century in a ferment of activity, with separatists setting the pace. Politicians and would-be politicians organised themselves, the language and literary movements flourished, the secret revolutionary movement revived, militant trade unionism came to Belfast, and women's suffragists began vigorously to press their demands.

In 1900, the Irish parliamentary party reunited, coming together with the Parnellite John Redmond as leader. The party had to reunite in order to survive: two years earlier, William O'Brien had formed an energetic peasant-based organisation, the United Irish League, in the west, which was threatening to displace the parliamentary party. Further, as Arthur Griffith's *United Irishman* scornfully recounted:

> The effect of the war in South Africa on the spirit of the Irish people has
> filled them with uneasiness. Day by day parliamentarism is becoming
> more discredited by the people whom it befooled for over twenty years...
> As the *Evening Herald*, Mr. Redmond's mouthpiece, explains, 'unity'
> was necessary because 'Funds have only empty boxes, American support
> had become estranged, and at home subscriptions for any purpose died a
> sudden death. *This state of affairs*,' adds our ingenuous contemporary,
> 'could not continue.'[49]

The reunited party absorbed the United Irish League, which became its
new constituency organisation. The party's leader, John Redmond, came
from the tiny Catholic upper class. His family were landowners and his
father was an MP, and Redmond graduated from the overwhelmingly
unionist Trinity College before training as a barrister. Then, through his
father, he obtained a post as a clerk in the House of Commons, before
himself becoming an MP in 1881. Redmond's nationalism was in the
conservative mould. He opposed Irish independence and advocated home
rule within an imperial federation. Redmond was also distinctly half-
hearted about social reform; he argued against workers forming independent
political organisations, and supported the control of education by the
Catholic church.

In the northeast, the leading constitutional nationalist was Joseph Devlin:
a barman in his youth, Devlin became MP for North Kilkenny in 1902,
then won the West Belfast seat in 1906, and remained an MP almost
continuously till his death in 1934. Devlin's political machine was the
Ancient Order of Hibernians, an exclusively Catholic organisation which
acted as a counterpart to the Orange Order, attempting to secure Catholic
interests in the face of Protestant political and economic dominance. Most
of Devlin's electors were working class, as he was himself, so he took up
their calls for improved living and working conditions, and appealed for
votes with the claim that, 'I hold the cause of Ireland and the cause of
Labour to be identical.'[50] At the same time Devlin needed the support of
the Catholic hierarchy and the small Catholic middle class. His newspaper,
the *Northern Star*, was anti-socialist, claiming that 'Catholics cannot be
socialists,' and was highly sectarian, for example describing Protestantism
as 'the religion of the muck-rake'. The paper also shared the small
businessman's dream of 'seeing the banking account... grow day by day
until it reaches colossal proportions'.[51]

Many nationalists, among them Alice Milligan, James Connolly, and
Padraic Pearse, deplored the growth of Catholic sectarianism, since the
identification of Catholicism and nationalism excluded Protestants from
the national movement, exacerbated the divisions in the working class,
and fostered bigotry and intolerance. Further, as the Ancient Order of
Hibernians spread into the south of Ireland, it employed unsavoury methods,

including bribery and intimidation, to advance the cause of the Irish parliamentary party.

Sinn Féin

The separatists, too, were gradually getting organised. In 1900 Arthur Griffith and other anti-Boer war activists and Fenians formed Cumann na nGaedheal. Among the founders were Maud Gonne, Boer war hero John MacBride, the veteran Fenian John O'Leary, and the former prisoners John Daly – now mayor of Limerick – and Tom Clarke, who was living in New York. Their plan was, as Gonne recalled, 'to link up all existing National societies into an open Separatist movement.'[52]

Their aim at the outset was to promote Irish economic resources, industry and culture. These concerns embraced those of the Celtic revivalists and also Griffith's interest in economic matters. Like many nationalists before him, he believed that Irish independence must be economic as well as political, and that Irish industry should be protected from British competition to allow it to grow. This could only be achieved by separate taxation systems, under which Ireland could tax British goods coming into the country, in order to prevent them undercutting Irish goods. Such 'tariff barriers' were the ambition of many in the Irish middle class, but were opposed by the big capitalists whose business depended on trade with Britain.

Soon Griffith began spelling out a directly political policy. In 1902 he called for the Irish parliamentary party to refuse to attend the British parliament and instead to 'remain at home to help in promoting Ireland's interests and to aid in guarding its national rights.'[53] Such calls had been made before by Irish leaders, but Griffith did not refer to them: instead, he pointed to the practical experience of Hungary. In the 1860s Hungarian deputies had abstained *en masse* from the imperial Austrian parliament at Vienna, and as a result had won the re-establishment of a separate Hungarian parliament. Austria and Hungary then became two separate entities linked by the emperor. Although himself a separatist, Griffith adopted this 'dual monarchy' arrangement as a possible model for the relationship between England and Ireland, because he believed it would win widespread support in Ireland.

In 1905 Griffith established a new body, later named Sinn Féin, to promote his ideas. Sinn Féin, meaning 'ourselves', implied self-respect and self-reliance: the name was suggested by a Gaelic League activist and cousin of Edward Carson, Máire de Buitléir. Griffith also established a new paper, likewise named *Sinn Féin*, which replaced the *United Irishman*. Various separatist organisations, including Cumann na nGaedheal and Inghinidhe na hÉireann, came together under the Sinn Féin banner. The

Sinn Féin policy, Griffith's brainchild, was attractively straightforward: the Irish MPs should withdraw from Westminster and, together with elected local councillors, should form a Council of 300 which would be a *de facto* Irish parliament. Its policies would be carried out by local councils. The Council of 300 would set up Sinn Féin courts, and an Irish civil service, stock exchange and bank, and would appoint consuls to represent Irish interests abroad.

In essence, Griffith envisaged an independent capitalist country. The socialist James Connolly had a different vision: he praised Sinn Féin's concept of self-reliance but criticised its economic outlook. He repeated one critic's judgement that 'the Hungary system was only fit for hungry men',[54] and wrote:

> Sinn Fein has two sides at least – its economic teaching and its philosophy of self-reliance. With its economic teaching... Socialists have no sympathy, as it appeals only to those who measure a nation's prosperity by the volume of wealth produced in a country, instead of by the distribution of that wealth amongst the inhabitants... But with that part of Sinn Fein which teaches that Ireland must rely upon herself, respect her own traditions, know her own history, preserve her own language and literature without prejudice to or denial of the worth in the language or literature of other people, stand erect in her own worth, and claim to be appraised for her own intrinsic value and not as part of the wheels and cogs of the Imperial system of another people – with that side of Sinn Fein Socialists may sympathise...[55]

Connolly also pointed out that Irish socialists responded to nationalism in different ways. Some saw no benefits in it for the poor, but others, like Connolly himself, saw an Irish socialist republic as their goal.

Cathleen ni Houlihan

Meanwhile the cultural movement continued to flourish, reaching even into Dublin Castle, heart of the British administration, where Lord and Lady Aberdeen, viceroy and vicereine from 1906-15 and supporters of home rule, sponsored Irish cottage industries such as lace-making and weaving, and featured Irish music and dancing at their parties. Mary Colum, who was a student in Dublin in the first decade of the century, described the atmosphere:

> there were movements for the restoration of the Irish language, for reviving native arts and crafts; for preserving ancient ruins, for resurrecting native costume, an array of political movements; there, too, were the theatres and the tearooms and pubs which corresponded to the café life of the Continental city. In the centre, too, were the headquarters of the clubs and societies... Between Abbey Street and College Green, a five minutes' walk, one could meet every person of importance in the life of the city at a certain time of the afternoon.[56]

Artists and craftspeople, influenced by the arts and crafts movement in England, brought neo-Celtic themes to a wide range of skills, from stained glass to weaving and printing. In 1902 Lilly and Elizabeth Yeats – the poet's sisters – set up a craft workshop, the Dun Emer Guild, with a carpet designer named Evelyn Gleeson. Lilly had worked as an assistant embroiderer with May Morris, William Morris's daughter, and Evelyn Gleeson had studied under Morris's followers. Elizabeth Yeats, an art teacher, set up the group's printing press. In 1903 Sarah Purser, a successful portrait painter, and Edward Martyn, a Catholic landowner, set up An Túr Gloine, 'the tower of glass', a stained-glass workshop. Both the Dun Emer Guild and An Túr Gloine, though run mainly by people from Protestant backgrounds, were to create many beautiful objects – stained glass, vestments, mosaics, and stone-carvings – for Catholic buildings, most notably Loughrea Cathedral and the Honan Chapel in Cork.

Most dynamic – and sometimes turbulent – was the theatre movement, its productions developing from 'tableaux' to full-scale plays. In 1899 Augusta, Lady Gregory, a poetry-lover and later a prolific playwright, widow of a landowner who had been governor of Ceylon, launched the Irish Literary Theatre, together with Edward Martyn and the poet W.B. Yeats. Their manifesto stated:

> We will show that Ireland is not the home of buffoonery and easy sentiment, as it has been represented, but the home of an ancient idealism. We are confident of the support of all Irish people, who are weary of misrepresentation.[57]

Their productions included Yeats' play *The Countess Cathleen* in 1899, and Alice Milligan's *The Last Feast of the Fianna* in 1900.

Further impetus came from two theatre enthusiasts, the brothers Frank and Willie Fay. In 1902 they staged Yeats' *Cathleen ni Houlihan*, a short play set in 1798. Maud Gonne played Cathleen: the old woman, representing Ireland, who visits a family as one of the sons is about to be married, and leads him away to fight for Ireland. As the old woman leaves, she is transformed into a young girl with 'the walk of a queen'. Yeats wrote afterwards that Maud Gonne 'played very finely, and her great height made Cathleen seem a divine being fallen into our mortal infirmity.'[58] Fay's company merged with the Irish Literary Theatre to form the Irish National Theatre Society, and in 1904 they acquired the Abbey Theatre: the building was bought and equipped for them by an English benefactor, Annie Horniman.

The Abbey's most famous – and, at the time, controversial – playwright was John Millington Synge. Born in 1891 into a Protestant professional family, Synge studied to become a classical musician in Ireland and Germany before turning to writing. He went to Paris – a Mecca for artists and intellectuals – where his studies ranged from socialism to old Irish literature. Here he met Yeats and Maud Gonne. On Yeats' advice, Synge visited the Aran Islands, off the west coast of Ireland: the islands provided the inspiration for his plays, passionate and eloquent dramas ostensibly based on peasant life.

Like Yeats, Synge idealised the peasantry, but while the Celtic revivalists depicted the peasants as fey and romantic, Synge showed them as wild and violent – characteristics he admired as embodying energy – and brought the sensuality of the old Gaelic poets to his love scenes. He also showed some of the unpleasant aspects of rural life, such as loveless marriages, unfaithful wives, brutality and boredom. This mix was too much for many nationalists: it seemed to them as if a playwright from an ascendancy background was reproducing the familiar derogatory English stereotypes. *The Shadow of the Glen*, about a peasant woman who ends up leaving her miserable and much older husband for a tramp, provoked a fierce debate in 1903 about what a truly national theatre should be. Yeats put the case for artistic freedom:

> A community that is opinion-ridden, even when those opinions are in themselves noble, is likely to put its creative minds into some sort of a prison.

He recalled that the idea for *Cathleen ni Houlihan* had come to him in a dream, and continued:

> But if some external necessity had forced me to write nothing but drama, with an obviously patriotic intention, instead of letting my work shape itself under the causal impulses of dreams and daily thoughts, I would have lost, in a short time, the power to write movingly upon any theme. I could have roused opinion; but I could not have touched the heart...[59]

The political activists took a sterner view. Griffith baulked at Synge's portrayal of an unfaithful wife, insisting:

> Irishwomen are the most virtuous women in the world. A play which leads those who witness it to form a contrary conclusion can only be a lie and nothing more.[60]

James Connolly thought that until Ireland was self-governing, the task of a national theatre was to restore national pride, and that in return for artistic freedom, dramatists should exercise responsibility.[61]

Maud Gonne's view was that Irish writers should write for 'the poor and the workers':

> if the Irish people do not understand or care for an Irish play, I should feel very doubtful of its right to rank as national literature, though all the critics in England were loud in its praise and though I myself might see beauty in it.[62]

Synge's *Playboy of the Western World*, staged in 1907, produced an even bigger furore. Many Dubliners were deeply offended. The *Irish Times* reviewer, while praising Synge for revealing 'truly terrible truths', observed: 'It is as if we looked in a mirror for the first time, and found ourselves hideous.'[63] People in the audience disrupted the performances with groans, cheers, whistles, and blasts from a penny trumpet, and there were riots in the surrounding streets.

St Enda's

The language revival influenced education. Colleges were set up to train teachers of Irish, and the language was taught in many Catholic schools. Gaelic League activists wanted to set up an 'Irish-Ireland' school with lay teachers, and in 1908 Padraic Pearse founded St Enda's, a school for boys in Dublin. Later he founded a girls' school, St Ita's, as he believed that women should have full educational opportunities. The socialist republican Desmond Ryan, who worked for a while as Pearse's secretary at St Enda's, recalled their first meeting:

> Outwardly he was shy, unassuming and very reserved... He strode forward, smiling his shy smile and talking in Irish. His voice was clear and persuasive. He always talked to his pupils in Irish, lapsing into the barest minimum of English until by twelve months his vocabulary had become the property of his young charges, and he laughed to himself as they flourished his own phrases and idioms as theirs.[64]

Pearse combined his Irish perspective with advanced educational theories, advocating 'direct method' language teaching, attention to science, and student involvement in shaping the curriculum. In a famous polemic titled *The Murder Machine*, Pearse flayed the existing education system:

> One of the most terrible things about the English education system in Ireland is its ruthlessness... It is cold and mechanical, like the ruthlessness of an immensely powerful engine. A machine vast, complicated... It grinds night and day; it obeys immutable and predetermined laws; it is as devoid of understanding, of sympathy, of imagination, as is any other piece of machinery that performs an appointed task. Into it is fed all the raw human material in Ireland; it seizes upon it inexorably and rends and compresses and remoulds...

Pearse offered a very different vision:

> In particular I would urge that the Irish school system of the future should give freedom – freedom to the individual school, freedom to the individual teacher, freedom as far as may be to the individual pupil... Our school system must bring, too, some gallant inspiration. And with the inspiration it must bring a certain hardening... I would boldly preach the antique faith that fighting is the only noble thing, and that he only is at peace with God who is at war with the powers of evil.[65]

Roger Casement

The language movement continued to draw in many activists who, like Pearse, would later take up directly revolutionary activity. One such was Roger Casement, an Ulsterman then working for the British Foreign Service as a consul. Casement's father was a Protestant with Fenian sympathies, and his mother was a Catholic. Both parents died when he was a child, and he was brought up by relatives in Ulster. In 1884, aged 20, he went out to West Africa and worked in various jobs. He felt a strong sympathy for the African people: in 1893, for instance, he wrote an angry poem after mercenary troops, working for Cecil Rhodes with the blessing of the British government, massacred Matabele fighters in east Africa who were resisting the takeover of their land:

> Prate not of England's valour in the field
> Her heart is sick with lust.
> The gold she wins is red with blood, nor can it shield
> Her name from tainted league with men of broken trust.[66]

In 1895 Casement was made a British consul in Portuguese East Africa. Three years later he was transferred to Portuguese West Africa, which bordered on the Congo Free State: this was in effect the private fiefdom of King Leopold of the Belgians, who was extracting vast sums of money from it through the exploitation of rubber. As Casement soon discovered, Leopold was running a grotesque – and highly profitable – system of forced labour. The native people were forced to collect rubber unpaid and at gunpoint, and were gruesomely punished if they refused. A missionary's report revealed:

> Each town and district is forced to bring in a certain quantity to the headquarters of the Commissaire every Sunday. It is collected by force; the soldiers drive the people into the bush. If they will not go, they are shot down, and their left hands cut off and taken as trophies to the Commissaire... these hands, the hands of men, women and children are placed in rows before the Commissaire who counts them to see that the soldiers have not wasted cartridges. The Commissaire is paid a commission of about 1d. a lb. on all the rubber he gets.[67]

In Britain, campaigners began trying to goad the government into action, but the Foreign Office preferred to appease Leopold, wanting to keep him as an ally amid European political rivalries. Finally in 1903 the foreign secretary allowed Casement to make an investigative tour of the Upper Congo. He found a huge decrease in population: one village of 5,000 had been reduced to 352, its people killed off by forced labour, cruel punishments and lack of food. He saw boys whose hands had been chopped off, and wrote in his diary of the 'terrible oppression of these poor people.'[68] The Foreign Office altered Casement's report without his consent, reducing its impact. Frustrated, he helped campaigners to set up the Congo Reform Association.

After his return from the Congo in late 1903, Casement spent much of the next 18 months in Ireland. He became enthusiastically involved in the language movement, joining the Gaelic League, donating money to various causes, and travelling to the west to learn Irish from native speakers. Casement saw parallels between Leopold's terrible 'Congo system' and Ireland's experience. In both, the people's problem had started with the expropriation of their land, and then its produce, by the colonisers. He often said that his knowledge of Irish history had helped him to understand what was happening in the Congo. He wrote to his friend, the historian Alice Stopford Green:

> I knew that the Foreign Office would not understand the thing, for I realised that I was looking at this tragedy with the eyes of another race of people once hunted themselves, whose hearts were based on affection as the root principle of contact with their fellow men, and whose estimate of life was not of something eternally to be appraised at its market 'price'.[69]

Living in northeast Ulster, Casement worked with activists such as Alice Milligan and Bulmer Hobson, a member of the IRB. He became a keen supporter of Sinn Féin, and contributed money and articles – unsigned, because he was still employed by the British government – to its paper. Casement later wrote that his months in Ireland 'moulded all my subsequent actions'.[70] He continued to take an interest after he was posted to South America in 1906.

In 1910, he was sent to the Putumayo region of the Upper Amazon on an investigation that proved horribly similar to his Congo experience. The Indians were being forced to collect rubber, and were tortured and murdered if they failed to do so. The rubber venture was being financed by a London-based company. The Foreign Office once again prevaricated, reluctant to press the humanitarian issue when wider diplomatic interests were at stake. Casement, by now honoured with a knighthood but thoroughly disillusioned, retired in 1913 to devote what were to be his three remaining years to the cause of Irish independence.

Constance Markievicz

Another person who was to desert her class for the revolution was Constance Markievicz, who arrived in Dublin in 1903. Markievicz had been born in 1868 into an ascendancy family, the Gore-Booths, who owned land in Sligo. Her first venture into politics had been to form, with her two sisters, the Sligo branch of the Irish Women's Suffrage and Local Government Association in 1896. They held a crowded and noisy public meeting that December, and Constance, presiding, told the audience:

> Now in order to attain to any Political Reform, you all know that the first
> step is to form societies to agitate and force the government to realize
> that a very large class have a grievance, and will never stop making
> themselves disagreeable till it is righted... silence is an evil that might
> easily be remedied, and the sooner we begin to make a row the better.[71]

The feminist impetus came in part from her sister Eva, who had recently
met the English suffragist Esther Roper, who had immediately inspired
her. Soon Eva moved to Manchester to join Roper, where both devoted
their lives to the cause of working-class women. Many years later Constance
referred to her espousal of equality for women as her 'first bite... at the
apple of freedom', from which she got on to 'freedom to the nation,
freedom to the workers.'[72] These three freedoms were to be the guiding
stars of her life.

In 1897, with the reluctant support of her parents, Constance went to
Paris to study art. Here she met her future husband, Casimir Dunin-
Markiewicz. (Unlike Constance, he spelt his name with a 'w'.) Casimir,
likewise an art student, was an impoverished and gregarious Polish count,
recently widowed. In 1903 they settled in Dublin and immediately became
involved in theatrical and artistic activities, mixing both in 'Castle' society
and with people such as Yeats and AE – the pen-name of George Russell,
the writer, mystic and advocate of agricultural co-operatives.

Constance became increasingly interested in nationalist politics, but her
ascendancy background was at first a barrier: when she expressed her
interest to Arthur Griffith, he was, she wrote later, 'very discouraging to
me'. She realised afterwards that he thought she was 'an agent of the
enemy'.[73] Constance nonetheless began attending Sinn Féin meetings,
and soon Helena Molony recruited her to the women's organisation,
Inghinidhe na hÉireann. She immediately became involved in preparing
its new journal, *Bean na hÉireann*, 'The Woman of Ireland', which
started in November 1908. The paper's launch coincided with the rise of
the suffragette movement, and its message combined feminism and
nationalism. Constance designed its masthead and, as an expert gardener,
contributed a column titled 'The Woman with the Garden', in which she
occasionally took the opportunity to make a political point:

> It is very unpleasant work killing slugs and snails, but let us not be
> daunted. A good Nationalist should look upon slugs in a garden much in
> the same way as she looks on the English in Ireland, and only regret that
> she cannot crush the Nation's enemies with the same ease that she can
> the garden's, with just one tread of her fairy foot.[74]

In England, the Boer war hero Robert Baden-Powell had started a boy
scout movement. This spread to Dublin, where 800 boys paraded before
the viceroy. Constance responded by starting up an Irish scout troop, the

Red Branch Knights. Helped by Helena Molony and others, she taught them signalling, drill and tracking on her front lawn.

Next, aided by a keen IRB member, Bulmer Hobson, who had earlier formed a youth organisation in Belfast, Markievicz transformed the Red Branch Knights into a full-scale scout organisation. They were renamed Na Fianna Éireann, after the young warriors of ancient Ireland, the name Hobson had used for his Belfast group. On joining, the boys declared: 'I promise to work for the Independence of Ireland, never to join England's armed forces, and to obey my superior officers.'[75] An excellent shot, Constance passed on her skills to the boys. Roger Casement sent a donation towards buying kilts for them. Soon the Fianna, with Constance at their head, became a nationwide organisation, and trained many future revolutionaries.

The IRB revives

Meanwhile the dormant underground movement, the Irish Republican Brotherhood, was gaining a fresh lease of life. This was spurred by young militant members in Belfast, among them Bulmer Hobson, who was a clerk, Denis McCullough, a piano-tuner, and Seán Mac Diarmada, a tram conductor. Hobson had been drawn into politics as a schoolboy through the 1798 centenary events; he had been an enthusiastic reader of the *Shan Van Vocht* and knew Ethna Carbery. He was from a Quaker background, and was keen on bringing together Orange and Green against English rule.

The young men were impatient with the older, more cautious IRB leaders. They persuaded older men and habitual drinkers to retire from the Ulster IRB. In 1905 they set up patriotic societies named the Dungannon Clubs, after the 1782 Volunteer convention in Tyrone. The young activists were harassed by the police and found it difficult to hold down jobs. A fellow IRB member, Patrick McCartan, described how Denis McCullough was going round the country tuning pianos, 'and the police call when he leaves a family or private house and make all sorts of enquiries about him in order to frighten the people out of employing him again.'[76]

In 1907 the veteran Fenian Tom Clarke returned to Dublin and aligned himself with the young men against the old guard. After his release from Portland prison in 1898, Clarke had gone to New York where he worked closely with John Devoy in Clan-na-Gael: with Clarke's return to Dublin, the Clan doubled its funding to the IRB. In New York, Clarke married another staunch republican, Kathleen Daly, niece of John Daly who had also been imprisoned in Portland. Back in Dublin, Clarke ran a small newsagent and tobacconist's shop near the centre of the city, which became a magnet for political activists. Constance Markievicz remembered:

> The thing that struck you first about him were his eyes they were so
> bright and so alert... afterwards you noticed the colour and found out
> how kindly they were... Interest in your schemes, encouragement for
> your hopes, support in your hours of despair was what you got from
> him.[77]

Clarke proved a powerful ally for the young progressives. One of them,
P.S. O'Hegarty, recalled:

> I can still remember the thrill of pleased surprise with which I saw him,
> after I first met him, stand for every proposal which the other men of his
> generation frowned at and would down.[78]

They founded a militant new paper, *Irish Freedom*, and at the end of
1911 they finally succeeded in wresting control of the organisation from
the old guard. The reinvigorated IRB began setting up hidden networks
within the open nationalist organisations, recruiting members of Sinn
Féin, the Fianna and the Gaelic League. This process signalled a shift
from cultural resistance towards revolution, but at the same time it pushed
many committed nationalists to the sidelines, excluding them from policy-
making, which was done in IRB caucuses.

Women were automatically excluded from the IRB, despite the fact that
IRB members were happy to work with them and encourage them. After
the IRB established a 'circle' in the Fianna, Constance Markievicz found
that though she was president she could not contribute to important
policy-making: this in practice was done by the IRB circle, which met
before every ard fheis (convention) to agree its line. At the ard fheis, other
views were outvoted or overruled. Markievicz disapproved of these secret
machinations, but had no choice but to accept the position.

Industrial turbulence

Growing alongside the nationalist movement, and intertwining with it,
were the two other great social movements of the first decades of the
century: the struggle of unskilled workers for trade union rights and better
wages, and the fight to win votes for women.

The new wave of industrial turbulence was part of an international
trend. Strikes and demonstrations swept across Europe – including Russia,
which was shaken by an abortive revolution in 1905 – and also hit the
USA and Australia.

In the industrialised imperialist countries, huge wealth confronted bitter
urban poverty; unskilled workers sought redress through militant trade
union action and in revolutionary theories such as Marxism and a new
variant, syndicalism. Typified by the USA's Industrial Workers of the
World, syndicalists held that if all workers were organised in one big
union they could bring capitalism to a standstill and usher in a brave new

world. There was also a drive to build political parties that would provide an independent voice for socialists and trade unionists. Up until then in Britain and Ireland the craft unions which dominated the labour movement had been content to use the Liberals or the Irish parliamentary party to make their needs felt.

In countries with flexible political systems, such as Britain and France, labour parties could win elections and exert some influence. Once in power, however, socialist politicians tended to swim with the establishment tide, disappointing their followers. At the opposite extreme was Russia, where the Tsarist autocracy made open political opposition impossible. There, socialists were driven into forming a clandestine party and working for the violent overthrow of the state. A feudal, economically backward country with a weak capitalist class, Russia was to prove especially vulnerable to revolutionary pressures.

In Ireland, the new phase of the 'new unionism' was personified by James Larkin, a big man with a powerful presence, an electrifying orator and dynamic strike leader. Born in Liverpool in 1874 to Irish parents, Larkin grew up in poverty and had little formal education, leaving school early when his father died of tuberculosis.

The young Larkin did a variety of jobs, then stowed away on a steamer to Montevideo and spent a year in South America before getting steady work as a foreman dock-porter in Liverpool. In the meantime he became a socialist, joining the Independent Labour Party: the ILP was formed in the 1890s by working-class leaders, formerly Liberal supporters, wishing to establish a separate party. He retained the Catholic faith of his family. He gave his scarce spare time to his family, to his socialist activities, and to helping the Liverpool poor, whose desperate condition deeply moved and angered him.

Larkin joined the National Union of Dock Labourers and, after losing his job during a dispute, became a full-time union organiser. In 1907 he went to Belfast as the first step in the union's plan to reorganise the Irish ports, where the branches built up in the previous decade had become moribund. His tempestuous association with Ireland had begun.

Belfast was a very wealthy city, boasting at least three millionaires, a grandiose new city hall, and flourishing garden suburbs. But the prosperity of the few was being won at the expense of the many: the unskilled workers who toiled in the mills, docks and shipyards, and those who transported goods to and from the docks in horse-drawn carts. For while skilled workers – overwhelmingly Protestant – were paid as much as their counterparts in Britain, unskilled workers were paid very much less: the effect of the endless supply of cheap labour from the Irish countryside.

Acute poverty and ill-health were rife. An official report in 1907 noted cases where infants, even those with working mothers, 'were constantly fed on bread soaked in tea', because the women could not afford to buy milk.[79] People earned scarcely enough to keep themselves, let alone their parents, so that many old people had to resort to the workhouse. In the shipyards, accidents were common, while in the mills consumption continued to mow down the workers, particularly young women.

The Belfast workforce was as divided on sectarian lines as ever, both in political aspirations and in their access to jobs. In the docks, for example, the regular jobs on the cross-channel quays were held by Protestants, who were paid 20 to 25 shillings a week for 67 or more hours, enough for bare survival. But the irregular jobs on the deep-sea quays were mainly taken by Catholics, who were hired by the day and often earned less than ten shillings a week: survival was only possible if their wives and children could find work in the mills.

The trade union movement was controlled by cautious Protestant-dominated craft unions, and trades council demonstrations sported loyalist bands and flags. But despite sectarian divisions, the times were favourable to union mobilisation. The home rule issue was on the back-burner, as the Liberals had won power with a huge majority in 1906 and had no need to curry favour with the Irish parliamentary party. Further, discontent among working class Protestants had split the Orange monolith.

Whereas the Irish nationalist party, and its Belfast MP Joe Devlin, went out of their way to woo working class voters with a labour programme, the Tory Party was unable to do this, and Protestant workers became disaffected. Many northern Protestants agreed with the Irish Party's stance on labour issues – but rejected their desire for home rule. So Protestant trade unionists pushed for a Labour Party attached to its British counterpart. The best-known exponent of this viewpoint was William Walker, a former shipyard worker and leading trade union official who described himself as a 'Unionist in politics'. Contesting West Belfast for Labour in 1905, Walker came under pressure from the Belfast Protestant Association, a militantly sectarian grassroots body, who questioned him on a series of issues.

Walker replied by saying he would oppose any Catholic succeeding to the throne, he would oppose home rule, and he would obtain a redistribution of Irish seats so that Protestants would have more MPs. 'Protestantism means protesting against superstition, hence true Protestantism is synonymous with labour,' Walker declared.[80] He nevertheless lost the election, and his sectarian stance prompted considerable criticism from Labour supporters in Britain, who tended to support home rule.

Members of the Belfast Protestant Association were themselves unhappy with the upper class leaders of Orangeism, but their discontent tended to manifest itself in complaints that the ascendancy was not Protestant enough.

In 1902 the leader of the Belfast Protestant Association, Tom Sloan, a shipyard worker and militant anti-Catholic, stood successfully for election in South Belfast against the Tory, a County Down landowner. As a result, Sloan was expelled from the Orange Order. Sloan and others then defiantly formed the Independent Orange Order, which took the part of Protestant workers against their bosses, but also asserted Protestant supremacy over Catholics. The new body softened its attitude to Catholics for a while under the influence of Lindsay Crawford, an Antrim-born journalist who had become friendly with nationalists while working in Dublin. In 1905 Crawford became grand master of the Independent Orange Order, and produced a remarkable document, the *Magheramorne Manifesto*. This urged Protestants 'to hold out the right hand of fellowship' to Catholics, and pointed out:

> No people suffered more at the hands of landlords than the Protestant tenant farmers, and none have done more to rivet the chain around their own necks by the return to Parliament of landlord representatives.[81]

Crawford told a cheering audience in Banbridge that, as the *Irish News* reported,

> The Independent Orange Institution was a revolt against landlord and clerical ascendancy and against the Orangeism that had been so long the willing and pliant tool of both... Hatred of their Roman Catholic countrymen was not the creed of Orangeism. They were taught as Orangemen, to regard their Roman Catholic neighbours as their brethren.[82]

The Belfast dock strike

Workers' militancy was already on the upswing by the time Larkin arrived in January 1907. The previous year, spinners in several mills had gone on strike and won a wage increase. Within three months of Larkin's arrival, most of the 3,000 dockers and all of the 1,500 carters had joined his union. Strikes began to break out among other unskilled workers, including workers at the Sirocco Engineering Works. The shipping companies began to prepare for a showdown, and alerted the owners' organisation, the Shipping Federation: this had been formed in 1891 to counter the first phase of 'new unionism', and had supplied strike-breakers to companies throughout Europe.

Initially, most employers recognised the Dockers' Union, but Thomas Gallaher, chairman of the Belfast Steamship Company, stood firm. 'Larkinism' was a serious threat to Gallaher, who was a major employer of unskilled labour: he had thousands of low-paid employees at his tobacco factory, the largest in Belfast. When union members at the Belfast

Steamship Company walked out on 6 May in a dispute over union recognition, Gallaher responded by locking them out and importing strike-breakers. More men then walked out, and tension began to rise. Strikers attacked strike-breakers, and Larkin denounced Gallaher as 'an obscene scoundrel', saying that 'although St. Patrick was credited with banishing the snakes, there was one he forgot, and that was Gallaher'.[83] Thousands attended mass meetings, including 1,000 women from Gallaher's tobacco factory who had been provoked into a walk-out. In mid-May troops were brought in. The militant mood spread to coal-heavers, sailors, firemen and iron-moulders. Thousands were laid off and roamed the streets.

Towards the end of June, the union called for a pay rise for dockers on the cross-channel quays. But the big British railway companies who owned most of the cross-channel services refused to give way, and the dockers came out on strike. Soon Belfast's 1,500 carters were also on strike, followed by coal quay workers.

By mid-July the strike was beginning to paralyse the city. Linen firms were closing, and coal and grain remained unloaded at the docks. Crowds attacked strike-breaking carters, and thousands attended strike meetings in the Protestant Shankill Road and Sandy Row, and the Catholic Falls.

But by now the strikers' weaknesses were showing. Union funds were running short, and employers were threatening to lock out new groups of workers. James Sexton, Liverpool-based leader of the Dockers' Union, was reluctant to commit large sums to the dispute: like Larkin, Sexton was of Irish parentage, but he was a cautious career trade unionist rather than a militant leader. The British Trades Union Congress, too, was hesitant: TUC officials arrived in Belfast and, in Larkin's absence, negotiated a disastrous settlement to the coal heavers' dispute, as a result of which trouble continued to flare.

Then the Belfast police mutinied. Towards the end of July, resentful of their strike-breaking duties, they demanded higher pay: when the commissioner banned their meetings, up to 800 of the 1,000-strong force defied him, and attended nonetheless. The authorities rushed more than 2,500 troops to Belfast to overawe them, and transferred 200 dissident policemen to other districts.

By early August there were more than 6,000 troops in the city, and the authorities, under pressure from the employers, saturated both Protestant and Catholic areas. On 9 August troops started guarding strike-breaking carters in the Falls, a highly provocative move in an area where people regarded the soldiers as an army of occupation. Days of serious rioting ensued. More than 2,000 troops, 80 cavalry and hundreds of police confronted rioters, many of them women, wielding paving stones and throwing boiling water.

During a tumultuous riot on the evening of 12 August, troops opened fire, killing two uninvolved passers-by, one a 23-year-old woman who had gone out to look for her young brother. The killings provoked widespread anger and concern, which extended to Britain. In East London, George Lansbury led 10,000 demonstrators in a march of mourning, and numerous labour movement bodies made protests to Augustine Birrell, the Irish secretary. Labour MPs at Westminster were more cautious, but later they pressed for a parliamentary enquiry, and the government agreed.

Although there was no fighting between Protestants and Catholics, the riots changed the atmosphere, reopening the gulf between the communities. The huge non-sectarian mass meetings were no more. Groups of strikers began to return to work, often on unfavourable terms: a process which was disastrously hastened in November by the Dockers' Union general secretary James Sexton, who was at loggerheads with Larkin. Sexton told dockers to return to work even though no agreement had been secured: many went back to be told that their places had been filled, while others had to leave the union or suffered pay cuts.

The strike which for months had convulsed Belfast had been defeated, but Larkin, undeterred, already had his eyes on Dublin, where a new Dockers' Union branch was recruiting rapidly. During 1908, however, Larkin's militant tactics put him increasingly at odds with James Sexton, who finally suspended him in December.

Larkin now took up the idea, which had been circulating for some months, of forming an Irish-based union for unskilled workers, and on 4 January 1909 the Irish Transport and General Workers' Union was officially founded, enroling some 1,200 members that first day. The new union held high the banners of Irish independence and a new social order. It asserted the need to cease 'grafting ourselves on the English trades union movement'; it argued that unskilled workers should be organised in a single union if they were to combat 'the power of the employing class'; and it put forward an ambitious programme:

> a legal eight hours' day; provision of work for all unemployed, and pensions for all workers at 60 years of age; adult suffrage; nationalisation of canals, railways and all means of transport; the land of Ireland for the people of Ireland. Our ultimate ideal: the realisation of an Industrial Commonwealth.[84]

Larkin's influence grew. When he was released from jail in October 1910 after spending three months inside on trumped-up charges, he was greeted by mass rallies in Dublin. Constance Markievicz, who heard him there for the first time, recalled:

> listening to Larkin, I realised that I was in the presence of something that I had never come across before, some great primeval force rather than a

man. A tornado, a storm-driven wave, the rush into life of spring, and the blasting breath of autumn, all seemed to emanate from the power that spoke. It seemed as if his personality caught up, assimilated, and threw back to the vast crowd that surrounded him every emotion that swayed them, every pain and joy that they had ever felt made articulate and sanctified.[85]

The ITGWU soon became a dynamic force in Dublin and other southern cities, but in Belfast its fate was very different. Whereas Dockers' Union members in Dublin transferred *en masse* to the new union, in Belfast they split along sectarian lines. Protestant cross-channel dockers stayed in the Dockers' Union, while Catholic deep-sea dockers joined the ITGWU. After an unsuccessful confrontation with the employers, the ITGWU branch collapsed; for its part, the Dockers' Union branch became moribund.

Non-sectarianism was also on the wane in the Independent Orange Order. Lindsay Crawford, who had strongly supported the Belfast strikers, was becoming an open advocate of home rule. His critics, led by the anti-Catholic Tom Sloan, succeeded in expelling him in May 1908. Seven entire lodges resigned in Crawford's support, and the brief progressive flurry in the history of Orangeism was over.

The ITGWU was followed in September 1911 by the formation of an all-women's union, the Irish Women Workers' Union, in the wake of a successful strike by 3,000 women at Jacob's biscuit factory in Dublin. The moving spirit behind the IWWU was Delia Larkin, James Larkin's sister. Prominent supporters included the suffragette Hanna Sheehy Skeffington and Constance Markievicz, who told the founding meeting, to cheers and laughter:

> Without organisation you can do nothing and the purpose of this meeting is to form you into an army of fighters... As you are all aware women have at present no vote, but a union such as has now been formed will not alone help you to obtain better wages, but will also be a great means of helping you to get votes... and thus make men of you all.[86]

Within a few months, the IWWU had recruited some 1,000 members.

The women's movement

Like the labour movement, the women's movement was rapidly gathering strength. It, too, was a product of nineteenth century capitalism, and spanned much of the world, from Europe and America – where it was closely linked to the anti-slavery movement – to China, where women would win the vote before their European sisters.

The gradual extension of the franchise during the 19th century first to middle-class men, and then to better-off workers – a process which began in Britain with the Reform Act of 1832 – stimulated demands for women to be given the vote. Middle-class women, aided by male advocates of their cause, also demanded equal access to education and professional employment, and an end to the legal restrictions which subordinated married women to their husbands, and made everything women owned – including their earnings – their husbands' property. For working-class women, condemned to ceaseless toil in grim factories, or to harsh poverty in the countryside, priorities were very different. Their most urgent need was to improve their wages and conditions of work, and many women in both Britain and Ireland played a militant part in the upsurge of 'new unionism'.

In Britain, the first women's suffrage organisation was formed in Manchester in 1865. Suffrage meetings were also held in many parts of Ireland, and in 1876 two Quakers, Anna and Thomas Haslam, formed the first Irish suffrage society in Dublin, which later became the Irish Women's Suffrage and Local Government Association. The IWSLGA's members were mostly middle-class and non-Catholics. Like their English equivalents, they concentrated on lectures, petitions, appeals to MPs – they focused on the Irish members – and letters to the press.

In 1870 hopes were high when a suffrage bill was carried on its second reading: but then Gladstone intervened personally to make sure it went no further. He did the same the following year, saying that the intervention of women in parliamentary election proceedings would be 'a practical evil of an intolerable character'.[87] From then on, a succession of attempts to change the law were met by implacable opposition from both Liberal and Tory governments.

Reforms were, however, conceded in areas such as married women's rights to property and to custody of their children. Women were also given the vote, subject to a property qualification, in local government elections, first in Britain and some years later in Ireland. But the vote in national elections was adamantly refused them. It became the issue symbolising all women's disadvantages, and many women believed that if the vote were won, they would have the power to change their lot.

Repeated parliamentary failure led to discouragement and a decline in the women's suffrage movement, but the opening of the new century brought new hope. Tory rule was approaching its end, and Labour – with which suffragists such as the Pankhursts were closely identified – was a growing force on the political scene.

In England, Mrs Emmeline Pankhurst, together with her daughters Christabel and Sylvia and others, formed the Women's Social and Political Union in 1903. They initially directed their energies at winning Labour's support: a task which would prove far from easy. The limitations of conventional campaigning became evident in 1905, when a bill for women's suffrage was 'talked out' in parliament: the discussion on the preceding bill, about lights on vehicles, was artificially extended so that no time was left for the suffrage bill. Then two months later, unemployed people held defiant demonstrations to pressurise the government into passing a bill improving their conditions. They were successful, and the women's suffrage campaigners drew the lesson: they, too, should resort to militant tactics. Members of the WSPU began heckling prominent liberals and disrupting their election campaign meetings. Arrests and imprisonment followed.

Year after year women's suffrage bills were blocked, often after being carried at their second reading. The women became more and more impassioned, and their numbers swelled till in 1908 the WSPU could muster a spectacular midsummer demonstration, more than 250,000-strong. Women tracked government ministers, accosting them at public meetings and private parties alike. They addressed the House of Commons from a steam launch on the river Thames; they flew kites above the House; they sailed over it in a dirigible balloon; they chained themselves to the grille in the ladies' gallery; and they threw stones through prime minister Asquith's windows.

The WSPU's militant approach inspired two young Irishwomen, Hanna Sheehy Skeffington and Margaret Cousins, backed by their ardently feminist husbands, to set up a new organisation, the Irish Women's Franchise League. The two women were both graduates, and around thirty years old. Hanna was the daughter of a Parnellite MP and one-time Fenian, David Sheehy. She became aware of the suffrage issue when she was an undergraduate, when Esther Roper organised a huge petition to the House of Commons. Hanna remembered how she

> was amazed and disgusted to learn that I was classed among criminals, infants and lunatics – in fact, that my status as a woman was worse than any of these.[88]

In 1903 Hanna married Francis Skeffington, and 'true to his feminist principles', as she put it, he adopted her surname, Sheehy, as part of his own.[89] Frank was a much-loved and somewhat eccentric figure, small and red-bearded. Padraic Pearse reportedly said of him:

> He had a thousand principles, from pacifism and women's suffrage to wearing knickerbockers, and would die at the stake for the least of them, even his right to wear knickerbockers.[90]

Hanna described him as 'a hater of all oppressions, whether of class, creed, sex or nation.'[91]

Margaret Cousins and her husband James were both from Protestant unionist families. Margaret's father was a government official, but she recalled: 'I belonged in my heart from the beginning to the fighters for freedom.'[92] James's family were working-class: his father was a coal-heaver on the Belfast docks. James left school at 12 years old, and eventually improved his job prospects when he found he had a talent for shorthand. His conversion to Irish nationalism came during a trip to England to take a shorthand examination. He remembered:

> For relaxation I took myself to a circus performance in the Crystal Palace. A "Review of the Nations" included Ireland as a conventional stage-Irishman riding round the ring on a pig shouting, "Begorra, bejapers, bedad, and hurroo" with a detestable Cockney accent. Something in me went wild. I jumped to my feet and protested loudly that the item was a lie and a gross libel on people that were as good as anybody there. I was "shooed" into red-hot silence by those around me... I returned to my orange environment in Belfast as green as grass, determined to do one man's work towards ridding the stage of such low caricatures of my people...[93]

James wrote poetry and plays, and became keenly involved in the theatrical side of the Gaelic revival. He met Margaret in Dublin where she was a music student and he was a clerk. He converted her to vegetarianism, and both took up theosophy and, like Yeats, engaged in occult experiments. Margaret wrote later:

> Probably my experiences in these years were typical of those with which the western world was being flooded just then. There was undoubtedly a stirring of the waters of the seeking mind... Ireland itself was a focal point in just those years, and we were right in the middle of it.[94]

Margaret first came into contact with the women' movement in 1906 in Manchester, where she had been invited to speak at a vegetarian conference. The National Council of Women was also holding a conference in the town, and she attended it. She wrote:

> It impressed me deeply with the possibilities that were latent in womanhood. It made me aware of the injustices and grievances which were taken for granted as the natural fate of my sex.[95]

On her return to Ireland she went to see the veteran suffragists Anna and Thomas Haslam, now nearly seventy and 'a remarkable old pair', and began attending and organising suffrage meetings. She eagerly followed news of the English suffragettes' activities through their paper *Votes for Women*. Then in late 1908 the Cousins and the Sheehy Skeffingtons decided it was time to form a militant suffrage society suited to Ireland's particular political situation, as 'a subject-country seeking freedom from England'.[96] The new group, wrote Hanna later, was to have the same aim – Votes for Women – as the English groups, but would

> work on independent Irish lines: that was essential, and we were strongly Irish-minded, most of us, realizing that, though the House of Commons was still the arbiter of Irishwomen's as well as Irishmen's destinies, we should have to adopt slightly different tactics and begin at once on our own M.P.s, pressing to have a clause embodying Votes for Women in our measure of Home Rule.[97]

On 11 November 1908 the Irish Women's Franchise League was founded. Only women could be members, but men – especially Francis and James – were to prove dedicated supporters. Margaret later summed up the stance of the new body:

> Its policy was to educate by all forms of propaganda the men, women and children of Ireland to understand and support the members of the League in their demand for votes for women, and to obtain pledges from every Irish Member of Parliament to vote for Women Suffrage Bills introduced in the British House of Parliament, and to include Women Suffrage in any Irish Home Rule Bill.[98]

The IWFL held public meetings, often in the open air, in many parts of Ireland, and organised poster parades and processions, chalking announcements of their activities on the pavements. Margaret wrote:

> Starting with a dozen enthusiasts, we grew to about fifty women whose hearts were in the movement, and who could be relied on to take their share in every kind of propaganda. We were a very mixed lot, a cross-section of all the classes, political parties, religious groups, and avocations open to women in those days.[99]

The women of Inghinidhe na hÉireann, who had been campaigning for years on national and cultural questions, shared the IWFL's aim of equality for women, but disagreed with their tactic of pressurising the British parliament. An editorial in their paper *Bean na hÉireann* in April 1909 responded to a critic by saying:

> we do not 'refuse to join the women's franchise movement'... but we decline to join with Parliamentarians and Unionists in trying to force a bill through Westminster. We prefer to try and organise a women's movement on Sinn Fein lines, or on lines even broader still. Freedom for our Nation and the complete removal of all disabilities to our sex will be our battlecry.

Constance Markievicz, who with her sisters had formed a suffrage society in Sligo in 1896, often spoke at IWFL meetings and helped them with publicity and fund-raising. She thought that the IWFL's demands did not go far enough, and urged women to become involved in the national struggle: they should argue for the cause, and they should get themselves elected to public bodies and influence them to support Irish industries. In a lecture to students in March 1909 she called on young women to

> regard yourselves as Irish, believe in yourselves as Irish. Arm yourselves with weapons to fight your nation's cause. Arm your souls with noble and free ideas. Arm your minds with the histories and memories of your country and her martyrs, her language, and a knowledge of her arts and industries. And if in your day the call should come for your body to arm, do not shirk that either.[100]

She saw England as the obstacle preventing both national freedom and equality for women, and wrote in *Bean na hÉireann* in July 1909:

> As our country has had her Freedom and her Nationhood taken from her by England, so also our sex is denied emancipation and citizenship by the same enemy. So therefore the first step on the road to freedom is to realize ourselves as Irishwomen – not as Irish or merely as women, but as Irishwomen doubly enslaved and with a double battle to fight.

The IWFL continued to pressurise Irish MPs to support bills that would extend the franchise, and worked alongside the English suffrage movement. In 1910 they brought Christabel Pankhurst to Dublin, and some 3,000 people packed into the Rotunda to see her.

In November 1910 Margaret Cousins joined English suffragettes in a demonstration at the House of Commons. The police violently attacked the women, injuring about 50 and arresting around 115. The women retaliated over the next few days, breaking windows in cabinet ministers' houses. Margaret and another Irish suffragette contributed by throwing potatoes through the window-panes of the chief secretary for Ireland, Augustine Birrell; they then threw pieces of broken flowerpot at the windows of Asquith and Lloyd George – the prime minister and chancellor of the exchequer – in Downing Street, and got arrested. As a result, they were imprisoned in Holloway: 'a species of living death because of the solitariness of the confinement', Margaret wrote of her month inside.[101]

The suffragettes had an immediate and warm response from male socialists and trade unionists such as James Larkin and James Connolly.

Towards the end of 1910 socialists, suffragists and 'advanced' nationalists came together in a campaign to get school meals provided for Irish children: an act enabling local authorities to do this had been passed in England in 1906, but had not been extended to Ireland. Maud Gonne raised the issue in *Bean na hÉireann*, describing the undernourishment of working-class children who went to school without breakfast and did not have time to go home for a mid-day meal. The Inghinidhe decided to set up a committee to start organising school dinners, hoping that this would force the authorities to act. They set up canteens in sympathetic schools, serving hundreds of dinners of Irish stew and rice pudding. Among the women who served the dinners were Maud Gonne herself, along with Hanna Sheehy Skeffington, Constance Markievicz, Helena Molony and Kathleen Clarke. Aided by James Connolly – who had returned from America in mid-1910 – and James Larkin, they began pressurising the politicians to change the law, and eventually succeeded in 1914.

8
The Conservative Revolt

In 1910 the political tide turned dramatically in favour of Irish nationalism. Since their return to power in 1906, Liberal policies in Ireland had resembled the Tories' strategy of 'killing home rule with kindness'. They had created an Irish national university, effectively for Catholics; they had improved land purchase provisions; and they had resettled thousands of evicted tenants. But they had made no moves towards home rule. Then in December 1909 the Liberals called a general election for the following month. Anticipating a close result, the Irish Party leader, John Redmond, threatened that the Irish in England would desert the Liberals unless Asquith, the prime minister, publicly committed himself to home rule. Asquith reluctantly gave in, declaring at an election rally at the Albert Hall in London that he would pursue

> a policy which, while explicitly safeguarding the supreme and indefeasible authority of the Imperial Parliament, will set up in Ireland a system of full self-government in regard to purely Irish affairs.

He added:

> There is not, and there cannot be, any question of separation. There is not, and there cannot be, any question of rival or competing supremacies. But, subject to those conditions, that is the Liberal policy.[1]

The election result was ideal for the Irish. The Liberals were once more returned to power, but whereas in 1906 they had had 400 MPs, now they had only 275 – just two more than the Conservatives. Labour, allies of the Liberals, held 40 seats. So for the first time in 15 years, the Irish nationalists, with 82 MPs, held the balance of power. Once again they would be able to demand home rule as the price of their support.

And there was a further vital change in their favour: the Liberals were planning to curtail the powers of the House of Lords. Asquith had called the election after the Lords had rejected Lloyd George's 'people's budget': its proposals had included a super-tax on the very rich to pay, among other things, for old age pensions. It was by no means the first time that the Lords had frustrated Liberal legislation: they were acting as the Tories' allies, winning for them the battles that could not be won in the Commons. In essence, the Lords and the Tories were conducting a rearguard action in defence of the privileges of the propertied, while the Liberals were the capitalists' left wing, gingerly bringing in reforms to placate their working-class voters and undermine the appeal of the Labour Party.

The Liberals were now determined to end the Lords' power to veto legislation. For the Irish, this would mean that the Lords would no longer be able to put a permanent block on home rule bills, as they had done in 1893. Home rule would be a serious possibility. The Liberals went to the country again in December 1910, focusing the election on the issue of the Lords' veto. The results were similar to the January election. This time the Liberals and Conservatives each had 272 seats, while Labour had 42. The Irish nationalists, with 84 MPs, still held the balance of power.

Next the Liberals brought in a Parliament Bill which would drastically cut back the Lords' powers. It would allow the Lords to hold up legislation for two years only; if a bill completed all its stages in the Commons three times, in successive sessions, and was each time rejected by the Lords, it would automatically become law. On 10 August 1911 the Lords passed the Parliament Bill by a small majority. They had been faced with a grim choice: either they vote away their own powers, or the king – himself under pressure from the Liberals – would create hundreds of new Liberal peers, who would end the Tory stranglehold on the upper house.

Eight months later, on 11 April 1912, as the price of retaining the Irish Party's backing, Asquith presented the third Home Rule Bill to the House of Commons. Even if the Lords exercised their delaying powers to the full, the Home Rule Bill could become law in mid-1914. The end of a long struggle seemed in sight. But already a motley alliance was mustering to thwart the bill.

Storm clouds gather

The years 1912 to 1914 were to be convulsed by a drama of great bitterness and extraordinary dimensions, as the Conservative party, guardian of the British establishment, jettisoned constitutional politics in a desperate effort to regain power. Pawns in their game were the unionists of northeast Ireland, whom the Tories encouraged to take up arms to resist the will of parliament by force. The Tories would also pressurise the king to help them, and, aided by top-ranking officers, would incite the army to disobey the government.

The Liberal government, like its predecessors, proposed to give the Irish a modest amount of autonomy, leaving Westminster in control of matters such as war and peace, and with a veto over laws passed by an Irish parliament. But however limited the measure, it would embody the aspirations of the Irish electorate as expressed in every election since the extension of the franchise in 1884. In eight general elections from 1885 onwards, more than 80 of the 103 Irish MPs had been nationalists.

But the wishes and welfare of the Irish people swiftly receded into insignificance as the power game developed between the Conservatives and Irish unionists on the one hand and the Liberals on the other. The Conservatives, frustrated by years out of office and infuriated by the emasculation of the House of Lords, were determined to force the Liberals to call an early general election, which they thought would bring a return to Tory rule. The Liberal majority meant that the Tories could achieve nothing within parliament, so they resorted to extra-parliamentary tactics, going to ever more extreme lengths. Irish home rule seemed the weak point the Tories could play on, and they did so with utter ruthlessness.

In reality, the Tories were not unanimously opposed to home rule: but they declared themselves so as a matter of expediency. In the autumn of 1910, some leading Tories had canvassed the idea of conceding home rule in return for a place in a Liberal-Tory coalition government. The *Times* had published articles inclining towards the idea; and one of those involved, F.E. Smith, a prominent Tory MP with a Liverpool seat, publicly a champion of the loyalist cause, wrote in a private letter that home rule was 'a dead quarrel for which neither the country nor the party cares a damn outside of Ulster and Liverpool.'[2]

Like Randolph Churchill in 1886, the Tories swiftly recognised that the 'Orange card' was the one to play. They had no thought of winning special treatment for the Protestants of the northeast: their class and family ties were generally with the ascendancy Protestants in the south. Rather, they aimed to use the threat of disorder in the north to scuttle both the Home Rule Bill and the Liberal government.

During the December 1910 election campaign, there were ominous signs of impending storms, as leading Tories made speeches prophesying violence if the Home Rule Bill were passed. Sir Edward Carson, one of the two MPs for Dublin University, and leader since February of the small band of Irish unionists at Westminster, warned that Asquith

> was playing with fire if he thought he was going to trifle with the loyal minority, who were as keen for King and Constitution as any Englishman.[3]

Now in his fifties, Carson was a formidable figure. A grim-visaged hypochondriac, he was a top barrister who had first come to prominence as a crown prosecutor relentlessly securing convictions against land-rights agitators during the Plan of Campaign of the late 1880s. For this he was rewarded with the post of solicitor-general for Ireland, and later became solicitor-general for England. In 1895 he won notoriety for his destruction of Oscar Wilde in the witness-box, when Wilde sued for libel after the Marquess of Queensberry, father of his lover Alfred Douglas, accused him of being a sodomite. Wilde made damaging admissions to Carson, and was later charged with homosexual offences and imprisoned.

On social issues Carson was an uncompromising reactionary, supporting landowners' interests, and opposing every measure that would improve workers' lives, including shorter hours for miners, trade union rights, old age pensions, and electoral reform.

Carson was against the idea of a separate parliament for Ulster, which would mean deserting his own people, the Protestants of the south. But he thought that the Protestants of the northeast could frighten the government into abandoning home rule altogether. In December 1910 he declared:

> It is my wish, and the wish of those with whom I act, to be law-abiding citizens; but, by heaven, I tell you this – from what I know of the men of the North of Ireland they will not yield their birthright, not one inch, without a struggle.[4]

Aligned with Carson was another leading Tory, Walter Long. From an English landowning family, Long was intimately connected with the Anglo-Irish ascendancy. His mother's father had been MP for Wicklow for 28 years, during which he had addressed the House of Commons only once, for three minutes, on the subject of pigeon-shooting. Long's wife was a daughter of the Earl of Cork and granddaughter of the Marchioness of Clanricarde. Long himself had briefly been chief secretary for Ireland in 1905, and had then been MP for South County Dublin for four years. He was also a keen anti-socialist. On 6 December 1910 Long told an election meeting in London, the *Times* reported,

> that if the Liberals tried to force Home Rule on Ireland there was a large section of the community – a minority, no doubt, but large, powerful, determined – who would resist their efforts with all the power and all the force they could command. Instead of bringing peace to Ireland they would bring trouble and controversy, and that which was first cousin to, if it was not actual, civil war. (Cheers.)[5]

Meanwhile at Lisburn a few miles south of Belfast, Captain James Craig, MP for East County Down, was saying that:

> Perhaps the time had arrived when they should change their tactics... and spend the money hitherto used in the sister counties in buying arms and ammunition... In a short time the Unionist Clubs would be reorganised, and he would advise all the young men of the countryside to join and to employ some old soldiers to train them in military tactics...[6]

Craig, who had fought in the Boer war, was the son of a self-made whiskey millionaire and Presbyterian from County Down. A massive, red-faced man with an alert mind, he would provide the organising skills behind the loyalist campaign.

Immediately after the election, on 24 December 1910, the *Spectator*, a leading Tory journal, published a leader appealing to the Protestants of northeast Ulster to put forward a claim for self-government, and overcome their reluctance to desert the cause of Protestants in the rest of Ireland. By doing this,

> they will almost certainly destroy the chances of a Home-Rule Bill being passed, and thus they will far better serve the interests of the minorities in the South than by refusing to make the demand in question.

The paper contended that if the Liberals agreed, the Irish nationalists would refuse the bill, because Ireland would go bankrupt if it could not tax 'the rich city of Belfast'; but if the Liberals refused, the people of northeast Ulster would have enormously strengthened their case for resisting a Dublin parliament:

> They will be able to say: "… What we will never admit is your moral right not only to separate us from Britain, but to place us under the oppressive rule of the Southern Irish. Such an act of oppression as that justifies us in exercising the ultimate right of insurrection which belongs to every free man."[7]

The Protestants of the northeast, however, remained reluctant to demand anything other than a total abandonment of home rule.

Many Tories and Irish loyalists, unlike the *Spectator*, claimed not just northeast Ulster, but the whole of Ulster, as Protestant territory. Yet in fact Protestants made up only 56 per cent of Ulster's one-and-a-half million people. Ulster MPs, too, were evenly balanced, with 17 Tories to 16 nationalists: a position that was reversed in 1913 when the nationalists and liberals put up a Protestant home rule candidate in a hard-fought by-election in Derry City and won the seat from the Tories.

Further, in only two counties, Antrim and Down, did the Protestants have large majorities, with 79.5 per cent and 68 per cent respectively. In counties Armagh and Derry (officially referred to as Londonderry) Protestants were 55 per cent and 54 per cent of the population. In the remaining five counties they numbered 45 per cent in Tyrone, 44 per cent in Fermanagh, 25 per cent in Monaghan, 21 per cent in Donegal, and 18.5 per cent in Cavan. Nor did Protestant-dominated areas form a single bloc: the communities were intermingled, and the nationalist majority in Tyrone cut a swathe across the middle of the province.

Unionists organise

The imminent Parliament Bill and the prospect of home rule spurred unionists in the northeast of Ireland to organise as they had not done since the 1890s. The Ulster Unionist Council began organising unionist clubs, which soon began practising military drill. Formed in 1905 when there were fears that the Conservatives might be weakening on home rule, the UUC brought together local unionist associations, Orange lodges and MPs in a single body. Clubs were soon formed in the Belfast shipyards, where skilled Protestant workers were intent on guarding their privileged position from Catholic encroachment. The owners of the big yards, however, had differing positions on home rule. Typical of Belfast businessmen was Sir George Clark of Workman and Clark, a convinced unionist who was to play an important practical role in the anti-home rule campaign. By contrast, Lord Pirrie, a director of Harland and Wolff, had abandoned unionism and become a Liberal home ruler.

In January 1911 an Ulster Women's Unionist Council was formed, with the Duchess of Abercorn as president. The women pledged:

> We will stand by our husbands, our brothers, and our sons, in whatever steps they may be forced to take in defending our liberties against the tyranny of Home Rule.[8]

The same month Captain James Craig announced in the *Morning Post*, a Tory paper, that

> there is a spirit spreading abroad which I can testify to from my personal knowledge – that Germany and the German Emperor would be preferred to the rule of John Redmond, Patrick Ford, and the Molly Maguires. [Patrick Ford was a leading Irish-American activist, while the Molly Maguires were a secret society of US coal miners in the previous century, who had used violence in pursuit of workers' rights.][9]

As the rank-and-file drilled, their leaders made apocalyptic speeches. In July 1911 Lord Londonderry, president of the UUC, warned the House of Lords that 'Ulster' had shown by its demonstrations 'it will not have Home Rule.' He predicted:

> if a Home Rule parliament is established on College Green there will be not only lawlessness and disorder, but bloodshed; and if blood is shed it will be upon the heads of His Majesty's Government... they will ruin Ireland and bring it to bankruptcy, and in all probability create civil war.[10]

On 8 August, during the debate on the Parliament Bill, Sir Edward Carson accused the government of aiming to pass home rule 'by a pure act of force', and went on: 'I may at least express my own hope, made most solemnly, that your act of force will be resisted by force.'[11]

Soon there were signs – though not in public – that the Liberal government was weakening. A committee of seven ministers had been considering the home rule question, in a desultory fashion, since the start of the year. They discussed the possibility of all-round devolution, with subordinate assemblies for England, Scotland and Wales, as well as Ireland: Winston Churchill even suggested dividing the UK into ten parts. But eventually the committee rejected the federal idea and returned to Gladstone's Home Rule Bill of 1893 for its model.

Irish nationalists remained unconcerned about what they dubbed 'Ulsteria', regarding the threatening speeches as a bluff. But Augustine Birrell, the chief secretary for Ireland and a supporter of home rule, was worried. He wrote to Winston Churchill at the end of August 1911:

> Ulster has cried 'Wolf' so often and so absurdly that one is inclined to ridicule her rhodomontade, but we are cutting very deep this time and her yells are genuine... Great ferment and perturbation of spirit exists – mainly fed amongst the poor folk by hatred of Roman Catholicism and amongst the better to do by the belief that under a Home Rule regime Ireland will become a miserable, one-horsed, poverty stricken, priest ridden, corrupt oligarchy.[12]

Birrell floated an idea for a compromise, suggesting that each Ulster county could be allowed to vote separately on whether it wished to be excluded from home rule, which would probably result in two counties opting out:

> were the question referred to Ulster county by county, it is probable that all Ulster save Antrim and Down would by a majority support Home Rule and it might then be suggested and agreed to that for the transitional period, say 5 years, Antrim and Down might stand out and that at the end of that time there should be a fresh referendum to settle their fate. If this was done, there could be no Civil War.[13]

In the autumn of 1911, the Ulster unionist campaign escalated. That July, Sir Edward Carson had written to Captain Craig seeking reassurance:

> What I am very anxious about is to satisfy myself that the people over there really mean to resist. I am not for a mere game of bluff & unless men are prepared to make great sacrifices which they clearly understand the talk of resistance is of no use.[14]

In response Craig organised a huge demonstration of more than 50,000 on 23 September. Orangemen and members of unionist clubs assembled in the centre of Belfast and marched to the grounds of Craigavon, Craig's large house on the shore of Belfast Lough. Carson addressed the crowd from a specially constructed platform on the top of a hill. Speaking in his Dublin accent, he bound his destiny with theirs:

> I now enter into a compact with you, and every one of you, and with the help of God you and I joined together... will yet defeat the most nefarious conspiracy that has ever been hatched against a free people.

He went on:

> We must be prepared – and time is precious in these things – the morning Home Rule passes, ourselves to become responsible for the government of the Protestant Province of Ulster.[15]

Carson announced that the Ulster Unionist Council would start planning a provisional government. Two days later 400 delegates assembled and the UUC set up a commission of five to draft a constitution for such a government.

Nationalists, too, were organising demonstrations: but now for the first time they were in effect on the side of the British government, defending the home rule policy against the threats of the hitherto loyal Protestants. Thousands rallied in County Fermanagh in August, while the Gaelic League held a huge procession in Dublin in September, and a very big home rule demonstration was held in Newry, County Down, in December. Prominent Belfast Protestants, too, gathered to press the home rule case, with Lord Pirrie of Harland and Wolff to the fore.

In November 1911 the anti-home rule forces gained a vital boost when Andrew Bonar Law, a Glasgow businessman, took over as leader of the Conservative party. His leadership bid was spearheaded by his friend Max Aitken, later Lord Beaverbrook, the millionaire Canadian financier and owner of the *Daily Express*.

Bonar Law brought a new and calculated virulence to the debate, telling the prime minister in February 1912: 'I am afraid I shall have to show myself very vicious, Mr. Asquith, this session. I hope you will understand.'[16] He would soon commit the entire Tory Party to an unprecedented campaign to undermine parliamentary democracy by backing a threatened insurrection against the government.

Though the main motive for Bonar Law's ruthlessness was his desire to oust the Liberal government, he also had a strong personal identification with the 'Ulster' loyalist cause. His father, a Presbyterian minister, was born in Coleraine, County Derry, and emigrated to New Brunswick, which later became part of Canada. Bonar, born in 1858, was sent to Scotland at the age of 12 and brought up by an aunt, eventually becoming a broker on the Glasgow iron market. His father became ill and returned to Ireland in 1877, where Bonar visited him nearly every weekend till his death five years later.

On becoming leader, Bonar Law soon gained another strong link with the Ulster unionists in the person of Lady Londonderry, wife of the UUC's president, an influential hostess who lost no time in cultivating him. Londonderry House became the social focus for the Conservative Party in London, and since Bonar Law's wife had died, Lady Londonderry entertained on his behalf.

The invitation to Churchill

The first showdown between Liberals and unionists came early in 1912 when the Ulster Liberal Association, with Lord Pirrie to the fore, invited Winston Churchill to speak in Belfast's Ulster Hall on 8 February, along with John Redmond, leader of the Irish Party, and the West Belfast MP, Joseph Devlin. Churchill's acceptance caused instant consternation among Belfast unionists, especially as he was to speak in the very hall where his father, Lord Randolph Churchill, had resoundingly backed the unionist cause. Violent disorders were widely prophesied. The Liberals asked for troops and police to protect the meeting. The Ulster Unionist Council caused a sensation in the press when it decided, on 17 January, that it would 'take steps to prevent its being held.'[17]

Speaking at a huge demonstration in Liverpool a few days later, Carson supported the UUC's decision and said that if he was doing anything illegal, he was 'prepared to take the consequences'.[18] Addressing the same meeting, Tory MP F.E. Smith raised the stakes, saying:

> he for one, speaking with a full sense of responsibility, went further and said there was no length to which Ulster would not be entitled to go, however desperate or unconstitutional, in carrying the quarrel, if the quarrel was wickedly fixed upon them.[19]

Then on 26 January Bonar Law, the new Tory leader, told 10,000 people at the Albert Hall that the party would support the 'minority' in Ireland against home rule.[20]

Meanwhile Belfast businessmen were rallying round the UUC and organising its finances. On 19 January Lord Dunleath, chairman of the Sir Edward Carson Unionist Defence Fund, wrote to Carson that 'the people connected with the Ulster industries will supply any money you may require in the course of the next two years.'[21]

The hostility to Churchill's meeting frightened the authorities. The chief secretary for Ireland, Augustine Birrell, received alarming prognostications from his officials, forecasting ferocious riots, perhaps sparked off by minor incidents. One official suggested that 6 to 8 o'clock in the evening was a dangerous time:

> The factory girls who are of all religions turn out at this time and are met by their young men, mostly a rather bad lot, as religious rancour is tuned up to a high pitch… A very harmless remark from one girl to another such as, 'Go along, you papist bitch', which would ordinarily pass unnoticed, would set them at one another; the young men would join in, and word would be sent to the forces of both sides that Protestants and Catholics were killing each other.[22]

The UUC clinched the matter by booking the Ulster Hall for the evening before the Churchill meeting and announcing they would pack it with supporters who would not leave. The authorities felt unable to intervene. Churchill agreed to ask the Liberals to change the venue. Birrell wrote to Churchill on 28 January: 'My own belief is that if you hold a midday meeting in a tent, no blood will be shed. But the moral is… Leave Ireland alone in future.'[23]

On 6 February the authorities nervously moved troops into the city, and at a cabinet meeting the same day Churchill and Lloyd George made a proposal on the lines of Augustine Birrell's idea, that predominantly Protestant counties should be given the option of contracting out of home rule. The cabinet rejected this, but supported another compromise, which Asquith summarised in a report to the king:

> (a) that the Bill as introduced should apply to the whole of Ireland;
> (b) that the Irish leaders should from the first be given clearly to understand that the Government held themselves free to make such changes in the Bill as fresh evidence of facts, or the pressure of British opinion, may render expedient;
> (c) that if... it becomes clear as the Bill proceeds that some special treatment must be provided for the Ulster counties, the Government will be ready to recognise the necessity either by amendment of the Bill, or by not pressing it on under the provisions of the Parliament Act.[24]

On 8 February Churchill duly braved large and menacing crowds at Larne and in Belfast, before going to the Celtic Park football ground, off the Falls Road, where he addressed 50,000 people in a marquee.

In this first trial of strength, the unionists had won. The Churchill incident proved to be a microcosm of the wider struggle over home rule. Now believing that the unionists were serious, the government decided to compromise rather than confront them.

A note of warning

Tension heightened as the introduction of the Home Rule Bill neared. On 31 March 1912 nationalists held an enormous demonstration in Dublin, which filled Sackville Street – now O'Connell Street – from end to end, and included a large contingent from Belfast. Among the speakers were John Redmond, Joseph Devlin, and the Gaelic League activist and founder of St Enda's, Padraic Pearse, who sounded a note of warning. Speaking in Irish, he said:

> Let us unite and win a good Act from the British; I think it can be done. But if we are tricked this time, there is a party in Ireland, and I am one of them, that will advise the Gael to have no counsel or dealings with the Gall [foreigner] for ever again, but to answer them henceforward with the strong hand and the sword's edge. Let the Gall understand that if we are cheated once more there will be red war in Ireland.[25]

In the north, loyalists were drilling with increasing earnestness, though as yet unarmed. By February 1912, according to police reports, some 12,000 men were involved. Leading Orangemen had spotted a legal loophole: training and drilling in the use of arms and in military exercises was legal if authorised by two justices of the peace, and the north's JPs proved co-operative.

During March and April the drilling intensified as loyalists prepared for a major demonstration to be held on Easter Tuesday, 9 April. Asquith, with the weakness that would characterise his response to the loyalists over succeeding years, took no action. A million miners were out on strike at the time, and in parliament on 1 April the socialist MP George Lansbury asked: 'If the Miners' Federation commenced to teach their men to drill would they be allowed to do so without the law being called in?' Asquith replied, to laughter: 'That is a hypothetical question, which I will answer when the case arises.'[26] Lansbury went on to draw attention to a leaflet that was, he reported,

> being circulated throughout Ulster informing the Ulster people that the officers of the British Army have assured their friends that they will refuse to order the troops to fire on the people of Ulster if they rebel against Home Rule...[27]

On 9 April, at the Agricultural Society's show grounds in Balmoral, a suburb of Belfast, a huge and theatrical demonstration sealed the alliance between the 'Ulster' Protestants and the British Conservative party. About 100,000 loyalists marched in military formation past a platform on which stood Andrew Bonar Law, Sir Edward Carson, Lord Londonderry and Walter Long, while some 70 British MPs looked on. At the centre of the scene was a 90-foot flagpole bearing the largest union jack ever woven. Carson ceremoniously persuaded the crowd to raise their hands and repeat after him: 'Never under any circumstances will we submit to Home Rule.'[28]

Bonar Law summoned up the resonant loyalist folk memory of the siege of Derry of 1689, which had started after the townsfolk prevented the governor, Robert Lundy, surrendering the city to the Catholic King James II:

> I say to you with all solemnity; you must trust to yourselves. Once again you hold the pass for the Empire. You are a besieged city. Does not the picture of the past, the glorious past with which you are so familiar, rise again before your eyes? The timid have left you, your Lundys have betrayed you, but you have closed your gates. The Government by their Parliament Act have erected a boom against you, a boom to cut you off from the help of the British people. You will burst that boom.[29]

Two days later, on 11 April 1912, Asquith introduced the third Home Rule Bill to a packed House of Commons. The bill offered Ireland limited autonomy, proposing an Irish parliament consisting of a Senate and a House of Commons, but reserving for the imperial parliament at Westminster matters such as war and peace. Westminster would have the power to nullify or amend any act of the Irish parliament. Irish MPs would still attend at Westminster, but the number would be reduced to 42. Asquith pointed out that:

> From the first moment the Irish people was granted an articulate political voice in 1885 it pronounced by a majority of four to one of its representatives in favour of Home Rule.[30]

Despite the cabinet's private decision in February to consider compromising with the northern unionists, Asquith remained firm in public, saying:

> we cannot admit, and we will not admit, the right of a minority of the
> people, and relatively a small minority – particularly when every possible
> care is being taken to safeguard their special interests and susceptibilities
> – to veto the verdict of the vast body of their countrymen.[31]

Bonar Law raised the spectre that Tories would evoke again and again in
coming months, of loyalist revolt and a government unable to tackle it.
Loyalists were ready 'to lay down their lives', he said, and asked:

> Do hon. Members believe that any Prime Minister could give orders to
> shoot down men whose only crime is that they refuse to be driven out of
> our community and be deprived of the privilege of British citizenship?[32]

The bill passed its first reading on 16 April by 360 votes to 266, and its
second reading went through on 9 May by 372 to 271.

The bill then went into its committee stage, when amendments could be
put forward. On 11 June 1912 came the first attempt to legislate for the
exclusion of part of Ulster when a young Liberal backbench MP named
Agar-Robartes, who represented a Cornwall constituency and had strongly
Protestant views, proposed the exclusion from the act of counties Antrim,
Armagh, Down and Derry.

Agar-Robartes saw his amendment as a practical way of defusing
Protestant opposition to home rule, which was, he said, partly based on
their 'strong and vigorous' feeling against 'the dreaded supremacy of the
Church to which the majority belongs'.[33] Agar-Robartes was not backed by
his party. Prime minister Asquith said: 'You can no more split Ireland into
parts than you can split England or Scotland into parts.'[34]

The Irish nationalists, predictably, strongly opposed the amendment. John
Redmond pointed out that the four counties did not form 'a homogenous
community' opposed to home rule. The area contained 315,000 Catholics
to less than 700,000 Protestants; four of its MPs were home rulers, and
many Protestants had voted for them. Redmond went on:

> This idea of two nations in Ireland is to us revolting and hateful. The idea
> of our agreeing to the partition of our nation is unthinkable. We want the
> union in Ireland of all creeds, of all classes, of all races, and we would
> resist most violently... the setting up of permanent dividing lines between
> one creed and another and one race and another.[35]

Joseph Devlin, the MP for West Belfast, said: 'I cannot understand why
any democrat should propose that you ought permanently to establish as a
force in a nation a minority.'[36] Devlin predicted that Ulster Protestants would
have 60 of the 160 members of an Irish parliament, and added that security
for a minority would be found

> in the readjustment of parties, in the union of the Protestant workers of the
> North with the Catholic labourer of the South, in the union of the privileged

classes of the North with the farmers and the tillers of the soil in the South.[37]

Both Irish unionists and Tories supported the Agar-Robartes amendment, but with varying motives. Sir Edward Carson supported it because he believed that 'If Ulster succeeds Home Rule is dead.'[38] He said he would never agree to leave out Tyrone and Fermanagh, but in any case he did not agree with the principle of the amendment:

> We do not accept this Amendment as a compromise of the question. There is no compromise possible. We believe that Home Rule would be disastrous for the rest of Ireland...[39]

He also stressed:

> Ulster will ask for no separate Parliament. .. she will try and remain in this Parliament .. that will be the best way of helping the people in the South and West of Ireland.[40]

The Tory leader Bonar Law, however, conceded that a compromise might be necessary if home rule were inevitable:

> We are, of course, opposed to Home Rule root and branch, but ... if there is to be Home Rule, I would rather have it under an arrangement by which civil war can be escaped.[41]

Bonar Law threatened the government:

> If you carry out your proposals to an end it will be a civil war in which you will use your forces, not to prevent, but to compel loyal citizens to leave their country.

The government knew, he asserted,

> that if Ulster is in earnest, that if Ulster does resist by force, there are stronger influences than Parliamentary majorities. They know that in that case no Government would dare to use their troops to drive them out... They are saying... "Convince us that you are earnest, show us that you mean to fight, and we will yield to you as we have yielded to everybody else."[42]

The Agar-Robartes amendment was defeated on 18 June by 320 votes to 251.

Women protest

The Home Rule Bill also came under fire from a different quarter: women, who were angered by its failure to promise them the vote. A fortnight before the Home Rule Bill was introduced, the Irish Party had deeply angered suffragettes both sides of the water by voting against the Conciliation Bill, which would have given the vote to women householders. A majority of Irish nationalist MPs were sympathetic to women's suffrage, though Redmond opposed it. But now the party leadership was worried that if the Conciliation Bill were passed, it could destabilise the government and consequently the chances of home rule. The Irish nationalist MPs duly voted as a bloc against the bill and were a crucial element in its defeat.

The leading English suffragette, Christabel Pankhurst, promptly sent a poster parade to Parliament Square, bearing the message, 'No votes for women, no home rule.' H.N. Brailsford, the journalist and dedicated suffrage supporter, protested: 'Mr. Redmond sullied the Irish flag by opposing one movement of liberation in the supposed interests of another. His methods are not a model to imitate.'[43]

The Irish suffragettes were outraged at the way their erstwhile supporters in the Irish Party had 'ratted' on them. They now stepped up their campaign for votes for women to be included in the Home Rule Bill. They were supported by James Connolly, who also called for two other democratising measures: proportional representation, and the removal of the proposed senate or upper house, which would be unelected.

At the great Dublin home rule demonstration on 31 March, members of the Irish Women's Franchise League paraded with sandwich boards. They were roughly treated by stewards – reputedly members of the Ancient Order of Hibernians – who forcibly removed their posters and tore them up.

In April women – including the great-granddaughter of Daniel O'Connell – attempted to attend a national convention organised by Redmond in Dublin to consider the Home Rule Bill. They were barred by police, and that night IWFL members painted 'Votes for women' on the offices of the United Irish League. Margaret Cousins wrote later of the Irish MPs:

> Those Irish politicians had no use for women citizens; they were sufficient for themselves and for the country. We measured them by principle and democracy and found them wanting... Looking back, facts have proved that our policy was right. The cause of Freedom is single and indivisible. No one facet of it can be sacrificed to expediency in favour of another without radical danger to the whole cause and to those who place expediency before principle.[44]

On 1 June 1912, women from all over Ireland assembled at a mass suffrage meeting in Dublin. The speakers included the nationalist Constance Markievicz, and Delia Larkin, founder of the new Irish Women Workers' Union and sister of James. Jennie Wyse-Power, vice-president of Sinn Féin, pointed out that her party had unanimously called for votes for women, and said:

> as an Irish Nationalist I cannot see why there should be any antagonism between the Irish women's demand for citizenship and the demand for a native Parliament. Our claim is that we shall not be debarred merely by sex from the rights of citizens.[45]

The meeting passed a resolution calling for the Home Rule Bill to be amended to include votes for women. Copies were forwarded to each cabinet minister and all Irish MPs, and were ignored. The Irish Women's Franchise League decided to take up militant action.

On 13 June eight IWFL members, including Hanna Sheehy Skeffington, were arrested for breaking the windows of government buildings in Dublin, and were jailed for refusing to pay their fines. The Dublin papers were loud in condemnation, prompting the IWFL paper, the *Irish Citizen*, to declare:

> it would be ludicrous, were it not shameful, to find Nationalists, whose history is a record of success gained by the use of violence and law-breaking and damage to property, condemning the smashing of a few panes of glass as if it were an unheard-of and unpardonable outrage; or to find Unionists, while vehemently applauding the resolve of Ulster to resist Home Rule by illegal methods, and encouraging them to drill for the purpose of armed resistance, at the same time condemning last Thursday's window-smashing in the name of Irish reputation for "sanity and sobriety in the conduct of their social and political affairs."[46]

Hanna Sheehy Skeffington, about to go to prison, attacked the critics with irony:

> men applaud the stone-thrower as long as the missile is flung for them and not at them.
>
> The novelty of Irish women resorting to violence on their own behalf is, I admit, startling to their countrymen who have been accustomed for so long to accept their services (up to and including prison, flogging at the cart-tail, death by torture) in furtherance of the cause of male liberties.[47]

There was more drama in mid-July, when Asquith visited Dublin. Two English suffragettes, Gladys Evans and Mary Leigh, flung a small hatchet into the coach in which Asquith was riding in a procession with his wife and John Redmond, slightly grazing Redmond's cheek. They then started fires with paraffin and gunpowder in the Theatre Royal, where Asquith was due to speak at a home rule meeting next day. Prompt action by patrons prevented serious damage, and the two women were arrested. Frank Sheehy Skeffington succeeded in infiltrating Asquith's meeting disguised as a clergyman, and was swiftly ejected when he started heckling about votes for women.

The English suffragettes' actions sparked off mob violence against women. The *Irish Independent* reported: 'Every woman respectably dressed went in danger of being singled out by the mob as a Suffragette, and a state of panic prevailed.'[48] The IWFL had organised an open-air rally to coincide with Asquith's meeting. The women were surrounded by an angry crowd shouting, 'Throw them in the river.' Several were hurt, including Constance Markievicz. Hanna Sheehy Skeffington later wrote of the English suffragettes' activities:

> unfortunately this time they did not leave the heckling in Irish hands (even the best-meaning English have blind spots where the Sister Isle is concerned)... The Irish Women's Franchise League did not repudiate, whatever our private opinion of the timeliness and manner of the act, because we naturally considered the women strictly within their rights.[49]

The English suffragettes were sentenced to five years' penal servitude, and went on hunger strike on 14 August, demanding to be treated as political prisoners. Four Irish suffragettes, also in Mountjoy, and nearing the end of their sentences, hunger-struck in sympathy. Hanna Sheehy Skeffington recalled:

> Hunger-strike was then a new weapon – we were the first to try it out in Ireland – had we but known, we were the pioneers in a long line. At first, Sinn Fein and its allies regarded the hunger-strike as a womanish thing; some held that politicals should take their medicine without whining and all that, others more sympathetic regarded the fast as a form of suicide and a waste of life. But the public was, at least, not apathetic, and a feeling began to be voiced that there was something unreasonable in refusing women the vote.[50]

Eventually, after being forcibly fed for 46 and 58 days respectively, Mary Leigh and Gladys Evans were released.

The Irish Party remained unmoved by the suffrage cause. In November 1912, the votes of 71 Irish nationalist MPs defeated the Women's Suffrage Bill and women's suffrage amendments to the Home Rule Bill. The following spring, the Irish Party caused a storm of protest when it supported the government's policy of forcible feeding, and also its notorious 'cat and mouse act', under which hunger-striking women were released on licence until they recovered, and were then rearrested.

In January 1913, as the second reading of the Home Rule Bill approached, Margaret Cousins and two other women decided to break the windows of Dublin Castle, 'the official seat of English domination', in order to draw attention to the exclusion of women from the bill.[51] The three were arrested and sentenced to a month's imprisonment. Held in Tullamore jail, County Offaly, they went on hunger strike for political status. Margaret Cousins recalled:

> I always had had a good appetite, and had never before gone without a meal in my life. But so strong was my faith in our cause… that I had no fear of failing in the hunger-strike. I felt even privileged in being in the historic line of the political prisoners of Ireland who fought for proper status, and I could not sell the pass they had won.[52]

They won their demand after a week, and completed their sentence 'in peace and honour'.[53]

Soon Margaret Cousins and her husband James would set off in search of employment, first to England and then India, where they found work in journalism and teaching through Annie Besant, the theosophist and campaigner for Indian home rule. In India the Cousins started a campaign for votes for women, which would succeed before its English equivalent. Margaret became India's first woman magistrate: she agreed in order to open the way for Indian women. In 1932 Margaret once again found herself in prison, this time for a year, for being the main speaker at a 1,000-strong meeting on Madras beach against the emergency laws imposed by the British, which banned free speech.

Pogroms in the shipyards

The growing tension over the Home Rule Bill erupted in violence against Belfast Catholics in July 1912. July was the height of the loyalist marching season, when sectarian bitterness always reached a peak. The spark was provided by exaggerated accounts of an incident at Castledawson, County Derry, on Saturday 29 June, when members of an Ancient Order of Hibernians procession attacked a Presbyterian Sunday school excursion.

Reports appeared in the Monday papers, and next day unionist shipyard workers went on the rampage in the Workman Clark yard, driving most of the 300 to 400 Catholic workers out and leaving several with serious injuries. More violence followed in Harland and Wolff's yard and other workplaces, directed against Protestant socialists as well as Catholics, and on 10 July the chief secretary for Ireland, Augustine Birrell, announced that 2,009 men had left work. The expelled workers included some 300 Protestants.

The persecution went on for months, spreading to many different businesses. A coffee-bar hand at an army canteen contractors told a newspaper how he had been driven out of his job:

> "The staff," said he, "were all of a different religion from me. I am a Catholic, and at meal times all the conversation was directed at me. Disparaging references were made to the Pope... I tried to ignore their taunts... Day after day they became worse and worse, and it was so unbearable that on Sunday week I left the employment, leaving a week's wages behind me. That will tell you how bad things were when I did not wait to get my wages.'[54]

At an extravagant demonstration on 27 July 1912 at Blenheim, the Duke of Marlborough's palace near Oxford, the Tories intensified their threats of unconstitutional resistance. Delegates came from Tory organisations all over the country. The *Times* reported:

> They came to the number of 3,000 in special trains... they were entertained to luncheon in a huge marquee; they were shown the treasures of the great mansion; and, finally, they marched in procession to the noble courtyard of Vanbrugh's ornate pile to hear the speeches of Mr. Bonar Law, Sir Edward Carson, and Mr. F.E. Smith.[55]

Also present was the Duke of Norfolk, England's leading Catholic layman.

The 10,000-strong crowd repeatedly cheered Bonar Law as he threatened the government:

> We regard them as a revolutionary committee which has seized by fraud upon despotic power. (Cheers.) In our opposition to them we shall not be guided by the considerations, we shall not be restrained by the bonds,

which would influence us in an ordinary political struggle. We shall use any means (loud cheers), whatever means seems to us to be most effective.

The audience gave him a standing ovation when he told them:

I can imagine no length of resistance to which Ulster will go in which I shall not be ready to support them and in which they will not be supported by the overwhelming majority of the British people.[56]

Carson declared:

We will shortly challenge the Government to interfere with us if they dare... They may tell us if they like that that is treason; it is not for men who have such stakes as we have at issue to trouble about the cost.[57]

The Tory campaign paid off, spreading unease through Liberal ranks. While Winston Churchill publicly lambasted Bonar Law and Carson for inciting the Orangemen to civil war, privately he wrote to Lloyd George and John Redmond urging a compromise. He wrote to Redmond on 31 August:

The opposition of three or four Ulster counties is the only obstacle which now stands in the way of Home Rule. The Unionist Party have now staked their whole power to fight Home Rule on this foundation. Remove it, and the path in my judgment is absolutely clear. I do not believe there is any real feeling against Home Rule in the Tory Party apart from the Ulster question, but they hate the Government, are bitterly desirous of turning it out, and see in the resistance of Ulster an extra-Parliamentary force which they will not hesitate to use to the full... my general view is just what I told you earlier in the year – namely, that something should be done to afford the characteristically Protestant and Orange counties the option of a moratorium of several years before acceding to the Irish Parliament.[58]

Two weeks later Churchill went public, calling for a scheme of federal devolution involving ten or twelve different legislatures.

The covenant

Brilliantly orchestrated by James Craig, the loyalist campaign intensified with a series of demonstrations across the north of Ireland. These climaxed on 28 September 1912 with a portentous ceremony in which Sir Edward Carson led the signing of a 'Solemn League and Covenant' pledging defiance to home rule. Industrial Belfast came to a halt for the occasion, crowds thronged the city centre and Orange bands played, as men queued to sign at the City Hall. The covenant read:

Being convinced in our consciences that Home Rule would be disastrous to the material well-being of Ulster as well as of the whole of Ireland, subversive of our civil and religious freedom, destructive of our citizenship and perilous to the unity of the Empire, we... do hereby pledge ourselves in solemn Covenant, throughout this our time of threatened calamity, to stand by one another in defending, for ourselves and our children, our cherished position of equal citizenship in the United Kingdom, and in using all means which may be found necessary to defeat the present conspiracy to set up a Home Rule Parliament in Ireland. And in the event of such a Parliament being forced upon us, we further solemnly and mutually pledge ourselves to refuse to recognise its authority.[59]

At the Ulster Hall the women signed a separate declaration associating themselves with the men's stance. Altogether over the next few days 237,368 men, mostly in Ulster but some elsewhere, signed the covenant, while 234,046 women signed the declaration.

Huge crowds cheered Carson as he left Belfast. He crossed the gangway to his boat to the sounds of a revolver salute mounted by unionist shipyard workers, and fireworks burst overhead as the steamer moved into the channel.

The covenant's signatories had committed themselves to oppose home rule for the whole of Ireland, but the unionist leaders soon showed signs that they might retreat to the north and salvage what they could rather than risk losing everything.

The first circuit of the Home Rule Bill was approaching its end: this was the only circuit in which amendments were permitted. In December 1912 Carson persuaded the Ulster Unionist Council to back an amendment which would exclude the province of Ulster – all nine counties – from the bill's scope. Carson moved the amendment on 1 January 1913, and again threatened violence. People asked him, he said, 'What are you going to fight, and who are you going to fight?' He continued:

Can any man measure beforehand – if you once try to drive people out of a Constitution they are satisfied with into another – where the forces of disorder if once let loose will find their objective, or what will be the end of it?[60]

Redmond protested: 'Ireland for us is one entity. It is one land.' He attacked the amendment as

a proposal which would create for all times a sharp, eternal dividing-line between Irish Catholics and Irish Protestants, and a measure which would for all time mean the partition and disintegration of our nation. To that we, as Nationalists, can never submit.[61]

The Liberal cabinet decided that no concessions should be made at this point, and the amendment was defeated by 294 votes to 197. But by now it was clear that senior Liberals, like Carson and the Ulster unionists, were looking for a compromise.

On 16 January the Home Rule Bill passed its third reading in the Commons by 367 to 257 votes. A fortnight later the Lords threw it out by 326 votes to 69. The same month, the Nationalists received a boost when they narrowly won Derry City in a by-election from the Unionists, giving them 17 of Ulster's 33 MPs to the Unionists' 16, and nailing the myth of the Protestant province.

The Ulster Volunteer Force

In January 1913 the Ulster Unionist Council raised the stakes by announcing at its annual meeting that the various clubs which had been drilling would be united into a single Ulster Volunteer Force. This, the UUC decided, would recruit up to 100,000 men aged between 16 and 65. The UUC leaders saw the UVF primarily as a propaganda weapon and did not envisage an actual fight. Lord Dunleath, a County Down landowner, recalled:

> The general idea in the minds of the men who promoted and organized this movement was to give as strong an expression as possible of their resolve to resist the policy of Home Rule. Speeches in and out of Parliament, and Monster Demonstrations in Ulster had apparently failed to interest the English and Scotch electors...[62]

By April 1913, according to police reports, the UVF had enrolled some 41,000 men, and by November it numbered more than 76,000. It was organised across the nine counties into regiments, battalions and sections, and big landowners played a key role. The brigadier commanding the crown forces in the area, Count Gleichen, recalled:

> The large landowners, almost to a man Unionists, and many of them ex-officers of the Regulars or late Militia, peers and commoners, rich men and well-to-do farmers, held local meetings and enrolled nearly all their men in the Volunteer force. They went round their properties night after night, superintending the organization and attending at the drill-halls to see that all was going well.[63]

Loyalists of all classes joined up. A *Yorkshire Post* correspondent, who accompanied Sir Edward Carson when he inspected Antrim volunteers in September 1913, wrote:

> There were in the ranks landowners, business men, mill hands, farmers and their sons, country peasants, gardeners, fishermen, plasterers, and shopkeepers, and in one contingent even... golf greenkeepers...[64]

While the men drilled and paraded, loyalist women mostly joined the nursing corps, though a few became signallers and motorcycle despatch riders.

The UVF's founders hoped that the 80-year-old imperial veteran, Field Marshal Lord Roberts of Kandahar, might become their commander-in-chief. Roberts was busy with other matters, but he helped by finding a distinguished retired officer to fill the post, Lieutenant-General Sir George Richardson. Richardson had been in the Indian Army – the British-officered force of Indian troops which guarded the northwest frontier – and had served under Roberts in his 1880 campaign against rebellious Afghans. He had also commanded the cavalry brigade of the multinational imperialist force that suppressed the Chinese nationalist 'Boxer' rising of 1900.

As soon as the UVF was founded, its leaders began importing arms. Charles Craig, MP for South Antrim and brother of James, said in March 1913 that:

> While it was incumbent on Ulstermen to do their best to educate the
> electorate, he believed that, as an argument, ten thousand pounds spent on
> rifles would be a thousand times stronger than the same amount spent on
> meetings, speeches, and pamphlets.[65]

Lord Leitrim, commander of the UVF's Donegal regiment, used his chauffeur to organise a weekly run of rifles and ammunition, bought in Birmingham and shipped from Glasgow to Derry.

The UVF's prime gun-runner was Major Frederick Crawford, the son of a Belfast chemical manufacturer, who had wandered the world and fought on the British side in the Boer war. Since the 1890s he had been plotting schemes for armed loyalist resistance. One of his unfulfilled projects had been to kidnap Gladstone and maroon him on a Pacific island. Crawford began importing rifles from Hamburg for the UVF. One of his helpers was the Conservative MP for Hammersmith, William Bull, who arranged the renting of the yard and stables of an old inn where Crawford stored several thousand rifles, until the premises were raided by the police.

On 23 September 1913 the Ulster Unionist Council, with Lord Londonderry in the chair, set up a 77-member provisional government which would take power if home rule became law. Carson was appointed chairman of the central authority, and a military council and various sub-committees were set up. The meeting also established an indemnity guarantee fund to compensate members of the UVF and their families for any loss or disability they might suffer in the loyalist cause. Belfast's wealthy businessmen underwrote the fund, which stood at over a million pounds by the end of the year.

The arms committee of the provisional government was known as the 'business committee'. Its chairman was George Clark, a partner in the big Workman and Clark shipbuilding firm. The committee set up a highly efficient gun-running organisation in Britain. Finances were organised through a Belfast stockbroking firm, and other businesses – bleach-works, chemical merchants, and Workman and Clark's yard – received the consignments of arms, which were disguised as industrial materials. In October the police reported to the chief secretary that the UVF had 10,000 rifles ready for issue. But this was nowhere near the number needed to arm all the recruits, and Crawford repeatedly argued that a whole shipload should be brought in at once.

By now the Home Rule Bill had swiftly completed its second circuit. It passed its third reading in the Commons on 7 July 1913 by 352 votes to 243, only to be rejected again by the Lords on 15 July by 302 to 64. The next parliamentary session would start in February 1914: that session would be crucial because, unless special action was taken, the Home Rule Bill would complete its third circuit and become law.

The Dublin lockout

Meanwhile Dublin was being convulsed by a titanic labour struggle in which James Larkin's 'new unionism' confronted Ireland's biggest businessman, William Martin Murphy.

Since 1910 a series of tumultuous strikes had gripped first Britain, then Ireland. In Britain, miners, tailors and tailoresses, seamen, dockers, carters, and railway workers struck in pursuit of union recognition and basic wage demands. In Ireland, strikers included mill girls in Belfast – organised by James Connolly – and women in Dublin's Jacob's biscuit factory, as well as dockers in Belfast and Dublin, foundry workers in Wexford, railway labourers, and numerous skilled tradesmen. Many won their demands, often as a result of the Irish Transport and General Workers' Union's use of the sympathetic strike: dockers refused to load ships with non-union crews, while carters refused to move goods to or from firms where disputes were in progress.

By the summer of 1913, the ITGWU had organised the majority of unskilled workers in Dublin. Two important companies remained untouched. There was the Guinness brewery, run with benevolent paternalism by Lord Iveagh, paying good wages, and providing cheap housing and medical care, and therefore impossible to organise because there was no discontent. And there was the Dublin United Tramways Company, owned by William Martin Murphy, where discontent was plentiful.

Murphy was a tycoon who had made his money constructing electric tramways in Britain, and financing railways in West Africa and South America. Then he turned to Ireland, again building railways and tramways, and buying Ireland's largest daily paper, the *Irish Independent*, as well as Dublin's most prominent hotel, the Imperial, and largest department store. Murphy regarded business as a fascinating game. He was a hard employer but did not believe in sweated labour. At the same time he would not tolerate any interference with his business by his workforce, and consequently was implacably opposed to the spread of the ITGWU. In 1911 he formed a 400-strong Dublin Employers' Federation to try to halt it.

The ITGWU began recruiting in the Tramways Company, and on 19 July 1913 Murphy summoned his employees and told them not to join Larkin's union. They could form a union of their own, he said, but they should not place themselves

> under the feet of an unscrupulous man who claims the right to give you the word of command and issue his orders to you and to use you as tools to make him the labour dictator of Dublin.

Murphy went on: 'I am here to tell you that this word of command will never be given, and if it is, that it will be the Waterloo of Mr. Larkin.'[66] Then on 21 August the company dismissed about 100 workers because they had joined the ITGWU. The union responded by calling the tramway workers out on strike.

Larkin carefully chose the moment for the start of the strike: the morning of 26 August 1913, the first day of the Dublin horse show, a gala event in the social calendar of Ireland's upper classes, when the city would be full of visitors. Just before ten o'clock, trams all over Dublin came to a halt as some 700 drivers and conductors – more than a third of the company's workers – walked off, leaving their passengers stranded.

Tension rose rapidly in the city, as Larkin made fiery speeches to vast crowds, and police fought with strikers. Police baton charges caused many injuries, and on the night of Saturday 30 August they fatally injured a man named James Nolan as he tried to get away. Larkin was arrested for making seditious speeches and then bailed. A public meeting was planned for Sunday 31 August, but the authorities banned it. Before a crowd of 10,000, Larkin burned the proclamation banning the meeting and promised he would speak there.

Larkin was staying with Constance Markievicz in her house in Rathmines, and on the Sunday morning Constance, her husband Casimir, and Helena Molony used their theatrical experience to disguise Larkin as an elderly clergyman. Rooms were booked for the 'clergyman' and his 'niece' – a role played by Nellie Gifford – at Murphy's Imperial Hotel overlooking Sackville Street. Minutes after Larkin appeared on a balcony of the hotel and began speaking, he was arrested. The police turned ferociously on the onlookers. Constance Markievicz was hit on the face and had the buttons torn off her blouse. She recalled:

> I saw a woman trying to get out of the way. She was struck from behind on the head by a policeman with his baton… I saw a barefooted boy with papers hunted and hit about the shoulders as he ran away.[67]

More than 430 people were treated in hospital for their injuries.

Two days later, on 2 September, the desperate condition of Dublin's poor was sharply highlighted when two four-storey tenement houses collapsed, killing seven and injuring many more. The buildings had shops on the ground floor and 16 rooms above, occupied by ten families, more than 40 people. Many of the victims had been in the doorway or street when the front wall fell, burying them.

William Martin Murphy galvanised the Employers' Federation and on 3 September 400 employers met and decided to lock out all their employees who were members of the ITGWU. Some had already begun doing this, including the owner of Jacob's biscuit factory, where 250 women were dismissed after refusing to take off their union badges. Coal merchants, builders, farmers, and timber and cement merchants all locked out workers who belonged to the union, so that by the end of the week some 25,000 workers were affected. Thousands of workers were sacked after refusing to sign a document which read:

> I hereby undertake to carry out all instructions given me by or on behalf of my employers, and further, I agree to immediately resign my membership of the Irish Transport and General Workers Union (if a member) and I further undertake that I will not join or in any way support this union.[68]

The union's headquarters, Liberty Hall, became the centre of a vast welfare operation, with Delia Larkin and Constance Markievicz in charge, to feed and clothe locked-out workers and their families. Liberty Hall had once been a hotel, and in its large basement kitchens Markievicz and a team of volunteers toiled from morning to night to produce food for thousands every day. Nora Connolly, James Connolly's daughter, recalled visiting the Liberty Hall kitchens during the lockout:

> Here the Countess de Markievicz reigned supreme – all meals were prepared under her direction. There were big tubs on the floor; around each were about half a dozen girls peeling potatoes and other vegetables. There were more girls at tables cutting up meat. The Countess kept up a steady march around the boilers as she supervised the cooking. She took me to another kitchen where more delicate food was being prepared for nursing and expectant mothers.[69]

Financial help arrived from workers all over the world, and the British Trades Union Congress made an initial contribution of two shiploads of food.

Writers and artists

The workers' cause awoke passionate sympathy among Irish writers and artists, including W.B. Yeats, AE, and, in London, George Bernard Shaw. In early October AE flayed the employers in an open letter 'to the masters of Dublin', accusing them:

> you determined deliberately, in cold anger, to starve out one-third of the population of this city, to break the manhood of the men by the sight of the suffering of their wives and the hunger of their children...
> Your insolence and ignorance of the rights conceded to workers universally in the modern world were incredible, and as great as your inhumanity.[70]

Most members of the Irish Republican Brotherhood, too, such as Tom Clarke, supported the workers, as did the IRB's paper *Irish Freedom*. The Irish-Ireland activist Padraic Pearse, who would soon join the IRB, and who had Larkin's two sons at his school, St Enda's, wrote:

> My instinct is with the landless man against the lord of the land, and with the breadless man against the master of millions. I may be wrong but I do hold it a most terrible sin that there should be landless men in this island

of waste yet fertile valleys, that there should be breadless men in this city where great fortunes are made and enjoyed.[71]

But Arthur Griffith, the founder of Sinn Féin, which was then in decline, was bitterly opposed to Larkin and showed little sympathy for the affected workers. While Larkin and the labour movement leaders saw English and Irish employers as the same, and expected support from fellow workers in Britain, Griffith discriminated on the basis of nationality, not class. He saw capital and labour as not antagonistic, but complementary, writing: 'the security of one and the efficiency of the other are essential to national prosperity'.[72] He grouped all the English together – imperialists and socialists alike – as bad, and all Irish people as good. In the end, both nationality and class would play a part.

The Irish Catholic hierarchy sided with the employers. Their chance to foment trouble came in mid-October, when three well-intentioned women, including the English suffragette Dora Montefiore, suggested a plan, to which Larkin agreed, to save strikers' children from starvation by sending them to homes in England. Archbishop Walsh of Dublin instigated a crusade against the plan, writing to the papers reminding Dublin Catholic mothers of their 'plain duty':

> I can only put it to them that they can be no longer held worthy of the name of Catholic mothers if they so far forget that duty as to send away their little children to be cared for in a strange land, without security of any kind that those to whom the poor children are to be handed over are Catholics, or indeed are persons of any faith at all.[73]

There were hysterical scenes as priests and laity patrolled railway stations and quaysides, seizing children who appeared to be destined for England.

James Connolly, who was himself unenthusiastic about the scheme, nevertheless rounded on the archbishop, writing that if he was 'as solicitous about the poor bodies of those children as we know you to be about their souls', then he should do everything in his power to make the employers of Dublin negotiate. Connolly announced the abandonment of the scheme, and demanded that the children be cared for in Dublin. He suspended the free meals at Liberty Hall, telling the people to ask the archbishop and the priests for food and clothing. Catholic organisations were flooded with demands, forcing the archbishop to issue urgent appeals for funds and for a settlement of the dispute. Having made his point, Connolly reinstated the free meals at Liberty Hall.

Meanwhile on 27 October 1913 Larkin had been jailed for sedition, and on 1 November 10,000 people gathered at London's Albert Hall to demand his release. Among the speakers was the suffragette Sylvia Pankhurst, who was herself in danger of arrest under the 'cat and mouse' act. She recalled:

> It was a tremendous meeting, crammed with Labourists, Socialists, Suffragists, reformers of every school; the miseries of Dublin had stirred the public heart.[74]

George Lansbury, who had tirelessly publicised the lockout through the *Daily Herald*, took the chair. The speakers – who, according to the *Times*, mostly addressed their audience as 'rebels' – included George Bernard Shaw, Delia Larkin, Dora Montefiore, AE, James Connolly, and the veteran socialist and suffragist Charlotte Despard.[75] Shaw pointed out the contrast, which was causing widespread anger, between the imprisoning of Larkin for sedition and Carson's freedom to organise an army against the government. AE ridiculed the Catholic bishops with bitter irony, saying:

> they have so little concern for the body at all that they assert it is better for children to be starved than to be moved from the Christian atmosphere of the Dublin slums. Dublin is the most Christian city in these islands. Its tottering tenements are holy. The spiritual atmosphere which pervades them is ample compensation for the diseases which are there and the food which is not there.[76]

Soon afterwards, Sylvia Pankhurst and her East London organisation were expelled from the Women's Social and Political Union by her mother and sister, Emmeline and Christabel. They did not like Sylvia's involvement with working class people, and her appearance at the Larkin release meeting was the final straw.

At the meeting, James Connolly had proposed that everyone vote against the Liberal government till Larkin was freed. This tactic bore fruit in by-elections at Linlithgow and Reading: in the first, the Liberals' majority was heavily reduced, while in the second they lost their seat. Larkin was speedily released after serving 17 days of his seven-month sentence.

The leadership of the Irish parliamentary party stood aside from the conflict. Most of the Irish MPs were property owners, and during the entire course of the lockout scarcely any showed the slightest concern for the workers' situation. As a result, the alliance of labour, intellectuals, and 'advanced' nationalists gained in popularity while Redmond, in the words of the London *Times*, was 'compelled to flit almost furtively through the city which he hopes to make the home of his future parliament.'[77] The *Times*' Dublin correspondent observed:

> the new Labour movement is assuming increased political importance… it is winning a good many recruits among the educated and leisured classes… The official Nationalists are seriously alarmed, for they are beginning to realise that the end of the strike will not mean the end of the revolt against the party machine. The new democratic movement has come to stay.[78]

But in the end the fate of the dispute lay in the hands of British trade unionists, whose funds kept the locked-out workers going, and who had the power to use – and in some cases did use – sympathetic strike action to increase the pressure on the Dublin employers.

Connolly and Larkin appealed to the British Trades Union Congress to institute a refusal to handle Dublin goods – some British workers had been doing this since early in the lockout – and also to stop the flow of strike-breakers across the channel. The TUC called a special meeting on 9 December 1913. Some 600 delegates attended, and tempers were high as Larkin attacked the trade union leaders. The ITGWU called for an ultimatum to the employers to settle within a specified time, or face an immediate boycott of Dublin goods. But the British trade union leaders, afraid of industrial war and of departing from the constitutional framework, overwhelmingly defeated the Irish demand. Connolly wrote bitterly later:

> We asked for the isolation of the capitalists of Dublin, and for answer the leaders of the British Labour movement proceeded calmly to isolate the Working Class of Dublin.[79]

The Dublin fighters had 'met their Waterloo' at the 9 December conference, he wrote.[80]

Soon the dispute was over. But though the workers were forced back to work on the employers' terms, it was, in Connolly's words, 'a drawn battle'.[81] The workers had gained a new sense of their own power, and the alliance forged between workers, intellectuals and 'advanced' nationalists was to have a great impact in the years ahead.

The Irish Citizen Army

In November 1913, in the midst of the lockout, two more unofficial armies were born in Ireland, both spurred by the example of the loyalist Ulster Volunteer Force in the north. One, the Irish Citizen Army, was a small force of workers established by the ITGWU. The other, the Irish Volunteers, or Oglaigh na hÉireann, was a much larger body set in motion by the hidden hand of the Irish Republican Brotherhood.

The brutal behaviour of the Dublin police had prompted Larkin and others to consider the need for the workers to arm in self-defence. Captain Jack White, an ebullient and impulsive rebel whose father, Field-Marshal Sir George White, was the famous defender of Ladysmith during the Boer war, offered to drill the strikers. Born in Antrim and educated at Winchester, Jack White had also fought in the Boer war on the British side and was awarded the DSO. Leaving the army some years later, he drifted through various jobs including teaching in Bohemia and logging in Canada, before fetching up in a 'Tolstoyan anarchist colony' in Gloucestershire in 1912.[82] From here he directed his first salvoes, in the form of letters to the press, against Ulster Unionism.

In December 1912 he spoke at a crowded home rule rally in London – hundreds were turned away for lack of space – along with George Bernard Shaw and Sir Arthur Conan Doyle, creator of Sherlock Holmes. He returned to Antrim and in October 1913 he organised an all-Protestant meeting in

Ballymoney against Carsonism. The other speakers were the former diplomat Sir Roger Casement, the historian Alice Stopford Green, and the local Presbyterian minister, the Reverend J.B. Armour, a home ruler widely known for championing tenants' rights. The same month, White was invited to speak in Dublin: there he was angered by the plight of the poor, and soon embraced the revolutionary socialist cause.

His offer to drill the locked-out workers was enthusiastically taken up, and on 13 November 1913, at a rally to celebrate Larkin's release from jail, James Connolly announced plans for a citizen army, saying:

> I am going to talk sedition, the next time we are out for a march, I want to be accompanied by four battalions of trained men. I want them to come with their corporals, sergeants and people to form fours. Why should we not drill and train our men in Dublin as they are doing in Ulster?[83]

Constance Markievicz was one of the first to join, and Roger Casement sent a telegram of support. Thousands enrolled, although many fewer turned out to practise drill. White succeeded in building 'a solid and reliable nucleus', which trained regularly in the grounds of Croydon Park, the union's estate, and defended strikers from police and strikers.

The Irish Volunteers

The young militants of the Irish Republican Brotherhood had their eye on revolution. As the rivalries between Britain and Germany over colonies moved inexorably towards war, IRB leaders saw a great opportunity for Ireland – in time-honoured fashion – to attempt to seize independence by siding with Britain's enemy. The mobilisation of the Ulster Volunteer Force in the north added a new urgency: a force to defend home rule was now necessary. More, the espousal of insurrection by a powerful section of the British establishment had a galvanising effect on nationalist Ireland, which had made no attempt to raise an army since the Fenian rising more than forty years earlier.

The boys of Na Fianna Éireann, the republican scouts, were drilling and marching with increasing proficiency under their new full-time organiser, Liam Mellows, a young member of the IRB. From mid-1913, Dublin IRB members practised military drill in secret under Fianna instructors. The IRB also began to buy a few rifles, but funds were limited.

When in September 1913 the loyalists established a provisional government in the north, the IRB decided it was time to launch an open movement. They wanted a respected figure as the focus, and found their chance when on 1 November the Gaelic League magazine, *An Claidheamh Soluis*, published an article titled 'The North Began', by Eoin MacNeill, a celebrated Celtic archaeologist and professor of early and medieval history at University College, Dublin. MacNeill examined developments in the northeast and observed:

> it appears that the British Army cannot now be used to prevent the
> enrolment, drilling, and reviewing of Volunteers in Ireland. There is
> nothing to prevent the other twenty-eight counties from calling into
> existence citizen forces to hold Ireland "for the Empire."[84]

Bulmer Hobson promptly approached The O'Rahilly, editor of *An
Claidheamh Soluis*, and proposed the formation of a national volunteer
force. O'Rahilly then asked MacNeill if he would preside at a meeting to
discuss forming such a body. MacNeill agreed, and the first of several
preliminary meetings was held on 11 November at Wynn's Hotel. A
provisional committee was set up. Twelve of its 30 members were in the
IRB, though their allegiance was not publicly known. Before three years
were out, six members of the committee – Roger Casement, Eamonn Ceannt,
Con Colbert, Tomás MacDonagh, Padraic Pearse, and Joseph Plunkett –
would be executed for their beliefs.

On 19 November the committee issued a circular announcing that a national
volunteer force was being launched: 'The purpose of the Irish Volunteers
will be to secure and maintain the rights and liberties common to all the
people of Ireland.'[85] The circular stated that enrolment would begin at a
public meeting at the Rotunda at 8 p.m. on 25 November.

The turnout at the Rotunda meeting was stupendous. Tom Clarke – who
had stayed tactfully in the background because he was such a well-known
Fenian – wrote to a Clan-na-Gael member in the USA:

> Such an outpouring of young fellows was never seen. They filled the
> Rink in the Rotunda Gardens (which holds 7,000), filled the adjacent
> garden, overflowed into the large Concert Hall in the Rotunda buildings
> and packed the street around the entrances and afterwards 5,000 people at
> least had tried to get up to the entrance and had to go back home… Then
> the drills – every drill hall packed since… then the class of fellows who
> are there – and the enthusiasm and the National note in the atmosphere!
> – 'tis good to be in Ireland in these times.[86]

Nine days after the Rotunda meeting, on 4 December, the Asquith
government, which had done nothing to stop tens of thousands of rifles
reaching the UVF, issued a ban on the importation of arms into Ireland.

Cumann na mBan

The Volunteers' manifesto had said, 'There will also be work for women to
do,' and had noted the signs that women were 'especially enthusiastic' for
the success of the new organisation.[87] But the women who tried to join met
an uncertain response. Those who attended the Rotunda meeting were
corralled in a special area. Jennie Wyse-Power, a veteran of the Ladies'
Land League, the Inghinidhe and Sinn Féin, recalled: 'The space reserved

for women was crowded to excess by well known women workers in the Irish Ireland cause'.[88]

Inghinidhe members gave in their names to join, but the Volunteers recruited only men. On 30 November Padraic Pearse wrote to Chrissie Doyle, a former Inghinidhe member:

> We have been so busy grappling with the immediate problem of organising and drilling the men... that we have not yet had time to consider in any detail the work of the women. First of all there will be ambulance and Red Cross work for them, and then I think a women's rifle club is desirable. I would not like the idea of women drilling and marching in the ordinary way but there is no reason why they should not learn to shoot.[89]

Women got together to plan a new organisation, and on 5 April 1914 some 100 women gathered at Wynn's Hotel, Dublin, for the inaugural meeting of the Irish Women's Council, soon to be known by its Irish title, Cumann na mBan. Four branches were formed in Dublin, soon followed by more elsewhere. In May Inghinidhe na hÉireann, presided over by Constance Markievicz, decided to work with Cumann na mBan. Thirty members enrolled, forming a separate branch. Their first joint activity was first aid classes.

While the Volunteers drilled, the women of Cumann na mBan set up a Defence of Ireland Fund to arm and equip the men. They were aided by a committee in London headed by the historian Alice Stopford Green. Later they added signalling, the use of weapons, and physical drill to their activities.

One of those who responded to their fund-raising appeal was Wilfrid Scawen Blunt, now 73 years old, who sent £10 along with a letter in which he advised:

> a long experience of British Imperial ways has taught me... that in dealing with British Governments, the best sort of moral force is always material force.[90]

The auxiliary role adopted by Cumann na mBan drew scathing criticism from the suffragists. Hanna Sheehy Skeffington accused the new body of being merely 'an animated collecting box for men', which

> has apparently no function beyond that of a conduit pipe to pour a stream of gold into the coffers of the male organisation, and to be turned off automatically as soon as it has served this mean and subordinate purpose.[91]

But it was the loyalist build-up in the north, coupled with pressure from the Tories and the king, that was causing the government to buckle.

Since May 1912 the Tories had been trying to persuade King George V to block the Home Rule Bill and bring down the government. This would mean a drastic breach with the conventions of constitutional monarchy, reviving powers which had lain dormant for many years. On 4 May 1912 Bonar Law told the king that when the Home Rule Bill was passed in 1914, he would have a choice:

> you must either accept the Home Rule Bill or dismiss your Ministers and choose others who will support you in vetoing it – and in either case half your subjects will think you have acted against them.[92]

At this, the king reportedly 'turned red', and Bonar Law said afterwards: 'I think I have given the king the worst five minutes that he has had for a long time.'[93] In September Bonar Law repeated his advice in a memorandum to the king.

The king became increasingly agitated as the Tories bombarded him with complaints and advice. In July 1913 Bonar Law and Lord Lansdowne – a senior Tory with huge estates in the south and west of Ireland – increased the pressure. They sent him a memorandum suggesting he urge Asquith to dissolve parliament: if Asquith refused, the king should dismiss him and replace him with someone more amenable. The king – who was becoming ill with worry – took their advice, and addressed lengthy memoranda to Asquith setting out the Tory arguments and stressing the difficulties of his position. He also asked whether Asquith proposed to use the army to suppress disorder. Pointing out that soldiers 'may have strong feelings on the Irish question', he asked:

> Will it be wise, will it be fair to the Sovereign as head of the Army, to subject the discipline, and indeed the loyalty of his troops, to such a strain?[94]

Asquith refused to dissolve parliament, but did decide to talk to the Tories to see if a compromise could be reached. Between October and December he had three meetings with Bonar Law. These focused on the possibility of excluding Ulster, or part of it, from the Home Rule Bill.

Leaving 'Ulster' out

By now senior Tories, including Bonar Law and Carson, were privately resigned to the fact that they could not oust the Liberal government nor stop the Home Rule Bill, but might be able to salvage Ulster, or part of it. They had intended the arming of 'Ulster' to be the means of blocking home rule throughout Ireland, but now 'Ulster' itself had become their goal. Carson wrote to Bonar Law on 20 September 1913:

> on the whole things are shaping towards a desire to settle on the terms of leaving 'Ulster' out. A difficulty arises as to defining Ulster and my own view is that the whole of Ulster should be excluded but the minimum would be the 6 Plantation counties and for that a good case could be made. The South and West would present a difficulty and it might be that I could not agree to their abandonment though I feel certain it would be the best settlement if Home Rule is inevitable...[95]

Asquith and Bonar Law discussed various schemes for excluding 'Ulster' – 'the actual definition of Ulster for this purpose being for the moment postponed', as Asquith put it.[96] While Asquith favoured excluding only the four northeastern counties, Bonar Law hinted that the Tories would accept a minimum of six counties. Bonar Law specifically rejected 'home rule within home rule' – the area having its own parliament subject to a Dublin parliament – and insisted that Westminster should legislate for the excluded area. He opposed the idea of 'Ulster' being automatically included in a home-ruled Ireland after a certain number of years: rather, the people of the area should be able to vote on the question after it had been excluded for at least ten years.

Within the Liberal cabinet, the balance was shifting in favour of exclusion. In mid-November Lloyd George proposed a scheme for the temporary exclusion of a certain area for five or six years, after which it would be automatically included. This plan, he argued, would 'knock all props from under Carson's rebellion'.[97] There would be no point in violent resistance to a change that was not coming for several years, and there would be two British general elections in the intervening period which would give a chance of reconsidering the automatic inclusion of the area.

Next Asquith met Sir Edward Carson, and tried unsuccessfully to persuade him to accept a hybrid scheme in which an undefined area, 'statutory Ulster', would have special powers of veto in the Irish parliament. Its MPs would be able to prevent Irish laws from applying in the area, subject to the approval of the Westminster government. Asquith's aim was to formulate an exclusion scheme that would be palatable to the Irish nationalists. He wrote later to Carson that his 'statutory Ulster' suggestions

> were conceived with the double purpose of giving to the Ulster majority the substance of what they claim, while doing as little violence as possible to Nationalist sentiment. They amounted roughly (as we said in conversation) to 'veiled exclusion.'[98]

Carson refused to have any truck with Asquith's idea on the grounds that, however guarded, the basis was the inclusion of Ulster in the Irish parliament. What Carson wanted was, in Asquith's phrase, 'naked exclusion'.[99] On 10 January 1914 Carson stressed in a letter to Asquith:

> I thought that it was always apparent that when the exclusion of Ulster was discussed, I meant that Ulster should remain as at present under the Imp. Parlmt. & that a Dublin Parlmt. should have no legislative powers within the excluded area. Ulster wd. therefore send no members to the Dublin Parlmt., but would continue as at present to send members to the Imp. Parlmt.[100]

Asquith's negotiations with the Tories came to nothing, but the course was now set firmly towards a compromise based on exclusion. Only the Irish nationalists stood in the way. In mid-November 1913 Asquith had tried to persuade Redmond of the need for a compromise, saying he feared a 'baptism of blood' for home rule.[101] Redmond rejected Lloyd George's exclusion plan, but said he might accept 'home rule within home rule'. He insisted that the government should not offer a compromise, arguing that

> I feel strongly that it is cruel to Ireland, and cruel even to the Orangemen, to give them the impression that their movement has the power of intimidating English opinion.[102]

On 2 February 1914 Asquith increased the pressure on Redmond by revealing that the Tories were recklessly plotting to obstruct the passage of the army annual bill unless they were assured that the army was not going to be used against 'Ulster'. This bill was passed each year: if it failed to go through, the government would be unable to control or pay the army. Such a crisis, Asquith suggested, would probably result in a general election, which the Tories would win, and home rule would be postponed for many years.

Though Asquith himself probably did not expect the Tories to carry the plot through, he found the threat an effective means of intimidating Redmond, saying he 'shivered visibly and was a good deal perturbed' when told the news.[103]

Soon afterwards Lloyd George revived his exclusion scheme, this time with a refinement that became known as the 'county option': if one-tenth of the voters in any Irish county demanded it, that county would be able to vote itself out of home rule 'for X years'. At the end of that period, the county would automatically be incorporated under a Dublin parliament unless the Westminster parliament decided otherwise. This plan became the basis of the government's thinking, replacing Asquith's earlier preference for some form of 'home rule within home rule'.

The Irish nationalist leaders, however, were not happy. Joseph Devlin, MP for West Belfast and leader of the Ulster nationalists, made an offer – originally suggested by Sir Horace Plunkett – to allow 'Ulster' 'to claim exclusion after, say, ten years if her representatives were not satisfied with their treatment in the Irish Parliament.'[104] Devlin also offered 'Ulster' extra representation in an Irish parliament.

But on 2 March, under further pressure from Asquith, Redmond took the fateful step of conceding the principle of exclusion. He accepted the 'county option', with the period of exclusion 'limited to three years, covering the period when a General Election must take place'.[105] Joseph Devlin travelled to the north of Ireland and persuaded Catholic bishops and other influential people to support the three-year exclusion plan. The three-year exclusion period was a cynical bait for the nationalists, and foredoomed to rejection by the Tories. The king wrote to Asquith protesting:

> I must confess that I have grave fears that the proposed limit .. will not be acceptable to Ulster. This will make Sir Edward Carson's position an almost impossible one…[106]

Asquith then deputed Augustine Birrell, the chief secretary for Ireland, to tell Redmond the period must be extended. Redmond reluctantly agreed first to a five-year exclusion period, then, after more pressure, to six years. Six years was essential, Asquith argued, to ensure that a general election would intervene before the opted-out counties were automatically included under a Dublin parliament. The reasoning behind this was that a new government could halt the process, making exclusion permanent.

The government decided to incorporate the exclusion proposal not into the Home Rule Bill itself, which might give the Tories an opportunity to wreck the whole bill, but into a separate amending bill, so that even if the amending bill were rejected, the Home Rule Bill could still go ahead.

On 9 March 1914 Asquith moved the second reading of the final circuit of the Home Rule Bill. Alterations were necessary, he said, because home rule as embodied in the bill brought 'the prospect of acute dissension and even of civil strife' in Ulster, while if the bill were shipwrecked, there was 'at least an equally formidable outlook' in Ireland.[107] Asquith said that he himself would have preferred the 'home rule within home rule' option, or Sir Horace Plunkett's proposal to allow a dissatisfied 'Ulster' to exclude itself after 10 years. But his efforts at compromise, and Redmond's sacrifice, were in vain, since the Tories rejected them out of hand.

Carson reiterated the 'loathing of every Unionist' throughout Ireland for the Home Rule Bill, but then conceded:

> I frankly admit we have made some advance this afternoon by the acknowledgment of the principle of exclusion. That, in my opinion, is an important matter, because the moment you admit the principle of exclusion the details of the principle may be a matter that may be worked out by negotiation...

But he went on to dismiss outright the six-year time limit: 'Ulster wants this question settled now and for ever. We do not want sentence of death with a stay of execution for six years.'[108]

There was considerable dismay in Ireland at Redmond's concession of exclusion, especially among 'advanced nationalists' and socialists, and among nationalists in the north, who would be the most drastically affected.

Redmond was already doing his utmost to suppress the rising tide of militancy among northern nationalists. At the end of February he had succeeded in persuading Derry nationalists, against their better judgement, to call off a great public meeting planned for 14 March. Then on 19 March he heard that the Irish Volunteers were to march two days later in Derry City, and fired off telegrams begging – successfully – for the parade to be abandoned. Meanwhile up and down the country the United Irish League and the Ancient Order of Hibernians, which supported the Irish parliamentary party, organised resolutions backing the exclusion proposal.

But militant nationalists felt very differently. The Irish Republican Brotherhood's paper, *Irish Freedom*, thundered:

> If this nation is to go down, let it go down gallantly as becomes its history, let it go down fighting, but let it not sink into the abjectness of carving a slice out of itself and handing it over to England.[109]

Arthur Griffith's paper *Sinn Féin* argued vehemently and at length against partition, advising:

> The best thing Ireland can do… is to make it manifest that no partition of Ireland, disguised as Home Rule, will be quietly submitted to… Irish Nationalism is based on the indissoluble unity of the whole people of this island in one community.[110]

James Connolly, who as the ITGWU organiser in Belfast had experienced at first hand the bigotry of Orangeism and the profound divisions in the working class, protested bitterly against the prospect of partition. He organised meetings in Belfast, and on his initiative the Irish Trades Union Congress passed a resolution stating that partition would

> intensify the divisions at present existing and destroy all our hopes of uniting the workers of Ulster with those of Munster, Leinster and Connaught on the basis of their industrial and economic interests.[111]

The ITUC organised a demonstration, and sent deputations to plead in vain with the chief secretary, Augustine Birrell, and with John Redmond. It also urged the British Labour Party to oppose exclusion, again without success, leading Connolly to condemn 'the love embraces which take place between the Parliamentary Labour Party and our deadliest enemies – the Home Rule Party'.[112]

Connolly contributed a stream of articles to socialist newspapers warning of the appalling consequences of partition, and denouncing 'the depths of betrayal to which the so called Nationalist politicians are willing to sink.'[113] Writing in the *Irish Worker* of 14 March, he attacked the 'trusted guardians of the people' for agreeing

> to sacrifice to the bigoted enemy the unity of the nation and along with it the lives, liberties and hopes of that portion of the nation which in the midst of the most hostile surroundings have fought to keep the faith in things national and progressive.

He continued:

> Such a scheme as that agreed to by Redmond and Devlin, the betrayal of the national democracy of industrial Ulster would mean a carnival of reaction both North and South, would set back the wheels of progress, would destroy the oncoming unity of the Irish Labour movement, and paralyse all advanced movements whilst it endured.

The Citizen Army reorganised

The Irish Citizen Army had lost impetus when the Dublin lockout ended, but the quickening political pace now prompted a reorganisation. A committee was elected, with the impetuous Captain Jack White as chairman: he soon left 'in a huff', as he put it, and joined the Irish Volunteers, and James Larkin was elected to replace him. The future playwright Sean O'Casey, a former IRB member and somewhat cantankerous figure, was secretary, and Constance Markievicz was one of the treasurers. A constitution, drafted by O'Casey, was adopted, which established:

> That the first and last principle of the Irish Citizen Army is the avowal that the ownership of Ireland, moral and material, is vested of right in the people of Ireland.
>
> That the Irish Citizen Army shall stand for the absolute unity of Irish nationhood, and shall support the rights and liberties of the democracies of all nations.
>
> That one of its objects shall be to sink all differences of birth, property and creed under the common name of the Irish People.[114]

On 22 March a public meeting was held at Liberty Hall, presided over by Jim Larkin, who expressed the hope that all members of the ITGWU would immediately join the Irish Citizen Army. Uniforms were acquired – dark green with a slouch hat fastened with the union's 'red hand' badge – and a banner bearing the design of the starry plough. Drilling, rifle-training and numerous social events proceeded at Croydon Park, while recruitment meetings in and around Dublin steadily built up the organisation, till it was a thousand strong.

Larkin was soon to leave the Irish scene. In late 1914 he travelled to the USA for a lecture tour. It was meant to be a short trip, but he did not return till 1923. After he left, James Connolly became the key figure in the Irish labour movement, and took over the command of the Irish Citizen Army. Larkin lived in poverty in the USA, lecturing, working as a union organiser, and passionately backing the Bolshevik revolution of 1917. In late 1919, during the 'red scare', he was arrested for allegedly advocating the violent overthrow of the US government. Convicted the following spring, he was imprisoned till January 1923, and returned to Ireland soon afterwards.

The Curragh mutiny

The Tories' rejection of a compromise based on exclusion set off a chain of events, part high drama and part farce, that became known as the 'Curragh mutiny'. The government began to make moves – albeit tentative and unco-ordinated – to limit the loyalist mobilisation. In the process, they put the army's loyalty fatally to the test.

Since the introduction of the Home Rule Bill in May 1912, the Tories had been prophesying that the army would not or could not be used against 'Ulster', and had in effect been inciting them to refuse to move. There was widespread sympathy in the officer class, from the highest reaches of the War Office downwards, for the loyalist cause. In July 1913 the editor of the

Times asked his military correspondent to look into the effects of the government's Irish policy on army morale, noting:

> I hear already of officers preparing to go and fight for Ulster, and others preparing to send in their papers and get out of the whole business, and of others arguing that it is the business of a soldier to obey constituted authority...[115]

In September 1913 Brigadier John Gough, whose brother Hubert was commanding the Third Cavalry Brigade at the Curragh Camp near Dublin, was asked his views by the king's private secretary. He replied that he thought perhaps 40 to 60 per cent of officers would refuse to serve against 'Ulster'. He personally objected not to home rule as such, but to the type of government he believed the nationalists would bring in: it would not be loyal or honest, and it would be priest-ridden. He noted:

> The idea of these disloyal men becoming our rulers was an outrage to every decent feeling I possessed... we would have corruption & graft, & probably the country would be inundated with unscrupulous Irish American low class politicians... I could not tolerate the possibility of having a priest-ridden government.[116]

Within the War Office, the loyalists' key ally was Major-General Henry Wilson, director of military operations. From an Anglo-Irish family, Wilson was described by Asquith as 'voluble, impetuous, and an indefatigable intriguer.'[117] In November 1913 Wilson recorded in his diary that he had told Sir John French, the commander of the imperial general staff, 'that I could not fire on the North at the dictation of Redmond'. Next day Wilson told the Tory leader Bonar Law 'that if we were ordered to coerce Ulster there would be wholesale defection.'[118]

On Wednesday 11 March 1914, two days after the Tories rejected exclusion, the Liberal cabinet met and was presented with police reports estimating that the UVF had 80,000 men and 17,000 weapons. The cabinet considered what to do about rumours that the UVF was planning to raid arms depots in the north, and decided to set up a sub-committee to formulate a response. In practice, the committee consisted of Colonel John Seely, the flamboyant secretary of state for war, and Winston Churchill, first lord of the admiralty.

On 14 March Churchill raised the temperature with a belligerent speech which was widely interpreted as a declaration of war on 'Ulster'. There were, he said, 'worse things than bloodshed even on an extended scale'. He went on:

> if the Government and the Parliament of this great country and greater Empire are to be exposed to menace and brutality... then I can only say to you, 'Let us go forward together and put these grave matters to the proof!'[119]

Also on 14 March the War Office sent a letter to Lieutenant-General Sir

Arthur Paget, commander-in-chief in Ireland, instructing him that because

> attempts may be made in various parts of Ireland by evil-disposed persons
> to obtain possession of arms, ammunition, and other Government stores,
> it is considered advisable that you should at once take special precautions
> for safeguarding depots and other places where arms or stores are kept...
>
> It appears from the information received that Armagh, Omagh,
> Carrickfergus and Enniskillen are insufficiently guarded, being specially
> liable to attack.[120]

Paget's reply indicated that he was responding hesitantly to the instructions, so he was summoned to London for meetings on 18 and 19 March. At these, it was decided that troops should immediately be sent to reinforce six towns: Dundalk and Newry were added to the earlier list.

By now, Carson and the Tories were thoroughly roused, kept abreast of the situation by General Henry Wilson. In the House of Commons on 19 March, Carson denounced the government's plans to deploy troops against 'Ulster'. To resounding Tory cheers, he stalked out dramatically and headed for the boat-train at Euston amid rumours that he was about to set up a provisional government in Belfast.

The same day Winston Churchill ordered a spate of naval movements. He sent two warships from Bantry Bay to the northeast of Ireland, and telegraphed the vice-admiral commanding the third battle squadron off the coast of Spain, ordering the squadron to proceed to Lamlash on the island of Arran, on Scotland's west coast and only some 60 miles from Belfast.

Also on a train to Ireland on the night of 19 March 1914 was the agitated commander-in-chief, Sir Arthur Paget, heading for Dublin. Paget had extracted an unwritten commitment from Colonel Seely, the secretary of state for war, that, in Seely's words:

> in the few exceptional cases where officers have direct family connection
> with the disturbed area in Ulster, so that in the event of serious trouble
> arising their future private relations might be irretrievably compromised
> if they were engaged with our troops, they should be permitted to remain
> behind...
>
> In all other cases... any officer hesitating to comply with orders or
> threatening to resign should be removed.[121]

Paget met seven senior officers on 20 March in Dublin, and presented the situation in highly alarmist terms, talking of the whole country being 'ablaze' in 24 hours. He informed them of the concession for officers with families in Ulster, and said that the rest must let him know whether they would prefer to do their duty or accept dismissal.

Brigadier-General Hubert Gough telegraphed his brother Johnnie in England:

> Have been offered dismissal service or undertake operations against Ulster.
> Two hours to decide. First means ruin of army as others will follow... Am
> taking first contingency.[122]

Gough relayed Paget's message to his cavalry officers at the Curragh, and about 60 of them decided to resign along with him. Some 60 infantry officers wanted to resign too. Officers' messes throughout Ireland were gripped by near-hysteria. A second lieutenant in the King's Own Scottish Borderers, based in Dublin, wrote to his father of the reaction to the ultimatum:

> We all sat for an hour and a half in the ante room discussing the situation and trying to make up our minds. We all loathed the idea of going to Ulster for the sake of a few dirty Nationalists who loathe the army and are most unloyal to anything to do with Britain & yet we wondered what on earth we should do if we left.[123]

The alarmed politicians and military chiefs in London ordered Hubert Gough and his three colonels to come at once. They did so, but Gough, advised by his brother Johnnie and General Henry Wilson, and supported by the Tory leader Bonar Law, swiftly outmanoeuvred the government. Summoned to the War Office on Monday 23 March, Gough refused to go back to Ireland and resume normal duties unless he was provided with a written guarantee that the army would never be used to impose home rule on 'Ulster'. Colonel Seely eventually agreed. A draft statement was produced, and amended by Asquith. This merely stated that the cavalry officers' resignations had been due to a misunderstanding, that it was 'the duty of all soldiers to obey lawful commands', and that the officers had never intended to disobey such commands. But Seely then added two paragraphs of his own, without consulting Asquith:

> His Majesty's Government must retain their right to use all the forces of the Crown in Ireland, or elsewhere, to maintain law and order and to support the civil power in the ordinary execution of its duty.
>
> But they have no intention whatever of taking advantage of this right to crush political opposition to the policy or principles of the Home Rule Bill.[124]

Next General Henry Wilson and Gough drafted a note of clarification which Gough added to the bottom of the document:

> We understand the reading of the last paragraph to be that the troops under our command will not be called upon to enforce the present Home Rule Bill on Ulster, and that we can so assure our officers.

Sir John French, chief of the imperial general staff, added: 'This is how I read it.'[125]

When Asquith saw the new paragraphs, he demanded that they be struck out. But it was too late: Gough had already left for Ireland. Gough thwarted attempts to retrieve the document by depositing it with a solicitor and putting it in trust for his eldest daughter.

The government's apparent capitulation to Gough and his colonels provoked bitter attacks in the House of Commons. One of their most vociferous critics was Labour MP John Ward, who declared on Monday 23 March:

> This Debate is the best illustration that we workmen have ever had in this House that all the talk about there being one and the same law for the rich and the poor is all a miserable hypocrisy. Hon. Gentlemen belonging to the wealthy classes have no more intention of obeying the law that is against their interests than they have of flying to the moon.[126]

Ward returned to the attack next day, going to the heart of the matter:

> We have here and now unquestionably to decide whether we are going to maintain the discipline of the army as a neutral force… or whether for the future this House, when elected by the people, must go to a committee of officers and ask that military junta whether this is a subject that will be allowed to be put into execution…[127]

Himself a former soldier, Ward went on to read out a syndicalist manifesto addressed to British troops:

> "Often you are called upon to fire on unarmed and defenceless crowds of men and women. You are asked to do so in order that your own flesh and blood may be bought and sold cheap that others may be rich. We therefore ask you now to resolve that from this day forward you will never fire a shot against your own class, that you will follow the example of the generals and other officers in Ireland who have refused to take risks against their class interests."[128]

The Labour MP for Derby, J.H. Thomas of the Railway Servants' Union, said that if the Tories' doctrine held good, his duty would be to tell the railwaymen to spend the union's half-million of capital on arms and ammunition. Such speeches were enthusiastically received by the Liberals, and reportedly aroused much sympathy in the rank and file of the army.

To save his government, Asquith repudiated the added paragraphs, and French and Seely resigned, as did the adjutant general. But the damage was already done. The government's inability to use the army against the loyalists was now patently clear.

Gough's stand had won support throughout the officer class, from the War Office downwards, and across England and Scotland as well as Ireland. In coming months, disaffection remained widespread. In mid-April Major-General Sir Charles Fergusson reported that the troops 'are not to be depended on to coerce Ulster into accepting the Home Rule Bill.'[129] From now on, troops would be used only against nationalists.

The Tory-loyalist-military alliance had defied the government and spurned the conventions of parliamentary politics, and by doing so they had achieved their aims. The Russian revolutionary Vladimir Ilyich Lenin dramatically declared that the Curragh incident would mark

> a world-historical turning point, when the noble landlords of England, smashing the English Constitution and the English law to atoms, gave an excellent lesson in class struggle.[130]

For the leaders of the Irish Volunteers the message was clear. As Eoin MacNeill and Roger Casement pointed out in a letter published in the *Irish Independent* on 28 March 1914, the Irish people would now have to face the fact that they could not hope to get their independence from England: they would have to take it.

Arson

Ironically the only group actually to take to open warfare in Ireland in the tempestuous spring of 1914 was neither loyalists nor nationalists, but militant women. Suffragettes in the north of Ireland were outraged because Sir Edward Carson had reneged on earlier promises to them. In September 1913 Carson and the Ulster Unionist Council had promised that under an Ulster government women would have the right to vote, and had been lavishly praised by Christabel Pankhurst and other suffragettes. But in March 1914 matters changed.

On 6 March a deputation of women from the north of Ireland travelled to London to see Carson. They were led by Dorothy Evans, Belfast organiser for the Women's Social and Political Union, and a former physical culture teacher in England. After the women had sat on Carson's doorstep from Friday to Monday, he finally admitted them, but only to tell them that he would not introduce votes for women because his colleagues disagreed on the issue.

Spurred by the militant lawlessness of the Tory-loyalist camp, and angered that the loyalists, unlike themselves, enjoyed immunity from punishment, the women followed the example of their sisters in England and embarked on a major campaign of arson. Unlike the Dublin suffragettes, they attacked private rather than government property. Between 27 March 1914 and the end of July, they burned down several large houses, a tea house, a sports pavilion and a race stand, mainly around Belfast and in County Down. They exploded a bomb in Lisburn's Protestant cathedral, which resulted in a mob attacking the house of a local suffragette, Mrs Metge. They even set fire to hospitals set up for the use of the Ulster Volunteer Force in the event of civil war.

Huge sums were paid out in damages. Major-General Sir Hugh McCalmont, the former MP for East Antrim, in whose grounds the UVF had been drilling, received £11,000 for the destruction of his home, Abbeylands. The executors of the deceased Catholic bishop of Down and Connor were awarded £20,000 for his palace, Orlands House, which had also been burned down. Ballymenoch House, near Belfast, burned down on 3 July, was also valued at £20,000. Altogether County Antrim paid out £92,000.

After the attempt to burn Lisburn Cathedral, Dorothy Evans and another suffragette, Maud Muir, were taken to court on 8 April charged with possession of explosives. They disrupted the court proceedings by struggling to leave and by constant speech-making, demanding to know why Carson and his friends were not arrested, since they were obviously guilty of the same offence. They added hunger-striking to their obstructive techniques, and when released they resumed their militancy.

The arch-rebel Carson was given police protection from the suffragettes when he visited the north of Ireland, as were loyalist demonstrators in London, who were mobbed by women angry that the loyalists, but not themselves, were allowed to rally in Hyde Park.

The Larne gun-running

The loyalists' immunity in the wake of the Curragh mutiny was dramatically illustrated when the authorities turned a blind eye to a substantial gun-running operation in April 1914.

The Ulster Volunteer Force by now numbered some 90,000 and was highly organised, but there were far too few guns to go round. On 20 January 1914 Sir Edward Carson convened a meeting in Belfast to discuss the arms question. The meeting considered a plan suggested by the gun-runner Major Fred Crawford to buy at least 20,000 rifles and two million rounds of ammunition in Hamburg and smuggle them into Ireland in one boatload. Carson gave his blessing to the plan, leaving James Craig in charge of putting it into effect. In February Crawford called on Carson at his London home, 5 Eaton Place, to make certain of his support. Crawford later described the meeting:

> We were alone. Sir Edward was sitting opposite to me. When I had finished his face was stern and grim; and there was a glint in his eye. He rose to his full height, looking me in the eye; he advanced to where I was sitting and stared down at me, and shook his clenched fist in my face, and said in a steady, determined voice, which thrilled me and which I shall never forget: "Crawford, I'll see you through this business, if I should have to go to prison for it." I rose from my chair; I held out my hand and said, "Sir Edward, that is all I want. I leave tonight."[131]

Some of the money for the scheme almost certainly came from a substantial fund raised by Lord Milner, a leading imperialist, from his wealthy friends. Donors included Rudyard Kipling, who sent £30,000, as well as Lords Iveagh and Rothschild, and the Duke of Bedford. Crawford's expedition would cost some £60,000 to £70,000.

In Hamburg, Crawford arranged to buy 20,000 rifles plus ammunition from his regular supplier, a Jewish businessman named Bruno Spiro, who was later to die in a Nazi concentration camp. He also arranged to take 4,600 rifles which Spiro was holding for him. It seems likely that the German government connived at the operation, glad to see Britain in difficulty.

Loyalist leaders had expressed pro-German sympathies, and German military strategists saw the loyalists as potential allies in the enemy's camp in the event of war.

Crawford began the complicated task of shipping the guns to Ireland, aided by a ship's captain and chief engineer who had been specially released by their employers, the Antrim Iron Ore Steamship Company. The smuggling operation was fraught with adventures and mishaps, and was bathed in a glare of publicity almost as soon as it began. On 31 March 1914 near the Baltic island of Langeland, the rifles were transferred from a lighter that had carried them through the Kiel Canal to the *Fanny*, the steamer Crawford had acquired. The Danish authorities grew suspicious and removed both vessels' papers. The *Fanny* and the tug-drawn lighter departed in secret, paperless, next morning, but made headlines in the British press.

On the night of 19 April in the Irish Sea the guns were transferred from the *Fanny* to a less conspicuous boat, the *Clydevalley*, which Crawford renamed the *Mountjoy II* after the ship that broke the blockade at the siege of Derry in 1689.

On the night of Friday 24 April, the *Mountjoy II* landed the guns at Larne. A vast mobilisation of the UVF took place that night, and telegraph and telephone connections to the town were broken by earthing the wires. Police and coastguards were shut into their barracks and guarded. Lord Massereene threw a UVF cordon right round the town, while a huge convoy of cars assembled at Lord Templetown's estate before leaving to collect the guns. The arrangements for the landing were made by the chairman of the company which owned the harbour, who was also a UVF battalion commander. Some 11,000 rifles were unloaded by crane onto the quayside, then picked up by the waiting cars. The remainder of the guns were taken by the *Mountjoy II* and two other boats to Donaghadee, Belfast and Bangor. The authorities did nothing to interfere with the huge operation, and the guns were safely dispersed across the north. Count Gleichen, commander of the 15th Infantry Brigade at Belfast, recalled:

> [General] Macready turned up from the War Office on the Sunday evening, full of desire to make the Ulster Volunteer Force laugh on the wrong side of their mouths. But after talking it over with us, I think that he was not quite so cocksure of being able to do it.. I pointed out... that it was not the business of us soldiers to stop gun-running or smuggling...[132]

Gleichen evidently found the gun-running quite amusing, telling later how

> in spending a week-end at Antrim Castle I went to fetch some lawn-tennis balls from the long box in the hall in which they were usually kept. But their place had been taken by something much more reprehensible. I shall never forget the noble owner's face when I acquainted him with the result of my search![133]

In London on four successive mornings the cabinet discussed what to do, and then did nothing, except send a cruiser and 18 destroyers to patrol the Irish Sea. The socialist James Connolly commented scathingly:

> Can anyone believe that if railway stations were seized, roads held up, coastguards imprisoned and telegraph systems interfered with by Nationalists or Labour men, that at least 1000 arrests would not have been made the next morning? Evidence is difficult to get, they say. Evidence be hanged! If Nationalists or Labour men were the culprits, the Liberal Government would have made the arrests first and looked for evidence afterwards.[134]

Amending the amending bill

The twin incidents of the Curragh mutiny and the Larne gun-running confirmed the government's inability to coerce 'Ulster'. In effect, where before the government had been armed and the loyalists unarmed, the opposite was now the case. In May 1914 General Sir Nevil Macready, now overseeing the north but based at the War Office in London, went to see Asquith seeking instructions on how to handle the rising tension: Asquith told him to do nothing if Carson declared a provisional government or if the mayor of Belfast deployed the UVF.

Asquith once again began trying to reach a compromise with the Tories, and secretly met Carson and Bonar Law. On 12 May he announced that a bill to amend the Home Rule Bill would be introduced in the House of Lords. On 25 May, after stormy debates, the Home Rule Bill passed its third reading in the House of Commons. Its final circuit was complete, and unless exceptional circumstances intervened it would become law.

On 23 June Lord Crewe introduced the promised amending bill in the House of Lords. It embodied Asquith's previous proposal: Ulster counties should be allowed to vote themselves out of home rule for six years. At the end of that period, parliament would consider whether any change should be made – there would be no automatic inclusion. But the Tory lords, led by William Waldegrave Palmer, the Earl of Selborne, and by the Marquess of Lansdowne, a former foreign secretary who had huge estates in the south of Ireland, proceeded to wreck the bill. They amended it so that it proposed the permanent exclusion of all nine counties of Ulster, a position that a majority in the Commons would certainly reject.

Asquith now faced a serious problem. The Home Rule Bill would shortly become law, but how was it to be implemented? The government could hardly attempt to force home rule on the loyalists when it had publicly accepted the idea of some form of exclusion. Hysterical speculation about imminent civil war in Ireland, and rising tensions in Europe, made a solution all the more urgent.

Asquith initiated a web of private meetings, with government representatives seeing Redmond and Carson separately, in an effort to get agreement in advance of a formal conference. Asquith tried to narrow the issue to geography. Bending to loyalist demands, he was willing to abandon the six-year time limit and the county-by-county vote, and hoped that all parties might agree to the exclusion of a five or five-and-a-half county bloc. This would require agreement on partitioning Tyrone or Fermanagh, which had Catholic majorities of 55 per cent and 56 per cent respectively.

The king had been pressing Asquith to bring Redmond and Carson together, and on 16 July Asquith suggested to the king that a conference should be held at Buckingham Palace. The conference ran from 21 to 24 July, ending in deadlock. It was attended by Asquith and Lloyd George for the Liberals, John Redmond and John Dillon for the Irish Nationalists, and Bonar Law, Lord Lansdowne, Sir Edward Carson and James Craig for the Tories and loyalists. Suffragettes picketed the conference with posters declaring, 'The King must call a conference on Votes for Women'.

The meeting decided to discuss two subjects: first area, then time limit. But it swiftly ran into insuperable difficulties on the first, and got no further.

For Asquith, the problem resolved into just one issue, and he was disdainfully impatient towards the failure of the Irish parties to agree. On 22 July he wrote to his confidante, Venetia Stanley:

> We sat again this morning for an hour and a half, discussing maps and figures, and always getting back to that most damnable creation of the perverted ingenuity of man – the County of Tyrone. The extraordinary feature of the discussion was the complete agreement (in principle) of Redmond & Carson. Each said 'I must have the whole of Tyrone, or die; but I quite understand why you say the same.' The Speaker who incarnates bluff unimaginative English sense, of course cut in: 'When each of two people say they must have the whole, why not cut it in half?' They wd. neither of them look at such a suggestion.[135]

But for both Redmond and Carson the issue was more complicated. After each session, Redmond dictated a detailed account, and on 22 July he noted:

> Sir Edward Carson repeatedly stated that, so far as Tyrone was concerned, he was unable... to agree to the INclusion of any part of the county in the jurisdiction of the Home Rule Parliament.
>
>   Mr. Redmond made a similar declaration with reference to the EXclusion of any part of Tyrone.
>
>   The same situation, in substance, arose with regard to county Fermanagh and, eventually Sir Edward Carson substituted, for his demand for the EXclusion of the whole of Ulster, the EXclusion of a block consisting of the Six Counties: Antrim, Down, Armagh, Derry, Tyrone and Fermanagh, INcluding Derry City and Belfast: all to vote as One Unit.
>
>   Mr. Redmond intimated that he could not seriously consider this proposal, any more than the proposal for the total EXclusion of Ulster.[136]

Next day Asquith proffered a suggestion of his own, which Redmond summed up:

> The EXcluded area would consist of the whole of Antrim and the whole of Belfast; of North and Mid Armagh; North, East and West Down; the whole of Derry; Derry City, South Tyrone and North Fermanagh.[137]

This area would vote either *en bloc* or by constituencies or counties on whether it would go into the Irish parliament, and would vote again on the issue after some years. This proposal was flatly rejected by both the Tories and the Irish nationalists, and the conference broke up.

The Irish Volunteers

Until recently nationalists had been generally confident that home rule was on the way, and had tended to dismiss the loyalist mobilisation as a laughable charade. But Redmond's concession of exclusion, rapidly followed by the Curragh and Larne incidents, raised widespread fears and suspicions. James Connolly wrote after the gun-running:

> My firm conviction is that the Liberal Government wish to betray the Home Rulers, that they connive at these illegalities that they might have an excuse for their betrayal, and that the Home Rule party through its timidity and partly through its hatred of Labour in Ireland is incapable of putting the least pressure upon its Liberal allies...
> Who can forecast what will come out of such a welter of absurdities, betrayals and crimes?[138]

After the Curragh mutiny, alarmed nationalists flocked to join the Irish Volunteers, which began expanding rapidly. The Larne gun-running brought another big influx of recruits, and more came after Asquith's promise of an amending bill. Faced with loyalists parading with their new weapons, younger nationalists believed Redmond had been completely outwitted; they were impatient to follow the loyalists' example and assert their right to arm. At the start of 1914, the Irish Volunteers had been barely 10,000 strong, but by the end of May they numbered 129,000. Tom Clarke wrote to John Devoy, the Clan-na-Gael leader in New York:

> The country is electrified with the volunteering business – never in my recollection have I known in any former movement anything to compare with the spontaneous rush that is being made all over to get into the movement and start drill and get hold of a rifle. John E. Redmond and Co. were panic-stricken at what was happening...[139]

A third of the Volunteers were in Ulster, where the nationalist rank and file were particularly restless and apprehensive, seeing themselves about to be excluded from the Irish parliament that they had demanded for thirty years.

Eoin MacNeill, the history professor and chairman of the Volunteers, made approaches to the Irish Party to try to get Redmond's blessing for the organisation. John Redmond and the West Belfast MP Joseph Devlin, concerned about the movement burgeoning outside their control, took advantage of MacNeill's move to try to bring the Volunteers under their supervision. Soon Redmond began pressing for his own nominees to be included on the Volunteers' committee, and threatened that the alternative would be to create a second Volunteer organisation.

MacNeill tried and failed to reach a compromise, and on 9 June Redmond issued a public statement demanding that 25 Irish Party nominees should be added to the committee: he thought it already had 25 members, though in fact it had 30. In order to avoid a split, the Volunteers' committee reluctantly acquiesced, with 18 members voting in favour and nine against. Most of those against, including Padraic Pearse, Sean Mac Diarmada and Liam Mellows, were members of the Irish Republican Brotherhood: they decided to continue to work in the Volunteers despite the decision. Bulmer Hobson, who supported Redmond's proposal in the interests of unity, lost the confidence of his IRB colleagues and had to resign as editor of *Irish Freedom*.

Redmond and Devlin began buying guns and sending them to Belfast, and Pearse and the other original members of the committee found themselves resisting attempts to focus all effort in Ulster, and to turn the Volunteers into a 'pro-Asquith and anti-Carson' movement.

The Howth gun-running

Meanwhile plans were afoot, initiated by Sir Roger Casement, to run guns into Dublin. Casement had been spearheading the Volunteers' recruiting campaign, touring Ireland holding crowded and enthusiastic rallies. The Curragh mutiny had convinced him that independence would not be won without the threat of force. There would be an additional advantage in obtaining weapons: whoever controlled them, he believed, would control the Volunteers, regardless of whether Redmond controlled the committee. The gun-running plans were set in motion in May 1914 by a loose committee of upper class Anglo-Irish enthusiasts in London, organised by Casement's close friend, the historian Alice Stopford Green, a charming and clever woman, now in her sixties. They raised £1,500 between them. Among the members were Erskine Childers and his American wife Molly, who was the committee's secretary, and the Honourable Mary Spring Rice, all of whom would play key roles in the gun-running.

Erskine Childers, now in his forties, was the son of an English father and an Anglo-Irish mother from Wicklow. He became committee clerk to the House of Commons in 1895, and fought for ten months as a volunteer on the British side in the Boer war: an experience which, he said later, changed him from a unionist and imperialist to a liberal and nationalist. He was an expert sailor and used his experience to write a classic thriller, *The Riddle of the Sands*, aiming to alert the British authorities to gaps in their naval defences. Then in 1910 he threw up his House of Commons post to dedicate himself to the cause of Irish freedom, speaking and writing in favour of home rule.

Mary Spring Rice was a Gaelic League supporter, daughter of an Anglo-Irish landowner, Lord Monteagle, and first cousin of the British ambassador to Washington. Mary Colum described her as 'a dowdy, pleasant young woman... Shy as a rabbit, she had the courage and fighting spirit of several Bengal tigers, and the competency of a few field marshals.'[140]

Mary Spring Rice suggested that the guns be brought from the continent in a fishing smack skippered by Erskine Childers. He adapted this idea, deciding to use his and his wife's yacht, the *Asgard*: a wedding present from Molly's parents, the *Asgard* was built in Norway and its name was Old Norse for 'home of the gods'. Two other yachts were also used: the *Kelpie*, which belonged to Conor O'Brien, a cousin of Mary Spring Rice, and the *Chotah*, a steam-yacht owned by Sir Thomas Myles, a prominent Dublin surgeon.

Childers and a young Anglo-Irish writer named Darrell Figgis – described by Mary Colum as 'a gay adventurer... charming, cultivated, self-important'[141] – travelled to the continent in search of weapons. In Hamburg, they bought 1,500 second-hand Mauser rifles and 45,000 rounds of ammunition. Figgis chartered a tug in Hamburg and brought the guns to a rendezvous in the North Sea, where 900 rifles were transferred to the *Asgard* and 600 to the *Kelpie*. The *Asgard* then headed for Howth harbour near Dublin, while the *Kelpie* went to the Welsh coast where the cargo was transferred to the *Chotah* and then taken to Kilcoole in County Wicklow.

On board the *Asgard* were Erskine and Molly Childers, Mary Spring Rice, an English officer named Gordon Shephard, and two fishermen from Donegal, Patrick McGinley and Charles Duggan. Mary Spring Rice wrote a vivid account in her diary of their four weeks at sea, amid guns, grease and gales. They had a narrow escape on 16 July:

> After dinner a fresh breeze sprang up and we beat along past Devonport, and, to my horror, got in among the fleet. They seemed to be executing some night manoeuvres and were all round us with their great lights towering up... There was one awful moment when a destroyer came very near. I stood holding up the stern light on the starboard side watching her get nearer and nearer, with my heart in my mouth, then mercifully at the last moment she changed her course and passed us by.[142]

Molly Childers wrote to Alice Stopford Green on 24 July:

> The whole boat except foc'sle is evenly full of guns. One can't stand; one crawls on one's knees, or walks doubled up, very low down. Mary and I are covered with black bruises!... It is all very funny and not so bad as it sounds... We lie, like the ancient Romans, at our meals, only twisted

Romans, for we are generally clinging to something to prevent tobogganing across the table which is now our floor.[143]

The *Asgard* landed the guns as planned at Howth on 26 July in broad daylight: a move thought up by Bulmer Hobson who calculated that a spectacular landing would increase financial support for the Volunteers, and hence their chance of buying more weapons.

Some 800 Volunteers marched to Howth as if they were on a regular route march, and collected the rifles. But as they marched triumphantly back towards Dublin, trouble began. The assistant commissioner of the Dublin police, H.V. Harrel, called out police and two companies of the King's Own Scottish Borderers. They blocked the Volunteers' route at Clontarf, but Darrell Figgis and Thomas MacDonagh distracted Harrel by arguing with him, and most of the Volunteers got away with their rifles. Worse followed, when a company of KOSBs returning to barracks was hooted and stoned by an angry crowd of civilians. At Bachelor's Walk on the Dublin quayside the soldiers opened fire, killing three and wounding 38, one of whom died later.

The reaction in Ireland combined horror and indignation, as people contrasted the authorities' behaviour with their attitude to the loyalists, who had been allowed not only to run guns with impunity, but also to parade openly with arms through Belfast on 25 July. Among the many people horrified by the news was the English suffragette Sylvia Pankhurst, who went to Dublin to investigate. She wrote later of visiting 'the homes of suffering and bereavement':

> a little boy of ten shot in the back; a schoolgirl with ankle shattered; a good father lost to his home.... The town was seething with anger. At the inquest the military were censured. Resolutions of censure were tabled for the City Council. They were never debated – War had been declared.[144]

9
The Easter Rising

As July 1914 ended, war in Europe was imminent. It was born out of the economic rivalries between the big powers, which since 1900 had aligned themselves in two blocs: France, Britain and the Russian empire on one side, and Germany and the Austro-Hungarian empire – which covered much of central Europe – on the other. Anglo-German competition was particularly fierce, as Germany increasingly threatened Britain's dominance of world trade. The two countries raced to build up their navies, and all the big European powers increased the strength of their armies.

But the flashpoint was Serbia, a Russian satellite which Germany was concerned about because of its position on the route of a planned Berlin-Baghdad railway, and which Austria wanted to crush because it was encouraging rebellion in the Slav regions of the Austro-Hungarian empire. The assassination of an Austrian archduke at Sarajevo on 28 June 1914 prompted Austria to declare war on Serbia on 28 July. A week later, all the big powers were at war.

Britain's entry was propelled by its fear of Germany dominating Europe; its opportunity to declare war came when Germany invaded Belgium on 4 August and refused to withdraw. This circumstance provided the British government with the invaluable pretext that it was going to war for 'the defence of small nations': an emotive theme that would rally much of the population of Britain and Ireland behind the war effort, and send nearly a million citizens of the British empire to their deaths.

John Redmond's instinct was whole-heartedly to support Britain in the coming war. As a home ruler, he wanted Irish self-government within the British empire, and he believed passionately that the empire must survive. On 3 August 1914, the day before Britain formally joined the war, Redmond made a speech in the House of Commons offering Ireland's backing. Recalling how in the eighteenth century the Irish Volunteers had sprung up to defend Ireland from foreign invasion, Redmond envisaged the Ulster Volunteer Force and the Irish Volunteers coming together now for the same purpose. He declared:

> if the dire necessity is forced upon this country we offer to the Government of the day that they may take their troops away, and that if it is allowed to us, in comradeship with our brethren in the North, we will ourselves defend the coasts of our country.[1]

The Commons met his speech with cheering, but in Ireland the response was mixed. Many Irish people sympathised with him, their hostility to Britain lessened by the belief that home rule was on the way, and their concern roused by the plight of another small Catholic nation, Belgium. But to many others, especially separatists and socialists, matters looked quite different. Arthur Griffith's paper *Sinn Féin* proclaimed,

> Ireland is not at war with Germany: it has no quarrel with any Continental Power... England wants our aid and Mr. Redmond, true to his nature, rushes to offer it – for nothing... We are Irish Nationalists and the only duty we have is to stand for Ireland's interests... Let it [the Government] withdraw the present abortive Home Rule Bill and pass... a full measure of Home Rule and Irishmen will have some reason to mobilize for the defence of their institutions. At present they have none.[2]

Irish Freedom, paper of the Irish Republican Brotherhood, printed mottoes such as 'Germany is not Ireland's enemy' across its pages, and predicted, 'The time will quickly come, perhaps in a month, when Ireland's honour and Ireland's cause will demand action.'[3]

Most outspoken of all was the socialist leader James Connolly. European socialist movements – and feminists likewise – had swiftly and deeply divided over the war. Many were swept along on the wave of patriotism, while others, like Lenin in Russia, Rosa Luxemburg in Germany, John Maclean in Scotland, Sylvia Pankhurst in England and Connolly in Ireland, bitterly denounced the war as a quarrel between profit-seeking capitalists in which workers would be needlessly sacrificed. The solution, they contended, was for the workers to rise in revolution. In the *Irish Worker* Connolly lashed Redmond for declaring

> that the Irish slaves will guarantee to protect the Irish estate of England until their masters come back to take possession – a statement that announces to all the world that Ireland has at last accepted as permanent this status of a British province.[4]

In the Glasgow paper *Forward* he asserted,

> The war of a subject nation for independence, for the right to live out its life in its own way may and can be justified as holy and righteous; the war of a subject class to free itself from the debasing conditions of economic and political slavery should at all times choose its own weapons, and hold and esteem all as sacred instruments of righteousness, but the

war of nation against nation in the interest of royal freebooters and cosmopolitan thieves is a thing accursed.[5]

With the outbreak of war, Connolly decided that it was time to organise an insurrection. At a meeting in Dublin on 30 August in memory of three people killed in the Dublin lockout, he declared,

> If you are itching for a rifle, itching to fight, have a country of your own; better to fight for our country than for the robber empire. If you ever shoulder a rifle let it be for Ireland... Make up your mind to strike before your opportunity goes.[6]

Some IRB leaders, notably the veteran Tom Clarke, had also rapidly concluded that it was time to begin planning a rising. The IRB at this time had about 1,660 members in Ireland, with a further 250 in Scotland and 117 in England. The IRB's supreme council met in August and – though some members at first demurred – decided an insurrection should be held before the war ended. Tom Clarke and Seán Mac Diarmada took on the task of developing the project, and apparently operated without further reference to the supreme council.

The IRB held discussions with other 'advanced nationalists' at the Gaelic League building in Dublin's Parnell Square on 9 September 1914. Those present included Tom Clarke, Seán Mac Diarmada, Padraic Pearse, Joseph Plunkett and Eamonn Ceannt of the IRB; Arthur Griffith of Sinn Féin; and James Connolly and William O'Brien of the ITGWU and Citizen Army. A participant, Seán T. Ó Ceallaigh, recalled:

> it was decided that a Rising should take place in Ireland – if the German army invaded Ireland; secondly, if England attempted to force conscription on Ireland; and thirdly, if the war were coming to an end and the Rising had not already taken place, we should rise in revolt, declare war on England and, when the conference was held to settle the terms of peace, we should claim to be represented as a belligerent nation.[7]

Meanwhile in New York lost no time in approaching the German ambassador and asking for Germany to supply arms and 'capable officers' to help with the projected rising. On 21 August a Clan emissary left New York to deliver the same request to Berlin, while Sir Roger Casement, who was in the USA to raise funds for the Irish Volunteers, composed an address to the Kaiser. Signed by the Clan executive, the address expressed hope for a German victory, pointed out the strategic importance of Ireland to Britain's 'mastery of the seas', and concluded:

> We pray for that triumph for Germany; and we pray with it Your Majesty may have power, wisdom and strength of purpose to impose a lasting peace upon the seas by effecting the independence of Ireland and securing its recognition as a fixed condition of the terms of final settlement between the great maritime Powers.[8]

Home rule on the statute book

Redmond assumed that Asquith would respond to his offer of Irish support in the war by immediately making the Home Rule Bill law. But Asquith was hesitant. Redmond wrote repeatedly pressing the case, and warning of the dire consequences that would otherwise follow: Ireland would be 'divided and distracted', and Irish-Americans would become pro-German. Redmond feared that if home rule were not granted, Irish people would feel betrayed and humiliated, and it would be impossible to win enthusiastic support for the war. His anxiety intensified when Lord Kitchener, the new secretary of state for war, refused to arm the Irish Volunteers, a move which Redmond believed would encourage recruiting.

But Carson and Bonar Law bombarded Asquith with letters and memoranda putting the opposite case, and Asquith stalled, writing in his diary on 31 August:

> The Irish on both sides are giving me a lot of trouble just at a difficult moment. I sometimes wish we could submerge the whole lot of them and their island for, say, ten years under the waves of the Atlantic.[9]

Eventually the cabinet decided on a compromise, which was presented to the Lords on 14 September and to the Commons next day. The Home Rule Bill would be allowed to pass onto the statute book, but at the same time a Suspensory Bill would be passed preventing home rule being put into operation for a minimum of 12 months, or till a later date if the war continued. Asquith also promised that an amending bill would be introduced before the Home Rule Bill could come into operation, and pledged that force would not be used against 'Ulster':

> in our view, under the conditions which now exist – we must all recognise the atmosphere which this great patriotic spirit of union has created in the country – the employment of force, any kind of force, for what you call the coercion of Ulster, is an absolutely unthinkable thing.[10]

Bonar Law responded with a bitter speech, then led the Tories out of the Commons: a sight which Asquith described as

> not really a very impressive spectacle, a lot of prosaic and for the most part middle-aged gentlemen, trying to look like early French revolutionists in the tennis court.[11]

Redmond, relieved, launched immediately into the recruiting campaign he had longed to start but had felt bound to postpone till the Home Rule Bill was assured. He attacked those campaigning against enlistment as 'our bitterest enemies', publishing 'little wretched rags', and told the Commons:

> For the first time – certainly for over one hundred years – Ireland in this War feels her interests are precisely the same as yours... She knows that

this is a just War. She knows, she is moved in a very special way by the fact that this War is undertaken in the defence of small nations and oppressed peoples...

I say that the manhood of Ireland will spring to your aid in this War... it is their duty, and should be their honour, to take their place in the firing line in this contest.[12]

Three days later, on 18 September 1914, the Government of Ireland Bill, fruit of nearly 30 years' campaigning, received the royal assent. MPs cheered, but in Ireland advanced nationalists were already warning of peril ahead. Sinn Féin admonished,

If the Home Rule Bill be signed, but not brought into immediate operation *by the appointment of a Home Rule Executive Government,* Ireland is sold and betrayed. Let every Irishman get that into his head and keep it there.[13]

James Connolly acidly denounced the government's move as 'ruling by fooling': its problem had been 'not how to defeat a nation in arms battling for all that makes life worth having, but how to fool a nation without arms into becoming the accomplice of its oppressor'. Home rule, he wrote, had been postponed till after the war when the game would be in Carson's hands, since Asquith had promised no 'coercion of Ulster':

Meanwhile the official Home Rule press and all the local J.P.'s, publicans, land-grabbers, pawnbrokers and slum landlords who control the United Irish League will strain every nerve in an endeavour to recruit for England's army, to send forth more thousands of Irishmen and boys to manure with their corpses the soil of a foreign country... to expend in the degradation of a friendly nation that magnificent Irish courage which a wiser patriotism might better employ in the liberation of their own. 'Yes, ruling by fooling is a great British art – with great Irish fools to practise on.'[14]

Thirty years of constitutional campaigning had produced a fragile and uncertain result. Soon disillusionment with parliamentary politics, coupled with the opportunity and atmosphere engendered by the war, would bring a return to insurrectionary methods for the first time since the 1880s.

Towards the Battlefields

Redmond now threw all his energies into the recruiting campaign for the war. The original members of the Irish Volunteers' committee strongly opposed his stance, and matters came to a head when he spontaneously addressed a parade of Volunteers at Woodenbridge near his Wicklow home on 20 September, urging them to

account yourselves as men, not only in Ireland itself, but wherever the firing line extends, in defence of right, of freedom, and of religion in this war.[15]

The original committee met to consider his speech, and 20 of its members issued a manifesto repudiating his policy. The signatories included the chairman, Eoin MacNeill, as well as several of those who were already considering a rising: Seán Mac Diarmada, Padraic Pearse, Eamonn Ceannt, Thomas MacDonagh and Joseph Plunkett. They stated that Redmond's nominees would no longer be regarded as members of the committee, and declared that the Volunteers' policy should be

> To oppose any diminution of the measure of Irish self-government which now exists as a Statute on paper... To repudiate any undertaking, by whomsoever given, to consent to the legislative dismemberment of Ireland... To declare that Ireland cannot, with honour or safety, take part in foreign quarrels otherwise than through the free action of a National Government of her own... To demand that the present system of governing Ireland through Dublin Castle and the British military power... be abolished without delay, and that a National Government be forthwith established in its place.[16]

Redmond pushed the recruiting campaign forward with a public meeting at Dublin's Mansion House on 25 September, addressed by himself and Asquith. Connolly gathered a group of armed men with the aim of seizing the Mansion House in advance and preventing the meeting being held: the plan was called off when they discovered that English troops armed with machine guns were already holding the building. Instead, a wagonette carrying Connolly, Constance Markievicz and James Larkin led a parade of Citizen Army members – a hundred of them carrying rifles with fixed bayonets – from the union headquarters at Liberty Hall to the streets near the Mansion House. In the *Irish Worker* Connolly prophesied:

> We may now confidently expect the Redmondites to make the fight of their lives to resume control of the Volunteer movement... It is a fight to a finish.
> For some of us the finish may be on the scaffold, for some in the prison cell, for others more fortunate upon the battlefields of an Ireland in arms for a real republican liberty.[17]

The Volunteers split into two bodies. The vast majority, some 184,000, followed Redmond and called themselves the National Volunteers, while about 11,000 stayed with Eoin MacNeill. Most of Redmond's Volunteers went on to join the British army. The executive of the women's organisation, Cumann na mBan, overwhelmingly rejected Redmond's pro-recruiting stance and backed MacNeill's Irish Volunteers.

Some 35,000 men from all parts of Ireland enlisted in the first two months of the war, doubling the number of Irishmen in the British army. But the British authorities, in particular Lord Kitchener, seemed determined to frustrate Redmond's recruiting efforts, and disillusionment soon set in.

At the start of September, Sir Edward Carson announced that the War Office had agreed to allow members of the Ulster Volunteer Force to form a division of their own, with their own officers, training in 'Ulster' camps. But the War Office refused to grant the same privileges to nationalist regiments: the new Irish division based at the Curragh was not even permitted a special badge in recognition of its national identity. Its colonels were all Protestants, and the general in charge repeatedly refused applications from nationalists, including MPs, for commissions. At the Mansion House on 25 September, Asquith promised that an Irish Army Corps would be formed, but this promise was never fulfilled. Nor would the government recognise or equip the National Volunteers.

Resentment mounted when the authorities began harassing anti-war campaigners. On the outbreak of war, two Defence of the Realm Acts were passed, giving the authorities drastic powers to suppress dissent, including authorising the trial of civilians by courts-martial – military courts – for aiding the enemy. The two acts were followed by a succession of bills to amend and consolidate them: these included the authorisation of the death penalty for anyone found guilty by a court-martial of intending to assist the enemy. In effect, Britain and Ireland were put under martial law.

In Ireland, 'seditious' papers were suppressed and civil servants who belonged to the Irish Volunteers were sacked. The military authorities warned printers of campaigning papers that if they printed any criticism of the government, or articles against recruiting, their premises would be closed and they would be arrested. Consequently the 5 December issue of the *Irish Worker*, the ITGWU's paper edited by James Connolly, appeared with blank spaces in place of an editorial.

On 4 December the military raided the works where the *Irish Worker* was printed, and dismantled and took away part of the plant and type. Two weeks later police removed the banner which stretched across the front of Liberty Hall proclaiming, 'WE SERVE NEITHER KING NOR KAISER BUT IRELAND'. A substitute paper was printed in Glasgow until it too was suppressed, and in May 1915 Connolly set up a press in Liberty Hall, where he produced another paper – named the *Workers' Republic*, like his paper of the 1890s – under an armed Citizen Army guard. Other oppositional papers were also suppressed, including Arthur Griffith's paper *Sinn Féin*. He went on to produce first a compilation from other papers called *Scissors and Paste*, which was suppressed after a month, and then *Nationality*, which was printed in Belfast.

Irish distress increased as the government's mishandling of the war led to catastrophic casualties, and, to add insult to injury, the heroism of Irish regiments went unacknowledged in official dispatches. In the retreat from

Mons at the end of August 1914, the second battalion of the Royal Munster Fusiliers fought an epic last stand and were virtually exterminated. Then in April 1915 the Munsters and the Dublin Fusiliers were thrown into another massacre, this time in the ill-planned assault on the Gallipoli peninsula in the strategically placed Dardanelles straits, which link the Black Sea and the Mediterranean.

It was Winston Churchill, the determined and argumentative first lord of the admiralty, who pressed for the attack on the Dardanelles, but he forced the pace and the campaign was mishandled. The British fleet launched a major bombardment in March, but then a month passed before landings were attempted, by which time the Turks had thoroughly fortified the area. On 25 April the allies tried to land, and soldiers were swept with fire as they waded ashore or sat trapped in open boats. By 8 May over 6,000 allied soldiers had been killed and some 14,000 injured, out of a total force of 70,000. In the official dispatch the Dublins and Munsters, who had been at the heart of the slaughter, were not mentioned by name, though all the other regiments were.

The Gallipoli disaster contributed to bringing down the Liberal government in mid-May. Faced with the threat of a damaging attack from the Tories, Asquith agreed to form a coalition government. This became another source of Irish anger, for the new cabinet was laden with Tories who had led the loyalist campaign against home rule, and who continued to pledge that they would repeal the Home Rule Act. The new cabinet included Bonar Law, Lord Lansdowne, and – the worst cut of all – Sir Edward Carson, who was made attorney-general, the chief law officer of the United Kingdom.

Redmond was pressed to join the new government, but knew that it was politically impossible for him to accept. Silent on any issue except the war, he became increasingly isolated and unpopular in Ireland. His National Volunteers declined, while the rival Irish Volunteers grew. Northern nationalists lost all confidence in his ability to protect them. In July 1915, the Dublin Corporation and other public bodies tried to persuade him to press for the Home Rule Act to be put into operation, but he refused.

Grand plan for a rising

As Redmond's popularity waned, the credibility of the advanced nationalists grew. The IRB pressed ahead with their preparations, backed by funds from Clan-na-Gael in the USA.

In October 1914 Sir Roger Casement left New York for Germany. He had three aims: to secure military help for Ireland, to educate German public opinion so that the people would back their government in aiding Ireland, and to organise Irish prisoners of war in Germany into a military unit to take part in the fight for freedom. Casement's mission was one element in a grand plan drawn up by the IRB for a nationwide rising made possible by a German-backed invasion. The invasion force would consist of both Irish prisoners of war and also Irish-American soldiers, who would travel in German naval ships. They would land in parts of the country left weakly garrisoned by Britain because of war-time commitments elsewhere. The main force would disembark at Limerick.

The aim was to secure a line west of the Shannon. Ports on the west coast would be seized, and the German fleet would establish its new Atlantic headquarters at Lough Swilly, on the northern coast of Donegal. Volunteers in many parts of Ireland would destroy transport and communication links, to prevent the movement of British troops and loyalists. Rebels in Dublin would seize key buildings, and would hold out for a week or ten days till the invasion force arrived to relieve them. British military personnel and officials would be arrested, and a military governor would be installed.

The IRB plan went into great detail about the numbers of British troops stationed in different parts of the country, and the weapons at their disposal. Joseph Plunkett – who was suffering from terminal tuberculosis – committed the plan to memory and travelled in the spring of 1915 via Switzerland to Berlin, where he delivered the plan to the German High Command, dictating it to typists. In the event, the Germans chose not to attempt the plan, giving a fraction of the support the IRB wanted.[18]

On 29 June 1915 Jeremiah O'Donovan Rossa, the last of the original Fenians, died aged 83 on Staten Island in the USA after a long illness. Many months earlier his wife Mary had written to John Devoy:

> I could sit and cry for him, poor old faithful banner-bearer, poor old wolfhound of the cause of Ireland, fading away slowly in mental decline, while the mutterings of the longed-for storm beat on deaf ears.[19]

Half a century before in 1861, the funeral of the Young Irelander Terence Bellew McManus had marked the reawakening of Irish nationalism and helped to launch the Fenian movement. Now John Devoy saw that Rossa's funeral could do the same for the new generation of militant nationalists.

Rossa was given a great funeral on Staten Island before his body was shipped to Ireland. In Dublin the remains lay in state at City Hall and people thronged to pay their respects. The funeral arrangements were made by a committee of more than 50 members representing all shades of advanced nationalism: among them were Tom Clarke, Thomas MacDonagh, James Connolly, Constance Markievicz and Arthur Griffith. On Sunday 1 August many thousands of people from all over Ireland joined the funeral procession to Glasnevin cemetery. The Irish Volunteers, the Citizen Army and Cumann na mBan marched in uniform. At the graveside, Padraic Pearse gave an oration which would resound across future generations, declaring:

> Our foes are strong and wise and wary; but, strong and wise and wary as they are, they cannot undo the miracles of God who ripens in the hearts of young men the seeds sown by the young men of a former generation. And the seeds sown by the young men of '65 and '67 are coming to their miraculous ripening to-day. Rulers and Defenders of Realms had need to be wary if they would guard against such processes. Life springs from death; and from the graves of patriot men and women spring living nations. The Defenders of this Realm have worked well in secret and in the open. They think that they have pacified Ireland. They think that they have purchased half of us and intimidated the other half. They think that they have foreseen everything, think that they have provided against everything; but the fools, the fools, the fools! – they have left us our Fenian dead, and while Ireland holds these graves, Ireland unfree shall never be at peace.[20]

The nationalist military bodies – the Irish Volunteers, Cumann na mBan, the Fianna boy scouts and the Citizen Army – were training intensively. The Citizen Army drilled daily, and Connolly wrote a series of articles on insurrectionary warfare for the *Workers' Republic*. In September 1915 twelve hundred Volunteers marched openly with their arms through Dublin, and past midnight on 6 and 24 October, men and women of the Citizen Army, most carrying rifles, took part in manoeuvres around Dublin Castle, the complex of buildings which formed the heart of the British administration. Police reports stated that 85 members turned out on the first occasion, and about 140, including 12 women and 20 Fianna scouts, on the second.

The British authorities in Dublin made no attempt to prevent such activity or disarm the organisations, because they believed that to do so without also moving against the other volunteer bodies, loyalist and nationalist, would alienate nationalist opinion and weaken recruitment. They also thought that the Volunteers would forcibly resist disarmament, resulting in bloodshed.

Leading the Citizen Army's manoeuvres alongside James Connolly was Countess Markievicz, who in a speech on 12 October to the Irish Women's Franchise League declared that

> What distinguished Ireland chiefly of old was the number of fighting women who held their own against the world, who owned no allegiance to any man, who were super-women – the Maeves, the Machas, the warrior-queens.[21]

Markievicz was also president of Cumann na mBan, the Volunteers' women's wing, but she deplored their subservient role, saying,

Today the women attached to national movements are there chiefly to collect funds for the men to spend. These Ladies' Auxiliaries demoralise women, set them up in separate camps, and deprive them of all initiative and independence. Women are left to rely on sex charm, or intrigue and backstairs influence.[22]

She advised,

Don't trust to your 'feminine charm' and your capacity for getting on the soft side of men, but take up your responsibilities and be prepared to go your own way depending for safety on your own courage, your own truth, and your own common sense, and not on the problematic chivalry of the men you may meet on the way. The two brilliant classes of women who follow this higher ideal are Suffragettes and the Trades Union or Labour women. In them lies the hope of the future.[23]

Women in the Citizen Army, she later recorded,

were absolutely on the same footing as the men. They took part in all marches, and even in the manoeuvres that lasted all night. Moreover, Connolly made it quite clear to us that unless we took our share in the drudgery of training and preparing, we should not be allowed to take any share at all in the fight. You may judge how fit we were when I tell you that sixteen miles was the length of our last route march.[24]

Meanwhile the war in Europe continued to sap the constitutional nationalists' support. Consternation spread throughout Ireland when the news filtered through of a second ghastly tragedy in the Dardanelles, in early August. Again the generals had hopelessly bungled, sending tens of thousands of soldiers, many of them Irish or Australian, to their deaths. Again, the Irish soldiers received no official recognition for their heroic efforts, and bitter letters from their parents and relations filled the Dublin papers.

Till now recruitment to the British forces had been voluntary, but in the autumn of 1915 the pro-war lobby in Britain whipped up a campaign for compulsory military service, though this was not yet essential to fill the gaps left by the dead and wounded. In Ireland, the threat of conscription gave a weapon to the advanced nationalists. In the *Workers' Republic*, Connolly inveighed bitterly against the war:

All these mountains of Irish dead, all these corpses mangled beyond recognition, all these arms, legs, eyes, ears, fingers, toes, hands, all these shivering, putrefying bodies, once warm, living and tender parts of Irish men and youths – all these horrors buried in Flanders or the Gallipoli Peninsula, are all items Ireland pays for being part of the British Empire...

Ireland is rotten with slums, a legacy of Empire. The debt of this war will prevent us getting money to replace them with sound, clean, healthy homes. Every big gun fired in the Dardanelles fired away at every shot the cost of building a home for a working class family.

Ireland has the most inefficient educational system, and the poorest schools in Europe. Empire compels us to pay pounds for blowing out the brains of others for every farthing it allows us with which to train our own.[25]

Redmond found himself in a distressing position, forced by circumstances to argue against conscription. On 15 November he warned Asquith:

> Recruiting is now going on at a greater rate than ever in Ireland, and it would be a terrible misfortune if we were driven into a position on the question of conscription which would alienate that public opinion which we have now got upon our side in Ireland.
>
> The position would indeed be a cruel one if conscription were enacted for England and Ireland excluded.
>
> On the other hand, I must tell you that the enforcement of conscription in Ireland is an impossibility.[26]

The chief secretary for Ireland, Augustine Birrell, wrote worriedly to Redmond on 19 December about

> the real condition of the country at the present moment, which *I am sure*, largely owing to this thrice damnable conscription scare, is very bad and may fairly be called *alarming*.

He continued:

> During the last few *weeks* I have been reading nothing but uncomfortable figures about the Irish Volunteers, who are steadily month by month *increasing*, here and there, in this place and that. Wherever there is a plucky priest and two or three men with a little courage the *movement* is *stamped out*, but unluckily such priests and laymen are not always to be found. I am afraid it is no exaggeration to say that there are now nearer 14,000 than 13,000 of these Volunteers, and though many of them are men of *straw* and *wind*, still wherever there is an organization it is a centre of sedition, both to Dublin Castle and the Government, and the *revolutionary* propaganda grows in strength and, I think, in sincerity of purpose. How many rifles they have I don't know – some few thousands, I am certain... Shot-guns and revolvers abound on all sides, and great efforts are being made to *smuggle* in arms and ammunition, and this requires *most careful watching*.[27]

The government heeded the warnings, and when conscription was introduced early in 1916, Ireland was left out.

By now, the storm was gathering. The IRB's military command – Padraic Pearse, Joseph Plunkett, Eamonn Ceannt, Tom Clarke and Seán Mac Diarmada – had been planning a rising for some time. In January 1916 the IRB's supreme council formally decided – against some opposition – that a rising would be held. The IRB planned to use the Irish Volunteers to carry out the rising. Then about 1,000 strong, the IRB had a network of members within the Volunteers, while Plunkett was their director of military operations. But the IRB did not inform those Volunteer leaders whom they knew would not agree with their plans. These included Eoin MacNeill, the chief of staff, who believed there should not be a rising unless it had a real chance of success, or unless the government attempted to enforce conscription or arrest or disarm the Volunteers.

Meanwhile James Connolly, unaware of the IRB's plans, was becoming increasingly impatient. He told a meeting at Liberty Hall in November 1915, *Workers' Republic* reported,

> that the saying that "England's difficulty is Ireland's opportunity," had been heard on a thousand platforms in Ireland when England was in no difficulty, but since England got into difficulties the phrase had never been heard or mentioned. If Ireland did not act now the name of this generation should in mercy to itself be expunged from the records of Irish history.[28]

Then between 19 and 22 January Connolly disappeared, taken away for secret discussions by the IRB's military council. They briefed him on their plans for a rising, and made him one of their members. Later the poet and lecturer Thomas MacDonagh, the Volunteers' director of training, also joined the military council, bringing it to its final complement of seven.

The IRB sent a message to Clan-na-Gael in New York saying that they could not expect the British government to remain inactive much longer, so they had 'decided to strike on Easter Sunday, April 23'.[29] They asked Clan to send a shipload of arms between 20 and 23 April. John Devoy contacted the German embassy, who passed on the message to Berlin. The Germans replied in March that they would send 10 machine-guns, 20,000 rifles, ammunition and explosives to Tralee Bay off County Kerry.

A host of other preparations went ahead. Revolvers and pistols were smuggled in from England. A Glasgow schoolteacher, Margaret Skinnider, brought in detonators, and went with Constance Markievicz to the Wicklow Hills to practise with them. Ammunition was prepared and hand grenades were made. Red Cross packages of bandages and iodine were made up. James Connolly gave lectures on street fighting, and Dr Kathleen Lynn gave first aid classes.

The cause of Ireland

Police reports noted that parts of Ireland were very disturbed and that insurrection had been openly suggested in the press, but the chief secretary, Birrell, refused to take the warnings seriously. On St Patrick's Day, 17 March 1916, 4,500 Volunteers paraded in the centre of Dublin, 1,800 of them armed, holding up the traffic for two hours. A week later the police raided various premises to confiscate a paper called the *Gael*. When they arrived at a shop run by the ITGWU adjoining Liberty Hall, James Connolly threatened them with a revolver. Fearing a general suppression was planned, Connolly issued an order mobilising the Citizen Army.

From then on, Liberty Hall was guarded day and night. On 3 April Padraic Pearse, as the Volunteers' director of organisation, issued 'general orders' for manoeuvres at Easter, which were to last three days.

Tension rose further when Birrell, under pressure from the Tories, reluctantly agreed to deport two Volunteer organisers, Ernest Blythe and Liam Mellows, to England. This provoked a spate of protest meetings, and on 9 April some 1,300 Volunteers demonstrated in Dublin. Aided by James Connolly's daughter Nora, Mellows soon returned to Ireland disguised as a priest.

On 8 April Connolly announced in the *Workers' Republic* that on Palm Sunday the Citizen Army would hoist the green flag of Ireland over Liberty Hall. He declared:

> Where better could that flag fly than over the unconquered citadel of the Irish Working Class, Liberty Hall...
> We are out for Ireland for the Irish. But who are the Irish? Not the rack-renting, slum-owning landlord, not the sweating, profit-grinding capitalist, not the sleek and oily lawyer, not the prostitute pressman – the hired liars of the enemy. Not these are the Irish upon whom the future depends. Not these, but the Irish Working Class, the only secure foundation upon which a free nation can be reared.

He continued:

> The Cause of labour is the Cause of Ireland, the Cause of Ireland is the Cause of labour. They cannot be dissevered. Ireland seeks Freedom. Labour seeks that an Ireland Free should be the sole mistress of her own destiny, supreme owner of all material things within and upon her soil.[30]

Connolly, who was acting general secretary of the ITGWU, had made his announcement without reference to the union's committee, and met considerable opposition. He overcame this by letting one of the strongest opponents into the secret of the planned rising.

The green flag with a gold harp was duly raised by 15-year-old Molly O'Reilly – already a veteran republican – amid much ceremony on 16 April. That evening Connolly told the Citizen Army:

> The odds are a thousand to one against us, but in the event of victory, hold on to your rifles, as those with whom we are fighting may stop before our goal is reached. We are out for economic as well as political liberty. Hold on to your rifles.[31]

As envisaged at this stage, the rising would have presented the British authorities with a considerable challenge. Volunteers – who numbered some 3,000 in Dublin, including the 200-strong Citizen Army, and 13,000 in the provinces – were to muster all over Ireland, and a large supply of arms was to arrive from Germany. A widespread insurrection, with guerrilla warfare in the countryside accompanying a rising in Dublin, was a serious possibility.

But key elements in the plan were to go badly wrong. In late March preparations had begun in Germany to send a ship, renamed the *Aud* for the occasion and disguised as a Norwegian tramp steamer, to Ireland with a secret hold full of arms. The *Aud* sailed on 9 April captained by a young naval officer, Karl Spindler, and three days later Roger Casement followed in a submarine. Believing that the German arms were insufficient for the rising, Casement secretly planned to try to persuade the leaders to call it off, or, if he failed, to join it himself.

The *Aud* arrived in Tralee Bay as planned on 20 April, but found no-one to meet it. Spindler said later: 'This was the greatest disappointment I ever had in my whole life.'[32] The military council had sent a message to Germany changing the date for the landing to Easter Sunday, 23 April, but the *Aud* had no wireless equipment and could not receive it. Spindler stayed in Tralee Bay as long as he could – and successfully hoodwinked a British ship into believing they were Norwegians – but on leaving the bay the *Aud* was intercepted by British cruisers and forced to go to Queenstown. Approaching Queenstown harbour, Spindler and his crew blew up their ship and escaped in the lifeboats. Spindler subsequently spent two years in prisoner-of-war camps in England.

Meanwhile the U-boat carrying Casement arrived at Tralee Bay on the evening of 20 April. Finding no-one to meet them, and wanting to leave before daylight, the captain put Casement and his two Irish companions ashore in a dinghy on Banna Strand. Casement was ill and exhausted, and his companions left him in the shelter of an ancient fort while they went for help. The dinghy floating in the sea and weapons on the shore gave him away, and he was found by a local farmer and a policeman, who arrested him.

Casement's capture triggered a further setback for the planners of the rising. Eoin MacNeill, chief of staff of the Volunteers, learnt to his dismay on 20 April that a rising was imminent. He threatened to issue orders countermanding the Easter manoeuvres, but was dissuaded when he was told that a German ship was on its way with arms. But late on the night of Easter Saturday, 22 April, MacNeill learnt that the *Aud* had been sunk and Casement arrested. Now he sent out orders countermanding the rising, and published a notice in the *Sunday Independent* of Easter Sunday forbidding all Volunteer movements for that day.

There was now great confusion in the Volunteer ranks to add to the problem of the lack of arms. But the military council, though deeply doubtful of the chances of success, decided nonetheless to go ahead with the rising, postponing it for a day till Easter Monday at noon. They believed – rightly – that the authorities would soon move to arrest them, and also felt it would be better to give their lives in a symbolic protest than to call off the enterprise now.

Easter Monday

To all but the participants, the rising on Easter Monday, 24 April 1916, came as a total surprise. The opera singer Sir Henry Lytton, in Dublin to perform Gilbert and Sullivan, recalled:

> To the outsider the 'trouble' was extremely well organized. On the day it began a brilliant sun was shining in the sky, and, it being a Bank Holiday, everyone went off in the early morning for a day in the country or somewhere to enjoy themselves. It seemed like a normal public holiday, and yet everything had been arranged.[33]

A sternly unsympathetic commentator wrote soon afterwards:

> Sheer madness was this Rising, but like Hamlet's aberration, there was method in it. There was a stroke of genius even in the time chosen for its inception. People are little inclined to suspect mischief in others when in a holiday frame of mind... nobody troubled about the little bodies of Irish Volunteers as they wended their way, towards noon, with full accoutrements, to their allotted posts. Happy in their unsuspicion, most of the Military officers had gone to Fairyhouse Races. The good-humoured giants of the Dublin Metropolitan Police merely smiled at the spectacle.[34]

The authorities, too, were taken unawares. Events surrounding Casement and the *Aud* had alerted them to the intended insurrection, and they were planning to arrest the leaders. But MacNeill's countermand had lulled them into believing there was no immediate hurry.

At nine o'clock that morning the seven members of the military council of the Irish Republican Brotherhood – which was still a secret organisation, unknown to most of those who were soon to mobilise – had met at Liberty Hall. They appointed Padraic Pearse president of the provisional government and commandant-general of the army of the Irish republic, and designated James Connolly vice-president and commandant-general of the Dublin division.

At 11.30 some 210 men and women of the Citizen Army fell in at Liberty Hall. William O'Brien recalled,

> Shortly before noon, Connolly came down the stairs and spoke to me on the landing. Putting his head close to mine, and dropping his voice, he said: "We are going out to be slaughtered." I said: "Is there no chance of success?" and he replied: "None whatever."[35]

At noon the republican forces, numbering some 1,500, including more than 100 women, occupied buildings in the centre of Dublin, with the General Post Office as their headquarters. They also occupied a chain of buildings across the southern suburbs, aiming to control the main routes by which the military would enter the city. But the original plan had called for 3,000 people, and the effect of MacNeill's countermand had been to halve the number.

Desmond Ryan, who mustered at Liberty Hall, made notes soon afterwards recalling the excitement of the day:

> Admitted to Larkin's palace we swarm upstairs. The Volunteers are 'out' and Ireland is rising. It is evident from the excited shouts to keep 'a watch on the railway line' and 'fill all vessels with water.' Rifles and flushed faces. A feeling of momentary sickness, then wonder.[36]

The republicans cut the telegraph wires linking Dublin to the outside world, and later blew up a railway line which could carry troops. First to die was a policeman, shot at the gates of Dublin Castle soon after midday by a member of the Citizen Army.

On the steps of the GPO, Padraic Pearse read out a proclamation declaring the establishment of the Irish republic. Signed by the seven members of the military council, and addressed to 'Irishmen and Irishwomen', the proclamation stated:

> We declare the right of the people of Ireland to the ownership of Ireland, and to the unfettered control of Irish destinies, to be sovereign and indefeasible... In every generation the Irish people have asserted their right to national freedom and sovereignty; six times during the past three hundred years they have asserted it in arms.

Influenced by Connolly's socialist ideals and by the feminist movement, and firmly non-sectarian, the proclamation avowed,

> The Irish Republic is entitled to, and hereby claims, the allegiance of every Irishman and Irishwoman. The Republic guarantees religious and civil liberty, equal rights and equal opportunities to all its citizens, and declares its resolve to pursue the happiness and prosperity of the whole nation and of all its parts, cherishing all the children of the nation equally, and oblivious of the differences carefully fostered by an alien government, which have divided a minority from a majority in the past.

Dubliners reacted to the rising with surprise and curiosity. Among the many who ventured out to see what was happening was Mrs Norway, wife of the secretary of the post office in Ireland. Soon after four o'clock she went with her 17-year-old son Nevil – later well known as the novelist Nevil Shute – to see the GPO, where her husband had his office. She wrote in a letter immediately afterwards:

> Over the fine building of the G.P.O. floated a great green flag with the words "Irish Republic" on it in large white letters. Every window on the ground floor was smashed and barricaded with furniture, and a big placard announced "The Headquarters of the Provisional Government of the Irish Republic." At every window were two men with rifles, and on the roof the parapet was lined with men.[37]

There were also scattered risings in the provinces, but it was here that MacNeill's countermand and the failure to land the German arms had their most disabling effect. Messages from Dublin took time to arrive.

Warned by events in Dublin, the police and military arrested republicans before they could take action. But in north County Dublin, Volunteers under Thomas Ashe captured police barracks, broke the Belfast-Dublin railway line, and fought a five-hour battle against armed police. In County Wexford some 600 Volunteers occupied the town of Enniscorthy while in Galway some 1,000 Volunteers under Liam Mellows cut telegraph wires, attacked barracks, and occupied the town of Athenry.

In Cork, however, to the intense disappointment of the local leaders, Tomás Mac Curtain and Terence MacSwiney, the news that the rising was going ahead came too late to re-mobilise the Volunteers, who had dispersed after MacNeill's countermand. But in East Cork three brothers called Kent decided to resist when police came to arrest them: in the ensuing gunbattle, a head constable was shot dead. Richard Kent died of his wounds, and Thomas Kent was later court-martialled and executed.

Belfast Volunteers, too, ended up in frustration. James Connolly instructed the Belfast leader, Denis McCullough, that not a shot was to be fired in Ulster: they must go to Tyrone to join up with the Volunteers there, then go on to Connacht. On Easter Saturday, 132 Volunteers set off from Belfast for Coalisland, but the plan did not work out and they returned home next day.

Those who rose in Dublin were overwhelmingly drawn from the working class. Many were tradesmen – such as electricians, tailors, carpenters, compositors, and plumbers – while others were clerks, shop assistants and labourers. The women included teachers, seamstresses, and office and shop workers. In the countryside, most of the insurgents were tradesmen, small farmers and agricultural labourers. Few middle-class people were involved, though three of the seven members of the military council – Padraic Pearse, Thomas MacDonagh and Joseph Plunkett – were writers and leaders of the cultural revival.

Eighty or more volunteers, mainly of Irish origin, travelled over from London, Liverpool, Manchester and Glasgow to join the rising. Among them were seven women from Cumann na mBan in Liverpool.

Some 150 women took part in Dublin – 30 or more of them stationed in the GPO – and about 50 in the provinces. At St Stephen's Green, Constance Markievicz and Margaret Skinnider of the Citizen Army were involved in the fighting. Skinnider was shot and badly wounded when trying to set fire to a house to cut off the retreat of some British soldiers. Some women used revolvers to hold up bread vans to obtain food for the commissariat. Dr Kathleen Lynn was chief medical officer of the Citizen Army, and was attached to the City Hall garrison. The Citizen Army proved much keener to involve women than the Volunteers, and some women had to be very persistent before Volunteer leaders would allow them to participate. But in the end only one commander, Eamon de Valera, who was in charge at Boland's Mill, refused to allow any women to join him.

Many of the women worked as nurses, cooks or couriers: a highly dangerous occupation which involved braving rifle fire to carry dispatches, arms, ammunition or explosives. Margaret Skinnider recalled taking a message by bicycle:

> Soldiers on top of the Hotel Shelbourne aimed their machine-gun directly at me. Bullets struck the wooden rim of my bicycle wheels, puncturing it, others rattled on the metal rim or among the spokes.[38]

The British counter-attack

At the start of the rising, the British government had more than 6,000 troops in Ireland, of whom some 2,500 were in Dublin, as well as 9,500 members of the Royal Irish Constabulary armed with carbines. Reinforcements were rapidly brought into Dublin. A column of 1,600 troops came in from the Curragh, soon followed by more. Within 48 hours, 2,000 British troops landed at Kingstown harbour. The republican forces were heavily outnumbered, and, especially as the British had artillery, massively outgunned. The British strategy was simple: to throw a cordon around the Irish positions and then close in on the GPO. They also drove a line of troops and fire roughly along the river Liffey, dividing the Irish positions on either side.

Tuesday saw fierce fighting and many casualties. British troops raked St Stephen's Green with machine-gun fire, forcing the republicans to retreat to the College of Surgeons down the road, and British artillery began shelling republican barricades.

Then on Wednesday morning the gunboat *Helga*, a former fishery patrol vessel, stopped in the river Liffey and at eight o'clock began bombarding Liberty Hall at a few hundred yards' range. Fortunately the only person in the building was the caretaker, who quickly escaped.

Some two hours later, little more than a mile away across the city, one of the worst outrages of the rising took place, when on the orders of an Irish officer in the British army, the tireless and much loved activist Francis Sheehy Skeffington and two journalists were shot dead. Since Monday, the absence of police had provoked the poor of the Dublin slums into a celebratory orgy of looting: hats, boots, bikes, umbrellas, toys, fruit, and especially sweets were triumphantly carried away, often by women and children. The looting, however, allowed the press to smear the insurgents as a rabble mob, and Francis Sheehy Skeffington – who sympathised with the aims of the rising, although, as a pacifist, he disapproved of violence – tried to organise a citizens' force to prevent it.

On his way home on the Tuesday evening he was arrested and taken to Portobello Barracks. That night an officer at the barracks, Captain Bowen-Colthurst, took him out, with his hands bound behind his back, as a hostage on a patrol: if the republicans shot at the soldiers, Sheehy Skeffington would be shot in return. On the way, he saw Bowen-Colthurst shoot dead a 17-year-old boy named Coade. Soon afterwards Bowen-Colthurst arrested two editors of loyalist papers named Thomas Dickson and Patrick MacIntyre, and brought them to the barracks as well.

Soon after ten o'clock next morning, Wednesday, on Bowen-Colthurst's orders, Sheehy Skeffington and the two journalists were taken into the barracks yard and shot dead. Their bodies were buried in sacks in the barracks yard that night.

Sheehy Skeffington's family were not told of his fate. Instead, on the Friday morning soldiers raided his home in a vain attempt to find incriminating material that would justify the murder. They fired through the windows and put Hanna and their seven-year-old son Owen under arrest as they ransacked the house. The truth began to come out after the killing was reported by another Irish officer at the barracks, Major Sir Francis Vane, who before the war had sympathised with the socialist movement. Vane was sacked for exposing the incident. But the full story only emerged after a tenacious campaign by Hanna Sheehy Skeffington, who wrote many years later that what most shocked her in retrospect was

> not the brutality of the British Army in action against a people in revolt (we learned to take this for granted, and indeed it is part of war everywhere), but the automatic and tireless efforts on the part of the entire official machinery, both military and political, to prevent the truth being made public...[39]

Bowen-Colthurst was court-martialled in June and found guilty of the three murders but insane. He was detained in an asylum and released 20 months later. He then settled in Canada on a military pension and lived there till his death in 1965.

That Wednesday, the British took their heaviest casualties of the rising when a dozen republicans at Mount Street Bridge on the canal fired for much of the day on reinforcements advancing into the city. An eye-witness wrote:

> The Sinn Féiners had got Clanwilliam House – a corner residence – wonderfully barricaded... Clanwilliam House not only dominated the bridge, but also the whole of Northumberland Road.
>   Along this road the troops had to pass, and they crouched down in long rows of heads – like great khaki caterpillars – in a most terribly exposed order, so that if the rebel shot failed to hit the first head it was bound to hit the second head, provided the rifle was anywhere in the vertical line...

> I arrived on the scene a few minutes after the start of the engagement, but already one could see the poor fellows writhing in agony in the roadway, where the advanced line had been sniped by the terrible leaden bullets of the Sinn Féiners.[40]

The British forces finally broke through, killing four republicans, but they had lost six officers killed and 21 wounded, and more than 200 other ranks killed or wounded.

The crisis came on Thursday and Friday, when the British launched a massive and continuous artillery bombardment of the city centre, causing an immense conflagration and reducing many of Dublin's principal streets and buildings to ruins, a scene which many likened to Ypres or Flanders. Mrs Norway, who watched from her hotel window in Dawson Street, wrote:

> It was the most awe-inspiring sight I have ever seen. It seemed as if the whole city was on fire, the glow extending across the heavens, and the red glare hundreds of feet high while above the roar of the fires the whole air seemed vibrating with the noise of the great guns and machine-guns. It was an inferno![41]

Desmond Ryan described how Pearse sat beside him in the GPO as the fires glared in:

> The volleys rolled away, and Pearse watched the flames. "All the boys were safe," he said, with a sigh of relief. Then he suddenly turned and asked me, casually but with a certain abruptness: "It was the right thing to do, wasn't it?" "Yes. Failure means the end of everything, the Volunteers, Ireland, all!" And the tone showed the agony of his mind, but an agony flaming to final conviction. Outside the flames grew brighter and there was a terrific burst of gunfire away in the darkness. Pearse paused and continued with deep enthusiasm and passionate conviction in his words: "Well, when we are all wiped out, people will blame us for everything, condemn us, but only for this protest the war would have ended and nothing would have been done. After a few years, they will see the meaning of what we tried to do."[42]

That Thursday prime minister Asquith announced in parliament that General Sir John Maxwell was being sent to Ireland with plenary powers under martial law over the whole country. On behalf of the Irish nationalist party, John Redmond expressed 'detestation and horror' at the rising.[43] That day, too, James Connolly was badly wounded in the ankle on his way back to the GPO after he had accompanied an expedition a short way out of the building.

By Friday, the British bombardment had isolated the GPO from the other rebel positions. British troops fought their way in from house to house, shooting or bayoneting several civilians out of hand as they went. That night, the republicans evacuated the blazing GPO under heavy fire, taking James Connolly on a stretcher. On Saturday morning, James Ryan recalled,

> we moved from house to house through bored walls. The openings were small and Connolly's stretcher would not pass through. We had to put him in a sheet and so carry him northwards. He must have suffered torture during that journey but he never complained.[44]

That day, to avoid further loss of life, the leaders decided on surrender. Elizabeth O'Farrell, a nurse, acted as intermediary between Padraic Pearse and the British commander, General Lowe. At 3.30 Pearse met Lowe and handed over his sword. Elizabeth O'Farrell spent the rest of Saturday and all of Sunday braving the firing to carry the surrender instructions to the republican posts.

As the republicans surrendered and were marched away by British troops, people in the richer areas reacted with hostility, but among the poor there was considerable sympathy. F.A. McKenzie, a Canadian journalist, wrote:

> As I was passing through a street near the Castle cheer after cheer could be heard. I looked ahead. A regiment was approaching. People were leaning from their windows waving triangular flags and handkerchiefs. "They are cheering the soldiers," I said to my companion… As the main body approached I could see that the soldiers were escorting a large number of prisoners, men and women, several hundreds in all. The people were cheering not the soldiers but the rebels...

> I spoke to a little group of men and women at the street corner. "Shure, we cheer them," said one woman. "Why shouldn't we? Aren't they our own flesh and blood?"[45]

McKenzie – a supporter of the British empire with a reluctant admiration for the rebels – summed up the reaction:

> I have read many accounts of public feeling in Dublin in these days. They are all agreed that the open and strong sympathy of the mass of the population was with the British troops. That this was so in the better parts of the city, I have no doubt, but certainly what I myself saw in the poorer districts did not confirm this. It rather indicated that there was a vast amount of sympathy with the rebels, particularly after the rebels were defeated.[46]

The rising had cost 450 people dead – about 116 soldiers, 16 policemen, 64 republicans and 254 civilians – and more than 2,600 wounded. Further, the British bombardment had done some £2,500,000 worth of damage to the city. A member of Cumann na mBan recalled:

> Monday afternoon, May 1, some of us girls went through North King Street and the deadhouses in the Richmond Union hospitals. It was a gruesome sight to see the dead piled on top of each other in the morgues where there were not enough marble slabs on which to place the bodies.

Some lay in their clothes just as they had fallen, and so close to each other that one had to go sideways to pass through. It was pitiful to see the women going around from one house of death to another and to the hospitals looking for husbands, fathers or brothers, not knowing where they were or where to look for them. Then the shock when one lifted the cloth from the face of some prostrate form and recognized the features of a dear friend.[47]

In the aftermath, 3,430 men and 79 women were arrested. Many of them, including Eoin MacNeill and several trade union leaders, had not been involved in the fighting. Of those arrested, 1,836 men and five women were swiftly shipped to England and Scotland, where they were interned. Others were subsequently sentenced. The male internees were sent to detention barracks in Knutsford in Cheshire, Stafford, Wakefield, Wandsworth in London, Woking, Lewes, Glasgow and Perth, while the women went to Aylesbury. Later most of the men were transferred to Frongoch camp in North Wales, which had previously housed German prisoners of war. Desmond Ryan made notes about the internees' journey:

Heaped together in the darkened and stuffy hold with life-belts for pillows... We dozed fitfully in the darkness while the sea gurgled beneath us, prepared for anything from a watery exit from some prowling German submarine's torpedo to an awakening in France... Holyhead at dawn and the gulls and the Welsh hills... The train jolts onward, packed. The light shows us grime-faced and weary-eyed. No conveniences for deportees, hold on boys or soak your breeches. Mostly we hold on and fall asleep.[48]

Executions

The leaders faced a more terrible fate. As soon as the rising was over, General Maxwell set in motion a series of secret courts-martial. On the morning of Wednesday 3 May came a bald official announcement:

Three signatories of the notice proclaiming the Irish Republic,

P.H. Pearse
T. MacDonagh, and
T.J. Clarke,

have been tried by Field General Courts-martial and sentenced to death. The sentence having been duly confirmed the three above-mentioned men were shot this morning.[49]

Redmond, who two days earlier had written that the 'real ringleaders' would 'have to be dealt with in the most severe manner possible', now wrote anxiously to Asquith: 'I wd. most earnestly beg of you to prevent any wholesale trials of this kind – wholesale executions wd. destroy our last hopes.'[50]

After condemning Pearse to death, General Blackader, president of the courts-martial, visited Lady Fingall, who recalled,

He came to dinner one night greatly depressed. I asked him: "What is the matter?" He answered: "I have just done one of the hardest tasks I have ever had to do. I have had to condemn to death one of the finest characters I have ever come across. There must be something very wrong in the state of things that makes a man like that a Rebel. I don't wonder that his pupils adored him!"[51]

But the courts-martial went remorselessly on, and day after day curt official notices announced more executions. On Thursday 4 May, Joseph Plunkett, Edward Daly – brother of Tom Clarke's wife Kathleen, William Pearse – brother of Padraic, and Michael O'Hanrahan were shot. Plunkett's death was given a bitter poignancy by his marriage the night before to the artist Grace Gifford. She recorded:

I entered Kilmainham Jail on Wednesday, May 3rd, at 6 pm., and was detained there till about 11.30 p.m., when I saw him for the first time in the prison chapel, where the marriage was gone through and no speech allowed. He was taken back to his cell, and I left the prison... I went to bed at 1.30, and was wakened at 2 o'clock by a policeman, with a letter from the prison Commandant – Major Lennon – asking me to visit Joseph Plunkett. I was brought there in a motor, and saw my husband in his cell, the interview occupying ten minutes. During the interview the cell was packed with officers, and a sergeant, who kept a watch in his hand and closed the interview by saying: 'Your time is now up.'[52]

On Friday John MacBride was shot. On Saturday came a moment of hope, with the announcement that a number of those sentenced to death would now be imprisoned for life instead, including Countess Markievicz who had been reprieved 'solely and only on account of her sex.'[53] But on Monday, 8 May, came the executions of Eamonn Ceannt, Cornelius Colbert, Seán Heuston, and Michael Mallin. On 9 May Thomas Kent was executed in Cork. The Irish public was profoundly shocked. Lady Fingall remembered:

To the Irish people, being told of these executions in barrack yards, it was, as someone wrote: "As though they watched a stream of blood coming from beneath a closed door."[54]

George Bernard Shaw wrote to the *Daily News*:

My own view... is that the men who were shot in cold blood after their capture or surrender were prisoners of war, and that it was, therefore, entirely incorrect to slaughter them...

Until Dublin Castle is superseded by a National Parliament and Ireland voluntarily incorporated with the British Empire... an Irishman resorting to arms to achieve the independence of his country is doing only what Englishmen will do if it be their misfortune to be invaded and conquered by the Germans in the course of the present war...

It is absolutely impossible to slaughter a man in this position without making him a martyr and a hero, even though the day before the rising he may have been only a minor poet. The shot Irishmen will now take their

places beside Emmet and the Manchester Martyrs in Ireland, and beside
the heroes of Poland and Serbia and Belgium in Europe; and nothing in
heaven or on earth can prevent it.[55]

In the House of Commons on 11 May John Dillon, Redmond's deputy,
who had been in Dublin during the rising, and who likewise had not
opposed the idea of executing the leaders, bitterly attacked the executions.
He told the government,

> It is the first rebellion that ever took place in Ireland where you had a
> majority on your side. It is the fruit of our life work. We have risked our
> lives a hundred times to bring about this result... and now you are
> washing out our whole life work in a sea of blood.

He continued:

> What is happening is that thousands of people in Dublin, who ten days
> ago were bitterly opposed to the whole of the Sinn Féin movement and to
> the rebellion, are now becoming infuriated against the Government on
> account of these executions, and, as I am informed by letters received
> this morning, that feeling is spreading throughout the country in a most
> dangerous degree.

He went on: 'This series of executions is doing more harm than any
Englishman in this House can possibly fathom.'[56]

English voices too, including the *Manchester Guardian*, were calling
for mercy. And in Wales the former Citizen Army organiser Captain Jack
White was arrested and jailed for trying to get the Welsh miners out on
strike to prevent Connolly being shot: his idea was to obstruct the coal
supply to the British fleet. But back in Ireland the *Irish Independent*,
owned by William Martin Murphy who had confronted Connolly in the
Dublin lockout of 1913, ran editorials demanding more blood. Young
people and the rank and file should be dealt with leniently, the paper
argued on 10 May, then added:

> When, however, we come to some of the ringleaders, instigators, and
> fomentors not yet dealt with, we must make an exception... Weakness to
> such men at this stage may be fatal... Let the worst of the ringleaders be
> singled out and dealt with as they deserve...[57]

Then on Friday 12 May James Connolly and Seán Mac Diarmada were
executed, and the *Independent* was at last satisfied, saying that

> The total executions to date number 15, and the penalty of capital
> punishment should not, we think, be inflicted in any other case except
> where actual cool murder... has been committed.[58]

The execution of Connolly, wounded as he was, proved especially
shocking. Since the surrender he had been held in the hospital at Dublin
Castle, where his wife Lillie and daughter Nora visited him. Nora recalled
their last visit, at midnight on 11 May:

When we entered the room Papa had his head turned to the door watching for our coming. When he saw Mamma he said:

"Well, Lillie, I suppose you know what this means?"

"O James! It's not that – it's not that?" my mother wailed.

"Yes, Lillie," he said. "I fell asleep for the first time to-night and they wakened me at eleven and told me that I was to die at dawn."

My mother broke down, laid her head on his bed and sobbed heartbreakingly.

My father patted her head and said, "Don't cry, Lillie, you'll unman me."

"But your beautiful life, James," my mother sobbed. "Your beautiful life."

"Well, Lillie," he said. "Hasn't it been a full life, and isn't this a good end?"[59]

Soon afterwards, at about three in the morning, accompanied by Father Aloysius, a Capuchin priest, Connolly was carried down on a stretcher to an ambulance which took him to Kilmainham jail. There he was carried to the grim jail yard, put on a chair, and shot.

Altogether 183 people were court-martialled, of whom 15 were shot, 145 were imprisoned, and 23 acquitted.

Constance Markievicz, whose death sentence had been commuted to penal servitude for life, was held in Mountjoy jail before being transferred to England. On 12 May, the day of Connolly's execution, her sister Eva Gore-Booth, with her friend Esther Roper, visited her. Esther remembered being shown into

a bare white-washed room at the end of which was a small barred window opening. Crossing outside this was a narrow passage on the opposite side of which was another barred opening, and it was behind this grille that Con's face at last appeared, looking ghost-like.

A wardress walked up and down the passage between the two grilles. After greeting us, Con asked almost at once whether Connolly had been shot. We had been warned that on no account must we answer this question. Though no word was spoken she must have seen the answer in our faces, for with the tears running slowly down her cheeks she said, 'You needn't tell me, I know. Why didn't they let me die with my friends?' It was a terrible moment. Under all other circumstances in prison she kept gay and brave... It was a ghastly story, and for a moment she was overwhelmed. Soon she drew herself up and said, 'Well, Ireland was free for a week.'[60]

Transformation

The Easter rising was a watershed, transforming the political situation in Ireland. From the start of the world war there had been growing discontent with Redmond's party and parliamentary politics, but now the rising, and the ferocity of Britain's response, changed dissatisfaction to alienation, and a tide of sympathy for the insurgents swept across the country. Douglas Goldring, an English writer who spent several months in Dublin after the rising because he wanted to find out what had inspired the rebels, wrote:

> no one could be in the city for twenty-four hours without discovering what was the general feeling of the mass of the population about the Sinn Feiners. Picture postcards of the executed rebels were displayed in almost every shop window, and their faces were gazed upon with silent veneration by the passers-by. A large photogravure of P.H. Pearse, produced by some enterprising firm, attracted crowds wherever it was displayed. Up and down Sackville Street urchins ran selling broad sheets purporting to contain, "The last and inspiring speech of Thomas MacDonagh."… So far as one could tell, except among the shopkeepers who had not received compensation for their losses and among the upper classes, all resentment against the Sinn Feiners had died away.[61]

There was even some sympathy in the Catholic hierarchy. While several Catholic bishops vehemently condemned the rising, and General Maxwell expressed his 'high appreciation' of the 'services rendered' by the clergy of Dublin, the bishop of Limerick, Dr O'Dwyer, broke ranks. Maxwell asked the bishops to remove priests who had shown sympathy to the insurgents, but O'Dwyer refused, accusing Maxwell in an open letter on 17 May:

> You took great care that no plea for mercy should interpose on behalf of the poor young fellows who surrendered to you in Dublin. The first intimation which we got of their fate was the announcement that they had been shot in cold blood. Personally, I regard your action with horror, and I believe that it has outraged the conscience of the country… altogether your regime has been one of the worst and blackest chapters in the history of the misgovernment of the country.[62]

The poets expressed the transformation in popular feeling. AE wrote:

> Their dream had left me numb and cold,
> But yet my spirit rose in pride,
> Refashioning in burnished gold
> The images of those who died,
> Or were shut in the penal cell.
> Here's to you, Pearse, your dream not mine,
> But yet the thought, for this you fell,
> Has turned life's water into wine.[63]

Abroad, the rising had its biggest impact in the USA, where the execution turned Irish-American opinion massively against Britain. The president of the United Irish League of America cabled Redmond on 15 May:

> Irish executions have alienated every American friend and caused resurgence of ancient enmities. Your life-work destroyed by English brutality. Opinion widespread that promise of Home Rule was mockery.[64]

But socialists in the United States and Europe had difficulty understanding the thinking behind the rising – a reaction that Connolly had predicted. The British Independent Labour Party and American De Leonites condemned Connolly's involvement, and Russian social democrats dismissed the rising as a 'putsch'. There were, however, some exceptions. Sylvia Pankhurst, always a friend of Ireland's socialist republicans, wrote warmly in the *Woman's Dreadnought* of the 'reckless bravery' of the rebels, and said,

> mistaken though they may have been, their desperate venture was undoubtedly animated by high ideals.[65]

And the Russian revolutionary V.I. Lenin reproved those who belittled the rising, declaring,

> Whoever calls such an uprising a 'putsch' is either a hardened reactionary, or a doctrinaire hopelessly incapable of picturing a social revolution as a living thing.[66]

The rising prompted a swift political reaction from the British government. The chief secretary, Augustine Birrell, resigned. On 30 April he had written gloomily to Asquith: 'Nobody can govern Ireland from England save in a state of siege.'[67]

Then on 11 May Asquith left for Ireland to investigate the situation. He returned a week later convinced of the urgent need for a settlement, and appointed Lloyd George to negotiate with Redmond and Carson. Lloyd George saw a settlement, however temporary, as vital to the war effort. Otherwise, he told Carson,

> The Irish-American vote will go over to the German side. They will break our blockade and force an ignominious peace on us, unless something is done, even provisionally, to satisfy America.[68]

Lloyd George won what appeared to be agreement between Redmond and Carson that home rule should be brought in with six counties – Antrim, Down, Armagh, Tyrone, Fermanagh, and Derry – excluded as a block. In agreeing to this, Redmond dropped his earlier demand for a county by county vote on the issue, and also the expectation that only four counties – not Tyrone and Fermanagh – would be excluded.

But Lloyd George had achieved agreement by a characteristic act of duplicity: he told Carson that exclusion would be permanent, and Redmond that it would be temporary. On 29 May he wrote to Carson: 'We must make it clear that at the end of the provisional period Ulster does not, whether she wills it or not, merge in the rest of Ireland.'[69]

But the draft agreement reached with the nationalists stipulated: 'During the war emergency period six Ulster counties to be left as at present under the Imperial Parliament.' After the war, an 'imperial conference' would be held to consider the future government of the Empire, including the question of the government of Ireland.

Immediately after the Conference... the permanent settlement of all the great outstanding problems, such as the permanent position of the six exempted counties... would be proceeded with.[70]

Both Carson and Redmond had great difficulty persuading their followers to accept the proposals. On 6 June Carson told the Ulster Unionist Council that this was the only way to get the Home Rule Act off the statute book, and explained the arithmetic of the exclusion plan. If they got the whole of Ulster, he said, with 896,000 Protestants and 700,000 Catholics, in their parliamentary representation they would be in a minority of one; but in the six counties, with 825,000 Protestants and 432,000 Catholics, they would have a parliamentary majority of seven. Further, he continued, there would still be an area with over 1,250,000 people 'governed absolutely independent, both legislatively and executively, of the Parliament in Dublin.'[71]

At a subsequent meeting, the delegates of Monaghan, Donegal and Cavan – the Ulster counties that would be left out of the excluded area – agreed with great reluctance to the proposal, on the grounds that a 'strong haven of refuge' in the six counties was better than a weak and precarious Ulster.[72]

For Redmond, the main problem was the northern nationalists. A conference was planned for 23 June to discuss the issue, and at preliminary conferences the nationalists of Derry, Tyrone and Fermanagh gathered to protest against any proposals to exclude any part of the nation, permanently or temporarily. The northern Catholic bishops were implacably opposed to the scheme. Dr MacHugh, the bishop of Derry, wrote,

what seems to be the worst feature of all this wretched bargaining is that Irishmen, calling themselves representatives of the people, are prepared to sell their brother Irishmen into slavery to secure a nominal freedom for a section of the people... was coercion of a more objectionable or despicable type ever resorted to by England in its dealings with Ireland than that now sanctioned by the men whom we elected to win us freedom?[73]

On 23 June, 776 delegates from nationalist bodies in the six counties assembled in Belfast. The strongest voices against exclusion came from Armagh, Derry, Tyrone and Fermanagh. The *Manchester Guardian* reported:

It was from the districts in which, although in the excluded area, the Nationalists are in power in local government that the main opposition came. It was based on two grounds. One was the sentiment of an Ireland united as a nation, the stronger of the two, and the other was a fear that Nationalists might be oppressed by an overwhelming majority of Unionists in the excluded area.[74]

Redmond threatened to resign the party leadership if the conference refused to endorse the exclusion policy, and the West Belfast MP Joseph Devlin eloquently supported him. Their combined weight was decisive: the delegates voted by 475 to 265 to accept Lloyd George's proposals 'for the temporary and provisional settlement of the Irish difficulty'.[75] Of the 270 delegates from Fermanagh, Tyrone and Derry City, 183 voted against exclusion. There were allegations that the majority in favour had been achieved by Joe Devlin's supporters packing the meeting and spinning out their speeches to prevent delegates who wanted to catch the last train home from voting.

But Carson predictably refused to accept temporary exclusion, and leading conservatives with southern Irish connections, including Walter Long and the Kerry landowner Lord Lansdowne, protested vociferously against the whole plan. Under this pressure, the government opted for permanent exclusion and demanded that the number of Irish MPs at Westminster be cut by more than half. Redmond could not, of course, accept these conditions, and the negotiations irretrievably broke down. On 24 July Redmond denounced the government:

> They have disregarded every advice we tendered to them, and now in the end, having got us to induce our people to make a tremendous sacrifice and to agree to the temporary exclusion of six Ulster counties, they throw this agreement to the winds and they have taken the surest means to accentuate every possible danger and difficulty in the Irish situation.[76]

The fiasco further intensified Irish disillusionment with the home rulers, and the gainer was Sinn Féin, the tiny 'advanced nationalist' party which had played no part in the Easter rising, but had been instantly and widely credited with it.

In the north, the decision to back exclusion destroyed the confidence of many nationalists in the Irish Party. Most Fermanagh nationalists, for instance, were strongly opposed to the idea, and in August 2,000 gathered in Enniskillen to condemn the Irish Party and even their own MP. Dissatisfied Fermanagh nationalists turned towards the Irish Nation League, formed by northern nationalist lawyers to opposed partition, and then to Sinn Féin.

Casement on trial

Meanwhile the final tragedy of the Easter rising was being played out. Sir Roger Casement, captured on Good Friday, was brought to London and imprisoned first in Brixton and then in the Tower of London. Here he had a hellish existence, with two soldiers always in his cell, the light on all night, still wearing the clothes in which he had landed, and his friends barred from visiting him for the first two weeks. First to see him was his solicitor, George Gavan Duffy, son of the Young Ireland leader. Casement was usually impeccably groomed, handsome and self-possessed, and Gavan Duffy was shocked by the encounter. Immediately after the visit he spoke to Casement's cousin and close friend Gertrude Bannister, who wrote:

> He said that he was not sure that it was really Roger (though he knew him well), that he was terribly changed, that his clothes were dirty, his face unshaven (he had shaved his beard off in Germany and it was half grown) and his eyes red around the rims and bloodshot; his manner hesitating, and he was unable to remember names or words. His tie, bootlaces and braces had been taken away from him and his boots were hanging round his ankles; he was collarless and he had to hold up his trousers. I discovered afterwards that his cell in the Tower was verminous, and his poor arms, head and neck were all swollen with bites. Thus does England chivalrously treat her enemies.[77]

On 15 May Casement appeared at Bow Street magistrates' court, charged with high treason, and was moved to Brixton, where conditions were somewhat better. On 26 June he went on trial at the Old Bailey: the prosecutor was the attorney-general Sir Frederick Smith, formerly F.E. Smith, leading promoter of the loyalist mobilisation against home rule. Casement's defence was funded by Clan-na-Gael in the USA, who scraped together what they could since he would otherwise have gone undefended. Among the friends and sympathisers who attended the trial were Eva Gore-Booth and Esther Roper, and the Irish-Irelander Alice Milligan. On 29 June the jury found Casement guilty. He made a long and passionate statement from the dock, declaring:

> Self-government is our right, a thing born in us at birth; a thing no more to be doled out to us or withheld from us by another people than the right to life itself – than the right to feel the sun or smell the flowers, or to love our kind... Where all your rights become only an accumulated wrong; where men must beg with bated breath for leave to subsist in their own land, to think their own thoughts, to sing their own songs, to garner the fruits of their own labours – and even while they beg, to see things inexorably withdrawn from them – then surely it is braver, a saner and a truer thing, to be a rebel in act and deed against such circumstances as these than tamely to accept it as the natural lot of men.[78]

Then, the journalist Henry Nevinson, who campaigned for Casement, recorded:

> Looking to the judges, I saw that clerks had put soft black things, like battered college-caps upon the head of each, and I heard the usher command silence while sentence of death was passed.[79]

A formidable campaign got under way on Casement's behalf to try to halt his execution. To the fore were his old friends, including Alice Stopford Green and Gertrude Bannister. Pleas for clemency poured in from an array of influential Irish-Americans, as well as Irish Party MPs and Irish archbishops and bishops. On 29 July the US Senate passed a resolution expressing 'the hope that the British Government may exercise clemency in the treatment of Irish political prisoners'.[80] The Negro Fellowship League in the USA and the president of Colombia added their voices, recalling Casement's heroic work to publicise the horrific treatment of rubber workers in the Congo and the Amazon. In England, Sir Arthur Conan Doyle organised a petition which was signed by Galsworthy, Chesterton and other Liberal writers. The Women's International League for Peace and Freedom, formed to oppose the 'great war', also protested.

But their efforts were undermined by an unscrupulous campaign of character assassination conducted by the government. After Casement was arrested, his diaries were found in his London lodgings. Like others of his class and era, Casement was a compulsive diarist, noting every detail of his life, from the people he met to the things he bought and the books he read. He also recorded, in elliptical but nonetheless revealing detail, his many sexual encounters with young men.

To the society of the day, homosexuality was a shameful and illegal vice. Casement himself appears to have had a divided attitude: his diaries reveal both that he regarded his sexual adventures as a delightful pastime, and that he saw homosexuality as a 'terrible disease'. He wrote in a poem:

> I sought by love alone to go
> Where God had writ an awful no...
> I only know tis death to give
> My love; yet loveless can I live?[81]

His friends had no inkling of his secret life, and, along with many Irish people, refused to believe that the diaries were anything other than British forgeries. In a smear campaign run from the home office, photographic copies of parts of the diaries were made, and circulated among MPs, churchmen and journalists, and through the London clubs, where men of power and influence congregated. King George V was shown the material, as was John Redmond, who decided to have nothing to do with the reprieve campaign. Asquith asked the US ambassador, Walter Page, if he had seen it. When Page said that he had, Asquith remarked: 'Excellent, and you need not be particular about keeping it to yourself.'[82]

The cabinet discussed Casement's sentence at length at four meetings. On 5 July they decided to submit the diaries to an 'alienist', as specialists in mental disorder were then known. Asquith wrote:

> Several members of the Cabinet... were strongly of opinion that it would be better (if possible) that he should be kept in confinement as a criminal lunatic than that he should be executed without any smirch on his character and then canonized as a martyr both in Ireland and America.[83]

The alienist, however, decided that Casement was 'abnormal but not certifiably insane' and the cabinet decided that he should be hanged. They could afford to ignore the pleas flooding in on his behalf, secure in the knowledge that his reputation could later be destroyed.

On 27 July, Gertrude Bannister visited Casement, now in Pentonville prison, for the last time. Both wept. He told her not to delude herself that he could still be saved, and said,

> "they want my death, nothing else will do. And, after all, it's a glorious death to die for Ireland – and I could not stand long in a place like this – it would destroy my reason."

Gertrude's memoir continued:

> The warder broke off the interview and marched him out. I stood up and stretched out my hands to him; he turned at the door and said, "Good-bye God bless you" – I went out and in the corridor outside I simply abandoned myself to my grief.[84]

On 3 August Casement was hanged in Pentonville prison and buried in quicklime in the prison yard. Nearly 50 years later the British government finally permitted the removal of his remains to Ireland.

Disaster on the Somme

Meanwhile the 'great war' was now being fought in the Middle East, Africa and the Atlantic ocean, although Europe was still the main battleground. In northern France, huge armies were bogged down in the trench warfare that had begun in 1914, with each side making costly but unsuccessful attempts to break through.

Most notorious of the allies' assaults was the battle of the Somme in 1916. The attack was purposeless, since there was no strategic gain to be made on the Somme, but the British commander-in-chief, Sir Douglas Haig, was convinced that a powerful offensive, even here, would win the war. On 1 July, 13 British divisions left their trenches and went 'over the top', attacking the German lines in regular waves, only to be mown down by machine-guns and artillery. The slaughter was terrible: 20,000 British soldiers were killed and 40,000 wounded in a single day. The attack was a total failure. For the loyalists of the north of Ireland, the Somme was a catastrophe. The *36th (Ulster) Division*, formed from the Ulster Volunteer Force, took the fourth highest casualties of all the British divisions. Of its 17,000 men, 2,000 or more were killed on 1 July alone, while about 3,000 were injured.

Back in Ireland, Protestant communities were devastated. An Orangeman in Lurgan wrote to a friend:

> There is hardly a house in Hill Street in which at least one member of the family has not been killed or wounded. It is terrible, terrible hard news to

bear with equanimity, for however just and right a cause it may be, the death of so many young men leaves our land that much the poorer.[85]

Orange parades were cancelled on 12 July; instead, people stood still for a five-minute silence at noon.

The generals allowed the futile slaughter on the Somme to continue till mid-November, by which time British losses were 420,000. In Britain, enthusiasm for war was replaced by disillusionment.

Frongoch camp

Differences within the establishment over the conduct of the war led Lloyd George, backed by the Conservatives and a section of the Liberal Party, to challenge Asquith, who resigned. On 7 December 1916 Lloyd George became prime minister in his place, at the head of a new, predominantly Conservative, coalition government.

The Irish separatist movement – now commonly described as Sinn Féin – was meanwhile developing apace. In Ireland, the middle classes shifted their allegiance from Redmond's Home Rule Party, while the jails and internment camps in Britain became universities for a new generation of revolutionaries. Frongoch internment camp in North Wales proved particularly significant. Here volunteers from all over Ireland were brought together: 1,850 of them at first, till large-scale releases at the end of July reduced the number to about 600.

The Volunteers – now becoming known as the Irish Republican Army – organised a military staff to run the camp. Mornings were taken up with military training and drill, and the afternoons with a variety of classes, such as languages, including Irish, mathematics and shorthand.

The prisoners repeatedly clashed with the authorities over the issue of prison work. One of the internees, Michael Collins, wrote to his sister on 25 August:

> It is a custom to appoint a fatigue of 8 men every day, for general scavenging & removing ashes, *inside the wires*. About 8 or 10 days ago the particular party that was on for the day was ordered outside the wires to do scavenging &c for the soldiers. Of course they refused. They were immediately sent to cells and since then have been interned in the northern portion of this camp being deprived of their letters, newspapers, smoking materials. Every day since 8 men have been given the same treatment, & the affair still goes on.[86]

Several weeks later the Home Office caved in, conceding that the soldiers could clear their own rubbish.

On the outside, women organised a Dependants' Fund for the prisoners, raising money, organising food parcels and supporting the prisoners' relatives. To the fore were relatives of the executed 1916 leaders, including

Tom Clarke's widow Kathleen. She had suffered especially grievously as a result of the rising, not only losing her husband and brother, and being left with three young children to care for, but also having a miscarriage soon afterwards. But she fought back indomitably, not only organising support for the prisoners, but also beginning the reorganisation of the secret Irish Republican Brotherhood. Other women, including Hanna Sheehy Skeffington and Nora Connolly, toured the USA speaking at hundreds of meetings to publicise the cause of Irish independence and raise money for the prisoners.

Frongoch camp

A second body, the Irish National Aid Association, also raised funds for the prisoners. Organised by respectable public figures, it attracted sizeable donations from priests, doctors and solicitors, as the professional classes moved to support militant nationalism.

Reorganising the IRB

Frongoch provided fertile conditions not only for the development of the IRA, but also for reorganising the Irish Republican Brotherhood, which recruited in the camp and formed a secret network holding key positions in the IRA. Central to the reorganisation was Michael Collins, an energetic, ebullient and quick-tempered personality in his mid-twenties, and a highly efficient organiser. The son of a Cork tenant farmer, Collins had spent several years in London, working as a clerk in various offices. He joined the Gaelic League, the IRB and the Volunteers, and then returned to Ireland in 1916 and spent the Easter rising in the GPO. He appraised the rising without sentiment, writing to a friend:

> I think the Rising was bungled terribly costing many a good life. It seemed at first to be well organised, but afterwards became subjected to panic decisions and a great lack of very essential organisation and co-operation.

He commented:

> Of Pearse and Connolly I admire the latter the most. Connolly was a realist, Pearse the direct opposite. There was an air of earthy directness

about Connolly. It impressed me. I would have followed him through hell had such action been necessary. But I doubt very much if I would have followed Pearse – not without some thought anyway.[87]

The IRB was simultaneously being reorganised in Dublin by Kathleen Clarke, and a provisional governing body was established in August 1916. At Christmas the bulk of the prisoners were released – Lloyd George wanted to appease American opinion in order to gain support for Britain in the war – and soon the IRB replaced the provisional body with a supreme council. Michael Collins was among its members, and the president was another veteran of the rising, Thomas Ashe.

Growing support for republicanism began to be reflected at elections. In February 1917 advanced nationalists challenged the Redmondites in a by-election in North Roscommon by putting up an independent candidate, Count Plunkett, father of Joseph Plunkett, executed in 1916. Count Plunkett won easily and, following Arthur Griffith's 'Sinn Féin' policy, refused to take his seat at Westminster. The authorities responded to Plunkett's victory by arresting 26 leading republicans and deporting ten of them, and by charging people for minor acts of disaffection such as singing disloyal songs.

In April on the anniversary of the Easter rising, the Volunteers organised parades, including one in Belfast's Falls Road. In Dublin the police struggled to remove the tricolour which flew at half mast over the ruins of the GPO, and members of the Citizen Army postered the walls with copies of the proclamation.

Differences now surfaced among non-Redmondite nationalists about what direction the movement should take. Should it adopt the full-blown republicanism and physical force methods of the leaders of the Easter rising? Or should it follow the more moderate policies of Sinn Féin's founder, Arthur Griffith? Sinn Féin was now moribund but was popularly identified with the rising, and Griffith had kept his credibility because he had been interned afterwards, despite the fact that he had not participated – though he had offered to do so.

To clarify the issues, Count Plunkett called a convention in Dublin on 19 April, where a wide range of opinion was represented, from mild nationalists vaguely dissatisfied with Redmond's party to outright advocates of an Irish republic. The meeting was heated, but eventually agreed to set up a Mansion House Committee which would put forward Ireland's claim to independence at the international peace conference which would follow the 'great war'.

The separatists decided to challenge Redmond's party at a by-election in May in South Longford, and put up an uncompromising candidate: Joseph McGuinness, then a prisoner in Lewes jail in England. John

Dillon, speaking for the Redmondite candidate, said that the issue was now clear:

> they were asked to abandon the demand for Home Rule or any form of self-government involving a continued connection with Great Britain and to substitute a demand for sovereign independence – an Irish Republic, and complete separation from the British Empire.[88]

The campaign was vigorously fought. The London *Times* reported:

> The organization of the Sinn Feiners was excellent. Speakers poured into Longford from every part of Ireland. There was a lavish expenditure of money. The roads for miles around Longford were littered with posters and appeals. Fleets of motor-cars appeared from every quarter.[89]

'Put him in to get him out!' was one of the slogans, but the issue that tipped the balance in McGuinness' favour was partition. On the eve of the election a manifesto was issued signed by three Catholic archbishops and fifteen bishops, and three Protestant bishops, stating:

> To Irishmen of every creed and class and party the very thought of our country partitioned and torn as a new Poland must be one of heart-rending sorrow.

McGuinness won narrowly, by 37 votes, and the *Times* opined:

> The fact of immediate' importance is that the Nationalist Party, at one of the most critical moments in its career, has suffered a most damaging defeat... The result of the election... is another warning that no settlement based on the temporary or permanent partition of Ireland can have the smallest chance of success.[90]

Count Plunkett had set up an organisation called the Liberty Clubs, probably sponsored by the IRB, which came into competition with the burgeoning network of Sinn Féin clubs. The separatist movement was in danger of splitting into factions, so Cathal Brugha and others held a meeting with Arthur Griffith. They suggested that Griffith hand over Sinn Féin to the Volunteers, but he refused; so the republicans, unwilling to risk starting a new organisation, decided to take over Sinn Féin on conditions which Griffith would agree with. Griffith agreed to propose to the Sinn Féin executive, known as the National Council, that half its members should retire and make room for six representatives of the Liberty Clubs and the Mansion House Committee – a move that was soon carried out.

Meanwhile, thoroughly alarmed by the way their support was draining to Sinn Féin, the Irish Party pressed the government on 17 March 1917 to bring in home rule 'without further delay'.[91] Lloyd George said he would do so, but the northeast would be excluded. Redmond immediately rejected this, warning:

there are men in Ireland, serious men… who are bent on the enterprise of smashing the constitutional movement. I say that the action taken by the Government tonight plays directly into the hands of these men… if the constitutional movement disappears, I beg the Prime Minister to take note that he will find himself face to face with a revolutionary movement, and he will find it impossible to preserve… any of the forms even of constitutionalism. He will have to govern Ireland by the naked sword.[92]

Then in May, under pressure from the USA and also wanting to get the Irish MPs on his side in his battle with the 'Asquithites', Lloyd George again embarked on a political initiative. He wrote to Redmond outlining the government's proposals:

Firstly, they would introduce a Bill for the immediate application of the Home Rule Act to Ireland, but excluding therefrom the six counties of North-east Ulster, such exclusion to be subject to reconsideration by Parliament at the end of five years, unless it is previously terminated by the action of the Council of Ireland, to be set up as hereinafter described.

Secondly… the Bill would provide for a Council of Ireland to be composed of two delegations, consisting, on the one hand, of all the Members returned to Westminster from the excluded area, and, on the other, of a delegation equal in numbers from the Irish Parliament.[93]

Lloyd George also suggested a fall-back plan: 'that of assembling a Convention of Irishmen of all parties for the purpose of producing a scheme of Irish self-government.'[94]

Redmond again rejected the home rule-plus-exclusion scheme, but agreed to the proposal for an all-Ireland convention.

Sinn Féin, which was rapidly becoming the most potent political force in the country, refused to take part in the convention unless the members were 'freely elected by adult suffrage in Ireland' – a move which would have reflected the strength of the demand for independence and unity.[95] But the government decreed that the members be hand-picked, so Sinn Féin, offered five places out of a total of 100, stayed away.

Amnesty

In June 1917, to ease the start of the convention, the government amnestied the remaining 160 prisoners held since the rising. They were released to a tumultuous welcome. Esther Roper described travelling to Dublin with Constance Markievicz:

We zigzagged across the water, and at last arrived at Kingstown Harbour, where the people were delirious with excitement and pleasure. It was difficult to reach the train for Dublin. Arriving there, we gave up any effort to hurry. Stepping down from the train was like plunging into the waves of the Atlantic – we were swallowed up… Constance and Eva were in Dr. Kathleen Lynn's car… Constance had to stand nearly all the time so that she could be seen by the vast crowds.[96]

Sinn Féin was growing rapidly, and soon there was more evidence of its popularity. In June Redmond's brother, Major Willy Redmond, was killed in Flanders, leaving his parliamentary seat vacant in East Clare. The by-election was held on 10 July, and Eamon de Valera went forward as the Sinn Féin candidate. He was the senior surviving commandant of the Easter rising and had just been released from Pentonville prison. He won a resounding victory against the Redmondite candidate, with 5,010 votes to 2,035. The Irish Party was stupefied and popular rejoicing swept the country.

Then in his mid-thirties, de Valera had been born in New York: his mother was Irish, daughter of a farm labourer and working as a domestic servant, and his father was a Spanish music teacher. His father died and his mother had to work, so the two-year-old Eamon was sent to Ireland to be brought up by his grandmother in an agricultural labourer's cottage in County Limerick. Later he went to college and became a mathematics teacher, joining the Gaelic League and then the Volunteers. He was one of the 90 sentenced to death after the rising; his sentence was commuted to life imprisonment. A competent and conscientious organiser, de Valera was not a profound political thinker: he had none of the ideological fire of Pearse nor the socialist and feminist idealism of Connolly. Like Michael Collins, he represented the new wave of pragmatic revolutionary leaders.

In his Clare election campaign, de Valera declared that he stood for the 1916 proclamation of the republic, but he did not take a doctrinaire position, saying:

> We want an Irish Republic because if Ireland had her freedom, it is, I believe, the most likely form of government. But if the Irish people wanted to have another form of government, so long as it was an Irish government, I would not put in a word against it.[97]

The convention first met at Trinity College, Dublin, on 25 July. It had 95 members, all prominent men, a fifth of them northern loyalists. The chairman was Sir Horace Plunkett, the eminent pioneer of the agricultural cooperative movement. Its deliberations continued for nine months, and predictably came to grief on the question of the northeast.

For the first time, southern Anglo-Irish aristocrats broke seriously from the northern loyalists. Recognising that home rule was inevitable, the southerners wanted to make it as harmless to themselves as possible: they wanted to avoid partition, which would leave them in a tiny minority, and to maintain links with the British empire. They were traumatised by the Easter rising, and were coming to believe that they should encourage the moderate nationalists. Viscount Powerscourt wrote that the upper classes should no longer ridicule patriotic sentiment, because this allowed it to fall 'into the hands of unprincipled organisers'. Instead,

> If Irish national sentiment became respectable and was organised by
> respectable people, who would introduce sound principles into it, it
> would be a great power for good in our country...[98]

The southern loyalists won Redmond's agreement to a home rule scheme
which offered the loyalists, who were about a quarter of Ireland's
population, 40 per cent of the seats in an Irish House of Commons: the
southerners' seats would be filled by nomination and the northerners'
through election, with extra northern members elected by special
constituencies representing commercial and agricultural interests.

A majority of the convention – 66 members, including 10 southern
loyalists and US nationalists – agreed to this plan, but the northern
loyalists refused to accept it, demanding instead the exclusion of all nine
counties of Ulster.

In March 1918, broken in health through repeated political
disappointments, John Redmond died, and the following month the
convention came to an end.

The convention had served the British government by keeping the Irish
issue off the international political agenda. Within Ireland, however, it
was widely scorned and outside its doors disaffection continued to rise.

In August 1917 there had been yet another Sinn Féin election triumph,
when William Cosgrave, like de Valéra a veteran of the rising and
recently released from prison, won Kilkenny City from the Redmondite
candidate.

The authorities continued their petty harassment of the Irish Volunteers,
carrying out arms raids and arrests, while leaving the loyalist Ulster
Volunteer Force alone. That August, 84 republicans were arrested. One of
them was Thomas Ashe, a hero of the rising, recently amnestied, and
president of the IRB. Ashe was charged with 'speeches likely to cause
disaffection' and sentenced by court-martial to a year's hard labour. Sent
to Dublin's Mountjoy jail, he and some 13 other republicans went on
hunger strike demanding to be treated as prisoners of war. He was forcibly
fed and died as a result on 25 September.

Ashe's funeral became the occasion for an enormous demonstration of
republican feeling. The procession was led by armed Volunteers and
nearly 200 priests, and representatives of the whole range of advanced and
constitutional nationalist organisations and the ITGWU. Thirty thousand
people followed, and many more lined the streets.

Three volleys were fired over Ashe's grave, and Michael Collins, in
Volunteer uniform, made a terse and celebrated oration, saying in English
and Irish,

> Nothing additional remains to be said. That volley which we have just
> heard is the only speech which it is proper to make above the grave of a
> dead Fenian.[99]

Sinn Féin transformed

At the end of October 1917 Sinn Féin held its ard fheis – annual conference – at which it was transformed into a new organisation. Held at Dublin's Mansion House, the ard fheis was attended by over 1,000 people. Arthur Griffith and Count Plunkett stood down from the contest for the presidency, leaving the field clear for Eamon de Valera, who was unanimously chosen. Michael Collins organised a secret slate of IRB candidates for the national executive, but most of them were beaten.

The new Sinn Féin was in effect a coalition embracing nationalists with widely differing political views, especially on whether or not the new Ireland should be a republic. The battle over the constitution was fought out before the conference, and de Valéra succeeded in papering over the cracks with a formula which stated:

> Sinn Féin aims at securing the International recognition of Ireland as an independent Irish Republic.
>   Having achieved that status the Irish people may by referendum freely choose their own form of Government.[100]

In his presidential speech to the ard fheis, de Valéra again took pains to defer any discussion about the form of a future Irish state, saying,

> This is not the time for discussion on the best forms of government. But we are all united on this – that we want complete and absolute independence. Get that and we will agree to differ afterwards.

He did not rule out a monarchy, saying instead that there was 'no contemplation... of having a Monarchy in which the Monarch would be of the House of Windsor.'[101]

The constitution pledged Sinn Féin to developing Irish industries and commerce, and transport and fisheries, and also to reforming education, and setting up a national civil service and Sinn Féin courts. Its last section nodded towards workers and women.

The women's clause was won by pressure from Dr Kathleen Lynn and Jennie Wyse-Power, backed by Seán T. Ó Ceallaigh. It stated: 'That the equality of men and women in this organisation be emphasised in all speeches and leaflets.'[102] Four women – Constance Markievicz, Dr Kathleen Lynn, Kathleen Clarke and Grace Plunkett – were included on the new 24-member executive.

The workers' clause stated simply: 'Sinn Feiners should make it their business to secure that workers are paid a living wage.'[103] Sinn Féin leaders repeatedly declared their sympathy with labour, but the labour organisations refused to become formally involved, allowing Sinn Féin's commitment to the workers' cause to remain weak and ill-defined.

With James Connolly dead, the new labour movement leadership had an ambiguous relationship to the national question. While Connolly had vigorously tried to thrust labour to the forefront of the independence struggle, the new leaders such as William O'Brien – who had been a close colleague of Connolly's in the ITGWU – believed that the labour movement and the newly formed Labour Party should stand aside from the national issue and allow other parties to take the lead. Labour's role, they considered, was to concentrate on expanding the union organisation: like Larkin and Connolly, they held the syndicalist view that industrial organisation was the key to the triumph of the working class.

Consequently William O'Brien had refused an invitation from Arthur Griffith in January 1917 for labour to become involved in forming the advanced nationalist coalition that later became the reconstituted Sinn Féin; and in April all the labour organisations invited to Count Plunkett's convention had refused to attend. But at the same time O'Brien and other ITGWU activists were committed to the cause of Irish independence. O'Brien supported Sinn Féin in its by-election campaigns, and participated in Plunkett's convention. The new labour paper *Irish Opinion* – later renamed the *Voice of Labour* – nailed its colours to Connolly's mast. De Valera had pledged, 'when Labour frees this country – helps to free it – Labour can look for its own share of its patrimony.' *Irish Opinion* riposted,

> What Mr. de Valera asks in effect is that Labour should wait till freedom is achieved before it claims "its share of its patrimony." There are free countries, even Republics, where Labour claims "its share in its patrimony" in vain. We can work for freedom, and we will, but at the same time we'll claim our share of our patrimony when and where opportunity offers.[104]

The Irish Volunteers had expanded rapidly over the previous few months, and now numbered some 50,000 to 60,000 young men, organised over much of the country. Immediately after the Sinn Féin ard fheis they held a convention, and de Valéra was elected president of that body too. The IRB was more successful than it had been with Sinn Féin, capturing nearly all the seats on the Volunteer executive, with Michael Collins becoming director of organisation. The existence of this secret organisation-within-an-organisation promised trouble ahead. Not only was de Valéra not in the IRB, though he had briefly belonged, but nor was Cathal Brugha, the Volunteers' chief of staff. Both de Valéra and Brugha believed that a secret body was no longer necessary, and could indeed be harmful.

Cumann na mBan held its own convention in the autumn of 1917, and Constance Markievicz was reconfirmed as president. Since the rising, there had been an influx of militant recruits, and Cumann na mBan began to see itself as more than a mere support organisation for the Volunteers: its new policy declared that funds collected were to be devoted 'to the arming and equipping of the men and women of Ireland.'[105]

That winter, famine seemed imminent in Europe, but cattle, oats and butter continued to pour out of Ireland to England in response to high prices, regardless of Irish needs. Sinn Féin set up a food committee which attempted to discourage exports, while in the west of Ireland, to the discomfort of the city-based leaders, Sinn Féin militants organised the takeover of parts of large estates: they removed the cattle and leased the land as allotments to labourers, paying the rent to the landowners.

Widespread arms-raiding and cattle-driving prompted the British authorities to ban the carrying of arms by unauthorised persons, and on 27 February they proclaimed County Clare a special military area. A brigadier-general was put in charge, extra troops were sent in, censorship was imposed on letters and newspapers, and the military issued or refused passports to people wishing to enter the county. Tension built up throughout the country as hundreds were arrested, and papers were suppressed or banned from issuing foreign editions.

Conscription

In early 1918 Sinn Féin lost three by-elections in a row to the Irish Party, but its fortunes were soon massively boosted when the government announced that conscription would be applied to Ireland. To compensate for the huge casualties being taken on the western front, the government's man-power committee recommended that 250,000 more men be recruited in 1918. Lloyd George considered that he would not be able to persuade the trade unions to accept a raising of the age limit for conscription from 42 to 50 unless he extended conscription to Ireland.

But the decision was made in the face of stern warnings. The chiefs of the army and police in Ireland prophesied in a memorandum on 27 March:

> Conscription can be enforced, but with the greatest difficulty. It will be bitterly opposed by the united Nationalists and the clergy... Some of the difficulties would be organised strikes dislocating the life of the country... to render it feasible... the country must be put under some kind of military control...[106]

On 9 April 1918 Lloyd George introduced the Military Service Bill, which raised the age limit in Britain and provided for conscription in Ireland. At the same time he promised a home rule bill. The reaction of nationalist Ireland to the Conscription Bill was instantaneous and furious. Sections of society who had earlier supported Britain's war effort, such as the Irish parliamentary party and the Catholic hierarchy, were unanimously hostile. In the Commons, William O'Brien denounced the bill as 'a declaration of war against Ireland,' while Joseph Devlin accused Lloyd George of adopting 'the methods of Prussia'.[107] Even working class loyalists protested: on 14 April a huge crowd of 8,000 or more gathered on the Custom House steps in Belfast to condemn the bill at a meeting addressed by trade union leaders.

The Commons passed the bill on 16 April by 301 votes to 103. The Irish Nationalist MPs walked out as a bloc in protest, and crossed to Ireland to organise resistance. Desmond Ryan described the atmosphere there:

> Feeling at white heat. Dublin has been lit with an electric resentment. Insurrection permeates the atmosphere. Not since 1916 has there been such feeling abroad.[108]

At the same time the government set up an Irish Committee, chaired by Walter Long and with no Irish members, to draft a home rule bill. The committee's discussions focused on the possibility of a federal solution, strongly urged by Long. This envisaged regional parliaments for England, Scotland, Wales and Ireland, all subject to the imperial parliament at Westminster. For the Conservatives, the scheme had the attraction of conceding a measure of self-government to Ireland, but under the guise of merely reorganising the United Kingdom. As the anti-conscription campaign mounted, however, the committee soon concluded that the priority was to 'restore respect for government' and 'enforce the law', and that the early introduction of a home rule bill was an impossibility.[109]

On 18 April, Nationalist, Sinn Féin and Labour leaders assembled at Dublin's Mansion House and condemned the Conscription Bill as being 'in direct violation of the rights of small nationalities to self-determination'. Their statement continued:

> The attempt to enforce it will be an unwarrantable aggression, which we call upon all Irishmen to resist by the most effective means at their disposal.[110]

A delegation from the conference went that afternoon to Maynooth, where the Catholic bishops were meeting. The 27 bishops signed a statement pronouncing,

> we consider that conscription forced in this way upon Ireland is an oppressive and inhuman law, which the Irish people have a right to resist by all means that are consonant with the law of God.[111]

The bishops instructed the clergy to celebrate masses 'to avert the scourge of conscription', and to announce public meetings at which people would sign a pledge to resist it. The following Sunday, 21 April, some two million people signed the pledge. Dublin Protestants, too, organised a petition.

The trade union movement went spectacularly into action. On 20 April, 1,500 delegates attended a special congress at the Mansion House and backed a call from the national executive of the Irish Trade Union Congress and the Labour Party for a general strike on 23 April. The strike brought virtually the whole of Ireland to a standstill except the loyalist areas of the northeast. Desmond Ryan wrote: 'Labour Day comes and there are no trains, trams, bread, papers, no shops open. The very clouds scarcely moved.'[112]

The women of Cumann na mBan, the Irish Women Workers' Union, and the Irish Women's Franchise League threw their energy into the campaign. On 9 June a national women's day was held, and women throughout the country signed a pledge that they would not take jobs vacated by men being conscripted. Esther Roper's brother went to Dublin, and she wrote:

> He saw people of all sorts, from 'AE' and James Stephens to Sinn Féin women, preparing lint and other materials which would be needed for Red Cross work if force was used. Constance of course was in the thick of the fight.[113]

Ernie O'Malley was sent by Michael Collins to organise a Volunteer brigade in Offaly, and recalled,

> In daytime I could now enter a town to practise quick mobilization. Shop boys, carpenters, shop owners, clerks, fell into line quickly. They practised bayonet fighting with brush handles up and down streets; they sat on pathways or in halls to listen to my talks from the destruction of railway plant to street fighting... Jewellers and locksmiths made revolver springs... Telegraphic clerks held classes with buzzers and tappers... Cumann na mBan sewed signalling flags and haversacks... Shops were raided for cartridges and detonators, quarries for explosives.[114]

The 'German plot' arrests

The immense wave of fury alarmed the government and conscription was never implemented. Fearing another rising, the authorities moved to suppress Sinn Féin. On 25 April the government extended the provisions of the Defence of the Realm Act to allow for the internment of Irish people, and in May machine guns were mounted on the Bank of Ireland in the centre of Dublin.

Then on the night of 17 May, there was a wave of arrests of Sinn Féin leaders and Volunteer officers all over Ireland, and 73 were immediately deported to England and interned. The deportees included Arthur Griffith, Eamon de Valera, Constance Markievicz, Maud Gonne MacBride, and Kathleen Clarke. In a vain attempt to make the arrests acceptable to public opinion, especially in America, the authorities claimed to have uncovered a 'German plot'. Field Marshal Lord French, the tough, newly appointed lord lieutenant, issued a proclamation declaring that

> certain subjects of His Majesty the King, domiciled in Ireland, have conspired to enter into and have entered into treasonable communication with the German enemy...[115]

The arrests and the general crackdown that followed only intensified antagonism to British rule, and cemented Sinn Féin's position as the voice of nationalist Ireland. Constance Markievicz wrote to her sister Eva from Holloway prison: 'Sending you to jail is like pulling out all the loud stops on all the speeches you ever made or words you ever wrote!'[116]

On 21 June Arthur Griffith, in prison in Gloucester, was elected Sinn Féin MP for East Cavan, defeating his Nationalist opponent by 1,200 votes in a result which was celebrated throughout the country.

Police activity against 'disloyally affected persons' was stepped up, and in June many areas were 'proclaimed' and subjected to special laws. Then on 3 July 1918 Lord French issued a proclamation declaring Sinn Féin, the Irish Volunteers, Cumann na mBan and the Gaelic League to be dangerous associations, 'designed to terrorise the peaceful and law-abiding subjects of His Majesty in Ireland'.[117] Their meetings were declared illegal, and people organising or attending them could be prosecuted.

On 9 July the military commander-in-chief issued an order under the Defence of the Realm Act banning all meetings and processions in public places in the whole of Ireland. Concerts, hurling matches, and literary competitions were suppressed. The people responded with defiance: 1,500 hurling matches were played on 4 August, and on 15 August hundreds of public meetings were held, with speakers being jailed as a result. Between mid-May and mid-December, there were more than 500 political arrests. Ireland was now being treated blatantly as hostile territory, governed by force and not by constitutional means. Michael Collins and Cathal Brugha had escaped arrest and gone 'on the run', concentrating on organising the military side of the movement. By November 1918 the authorities were alarmed: the chief secretary told parliament that the Volunteers were dominated by the Irish Republican Brotherhood and were preparing for 'violence of the most serious description'. He continued:

> only last week at one of their headquarters there was seized sufficient of high explosives, with fuses all prepared... sufficient to have blown up the whole of Belfast and Dublin.[118]

At 5 o'clock on the morning of 11 November 1918 the Germans signed the armistice, bringing the first world war to an end six hours later.

The devastation was almost unimaginable. Some seventeen million had died – around ten million in the fighting, and the rest of hunger and disease. Millions more were left permanently injured by wounds or gas. There was huge economic damage, and starvation was rife over much of Europe. Of the dead, about 700,000 were from England, Scotland and Wales, and 250,000 from elsewhere in the British empire, nearly a third of them Indians. Some 49,000 Irishmen had been killed, of the more than 300,000 – five-sixths of them Catholics – who had served with the British forces.

10
The War of Independence

On 14 December 1918, a month after the armistice, a general election was held. In Ireland, Sinn Féin made the election a plebiscite on the country's future.

Lloyd George and a section of the Liberal Party fought the election alongside the Tories as a coalition, and their manifesto was firmly negative on the Irish question:

> there are two paths which are closed – the one leading to a complete severance of Ireland from the British Empire, and the other to the forcible submission of the six counties of Ulster to a Home Rule Parliament against their will.[1]

While the Irish parliamentary party still stood for dominion home rule, Sinn Féin declared that it aimed to secure the establishment of the Irish republic,

> 1. By withdrawing the Irish Representation from the British Parliament and by denying the right and opposing the will of the British Government or any other foreign Government to legislate for Ireland.
> 2. By making use of any and every means available to render impotent the power of England to hold Ireland in subjection by military force or otherwise.[2]

Sinn Féin also said it would set up a constituent assembly, and send an appeal to the post-war peace conference 'for the establishment of Ireland as an independent nation.' Sinn Féin stood candidates in all but two of the 103 parliamentary seats. They were reportedly selected by Michael Collins and two other members of the IRB, and many of them were still in jail following the 'German plot' arrests.

The Irish parliamentary party – the Nationalists – had been deserted by their supporters, especially the younger ones. Demoralised and facing certain defeat, they surrendered 25 seats to Sinn Féin without a fight. Sinn Féin, by contrast, despite the fact that it was a banned organisation with many of its leaders in jail, was full of vigour. Ernie O'Malley recalled:

There was no dearth of workers; canvassers, bill posters, motor drivers, boys with whitewash to decorate bridge parapets and dead walls... Republican flags hung from old castles, until the peelers, in despair, tired of trying to take them down. Successive directors of elections were arrested, but others took their places. Through all their work was eagerness, talk, and gaiety.[3]

Women played a major part in Sinn Féin's campaign. In February 1918 the Representation of the People Act had given the vote to women of 30 years old, with a property qualification. Both the Irish parliamentary party and Irish Unionists tried to prevent the act being extended to Ireland, because they feared the new voters.

That November, an act was brought in enabling women to stand for parliament, and 17 stood in all. In Ireland, Cumann na mBan called on constituencies to select women candidates to stand for Sinn Féin, while the Irish Women's Franchise League appealed to all the Irish political parties. But only two women candidates went forward, both for Sinn Féin: Constance Markievicz, then in Holloway prison, who stood for St Patrick's division in Dublin, and Winifred Carney, formerly James Connolly's secretary and also a veteran of the rising, who stood for the Victoria division in Belfast with her own electoral programme calling for a workers' republic. Hanna Sheehy Skeffington was offered a seat but refused. The women of Cumann na mBan and the IWFL threw themselves into the election campaign, organising, canvassing and speaking. The campaign for Markievicz, in particular, was run largely by women.

In a move that would provoke controversy long into the future, the Labour Party, which had earlier announced it would stand candidates in the next parliamentary election, now decided it would withdraw. In its election manifesto, issued in September, Labour adopted a position of cautious support for both self-determination and abstentionism: but this proved too nationalistic for loyalist-dominated labour organisations in the northeast, which declined to put forward Labour candidates, and insufficiently outspoken for many in the labour movement elsewhere, whose sympathies lay with Sinn Féin.

Labour aimed to stand in four Dublin constituencies and several elsewhere. But it came under considerable pressure both from its own supporters and from Sinn Féin to stand down and avoid splitting the vote, which would allow the old Irish Party to slip through the middle. At the same time, Sinn Féin offered to allow Labour to stand unopposed in the four Dublin constituencies, provided its candidates pledged support for an independent Irish republic and that they would abstain from the Westminster parliament. At least three of the four Labour candidates would probably have signed the pledge, but the issue was brought to a head on 1 November when a special

Labour conference convened. That morning the national executive decided to recommend that the party withdraw from the election,

> in the hope that the democratic demand for self determination to which the Irish Labour Party and its candidates give unqualified adherence will thereby obtain the greatest chance of expression at the polls.[4]

The conference backed the decision to withdraw by 96 votes to 23.

Many socialists subsequently felt that by standing aside at this point, and not following James Connolly's example, the labour movement gave away its chance of playing an influential role in the Ireland of the future. The socialist republican Peadar O'Donnell, asking why the Labour leaders had acted as they did, considered that they had responded to the conflicting pressures from republican and loyalist workers:

> The simplest explanation is, like as not, the true one – Labour leaders could not make up their minds what road to take. They were a bothered lot of men who gave themselves one task above every other, to hold the branches of the trade unions together in a period of high controversy.

If union officials took the Sinn Féin side, wrote O'Donnell,

> their Protestant members, almost to a man, would stampede into a sectarian trade union in the shelter of the Orange lodges... On the other hand, a decision by trade union officials to put forward Labour candidates who would take their seats in the British Parliament would have caused an uproar.[5]

Meanwhile in the northeast, loyalist leaders, aiming to retain the support of Protestant workers in the face of widespread working-class unrest, had set up the Ulster Unionist Labour Association. Sir Edward Carson was its first president, while its chairman was the head of a large linen firm. The UULA put up three 'Labour Unionist' candidates for the election. During the campaign, they supported the demand for a cut in the working week to 44 hours; but once elected, they acted simply as Unionists, and did not take up the workers' grievances.

Polling was on 14 December 1918, but the votes were not counted till two weeks later. The result was a spectacular victory for Sinn Féin, and the old Irish Nationalist Party was obliterated. Sinn Féin won 73 of the 105 seats, while the Irish Party, which had previously held 80 seats, won only two outright – one of them Joseph Devlin's in West Belfast – and took a further four by agreement with Sinn Féin. The Unionists took 26 seats, including the three nominally Labour ones in Belfast, increasing their total by six. Constance Markievicz, who polled more than twice as many votes as her Irish Party opponent, was the only successful woman candidate in Ireland or Britain, and became the first woman ever elected to the Westminster parliament.

The *Irish Times* bemoaned the result:

> *Sinn Fein* has swept the board... The defeat of the Nationalist Party is crushing and final. If Mr. Asquith's Liberals could go back to Parliament on a big aeroplane, the Nationalists could go back on an Irish jaunting-car.[6]

The London *Times* conceded:

> after 10 years of obscure agitation and two or three of noisy turbulence, Sinn Fein is at last in the saddle, and in practically unchallenged political control of three-fourths of Ireland... Sinn Fein has won a tremendous political victory.[7]

Overall, Sinn Féin had received 47 per cent of the just over one million votes cast, while the Unionists took 28 per cent and the Nationalists 23 per cent. In addition, Sinn Féin had taken 25 seats unopposed, in which there were some 475,000 potential voters. The turnout had been about 70 per cent.

The Unionists' seats were concentrated in northeast Ulster. They had won a majority of votes in only four of the nine Ulster counties: Antrim, Down, Armagh and Derry – though Sinn Féin won Derry city. They were a minority in Tyrone and Fermanagh, while in Donegal, Cavan, and Monaghan no Unionist was returned.

The first Dáil

Michael Collins summed up the years from 1918 to 1921 as

> a struggle between our determination to govern ourselves and to get rid of British government and the British determination to prevent us doing either. It was a struggle between two rival Governments, the one an Irish Government resting on the will of the people and the other an alien Government depending for its existence upon military force – the one gathering more and more authority, the other steadily losing ground and growing ever more desperate and unscrupulous.[8]

On 7 January 1919 the newly elected republicans met at the Mansion House and issued an invitation to all representatives elected by Irish constituencies to attend the opening of Dáil Eireann, the parliament of Ireland.

The first Dáil met amid much excitement on the afternoon of 21 January. The Mansion House was packed with the public and with journalists from overseas, and cheering greeted the deputies as they arrived. Frank Gallagher described the proceedings:

> The roll of Deputies was called. To many names the clerks gave answer "Fe ghlas ag Gallaibh" – in foreign prisons. So often was that answer given that it became a refrain, a menacing refrain, which ever afterwards rang in the mind as that day was recalled. To other names the answer was simply "Absent." One of these names was Sir Edward Carson. For a moment the audience laughed and then it was realised that Dáil Éireann

was the assembly of Ireland, embracing all whom the people chose, and that Unionists had the same right to be there as Republicans, and the laugh died out and was not repeated.[9]

The new deputies were youthful and drawn largely from the urban lower middle class: most were journalists, teachers, shopkeepers, and office workers. Landowners and businessmen were now unrepresented, and there were few farmers. Nor had the working class won a place at the table, because labour had stood aside.

The Dáil did, however, acknowledge working-class interests by adopting a 'democratic programme' which owed much to the teachings of Pearse and Connolly. The original draft, drawn up by the Liverpool-born trade union leader Thomas Johnson, echoed the Communist Manifesto, and committed the new republic to aiming at 'the elimination of the class in society which lives upon the wealth produced by the workers of the nation but gives no useful social service in return',[10] Such clauses were removed by Seán T. Ó Ceallaigh at the insistence of Michael Collins, for fear of alienating the socially conservative members of the Dáil. But the final document still had a strong radical thrust, declaring that

the Nation's sovereignty extends not only to all men and women of the Nation, but to all its material possessions, the Nation's soil and all its resources, all the wealth and all the wealth-producing processes within the Nation, and... we reaffirm that all right to private property must be subordinated to the public right and welfare.[11]

The press censor at Dublin Castle issued a notice to all Irish papers forbidding publication of the democratic programme and the declaration of independence. The lord lieutenant, Lord French, described the Dáil's first meeting as 'a ludicrous farce'.[12]

Soon afterwards, the Irish cause won a sympathetic response at the international socialist conference held at Berne in Switzerland. The Irish and British delegations at first put forward conflicting resolutions: the Irish wanted recognition of their right to self-determination and a republic, while the British, led by Ramsay MacDonald, called for Irish home rule within the empire. The two sides compromised, with the British agreeing to support self-determination if the Irish omitted mention of the republic, and the resulting resolution was passed by the conference.

But attempts to press Ireland's claim at the post-war peace conference at Paris were less successful. Efforts to obtain a hearing continued over several months, but ultimately proved fruitless because of lack of support from the US government. Despite substantial and clamorous pressure from Irish-Americans, backed up by votes in the House of Representatives and the Senate, US president Wilson refused to press the Irish case: it was more important to him to have British co-operation in his efforts to create the

League of Nations. Wilson had strongly espoused the idea of national self-determination, and the British government too paid lip-service to it, but in the case of the Irish, as of the many other subjugated nationalities, principle swiftly fell victim to expediency. The government of the Soviet Union became the only one to recognise the 1919 republic.

The Egyptians likewise fell foul of British imperial self-interest. The British authorities refused to allow a nationalist delegation to attend the peace conference, or even to hear the Egyptian premier. The Egyptians were outraged, and strikes and violence followed. In a debate on the rebellion, Lord Curzon told the House of Lords,

> We should, indeed, have been quite ready to have heard Zaglul Pasha [the nationalist leader] and his friends if they had not opened the proceedings by demanding our complete retirement from the country. This was an impossible condition, which did not even provide a basis for reasonable discussion.[13]

Soloheadbeg

The day the first Dáil met came an incident that would later be regarded as the opening move in a two-and-a-half year guerrilla war. That morning nine Volunteers, led by Dan Breen and Seán Treacy, ambushed a small convoy taking gelignite by horse-and-cart from Tipperary town to Soloheadbeg quarry. The Volunteers called on the two armed policemen escorting the convoy to surrender: they refused and were shot dead, and the Volunteers took the cart and explosives.

There had been numerous raids for arms during the previous year, and the occasional ambush, but the policemen were the first members of the British forces to be killed since the Easter rising. The timing of the raid was a coincidence: the Volunteers had expected the convoy to arrive earlier, and had lain in wait for five days. But Breen and Treacy had decided in advance to shoot the police escort if necessary, in order to escalate the military side of the struggle, which they felt was being allowed to atrophy at the expense of political activity. Work for the 1918 election, wrote Breen,

> had had a serious effect on our army. Many had ceased to be soldiers and had become politicians. There was a danger of disintegration... I was convinced that some sort of action was absolutely necessary... I knew that if we once showed them the way, there were plenty of fine fellows on whom we could rely.[14]

The ruthlessness of the Soloheadbeg incident shocked Ireland and made many Sinn Féiners uneasy, but the Volunteer leadership retrospectively gave its backing. Their paper, *An t'Oglach*, declared on 31 January 1919 that Volunteers were entitled to use all legitimate methods of warfare against the soldiers and policemen of the English usurper, and to slay them if it is necessary to do so to in order to overcome their resistance.

In the wake of Soloheadbeg, the authorities declared the south riding of Tipperary a special military area, and repression was widespread. Sporadic republican violence continued, mostly directed at seizing arms, accompanied by a vigorous campaign for the release of the Sinn Féin prisoners in England. On 3 February, in a coup aided by Michael Collins and Harry Boland, Eamon de Valera escaped from Lincoln prison. In March the government released the remaining internees to an ecstatic welcome. Meeting at the start of April, the Dáil declared de Valera elected president. He in turn appointed ministers, including Arthur Griffith for home affairs, Cathal Brugha for defence, and Constance Markievicz for labour: she became the second woman cabinet minister in Europe, after Alexandra Kollontai who had been made a commissar in the Soviet government established after the 1917 revolution. Michael Collins was made minister for finance, and set about organising the issue of bonds to raise a loan to finance the new republic.

The Limerick soviet

Meanwhile working class militancy continued in the cities. In late January thousands of Belfast workers went on strike for a 44-hour week, and stayed out for nearly four weeks. The strikers were from the shipyards and engineering plants, and also gas and electricity stations, and they rapidly paralysed the city. The strikers were overwhelmingly loyalist, and were undermined by accusations from the unionist élite that the strike was inspired by Sinn Féiners and Bolsheviks, and would help the 'enemies of Ulster'. Nor did they want a confrontation with the state, and when the authorities moved troops into the gas works and electricity station, the strike was soon called off.

In April in Limerick, by contrast, workers took a different course, marrying the labour and republican causes in a protest against the authorities which, in keeping with the times, was soon dubbed the 'Limerick soviet'.

The sequence of events began on 6 April 1919, when Volunteers tried to rescue one of their imprisoned members, a trade unionist named Robert Byrne, who was leading a hunger strike for political status and had been transferred to Limerick Workhouse Hospital. In the rescue attempt, a constable was shot dead and another was mortally wounded, while Byrne himself was fatally injured. The authorities responded by declaring that Limerick city and an area around it would be made a special military area, and that anyone wishing to enter it would have to produce a permit issued by the military.

More than 5,000 workers would be directly affected by the restrictions, and on Sunday 13 April the Limerick trades council called a general strike from the next day till the ending of martial law. More than 14,000 workers went on strike, supported by small shopkeepers, while the Catholic bishop and even the Chamber of Commerce – which represented the large businessmen – condemned the permit system. The trades council became the strike committee, and organised publicity, food distribution, and skeleton staffs to maintain gas, electricity and water supplies. To meet the shortage of money, the strike committee printed its own currency. A strike committee member wrote,

> It was generally admitted that the city was never guarded or policed so well previously. The people, for once, were doing their own work, and doing it properly. There was no looting, and not a single case came up for hearing at the Petty Sessions.[15]

But their efforts were fatally hampered by the leaders of the British and Irish labour movements. The British Trades Union Congress instructed unions to refuse strike pay to those involved, on the grounds that the strike was political; while the national executive of the Irish Labour Party and Trade Union Congress refused to recommend a national general strike, instead suggesting the complete evacuation of Limerick. A national strike could anyway be only for a few days, said the ITUC's vice-president, because 'under the existing state of affairs they were not prepared for the revolution'.[16]

The Sinn Féin mayor and the bishop met the British commander, who offered concessions. Under pressure, the strike committee brought the strike to an end between 25 and 27 April; a week later the authorities announced the withdrawal of the martial law proclamation and the ending of the permit order.

Open rebellion

On 1 May workers throughout Ireland, with the exception of the Belfast area, downed tools to celebrate the newly established 'workers' holiday'. The Irish Labour Party and TUC announced on posters:

> All work will be suspended for that day to demonstrate that the Irish working-class joins with the INTERNATIONAL LABOUR MOVEMENT in demanding a DEMOCRATIC LEAGUE OF FREE NATIONS as the necessary condition of permanent peace based upon the SELF-DETERMINATION of all peoples including the PEOPLE OF IRELAND.[17]

Antagonism between the people and the authorities continued to grow. A three-person Irish-American delegation visited Ireland in May, and reported:

> we witnessed numerous assaults in public streets and highways with bayonets and clubbed rifles upon men and women known to be republicans, or suspected of being in favor of a republican form of government.[18]

Then on 13 May Volunteers led by Seán Treacy and Dan Breen shot and fatally wounded two constables while rescuing Seán Hogan, who had been arrested after the Soloheadbeg incident, from his guard at Knocklong station in County Limerick. On 22 May Lord Birkenhead – formerly F.E. Smith, leading sponsor of the loyalist revolt – told the House of Lords:

> There is no use closing our eyes to the fact that a great majority of Irishmen to-day are in open rebellion against the people of this country. Murder is not only common, but it is commonly approved. It excites no reprobation among an overwhelming number of the supporters of the Sinn Feiners.[19]

The succeeding months of 1919 saw widespread repression by the authorities and escalating republican guerrilla warfare. Troops and police were everywhere: in June, the *Freeman's Journal* described the Dublin quays as 'jammed with tanks, armoured cars, guns, motor lorries and thousands of troops, as if the port was a base of a formidable expeditionary force.'[20] By now, the British army in Ireland was costing half the total cost of maintaining the army throughout the empire: an area 357 times larger than Ireland, and with 90 times its population.

On 23 June District Inspector Hunt of the RIC was shot dead in broad daylight in Thurles, County Tipperary, prompting Lord French to ban Sinn Féin and like-minded organisations in that part of the county. On 24 June the Irish bishops blamed the violence on the British regime, which they described as 'the rule of the sword, utterly unsuited to a civilised nation, and provocative of disorder and chronic rebellion.'[21]

From her prison cell in Cork, to which she had been consigned for making a seditious speech, Constance Markievicz wrote in August to her sister of a recently reported incident involving Hanna Sheehy Skeffington, who had been 'awfully knocked about':

> She interfered with the police who continued to hammer an unconscious man with clubbed rifles and she was clubbed over the head. She lost a lot of blood and will have to keep quiet for a bit.[22]

During 1919, thousands of houses were raided. Meetings, fairs, Irish language classes, concerts, exhibitions of Irish produce – all were casualties. A man was jailed for singing 'The Felons of Our Land', while others were imprisoned for reading Sinn Féin's manifesto at meetings.

Led by Michael Collins, Cathal Brugha, and others, the Volunteers became a highly organised force, run on military lines. In August they began a co-ordinated campaign of guerrilla warfare, with systematic attacks on police barracks in many parts of the country. As a result, the RIC began to abandon outlying areas. At the same time, Collins began to organise the elimination of a key element in the British authorities' intelligence system: the detectives of the Dublin Metropolitan Police's political section, 'G' Division. Collins explained later that while England could always replace soldiers, spies were less easily replaced. He went on,

> To paralyse the British machine it was necessary to strike at individuals.
> Without her spies England was helpless... The most potent of these spies
> were Irishmen enlisted in the British service...[23]

In the summer of 1919 Collins organised a group of hitmen known as 'the
Squad' to kill the 'G men', as the detectives were known. Collins had agents
among the detectives in Dublin Castle itself, who provided the intelligence
necessary for the assassinations. Then, as one of the Squad, Bill Stapleton,
recalled,

> Two or three of us would go out with an Intelligence Officer walking in
> front of us, maybe about ten or fifteen yards. His job was to identify the
> man we were to shoot... He would take off his hat and greet the marked
> man. Of course, he didn't know him. As soon as he did this we would
> shoot.[24]

By the end of 1919, five of the ten or so detectives working on political
intelligence had been killed or wounded, while the chief commissioner was
petitioning London to find a job in Britain for his best detective before he
too was shot. Lord French wrote despairingly, 'Our Secret Service is simply
non-existent. What masquerades for such a Service in nothing but a delusion
and a snare.'[25]

On Sunday 7 September 1919 the IRA's Cork No. 2 brigade, commanded
by Liam Lynch, struck in Fermoy, the most important British military base
in the south of Ireland. In a carefully planned operation, some 25 Volunteers
attacked a party of 17 soldiers on their way to church, aiming to seize their
rifles. In the mêlée, a soldier was killed and three others wounded. Next day
an inquest jury found that, 'these men came for the purpose of getting rifles,
and had no intention of killing anybody.'[26] The jury's failure to bring a
murder verdict infuriated troops in the town, and that night, in the words of
the *Times*,

> some of the soldiers broke bounds, rioted through the town, sacked a
> number of shops – first among them apparently that of the foreman of the
> jury – and indulged in indiscriminate loot.[27]

Two days later Lord French, given virtually a free hand by an uninterested
cabinet, banned Dáil Éireann: a move which only served to increase the
combativeness of the population, and to spur the Irish campaign in the
USA, where Eamon de Valera had been touring since June. On 20 September
all republican papers were suppressed, followed in October by 22 journals
which publicised the Dáil loan.

The republicans responded by launching on 11 November 1919 a stencilled
information sheet titled the *Irish Bulletin*, which would appear every weekday
without fail for the duration of the war. Hundreds of copies of the *Bulletin*
were distributed to journalists and politicians in Ireland and abroad, including,

as Frank Gallagher, one of the publication's mainstays, recalled, 'India, Egypt and other nations asserting their right to freedom.'[28] Kathleen McKenna, who typed, duplicated and distributed the *Bulletin*, wrote,

> In our *Bulletin* was incorporated secret and incriminating information obtained by the armed raids carried out by themembers of the Irish Republican Army on British confidential mails, or from our secret helpers actually inside Dublin Castle and British governmental offices... We published sworn statements made by victims of assaults, arson and other atrocities committed by crown terrorists; and affidavits made by witnesses of murders, masked raids, tortures and other outrages.[29]

Constantly pursued by the authorities, the *Bulletin*'s staff 'flitted' from house to house with their equipment.

'Universal terrorism'

The last months of 1919 saw growing chaos as British law broke down and guerrilla war took hold in the south and west. An official report noted that in West Cork, already 'in a disturbed condition',

> matters have got worse... A system of universal terrorism exists, and this prevents the law-abiding section of the community from asserting itself or even assisting the authorities in maintaining the supremacy of the law and bringing offenders to justice. The principal efforts of Sinn Fein and the Irish Volunteers are directed against the R.I.C., whom they regard as the chief obstacle in their path, and who are now working under a strain which is almost unbearable... The ordinary processes of the law are useless now. The people in general will not give evidence in criminal cases, fearing attack. The result is that the lawless section commit crime and outrage with comparative impunity...[30]

The authorities began planning to reinforce the RIC by recruiting ex-servicemen from Britain, demobilised after the 'great war'. Recruiting offices were set up in London, Glasgow and Birmingham, and the first ex-servicemen were appointed in January 1920, arriving in Ireland two months later. Issued with ad hoc outfits made up from parts of army and police uniforms, they were soon dubbed the 'Black and Tans' – a name that would become notorious – after a well known pack of foxhounds.

In December 1919 the London *Times* ran a series of articles on 'The State of Ireland' by a special correspondent. He noted the 'moral ascendancy' of Sinn Féin, and criticised Lord French's policy of trying 'simply or solely either to defeat or destroy' the organisation. He went on: 'The citadel of Sinn Fein is in the minds of the young... The prospect of dying for Ireland haunts the dreams of thousands of youths to-day'.[31]

On 15 December police and soldiers stopped publication of the Dublin *Freeman's Journal* by taking away vital parts of its machinery, and next day a *Times* leader censured 'the present policy of coercion', saying, 'we deplore the fact that the authority of the British name in Ireland has come to rest upon military power'.[32]

Then on 19 December the IRA traumatised the establishment by narrowly failing to kill the lord lieutenant, Lord French, in an ambush at Ashtown, where he had left his train en route for his residence at Phoenix Park. In response, the army was given drastic powers to deport, intern and search. Plans were made for the mass arrest of IRA leaders, and destroyers were put on standby to carry deportees to Britain.

There was disarray among British civil servants and politicians as to how to deal with the situation on the ground. Should force alone be used, as Lord French advocated, or should Sinn Féin be negotiated with, as the *Times* believed? Sir Warren Fisher, a civil servant sent to investigate the Dublin Castle administration in 1920, wrote later that Lord French and others

> had convinced themselves that the only cure for the (then) sporadic and infrequent exhibitions of force in Ireland was the total excommunication of Sinn Fein as such with bell, book and candle. The fact that Sinn Fein was a political creed... escaped the notice of these gentlemen. They merely regarded it as a convertible term with the physical force faction... they decided that the Irish problem would be settled if the majority of the people in Ireland were forbidden to think, discuss, talk, write or speak the political views which they favoured...[33]

But at the level of long-term policy British Tories and Liberals were now agreed: Ireland should have home rule – with special arrangements for 'Ulster' – but it should on no account be allowed to leave the empire. There would be no republic, and not even the dominion status accorded to the other 'white' colonies, Canada, Australia, New Zealand and South Africa. As Lloyd George had put it,

> The demand for Dominion status was really a demand for the right of secession, since the Dominions were virtually independent States and could secede at any time if they chose...[34]

Ireland's strategic position was at the root of British opposition to its independence. Lloyd George told parliament on 22 December 1919 that if Ireland had been 'a separate unit' during the recent war, the Allies could have suffered:

> A hostile republic there, or even an unfriendly one, might very well have been fatal to the cause of the Allies... if we had had there a land over whose harbours and inlets we had no control, you might have had a situation full of peril... The area of submarine activity might have been extended beyond the limits of control, and Britain and her allies might have been cut off from the Dominions and from the United States of America.[35]

Ireland and the empire

Leading establishment figures saw Ireland as a vital link in the chain that bound the British empire together, so that to lose Ireland would mean to lose the empire. The empire in 1919 was in a highly volatile state, and its component countries influenced one another. During the 'great war' the colonies' hopes had been raised both by US president Wilson's talk of self-determination, and by Britain's intimations that support in the war would be rewarded by self-government. But now hopes had been dashed, and anger and violence followed.

India, most prized of Britain's possessions, which had sent 139,000 soldiers to fight in the trenches, was inflamed by a new militancy. Mahatma Gandhi organised *hartals* – mourning rituals – in protest against repressive legislation. Then in April 1919 India was overwhelmed by anger and grief by the Amritsar massacre, when General Dyer ordered Gurkha troops to fire on thousands of people assembled for a banned meeting in the Jallianwala Bagh – an enclosed square – in the Sikh city, killing hundreds of men, women and children. According to official figures, compiled months later, the soldiers killed 379 and wounded more than 1,200, while Indian survivors estimated that 500 to 1,000 had died. News of the full horror of the massacre did not percolate through to England till some eight months later.

Dyer compounded Indian fury by instituting martial law, under which many people were arrested and tortured or publicly flogged. Many bizarre and humiliating punishments were introduced, most notoriously Dyer's 'crawling order', which decreed that people passing through a lane where a white woman missionary had been assaulted must move on all fours: in fact they had to squirm along on their stomachs, because soldiers stood over them prodding them if they lifted their legs or arms. Outrage at the massacre and its aftermath swung Indian opinion away from constitutional nationalism and towards Mahatma Gandhi's new movement of non-co-operation with the British authorities.

As well as being spurred by the same post-war political conditions, the nationalist movements of India, Egypt and Ireland influenced each other both at a distance – they observed and drew lessons from each other's experiences – and directly. In the early years of the century, Irish, Indian and Egyptian revolutionaries had come together in Europe for training in the use of arms, and had assisted one another at international socialist conferences. The Indian home rule campaign drew on Irish models, and a key figure in it was the remarkable Annie Besant, who though born and brought up in Britain had an Irish mother and half-Irish father. She declared,

> It has always been somewhat of a grievance to me that I was born in London, "within the sound of Bow Bells," when three-quarters of my blood and all my heart are Irish.[36]

Another woman of Irish background who won an honoured place in Indian history was Margaret Noble, also known as Sister Nivedita, the name given her by a Hindu religious order. Brought up in Dungannon till the age of 9,

Margaret Noble was the daughter of a Wesleyan minister, and her grandparents had supported the Irish nationalist movement. In London Margaret met a well-known Hindu teacher, Swami Vivekananda, whose thinking was deeply imbued with the need to regenerate India and alleviate the sufferings of the poor. In 1898 Margaret joined him in India, where she stayed – apart from trips to Europe and the USA, where she lectured on Hinduism and Indian life – until her death in 1911. She founded a girls' school in Calcutta, and went on to become a famous figure in the home rule movement, associated with its revolutionary wing. She believed passionately in the need for India to rediscover and build on its own traditions, cultural and political, and wrote in a letter:

> I have no interest in anything done by the Government of India. To my mind, what a people do not do for themselves is ill-done, no matter how brilliant it seems...[37]

In the anti-imperialist upsurge of 1919 and 1920, Irish and Indian organisations worked closely together, especially in the USA. There, representatives spoke together at meetings, and Indians contributed to Irish papers. In 1919 Irish-Americans on the west coast protested against the deportation of Indians, and the Ghadar Party – an organisation of Indian workers in the US dedicated to the armed overthrow of the British raj – presented Eamon de Valera, president of the Irish republic, with an engraved sword and an Irish flag. In February 1920 de Valera delivered a rousing speech to a dinner in New York given by the Friends of Freedom for India. Lambasting the record of the British 'imperial system' in India and Ireland, and advocating the use of physical force to remove it, he declared:

> we of Ireland and you of India must each of us endeavor, both as separate peoples and in combination, to rid ourselves of the vampire that is fattening on our blood, and we must never allow ourselves to forget what weapon it was by which Washington rid his country of this same vampire.[38]

That March a large contingent of Indians in traditional dress joined the St Patrick's Day parade in New York. Meanwhile Irish republican sailors carried communications between Indian nationalists at home and overseas.

In early 1920 a Home Office intelligence report to the British cabinet stated that there was evidence that the Irish Republican Brotherhood was 'in direct touch with the Soviet Government in Russia through an address in Paris,' and was 'also in touch with the Egyptian extremists'.[39]

Plans for home rule

The Government of Ireland Act of 1914, giving home rule to all of Ireland under a single parliament, was due to come into effect automatically on the ratification of the last of the peace treaties following the 'great war'. In the autumn of 1919 the British cabinet decided that this prospect must be averted, since the bill 'was not acceptable to any of the interests concerned'.[40] The cabinet appointed a committee under the chairmanship of Walter Long to advise the government which Irish policy to adopt. Like the cabinet, the committee was dominated by Tories and without a single Irish member. They stated on 4 November 1919 that

> they found themselves limited in two directions. On the one hand, the Government was committed against any solution which would break up the unity of the Empire. On the other, it was committed that Ulster must not be forced under the rule of an Irish Parliament against its will. The first condition, therefore, excludes any proposal for allowing Ireland or any part of Ireland to establish an independent republic; the second precludes them from again attempting what has so often failed in the past, the establishment by the action of the Imperial Parliament of a single Parliament for all Ireland on the lines of the Home Rule Acts of 1886, 1893 and 1914.[41]

The committee rejected the idea of an all-Ireland home rule parliament with some part of 'Ulster' excluded, and also the idea of an all-Ireland parliament with 'Ulster' given special weighting within it, either through an Ulster Committee or through having an artificially large number of MPs. Instead, they recommended a third course of action:

> to establish one Parliament for the three Southern provinces and a second parliament for Ulster, together with a Council of Ireland... mainly to promote as rapidly as possible... the union of the whole of Ireland under a single legislature.[42]

This was the first time that two home rule parliaments had been proposed, and the committee argued that this plan would

> enormously minimise the partition issue. The division of Ireland becomes a far less serious matter if Home Rule is established for both parts of Ireland than if the excluded part is retained as part of Great Britain.[43]

When it came to drawing the dividing line,

> reasons of administrative convenience ought to be a principal consideration... The Committee are advised that from the administrative point of view, the retention of the historic boundaries between Ulster and the three other provinces would be far the most convenient... This arrangement has the further advantage that it minimises the division of Ireland on purely religious lines. The two religions would not be unevenly balanced in the Parliament of Northern Ireland.[44]

The committee added that they attached 'the greatest importance to doing everything possible to promote Irish unity.' To this end, they recommended that for one year only

> certain services which it is specially undesirable to divide, notably agriculture, technical education, transportation, old age pensions, health and unemployment, insurance and labour exchanges, should be reserved

to the Imperial Parliament, and that a Council of Ireland should be established consisting of twenty representatives from each Parliament...[45]

As under the 1914 act, substantial powers would be reserved to the imperial parliament, including peace and war, the armed forces, foreign relations and international trade.

The 'Ulster' question

At its meeting on 11 November 1919 the cabinet considered the report and decided that the Irish committee should draft a bill based on the scheme. Resuming the discussion on 3 December, the cabinet reached general agreement on the ultimate aim of government policy. The minutes summed up:

> While some views were expressed in favour of keeping Ulster, or at any rate the six Counties, permanently separate from the remainder of Ireland, the general feeling was that the ultimate aim of the Government's policy in Ireland was a united Ireland with a separate Parliament of its own, bound by the closest ties to Great Britain, but that this must be achieved with the largest possible support, and without offending the Protestants in Ulster...[46]

But while the Ulster Unionists accepted the idea of two home rule parliaments in Ireland – although without enthusiasm – they fought back over the question of how large the northeastern area should be. On 10 December the cabinet was told that

> the trend of opinion among responsible Ulster politicians was in favour of limiting the scheme to the Six Counties, since the idea of governing the three Ulster Counties which had a Nationalist majority was not relished.[47]

The cabinet heard the same message on 15 December, and was also told that Sir James Craig had proposed a boundary commission which would take a vote in the areas along the Six County border as to whether the inhabitants would prefer to be in 'the Northern or the Southern Parliamentary Area.'

On 19 December Sir James Craig saw Lloyd George and again expressed his strong opinion in favour of confining the Northern Parliament of Ireland to the Six Counties. Later that day the cabinet held a long discussion on the issue and began to lean towards the Six Counties proposal, on the grounds that while

> the jurisdiction of the Northern Parliament over the whole of Ulster as a geographical unit was more logical and in many ways easier to defend in Parliament, it was generally felt that it was even more important to get a scheme which, even though theoretically less perfect, would meet with more general acceptance... It would be difficult for the Government to force through a scheme which was unacceptable both to their friends and to their critics.[48]

On 22 December 1919 Lloyd George presented the government's plans to the Commons, proposing two home rule parliaments plus a Council of Ireland, and leaving open the size of the area to be partitioned.

Arguments over the size of the northeastern area continued over succeeding months. Walter Long went to the north of Ireland to assess Unionist opinion, and reported on 3 February:

> Most of the people with whom I discussed this question were of opinion that the whole of the province should be excluded; but on the other hand, the people in the inner circles hold the view that the new province should consist of the six counties, the idea being that the inclusion of Donegal, Cavan and Monaghan would provide such an access of strength to the Roman Catholic party, that the supremacy of the Unionists would be seriously threatened.[49]

But Long's committee nevertheless stuck to the view that 'the whole of the Province of Ulster should be included in the Northern Parliament.'[50]

The Conservative leader A.J. Balfour immediately weighed in on the opposing side, stressing,

> If you have a Hibernia Irredenta within the province of Ulster, you will greatly add to the difficulties of the Ulster Parliament; you will reproduce on a small scale all the troubles which we have had at Westminster during the forty years between the advent of Parnell on the political stage in 1878, and the blessed refusal of the Sinn Feiners to take the oath of allegiance in 1918...[51]

On 24 February 1920 the cabinet finally committed itself to the six county plan, stating:

> The area of Northern Ireland shall consist of the Parliamentary counties of Antrim, Armagh, Down, Fermanagh, Londonderry and Tyrone and the Parliamentary boroughs of Belfast and Londonderry.[52]

Next day the Government of Ireland Bill was formally introduced in the Commons.

Four years later, just before he died, Walter Long revealed that during 1920 the government had gone further, secretly pledging that the boundaries of the six county unit would remain virtually untouched. Long wrote to Lord Selborne that while trying to win support for the bill – which had virtually no backing in any party – he had spoken to Carson and Craig:

> I came to the conclusion that it would be possible to arrange some plan with the Ulster Members on one condition and one alone, and that was they should receive a definite pledge from me on behalf of the Cabinet to the effect that if they agreed to accept the Bill and to try to work it when passed, it would be on the clear understanding that the Six Counties, as settled after the negotiations, should be theirs for good and all and there should be no interference with the boundaries or anything else, excepting such slight adjustments as might be necessary to get rid of projecting bits, etc.

Long recommended that the cabinet 'authorize me to give this definite promise, which on their agreeing unanimously, I did'.[53] Long told Lord Londonderry,

> It was on this distinct pledge that we were able to pass the Bill with the aid of the Ulstermen; they did not care for it and they did not want it, as you know, but they realized the difficulties of the situation and were prepared to take the Measure of self-government and make the best of it provided they were independent of the Free State.[54]

In the north of Ireland, leading Unionists did their sums. They worked out that a six-county parliament would probably consist of 32 Unionists and 20 Nationalists, or perhaps 31 Unionists and 21 Nationalists: but in a nine-county parliament there were likely to be 33 Unionists and 31 Nationalists, or – even worse – 32 of each. So, despite the unhappiness of Unionists from Monaghan, Cavan and Donegal, the Ulster Unionist Council decided on 10 March 1920 to back the six-county formula. As Belfast MP Tom Moles argued,

> In a sinking ship, with lifeboats sufficient for only two-thirds of the ship's company, were all to condemn themselves to death because all could not be saved?[55]

The second reading of the Government of Ireland Bill began on 29 March 1920, and the Irish Unionists restated their reasons for reluctantly accepting it. Captain Charles Craig, brother of James, bluntly dismissed the idea that the bill lent itself to 'the union of Ulster and the rest of Ireland', saying,

> I would not be fair to the House if I lent the slightest hope of that union arising within the lifetime of any man in this House. I do not believe it for a moment.[56]

By giving 'Ulster' a parliament of its own, the bill, he said, 'sets up a state of affairs which will prevent, I believe, for all time Ulster being forced into a Parliament in Dublin without its own consent'.[57] If Labour and Asquith's Liberals came to power, they might try to push the Unionists out of the United Kingdom: their best protection against that would be to have their own parliament. Craig said:

> we have many enemies in this country, and we feel that an Ulster without a Parliament of its own would not be in nearly as strong a position as one in which a Parliament had been set up where the Executive had been appointed and where above all the paraphernalia of Government was already in existence.[58]

Craig went on:

> we believe that once a Parliament is set up and working well… we should fear no one, and we feel that we would then be in a position of absolute security…[59]

A six-county area was essential because

the majority of Unionists in the nine counties' Parliament is very small indeed. A couple of Members sick, or two or three Members absent for some accidental reason, might in one evening hand over the entire Ulster Parliament and the entire Ulster position... to the hon. Member and his friends [Irish nationalists], and that, of course, is a dreadful thing to contemplate.

He added: 'We quite frankly admit that we cannot hold the nine counties.'[60]

Sir Edward Carson, one-time leader of the loyalist revolt, reiterated his 'opposition to the very end' to home rule,[61] but said that, though many of his old friends in Ireland would call him a traitor, he would not fight the bill. He explained,

if I help to kill this Bill, I bring into force automatically the Act of 1914... what a nice leader I would be to go up to Belfast and call the people there together, and say, "Look here, you made a ; go and get your rifles again, and come out and drill and fight." For what? For the six counties that are offered in a Bill which I could have got without fighting at all. No one but a lunatic would undertake such a performance.[62]

Opponents of partition warned of disaster ahead. Since the 73 Sinn Féin MPs were abstaining from Westminster, it was left to the six Irish Nationalists, backed by a few Liberal and Labour members, to put the anti-partition case. J.R. Clynes, leader of the 60 Labour MPs, told the Commons:

we oppose this scheme of self-government, because it provides a form of partition founded on a religious basis and recognises neither the historic unity of the province of Ulster nor of Ireland as a whole. It gives to Ulster complete control over the fortunes of the rest of Ireland by giving to the Ulster Parliament the right to veto on the assumption of any powers by the Central Irish Council.[63]

He asked,

Are you... to place the minority of Catholics in the six Protestant counties in the keeping of their Protestant fellow-countrymen on conditions that would leave them in a state of permanent minority and helplessness so far as the work of the Northern Parliament was concerned?[64]

Labour, for its part, would offer Ireland limited independence: 'the maximum of national self-government compatible with the unity of the Empire and the safety of the United Kingdom in time of war'.[65]

T.P. O'Connor, the Liverpool Irish Nationalist MP, fiercely criticised the proposal to give the six counties their own parliament and judiciary, saying, 'Here you have every inducement to create vested interests and to make that partition permanent'.[66] The bill, he declared, treated the Orangemen

as super-men with higher rights than men of other creeds or other politics... Nietzsche in his wildest moments never though of creating a super-man like the Orangeman. What is he? He is at once a minority which must be protected and a majority though he is in a minority.[67]

Captain William Redmond protested bitterly that he and tens of thousands of Irishmen who had fought for Britain against Germany had been betrayed:

> Public pledges were given to three-fourths of Ireland when War broke out in 1914, in order to enlist the young life-blood of Nationalist Ireland in the struggle for the liberty of the world. Yes, Irishmen were very useful in those days.[68]

Asquith, the former Liberal prime minister, who by now favoured dominion home rule, said that, 'It is left to an Ulster minority for all time to veto, if it pleases, the coming into existence of an Irish Parliament.'[69] He continued,

> Under this Bill the position as regards Ulster is really this, that they are having thrust upon them a Parliament which they do not want, by way of compensation and make-weight for simultaneously thrusting upon the south of Ireland a Parliament which it does not want... In the annals of constitution-making, which contain the story of many strange and bizarre experiments, surely there is no record more paradoxical than this![70]

Joseph Devlin, the Nationalist MP for West Belfast, pointed out,

> The Catholics in the six counties – we may take it they are all Nationalists – number 430,161 out of a total of 1,250,000. The Catholics in the six counties constitute 34 per cent. of the population... We shall be in a permanent minority.[71]

The new parliament, said Devlin, would be 'practically an enlarged edition of the Belfast Town Council,' which had recently thrown three Catholics off a technical committee simply because they were Catholics.

But the protests of the anti-partitionists were in vain in the face of the huge government majority, and the second reading was carried on 31 March by 348 votes to 94. The bill passed its third reading on 11 November, and on 23 December 1920 it received the royal assent and became law.

Tanks and armoured cars

The year 1920 saw most of Ireland, outside the northeast, consumed in an ever more violent struggle between the IRA and the British forces, while in Belfast loyalists turned on nationalists in a pogrom of unprecedented horror. At the same time, Sinn Féin's moral and practical authority rapidly increased, and by the middle of the year the king's writ had ceased to run in much of the country.

The local elections in January demonstrated once again the popular demand for national independence, with Sinn Féin and Labour taking 72 out of 127 town councils and displacing many Nationalist councillors. Overall Sinn Féin returned 422 candidates, Labour 324, the Nationalists 213, the Unionists 297, and independents 128. Several women were elected, including five

Sinn Féin representatives in Dublin – among them Kathleen Clarke and Hanna Sheehy Skeffington – and two Unionists in Belfast.

Many councils – including Wexford's Labour council – pledged allegiance to Dáil Éireann and broke off relations with the Local Government Board. Dublin corporation chose as its lord mayor Sinn Féin alderman Thomas Kelly, who was in Wormwood Scrubs prison, while Cork elected the local IRA commandant Tomás Mac Curtáin, with his fellow republican Terence MacSwiney as his deputy.

In Belfast, the Unionists received a serious setback, with their block of 52 councillors reduced to 29. Unsettled by post-war unemployment, voters turned instead to several varieties of Labour candidates, including Labour Unionists, while Sinn Féin and the Nationalists each won 5 of the 60 seats.

But the Unionists had their biggest shock in Derry City, central to their mythology as the site of the siege of 1689 when the Protestant defenders held out successfully for King William of Orange against his Catholic father-in-law King James. Now for the first time in 230 years, after a cliff-hanging poll, the city had a Nationalist corporation and mayor, who promptly declared allegiance to Dáil Éireann.

Across the country, the repression continued. A British Labour Party mission to Ireland arrived in Thurles, County Tipperary, on 21 January 1920 just after a policeman had been shot and wounded. They issued a statement saying that

> in order to avenge their comrade it was evident that the police had run amok. About a dozen houses were fired into and a number of prominent residents were questioned. One man had retired for the night with his family. Shots came through the bed-room, and they had to take refuge in the basement.[72]

Constance Markievicz, on the run with, as she put it, 'the English Man-Pack in full cry' after her, wrote to her sister:

> Night after night they wake people up and carry off someone, they don't seem to mind who... When they could not find Mick S—, they took his old father, aged 60, and his baby brothers![73]

In March 1920 Erskine Childers described 'a typical night in Dublin' in an article for the London *Daily News*:

> As the citizens go to bed, the barracks spring to life. Lorries, tanks and armoured searchlight cars, muster in fleets, lists of "objectives" are distributed, and, when the midnight curfew order has emptied the streets – pitch-dark streets – the strange cavalcades issue forth to the attack... A thunder of knocks: no time to dress (even for a woman alone) or the door will crash in. On opening, in charge the soldiers – literally charge – with fixed bayonets and in full war-kit. No warrant shown on entering, no apology on leaving...[74]

On 19 March a policeman was shot near Cork, and in the early hours of the following morning men with blackened faces burst into the home of Tomás Mac Curtáin, the newly elected lord mayor of Cork, and shot him dead. The British authorities spread rumours that he had been killed by members of Sinn Féin, but the coroner's jury reflected the general opinion when it returned a verdict of 'wilful murder' against Lloyd George, the lord lieutenant Lord French, the chief secretary Ian Macpherson, three named RIC officers and unknown members of the RIC.

Terence MacSwiney replaced Mac Curtáin as lord mayor, and in his inauguration speech, which would echo across succeeding generations, he said:

> This contest on our side is not one of rivalry or vengeance, but of endurance.
> It is not those who can inflict the most, but those that can suffer the most who will conquer...[75]

A week after Mac Curtáin's death came another shock, this time for the establishment, when the IRA took an elderly magistrate named Alan Bell off a Dublin tram and shot him dead in the street. Bell was in charge of trying to find out which banks republican funds were held in; he was also high up in Dublin Castle's intelligence operation, helping to organise its network of secret agents.

Among the many imprisoned was the trade union leader William O'Brien, who had upset the authorities by putting a resolution to the Dublin corporation which, in the words of the *Times*, directed the officials

> to remove the sword and mace to the muniment room as they were only relics of barbarism originating in the desire of tyrannical monarchs to parade their power before the eyes of a subject people.[76]

O'Brien was arrested on 4 March 1920 and taken to Wormwood Scrubs prison in London, where he was held along with some 70 other Irish republican prisoners. A by-election was due in Stockport on 27 March, and members of the Irish Self-Determination League there, unhappy with the Labour Party's refusal to endorse full Irish independence, nominated O'Brien, who stood as an Irish Workers Republican candidate. Though he came bottom of the poll, he nevertheless received 2,336 votes: this was a worrying development for the Labour Party, whose candidate had lost by just over 6,000 votes. Nine days before polling day O'Brien went on hunger strike, following a decision made by other republican prisoners in the Scrubs. The others soon gave up, but O'Brien persisted. On 26 March Bonar Law admitted in parliament that O'Brien was 'in a precarious condition', and said, in line with the policy adopted by the cabinet the previous December,

> His Majesty's Government... have definitely decided they will not release him, even though he should in consequence commit suicide by refusing to take food.[77]

Worried by O'Brien's ill-health, the authorities moved him to a nursing home where he was held under police guard; he resumed eating, but insisted that if he was brought back to the Scrubs he would restart his hunger strike. Eventually in early May he was released.

Meanwhile on Easter Monday, 5 April, in a dramatic move, 88 prisoners in Dublin's Mountjoy jail had also gone on hunger strike, demanding that they be treated as prisoners of war or released. In a wave of popular sympathy, tens of thousands gathered outside the prison, singing and praying. Among the many who visited the prisoners was the Bishop of Killaloe, who told journalists:

> It affected me profoundly... to look upon them stretched exhausted, calmly awaiting death should that be necessary for the sake of principle. They are absolutely inflexible in their resolution to die rather than submit to what they regard as the terrible outrage on common humanity and justice.[78]

On 12 April the national executive of the Irish Labour Party and Trades Union Congress called a general strike, issuing a resounding statement:

> To the Workers of Ireland:
> You are called upon to act swiftly and suddenly to save a hundred dauntless men. At this hour, their lives are hanging by a thread in a Bastille. These men – for the greater part our fellow workers and comrades in our Trades Unions – have been forcibly taken from their homes and their families and imprisoned without charge, or, if charged, tried under exceptional laws for alleged offences of a political character, in outrageous defiance of every canon of justice.
> They are suspected of loving Ireland and hating her oppressors – a heinous crime in the sight of tyrants, but one of which hundreds of thousands of Irish working men and women proudly acclaim their guilt.[79]

The response to the strike call was instantaneous and decisive. Frank Gallagher, himself one of the hunger strikers, later described how

> The General Strike had not only paralysed all work: it had paralysed the official mind: they could not telephone, or post a letter; they could not call a taxi or board a train; they could not eat a meal in their exclusive clubs or be sure of to-morrow's dinner behind their castellated towers...[80]

Two days later Lord French capitulated and released the hunger strikers, and shortly afterwards the authorities declared that

> persons arrested and imprisoned for political offences shall be treated as political prisoners, and shall be entitled to be differently treated, both as regards place of confinement and treatment therein, to persons arrested and imprisoned for ordinary criminal offences.[81]

A wide range of offences, however, were deemed not to be political, including homicide, riot, unlawful assembly, and incitement to commit such offences.

Meanwhile in the countryside IRA attacks on the police were multiplying, forcing them to evacuate many smaller barracks and abandon substantial rural areas. The *Constabulary Gazette* lamented on 20 March 1920:

> There is no denying the fact that the number and frequency of Police tragedies that have recently occurred are calculated to appal the stoutest heart. No man going forth in the morning can be sure that he will return to his home or to his Barrack. In the hotel, on the roadside sheltering from the storm, within the barrack walls, leaving the church after worship – it is all the same... Callously and in cold blood Policemen are being shot down as men shoot game.

In the first six months of 1920, the IRA killed 66 policemen and wounded 79. They destroyed 15 occupied barracks and damaged 25, and they burned down 456 abandoned ones to prevent them being reoccupied – some 300 of them in a co-ordinated operation to mark the anniversary of the Easter rising. They also burned courthouses and Inland Revenue offices. The *Irish Times* warned the authorities on 1 May that they had 'hitherto been fighting a losing battle', and continued,

> the forces of the Crown are being driven back on their headquarters in Dublin by a steadily advancing enemy... The King's Government virtually has ceased to exist south of the Boyne and west of the Shannon. If every besieged or destroyed police barrack and the scene of every other major outrage were marked with a black dot, most of the counties of Leinster, Munster, and Connaught would be spotted like the pard.[82]

Sinn Féin extends its hold

In rural elections in June, Sinn Féin further consolidated its position, gaining 71 per cent of the seats, with Republican Labour candidates gaining a further ten per cent. With Labour's support, Sinn Féin won 29 of the 33 county councils, while the Unionists won four: Antrim, Derry, Down and Armagh. Sinn Féin also won 172 of the 206 rural councils. In Ulster, only 19 of the 55 rural district councils returned Unionist majorities. All councils outside Ulster pledged allegiance to the government of the Republic, as did 31 councils in Ulster. People paid their rates to the republican councils, which strove to administer their areas despite the fact that many of their members were 'on the run' and their meetings were forbidden.

Sinn Féin rapidly began to take over the justice system too, setting up its own courts in opposition to the official ones. On 28 June the *Times* reported that this had caused 'increasing confusion and alarm in legal circles in' Ireland because barristers and solicitors were 'confronted with the near prospect of an almost total loss of normal business.'[83] But soon the lawyers began appearing in the Sinn Féin courts.

Sinn Féin first set up land courts, hoping to put a stop to a wave of land seizures in western counties in the spring of 1920. The land issue caused the first serious internal problem in the Dáil, bringing out the differences between those, like Constance Markievicz, who saw themselves as representing the working class and landless poor, and those whose instincts were to maintain existing arrangements for the ownership of property. In April 1919 Markievicz and another deputy had put a resolution – which they withdrew after discussion – demanding

> That this Assembly pledges itself to a fair and full redistribution of the vacant lands and ranches of Ireland among the uneconomic holders and landless men.[84]

The Dáil was dominated, however, by more conservative voices. In 1920 it issued a proclamation to deter claims to land, declaring,

> That the present time when the Irish people are locked in a life and death struggle with their traditional enemy, is ill-chosen for the stirring up of strife amongst our fellow countrymen...[85]

In the majority of cases the courts came down in favour of the landlords, winning praise from the Unionist gentry and the British press. The IRA was used as a police force to enforce court decisions: punishments included fines, detention in remote places, and beatings. The IRA also kept order at race meetings, made sure pubs closed on time, and suppressed the distilling of poteen, the illegal liquor. Such uses of the IRA caused some disquiet. The radical republican Peadar O'Donnell recalled that many an IRA man had later

> cursed his use as a defender of pure ideals to patrol estate walls, enforce decrees for rent, arrest and even order out of the country leaders of local land agitations.[86]

In June 1920 the Dáil took a further step towards displacing the British administration by deciding to set up a full network of civil and criminal courts. In July the authorities began trying to suppress the courts, raiding hearings and arresting participants. The courts continued to meet, but in secret. Kathleen Clarke, who was chairman of the judges in North City, Dublin, remembered:

> Running the courts was not easy. We had no special place to hold them in, and we were likely to be raided by British military or Black and Tans, and that made it difficult to rent places to hold the Court in.[87]

Women played an important part in running the courts – not least because many men were preoccupied with the IRA – and special arrangements were made for women defendants. In the circuit court, when a case involved a woman, a woman judge usually sat with the court judge. In one case, when an unmarried mother was appealing for medical expenses, the judge decided that English law was retrograde on the issue, and therefore applied the traditional Irish Brehon law, finding in favour of the young woman. In general, however, except for the absence of judicial robes, the courts followed the British system.

Strikes against the military

At the end of May, the conflict gained a new dimension when first dockers, then railway workers, went on strike, refusing to handle war material or carry soldiers and police. The initiative came from Dublin dockers, who were following the example of British dockers who had refused to load munitions which were destined to help Poland in its war with the Soviet Union. They were backed by the Irish Transport and General Workers Union – once again headed by William O'Brien, just released from jail in England – and by the Irish Labour Party and Trades Union Congress. But the British trades unions, who had supported the action against munitions for Poland, proved divided and hesitant when it came to Ireland, and took no supporting action. The railway workers' embargo was particularly effective. Major C.J.C. Street, supervisor of Dublin Castle's publicity section, described the first serious incident:

> On June 21st a party of police… boarded the 7.30 a.m. train from Cloughjordan, County Tipperary. The engine-driver refused to proceed until the police left the train. The police received instructions to remain in their carriages, and the train remained in the station… The engine-driver was summoned to Dublin by the officials of the G.S. and W. Railway Company, and was dismissed.[88]

Thomas Farren, a leading trade unionist, told how the military responded:

> It was a common practice for the military authorities to get up upon the footplate of an engine and say to the driver, 'you have got to drive this train,' put a revolver to his head and say, 'you will get the contents of this if you don't drive,' and to the everlasting credit of the railwaymen they said no.[89]

By August 1920, almost 1,500 railway workers had been dismissed: soon Ireland's main railway lines came to a standstill. General Macready, Britain's commander-in-chief in Ireland, summed up the effects on the British war effort:

> These strikes delayed the activities of the troops for several months, the work at the docks falling upon fatigue parties of soldiers, and much of the motor transport which should have been employed on tactical work being diverted to supplying stations which had been cut off by the railway strike. This state of affairs, lasting over six months, was a serious set-back to military activities during the best season of the year.[90]

The strike continued till December, by which time many strikers were desperately short of funds, and violence and chaos were engulfing the country.

The Connaught Rangers' mutiny

Meanwhile across the world in India another drama was unfolding. In late June 1920 some 300 soldiers of the Connaught Rangers stationed at Jullundur and Solon in the Punjab mutinied in protest at British atrocities in Ireland. Most were Irish but a few were English, and they were already disaffected by being made to do strenuous training exercises in the sweltering heat. The leaders of the mutiny were also sympathetic to the Indian independence movement then underway.

A regiment of the British army, the Connaught Rangers recruited mainly in the west of Ireland, and were first formed there in 1793 by a brother of the ascendancy landowner Lord Clanricarde.

Within days the mutineers were disarmed and imprisoned. At the end of August more than 70 were court-martialled. Of these, 60 were sent to serve prison sentences in England, while 22-year-old James Daly was executed, on 2 November 1920. Daly, from Westmeath, had led the Solon mutineers in an unsuccessful raid on the magazine.

Pogroms in Belfast

In the northeast of Ireland, the political situation had created a tinderbox atmosphere. Fear of republican political and military successes in the south, coupled with widespread unemployment and the belief of Protestant ex-servicemen that Catholics had taken their jobs, led loyalist workers to turn viciously on nationalists. In mid-June 1920, loyalists went berserk in Derry, pouring rifle and revolver fire into nationalist districts, and provoking ferocious disturbances which left 18 or more dead – several of them killed by British troops – within a few days.

Even worse was to follow in Belfast, as Unionist leaders fanned the flames of sectarian division. They aimed to dissuade Protestant workers from developing socialist and nationalist sympathies, and so to maintain a solid bloc against Sinn Féin. Upper-class conservatives, including the loyalist leader Sir Edward Carson, saw Britain and Ireland menaced by a world-wide revolutionary conspiracy to bring down the British empire, and claimed that 'Sinn Féin was financed and helped by the Bolshevists in different parts of the world.'[91]

On 12 July, anniversary of the battle of the Boyne and high point of the loyalist marching season, Carson raised the temperature with a speech warning that the 'Sinn Feiners'' ambition was to 'take possession of the greatest part of Ulster.' Their 'insidious methods', he said, included 'posing as the friends of Labour'. He then declared,

> we in Ulster will tolerate no Sinn Fein – (cheers) – no Sinn Fein organisation, no Sinn Fein methods... we tell you (the Government) this – that if, having offered you our help... you are yourselves unable to

protect us from the machinations of Sinn Fein, and you won't take our help; well, then, we tell you we will take the matter into our own hands. (Cheers.)[92]

His speech was followed by a spate of letters to the *Belfast News-Letter* urging Protestants to 'rouse themselves to action' to stop Catholics taking over 'Ulster'.[93]

Loyalist tension rose further when on 17 July the IRA shot dead Colonel Smyth, an RIC commissioner, in Cork. Smyth was a native of Banbridge in County Down, and loyalists there attacked Catholic shops and houses, and drove Catholics out of factories and mills. Then on Wednesday 21 July, the day of Smyth's funeral, posters appeared in the Belfast shipyards summoning 'Unionist and Protestant' workers to a mass meeting at 1.30. Two thousand or more attended the meeting, many reportedly armed with sticks and other weapons. Several hundred then made their way to Harland and Wolff's east yard, where they proceeded to drive out Catholics and socialist Protestants. The *Irish News* reported:

> A number of workers received timely warning that a "purge" of the yard was about to commence, and made good their escape. Those who were not so fortunate received grievous maltreatment. They were attacked, beaten, and kicked, and at least two or three were compelled to take to the water and swim for their lives, and one man, who actually reached the opposite side of the channel, was driven back again into the water... several non-swimmers were compelled to stand in the water and crave for mercy from their attackers. About twenty men in all received injuries which necessitated their removal to the hospital.[94]

Many more, the paper noted, were injured but did not go to hospital.

Mayhem followed, as angry crowds gathered. Nationalists armed with stones attacked tramloads of loyalist shipyard workers returning home. That night, loyalists wrecked and looted Catholic shops in Ballymacarrett – concentrating on the 'spirit groceries' which were licensed to sell alcohol – and there was sectarian rioting around the Falls Road, where the military opened fire. By morning, three Catholics were dead: two men, victims of army rifle-fire, and a woman who was carrying a baby when she was hit by a bullet fired by a policeman.

Fierce disturbances continued until the weekend, with loyalists driving Catholics out of engineering firms, factories, warehouses and shops. In the Short Strand district, as the *Irish News* reported, shipyard workers invaded the Sirocco engineering works

> and evicted the Catholic employees, many of whom had to climb the railings and jump for safety into the backyards of adjacent houses. The women folk attempted reprisal, and made an effort to invade the works.[95]

Drunken loyalist mobs left a trail of destruction. The *Irish News* reported that on the Wednesday night and early hours of Thursday morning about 75 per cent of the spirit groceries in Ballymacarrett were wrecked and looted, and the district was 'in a very demolished state':

> It is nothing but a trail of smashed and looted shops, with the street strewn with broken glass, flour, flake meal, sugar, and other contents of spirit groceries, grocery shops, etc.[96]

John Redmond, Protestant vicar of Ballymacarrett, recalled going down the Newtownards Road, where

> I found Mr. Dick's boot shop... in the last stages of being looted. Men were coming out with arms filled with boots and shoes and women with aprons filled.[97]

On the Thursday night, loyalists drove Catholics out of their homes in Bombay Street, on the dividing line between the Falls and Shankill districts. The military opened fire in the area with machine-guns and rifles, leaving seven dead including a lay brother of the Redemptorist Order, who was apparently carrying a jug of water along the corridor of the Clonard Monastery when he was shot. Another five were killed elsewhere that night, and many were wounded.

In east Belfast, thousands of loyalists attacked St Matthew's church in the Short Strand with stones and bottles, and the next night attacked the neighbouring convent.

On the Friday, 23 July, mobs evicted Catholics from their homes in various districts. The *Irish News* reported: 'Families were expelled wholesale, and furniture flung into the streets, and smashing, burning, and pillage went on apace'.[98]

By the weekend 18 had died, some 300 had been wounded, and there was a serious refugee problem. Six of the dead were buried on the Saturday in Milltown cemetery, and the people of the Falls turned out *en masse* to join the vast cortège. The rioting died down in Belfast, but neighbouring towns were now afflicted.

Some 5,000 workers – Catholics and socialist Protestants – had by now been driven out of their jobs. Loyalist workers – led by members of the Ulster Unionist Labour Association – were determined to prevent them being reinstated, and held meetings in many places to make their views clear. Thousands of workers at Workman and Clark's shipyard passed a resolution saying

> that in all future applications for employment we respectfully suggest that first consideration be given to loyal ex-Service men and Protestant Unionists.[99]

Workers at Harland and Wolff's and other places demanded that Catholics be excluded from employment unless they signed a declaration that they were not members or supporters of Sinn Féin. Fr John Hassan, a curate who compiled a dossier on the pogroms, described the declaration as a 'crawling order': a reference to General Dyer's edict at Amritsar the previous year.[100]

The rioting died down, only to be renewed within weeks after the IRA killed RIC District-Inspector Swanzy in Lisburn on Sunday 22 August 1920 as he returned from morning service. Swanzy was an important target for the republicans because of his alleged involvement in the killing of Tomás Mac Curtáin, lord mayor of Cork, in March. Loyalist mobs in Lisburn immediately went on the rampage against Catholics, looting and wrecking their shops and pubs, and burning their homes. The *Belfast News-Letter* reported next morning:

> As darkness fell upon the scene the flames of burning houses lit up the sky, and the efforts of the local fire brigade made but little effect on the conflagration... in Bow Street several large establishments were a seething mass of fire, while great clouds of red tinted smoke hung overhead, and as roofs and floors fell in the air was filled with sparks falling to the ground like thick showers of crimson snow. It looked a veritable inferno.[101]

Within days, Lisburn's entire Catholic population – some 1,000 people – fled the town. Hugh Martin of the London *Daily News* reported:

> Refugees are pouring into Belfast by road and rail... Since the early days of the German invasion of Belgium... I have seen nothing more pathetic than this Irish migration... I found two mothers who each with a family of five small children had tramped the eight miles from Lisburn to Belfast, coming by the solitary road over the Black Mountain for safety's sake. They had slept on the hill and gone without food from Friday afternoon till Saturday mid-day.[102]

The 'war on Catholics', wrote Martin, 'is a deliberate and organised attempt, not by any means the first in history, to drive the Catholic Irish out of North-East Ulster'.[103]

The violence spread quickly to Belfast, with the tiny Catholic enclave in Ballymacarrett again the focus of loyalist fury. Hugh Martin reported: 'Except in an odd case, the military and police remain inactive, watching the mob burning and destroying property'.[104]

Ferocious battles broke out in other areas. Martin described the scene in York Street, near the city centre, where five people died on 30 August:

> Fully a thousand men were engaged at one time, and thousands of pounds' worth of damage was done, mainly to plate glass windows. Women fought ferociously, and supplied the men with ammunition torn up from the cobble-paved side streets. The Orangemen fought around two immense Union Jacks.[105]

Martin castigated the failure of the authorities to check the pogrom, declaring, 'By their apathy the Government must be reckoned aiders and abetters of a crime that has already reached appalling proportions.'[106]

On 31 August the authorities finally took action, putting Belfast under a curfew which confined people indoors between 10.30 p.m. and 5 a.m., and lasted till 1924. The violence nevertheless continued into the autumn, and 23 people were killed in September.

Efforts by trade unionists to get the 8,000 or so expelled workers reinstated came to nothing. With the dramatic exception of the carpenters' union, the response of the British trade unions – to which most of the expelled workers belonged – was half-hearted and ineffective. The carpenters' union had had several hundred of its members expelled from the shipyards, but it also had members among their persecutors. Despite its divided membership, it took a decisive stand. On 24 August members of its executive committee met the management of Harland and Wolff and demanded the reinstatement of the expelled workers. The management prevaricated, and the union decided to act. On 18 September they instructed all their members remaining in the shipyards and in other firms affected by the expulsions to come out on strike. They explained that it was a 'gross violation' of the rules agreed between the Belfast members and the employers

> for employers to allow men to be driven from their employ because they are suspected of not holding certain political or religious opinions... If the employers elect to discriminate between our members, then we have no option but refusing to allow them the use of the labour of *any* of our members...[107]

Six hundred of their members duly came out on strike, but 2,000 did not. The union promptly expelled the strike-breakers. Many British branches of the union passed resolutions supporting its stand, but the British TUC proved less helpful. The TUC sent a three-person delegation to Belfast in December 1920 to formulate a plan for reinstating the victimised workers, but the delegates' sympathies leaned towards the loyalist workers who had carried out the expulsions, and they recommended that the carpenters' union readmit the strike-breakers. The TUC took up this recommendation, but despite the pressure the carpenters' union leaders refused to comply.

The Belfast boycott

Angry and desperate nationalists had meanwhile turned to another means of pressurising the loyalists. Adapting a weapon long familiar in the countryside, they boycotted Belfast goods. Some local councils had begun such a boycott early in 1920, aiming to show Belfast businessmen the folly of partition by demonstrating the importance of the southern market. The July pogroms provided a powerful impetus, and boycotting spread. On 6 August 1920 the Dáil heard an appeal from Belfast Sinn Féin councillors and other prominent Belfast nationalists to stand by them in their struggle against the 'war of extermination' being waged against them and to make the boycott 'national and thorough.'[108] The Dáil was divided on the boycott proposal, with some deputies expressing the fear that, in the words of Constance Markievicz, it 'would be playing into the hands of the enemy and giving them a good excuse for partition.'[109]

On 11 August the Dáil cabinet agreed to support a boycott of Belfast-based banks and insurance companies, and later the Irish TUC and Labour Party gave their backing.

The boycott movement grew – with some southern towns very enthusiastic and others less so – and soon hit the banks hard. Boycott committees were set up, with women playing a large part, and the IRA and Cumann na mBan enforced the boycott. Major C.J.C. Street, a top official in the Dublin Castle publicity department, recorded:

> Travellers representing Ulster firms were expelled from Nationalist and Sinn Féin districts, bread vans belonging to Ulster distributors were destroyed, and a series of attacks were made on property belonging to Ulster business houses. A serious outrage of this character was perpetrated in Dundalk on the morning of the 27th [of August], when a large drapery establishment was set on fire and three shop assistants sleeping in the building were burnt to death.[110]

The boycott caused considerable damage to Belfast businesses, particularly banks and wholesalers, and probably halved Belfast's trade with the south. Unionists were publicly dismissive of its effects, pointing out that much of Belfast's output – including all its shipbuilding – was sold outside Ireland. But by April 1921 the chairman of the Belfast Wholesalers, Manufacturers and Merchants Association was admitting that, 'this Association, like all the others had been hard hit by the boycott, five sixths of the trade having gone off'.[111]

The Black and Tans

The last half of 1920 saw the war in the country at large reach new heights of viciousness. The new recruits to the Royal Irish Constabulary, the 'Black and Tans', demobbed soldiers who had served in the 'great war', had begun arriving in Ireland in March 1920. Recruitment rose to 600 a month in the summer and to 1,000 a month in the autumn.

In May 1920 Major-General Hugh Tudor, an artillery officer and friend of the belligerent secretary for war, Winston Churchill, was given overall command of the police in Ireland. Tudor swiftly set about recruiting a new force, made up of former British army officers. Named the Auxiliary Division, Royal Irish Constabulary, the new body numbered around 1,000 men by the end of the year.

The police force was now a curious hybrid. Former soldiers had been recruited into an organisation which lacked the disciplinary structures to control them. General Sir Nevil Macready, commander-in-chief of the British army in Ireland, thought it would have been better to raise special military battalions, and recalled critically:

> The men were good material, but many had little military training beyond what was required for trench warfare... The majority of officers under whom they served belonged to the R.I.C., and had scant experience in handling at short notice the class of man who was enrolled, nor, where discipline was concerned, had they as police officers the powers necessary to control the more turbulent spirits.[112]

Macready added:

> As policemen they were useless. The value of a policeman lies in his knowledge of a locality and its inhabitants, of which the R.I.C. recruits were necessarily ignorant.[113]

The Auxiliaries he described bluntly as 'a tough lot'.[114]

As 1920 continued, the Black and Tans and Auxiliaries rapidly earned a fearsome reputation as they launched into a series of acts of violence that became known as 'the terror'. When the IRA killed policemen or soldiers, the Tans and 'Auxies', and the regular military as well, took revenge through reprisals: they burned creameries, looted and burned towns, and inflicted general brutality on the populace.

Publicised by Sinn Féin's *Irish Bulletin* and by sympathetic journalists, news of the atrocities prompted questions in parliament and brought a succession of delegations from Britain to investigate: the Quakers in September, the Women's International League – formed by suffragettes opposed to the 'great war' – in October, and the Labour Party in December. An influential organisation, the Peace with Ireland Council, was formed in London, and a commission of enquiry was set up in the United States. Eventually the controversy would help to sicken British liberal opinion with the war and lead to pressure for a negotiated peace.

July and August 1920 saw a sharp rise in major incidents of violence by the police. The *Irish Bulletin* documented how they 'shot up' towns and villages, looting and wrecking. The English journalist Hugh Martin arrived in Ireland in mid-August and visited Limerick a few days after the Black and Tans had run amok, taking revenge for an incident in which two of their number had been set upon in a park and tied to a tree. Martin described how the Tans had attacked Carey's Road, 'a wide street of one-storey cabins', smashing the windows of over 100 cottages and wrecking many interiors. He noted that, 'Countless china ornaments of the sort with which the Irish poor crowd their shelves were broken and pictures destroyed.'[115]

The Tans also attacked the centre of Limerick, bringing a motorcar loaded with tins of petrol and setting the place alight, leaving five shops and houses burnt to the ground. Police and soldiers also burned down cooperative creameries – dairies which handled the milk produced by local farmers. Mostly run by the Irish Agricultural Organisation Society, the creameries were of major economic importance to their communities. Martin described how in July 1920 soldiers attacked Newport creamery in County Tipperary after local men had cut off the hair of an 18-year-old girl with a pair of shears, charging her 'with the crime of "walking out" with English soldiers.'[116] Martin saw the ruins of the Newport factory, 'built only two years ago and packed with valuable machinery', and related what had happened:

> A score of young soldiers, after firing a number of shots into the air, stormed the building, and set the place alight at a number of points. When Mr. Denis Ryan, the manager, tried desperately to put out the flames he was driven off, and the cheese house, containing at the time £2,000 worth of cheese, was set on fire.[117]

The authorities publicly condemned the reprisals but tacitly condoned them. Indeed the *Times* said later in the year that the policy of reprisals was 'now generally admitted in Ministerial circles to have been conceived and sanctioned in advance by an influential section of the Cabinet.'[118] Reprisals were the product of indecision in government policy towards Ireland. There were deep disagreements among politicians, top officials and military men as to whether the turmoil should be solved through conciliation or open military repression. Sir Hamar Greenwood, the new chief secretary for Ireland, told the cabinet on 31 May: 'I have the greatest possible reluctance to apply martial law at present… I had rather… go on trying to get moderate opinion on our side.'[119] He explained,

> The difficulty behind martial law is that you would put certain people in prison and they would hunger-strike. What would the people in England say? Could you go through with it to the death? Imprisoned men cannot be held indefinitely. Will they return as martyrs?[120]

By contrast Field-Marshal Sir Henry Wilson, who was now chief of the imperial general staff, advocated open and extreme coercion. Top civil servant Sir Maurice Hankey, secretary to the cabinet, recorded in his diary on 23 May 1920 that Wilson

> wants to collect the names of Sinn Feiners by districts; proclaim them on the church doors all over the country; and, whenever a policeman is murdered, pick 5 by lot and shoot them![121]

But Lloyd George sanctioned a covert reprisals policy, privately assuring Major-General Tudor, the chief of police, on 6 June 1920 of his full support. He was backed by Winston Churchill, who wanted full-blown repression, including tribunals with powers to summarily hang people, and the raising of a force of 30,000 loyalists in Ulster.

Lloyd George approved of the police carrying out assassinations of Sinn Féiners, though not of the burning of houses. Hankey recorded in September that Lloyd George 'strongly defended the murder reprisals... He showed that these had from time immemorial been resorted to in difficult times in Ireland'.[122]

Police chief Major-General Tudor gave the Black and Tans the go-ahead for reprisals through the pages of the *Weekly Summary*, a police bulletin which began publication on 13 August 1920. The third issue, for example, declared that the Black and Tans

> will go on with their job – the job of making Ireland once again safe for the law-abiding, and an appropriate hell for those whose trade is agitation and whose method is murder.[123]

Terence MacSwiney

Also in August 1920 the government brought in sweeping emergency powers through the Restoration of Order in Ireland Act. This allowed the authorities to imprison without charge or trial, for an indefinite time, anyone suspected of being connected with Sinn Féin. Prisoners could be tried by secret military courts; potential witnesses could be imprisoned or heavily fined for refusing to give evidence against a suspect; grants to local councils which did not support the Crown could be stopped; and coroners' inquests could be suppressed and replaced by military courts of enquiry.

The tension was heightened when Terence MacSwiney, the lord mayor of Cork, a 40-year-old IRA commander and former teacher, went on hunger strike in Cork jail after being arrested on 12 August. He was charged with sedition for possessing documents – including intercepted police ciphers – deemed 'likely to cause disaffection to His Majesty'. MacSwiney was swiftly court-martialled, convicted, put on a warship and taken to Brixton prison in London, where he continued his hunger strike. His condition rapidly deteriorated, inspiring worldwide sympathy. Thousands of people – many of them London Irish – gathered to protest at the prison gate, in meetings co-ordinated by the British-based Irish Self-Determination League, launched the year before. The ISDL also briefed the press on MacSwiney's condition and took care of his visiting friends and relatives.

The British government was inundated with protests, but refused to release him. In response to an appeal from the Labour Party, the government declared:

> Surely the sympathy which has been given in such full measure to the Lord Mayor, whose condition has been brought about by his own deliberate act, is due rather to the bereaved widows – and families of the murdered Irish Policemen.[124]

Delegations from Britain

Concerned by 'the disturbed condition of Ireland',[125] the British Society of Friends – the Quakers – sent a deputation to Ireland in mid-September 1920 to investigate the situation. The group – two men and a woman – visited Dublin, Belfast, Lisburn, Limerick and Cork, as well as several smaller places. Their impressions were shocked and vivid. One of the small towns they visited after an attack by the Black and Tans was Milltown Malbay in County Clare,

> where the burnt houses were still smoking, the people were still sleeping out in the fields and woods in terror of a renewal of the attack, the blood of one victim still red on the white wall of a burnt house, the funerals both of police and of those slain in revenge for them passed before our eyes, and the uncoffined and unrecognisable remains of an unknown person burnt in one of the cottages were still lying hidden in a calf shed in the rear.[126]

A member of the delegation, John Barlow, wrote an account which appeared in the London *Times*, ending by suggesting 'a liberal measure of self-government for Ireland'.[127] The Society reprinted the article in pamphlet form and distributed nearly 25,000 copies.

It was not till what became known as 'the sack of Balbriggan' that the reprisals hit the headlines in Britain. Balbriggan, a small town, is only some 20 miles from Dublin – possibly the reason for the press attention, for many newspaper correspondents were based in the capital. Two police officers were shot in the town, one of whom died, and on 20 September 1920 some 100 to 150 regular policemen descended to take revenge, killing two young men, wrecking around 25 houses and burning down a hosiery factory. The *Manchester Guardian* wrote that

> To realise the full horrors of the night one has to think of bands of men inflamed with drink raging about the streets, firing rifles wildly, burning houses here and there, and loudly threatening to come again to-night and complete their work.[128]

British officials were less concerned. Mark Sturgis, an English civil servant at Dublin Castle, wrote in his diary: 'Worse things can happen than the firing up of a sink like Balbriggan.'[129]

In early October ten women representing the British section of the Women's International League for Peace and Freedom arrived in Ireland, aiming 'to collect first-hand evidence of the condition of the country, and come back to tell British people what was being done in their name.'[130]

The WIL had been founded in The Hague in 1915 by suffragettes opposed to the 'great war': an issue which had split the suffrage movement in Britain. The British section, with over 4,000 members in 1920, had consistently shown concern about Ireland – for example calling for the reprieve of Roger

Casement – and liaised closely with Louie Bennett, secretary of the Irishwomen's International League.

It was the WIL's Manchester branch – which had been holding 'enthusiastic meetings' in support of Irish self-determination and against the imprisonment of Terence MacSwiney – that put forward the idea for a deputation to Ireland. The group that travelled included several prominent feminists, among them the WIL's chairman, Helena Swanwick. Then in her fifties, Swanwick was also a member of Richmond Labour Party, and deplored Labour's inactivity on Ireland. On their return from Ireland, the women called for:

> the immediate liberation of Irish political prisoners and the offering of a truce during which all armed force shall be withdrawn and the keeping of order be placed in the hands of Irish local elected bodies, thus creating conditions under which the Irish people may determine their own form of government.[131]

The women spoke at many meetings throughout Britain, sometimes sharing platforms with members of the Quaker delegation. They often showed lantern slides 'of the devastation committed during reprisals and raids',[132] and Helena Swanwick recalled:

> They did more than any words could do. Audiences that were cool before, broke out into cries and groans when they saw the ruined homes of Tuam, the roofless cottages of a whole street in Balbriggan, the wrecked shops and creameries and town halls of Cork and Mallow, the paralysed old women being rescued. "Why, it's like Belgium!" was the commonest of all the remarks one heard.[133]

They sent a deputation to the Labour Party, and two members of the delegation travelled to Washington to give evidence to a high-powered American commission on conditions in Ireland.

In the last months of 1920, reprisals fell fast and furious on the towns and villages of Ireland. On 20 October Arthur Henderson, deputy leader of the British Labour Party, moved a motion in the House of Commons calling for an investigation into reprisals and deploring

> the present state of lawlessness in Ireland and the lack of discipline in the armed forces of the Crown, resulting in the death or injury of innocent citizens and the destruction of property...[134]

The chief secretary for Ireland, Sir Hamar Greenwood, staunchly defended the Black and Tans, recalling their role in the 'great war': 'I protest with all the vigour that I can command against the suggestion that these heroes of yesterday to everybody have become murderers to-day.'[135] Men who 'acquiesced in, connived at, condoned or supported' the murders of policemen had 'no right to complain of reprisals,' he said.[136] He declared:

> I submit that the immediate, pressing, and paramount duty of the Irish Government now is to break up this murder gang that has terrorised Ireland

and rendered the mass of the Irish people inarticulate while it carries out the murders of servants of the Crown.[137]

Henderson's call for an enquiry was defeated by 346 votes to 79.

Disquiet in England about reprisals led to protests from writers, academics and clergy. The journalist Henry Nevinson recalled that in mid-October

> a small party of us paraded Parliament Square with placards and posters bearing appropriate inscriptions, such as "We English Protest," "Stop Reprisals," and "Terrorism is not Government," amid an apathetic or hostile crowd of onlookers.[138]

Nevinson and others then formed a committee, later known as the Peace with Ireland Council, to work for an end to 'the attempt to solve the Irish problem by force' and 'to awaken public feeling in England on the subject'.[139] The Council had a distinguished membership spanning party lines, including leading Liberal women, several bishops, and intellectuals such as Sidney Webb and George Bernard Shaw. One of the executive was John Annan Bryce, a former Liberal MP. At the end of October, in a case that became a minor cause célèbre, his wife, who had founded the first convalescent home for officers in Ireland, was arrested as she landed at Holyhead in Wales on her way to address a meeting about reprisals, from which she personally had suffered. She was deported to Kingstown [now Dun Laoghaire], and held in prison for four hours before being released without charge.

Terence MacSwiney dies

As the 'terror' raged on, Ireland was shaken by a series of climactic events. On 25 October Terence MacSwiney died in Brixton prison on the seventy-fourth day of his hunger strike. Two days later the coffin was taken to Southwark Cathedral, where it lay, draped in a tricolour and guarded by young men in IRA uniforms, as thousands gathered to pay their respects. Next day, 28 October, a requiem mass was con-celebrated by an archbishop and two bishops before a packed congregation, and then a huge procession, more than a mile long and led by kilted pipers, accompanied the coffin to Euston station. The Belfast-born socialist Robert Lynd wrote in the *Daily News*,

> There have been few stranger or more impressive spectacles in London than this tribute to a dead Irish Republican...
>   When the funeral procession left the Cathedral about half-past two, the streets were lined with people as for the funeral of a Prince. Hawkers in the street with Cockney voices were selling mourning-cards with prayers for the dead man's soul, paper handkerchiefs with a program of the day's events, green flags with gold harps, and Republican rosettes. The windows along the route were filled with work-girls, photographers, families and their friends. For an hour before the procession started, trams and lorries could scarcely pass along Blackfriars-road.[140]

The coffin was put on a special train to travel to Holyhead and thence to Dublin, where a huge procession was certain. But the authorities intercepted the train at Chester, where troops removed the coffin and sent it direct to Cork. Henry Nevinson described the scene in Cork City Hall:

> I went with the Irish people who passed continuously two and two round the open coffin, guarded by Irish Volunteers, while outside, the streets were paraded by British regiments with armoured cars. The exposed face of the dead man was yellow-pale, wasted to extreme thinness, but fine and resolute – the face of a poet as well as a patriot. On the door of the Hall a large placard repeated the coffin's inscription: "Terence MacSwiney, murdered by the Foreign Enemy, in the Fourth Year of the Republic."[141]

Bloody Sunday

Just afterwards came another traumatic event, when on 1 November 1920 an 18-year-old medical student named Kevin Barry was hanged in Mountjoy jail as a huge crowd prayed at the gates. Barry had taken part in an IRA attack on a British army lorry in Dublin which resulted in the deaths of three British soldiers. Despite being violently interrogated, Barry refused to name his companions.

The atmosphere of crisis intensified with the events of 21 November 1920, soon dubbed 'Bloody Sunday'. At nine o'clock in the morning, in a cool and ruthless operation devised by Michael Collins, groups of IRA men entered eight hotels and houses in Dublin and shot dead 10 British officers, some in front of their wives and girlfriends, and wounded several more. They also killed two passing Auxiliaries and two civilians. Most, if not all, of the dead officers were working as undercover agents in the city: since the summer there had been an influx of such agents, who spied on republicans and sometimes tortured or shot them.

There was an immediate security clampdown. All trains out of Dublin were stopped, cars were searched at the exits of the city, and the streets were heavily patrolled by troops and armoured cars.

The afternoon saw more bloodshed. A big Gaelic football match was being held at Dublin's Croke Park ground, and as the military cordoned off the stadium to search the crowd for IRA members, Auxiliaries opened fire, leaving 12 men and women dead and many more injured, both by bullets and by the panic-stricken stampede. That night three prisoners being held in Dublin Castle – two IRA leaders and a young Irish-language scholar – were shot dead 'while attempting to escape'. Detectives sympathetic to the republican cause reported to Michael Collins that all three had been tortured, and their faces battered after death.

Within 48 hours over 500 people were arrested and interned: six months later there would be over 4,000 internees, held in camps in Ballykinlar, the

Curragh, and Bear Island. Seven IRA men were eventually hanged for the killings of the officers.

The day after Bloody Sunday there were furious scenes in the House of Commons as the West Belfast MP Joseph Devlin tried to raise the question of the Croke Park killings in the face of a torrent of condemnation of the IRA's killings. The London *Times* reported:

> There were very angry cries of "Sit down" and much uproar...
>   Suddenly Major Molson, sitting on the bench in front of him, put his arm round Mr. Devlin's shoulders, which were bent forward, and pulled him down head first over the back of the bench... Mr. Devlin struggled to free himself, and hit out blindly, as anyone would have done in that position. The temper of the House was very ugly, particularly below the gangway. Someone, beside himself, cried "Kill him." Mr. Devlin, having worked himself free, turned on Major Molson and they made to fight. All blows missed their aim, but an innocent neutral was hit across the mouth.[142]

Flying columns

Succeeding weeks saw violence escalating still further. The IRA was beginning to organise 'flying columns', mobile units which used classic guerrilla techniques. Tom Barry, a 23-year-old veteran of the 'great war' and leader of the legendary West Cork flying column, wrote later that 'strange as it may seem' the flying column's main objective should be 'not to fight, but to continue to exist,' because its existence would force the enemy to maintain large garrisons. But, Barry continued,

> the Flying Column would attack whenever there were good grounds for believing that it would inflict more casualties on an enemy force than those it would itself suffer. It would choose its own battleground, and when possible, would refuse battle if the circumstances were unfavourable.[143]

On 28 November 1920 Barry's 36-strong column mounted a spectacular attack on two lorry-loads of Auxiliaries as they travelled through bleak bogland near Kilmichael. In fierce fighting, 16 Auxiliaries were killed and also two IRA Volunteers. Crown forces carried out large-scale reprisals in the area, burning shops, homes and farm buildings.

The IRA also began a campaign in England, using locally based Irish people to carry out arson attacks on property, conceived as reprisals for the ravages of the Black and Tans.[144] On the night of 27 November 1920 several large cotton warehouses were burned down in Liverpool, while police interrupted an attempt to set fire to a timber warehouse in London's Finsbury district. Over 100 were arrested, including some women; some were given prison sentences, while others were deported to Ireland and interned. The authorities were thoroughly alarmed: barricades were put up around Downing

Street, and the usual practice of allowing visitors to see round the Houses of Parliament on Saturdays was suspended.

After a lull, the attacks restarted, now extending to burning haystacks in agricultural areas. February 1921 saw the IRA start fires in London and damage eight farms in the Manchester area, and also a short-lived episode when the Liverpool IRA was instructed to implement a Dáil directive banning people from emigrating without permission.

On 18 February 1921 just after midnight armed IRA men inveigled their way into three boarding houses full of shipping passengers about to leave for America, and removed passports and tickets from numerous young men – the women were reportedly left alone. This tactic proved ineffective – the authorities simply supplied the victims with replacement documents – and was soon discontinued.

11
Partition and Truce

A s the war raged on during 1920, and the Government of Ireland Bill made its way through parliament, the unionists in the northeast worked to secure their position against present dangers and future uncertainties. Agitated by IRA attacks and distrustful of the Royal Irish Constabulary, which was 70 to 80 per cent Catholic, they pressed the British government to recruit a force of Ulster loyalists. In areas where they felt particularly vulnerable, such as Tyrone, Fermanagh and parts of County Armagh, unionists spontaneously organised armed vigilante groups. In Fermanagh Sir Basil Brooke, a big landowner and former British army officer who later became prime minister of Northern Ireland, took the lead. He recalled:

> I stumped the County, explaining the vital necessity of having some organisation if loyalists were not to be terrorised as in the South. Such was the response that, by the autumn, we had 200 men...[1]

Brooke's Fermanagh Vigilance Force mounted night-time roadblocks and searched passers-by.

In Lisburn, the Unionist-controlled local council organised a special constabulary of several hundred 'loyal ex-servicemen', some of whom had participated in the anti-Catholic pogrom in the town. A few were brought to trial, provoking a mass walk-out by fellow members of the force. The rebellion was only defused when the head of the force promised to try and get further charges dropped.

In July 1920 the Unionist leaders Sir Edward Carson and Sir James Craig initiated the reorganisation of the Ulster Volunteer Force: it had ceased functioning after the 'great war', but its network remained, and those members who had survived the war now had military experience. Though the revived UVF was still illegal, it had the tacit approval of Lloyd George. Belfast newspapers carried advertisements for UVF meetings, and in the countryside prominent landowners organised recruitment. The UVF swiftly established close links with the military in several areas, cutting out the RIC. By October 1920 it had some 10,000 members in Belfast and a further 10,000 to 20,000 across the rest of the northeast.

But operating an illegal private army was inconvenient: it was difficult to provide arms, and because the men were unpaid and part-time it was hard to maintain regular patrols. There were also worries about how compensation would be paid for those killed or injured. To resolve these problems, the unionist leaders pressed the government to set up a special constabulary into which the UVF could be absorbed. They also asked for the appointment of an assistant under-secretary for the six counties: a step which would remove decisions about security policy from Dublin Castle, where officials were unsympathetic to arming the loyalists because they feared it would lead to increased sectarian violence, which would undermine efforts to reach a compromise with Sinn Féin.

In a belligerent memorandum to the cabinet on 1 September 1920, Sir James Craig – who would soon take over from Sir Edward Carson as leader of the Ulster Unionist MPs – warned that if the government failed to organise a special constabulary, the loyalist rank and file would take action themselves to check the spread of 'rebel influences', and 'civil war on a very large scale' would be 'inevitable'.[2]

Craig submitted detailed proposals for a force of 2,000 full-time armed special constables, plus a much larger part-time force based on the UVF. The government conceded Craig's demands immediately: a move which provoked misgivings among senior military figures, including General Macready, who feared

> that as the Constabulary would necessarily be confined to Protestants, it would, unless under the strictest control, probably sow the seeds of civil war between North and South and necessitate the intervention of the Army.[3]

The *Daily News* commented:

> It is not very surprising that the official proposal to arm "well disposed" citizens to "assist the authorities" in Belfast should have raised serious question of the sanity of the Government. It seems to us to be the most outrageous thing which even they have ever done in Ireland… a citizen of Belfast who is "well disposed" to the British Government is almost from the nature of the case an Orangeman, or at any rate a vehement anti-Sinn Feiner. These are the very people who have been looting Catholic shops and driving thousands of Catholic women and children from their homes.[4]

The new assistant under-secretary, Sir Ernest Clark, arrived in Belfast on 17 September and immediately began meeting UVF leaders to discuss the Special Constabulary. The UVF organisers in Tyrone reported to their commanders on their talks with Clark:

It is fully recognised that, at first at any rate, no Roman Catholics will respond... The Special Constables will be selected by a selection committee of loyalists... to counter the opposition of the Labour Party in England an appeal to all 'well-disposed citizens' is the only way this scheme can be put through and, as only loyal men will respond, this may be looked upon as camouflage.[5]

On 1 November 1920 advertisements for 'law abiding citizens' to apply for enrolment appeared in the Belfast papers.[6] There would be three classes of special constables: A, B and C. Class A would be full-time, paid, and armed to the same level as the Royal Irish Constabulary. Class B would be part-time, usually serving one night per week plus drills; they would be unpaid and usually armed. Class C would serve in emergencies only, would be unpaid, and organised and armed like Class B. All three classes would be entitled to compensation for death and injury on the same basis as the RIC.

The new force filled nationalists with dread. The *Fermanagh Herald* warned:

These "Special Constables" will be nothing more and nothing less than the dregs of the Orange lodges, armed and equipped to overawe Nationalists and Catholics, and with a special object and special facilities and special inclination to invent 'crimes' against Nationalists and Catholics... they are the very classes whom an upright Government would try to keep powerless...[7]

Nationalist fears proved well-founded. The UVF joined up *en masse*, providing many of the county and district commandants for the new force, and with many of its companies simply becoming 'B' Special sub-districts. By July 1921, more than 3,500 'A' Specials had been enrolled, and almost 16,000 'B' Specials. Virtually all were Protestants: recruitment of Catholics was not encouraged by officialdom and was opposed by Sinn Féin and the IRA, and in any case few Catholics wanted to join.

The Specials swiftly made their sectarian attitudes clear. In Enniskillen in mid-December 1920 a new recruit shot at a Catholic church, and next day others marched round the town singing the Orange ballad 'Dolly's Brae' and shouting 'To hell with the Pope'. In Newry, Joe Devlin MP complained, Specials were harassing people and firing wildly in the streets, and had burnt down a Sinn Féin hall.

This zealous sectarianism continued. The routine work alongside the RIC – which included ransacking nationalist houses for arms, and searching people attending Hibernian dances and Gaelic football matches – was supplemented by a succession of violent incidents. In the early hours of 23 January 1921, a group of 'A' Specials drove into Clones, just outside the six-county border, and broke into a public house. The Royal Irish Constabulary arrived and a gun-battle broke out which left one Special dead and several injured. The platoon was disbanded and some of the culprits were court-martialled. In late February 1921, Specials burned down eight or nine Catholic houses in the County Fermanagh village of Roslea, prompting the *Manchester Guardian* to comment:

> The embodiment of this partisan force was an act of folly... The Special Constabulary was nominally raised to protect life and property and to maintain order, not to become a force of terrorists exercising powers of death over their Catholic neighbours... It will be a bad beginning for the Ulster Parliament if its establishment coincides with the dragooning of the Catholic minority in the six counties by an armed Protestant force administering a sort of lynch law.[8]

Ireland partitioned

On 11 November 1920 the Government of Ireland Bill passed its third reading in the House of Commons, proposing home rule parliaments for 'Southern Ireland' and for 'Northern Ireland'. The Ulster Unionists had won on the question of area, and Northern Ireland was defined as 'the parliamentary counties of Antrim, Armagh, Down, Fermanagh, Londonderry and Tyrone, and the parliamentary boroughs of Belfast and Londonderry'.[9]

'With a view to the eventual establishment of a Parliament for the whole of Ireland,' a Council of Ireland was to be set up, with each of the two parliaments sending 20 members.[10] Alternatively, the two parliaments could establish a single Irish parliament and reunite the country.

In a move designed to protect the unionist minority in the south and the nationalist minority in the north, the bill decreed that both parliaments would be elected by proportional representation, though they could change this after three years. Both Sinn Féin and the Unionists had lost seats through PR in the 1920 local elections, but Sinn Féin nevertheless supported it, while the Ulster Unionists vehemently opposed it and promised to abolish it at the first opportunity.

Both parliaments would be subject to the Westminster parliament, requiring the lord lieutenant to approve bills on behalf of the king, and would not be allowed to make laws relating to peace and war, the armed forces, foreign affairs, or overseas trade. But it was highly unlikely that the Sinn Féin majority of Southern MPs would ever implement a parliament subject to Britain, so at the last minute the bill's framers added a clause saying that if less than half the MPs of either parliament were validly returned or took their seats, then the powers of government could be taken over by the lord lieutenant and a committee appointed by the Crown.

The bill began the practical process of detaching North from South by providing for separate taxation and judicial systems, though leaving a unitary police force for the time being.

Supporting the bill, Lloyd George reiterated his refusal to recognise 'the independence of Ireland as a Sovereign State', saying it would be 'a constant source of temptation to Ireland, and... to others who wanted to injure the United Kingdom'.[11] He refused to relinquish control over the harbours of Ireland, warning 'what a menace the creeks of Ireland could be to the security of the Empire'.[12] Nor could Ireland be permitted its own army or navy, which would be a peril' to Britain.[13] Nor could a people 'rootedly hostile to the United Kingdom' be allowed to control the customs.[14]

The veteran Unionist Sir Edward Carson welcomed the bill, hoping that it would lead in the long run to Ireland being 'one and undivided, loyal to this country and loyal to the Empire.'[15]

But the West Belfast Nationalist Joseph Devlin lamented the listlessness of MPs and the empty benches, and prophesied a bitter future for Catholics in the northeast.[16] The government had chosen completely the wrong way to extirpate religious rancour, he said, pointing out that they were placing the Protestant minority in 26 counties 'absolutely at the mercy of the Catholic majority', while the Catholic minority in the remaining six counties would be at the mercy of the Protestant majority. The new parliament would be 'a permanent barrier against unity', he warned, and forecast:

> This Bill means that I am to live under a government in Ulster that will never make the slightest attempt to conciliate labour... During the 20 years I have been here I have never known them vote for a single democratic measure in my life... I am determined that the House of Commons shall understand what they are doing and under what thraldom they are prepared to put our people.[17]

Cataloguing the 'saturnalia of persecution' meted out against Catholics, he protested:

> The right hon. Gentleman has not put a single Clause into his Bill to safeguard the interests of our people... It is a story of weeping women, hungry children, hunted men, homeless in England, houseless in Ireland. If this is what we get when they have not their Parliament, what may we expect when they have that weapon, with wealth and power strongly entrenched? What will we get when they are armed with Britain's rifles, when they are clothed with the authority of government, when they have cast round them the Imperial garb, what mercy, what pity, much less justice or liberty, will be conceded to us then?[18]

The bill was carried by 183 votes to 52 and, after minor amendments in the Lords, received the royal assent on 23 December 1920 and became law.

The resulting border was described by the British publicist, Major Street:

The ancient boundaries of the counties had been determined by the limits of the baronies, which for the most part depended upon no definite physical features, but merely upon the extent of the land owned by the large proprietors. As a result of this, the frontier of Ireland was an impossible one, from the standpoint of either politics or strategy.[19]

With hindsight, British politicians came to see the significance of the step that had been taken. Writing a few years later, Winston Churchill described the 1920 act as 'a decisive turning-point in the history of the two islands.' He went on:

Ulster, or rather its six predominantly Protestant counties, became a separate entity clothed with constitutional form, possessing all the organs of government and administration, including police and the capacity of self-defence for the purposes of internal order. From that moment the position of Ulster became unassailable... Every argument of self-determination ranged itself henceforward upon their side. Never again could any British Party contemplate putting pressure upon them to part with the Constitution they had reluctantly accepted.[20]

Contacts with Sinn Féin

On 30 November 1920, in an article beginning 'If only the people of England knew,' the London *Times* evoked a nightmarish picture of the sufferings of the 'law-abiding population' in Ireland, caught between 'the terrorism of Sinn Fein' and official reprisals:

Day after day and night after night – especially night after night – murder and violence and terrorism are knocking at their doors... Every night thousands of people sleep in the fields, under hedges, or haystacks, because they dare not sleep at home. Every night, if they stay in their houses, many thousands go to bed in fear and trembling, in a Christian land, in the 20th century, in a time of peace.

But while the government was pursuing a policy of repression, it was at the same time engaged in an almost continuous series of contacts with Sinn Féin, both directly and through intermediaries. From May 1920 Lloyd George had his own personal envoy at Dublin Castle, Andy Cope, charged with contacting Sinn Féin. Cope was a former detective in Customs, highly strung and feverishly hard-working, who had become close to Lloyd George while working at the Ministry of Pensions. Cope was part of a team, led by the under-secretary Sir John Anderson, who were sent into Dublin Castle to revamp the administration. These officials, along with the London-based assistant cabinet secretary, Tom Jones, put out feelers to find out what kind of political settlement Sinn Féin might accept. They established that Arthur Griffith and others would be willing to 'acquiesce' in a scheme for dominion status, though publicly they would not 'accept' it.[21]

Dominion status was a modified form of home rule. It would give more freedom than the model contained in the Government of Ireland Bill – in particular, control over finance – but at the same time it would keep Ireland in the British empire, with defence and ports remaining in Westminster's hands. In late July 1920 the Dublin Castle officials told Lloyd George that Sinn Féin might accept dominion status, and Tom Jones urged him to adopt this policy. Jones argued that as the army and police appeared to be breaking, and repression would not work, a compromise should be attempted. Lloyd George, said Jones, should offer Sinn Féin a choice between two alternatives: martial law, which would 'inevitably involve suffering, starvation, death to large numbers of innocent Irishmen, women, and children', or dominion home rule for the south and west 'with self-determination for Ulster'.[22]

The dominion status option – though without partition – also won the backing of representatives of the Irish business and professional classes, including Sir Horace Plunkett, and of British Labour leaders and the former Liberal leader, Asquith. But Lloyd George rejected it, arguing that it would give Ireland too much power.

From the autumn of 1920 onwards, significant sections of Sinn Féin showed their interest in negotiating a truce, including Arthur Griffith and Michael Collins. Dr Clune, the archbishop of Perth in Western Australia, took a truce offer from Lloyd George to Arthur Griffith and Michael Collins in early December. They were willing to agree a truce, but in the meantime peace overtures from Sinn Féin vice-president Father Michael O'Flanagan, and from some members of Galway County Council, persuaded Lloyd George that Sinn Féin was about to cave in, so that he did not need to be conciliatory.

In a hardline speech on 10 December 1920, Lloyd George told the Commons that the government had decided to adopt 'a double policy': on the one hand, martial law would be proclaimed in the southwest of Ireland, but at the same time, if the republicans surrendered their arms, the government would grant safe conducts to members of the Dáil to meet to discuss a peace settlement.

To the Sinn Féin leaders, a surrender of arms was out of the question: as Griffith wrote, 'this was not a Truce but a surrender, and there would be no surrender no matter what frightfulness was used.'[23]

General Macready, the British commander-in-chief, had doubts about Lloyd George's 'double policy'. He reported to his deputy on 10 December:

> The Prime Minister himself told me to-day that he was most anxious that, while we put the screw on the rebels to the greatest degree, we and the police should rather go out of our way not to be disagreeable to the unoffending inhabitants. I pointed out to him that in Ireland it is very difficult to distinguish between the offending and the unoffending article.

> You will gather from his speech that with one hand he intends to repress outrage, but with the other he is waving an olive branch, and so it will be up to us to try and play up to what seems to be a somewhat complicated policy.[24]

Lloyd George described his policy to the cabinet on 20 December 1920 as 'to crush the murder gang but whenever there is any opening for peace take it and do not be too rough on the purely political lot.'[25] Consequently the cabinet decided that Sinn Féin president Eamon de Valera, travelling home – in theory secretly – from the United States, should not be intercepted at Liverpool when he arrived in January 1921. Then Dublin Castle instructed General Macready that de Valera was not to be arrested: an instruction which displeased Macready, who complained: 'It is quite impossible to carry out a repressive policy if we have one hand tied behind our back'.[26]

Martial law

Martial law was initially brought in for counties Cork, Tipperary, Kerry and Limerick, but was soon extended to cover the southern third of the country. The proclamation issued on 10 December 1920 stated:

> Any unauthorised person found in possession of arms, ammunition or explosives will be liable on conviction by a Military Court to suffer Death...
>
> No person must stand or loiter in the streets except in pursuit of his lawful occupation.
>
> All meetings or assemblies in public places are forbidden and for the purpose of this Order six adults will be considered a meeting.
>
> All occupiers of homes must keep affixed to the inner side of the outer door a list of the occupants setting forth their names, sex, age and occupation.[27]

First to die after conviction by a military court was an IRA captain from Kerry, Cornelius Murphy, who was captured on on 4 January 1921, tried for possessing a loaded revolver, and shot on 1 February. General Macready complained later that 'only fourteen death sentences' of this type were carried out, because the 'rebels' frequently complicated matters by appealing to the British courts – despite their theoretical refusal to acknowledge such courts. In the spring of 1921 'drum-head' courts were introduced, allowing almost immediate execution of those caught with arms: such courts were used three times before peace intervened.

On 11 December 1920 came one of the most notorious episodes of the war, when Auxiliaries and Black and Tans set fire to much of the centre of Cork city, firing their rifles and looting valuables as they went. They burnt down about 300 buildings – including the City Hall, and the Carnegie Library with many precious volumes – and left damage estimated at £3 million, a huge sum at the time. Two members of a British Labour Party commission of enquiry then visiting Ireland went to Cork and reported:

> The most valuable premises in the town were utterly destroyed, large business houses and massively fronted shops were reduced to piles of smouldering débris, charred woodwork, and twisted iron girders.[28]

In October, the government had refused a Labour Party request for an independent enquiry into reprisals and violence. The party then sent its own commission, made up of seven members – including four MPs – plus advisers. They spent the first two weeks of December 1920 in Dublin and the southwest, and produced a damning report itemising the 'reign of violence' inflicted by the Crown forces on the populace.

There were differences within the Labour Party over Ireland. Radicals such as Sylvia Pankhurst believed the party should support full self-determination, which in practice would mean an Irish republic. But the leadership – trade union leaders and Fabians – thought Ireland should have self-determination only for 'exclusively Irish affairs'.[29] As the Fabian Sydney Webb put it:

> whilst they may be quite frank and sincere in offering Ireland complete self-determination for all Irish affairs, that did not mean they wanted Ireland to go spinning along the road like a motor hog, without regard to anyone else on the road.[30]

At the party's annual conference in June 1920, a resolution calling for unqualified self-determination was carried. The *Catholic Herald* – then an Irish community paper owned by Labour parliamentary candidate Charles Diamond – commented:

> The rank and file of Labour... clearly recognise what self-determination means, and they are prepared to see its application made unreservedly in Ireland. They lead their "leaders."... The Labour leaders who are disposed to trim and whittle down in regards to Ireland adopt such an attitude from a fear and a hope which alike are groundless. Their fear is that the British electorate will never entrust Ministerial power to a party which would consent to the severance of Ireland's present relations with the British Empire: their hope is that they may attain to power if they soothe and placate the "moderate" vote... Such Labour leaders are either devoid of principle or they stifle it.[31]

But the Labour leaders ignored the conference decision and formulated their own policy. Party chairman William Adamson told the House of Commons that an Irish constitution must be 'subject to two conditions':

> The first that it affords protection to the minority... The second... that the Constitution will prevent Ireland from becoming a military or naval menace.[32]

The Labour leaders persuaded the Irish Labour Party and Trade Union Congress to back their stance, promising in return a serious campaign on Ireland.

After the commission of enquiry's return from Ireland, its report was presented to a special Labour Party conference in London on 29 December 1920, attended by 800 delegates. Here a resolution presented by the leadership was passed – no amendments were permitted – calling for self-determination limited by the two conditions, and thus overturning the June conference decision. In January and February 1921 the Labour Party organised several hundred meetings in England and sold 20,000 copies of the commission's report, contributing to the widespread unease about government policy.

While contacts between the British government and Sinn Féin continued through an assortment of intermediaries, the war on the ground became increasingly bitter.

Officially sanctioned reprisals, first threatened by General Macready in September 1920, were given legal backing by the martial law regulations, which authorised military governors to carry out 'punishments' in response to 'outrages'.[33] The first such punishment – or 'official reprisal', as they were swiftly dubbed – was carried out on 1 January 1920 at Midleton in County Cork after an IRA ambush. Next day General Strickland, military governor of the martial law area, issued a statement declaring that he had decided

> that certain houses in the vicinity of the outrages were to be destroyed, as the inhabitants were bound to have known of the ambush and attack, and that they neglected to give any information either to the military or the police authorities.

The statement then listed seven men whose homes had been 'duly destroyed', and continued,

> Previous to the burnings, notice was served on the persons affected giving them one hour to clear out valuables, but not furniture. No foodstuffs, corn or hay were destroyed.[34]

Ironically, the houses in fact belonged to the Earl of Midleton, leader of the Southern Irish Unionists.

The veteran republican Kathleen Clarke described how, in one such official reprisal, troops and Black and Tans wrecked the home occupied by her mother, sisters and aunt in Limerick, on the grounds that another sister, absent in Dublin, had failed to warn the authorities of an ambush. The officer in charge gave them 15 minutes to leave the house, telling them they could take nothing but family portraits. Kathleen Clarke wrote:

> My aunt Lollie was over eighty years old, and with the shock of hearing that the house was to be burned down, she seemed to get paralysed. It

took some time to get her down from her room... For some reason unknown to us they did not burn the house, as they had said they had orders to do, but everything that would burn was removed to the road, and there petrol was thrown on them and a match put to it. It was a huge bonfire. Then with sledgehammers and other implements they set to work on the destruction of the house...

She added,

There they were, a group of five women, left homeless... They were sad to see it all going up in flames; nevertheless, they showed a proud front to the enemy, and we were very proud of them.[35]

Aid from America

Pressure on the British government was mounting on both sides of the Atlantic. Sympathisers in the USA sent shiploads of food and clothing to Ireland during the winter, and the newly formed American Committee for Relief in Ireland sent three million dollars in 1921, to aid those displaced by the pogroms in the northeast, and made homeless or orphaned by the war.

On 6 January 1921 Lloyd George met Father Michael O'Flanagan, joint vice-president of Sinn Féin, at 10 Downing Street. O'Flanagan was a radical priest and agitator on the land issue, who had been suspended by his bishop for his republicanism. According to cabinet secretary Thomas Jones, Lloyd George was 'very much impressed with O'Flanagan's personality', but 'insisted that O'Flanagan represented nobody but himself and that he must deal with someone who could deliver the goods'.[36] Soon afterwards, Dublin Castle put out feelers to de Valera, using Father O'Flanagan and Sir James O'Connor, Lord Justice of Appeal, as intermediaries.

In England, the clamour against reprisals grew. It was fuelled by the government's refusal to publish a report by General Strickland, military governor of the martial law area, into the burning of Cork, and by criticisms from county court judges of burning and destruction of property by soldiers and police. Looking into claims for malicious injuries in County Clare, Judge Bodkin found:

There were in all 139 cases in which it was proved that the criminal injuries were committed by the armed forces of the Government... In no case was there any evidence to suggest that the victims had been guilty of any offence.[37]

Many influential voices were raised against the government. Among them was the poet W.B. Yeats, who on 17 February 1921 passionately denounced the Black and Tan terror in an address to the Oxford Union.

The Union voted 219 to 129 in favour of a motion calling for complete self-government in Ireland and condemning reprisals.

Next day, three young Irishmen were found guilty at the Old Bailey of attempting to set fire to barrels of oil belonging to the Vacuum Oil Company in Wandsworth, South London. The judge asked why they had done this, and 19-year-old Thomas O'Sullivan, a cable operator, replied that,

> There was a lot of damage being done in Ireland. Protest meetings have been held here, but the general public took no notice, and we wanted to force them to take notice.[38]

Lady Sykes, a Conservative prominent in the Peace with Ireland Council, wrote to the *Times* calling for a truce. She described what she had heard and seen in a recent visit to Ireland of the destruction and 'brutal and frequent murders' carried out by the Crown forces, and asked,

> Is it not time for the people of England to rise up in their wrath, and insist that their elected representatives shall put an immediate end to these shameful deeds that are being done in their name?

She added:

> The legend that the attacks on the Crown forces are the work of a small gang of criminals is contrary to fact; they are done by members of the I.R.A., acting under military orders, impelled, however wrongly, by the sense that they are fighting for the liberation of their country.[39]

On 21 February 1921 Captain Wedgwood Benn, a Liberal MP, led a barrage of criticism in the Commons against government policy. He attacked it for being 'very costly', harmful to opinion abroad, and ineffective, and accused the government of 'systematic terrorism of the population for the purpose of attempting to restore order'.[40]

Next day in the Lords the Archbishop of Canterbury criticised the government's failure to give information about reprisals, warning: 'you cannot justifiably punish wrongdoing by lawlessly doing the like. Not by calling in the aid of the devil will you cast out devils, or punish devilry.'[41]

The government's problems were compounded by the news that on 19 February Brigadier-General Crozier, commandant of the Auxiliaries, had resigned. Crozier, described as an 'adventurer' by some contemporaries, had had a somewhat eccentric career. From an Anglo-Irish military family, he had at first been unable to join the British army because he was too small: instead he set off to Ceylon to become a tea-planter. Soon, however, he went off to fight in the Boer war and then in Nigeria: here he acquired a drink problem, which he later conquered, becoming a crusading teetotaller. He lived for a time in Canada, then trained the Ulster Volunteer Force in Belfast and fought with the Ulster Division on the Somme. In 1919 he was asked to help reorganise the Lithuanian army, then fighting on three fronts against Germans, Bolsheviks and Poles: a mission he described as 'a ghastly failure'.[42] In 1920 he offered his services to the police in Ireland.

Crozier had differences with his fellow generals, Macready and Tudor, and was sceptical about politicians. His resignation from the command of the Auxiliaries was sparked after an incident when Auxiliaries were involved in looting at Trim. Crozier immediately placed five men under arrest and suspended 21, sending them to England, a move which worried General Tudor. The suspended men, according to Crozier, used the threat of revealing the truth about the burning of Cork and other incidents to blackmail the authorities. Crozier later related,

> When my discharged Trim warriors arrived over in London, they proceeded to "play old Harry" with the pompous prudes in Parliament and the dying ducks in Downing Street, by categorically stating that unless they were sent back and reinstated at once they would have the Government out of office within a week; so *back they came!*[43]

Crozier – who was also angry that Lloyd George was apparently trying to make one of his officers a scapegoat for the burning of Cork – now resigned.

Killings and burnings

While the Crown forces executed republicans, killed civilians, destroyed farms and creameries, and cordoned off large areas of Dublin for house-to-house searches, the IRA attacked soldiers and policemen, shot spies and informers, and began burning 'big houses'. Between January and April, some 70 bodies were found with placards attached proclaiming them as spies or informers. One killing that caused a particular outcry was that of a 70-year-old woman, Mrs Lindsay, a loyalist landowner from County Cork. Mrs Lindsay had passed on information to troops about an impending ambush, and as a result six Volunteers were captured. The Cork IRA then kidnapped Mrs Lindsay and her chauffeur, and got her to write a letter to General Strickland saying that the IRA would kill her if the Volunteers were executed. The authorities nevertheless carried out the executions, and five days later the IRA executed Mrs Lindsay.

In mid-March 1921, Tom Barry's West Cork flying column, now over 100-strong, organised a spectacular ambush at Crossbarry of a large force of British troops who were attempting to surround them. About 35 British soldiers died, for three IRA Volunteers.

The Crown forces had been burning and wrecking republican homes since mid-1920, and in the spring of 1921 local IRA commanders began to order retaliation in kind. Ernie O'Malley, now commanding the North

Cork brigade, related how his divisional commander, Liam Lynch, reacted when Crown forces blew up several houses in reprisal for an ambush:

> The pupils of Liam's eyes blackened with rage... He stuttered: 'I'll bloody well settle that; six big houses and castles of their friends, the Imperialists, will go up for this. I don't know what G.H.Q. will do – but I don't give a damn.' We selected six houses and castles from the half-inch map, then sent off the order.[44]

In West Cork, the IRA informed the British military commander that for every republican home destroyed, the homes of two British loyalists would be burned to the ground. The British ignored the threat, and mayhem ensued. Tom Barry recalled:

> Castles, mansions and residences were sent up in flames by the I.R.A. immediately after the British fire gangs had razed the homes of Irish Republicans. Our people were suffering in this competition of terror, but the British Loyalists were paying dearly, the demesne walls were tumbling and the British Ascendancy was being destroyed.[45]

Soon the Cork loyalists, hitherto silent on the subject, began vociferously demanding that the British forces cease destroying republican homes.

On the night of 26 March 1921, the Auxiliaries finally found the house in Dublin where the Sinn Féin daily news-sheet, the *Irish Bulletin*, was produced. They raided the house, removing back-numbers of the paper, and the Gestetner duplicator and typewriters used to produce it, as well as a full list of the addresses to which it was sent. More than 2,000 copies of the *Bulletin* were now being circulated to the press and people of influence around the world. With its stream of exposés of British atrocities, and articulation of the republican point of view, the *Bulletin* was very damaging to Britain's image.

An officer on the staff of General Tudor, the police chief, decided to produce a forged version of the *Bulletin*, using the captured equipment. The bogus copies came out daily from 30 March: they were written in the style of the original, but with the content twisted to discredit Sinn Féin and undermine the *Bulletin*'s reputation for accuracy. The forgeries included wildly exaggerated claims that the British had murdered 'thousands' of people and ruined 'millions' of homes. They also carried statements such as, 'there is less crime in Ireland than in any country in Europe, except Bolshevik Russia,' and, 'in no single recorded case have the Republican Forces attacked a single policeman with the odds less than six to one.' The London *Daily News* commented:

> It is scarcely necessary to comment on the character of a Government organisation which permits itself to use this contemptible and dishonest means of confounding a nation. It fits in exactly with all our official dealings in Ireland.[46]

Kathleen McKenna – a mainstay of the *Bulletin*, whose activities included conveying seditious documents around Dublin 'in a series of spacious pockets sewn into an underskirt' – recalled how production was resumed in a tiny kitchen:

> Our fine expensive duplicator, and my beautiful little typewriter were things of the past. I was back once more to a typewriter with large type and an antiquated box duplicator. But we did not lose heart. I placed a wax sheet, as of old, in the typewriter, attached it to the hand mimeographing press placed on the kitchen stove, and rolled off the day's issue.[47]

The republicans stamped 'Official Copy' on their version in green ink – whereupon the British followed suit! After a month or so, the bogus version ceased production. Kathleen McKenna related:

> The short adventurous life of the bogus *Bulletin* came to an abrupt end when Mick Collins had bombs exploded in the Auxiliaries headquarters at the North Wall Hotel, alas bringing also to an unmerited end my beautiful little typewriter.[48]

'Chief figurehead of partition'

The British were losing the propaganda war anyway, and events in the real world were conspiring to force their hand. The Government of Ireland Act, which would partition Ireland and create two separate parliaments, both subservient to Westminster, was about to be introduced. Its provisions were phased in, starting in April 1921: one of the first to come into effect was the removal of the ban on Catholics becoming lord-lieutenant, and soon Lord French was replaced by an English Catholic, Lord FitzAlan, a former Tory MP. Nationalists were unimpressed by his religious affiliation: the Belfast *Irish News* dubbed him the 'Chief Figurehead of Partition in Ireland'[49] while Sinn Féin's *Irish Bulletin* commented acidly:

> Lord Edmund Talbot's political reputation – in so far as he can be said to possess such a reputation – is one of bitter hostility to the national claims of the Irish people... The actual effect of this appointment among Irish Catholics will be one of repulsion at the thought of a Catholic acting as the agent of a tyranny.[50]

The cabinet set the elections for May 1921 – having been advised by the generals that the rebellion would be sufficiently under control by then. A Sinn Féin victory was widely predicted: if this happened, their MPs would refuse to co-operate with Britain, and the British government would face a choice between imposing Crown Colony government – rule by government nominees – on the 26 counties, or coming to an accommodation with Sinn Féin. The *Manchester Guardian* declared:

The result is a foregone conclusion. Sinn Féin candidates will be elected in an enormous majority, and they will refuse to take the oath of allegiance. There will be no Southern Parliament, and its place will be taken by an Executive and a "Legislative Assembly" nominated by the Government and with all the resources of the Government at their back – that is, by force under a new form.

The Guardian continued:

In the North the results will be somewhat different, but neither there will there be any real progress... The Ulster Parliament will function after a fashion, but it will be little more than the rump of a Parliament, and it will carry no moral authority over a very large minority of the Ulster people. It will govern, but it also will be compelled to govern by force... The Ulster Volunteers, a kind of local Black-and-Tans, will become the arm of government in Northern Ireland. It is not a cheerful prospect.[51]

Foreseeing 'the gravest consequences', southern Irish landowners and businessmen, led by Lord Midleton, repeatedly lobbied the government to delay the elections and to negotiate with Sinn Féin. On 8 March, Lord Midleton warned Lloyd George and the chief secretary for Ireland, Sir Hamar Greenwood:

If the elections fail, what is the alternative? You will have to appoint a Council to assist the Lord Lieutenant and Chief Secretary. Every man on the Council will be a marked man. In such circumstances no-one will serve.[52]

Instead, Midleton recommended, a government representative should get round a table with representatives of Irish commerce, the Catholic church, and Sinn Féin.

The cabinet, however, decided to go ahead with the elections. Cabinet secretary Thomas Jones predicted, in a letter to Bonar Law,

In Ulster there will be bloodshed, and in the south the Sinn Feiners will be returned without contests. They will refuse to take the oath and the Government will have to decide whether to try some sort of truce or Constituent Assembly or Crown Colony.[53]

Jones added:

The tenacity of the I.R.A. is extraordinary. Where was Michael Collins during the Great War? He would have been worth a dozen brass hats... I'm sure the P.M. has a secret admiration for him... He'll be canonised some day.[54]

The cabinet had lengthy discussions on whether there should be a truce, and, after much mind-changing, rejected the idea on 12 May. Nine members – eight Conservatives plus Lloyd George – were against a truce, and five – all Liberals – in favour.

In general, Liberal ministers took a more conciliatory line than Conservatives. Liberals were keener not only on offering a truce, but also on going beyond the existing Government of Ireland Act to offer some form of dominion status, with more autonomy for Ireland on the questions of raising taxes and imposing customs duties. Lloyd George, for his part, continued to hope 'in his inmost heart', according to his secretary and mistress Frances Stevenson, 'that Southern Ireland might still be forced to work his Act without any additions whatsoever'.[55] He remained adamantly opposed to conceding an Irish republic, wanting above all to keep Ireland within the empire.

In public, Lloyd George mentioned the possibility of compromise – except on the questions of the union between Britain and Ireland, and the 'non-coercion of Ulster' – but remained deliberately vague as to what this might entail. In private, he indicated that he might consider some form of dominion home rule – though not as extensive as the version applied to Canada and Australia. He was unwilling to concede Ireland its own army and navy, or the right to appoint its own ambassadors. On the financial side, he did not want Ireland to be able to impose customs duties on British goods, and was particularly concerned that Ireland should pay 'its share' of the national debt incurred during the world war. Lloyd George repeatedly warned the cabinet against giving away too much too soon. On 27 April 1921 he told them,

> I am afraid that in our anxiety to put an end to a disagreeable business which brings no credit to the Government or to the country, we may pay a price which this country will regret later.[56]

Meanwhile the 'semi-official negotiations' – as Lloyd George described them – continued between the British government and Sinn Féin.[57] On 21 April 1921, Lord Derby, a former secretary for war and ambassador to France, arrived in Dublin under the alias of 'Mr Edwards', and met de Valera at a secret rendezvous. The visit was arranged with the help of Cardinal Logue, the Catholic primate of all-Ireland, and with a much put-upon Liverpool priest, Father Hughes, as go-between. De Valera wrote later that at the meeting, 'I made our position clear: that the Republic had been declared and that it would have to be accepted as a basic fact.'[58]

Derby relayed this to Lloyd George, and then wrote to de Valera:

> Mr. Lloyd George is speaking on the Irish question on Thursday and desires me to put the following question to you. 'Is he entitled to say that those controlling the Irish movement will not consent to meet him or any representative of the Government unless the principle of complete independence is first conceded?'[59]

De Valera neatly inverted the question in his reply:

> I would like to ask the British Premier a question: Will he not consent to meet me or any representative of the Government of Ireland unless the principle of complete independence be first surrendered by us?[60]

Later, de Valera assessed the visit as 'useful as the first important contact between the British and ourselves and... a breaking of the ice.'[61]

News of Lord Derby's visit swiftly leaked out, and the press had fun with the idea of such a large and well-known figure, slightly disguised by a pair of spectacles – which Lord Derby said afterwards were his reading glasses – masquerading as Mr. Edwards at the Gresham hotel.

On 5 May 1921 came another British-sponsored clandestine meeting, this time between de Valera and Sir James Craig, leader of the Ulster Unionists. The meeting was set up by Andy Cope at Dublin Castle and Judge O'Connor. Britain's aim was to seek harmony between the two parts into which they were dividing Ireland, but it was a tense and unproductive encounter. Lloyd George described the meeting to the cabinet, from Craig's viewpoint, a few days afterwards:

> They met somewhere – he was motored out – car changed, came upon a haggard creature, dried lips, very excitable, lectured Craig on Irish history and industries; and parted with no arrangement to meet a second time.[62]

At the meeting, de Valera was annoyed to discover, as he recalled later, that 'Craigavon had been told... that I had asked to see him and I was told that Craigavon had asked to see me.'[63] He wrote after the meeting to Sinn Féin vice-president Father O'Flanagan: 'I can really see no evidence whatsoever that the other side has any disposition towards peace. It is manoeuvring, nothing else. I'm done with it.'[64]

When Judge O'Connor again attempted to get de Valera to meet Craig, de Valera responded:

> I do not see any hope of securing the end of the struggle with England through a prior agreement with the Unionist minority. At bottom the question is an Irish-English one, and the solution must be sought in the larger general play of English interests.[65]

Partition elections

The elections for the new parliaments of 'Northern Ireland' and 'Southern Ireland' – as the Government of Ireland Act termed the new units – were to take place in May 1921. The South's 'House of Commons' was to have 128 members, and the North's 52. Additionally, the South was entitled to elect 33 Westminster MPs, and the North 13. Each area was also to have a senate, but these were not to be elected by the full electorate.

The Sinn Féin executive decided that the elections should be contested on an abstentionist basis. Their proposal was put to the Dáil on 11 March 1921. This was the first time partition had ever been mentioned in the Dáil, which had been meeting in secret at intervals throughout the war. While Catholics in the northeast were seriously alarmed by the prospect of partition, republicans outside the loyalist strongholds tended not to take it seriously. Maire Comerford, an activist of the time, wrote later:

> We laughed hard at the thought that the English could make a lasting partition of Ireland against the practically unanimous will of the Irish people. Alas we had no conception either of their great ability, or the depths to which they would descend when the Conference stage would be reached, their smile and their handshake more deadly than war.[66]

There was some concern among members of the Dáil that the executive had not thought it necessary for the Dáil to have a full discussion about whether or not to contest the elections. One view was 'that the effect of a contest would be to consolidate a solid Orange Block.'[67] But the Dáil accepted the executive's proposal, and on 10 May approved a resolution put by de Valera which stated:

> That all members duly returned at these elections be regarded as members of Dáil Éireann and allowed to take their seats on subscribing to the proposed Oath of Allegiance to the Republic.[68]

The Irish Labour Party decided to abstain from the elections, in order not to 'divide the democratic forces', and instead called on workers North and South

> to demonstrate their loyalty to Ireland and freedom by voting only for those candidates who stand for the ownership and government of Ireland by the people of Ireland...[69]

On 13 May, nominations were put forward for constituencies North and South. In the North, all the seats were contested, so the elections would go ahead as planned on 24 May. But in the South, Sinn Féin was the only party to stand, except for the candidates for the four Trinity College seats, who were likewise unopposed. With all the Southern candidates unopposed, no voting was necessary and the nominations became the elections. Sinn Féin swept the board, taking 124 of the 128 seats. This outcome evidently came as a shock to the British cabinet: Sir Hamar Greenwood, the chief secretary for Ireland, had reportedly led them to believe that seats would be contested in many counties.

The new Sinn Féin TDs – members of the Dáil – were mostly very young men from the towns; all but a handful had been imprisoned at some point, and about a third of them were currently interned or in jail. This time more women had been elected. Constance Markievicz – now imprisoned in Mountjoy – had been the only woman member of the First Dáil: now, to her delight, she was joined by five more, including Kathleen Clarke and Margaret Pearse, mother of Padraic Pearse, executed in 1916.

Foreboding in the North

In the northeast, nationalists viewed the approaching elections with foreboding, and organised a big campaign to mobilise the anti-partition vote. The anti-partitionists had no hope of victory. Though they were approaching 40 per cent of the population of the six counties, they were considered likely to win only 12 – or at most 15 – of the 52 seats in the Northern parliament. The *Manchester Guardian* informed its readers on 28 February 1921:

> It is natural that nowhere else should partition be so thoroughly detested as among the Catholic minority of the six counties. For the artificial boundaries of what the Act designates "Northern Ireland" are clearly designed to leave that minority powerless... the development among Nationalists of a tendency towards the policy of abstention – hitherto peculiar to Sinn Féin – is not surprising.

The new 'parliament of Carsonia' – as anti-partitionists sarcastically termed it – promised no good for the newly created minority. Joseph Devlin MP, leader of the northern Nationalists, inveighed against partition in speech after speech, and said of the Northern parliament:

> It is a Parliament not of a nation, not of a province, not even of a proportion of a province, but a parliament of a section of a portion of a province. They have imposed on us the simulacrum of a constitution which gives no freedom to all the people, divides some of the people, and leaves things fifty times worse than they were before. The Ulster Parliament will be smaller than a town council. It will be merely a family party of profiteers, puppets and placemen...[70]

On 4 April 1921, over 800 delegates from organisations in the six counties supporting the Nationalist Party gathered at a 'great Convention', as the *Irish News* described it, in St Mary's Hall, Belfast. They agreed that the elections should be fought on the policy of 'self-determination and anti-partition', with candidates pledged neither to recognise nor enter the Northern parliament. They passed resolutions stating that the Convention

> places on record its unalterable belief in the right of Ireland to determine its own destinies according to the aspiration of its own people; that we regard the establishment of a Parliament for a section of the province of Ulster as a menace to public unity and a danger to the lives and interests of our Northern citizenship, and we feel it our duty to declare that alone in a Constituent Assembly for all Ireland lies the hope of well-ordered freedom and a spirit of brotherhood and goodwill among Irishmen of all creeds and classes.[71]

Next day, Eamon de Valera and Joseph Devlin signed an agreement committing their parties to co-operate in fighting the elections. Each party would put up 21 candidates. Voting would be on the proportional representation system, using the single transferable vote, so in each constituency the candidates would form an 'anti-partition ticket'. The text of the agreement explained:

> Voters shall be asked to give their earlier preferences to the candidates of
> their own party, and their next immediate preference to all the candidates
> of the other party to this agreement.[72]

Nationalists and Sinn Féiners organised a vigorous succession of meetings
and demonstrations, with large numbers turning out, including many
women. They were suspicious and apprehensive about how the elections
would be run. They protested to Belfast Corporation that the location of
polling booths would disadvantage anti-partition candidates. An *Irish
News* correspondent explained:

> The facilities offered to the Catholic population for recording their votes
> in the constituencies East, North and South Belfast are simply scandalous.
> It is unnecessary to remind the general public that huge numbers of
> Catholics were forcibly driven out of these areas when the famous
> outbreak took place in July last. They dare never go back; but at this
> election (every fair play is of course being guaranteed by Lloyd George)
> they are to be asked to return to the streets out of which they fled for their
> lives last July to mark their ballot papers.[73]

Nationalists suspected that deeper moves were afoot. The *Irish News*
correspondent continued:

> It would be a splendid opportunity for the Carsonites to personate the
> absent Catholic voters and thus show by a false vote how much Belfast
> desired Partition.[74]

Day after day, the leader columns of the *Irish News* spurred on the anti-
partition campaign, warning urgently of the horrors that would follow the
'ghastly experiment in national dissection'.[75] The Nationalist candidates
issued an address to the electors, declaring:

> The scheme of Partition was rashly conceived, insufficiently considered,
> and hastily rushed through Parliament as a trumpery expedient to suit the
> political exigencies of the moment. Even in that puerile purpose it has
> magnificently failed. Northern Unionists regard the forthcoming
> Parliament as a white elephant. They would be delighted if some one
> would take it off their hands, and conveniently dispose of it. Were it not
> for the grim tragedy it so painfully adumbrates, the Partition scheme
> might justly be regarded as a triumph of Gilbertian humour – purporting
> to accomplish a great work of national appeasement by giving every
> section of the community what it most abhors.[76]

Unionist leader Sir James Craig, for his part, issued an utterly bland
manifesto in order to avoid antagonising voters, especially workers and
advocates of the prohibition of alcohol – Craig's family were directors of
Dunville's Distillery in Belfast. Craig focused his appeal on the need to
secure a loyalist majority against the threat of 'immediate submergement
in a Dublin Parliament'.[77] 'The fate of the Six Counties hangs in the
balance,' he declared, so it was the duty of loyalists 'to lay aside minor
issues, and if need be to sacrifice personal interests' to secure the election

of candidates who would represent 'the great cause which we all have at heart.'[78]

The nominations were on 14 May. For the 52 seats in the Northern parliament, the Unionists put forward 40 candidates – five of whom stood as 'Unionist Labour' – while Sinn Féin nominated 20 and the nationalists 13.

There were also five Independent Labour candidates. Three of these – James Baird, Harry Midgely and John Hanna – had been prominently associated with the British Independent Labour Party. They now declared themselves 'straight Labour, not "Unionist Labour"', and proclaimed: 'We stand for an unpartitioned Ireland based on the goodwill of all who love their native land'.[79] They announced that a 'great Labour meeting' would be held at the Ulster Hall on 17 May. But loyalist organisations put up notices in Ballymacarrett summoning shipyard workers to assemble that evening 'for the purpose of taking possession of the Ulster Hall and driving out the Sinn Feiners.'[80] The *Irish News* reported:

> Thousands of men out of both yards gathered at the appointed place and at the stated hour, and preceded by a brass band and a brake containing prominent Pogrom leaders, marched to the Ulster Hall, singing Orange airs and making use of obscene expressions at points touching upon Catholic districts.[81]

The shipyard workers rushed into the hall and occupied it, while their leaders took over the platform. The Labour candidates, discovered in the artistes' room, were told they could address the meeting only if they did not make any 'disloyal utterances': they decided it was wiser not to speak. Sir James Craig sent a message to the gathering: 'Well done, big and wee yards.'[82]

Next night, during a rowdy unionist demonstration in East Belfast, a Catholic who had fought in the 'great war' was shot dead, and serious rioting followed. The following morning, 19 May, some 250 to 300 Catholic workers – mostly girls and women – were prevented from entering Gallaher's tobacco factory in York Street.

Out in the country districts the campaign was also rough. The *Daily News* reported from Tyrone and Fermanagh on intimidation by the newly formed Special Constabulary – 'a coercive police force' of Protestant farmers and shop assistants 'armed and drilled at the Government expense':

> Sinn Féin election workers are being pursued and arrested. Election literature is seized. Harassing restrictions on the use of motor cars by Nationalist and Sinn Fein organisers are imposed, while Unionist organisers get all the permits they ask for, and a few more besides... There are districts in Fermanagh where no Nationalist election meeting will be held for fear of those attending it being marked down by the "specials".[83]

Polling day itself was a tumult of violence and intimidation, as loyalists strove to keep nationalists from the polls. The *Manchester Guardian* reported:

> It would be hard to find even in the rather corrupt history of Irish politics an election fought with such ruthlessness, such corruption and such unfairness as the election for the Northern Parliament which ended today.[84]

The paper summed up:

> Unionists assembled in crowds outside the voting booths and set upon the Catholic voters. The Catholic shipyard voters, who were driven from their work and homes by the Unionists last summer, were marked men when they returned to vote.
>   Anti-Partitionist personation agents were thrown out of several of the polling booths because they objected to the Unionist agents helping electors to vote. This left the Unionists free to personate all the voters who had not voted. One polling booth was closed by the military. Outside Belfast the corruption was just as bad.[85]

In Belfast, people returning to vote in districts they had been expelled from were knifed, beaten and kicked. Many ended up in hospital, while many others stayed away in fear. The *Irish News* described the situation in East Belfast, near the shipyards:

> For hours, not a single voter could visit the Saunders Street polling booth, but at 3 o'clock armed police on a motor lorry escorted taxi-cab loads to Saunders Street, the district at the time being practically in a state of siege, and crowded by a howling mob... An old man named Harry Crawford was one of the occupants of the taxi escorted by the police wagon. He alighted at Saunders Street, registered his vote, and on emerging from the station, was jumped on by a ferocious mob. The poor old chap was severely maltreated, knocked down, and kicked, sustaining scalp wounds.[86]

The northern election results delivered 40 seats to the Unionists and only 12 to the Nationalists and Sinn Féin, who each took six. The anti-partitionists should have done much better in Belfast, but their votes were divided across constituencies in such a way that they only won one seat. The *Irish News* lamented that

> the Nationalists of Belfast city, who constitute a fourth of the entire population (25 per cent.), have succeeded in securing only one-sixteenth of the city's representation (6.2 per cent.) under the operation of the P.R. system...[87]

But the Unionist victory was not as monolithic as it appeared. In Armagh, anti-partitionists won two of the four seats, with 45 per cent of the vote. In Fermanagh and Tyrone – two counties with nationalist majorities that formed one eight-seat constituency – the anti-partitionists did even better, taking 57 per cent of the vote to win four seats. Fermanagh nationalists celebrated their victory with a procession through Enniskillen. They believed that their desire to be included under a Dublin parliament, expressed in two successive general elections, must now be respected. But they were to be bitterly disappointed.

Deaths in Belfast

The new 'Parliament of Northern Ireland' was inaugurated in Belfast City Hall on 7 June 1921 amid little public interest. The Nationalist and Sinn Féin members stayed away.

Within three days, the city was once more engulfed in violence and death. Soon after midday on Friday 10 June, three policemen were fired on in the Falls Road. All were injured, one fatally. That night, a lorry-load of Auxiliaries raced up the Falls, firing indiscriminately and causing a panic- stricken flight. Other lorries followed, scouring the streets and taking prisoners. One lorry, with three prisoners, stopped when it met a huge crowd of loyalists in Conway Street, near the bottom of the Falls. The crowd pulled out the prisoners and kicked and beat them. In another incident, an arrested man, evidently trying to escape, jumped out of a Crossley tender but knocked himself unconscious and later died.

Next night, Saturday, serious rioting broke out between rival crowds in the York Street area near the docks, leaving several seriously injured with bomb and bullet wounds. Horror followed in the early hours of Sunday morning, 12 June, when one or more parties of armed men in lorries – clearly belonging to one or other branch of the British forces – visited houses in North Belfast and dragged away three Catholic men, riddling them with bullets and abandoning their bodies in lonely places. The three were Alexander McBride, a 30-year-old publican; Malachy Halfpenny, a 20-year-old postman; and William Kerr, a 26-year-old hairdresser.

On Sunday night, gun battles in the York Street area left three young Catholic men and a Special Constable dead. In a sinister incident nearby, two young Catholics, Patrick Milligan and Joseph Millar, were murdered in their homes by men in uniform, allegedly Specials. The Millar family suffered particularly bitterly: in the previous night's rioting, a bomb explosion had left Joseph's sister Sarah without an eye, and their uncle, William Kane, without a hand.

Tuesday 14 June saw more deaths, this time in West Belfast, as Specials opened fire on civilians, and republican and loyalist gunmen from the Falls and the Shankill opened up on one another. Altogether, these few days saw some 14 killed and 76 wounded, while about 150 Catholic families in West Belfast were driven from their homes by loyalist mobs.[88]

Strain on the British army

Meanwhile the wider war continued. The IRA stepped up its attacks in May, and Crown forces casualties soared. More than 160 soldiers and policemen would die between the start of May 1921 and early July – well over a quarter of the Crown casualties since the start of the war two-and-a-half years earlier.

In England, the IRA's campaign of arson and sabotage took a new turn on the night of 14 May 1921, when they raided the English homes of men who had joined the Black and Tans and Auxiliaries. Groups of armed IRA men entered houses in several parts of London, including Shepherds Bush, Lewisham and Battersea, and also numerous houses in Liverpool. Major C.J.C. Street, British publicist at Dublin Castle, described the method used:

> The usual ruse for getting the door opened was the announcement of a desire to deliver a very important message. The next move was to overpower the person who opened the door and cover with revolvers anybody who came to the rescue. Then paraffin was produced and carpets, clothing and curtains were saturated with the inflammable liquid...[89]

In Dublin on 25 May, in a spectacular gesture symbolising the collapse of the British administration, the IRA burned down the Custom House, a civil service headquarters and one of the city's outstanding buildings. Thousands assembled to watch the flames. Seven IRA men were killed and some 100 arrested during the operation.

By now General Sir Nevil Macready, the British commander-in-chief in Ireland, was deeply pessimistic. He was worried by the strain imposed by the conflict on both officers and ordinary soldiers, and urged the cabinet to go all out for a swift military victory, advising them:

> Unless I am entirely mistaken, the present state of affairs in Ireland, so far as regards the troops serving there, must be brought to a conclusion by October, or steps must be taken to relieve practically the whole of the troops together with the great majority of the commanders and their staffs.[90]

Field-Marshal Sir Henry Wilson agreed. He took Macready to see the secretary of state for war, noting in his diary:

> Macready absolutely backs up my contention that we must knock out, or at least knock under, the Sinn Feiners this summer or we shall lose Ireland, and he told S. of S. so in good round terms, and that it was not wise nor safe to ask the troops now in Ireland to go on as they are now for another winter.[91]

A crisis was looming for the government. The Southern parliament was due to assemble at the end of June, and the Government of Ireland Act provided that if less than half its MPs took their seats – as was bound to happen – then the parliament would be dissolved and the country would be run as a 'crown colony' by the lord lieutenant and a government-appointed committee. This meant that government by force would go on. The choice between continuing coercion and negotiating with Sinn Féin could not be left much longer.

On 26 May 1921 the cabinet's Irish Situation Committee was reconvened for the first time in nine months. The committee concluded that if the Southern parliament failed to function, martial law should be imposed throughout the 26 counties from 12 July. The cabinet agreed to this on 2 June, but changed the date to 14 July to avoid it coinciding with the anniversary of the battle of the Boyne.

But the government's commitment was less than whole-hearted. As General Macready noted regretfully in his memoirs, 'No sooner… had the decision been reached… than the usual wobblings began to make themselves felt.'[92] Macready was told on 3 June that all 'official reprisals' were to stop – a decision hastened by the fact that, as one MP put it, when the military burned a cottage, the IRA burned a mansion. He was also told that martial law in Ireland meant 'martial law that is supported by the House of Commons', which he saw as putting the army in an impossible position, by requiring them to obtain government permission before taking action. Further, the government refused to transfer internees from camps in Ireland to Britain or – another suggestion – to St Helena. This, wrote Macready, was 'a great blow',

> not only on account of the number of troops required to guard the internment camps, but also because these places became centres of disaffection… The internees spent their time in listening to Republican effusions from their leaders, or in planning escape with the connivance of their friends outside…[93]

By mid-June, Macready recalled, 'the political wobblings had reached such a pitch' that he and Henry Wilson were considering resigning their posts.[94]

British ministers were now considering detailed plans for all-out repression – though worrying about public opinion – while at the same time the government was secretly putting out peace feelers to Sinn Féin.

On 15 June the Irish Situation Committee discussed General Macready's proposals, which included making membership of Dáil Éireann treasonable, suppressing newspapers, applying economic punishments such as the closure of ports, and stopping legal proceedings against the Crown forces. Cabinet secretary Thomas Jones wrote in alarm to Lloyd George that at the meeting Macready made no concealment of his own personal belief... that the policy of coercion will not succeed, but will instead 'land this country in the mire'. But he insisted that half-hearted coercion made the position of the troops and police farcical. 'It must be all out or another policy.'[95]

Jones added:

> Throughout the discussion Macready reiterated his main point: Does the Cabinet realise what is involved? Will they go through with it? Will they begin to howl when they hear of our shooting a hundred men in one week?[96]

More gloom came soon afterwards, with a letter from Colonel Elles, head of the tank corps, to Sir Henry Wilson. Elles had just visited Ireland, and observed:

> To go from Dublin to Cork, one may fly, one may go by T.B.D. [destroyer] and be met by escort at the docks, or one may go – very slowly – by armed train...
> On the other hand, the population moves when, where and by whatever route it wishes. This is a curious situation for a force whose raison d'être in the country is to maintain order.[97]

Pressure to negotiate

The parlous military situation, the uncertain outcome of extending martial law, and the inevitability of a public backlash to it, meant that the British government was under heavy pressure to negotiate.

The republicans, on the other hand, were still full of fight and felt able to hold out for what they wanted, though they knew they could not continue the struggle indefinitely. IRA leaders varied in their estimates of how long they could go on, according to where they were based and their political outlook. Michael Collins, based in Dublin where the IRA was relatively fragile, was pessimistic. By contrast Tom Barry, the 23-year-old commandant in West Cork, was optimistic – and exaggerated his optimism when questioned by Eamon de Valera, because he feared that de Valera 'was about to end the struggle'. Barry recalled telling the president:

> that if large scale British reinforcements were not sent to Cork we would last at least another five years. At this reply the President sat bolt upright and said he thought I was rather optimistic, which in truth I knew only too well myself.[98]

On 14 June, Eamon de Valera wrote to Art O'Brien, president of the Irish Self-Determination League in Britain, that the British were trying to get in touch through intermediaries to see if the republicans would accept a settlement which included these points:

1. Fiscal autonomy for the whole of Ireland.
2. Senate of Southern Parliament to be elected.

3. Belfast Parliament to retain its present powers unless by mutual agreement with the rest of Ireland.

4. Free trade between England and Ireland.[99]

De Valera commented:

> The best line to pursue is to indicate that they are going on the wrong track, that the right way is to propose a treaty with Ireland regarded as a separate State. Irish representatives would then be willing to consider making certain concessions to England's fears and England's interest...[100]

An important new intermediary was General Smuts, the former Boer leader. Smuts was now prime minister of South Africa, which was a dominion of the British Empire, with considerable autonomy but still subject to the Crown. His view was that Ireland should likewise be given dominion status – a position that went too far for Lloyd George but fell short of the Irish claim to a republic. Smuts also thought that the new six-county unit should remain in place.[101] Smuts had been kept informed about the Irish situation by, among others, his friend Tom Casement – brother of Roger – who had fought alongside him in East Africa in the 'great war'. Smuts was due in London in June for a conference of imperial prime ministers, and several people, including Tom Casement and Sir Horace Plunkett, urged him to help in promoting an Irish settlement.

On 13 June, Smuts lunched with King George V and had a long talk. The king was anxious about the visit he was about to make to Belfast to open the new Northern Ireland parliament. Smuts pressed him – as other influential figures were also doing – to use the speech to bring a message of peace and hope to his Irish subjects. At the king's request, Smuts composed a draft declaration and sent it to Lloyd George. Smuts' draft was discussed by the Irish Situation Committee on 16 June, along with another by Sir James Craig. The Conservative Arthur Balfour then made a fresh draft, and the final version was produced by Lloyd George's private secretary, Sir Edward Grigg.

The king and queen arrived in Belfast on 22 June to a tremendous welcome from loyalists, while nationalists kept away. Lady Craig, wife of the new premier, wrote in her diary:

> The King and Queen have the most wonderful reception... even the little side streets that they will never be within miles of are draped with bunting and flags, and the pavement and lampposts painted red white and blue, really most touching, as a sign of their loyalty. Imagine Radicals in England thinking they would ever succeed in driving people like that out of the British Empire, or wanting to!... They drive up High Street, and Donegall Place, to the City Hall. Luckily it was not very far, and precautions had been taken of every description... Every alternate policeman faced the crowd...[102]

In his speech to the parliament, the king declared:

> I speak from a full heart when I pray that My coming to Ireland to-day
> may prove to be the first step towards an end of strife amongst her
> people, whatever their race or creed.

He concluded:

> May this historic gathering be the prelude of a day in which the Irish
> people, North and South, under one Parliament or two, as those
> Parliaments may themselves decide, shall work together in common
> love for Ireland upon the sure foundation of mutual justice and respect.[103]

The speech was warmly welcomed by the British press, and many
editorials urged the government to attempt a settlement.

Lloyd George, now under considerable pressure, told the cabinet on 24
June,

> I think it is fair to the King to follow up his appeal and send an invitation
> to Craig and De Valera to come over and discuss the situation and see
> whether we can arrive at an accommodation.[104]

Four days later, on 28 June, the 'parliament of Southern Ireland' met
ignominiously in Dublin. The British publicist Major Street wrote:

> The Council Room of the Department of Agriculture and Technical
> Instruction was chosen for the purpose, and the whole ceremony occupied
> but a few minutes. The only persons who obeyed the summons were, in
> the Upper House, the senators nominated by the Lord Lieutenant, and in
> the Lower House, the four members for Dublin University.[105]

This 'parliament' would meet once more, on 13 July, when it adjourned,
never to reassemble.

More evidence of England's desire for peace came on 2 July, when
some ten thousand people joined a demonstration through London's West
End organised by the Women's Freedom League. It was 'a beautiful and
impressive spectacle,' noted the *Irish News*. Speaking from one of three
platforms in Trafalgar Square, the veteran campaigner Charlotte Despard
told the throng that Britain should withdraw her arms: 'Let the great heart
of England respond to the great heart of Ireland and then there would be
peace.'[106]

Andy Cope, the indefatigable civil servant, took Lloyd George's
invitation to Dublin, but de Valera refused it, because to come to a
meeting with Craig also there would have been tacitly to accept partition.
Instead, de Valera invited Craig and representatives of Southern Unionists
to a conference in Dublin. Craig did not attend, but Lord Midleton and
three other Southern Unionists did.

The meeting opened at the Mansion House on 4 July, with the Stars and
Stripes flying in appreciation of the sympathy and aid given by the people
of the United States. De Valera declared himself willing to meet Lloyd
George provided that Craig was not present and a truce was first arranged.

Lord Midleton travelled to London to press these conditions on Lloyd George. At the same time Smuts went to Dublin and tried in vain to persuade de Valera to meet Lloyd George alongside Craig.

The cabinet readily agreed that de Valera could be met without Craig, but the truce issue proved more difficult. Only after Midleton had threatened the breakdown of all negotiations did Lloyd George agree to a truce. Midleton then returned to Dublin, and on the evening of 8 July 1921 General Macready arrived at the Mansion House to negotiate terms. He was cheered by the waiting crowd: a gesture he did not appreciate, commenting in his memoirs that

> It was a vivid picture of the unstable excitability of a populace who, with tears running down their cheeks, could cheer to the echo a man who a few hours before, and indeed afterwards, they would have rejoiced to hear had met his death at the hands of the gunmen.[107]

The truce brought an almost euphoric sense of relief to much of Ireland outside the northeast. Constance Markievicz, released from Mountjoy jail soon afterwards, wrote to her sister Eva:

> Life is so wonderful. One just wanders round and enjoys it.
> The children and the trees and cows and all common things are so heavenly after nothing but walls and uniformed people.
> It is so funny, suddenly to be a Government and supposed to be respectable! One has to laugh.[108]

'Bloody Sunday' in Belfast

Hostilities ceased at noon on 11 July 1921, and next day de Valera and a party of leading republicans set off to London to meet Lloyd George. But even as the truce was taking shape in Dublin, Belfast was being convulsed in the worst violence yet seen in the city. The truce coincided with 'twelfth week', anniversary of the battle of the Boyne and traditional highpoint of loyalist sectarianism. Trouble began on the night of Saturday 9 July, when a police raid on a street off the Falls ended with a policeman shot dead, and another policeman and a Special seriously wounded.

Next day became another 'Bloody Sunday', as Specials in lorries invaded nationalist districts, firing indiscriminately with rifles, revolvers, and sometimes machine-guns. Gun battles broke out across much of the Falls Road area, and then in North Belfast and around York Street. The *Irish News* reported:

> In certain districts the streets were literally swept by the fire of the rival snipers and the Crown forces, and it was absolutely unsafe for anyone to be out of doors... From five until seven o'clock the condition of affairs on the Falls and Grosvenor Roads and in the great network of intervening streets was simply appalling, and the ambulances were kept busily

engaged in conveying the dead and wounded to the hospitals, while many were also brought in private cars and taxis.[109]

At the same time, unionist mobs burned Catholic homes and shops along the borderlines of their territory, once again forcing hapless families to flee. The *Irish News* described the scene in a North Belfast street that Sunday night:

> Shortly after half-past eight there was a sudden and terrifying rush into the street... by a mob estimated by those on the spot at several thousands. Many of them carried petrol, paraffin, rags, and even small bundles of wood, such as are sold by street hawkers. They began operations on the house of an aged woman, a widow, named Mrs Knox. They hunted her from her home, and then proceeded to saturate the furniture with the inflammable liquids... both sides of the street were soon a mass of flame.[110]

By the end of the week, 23 civilians had been killed – 16 Catholics and seven Protestants – and many more injured. More than 200 Catholic houses had been destroyed. A delegation from the American White Cross relief organisation, visiting on 22 July, found a thousand homeless Catholics huddled together in schools, old stores and stables. It was a sorry pointer to the future.

12
Postscript

Treaty negotiations proper began in London on 11 October 1921. After two months of tense bargaining, Lloyd George threatened the Irish delegation that if they failed to sign, it would be 'war within three days'. In the early hours of 6 December, they put their names to the fateful document.

The two main sticking points had been Britain's desire to keep Ireland within the empire, and the partition of the country. At the end, the empire question remained the most significant problem for the republicans.

The treaty offered a form of dominion status and was ambiguous on partition. It was a formula that went further than Lloyd George had originally wanted, but which fell far short of the republic that so many Irish people had voted and fought for.

The Irish Free State, as the country would be known, would be part of the British Commonwealth. It would have its own parliament, whose members would have to swear that they would 'be faithful to H.M. King George V, his heirs and successors'. The king would be represented in Ireland by a governor-general.[1] The Free State would have control over its internal affairs and its own revenues, though it would also have to contribute to the United Kingdom's exchequer. It would be allowed a limited army. Britain would control certain ports and other facilities for defence purposes, and would patrol the coastline for the time being.

On the partition question, the loyalists had been the main obstacle. The Irish were willing to give local autonomy to the northeast under an all-Ireland parliament: Lloyd George tried to persuade Craig to accept this, but he obdurately refused.

Lloyd George finally managed to sideline the partition issue by postponing it. First, the Northern Ireland parliament was given the right to vote to exclude the six counties from the Irish Free State and keep the powers given to it under the Government of Ireland Act of 1920. Second, if exclusion were decided on, a boundary commission would be appointed to determine the boundaries of Northern Ireland 'in accordance with the wishes of the inhabitants, so far as may be compatible with economic and geographic conditions.'

The commission would consist of three people, one each appointed by the governments of the Irish Free State, Northern Ireland and Britain: the British appointee would be chairman. Lloyd George convinced the Irish delegates that such a commission would inevitably assign Fermanagh and Tyrone and some other areas to the Free State, leaving Northern Ireland as an unviable unit, which would then be absorbed under an all-Ireland parliament.

Civil war

Feelings in Ireland ran deep over the treaty. Many, especially in areas which had led the fight, felt the delegates should have accepted nothing less than a republic. Others, business people and church leaders to the fore, were pressing for peace. Partition was not an issue, because everyone except the unionists imagined it was temporary.

On 7 January 1922, after a long and bitter debate, Dáil Éireann ratified the treaty by just 64 votes to 57. Most of those who supported it, both inside and outside the Dáil, did so without enthusiasm: they felt it was the best that could be got in the circumstances, and they feared the British threat of renewed war.

In mid-January 1922 a provisional government, headed by Michael Collins, was installed in Dublin, and British regiments began to depart, to the music of their bands. Internees had already been released from the camps, and now sentenced political prisoners were freed under an amnesty. In June, a general election endorsed the treaty, with more pro-treaty than anti-treaty Sinn Fein TDs elected.

By now, the IRA had split, with the pro-treaty section forming the new Free State army, while the anti-treaty section established a separate headquarters in the Four Courts building in Dublin. Lloyd George and Winston Churchill insisted that the anti-treaty IRA be removed from the Four Courts. In the early hours of 28 June 1922 the Free State army, using artillery supplied by the British, began bombarding the republican headquarters. Civil war raged for ten months, ending in April 1923 with the republican army admitting defeat, and leaving lasting divisions in Irish politics.

In succeeding decades, life in the twenty-six counties was to be relatively peaceful, though deeply marked by the after-effects of colonialism and by partition. The six counties, however, would remain in a state of bitter conflict – sometimes open, sometimes suppressed – until the present day.

The Boundary Commission

The Irish Free State Act, ratifying the treaty arrangements, received the royal assent on 6 December 1922, and next day the Northern Ireland parliament contracted out, so that the six counties would remain under British rule.

Nationalists' hopes now rested mainly on the proposed boundary commission, but this proved a fiasco, betraying their expectations. The commission was chaired by Richard Feetham, an English-born South African judge, appointed by Britain. Feetham shared the British view that his task was to make minor modifications to the border. The other members were J.R. Fisher, a staunch Ulster Unionist – also appointed by Britain, because the Northern Ireland government refused to co-operate – and Professor Eoin MacNeill, the Free State's nominee, who proved singularly inadequate for his task.

The commission decided that part of the Inishowen peninsula in Donegal would go to Northern Ireland, while South Armagh would go to the Free State. Fermanagh and Tyrone, despite their nationalist majorities, would stay where they were. The proposals were leaked by a right-wing paper in November 1925, provoking an uproar in nationalist Ireland which prompted MacNeill to resign from the commission.

In December, the British and Free State governments agreed to abandon the Boundary Commission and to accept the existing border. Nationalists in the six counties were astounded and furious, and felt deeply betrayed. 'Forty years of rising hopes had been shattered in a few hours,' wrote Fermanagh historian Peadar Livingstone.[2]

A Protestant state

Even before Britain withdrew from the South, the new unionist rulers of the North had urgently set about safeguarding their position. They concentrated power in their own hands, and took every conceivable measure to deny nationalists any political influence, and to stamp on rebellion. They soon created 'a Protestant parliament and a Protestant state', as Lord Craigavon – formerly Sir James Craig – would boast in the 1930s.

The Northern Ireland parliament took over control of local government in late December 1921. Shortly beforehand, Tyrone county council refused to co-operate and declared its allegiance to Dáil Éireann. The police seized the council offices. The Northern parliament swiftly voted itself the power to dissolve dissident local authorities. Tyrone and Fermanagh county councils, and many other nationalist bodies, were swiftly closed down.[3]

Then in 1922 the Northern parliament abolished proportional representation in local government elections and gave itself the power to redraw electoral boundaries. A commissioner was appointed, who consulted local unionist politicians and redrew the boundaries so as to minimise the power of nationalist voters. This was done by drawing ward boundaries so that nationalist seats were won with huge majorities – 'wasting' votes – while unionists had small majorities over a larger number of seats. On Enniskillen Rural District Council, for instance, 9,817 Catholics could elect nine members, while 9,097 Protestants could elect 17. Another notorious example was Derry City Council, where as late as the 1960s some 20,000 Catholics were represented by eight councillors, while 10,000 Protestants had 12.

The overall result of this gerrymander – as the process was known – was devastating. Unionists gained control of many areas where nationalists were in the majority. Nationalists now controlled no local bodies at all in Fermanagh, and only two in Tyrone. They controlled only two substantial towns – Newry and Strabane – where their majority was so large it could not be gerrymandered away.

Unionist voting power was increased by the restricted franchise: only ratepayers and their wives and tenants could vote. This system disenfranchised about a quarter of the parliamentary electorate: the poorest people, who included a disproportionate number of Catholics. The wealthy, who were predominantly unionist, got additional advantages because landlords got votes according to the number of properties they owned, and because limited companies, depending on their value, had up to six votes, to be exercised by the directors.

When in 1945 the Labour government brought in universal suffrage for local elections in Britain, the Northern Ireland parliament passed a law not only retaining the restricted franchise, but actually extending it, taking away the vote from lodgers who were not ratepayers, and thus depriving many young married couples of the vote.

Once in virtually total control of local government, unionists had enormous power over the allocation of jobs and housing. Systematic and blatant discrimination against nationalists became the norm, openly encouraged by unionist politicians, who boasted of their own refusal to employ Catholics. Skilled, and hence better paid, jobs in the private sector had for a long time been in unionist hands. Now, unionist councils handed out the best jobs to their own kind, corralling Catholics in low-paid manual jobs – such as road-sweeping and street-cleaning – but excluding them almost completely from senior posts.

It was the same story with housing. To have a house meant to have a local government vote, so unionist councils often simply refused to allocate houses to Catholics, despite their greater housing need. Where they did house Catholics, unionist councils made sure to put them in areas where they were already in the majority.

Such discrimination helped to keep working-class Protestants loyal to the new regime, by making them more secure and better off than Catholics, and also kept the number of Catholics down, by forcing them to emigrate in disproportionate numbers.

The unionist regime – which was based from 1932 in a palatial new parliament building at Stormont, just outside Belfast – kept this apartheid-style system in place through naked force.

By March 1922, the Northern Ireland government had some 20,000 Specials, exclusively Protestant and armed with rifles, at its command. The A and C Specials were disbanded after the boundary question was settled in 1925, but the B Specials survived, with around 11,000 to 12,000 members, till 1969. In April 1922, the Royal Irish Constabulary was disbanded and replaced in the North by the Royal Ulster Constabulary, to be 3,000-strong. The RUC not only carried revolvers and carbines, but also had armoured cars and machine-guns.

Also in April 1922, the Northern Ireland parliament rushed into law the Civil Authorities (Special Powers) Act, commonly described as draconian, despotic or dictatorial. Soon hundreds of people were being interned in appalling conditions on an antiquated wooden prison-ship, the *Argenta*, in Belfast Lough, or being sent to prison and flogged for possession of a revolver.

The Special Powers Act conferred almost limitless repressive powers on the Northern Ireland minister of home affairs, and on the police and Specials. The minister was able to make new regulations at will, and a catch-all provision stated:

> If any person does any act of such a nature as to be calculated to be prejudicial to the preservation of the peace or maintenance of order in Northern Ireland and not specifically provided for in the regulations, he shall be deemed to be guilty of an offence against the regulations.

Under the act, and additional regulations made by the minister, many nationalists were arrested on suspicion, interrogated – often brutally – for many hours, and detained or interned indefinitely without right of appeal. Houses were constantly searched, often at night. The authorities imposed curfews, outlawed organisations, banned meetings and suppressed newspapers. They imprisoned people for possessing republican emblems. They issued people with exclusion orders banning them to a small and remote area of the six counties – a practice aimed at excluding them from the North altogether.

The Special Powers Act was originally a temporary measure, but it was regularly renewed and then made permanent in 1933. In 1935 the London-based National Council for Civil Liberties sent a high-powered commission of inquiry to the six counties to investigate. In a damning report, they concluded

> that the Northern Irish Government has used Special Powers towards securing the domination of one particular political faction and, at the same time, towards curtailing the lawful activities of its opponents... It is sad that in the guise of temporary and emergency legislation there should have been created under the shadow of the British Constitution a permanent machine of dictatorship...[4]

The Special Powers Act was eventually repealed in 1972, but only to be replaced by the Emergency Provisions Act.

Appeals to the British government to intervene and put an end to the abuses carried out by its satellite regime proved fruitless. A convention at Westminster dictated that the affairs of the Northern Ireland parliament were not discussed there. The Bishop of Down and Connor recorded in 1943 that for eight years Westminster had been refusing demands for an inquiry into the condition of Catholics in the North. He added:

> On 17th July, 1935, when Catholic homes were burning; when pitiable bits of Catholic furniture made bonfires on the streets of Belfast; when the campaign of terror against Catholic life and property was at its height, I sent an urgent telegram to Lord Craigavon asking him to take steps to put an end to the campaign. A letter from his secretary stated that he was "desired by the Prime Minister to acknowledge receipt of my telegram." No more. I wrote to Baldwin who was then Prime Minister of England. He passed it on to Simon – then Home Secretary – I was informed by him "that it is the Government of Northern Ireland that is responsible for the maintenance of law and order in the area within their jurisdiction." He was "not prepared to intervene."

Nor were the British media interested. The Bishop observed:

> Just try to get some of the facts about the North published in the English dailies or weeklies. There is a veiled, courteous censorship which is as impenetrable as a good stone wall.[5]

Civil rights

In the decades after partition, nationalists repeatedly attempted to assert their rights, both through publicity campaigns aided by people in the South and in Britain, and through periodic outbreaks of armed struggle. But they remained isolated, ignored by the powers-that-be in Britain and internationally.

In the late sixties, however, with much of the world in a ferment of excitement – as colonised nations demanded liberation, students demanded revolution, and black people in the USA demanded civil rights – the lid could be kept on the six counties no longer. The new wave of civil rights protests was unstoppable. Marchers demanding 'one man – one vote' were met by the violence of the RUC. Crisis point came in August 1969, when the RUC laid siege to the nationalist Bogside area of Derry. The British government ordered troops onto the streets of Derry and Belfast. Twenty-five years and more than 3,000 deaths later, they were still there.

Footnotes

Chapter 1: Conquest and Resistance

1. Arthur Young, *A Tour in Ireland*, 2nd ed., 1780, vol. 2, pp. 127-8.
2. Quoted in W.E.H. Lecky, *A History of Ireland in the Eighteenth Century*, 1892, p. 12.
3. Quoted in James Connolly, *Labour in Irish History*, 1967 edition, pp. 23-4.
4. Quoted in Thomas Mac Nevin, *The History of the Volunteers of 1782*, 1846, pp. 156-7.
5. *Ibid*, pp. 159-60.
6. *Ed.* William Theobald Wolfe Tone, *Memoirs of Theobald Wolfe Tone*, 1927, vol. 1, p. 34. Histories of the United Irishmen's times include Marianne Elliott, *Partners in Revolution*, 1969; Nicholas Furlong, *Fr John Murphy of Boolavogue*, 1991; *eds* Hugh Gough and David Dickson, *Ireland and the French Revolution*, 1990; Mary McNeill, *The Life and Times of Mary Ann McCracken*, 1960; Thomas Pakenham, *The Year of Liberty*, 1969; Kieran Sheedy, *Upon the Mercy of the Government*, 1988. Useful general histories which include this period are Jonathan Bardon, *Belfast: An Illustrated History*, 1982; Peter Berresford Ellis, *A History of the Irish Working Class*, 1972; Sean Cronin, *Irish Nationalism*, 1980; Edmund Curtis, *A History of Ireland*, 1961; The Rev. E.A. D'Alton, *History of Ireland*, 1910; Frank Gallagher, *The Indivisible Island*, 1957; Robert Hughes, *The Fatal Shore*, 1987 (about the settlement of Australia); T.A. Jackson, *Ireland Her Own*, 1976; *eds* T.W. Moody and W.E. Vaughan, *A New History of Ireland*, vol. 4, *Eighteenth Century Ireland*, 1986; Liam de Paor, *Divided Ulster*, 1971.
7. *Ed.* R. Barry O'Brien, *The Autobiography of Wolfe Tone*, 1893, vol. 1, pp. 50-1.
8. Wolfe Tone, journal entry for 1 March 1798, in *ed.* William Theobald Wolfe Tone, *Life of Wolfe Tone*, 1826, vol. 2, p. 464; Theobald Wolfe Tone, *Autobiography*, 1893, vol. 1, p. 105.
9. Dr R.R. Madden, *The United Irishmen*, 3rd series, vol. 1, 1846, p. 242.
10. W.E.H. Lecky, *A History of Ireland in the Eighteenth Century*, 1892, vol. 3, p. 37.
11. *Ibid*, pp. 48-9.
12. Quoted in John Ranelagh, *Ireland: An Illustrated History*, 1981, p. 173.
13. Quoted in W.E.H. Lecky, as above, vol. 3, p. 430.
14. Thomas Knox, 13 August 1796; quoted in W.E.H. Lecky, *Ireland in the Eighteenth Century*, as above, vol. 3, p. 437.
15. *Ed.* William Theobald Wolfe Tone, *Life of Tone*, as above, vol. 1, p. 128.
16. *Ibid*, vol. 2, pp. 194, 195.
17. *Ibid*, p. 260.
18. *Ibid*, p. 266.
19. Quoted in Jonathan Bardon, *Belfast: An Illustrated History*, 1982, p. 61.
20. Quoted in W.E.H. Lecky, *A History of Ireland in the Eighteenth Century*, vol. 4, 1892, p. 50.
21. *Ibid*.
22. *Ibid*, p. 52.
23. Quoted in E.P. Thompson, *The Making of the English Working Class*, 1970, p. 179.
24. *Ibid*, p. 188.
25. Quoted in John Ranelagh, *Ireland*, as above, p. 140.
26. Quoted in Thomas Pakenham, *The Year of Liberty*, 1969, p. 250.
27. *Ibid*

Chapter 2: The Act of Union

1. Earl Stanhope, *Life of William Pitt*, vol. 3, 1862, p. 173.
2. Quoted in Dorothy Macardle, *The Irish Republic*, 1968 edition, p. 38.
3. Quoted in John Ranelagh, *Ireland: An Illustrated History,* 1981, p. 145.
4. Quoted in W.E.H. Lecky, *Leaders of Public Opinion in Ireland*, vol. 1, 1912.
5. R.R. Madden, *The Life and Times of Robert Emmet Esq.*, 1847, p. 246. See also *ed.* John Finegan, *The Prison Journal of Anne Devlin*, 1968; Kieran Sheedy, *Upon the Mercy of the Government*, 1988 (about Michael Dwyer).
6. From 'Don Juan', quoted in *ed.* Christopher Hampton, *A Radical Reader*, 1984, p. 416.
7. From 'The Mask of Anarchy', quoted in *ibid*, p. 423. The following epigram comes from *Selected Poems of Byron*, 1913, p. 86.
8. Quoted in Emil Strauss, *Irish Nationalism and British Democracy*, 1951, p. 81. On this period see also Nicholas Mansergh, *The Irish Question 1840-1921*, 1975; Gearoid Ó Tuathaigh, *Ireland Before the Famine 1798-1848*, 1972; W.E.H. Lecky, *Leaders of Public Opinion in Ireland*, vol. 2, Daniel O'Connell, 1861; Ian Budge and Cornelius O'Leary, *Belfast: Approach to Crisis*, 1973; Charles Townshend, *Political Violence in Ireland*, 1983.
9. William Thompson, *An inquiry into the principles of the distribution of wealth most conducive to human happiness*, London 1824, p. xvi.
10. Quoted in Richard K.P. Pankhurst, *William Thompson: Britain's Pioneer Socialist, Feminist and Co-operator*, 1954, pp. 71-2. See also Richard K.P. Pankhurst, 'Anna Wheeler: A pioneer socialist and feminist', *The Political Quarterly*, April-June 1954, vol. xxv, no. 2, p. 133.
11. William Thompson, *Appeal of one-half of the human race, women, against the pretensions of the other half, men, to retain them in political, and thence in civil and domestic, slavery*, 1825, reprinted 1983, p. xxiii.
12. *Ibid*, pp. 207-8.
13. *Ibid*, pp. xxv-xxvi.
14. *Ibid*, p. xxviii.
15. Percy Bysshe Shelley, *An Address to the Irish People*, first pub. 1912, reprinted with *Proposals for an Association*, undated, p. 41.
16. Quoted in Newman Ivey White, *Shelley*, vol. 1, 1947, p. 220.
17. Percy Bysshe Shelley, *Proposals for an Association etc.*, as above, pp. 48-9.
18. *Ibid*, p. 50.
19. *Selected Poems of Byron*, 1913 edition, reprinted 1960, pp. 87-91.
20. British Parliamentary Papers 1825, vol. viii, p. 210.
21. Quoted in Sean Cronin, *Irish Nationalism*, 1980, p. 70.
22. 'Journey to Ireland (1835)', in Alexis de Tocqueville, *Journeys to England and Ireland*, ed. J.P. Mayer, 1958, p. 151.
23. Quoted in Emil Strauss, *Irish Nationalism and British Democracy,* as above, p. 99.
24. Alexis de Tocqueville, *Journeys*, as above, p. 132.
25. *Ibid*.
26. G. Poulett Scrope, *How Is Ireland to Be Governed?*, (first pub. 1834), London 1846, p. 29.
27. Quoted in Dorothy Thompson, *The Chartists*, 1986, p. 19.
28. Reproduced in G.M. Young and W.D. Hancock, *English Historical Documents XII (1) 1833-1874*, 1956, p. 448.
29. Quoted in George Spater, *William Cobbett: The Poor Man's Friend*, vol. 2, 1982, p. 472.
30. Quoted in *ed.* Denis Knight, *Cobbett in Ireland: A warning to England*, 1984, pp. 73-4. Also see Molly Townsend, *Not by Bullets and Bayonets: Cobbett's Writings on the Irish Question 1795-1835*, 1983.

31. Cobbett's *Weekly Political Register*, 4 October 1834.
32. *Ibid*, 18 October 1834.
33. *Ibid*, 25 October 1834.
34. *Third Report of the Royal Commission on the Condition of the Poorer Classes in Ireland*, Parliamentary Papers 1836, vol. XXX, p. 5.
35. Quoted in W.E.H. Lecky, *Leaders of Public Opinion in Ireland*, vol 2, *Daniel O'Connell*, 1912, p. 164.
36. Mary McNeill, *The Life and Times of Mary Ann McCracken, 1770-1866*, 1988, p. 242.
37. Quoted in Frank Gallagher, *The Indivisible Island*, 1957, p. 48.
38. Quoted in Jonathan Bardon, *Belfast: An Illustrated History*, 1982, p. 87.
39. Quoted in Henry Patterson, *Class Conflict and Sectarianism*, 1980, pp. xv-xvi.
40. Quoted in Jonathan Bardon, *Belfast*, as above, pp. 93-4.
41. W.E.H. Lecky, *Leaders of Public Opinion in Ireland*, vol. 2, as above, p. 248.
42. *Hansard*, 9 May 1843, cols. 24-5.
43. Karl Marx and Frederick Engels, *Ireland and the Irish Question*, 1971, pp. 33-5.
44. Quoted in James Connolly, *Labour, Nationality and Religion*, 1910, reprinted 1954, p. 13.

Chapter 3: The Famine

1. *Royal Commission on the Occupation of Land in Ireland* (Devon Commission), Parliamentary Papers 1845, vol. XIX, p. 35.
2. *Freeman's Journal*, 4 November 1845. As well as the sources cited below, see Cormac Ó Gráda, *The Great Irish Famine*, 1989; Stephen, J. Campbell, *The Great Irish Famine*, pub. The Famine Museum, Strokestown, 1994; *ed* Margaret Crawford, *Famine: The Irish Experience*, 1989; Austin Bourke, *The Visitation of God: The Potato and the Great Famine*, 1993.
3. D.J. Corrigan, *On Famine and Fever as Cause and Effect in Ireland*, 1846, p. 22.
4. *Ibid*, p. 26.
5. Quoted in Cecil Woodham-Smith, *The Great Hunger*, 1977 edition, p. 65.
6. *Ibid*, p. 72.
7. *Ibid*, p. 84.
8. *Ibid*, p. 86.
9. *Ibid*.
10. *Ibid*, p. 132.
11. Quoted in Robert Kee, *Ireland: A History*, 1980, p. 88.
12. From 'The Famine Year', reproduced in T.P. O'Connor, *The Cabinet of Irish Literature*, vol. IV, undated, pp. 81-2. Also see Joy Melville, *Mother of Oscar: The life of Jane Francesca Wilde*, 1994.
13. Quoted in Jonathan Bardon, *Belfast: An Illustrated History*, 1982, p. 97.
14. Dated 12 December 1846, quoted in *Creggan, Journal of the Creggan Local History Society*, vol. 1, no. 1, spring 1986, p. 27.
15. Quoted in Cecil Woodham-Smith, *The Great Hunger*, as above, pp. 150-1.
16. *Times*, 24 December 1846 .
17. Quoted in Cecil Woodham-Smith, *The Great Hunger*, as above, p. 149.
18. *The Census of Ireland for the Year 1851*, part V, p. 243, House of Commons Sessional Papers, 1856, vol. XXIX.
19. *Belfast News-Letter*, 20 July 1847.
20. Quoted in Cecil Woodham-Smith, *The Great Hunger*, as above, p. 221.
21. *Ibid*, p. 219.
22. Quoted in The Rev. E.A. D'Alton, *History of Ireland*, vol. V, 1910, p. 205 .
23. *Ibid*.

24. Quoted in Cecil Woodham-Smith, *The Great Hunger*, as above, 298.
25. Quoted in Robert Kee, *Ireland*, as above, p. 96.
26. *Arkansas Intelligencer*, 3 April 1847.
27. Quoted in Cecil Woodham-Smith, *The Great Hunger*, as above, pp. 310-11.
28. *Ibid*, p. 314.
29. *Ibid*, p. 315.
30. *Ibid*, pp. 315-6.
31. *Ibid*, p. 317.
32. Letter dated 31 March 1848, quoted in John Saville, *1848:The British state and the Chartist movement*, 1987, p. 95.
33. Quoted in Cecil Woodham-Smith, *The Great Hunger*, as above, p. 325.
34. *Ibid*.
35. Quoted in Sir Charles Gavan Duffy, *Four Years of Irish History*, 1883, p. 466.
36. *Ibid*, p. 479.
37. *Ibid*, p. 469.
38. *Irish Felon*, 24 June 1848.
39. *Ibid*.
40. *Irish Felon*, 8 July 1848.
41. 'To the Landowners of Ireland', 19 April 1847, reproduced in *ed*. John O'Leary, *The Writings of Fintan Lalor*, 1895, p. 26.
42. *Irish Felon*, 8 July 1848.
43. Quoted in Sean Cronin, *Irish Revolutionaries*, 1971, pp. 64-5.
44. Speech made on 4 June 1848, reported in *Northern Star*, 10 June 1848; reproduced in John Saville, *Ernest Jones: Chartist*, 1952, p. 105.
45. Quoted in Peter Fryer, *Staying Power*, 1984, pp. 408-9.
46. *Nation*, 29 July 1848; see Charles Gavan Duffy, *Four Years*, as above, pp. 94-5, 680-1.
47. *Times*, 31 December 1849, p. 5.
48. Quoted in Cecil Woodham-Smith, *The Great Hunger*, as above p. 369.
49. *Ibid*, pp. 371, 373.
50. *Ibid*, p. 373.
51. *Ibid*, p. 378.
52. *Ibid*, p. 379.
53. Quoted in Robert Kee, *Ireland*, as above, p. 101.
54. *The Census for Ireland for the Year 1851*, part V, p. 242, House of Commons Sessional Papers, 1856, vol. XXIX.
55. *Ed*. George Petrie, *The Petrie Collection of the Ancient Music of Ireland*, 1855, p. xii.

Chapter 4: The Fenians

1. John Denvir, *The Life Story of an Old Rebel*, 1910, reprinted 1972, p. 53.
2. *Ibid*, pp. 61-2.
3. 23 May 1856, in *Karl Marx and Frederick Engels on Ireland*, 1971, pp. 83-4.
4. Letter dated 29 November, quoted in *An Phoblacht/Republican News*, 7 February 1985.
5. John Denvir, *The Irish in Britain*, 1892, p. 181.
6. John Devoy, *Recollections of an Irish Rebel*, first pub. 1929, reissued 1969, p. 25. On this period also see John O'Leary, *Recollections of Fenians and Fenianism*, 1896, reissued 1969; ed T.W. Moody, *The Fenian Movement*, 1968.
7. *Ibid*, p. 33.
8. John Denvir, *The Irish in Britain*, as above, p. 179.
9. *Irish People*, 16 September 1865.
10. John Devoy, *Recollections*, as above, p. 87.
11. *Ibid*.

12. *Ibid*, p. 115.
13. Quoted in Peter Berresford Ellis, *The Rising of the Moon*, 1987, p. 604.
14. John Devoy, *Recollections*, as above, p. 112.
15. *Ibid*, p. 113.
16. *Ibid*.
17. *Ibid*, p. 186.
18. John Denvir, *The Irish in Britain*, as above, p. 216.
19. Quoted in John Denvir, *The Irish in Britain*, as above, pp. 216-17.
20. *Nation*, 9 March 1867.
21. *Freeman's Journal*, 18 February 1867.
22 John Denvir, *The Irish in Britain*, as above, p. 234. Also see Paul Rose, *The Manchester Martyrs*, 1970; *eds* William O'Brien and Desmond Ryan, *Devoy's Postbag*, 1953, reissued 1979.
23. *Reynolds's Newspaper,* 3 November 1867.
24. Quoted in Paul Rose, *The Manchester Martyrs*, 1970, p. 11.
25. *Ibid*, p. 92.
26. John Denvir, *The Irish in Britain*, as above, p. 240.
27. Quoted in Paul Rose, *The Manchester Martyrs*, as above, p. 112.
28. Quoted in Peter Berresford Ellis, *A History of the Irish Working Class*, 1972, p. 140.
29. 24 November 1967, *Marx and Engels on Ireland*, as above, p. 145.
30. 14 December 1867, *Marx and Engels on Ireland*, as above, p. 149.
31. Quoted in Patrick Quinlivan and Paul Rose, *The Fenians in England 1865-1872*, 1982, p. 108.
32. Montagu Williams QC, *Leaves of a Life*, 1890, p. 103.
33. *Ibid*.
34. *Ibid*, p. 115.
35. *Ibid*, p. 114.
36. Quoted in Patrick Quinlivan and Paul Rose, *The Fenians in England*, as above, p. 132.
37. *Reynolds's Newspaper*, 31 May 1868.
38. John Devoy, *Recollections*, as above, p. 250.
39. Speech at Southport, 19 December 1867, quoted in J.L. Hammond, *Gladstone and the Irish Nation*, p. 80.
40. *Hansard*, 31 May 1869, col. 1062.
42. Quoted in J.L. Hammond, *Gladstone and the Irish Nation*, as above, p. 112.
44. 12 October 1869, 25 November 1870, quoted in Charles Townshend, *Political Violence in Ireland*, 1983, pp. 58-9. On this period also see F.S.L. Lyons, *Ireland Since the Famine*, 1973; J.C. Becket, *Confrontations: Studies in Irish History*, 1972, pp. 152-9. See W.D. Handcock, *English Historical Documents*, XII (2), 1977, for extracts from the Irish Church Act 1869 and the Irish Landlord and Tenant Act 1870.
43. Patrick Quinlivan and Paul Rose, *The Fenians in England*, as above, p. 145.
44. *Marx and Engels on Ireland*, as above, p. 151.
45. *Ibid*, pp. 274-5. Also see Yvonne Kapp, *Eleanor Marx*, vol. 1, 1979, pp. 116-119; Patrick Quinlivan and Paul Rose, *The Fenians in England 1865-1872*, as above, p. 145.
46. *Ibid*, p. 281.
47. Quoted in Emil Strauss, *Irish Nationalism and British Democracy,* 1951, p. 156.
48. 21 February 1870, *Marx and Engels on Ireland*, as above, pp. 164-5.
49. *Marx and Engels on Ireland*, as above, p. 381.
50. *Ibid*, p. 290.
51. *Ibid*, p. 163.
52. *Ibid*, pp. 382-3. See also O'Donovan Rossa, *Irish Rebels in English Prisons*, 1991.
53. Article for *La Marseillaise* written 22 March 1870, in *Marx and Engels on Ireland*, as above, p. 394.
54. For the full story, see Seán Ó Luing, *Fremantle Mission,* 1965.

Chapter 5: 'Home Rule' and the Land League

1. Quoted in Rev. E.A. D'Alton, *History of Ireland*, half vol. V, 1910, p. 258. See also Isaac Butt's speech to the House of Commons, 30 June 1874.
2. Isaac Butt, *Irish Federalism*, 1874, p. 39.
3. John Denvir, *The Life Story of an Old Rebel*, 1910, reprinted 1972, p. 148.
4. *Ibid*, p. 190.
5. Quoted in T.W. Moody, *Davitt and Irish Revolution 1846-82*, 1982, p. 123. See also Leon Ó Broin, *Revolutionary Underground: The story of the Irish Republican Brotherhood 1858-1924*, 1976, pp. 7-8.
6. Quoted in J.C. Beckett, *The Making of Modern Ireland 1603-1923*, 1981, p. 381.
7. John Devoy, *Recollections of an Irish Rebel*, 1929, reprinted 1969, p. 284.
8. Quoted in Leon Ó Broin, *Revolutionary Underground*, 1976, p. 11.
9. *Hansard*, 30 June 1876, col. 808.
10. *Freeman's Journal*, 17 April 1877.
11. Quoted in F.S.L. Lyons, *Charles Stewart Parnell*, 1977, p. 65.
12. *Freeman's Journal*, 11 April 1878; also see A.L. Lloyd, 'On an unpublished Irish ballad', in *ed.* Maurice Cornforth, *Rebels and Their Causes: Essays in honour of A.L. Morton*, 1978, p. 181.
13. Quoted in F.S.L. Lyons, *Parnell*, as above, p. 80.
14. Quoted in T.W. Moody, *Davitt*, as above, p. 251.
15. *Ibid*, pp. 8-9.
16. *Irishman*, 9 November 1878.
17. *Irishman*, 11 January 1879
18. *Irishman*, 18 January 1879.
19. Quoted in T.W. Moody, *Davitt*, as above, p. 284.
20. *Ibid*, p. 289.
21. *Ibid*, p. 290.
22. Quoted in Tom Corfe, *The Phoenix Park Murders*, 1986, p.63.
23. *Hansard*, 27 May 1879, col. 1394.
24. Quoted in T.W. Moody, *Davitt*, as above, p. 305.
25. Quoted in *ed.* Edmund Curtis and R.B. McDowell, *Irish Historical Documents 1172-1922*, 1943, 1968, pp. 254-9.
26. Michael Davitt, *The Fall of Feudalism in Ireland*, 1904, pp. 217-18.
27. Quoted by Dr Donal McCartney in *Irish Times* special supplement on the Land League, 30 April 1979.
28. *Freeman's Journal*, 20 September 1880 .
29. Quoted in *Times*, 10 November 1880.
30. *Ibid*.
31. Quoted in T.W. Moody, *Davitt*, as above, p. 448.
32. *Times*, 12 November 1880.
33. *Times*, 13 November, 1880.
34. Quoted in Charles Townshend, *Political Violence in Ireland*, 1983, p. 134.
35. Reproduced in Senator Mrs. J. Wyse-Power, 'The Political Influence of Women in Modern Ireland', in *ed.* William G. Fitz-gerald, *The Voice of Ireland*, undated, c. 1920s, p. 158.
36. Katharine Tynan, *Twenty-five Years: Reminiscences*, 1913, pp. 96-7.
37. Senator Mrs. J. Wyse-Power, 'The Political Influence of Women in Modern Ireland', as above, p. 159.
38. Quoted in Proinnsias Ó Duigneain, *North Leitrim in Land League Times 1880-84*, undated, p. 20. On the London organisers, see Dave Russell, 'Some early Irish movements in South London', *South London Record*, no. 2, 1987.
39. Quoted in Rev. E.A. D'Alton, *History of Ireland*, vol. VI, 1910, p. 292.
40. Quoted in T.W. Moody, *Davitt*, as above, p. 440.
41. *Irish Times*, 22 April 1881.

42. Anna Parnell, *The Tale of a Great Sham*, 1986, p. 99.
43. Quoted in Emil Strauss, *Irish Nationalism and British Democracy*, 1951, p. 162.
44. Quoted in F.S.L. Lyons, *Charles Stewart Parnell*, 1978, p. 175.
45. Quoted in Anna Parnell, *Great Sham*, as above, p. 105.
46. Quoted in Proinnsios Ó Duigneain, *North Leitrim*, as above, pp. 22-3.
47. Katharine Tynan, *Twenty-five Years*, as above, p. 99. Also see William O'Brien, *Recollections*, 1905.
48. Anna Parnell, *Great Sham,* as above, p. 122.
49. Annie Besant, *Coercion in Ireland,* 1882, p. 7.
50. Anna Parnell, *Great Sham*, as above, p. 91.
51. Quoted in Proinnsios Ó Duigneain, *North Leitrim,* as above, p. 45.
52. Anna Parnell, *Great Sham*, as above, pp. 92-3.
53. Quoted in Margaret Ward, *Unmanageable Revolutionaries*, 1983, p. 30.
54. Quoted in Emil Strauss, *Irish Nationalism and British Democracy*, 1951, p. 164, and J.L. Hammond, *Gladstone and the Irish Nation*, 1964, p. 256.
55. Quoted in T.W. Moody, *Davitt*, as above, pp. 528-9.
56. Quoted in F.S.L. Lyons, *Parnell*, as above, p. 195.
57. Anna Parnell, *Great Sham*, as above, p. 136.
58. *Ibid*, p. 142.
59. Quoted in Tom Corfe, *The Phoenix Park Murders*, 1968, p. 208.
60. Anna Parnell, *Great Sham*, as above, pp. 148, 144.
61. Quoted in T.W, Moody, *Davitt*, as above, p. 532.
62. Anna Parnell, *Great Sham*, as above, p. 155. Also see Jane McL. Côté, *Fanny and Anna Parnell*, 1991.
63. *Ibid*, p. 173.
64. Quoted in T.W. Moody, *Davitt*, as above, p. 545.
65. Quoted in K.R.M. Short, *The Dynamite War: Irish-American bombers in Victorian Britain*, 1979, p. 38.
66. Eds William O'Brien and Desmond Ryan, *Devoy's Post Bag*, vol. II, 1953, reissued 1979, p. 52.
67. Quoted in K.R.M. Short, *The Dynamite War*, as above, p. 92.
68. *Ibid*.
69. John Devoy, *Recollections of an Irish Rebel*, 1st ed. 1929, reprinted 1969, p. 211.
70. *Ibid*, p. 210.
71. *Ibid*, pp. 211-12.
72. Detective-Inspector John Sweeney, *At Scotland Yard: experiences during twenty-seven years' service*, 1904, p. 51. On the 'public toilets' episode in London, see Christopher Andrew, *Secret Service*, 1986, p. 45.
73. John Devoy, *Recollections*, as above, p. 212.
74. Quoted in W.F. Mandle, 'The I.R.B. and the beginnings of the Gaelic Athletic Association', *Irish Historical Studies*, vol. 20, no. 80, Sept. 1977, p. 421.
75. W.B. Yeats, *Autobiographies*, 1926, pp. 116, 118. Also see Richard Ellmann, *Yeats: The man and the masks*, 1977, pp. 46-8.

Chapter 6: Parnellites and Loyalists

1. Winston Churchill, *Randolph Churchill*, vol. 1, 1906, p. 230.
2. Letter dated 14 October 1885, quoted in Winston Churchill, *Randolph Churchill*, vol. 2, 1906, p. 4.
3. *Nation*, 24 January 1885.
4. Quoted in T.W. Moody, 'Michael Davitt and the British Labour Movement 1882-1906', *Transactions of the Royal Historical Society*, fifth series, vol. 3, 1953, pp. 63-4.
5. Quoted in F.S.L. Lyons, *Charles Stewart Parnell*, 1978, p. 290.

6. Wilfrid Scawen Blunt, *The Land War in Ireland*, 1912, p. 1.
7. Letter dated 15 October 1885, quoted in F.S.L. Lyons, *Parnell*, as above, pp. 298-9.
8. Quoted in F.S.L. Lyons, *Parnell*, as above, p. 289.
9. *Ibid*, p. 302.
10. John Denvir, *The Irish in Britain*, 1892, p. 317.
11. *Marx and Engels on Ireland*, 1971, p. 348.
12. Quoted in T.W. Moody, 'Michael Davitt and the British Labour Movement 1882-1906', as above, p. 64.
13. *Nation*, 12 December 1885. For a summary of franchise changes, see Chris Cook and Brendan Keith, *British Historical Facts 1830-1900*, 1975.
14. Quoted in R.F. Foster, *Lord Randolph Churchill*, 1981, p. 240.
15. Wilfrid Scawen Blunt, *The Land War in Ireland*, as above, p. 5.
16. Quoted in J.L. Hammond, *Gladstone and the Irish Nation*, 1964, p. 458.
17. Quoted in F.S.L. Lyons, *Parnell*, as above, p. 308.
18. Quoted in Winston Churchill, *Lord Randolph Churchill*, vol. 2, as above, p. 31.
19. Wilfrid Scawen Blunt, *The Land War*, as above, p. 11.
20. *Hansard*, 26 January 1886, col. 416.
21. Quoted in Winston Churchill, *Lord Randolph Churchill*, vol. 2, as above, pp. 28-9.
22. Wilfrid Scawen Blunt, *The Land War*, as above, p. 31.
23. Quoted in Winston Churchill, *Randolph Churchill*, vol. 2, as above, p. 59.
24. *Northern Whig*, 10 August 1885; also see article by D.C. Savage in *Irish Historical Studies*, vol. XII, no. 47. For population figures, see eds W.E. Vaughan and A.J. Fitzpatrick, *Irish Historical Statistics: Population 1821-1971*, 1977. On the unionist mobilisation, also see Ian Budge and Cornelius O'Leary, *Belfast: Approach to Crisis*, 1973; D.C. Savage, 'Origins of the Ulster Unionist Party, 1885-6', in *Irish Historical Studies*, vol. XII, no. 47, March 1961; A.T.Q. Stewart, *The Narrow Ground*, 1977.
25. From a series of pamphlets published by the Irish Loyal and Patriotic Union, around 1886; quoted in Geoffrey Bell, *This We Will Maintain: Ulster Unionism and the Protestant Working Class, 1868-1972*, unpublished thesis.
26. *Ibid*.
27. Quoted in David Kennedy, 'Ulster and the antecedents of home rule, 1850-86', in T.W. Moody and J.C. Beckett, *Ulster Since 1800*, 1954, p. 91.
28. Paschal Grousset, *Ireland's Disease*, first published 1887, reprinted 1986.
29. *Report of the Belfast Riots Commission*, Parliamentary Papers, 1887, XVIII, p. 40. On segregation in 1901, see A.C. Hepburn and B. Collins, in ed Peter Roebuck, *From Plantation to Partition*, 1981, ch. 13.
30. *Times*, 21 August 1872, p. 10.
31. Quoted in Henry Patterson, *Class Conflict and Sectarianism*, 1980, p. xiv. See also John Gray, *City in Revolt: James Larkin and the Belfast Dock Strike of 1907*, 1985; Jonathan Bardon, *Belfast: An Illustrated History*, 1982.
32. Dr C.D. Purdon, *The Sanitary State of the Belfast Factory District*, Belfast 1877; quoted in D.L. Armstrong, 'Social and economic conditions in the Belfast linen industry, 1850-1900', *Irish Historical Studies*, vol. VII, no. 28, September 1951, p. 248.
33. Quoted in Peter Gibbon, *The Origins of Ulster Unionism*, 1975, p. 126.
34. Wilfrid Scawen Blunt, *The Land War*, as above, p. 51.
35. Quoted in Winston Churchill, *Lord Randolph Churchill*, vol. 2, as above, pp. 62-3. Also see articles by John A. Murphy and others, *Irish Times*, 9-12 June 1986.
36. *Hansard*, 8 April 1886, col. 1041.
37. *Ibid*, col. 1053.
38. *Ibid*, cols. 1088-9.
39. *Ibid*, col. 1095.
40. *Hansard*, 12 April 1886, cols. 1395-6.
41. *Ibid*, col. 1134.

42. *Dictionary of National Biography 1912-21*, p. 107.
43. *Hansard*, 9 April 1886, col. 1183.
44. *Ibid*, col. 1185.
44. *Ibid*, cols. 1194, 1206.
46. Quoted in James Anderson, 'Ideological Variations in Ulster During Ireland's First Home Rule Crisis', forthcoming.
47. *Ibid*.
48. *Ibid*.
49. *Ibid*.
50. Quoted in Winston Churchill, *Sir Randolph Churchill*, vol. 2, as above, p. 65.
51. Quoted in J.L. Hammond, *Gladstone and the Irish Nation*, as above, pp. 468-9.
52. Wilfrid Scawen Blunt, *The Land War*, as above, p. 141.
53. *Hansard*, 7 June 1886, col. 1183.
54. *Ibid*, col. 1239.
55. Quoted in Winston Churchill, *Lord Randolph Churchill*, vol. 2, as above, p. 117.
56. Quoted in Bernard Porter, *The Lion's Share*, 1975, p. 80.
57. Quoted in Ralph G. Martin, *Lady Randolph Churchill*, 1969, p. 268.
58. Wilfrid Scawen Blunt, *The Land War*, as above, p. 124.
59. *Ibid*, pp. 72-3.
60. *Ibid*, pp. 127-9.
61. Quoted in the *Annual Register* for 1886, p. 311. On the Scottish crofters' revolt, see Ian Bradley, 'The Highland Land War of the 1880s', *History Today*, December 1987, pp. 23-8; John Murdoch, *For the People's Cause*, 1986.
62. *Hansard*, 15 March 1887, col. 363.
63. *Hansard*, 28 March 1887, cols. 1650-8.
64. *Daily Telegraph*, 12 April 1887.
65. *Times*, 7 March 1887.
66. *Times*, 14 March 1887.
67. *Times*, 18 April 1887, p. 8. On the forgery affair, see F.S.L. Lyons, *Parnell*, as above; *Annual Register*, 1889, pp. 477-507; John Denvir, *The Irish in Britain*, 1892, pp. 329-61.
68. *Ibid*.
69. *Hansard*, 18 April 1887, col. 1225. Also see essay by David Cannadine in *eds* Eric Hobsbawm and Terence Ranger, *The Invention of Tradition*, 1983, pp. 101-64; John M. Mackenzie, *Propaganda and Empire*, 1984, p. 27; Jacqueline Van Voris, *Constance de Markievicz*, 1967, pp. 31, 51; Wilfred Scawen Blunt, *The Land War*, as above, pp. 277-8; *eds* William O'Brien and Desmond Ryan, *Devoy's Post Bag*, vol. II, 1953, reissued 1979, pp. 298-9.
70. Quoted in the *Annual Register* for 1887, p. 139.
71. *Times*, 22 June 1887.
72. *Times*, 10 September 1887.
73. *Ibid*.
74. Frederick J. Higginbottom, *The Vivid Life*, 1934, pp. 99-100.
75. *Hansard*, 12 September 1887, cols. 323, 327.
76. William O'Brien, *Evening Memories*, 1920, pp. 290-1.
77. *Ibid*, p. 215.
78. Wilfrid Scawen Blunt, *The Land War*, as above, p. 303.
79. William O'Brien, *Evening Memories*, as above, p. 297. On the 13 November events, also see Rodney Mace, *Trafalgar Square*, 1976, p. 179ff; Annie Besant, *An Autobiography*, 1893, p. 323ff.
80. Quoted in Yvonne Kapp, *Eleanor Marx*, vol. II, 1979, pp. 228-9.
81. Quoted in William O'Brien, *Evening Memories*, as above, p. 335.
82. Wilfrid Scawen Blunt, *The Land War*, as above, pp. 346, 352.
83. *Ibid*, p. 379.
84. *Ibid*, p. 406.

85. *Ibid*, p. 410.
86. Quoted in L.P. Curtis Jr., *Coercion and Conciliation in Ireland 1880-1892*, 1963, p. 223.
87. *Derry Journal*, 8 July 1889. Also see Raymond Postgate, *Life of George Lansbury*, 1951, pp. 34-5.
88. George Lansbury, *My Life*, 1928, p. 64.
89. *Ibid*, pp. 26-7.
90. *Ibid*, p. 65.
91. *Ibid*, p. 66.
92. Quoted in F.S.L. Lyons, *Ireland Since the Famine*, 1973, pp. 190-1.
93. Quoted in F.S.L. Lyons, *Parnell*, as above, p. 463.
94. *Ibid*, p. 487.
95. *Ibid*, p. 488.
96. Quoted in J.L. Hammond, *Gladstone and the Irish Nation*, 1964, p. 647.
97. *Belfast News-letter*, 18 June 1892, p. 5.
98. *Ibid*, p. 7.
99. *Belfast News-Letter*, 5 April 1893, p. 7.
100. Quoted in Patrick Buckland, *Irish Unionism*, vol. 2, 1973, p. 18.
101. *Hansard*, 6 April 1893, cols. 1619-20.

Chapter 7: The Irish Revival

1. Katharine Tynan, 'The Pursuit of Diarmuid and Grainne', from *Shamrocks*, 1887.
2. Ed. Roger McHugh, *W.B. Yeats: Letters to Katharine Tynan*, 1953, p. 26.
3. Richard Ellmann, *The Artist as Critic: Critical writings of Oscar Wilde*, 1970, p. 150.
4. W.P. Ryan, *The Irish Literary Revival*, 1894, p. 29.
5. *Ibid*.
6. W.B. Yeats, *Autobiographies*, 1926, p. 250.
7. Sir Charles Gavan Duffy *et al.*, *The Revival of Irish Literature*, 1894, pp. 117-61. Also see *ed.* Robert Hogan, *Macmillan Dictionary of Irish Literature*, 1980, pp. 302-6; Patsy McGarry, 'The Gaelic Dream of Douglas Hyde', *Magill*, July 1988, pp. 35-8; Tom Garvin, 'Home rule hiatus spawned drive to independence', *Irish Times*, 10 June 1986; Shaun Richards, 'Polemics on the Irish Past', *History Workshop*, Spring 1991, pp. 120-35.
8. *Irish Volunteer*, 7 February 1914.
9. Thomas J. Clarke, *Glimpses of an Irish Felon's Prison Life*, 2nd edition, 1970, p. 42. See also 'The Irish National Amnesty Association of Great Britain, 1892-99', *United Irishman*, 4 November 1899.
10. Maud Gonne MacBride, *A Servant of the Queen*, 1938, pp. 177-8. Also see *eds*. Anna MacBride White and A. Norman Jeffares, *The Gonne-Yeats Letters 1893-1938*, 1992; Elizabeth Coxhead, *Daughters of Erin*, 1979; Margaret Ward, *Maud Gonne*, 1990.
11. Maud Gonne MacBride, *A Servant of the Queen*, as above, p. 125.
12. *Ibid.*, p. 126.
13. *Ibid.*, p. 129.
14. *Northern Patriot*, 23 November 1895, pp. 30-1. Also see Bríghid Mhic Sheáin, *Glimpses of Erin: Alice Milligan: poet, Protestant, patriot*, pamphlet published with *Fortnight*, no. 326; Sheila Turner Johnston, *Alice: A Life of Alice Milligan*, 1994. On Ethna Carbery's father see Dr Mark Ryan, *Fenian Memories*, 1946, p. 181.
15. Maud Gonne MacBride, *A Servant of the Queen*, as above, p. 176.
16. Ed. Seumas MacManus, *The Four Winds of Eirinn*, 1918, pp. 149-50.
17. *We Sang for Ireland*, 1950, p. 42.
18. John Leslie, *The Irish Question*, first pub. in *Justice*, 1894; reprinted 1986.

19. Quoted in C. Desmond Greaves, *The Life and Times of James Connolly,* 1976, p. 75. Also see Samuel Levenson, *James Connolly,* 1977.
20. *Shan Van Vocht,* 2 August 1897, pp. 138-9.
21. *Shan Van Vocht,* 8 January 1897, pp. 7-8. Note: This quotation is taken directly from the *Shan Van Vocht* – later versions of the article are slightly different.
22. Quoted in James Morris, 'High Noon of Empire', in *The British Empire,* vol. 4, 1979, p. 212.
23. Quoted in C.C. Eldridge, *Victorian Imperialism,* 1978, p. 172ff.
24. *Daily Mail,* 22 June 1897, p. 4. See also James Morris, *Pax Britannica,* 1969.
25. *Daily Mail,* 23 June 1897, p. 4.
26. *Ibid.,* p. 5.
27. *Irish News,* 24 June 1897, p. 4.
28. *Irish News,* 23 June 1897, p. 5.
29. Maud Gonne MacBride, *A Servant of the Queen,* as above, pp. 273-4.
30. *Daily Mail,* 23 June 1897, p. 3.
31. Maud Gonne MacBride, *A Servant of the Queen,* as above, p. 274.
32. *Ibid.,* p. 275.
33. *Workers' Republic,* 13 August 1898, pp. 1-2.
34. Michael Davitt, *The Boer Fight for Freedom,* 1902.
35. *Workers' Republic,* 19 August 1899.
36. *United Irishman,* 2 September 1899.
37. *United Irishman,* 7 October 1899, p. 3.
38. 12 October 1899, printed in various issues of *United Irishman.*
39. Michael Davitt, *The Boer Fight for Freedom,* as above, preface.
40. *United Irishman,* 23 December 1899.
41. *Ibid.*
42. *Ibid.*
43. *Irish News,* 20 February 1900.
44. *United Irishman,* 10 March 1900.
45. Quoted in Sean Cronin, *The McGarrity Papers,* 1972, p. 39.
46. *United Irishman,* 7 July 1900.
47. Wilfrid Scawen Blunt, *My Diaries 1888-1914,* 1932, pp. 375-6.
48. The Rev. E. A. D'Alton, *History of Ireland,* half vol.VI, 1910, p. 469.
49. *United Irishman,* 3 February 1900.
50. *Irish News,* 11 January 1906, p. 4.
51. *Northern Star,* 31 August 1907, 3 August 1907, 6 July 1907; quoted in John Gray, *City in Revolt,* 1985, pp. 54-5.
52. Maud Gonne MacBride, *A Servant of the Queen,* as above, p. 317.
53. Quoted in F.S.L. Lyons, *Ireland Since the Famine,* 1973, p. 251.
54. *Harp,* April 1908.
55. *Irish Nation,* 23 January 1909. A useful essay on this period is Donal McCartney, 'From Parnell to Pearse', in *eds.* T.W. Moody and F.X. Martin, *The Course of Irish History,* 1967, pp. 294-312.
56. Mary Colum, *Life and the Dream,* revised edition 1966, p. 83.
57. Quoted in G.J. Watson, *Irish Identity and the Literary Revival,* 1979, p. 64. On the arts and crafts movement see Jeanne Sheehy, *The Rediscovery of Ireland's Past,* 1980.
58. W.B. Yeats, *Collected Works,* 1908, vol. IV, p. 241.
59. *United Irishman,* 10 October 1903.
60. *United Irishman,* 24 October 1903.
61. *Ibid.*
62. *Ibid.*
63. *Irish Times,* 30 January 1907.
64. Desmond Ryan, *Remembering Sion,* 1934, p. 91. Also see Ruth Dudley Edwards, *Patrick Pearse: The triumph of failure,* 1977.
65. P. H. Pearse, *The Murder Machine,* 1912, reissued 1976, pp. 8-9.
66. Quoted in Brian Inglis, *Roger Casement,* 1974, p. 34.
67. *Ibid.,* p. 47.

68. *Ibid.*, p. 76.
69. *Ibid.*, p. 131.
70. *Ibid.*, p. 156.
71. *Sligo Champion*, 26 December 1896.
72. Dáil debate, 2 March 1922; quoted in Diana Norman, *Terrible Beauty: A life of Constance Markievicz*, 1987, p. 235. Also see Jacqueline van Voris, *Constance de Markievicz: In the cause of Ireland*, 1967; Anne Haverty, *Constance Markievicz: An independent life*, 1988.
73. *Éire*, 18 August 1923.
74. *Bean na hÉireann*, vol. 1, no. 8, June 1909.
75. Quoted in Diana Norman, *Terrible Beauty*, as above, p. 65. Also see *ed.* F.X. Martin, *The Irish Volunteers 1913-1915*, 1963, p. 17ff.
76. Quoted in Sean Cronin, *The McGarrity Papers*, 1972, p. 26. Also see Leon Ó Broin, *Revolutionary Underground*, 1976; *eds.* William O'Brien and Desmond Ryan, *Devoy's Post Bag*, vol.2, 1953, reissued 1979.
77. *Éire*, 26 May 1923.
78. P. S. O'Hegarty, introduction to Thomas J. Clarke, *Glimpses*, as above, p. 6.
79. Quoted in John Gray, *City in Revolt*, as above, p. 9.
80. *Northern Whig*, 11 September 1905, p. 12.
81. Quoted in John Gray, *City in Revolt*, as above, pp. 48-9.
82. *Irish News*, 2 August 1905, p. 8.
83. *Northern Whig*, 18 May 1907, p. 12.
84. Preface to the Rules of the ITGWU, reproduced in Desmond Greaves, *The Irish Transport and General Workers' Union: The formative years*, 1982, pp. 327-8.
85. *Éire*, 16 June 1923.
86. Quoted in Mary Jones, *These Obstreporous Lassies: A history of the IWWU*, 1988, p. 1.
87. Sylvia Pankhurst, *The Suffragette Movement*, 1931, reissued 1977, p. 47.
88. Hanna Sheehy Skeffington, 'Reminiscences of an Irish Suffragette', in *eds.* Andree Sheehy Skeffington and Rosemary Owens, *Votes for Women*, 1975 (pamphlet), p. 12. Also see Rosemary Cullen Owens, *Smashing Times: A History of the Irish Women's Suffrage Movement 1889-1922*, 1984.
89. Biographical notice by Hanna Sheehy Skeffington, in Francis Sheehy Skeffington, *In Dark and Evil Days*, 1916.
90. Desmond Ryan, *Remembering Sion*, as above, p. 163.
91. Biographical notice in Francis Sheehy Skeffington, *In Dark and Evil Days*, as above.
92. James and Margaret Cousins, *We Two Together*, 1950, p. 25.
93. *Ibid.*, p. 21.
94. *Ibid.*, p. 105.
95. *Ibid.*, pp. 128-30.
96. *Ibid.*, p. 164.
97. Hanna Sheehy Skeffington, 'Reminiscences', as above.
98. James and Margaret Cousins, *We Two Together*, as above, p. 165.
99. *Ibid.*, p. 166.
100. Lecture to the Students' National Literary Society, Dublin, 28 March 1909; quoted in Jacqueline Van Voris, *Constance de Markievicz*, as above, p. 63.
101. James and Margaret Cousins, *We Two Together*, as above, p. 180.

Chapter 8: The Conservative Revolt

1. *Times*, 11 December 1909, p. 8. On the years from 1910, as well as the sources cited below, see George Dangerfield, *The Damnable Question*, 1977; George Dangerfield, *The Strange Death of Liberal England*, 1935; Frank Gallagher, *The Indivisible Island*, 1957; J.J. Horgan, *The Complete Grammar of Anarchy*, 1918; *Annual Register*.
2. Quoted in Second Earl of Birkenhead, *The Life of F.E. Smith, First Earl of Birkenhead*, p. 156.
3. Quoted in Ian Colvin, *The Life of Lord Carson*, vol. 2, 1934, p. 55.

4. *Ibid.*

5. *Times*, 7 December 1910, p. 6. See also Sir Charles Petrie, Bt., *Walter Long and his Times*, 1936; Patrick Buckland, *Irish Unionism*, vols. 1 and 2, 1972 and 1973.

6. Quoted in Ian Colvin, *Life of Carson*, as above, p. 57. See also Patrick Buckland, *James Craig*, 1980.

7. *Spectator*, 24 December 1910, p. 1120.

8. Quoted in Denis Gwynn, *The Life of John Redmond*, 1932, p. 199. On the shipyard workers, see Henry Patterson, *Class Conflict and Sectarianism*, 1980.

9. *Morning Post*, 9 January 1911.

10. *Hansard*, House of Lords, 20 July 1911.

11. *Hansard*, 8 August 1911, col. 988.

12. Quoted in Patricia Jalland, *The Liberals and Ireland: The Ulster question in British politics to 1914*, 1980, p. 58.

13. *Ibid.*, p. 59.

14. Letter dated 29 July 1911, quoted in St. John Ervine, *Craigavon: Ulsterman*, 1949, p. 185.

15. Quoted in Ian Colvin, *Life of Carson*, vol. 2, as above, pp. 77, 79.

16. Quoted in Robert Blake, *The Unknown Prime Minister*, 1955, p. 96.

17. Quoted in Ian Colvin, *Life of Carson*, as above, p. 88.

18. *Times*, 23 January 1912.

19. *Ibid.*

20. *Times*, 27 January 1912.

21. Quoted in Patrick Buckland, *Irish Unionism*, vol. 2, as above, p. 49.

22. Quoted in Leon Ó Broin, *The Chief Secretary: Augustine Birrell in Ireland*, 1970, p. 49.

23. *Ibid.*, p. 51. Also see Major-General Lord Edward Gleichen, *A Guardsman's Memories*, 1932, pp. 259-62.

24. Quoted in Roy Jenkins, *Asquith*, 1986, p. 277.

25. Quoted in Dorothy Macardle, *The Irish Republic*, 1937, reissued 1968, p. 78.

26. *Hansard*, 1 April 1912, col. 872.

27. *Ibid.*

28. Quoted in Denis Gwynn, *Life of Redmond*, as above, p. 201.

29. Quoted in Robert Blake, *The Unknown Prime Minister*, as above, p. 129.

30. *Hansard*, 11 April 1912, col. 1400.

31. *Ibid.*, col. 1401.

32. *Hansard*, 16 April 1912, cols. 296-7.

33. *Hansard*, 11 June 1912, col. 771.

34. *Hansard*, 11 April 1912, col. 787.

35. *Hansard*, 13 June 1912, cols. 1086-7.

36. *Ibid.*, col. 1155.

37. *Ibid.*, col. 1165.

38. *Ibid.*, col. 1076.

39. *Ibid.*, col. 1068.

40. *Ibid.*, col. 1076.

41. *Hansard*, 18 June 1912, col. 1559.

42. *Ibid.*, cols. 1559-60.

43. Quoted in Sylvia Pankhurst, *The Suffragette Movement*, 1977, p. 403. Also see Cliona Murphy, *The Women's Suffrage Movement and Irish Society*, 1989, p. 185ff; Rosemary Cullen Owens, *Smashing Times*, 1984; Margaret Mac Curtain, 'Women, the vote and revolution', in *eds*. Margaret Mac Curtain and Donncha Ó Corrain, *Women in Irish Society*, 1978.

44. James and Margaret Cousins, *We Two Together*, 1950, p. 186.

45. *Irish Citizen*, 8 June 1912.

46. *Irish Citizen*, 22 June 1912.

47. Hanna Sheehy Skeffington, 'The Women's Movement – Ireland', *The Irish Review*, July 1912, pp. 225-7.

48. *Irish Independent*, 20 July 1912.
49. Hanna Sheehy Skeffington, 'Reminiscences', 1941, in *ed.* Andree D. Sheehy Skeffington, *Votes for Women*, 1975, p. 22.
50. *Ibid.*, p. 23.
51. James and Margaret Cousins, *We Two Together*, as above, p. 188.
52. *Ibid.*, p. 191.
53. *Ibid.*, p. 194.
54. *Irish News* (quoting the *Dublin Evening Telegraph*,) 27 August 1912.
55. *Times*, 29 July 1912.
56. *Ibid.*
57. *Ibid.*
58. Quoted in Denis Gwynn, *Life of Redmond*, as above, p. 214.
59. Facsimile no. 206 in *Steps to Partition*, Public Records Office of Northern Ireland.
60. *Hansard*, 1 January 1913, col. 388.
61. Quoted in Denis Gwynn, *Life of Redmond*, as above, pp. 220-1. *Hansard's* version is slightly different.
62. Facsimile no. 208 in *Steps to Partition*, Public Records Office of Northern Ireland.
63. Major-General Lord Edward Gleichen, *A Guardsman's Memories*, p. 367.
64. *Yorkshire Post*, 22 September 1913.
65. Quoted in Denis Gwynn, *Life of Redmond*, as above, p. 224.
66. Quoted in Curriculum Development Unit, *Dublin 1913*, 1982, pp. 74-5.
67. Quoted in Jacqueline Van Voris, *Constance de Markievicz: In the cause of Ireland*, 1967, p. 106.
68. Quoted in Curriculum Development Unit, *Dublin 1913*, as above, p. 84.
69. Nora Connolly, *The Unbroken Tradition*, 1918, p. 2.
70. *Irish Times*, 7 October 1913.
71. Quoted in Sean Cronin, *The Revolutionaries*, 1971, p. 146.
72. Quoted in Padraic Colum, *Arthur Griffith*, 1949, p. 110.
73. *Freeman's Journal*, 21 October 1913.
74. Sylvia Pankhurst, *The Suffragette Movement*, as above, p. 502.
75. *Times*, 3 September 1913.
76. Quoted in W.P. Ryan, *The Irish Labour Movement*, 1919, p. 230.
77. *Times*, 20 November 1913.
78. *Times*, 21 November 1913.
79. *Forward*, 7 February 1914.
80. *Forward*, 14 March 1914.
81. *Irish Worker*, 28 November 1914.
82. Captain J.R. White, *Misfit: An autobiography*, 1930, p. 150.
83. *Freeman's Journal*, 14 November 1913.
84. Reproduced in F.X. Martin, *The Irish Volunteers*, 1963, p. 59.
85. *Times*, 20 November 1913.
86. Quoted in Sean Cronin, *The McGarrity Papers*, 1972, pp. 38-9.
87. Quoted in *ed.* F.X. Martin, *The Irish Volunteers*, as above, p. 100.
88. *Leabhar na mBan*, December 1919, quoted by Maire Comerford in *ed.* Pat McGlynn, *Éirí Amach Na Casca*, 1986, p. 40.
89. Quoted in Rosemary Cullen Owens, *Smashing Times*, as above, pp. 108-9. On the formation of Cumann na mBan, see Margaret Ward, *Unmanageable Revolutionaries*, 1983, p. 88ff.; Eithne ni Chumhaill, lectures on the history of Cumann na mBan, *An Phoblacht*, 8, 15, 21 April 1933.
90. Wilfrid Scawen Blunt, *My Diaries*, 1932, p. 838.
91. Letter in *Freeman's Journal*, 6 May 1914.
92. Quoted in Robert Blake, *The Unknown Prime Minister*, as above, p. 133.
93. *Ibid.*
94. Quoted in Roy Jenkins, *Asquith*, as above, pp. 285-6.
95. Quoted in Patricia Jalland, *The Liberals and Ireland*, as above, p. 147.

96. Quoted in Roy Jenkins, *Asquith*, as above, p. 291.
97. Quoted in Patricia Jalland, *The Liberals and Ireland*, as above, p. 167.
98. Quoted in Ian Colvin, *Life of Carson*, as above, p. 269.
99. *Ibid.*
100. *Ibid.*, p. 270.
101. Quoted in Roy Jenkins, *Asquith*, as above, p. 293.
102. Quoted in Denis Gwynn, *Life of Redmond*, as above, p. 237.
103. Quoted in Roy Jenkins, *Asquith*, as above, p. 301.
104. Quoted in Denis Gwynn, *The History of Partition*, 1950, p. 89.
105. Quoted in Denis Gwynn, *Life of Redmond*, as above, p. 268.
106. Quoted in Roy Jenkins, *Asquith*, as above, p. 303.
107. *Hansard*, 9 March 1914, col. 906.
108. *Ibid.*, 9 March 1914, col. 934.
109. *Irish Freedom*, April 1914.
110. *Sinn Fein*, 11 April 1914.
111. *Irish Worker*, 21 March 1914. Also see Arthur Mitchell, *Labour in Irish Politics 1890-1930*, 1974, pp. 42-6.
112. Quoted in C. Desmond Greaves, *The Life and Times of James Connolly*, 1976, p. 344.
113. *Irish Worker*, 14 March 1914.
114. Sean O'Casey, *The Story of the Irish Citizen Army*, 1980, p. 14.
115. Reproduced in *ed.* Ian F.W. Beckett, *The Army and the Curragh Mutiny*, 1986, p. 33.
116. *Ibid.*, p. 36.
117. The Earl of Oxford and Asquith, *Memories and Reflections*, vol. 2, 1928, p. 155.
118. Reproduced in *ed.* Ian F.W. Beckett, *The Army and the Curragh Mutiny*, as above, p. 41.
119. Quoted in Robert Blake, *The Unknown Prime Minister*, as above, p. 185.
120. Reproduced in *ed.* Ian F.W. Beckett, *The Army and the Curragh Mutiny*, as above, p. 57.
121. *Ibid.*, pp. 61-2.
122. *Ibid.*, p. 197.
123. *Ibid.*, p. 90.
124. *Ibid.*, p. 218.
125. *Ibid.*, pp. 218-19.
126. *Hansard*, 23 March 1914, col. 121.
127. *Hansard*, 24 March 1914, col. 251.
128. *Ibid.*, col. 253. Also see *Annual Register* 1914, pp. 59-60.
129. Reproduced in *ed.* Ian F.W. Beckett, *The Army and the Curragh Mutiny*, as above, p. 369.
130. V.I. Lenin, *Against Imperialist War*, 1974, p. 58.
131. Quoted in A.T.Q. Stewart, *The Ulster Crisis*, 1969, p. 177.
132. Major-General Lord Edward Gleichen, A *Guardsman's Memories*, 1932, p. 386.
133. *Ibid.*, p. 387.
134. *Forward*, 30 May 1914.
135. Quoted in Roy Jenkins, *Asquith*, as above, pp. 320-1.
136. Quoted in Denis Gwynn, *The History of Partition*, as above, p. 125.
137. *Ibid.*, p. 127.
138. *Forward*, 30 May 1914.
139. Letter dated 14 May 1914, reproduced in *eds.* William O'Brien and Desmond Ryan, *Devoy's Post Bag*, vol. 2, 1979, p. 444. On these events, also see Denis Gwynn, *Life of Redmond*, as above; *ed.* F.X. Martin, *The Irish Volunteers*, as above; Desmond Greaves, *Liam Mellows and the Irish Revolution*, 1971, p. 62ff; Piaras Beaslai, 'How the fight began!', in *Dublin's Fighting Story*, c. 1948.
140. Mary Colum, *Life and the Dream*, 1966, p. 164.

141. *Ibid.*, p. 166.
142. Ed. F.X. Martin, *The Howth Gun-Running*, 1964, p. 86.
143. *Ibid.*, p. 106.
144. Sylvia Pankhurst, *The Suffragette Movement*, as above, p. 590.

Chapter 9: The Easter Rising

1. *Hansard*, 3 August 1914, col. 1829.
2. Quoted in R.M. Henry, *The Evolution of Sinn Fein*, c. 1920, pp. 164-5.
3. *Irish Freedom*, September 1914.
4. *Irish Worker*, 8 August 1914. Also see Connolly's article from *International Socialist Review*, March 1915, reproduced in James Connolly, *Collected Works*, vol. 2, 1988. p. 55ff.
5. *Forward*, Glasgow, 22 August 1914.
6. *Irish Worker*, 5 September 1914.
7. *An Phoblacht*, 30 April 1926. On these events also see C. Desmond Greaves, *The Life and Times of James Connolly*, 1976; Dorothy Macardle, *The Irish Republic*, 1937, reissued 1968; William O'Brien, introduction to 'Labour and Easter Week', in James Connolly, *Collected Works*, vol. 2, p. 1ff; Leon Ó Broin, *Revolutionary Underground*, 1976; P.S. O'Hegarty, introduction to Thomas J. Clarke, *Glimpses of an Irish Felon's Prison Life*, 1970.
8. Quoted in John Devoy, *Recollections of an Irish Rebel*, 1929, reissued 1969, p. 406.
9. The Earl of Oxford and Asquith, *Memories and Reflections*, vol. 2, 1928, p. 29.
10. *Hansard*, 15 September 1914, col. 892.
11. Quoted in Robert Blake, *The Unknown Prime Minister*, 1955, p. 229.
12. *Hansard*, 15 September 1914, col. 911.
13. *Sinn Fein*, 12 September 1914.
14. *Irish Worker*, 19 September 1914.
15. Quoted in Denis Gwynn, *The Life of John Redmond*, 1932, p. 392.
16. Reproduced in *ed.* F.X. Martin, *The Irish Volunteers 1913-1915*, 1963, p. 154.
17. *Irish Worker*, 3 October 1914. Also see Frank robbins,*Under the Starry Plough*, 1977; *Dublin's Fighting Story*, c. 1940s.
18. The documents, held in the German military archives, were discovered by Irish historian Lt. Col. J.P. Duggan and made public in 1991. *The Sunday Press*, 31 March 1991, carried a detailed account.
19. *Eds.* William O'Brien and Desmond Ryan, *Devoy's Post Bag*, vol. 2, 1979, p. 418.
20. Padraic H. Pearse, *Political Writings and Speeches*, 1952, pp. 136-7.
21. *Irish Citizen*, 23 October 1915. Also see *Sinn Fein Rebellion Handbook*, 1917.
22. *Ibid.* On Cumann na mBan also see lecture by Eithne ni Chumhaill, printed in *An Phoblacht*, 15, 18, 21 April 1933; Senator Mrs J. Wyse-Power, 'The political influence of women in modern Ireland', in *ed.* William G. Fitz-Gerald, *The Voice of Ireland*, 1923, pp. 170-3.
23. *Ibid.*
24. Quoted in *Prison Letters of Countess Markievicz*, first published 1934; reissued 1987, p. 36.
25. *Workers Republic*, 20 November 1915.
26. Quoted in Denis Gwynn, *John Redmond*, as above, p. 462.
27. *Ibid*, pp. 459-60.
28. *Workers' Republic*, 27 November 1915.
29. John Devoy, *Recollections of an Irish Rebel*, 1969, p. 458.
30. *Workers' Republic*, 8 April 1916. Also see Leon Ó Broin, *The Chief Secretary*, 1970.
31. Quoted in Donal Nevin, 'The Irish Citizen Army', in *ed.* Owen Dudley Edwards and Fergus Pyle, *1916: The Easter Rising*, 1968, p. 129.

32. *The Irish World*, 11 April 1931. On plans for the rising, also see J.J. Lee, *Ireland 1912-25*, 1989, pp. 24-5; introduction and Robert Monteith's story, in *ed.* Roger McHugh, *Dublin 1916*, 1976; Dorothy Macardle, *The Irish Republic*, 1968 edition, pp. 144-5; Karl Spindler, *Gun Running for Casement in the Easter Rebellion*, 1921; Brian Inglis, *Roger Casement*, 1974; Frau Dr. Agatha M. Bullitt-Grabisch, 'Roger Casement and the "German Plot"', in William G. Fitz-Gerald, *The Voice of Ireland*, 1923, p. 122ff; Eunan O'Halpin, 'British Intelligence in Ireland, 1914-21', in *eds.* Christopher Andrew and David Dilks, *The Missing Dimension*, 1984, pp. 54-77; Henry W.Nevinson, *Fire of Life*, 1935, p. 333.
33. Sir Henry Lytton, *A Wandering Minstrel*, London 1933, p. 111.
34. Quoted in *Dublin and the Sinn Fein Rising*, 1916, p. 16.
35. William O'Brien, introduction to 'Labour and Easter Week', in James Connolly, *Collected Works*, vol. 2, 1988, p. 21.
36. Desmond Ryan, *Remembering Sion*, London 1934, p. 197.
37. Mrs Hamilton Norway, *The Sinn Fein Rebellion As I Saw It*, 1916, p. 10.
38. Margaret Skinnider, *Doing My Bit For Ireland*, New York 1917, p. 121. On the women's mobilisation, also see article by Michael G.P. Maguire, *Irish Post*, 10 April 1982; letter from Bernard Morgan, *Irish Post*, 8 May 1982; R.M. Fox, *Green Banners*, 1938, ch. 22; article by Eilis Bean Ui Chonail, *Capuchin Annual*, 1966, p. 271ff.
39. Quoted in article by Owen Sheehy Skeffington in *eds.* Owen Dudley Edwards and Fergus Pyle, *1916: The Easter Rising*, as above, pp. 147-8. On the killing of Francis Sheehy Skeffington, also see *Sinn Fein Rebellion Handbook*, as above; biographical notice by Hanna Sheehy Skeffington in Francis Sheehy Skeffington, *In Dark and Evil Days*, 1916; interview with Hanna Sheehy Skeffington in Hayden Talbot, *Michael Collins' Own Story*, 1923.
40. L.G. Remond-Howard, *Six Days of the Irish Republic*, 1916, pp. 31-2.
41. Mrs Hamilton Norway, *The Sinn Fein Rebellion As I Saw It*, as above, p. 34.
42. Desmond Ryan, *Remembering Sion*, as above, pp. 200-1.
43. *Hansard*, 27 April 1916, col. 2512.
44. *Capuchin Annual*, 1966, p. 177.
45. F.A. McKenzie, *The Irish Rebellion: What happened and why*, 1916, pp. 92-3.
46. *Ibid*, p. 105. For a survey of reactions to the rising, see J.J. Lee, *Ireland 1912-25*, as above, pp. 28-36.
47. *Gaelic American*, 18 November 1916. For the casualty figures, see *Documents Relative to the Sinn Fein Movement*, PRO, Cmd. 1108, p. 14, 1921, vol. 29.
48. Desmond Ryan, *Remembering Sion*, as above, pp. 208-9. Also see Seán Ó Mahony, *Frongoch*, 1987.
49. *Sinn Fein Rebellion Handbook*, as above, p. 62.
50. Letter of 3 April, reproduced in Denis Gwynn, *Life of Redmond*, as above, see pp. 475-6, 482.
51. Elizabeth, Countess of Fingall, *Seventy Years Young*, 1937, p. 376.
52. Quoted in R.M. Fox, *Rebel Irishwomen*, 1967, p. 42.
53. Quoted in Jacqueline Van Voris, *Constance de Markievicz: In the Cause of Ireland*, 1967, p. 210.
54. Elizabeth, Countess of Fingall, *Seventy Years Young*, as above, p. 375.
55. *Daily News*, 10 May 1916.
56. *Hansard*, 11 May 1916, cols. 940, 948, 951.
57. *Irish Independent*, 10 May 1916.
58. *Irish Independent*, 13 May 1916. For analyses of press coverage of the rising, see Nollaig O Gadhra, 'Public reaction to the 1916 rising', *An Aisling*, 1976; appendices I and II in *eds.* Owen Dudley Edwards and Fergus Pyle, *1916: The Easter Rising*, as above; C.L. Mowat, 'The Irish question in British politics (1916-1922)', in *ed.* T. Desmond Williams, *The Irish Struggle 1916-1926*, 1966.

59. Nora Connolly, *The Unbroken Tradition*, 1918, p. 184. Also see 'Experiences of a V.A.D. at Dublin Castle', in *Blackwood's Magazine*, December 1916, reproduced in *Sinn Fein Rebellion Handbook*, as above, p. 16ff. Also recollections by Father Aloysius, *Capuchin Annual*, 1966.

60. *Prison Letters of Countess Markievicz*, p. 54.

61. An Englishman [Douglas Goldring], *Dublin Explorations and Reflections*, 1917, p. 33.

62. Quoted in Cathal Ó Háinle, *Promhadh Pinn*, 1978, p. 176.

63. From 'To the memory of some I knew who are dead and who loved Ireland', reproduced in *eds.* Owen Dudley Edwards and Fergus Pyle, *1916: the Easter Rising*, as above, p. 220.

64. Quoted in Denis Gwynn, *Life of Redmond*, as above, p. 500.

65. *Woman's Dreadnought*, 6 May 1916.

66. V.I. Lenin, *The discussion of self-determination summed up*, reproduced in *eds.* Owen Dudley Edwards and Fergus Pyle, *1916: The Easter Rising,* as above, pp. 192-4.

67. Quoted in Leon Ó Broin, *Dublin Castle and the 1916 Rising*, 1966, p. 122.

68. William O'Brien, *The Irish Revolution*, p. 273. Also see D.G. Boyce in *ed.* A.J.P. Taylor, *Lloyd George: Twelve Essays*, 1974, pp. 138-9.

69. Quoted in Ian Colvin, *The Life of Lord Carson*, vol. 3, 1936, p. 166.

70. Denis Gwynn, *The History of Partition*, 1950, pp. 151-2.

71. *Ibid.* p. 153.

72. Ian Colvin, *Life of Carson*, as above, p. 168.

73. Quoted in Seán Ó Mahony, *Frongoch*, 1987, p. 155.

74. *Manchester Guardian*, 24 June 1916.

75. *Irish News*, 24 June 1916. Also see T.J. Campbell, *Fifty Years of Ulster 1890-1940*, 1941, p. 48; R.B. McDowell, *The Irish Convention 1917-1918*, 1970, p. 54; Peadar Livingstone, *The Fermanagh Story*, 1969, pp. 280ff.

76. *Hansard*, 24 July 1916, col. 434.

77. Memoir of Gertrude Parry (formerly Bannister), reproduced in *ed.* Roger McHugh, *Dublin 1916*, as above, 1976, p. 292. For a summary of the trial, see *Sinn Fein Rebellion Handbook*, as above 1917, pp. 128-50.

78. Reproduced in Brian Inglis, *Roger Casement*, 1974, pp. 430-1.

79. H.W. Nevinson, *Fire of Life*, 1935, p. 337.

80. Quoted in *eds.* Owen Dudley Edwards and Fergus Pyle, *1916: The Easter Rising*, as above, 1968, p. 159. On the Women's International League's stance, see Helena Swanwick, *I Have Been Young*, 1935, p. 283.

81. Quoted in Brian Inglis, *Roger Casement*, as above, p. 399.

82. *Ibid*, p. 381. See also Henry W. Nevinson, *Fire of Life*, as above, 1935, pp. 338-9.

83. Quoted in Roy Jenkins, *Asquith*, 1964, p. 403.

84. Reproduced in *ed.* Roger McHugh, *Dublin 1916*, as above, 1976, p. 305.

85. Quoted in Philip Orr, *The Road to the Somme*, 1987, p. 198.

86. Quoted in Margery Forester, *The Lost Leader*, 1971, p. 56. On support for the prisoners, see Margaret Ward, *Unmanageable Revolutionaries*, 1983, p. 117ff; Kathleen Keyes MacDonnell, *There is a Bridge at Bandon*, 1972; Kathleen Clarke, *Revolutionary Woman*, 1991.

87. Letter of 6 October 1916, quoted in Rex Taylor, *Michael Collins*, 1970, p. 57. See also Hayden Talbot, *Michael Collins' Own Story*, 1923; Tim Pat Coogan, *Michael Collins*, 1990.

88. Quoted in Dorothy Macardle, *The Irish Republic*, 1968 edition, p. 201. See also Thomas Dillon, 'Birth of the new Sinn Fein and the Ard Fheis 1917', *Capuchin Annual*, 1967, pp. 39409.

89. *Times*, 11 May 1917.

90. *Ibid.*

91. *Hansard*, 7 March 1917, col. 425.

92. *Hansard*, 7 March 1917, cols. 477-8.
93. Quoted in Denis Gwynn, *Life of Redmond*, as above, p. 548. See also R.B. McDowell, *The Irish Convention 1917-18*, 1970; Frances Stevenson, *Lloyd George*, 1971, p. 155; David G. Boyce, 'British opinion, Ireland and the war, 1916-1918', in *Historical Journal*, vol. 17, 1974, pp. 575-593; Alan J. Ward, *Ireland and Anglo-American Relatioons 1899-1921*, 1969, ch. 7.
94. *Ibid*.
95. Quoted in Dorothy Macardle, *The Irish Republic*, as above, p. 204.
96. *Prison Letters of Countess Markievicz*, as above, pp. 72-3.
97. Quoted in Dorothy Macardle, *The Irish Republic*, as above, p. 209. See also The Earl of Longford and Thomas P. O'Neill, *Eamon de Valera*, 1970.
98. Quoted in Patrick Buckland, *Irish Unionism*, vol. 1, 1972, p. 86. See also Denis Gwynn, *The History of Partition*, as above, ch. 6; Michael Laffan, *The Partition of Ireland*, 1983, p. 56; letter from Sir Horace Plunkett to the prime minister, reproduced in *eds*. Arthur Mitchell and Pádraig Ó Snódaigh, *Irish Political Documents 1916-1949*, 1985, pp. 36-41; *Report of the Proceedings of the Irish Convention*, 1918, cmd. 9019.
99. Tim Pat Coogan, *Michael Collins*, as above, p. 74.
100. Reproduced in Dorothy Macardle, *The Irish Republic*, as above, appendix 4, pp. 838-9. Also see F.S.L. Lyons, *Ireland Since the Famine*, 1973, p. 391.
101. *Ibid*, p. 841.
102. *Ibid*, pp. 838-9.
103. *Ibid*, p. 839.
104. Irish Opinion, 1 December 1917, p. 4. Also see Arthur Mitchell, *Labour in Irish Politics 1890-1930*, 1974, p. 80ff.
105. Quoted in Margaret Ward, *Unmanageable Revolutionaries*, as above, p. 127. On this period, see also Florence O'Donoghue, 'Re-organisation of the Irish Volunteers 1916-1917', *Capuchin Annual*, 1967, pp. 380-5.
106. Quoted in David Lloyd George, *War Memoirs*, vol. 5, 1936, pp. 2665-6.
107. *Hansard*, 9 April 1918, cols. 1362, 1372.
198. Desmond Ryan, *Remembering Sion*, as above, p. 251.
109. Minutes of the Irish Committee's meeting on 9 May 1918, cited in Thomas Jones, *Whitehall Diary*, vol. 3, Ireland 1918-1925, 1971, p. 9.
110. Reproduced in *eds*. Arthur Mitchell and Pádraig Ó Snódaigh, *Irish Political Documents*, as above, p. 42.
111. *Ibid*, pp. 42-3. Also see Tomás Ó Fiaich, 'The Irish bishops and the conscription issue 1918', *Capuchin Annual*, 1968, pp. 351-68; William O'Brien, *Forth the Banners Go*, 1969, p. 164ff.
112. Desmond Ryan, *Remembering Sion*, as above, p. 251.
113. *Prison Letters of Countess Markievicz*, as above, p. 87.
114. Ernie O'Malley, *On Another Man's Wound*, 1979, p. 79. See also Florence O'Donoghue, 'Volunteer "Actions" in 1918', *Capuchin Annual*, 1968, pp. 340-4.
115. Statement issued on 16 May 1918, published in *Irish Times*, 18 May 1918, p. 5.
116. *Prison Letters of Countess Markievicz*, as above, p. 179.
117. Reproduced in *eds*. Arthur Mitchell and Pádraig Ó Snódaigh, *Irish Political Documents*, as above, p. 46.
118. *Hansard*, 5 November 1918, col. 1984.

Chapter 10: The War of Independence

1. *Times*, 22 November 1918.
2. Reproduced in *eds*. Arthur Mitchell and Padraig Ó Snodaigh, *Irish Political Documents 1916-1949*, 1985, p. 48.

3. Ernie O'Malley, *On Another Man's Wound*, 1979, p. 95. Also see Thomas P. O'Neill, 'The General Election 1918', *Capuchin Annual 1968*, p. 401; Senator Mrs. J, Wyse-Power, 'The political influence of women in modern Ireland', in *ed.* William G. Fitz-Gerald, *The Voice of Ireland*, 1923, p. 172.

4. Reproduced in *eds.* Arthur Mitchell and Padraig Ó Snodaigh, *Irish Political Documents*, as above, p. 52. Also see Arthur Mitchell, *Labour in Irish Politics 1890-1930*, 1974, p. 91ff.; Brendan Halligan, 'Triumph of the green flag', *Irish Times*, 5 July 1982; J.D. Clarkson, *Labour and Nationalism in Ireland*, 1925, p. 337ff.; D.R. O'Connor Lysaght, *The Making of Northern Ireland*, undated, p. 23ff.

5. Peadar O'Donnell, *There Will Be Another Day*, 1963, pp. 16-17. Also see Henry Patterson, *Class Conflict and Sectarianism*, 1980, p. 97ff.

6. *Irish Times*, 30 December 1918.

7. *Times*, 17 January 1919. Also see *Times*, 4 January 1919; T.J. Campbell, *Fifty Years of Ulster, 1890-1940*, 1941, p. 99.

8. Michael Collins, *The Path to Freedom*, 1968, p. 65.

9. Frank Gallagher [pseudonym David Hogan], *The Four Glorious Years*, as above, p. 60.

10. Reproduced in Brian Farrell, *The Founding of Dáil Éireann*, 1971, pp. 87-9. Also see J.J. Lee, *Ireland 1912-1985*, 1989, p. 41; Arthur Mitchell, *Labour in Irish Politics*, as above, pp. 107-10; J.L. McCracken, *Representative Government in Ireland*, 1958, pp. 30-4.

11. Reproduced in *eds.* Arthur Mitchell and Padraig Ó Snodaigh, *Irish Political Documents*, as above, pp. 59-60.

12. French to Long, 23 January 1919; quoted in Eunan O'Halpin, *The Decline of the Union*, 1987, p. 185.

13. *Hansard*, House of Lords, 15 May 1919, col. 677. Also see A.P. Thornton, *The Imperial Idea and Its Enemies*, 1959.

14. Dan Breen, *My Fight for Irish Freedom*, 1924, pp. 32-3.

15. Quoted by James Kemmy in 'The Limerick Soviet', *Irish Times*, 9 May 1969.

16. Thomas Farren quoted in D.R. O'Connor Lysaght, *The Story of the Limerick Soviet*, 2nd ed., c. 1984, p. 17. Also see Liam Cahill, *Forgotten Revolution*, 1990; Arthur Mitchell, *Labour in Irish Politics*, a above; Maire Comerford, *The First Dail*, 1969, p. 70ff.

17. Reproduced in ITGWU, *Fifty Years of Liberty Hall*, 1959.

18. Quoted in Jacqueline Van Voris, *Constance de Markievicz: In the cause of Ireland*, 1967, p. 261.

19. *Hansard*, House of Lords, 22 May 1919, col. 812.

20. *Freeman's Journal*, 10 June 1919.

21. Quoted in Dorothy Macardle, *The Irish Republic*, first pub. 1937, 1968 edition, p. 277.

22. *Prison Letters of Countess Markievicz*, first pub. 1934, reissued 1987 p. 237.

23. Quoted in Dorothy Macardle, *The Irish Republic*, as above, p. 283.

24. Quoted in Ulick O'Connor, *A Terrible Beauty is Born*, 1981, pp. 133-4.

25. Quoted in Christopher Andrew, *Secret Service*, 1986, p. 364.

26. *Times*, 9 September 1919. Also see Florence O'Donoghue, *No Other Law*, 1954, p. 48ff.

27. *Times*, 10 September 1919.

28. Frank Gallagher, *The Four Glorious Years*, as above, p. 86.

29. Kathleen McKenna, 'The Irish Bulletin', *Capuchin Annual*, 1970, p. 508.

30. Quoted in Cecil John Charles Street [pseudonym I.O.'], *The Administration of Ireland 1920*, 1921, pp. 65-6. Also see Charles Townshend, *The British Campaign in Ireland 1919-1921*, 1975.

31. *Times*, 13 December 1919.

32. *Times*, 16 December 1919.

33. Quoted in Eunan O'Halpin, *The Decline of the Union*, as above, p. 190.
34. April 1918; quoted in D.G. Boyce, 'How to settle the Irish question', in *ed.* A.J.P. Taylor, *Lloyd George: Twelve Essays*, 1971, p. 151.
35. *Hansard*, 22 December 1919, col. 1174.
36. Annie Besant, *An Autobiography*, 1893, p. 13.
37. Quoted in Pravrajika Atmaprana, *Sister Nivedita*, 2nd ed., 1967, p. 126.
38. Eamon de Valera, *India and Ireland*, 1920, p. 24. Also see Desmond Greaves, *Liam Mellows and the Irish Revolution*, 1971, pp. 205, 216; Ramesa-Chandra Majumdar, *History of the Freedom Movement in India*, vol. 2, pp. 387-91, 398-402; Janice R. and Stephen R. MacKinnon, *Agnes Smedley*, 1988, pp. 37, 59.
39. 15 January 1920, Cab 24/96, CP 458.
40. Cabinet conclusions, 25 September 1919, Cab 23/12.
41. First Report of Cabinet Committee on the Irish Question, 4 November 1919, Cab 27/68, CP56, para. 3.
42. *Ibid.*, para. 4(c).
43. *Ibid.*, para. 11.
44. *Ibid.*
45. *Ibid.*, para 12.
46. Cabinet conclusions, 3 December 1919, Cab 23/18, para. 4.
47. Cabinet conclusions,10 December 1919, Cab 23/18.
48. Cabinet conclusions, 19 December 1919, Cab 23/18.
49. Quoted in D.G. Boyce, *Englishmen and Irish Troubles*, 1972, p. 109.
50. Cabinet, Committee on Ireland, Report by Mr Bonar Law, 17 February 1920, Cab 27/68, CP 664.
51. Note by Mr Balfour, 19 February 1920, Cab 24/98, CP 681.
52. Cabinet conclusions, 24 February 1920, Cab 23/20.
53. Long memorandum to Selborne, Long papers, Wiltshire County Record Office, 947/352; also see *Times*, 30 September 1924.
54. Long to Londonderry, 28 August 1924, Long papers, Wiltshire County Record Office, 947/290.
55. Quoted in Ian Colvin, *The Life of Lord Carson*, vol. 3, London 1936, p. 384. Also see Patrick Buckland, *Irish Unionism, vol. 2*, 1973, p. 115ff.
56. *Hansard*, 29 March 1920, cols. 984-5.
57. *Ibid.*, col. 986.
58. *Ibid.*, col. 989.
59. *Ibid.*, col. 990.
60. *Ibid.*, col. 991.
61. *Hansard*, 31 March 1920, col. 1288.
62. *Ibid.*, col. 1292.
63. *Hansard*, 29 March 1920, col. 949. On Labour policy see Geoffrey Bell, *Troublesome Business*, 1982.
64. *Hansard*, 29 March 1920, col. 950.
65. *Ibid.*, col. 951.
66. *Ibid.*, col 973.
67. *Ibid.*
68. *Ibid.*, cols 1005-6.
69. *Hansard*, 30 March 1920, col. 1113.
70. *Ibid.*, col. 1115.
71. *Ibid.*, col. 1147.
72. *Times*, 22 January 1920. See also John MacLean, *The Irish Tragedy: Scotland's Disgrace*, 1920.
73. *Prison Letters of Countess Markievicz*, as above, p. 219.
74. *Daily News*, 29 March 1920.
75. Quoted in Dorothy Macardle, *The Irish Republic*, as above, p. 351.
76. *Times*, 31 January 1920.

77. *Hansard*, 26 March 1920, col. 767. Also see cabinet minutes, 2 December 1919, Cab 23/18.
78. Quoted in Frank Gallagher, *The Four Glorious Years*, as above, p. 174. Also see Frank Gallagher's diary of the hunger strike, *Days of Fear*, 1967.
79. *Ibid.*, pp. 177-8. Also see William O'Brien, *Forth the Banners Go*, 1969, pp. 190-2.
80. *Ibid.*, p. 187.
81. Statement issued by the Irish government on 20 April 1920, reproduced in C.J.C. Street, *The Administration of Ireland 1920*, as above, p. 448.
82. *Irish Times*, 1 May 1920.
83. *Times*, 28 June 1920. Also see Conor A. Maguire, 'The Republican Courts', in *Capuchin Annual*, 1969, p. 378ff.; Sir Edward Carson's reaction, *Hansard*, 22 July 1920, col. 705ff.
84. Quoted in Maire Comerford, *The First Dáil*, as above, p. 59.
85. Quoted in Frank Gallagher, *The Four Glorious Years*, as above, p. 73.
86. Peadar O'Donnell, *There Will Be Another Day*, 1963, pp. 19- 20.
87. Kathleen Clarke, *Revolutionary Woman*, 1991, p. 176.
88. C.J.C. Street, *The Administration of Ireland 1920*, as above, p. 245.
89. Quoted in Arthur Mitchell, *Labour in Irish Politics*, as above, p. 121.
90. General Sir Nevil Macready, *Annals of an Active Life*, 1924, p. 472.
91. Report of a statement by the Duke of Northumberland at a meeting in the House of Commons, *Times*, 30 July 1920.
92. *Belfast News-Letter*, 13 July 1920.
93. *Belfast News-Letter*, 15, 16 July 1920.
94. *Irish News*, 22 July 1920.
95. *Irish News*, 23 July 1920.
96. *Ibid.*
97. Rev. John Redmond, *Church: State: Industry 1827-1929 in East Belfast*, 1960, p. 12. On the pogroms also see Michael Farrell, *Arming the Protestants*, 1983; Andrew Boyd, *Holy War in Belfast*, 1987; Fr John Hassan [pseudonym G.B. McKenna], *Facts and Figures of the Belfast Pogrom 1920-1922*, 1922; Henry Patterson, *Class Conflict and Sectarianism*, 1980.
98. *Irish News*, 24 July 1920.
99. *Times*, 29 July 1920.
100. Fr John Hassan, *Facts and Figures*, as above, p. 40.
101. *Belfast News-Letter*, 23 August 1920.
102. *Daily News*, 30 August 1920.
103. *Ibid.*
104. *Daily News*, 28 August 1920.
105. *Daily News*, 31 August 1920.
106. *Daily News*, 30 August 1920.
107. Quoted in Geoffrey Bell, 'The TUC and Ireland', *Socialist Outlook*, no. 4, November/ December 1987, p. 34.
108. Dáil Éireann, *Minutes of the Proceedings of the First Parliament of the Republic of Ireland 1919-1921*, p. 191.
109. *Ibid.*, p. 193.
110. C.J.C. Street, *The Administration of Ireland 1920*, as above, p. 350.
111. Quoted in D.S. Johnson, 'The Belfast boycott, 1920-1922', in *eds*. J.M. Goldstrom and L.A. Clarkson, *Irish Population, Economy and Society*, 1981, p. 293.
112. General Sir Nevil Macready, *Annals of an Active Life*, vol. 2, 1924, p. 481.
113. *Ibid.*, p. 482.
114. *Ibid.*, p. 483.
115. Hugh Martin, *Ireland in Insurrection*, 1921, p. 61.
116. *Ibid.*, p. 68.

117. *Ibid.*, pp. 68-9. On Black and Tan attacks on creameries, see Labour Party, *Report of the Labour Commission to Ireland*, 1921, p. 90ff; 'AE', *A Plea for Justice*, 1920 or 1921, pamphlet.
118. *Times*, 1 November 1920.
119. Thomas Jones, *Whitehall Diary*, vol. 3, 1971, p. 18.
120. *Ibid.*, pp. 19-20.
121. Stephen Roskill, *Hankey: Man of Secrets*, 1972, p. 153.
122. *Ibid.*, p. 196.
123. *Weekly Summary*, No. 3; quoted in *Women's International League Monthly News Sheet*, November 1920.
124. C.J.C. Street, *The Administration of Ireland 1920*, as above, p. 108.
125. *Times*, 5 October 1920.
126. *The Friend*, 8 October 1920, p. 635.
127. *Times*, 5 October 1920. Also see Minutes and Proceedings of London Yearly Meeting of Friends, 1921, pp. 84-5.
128. *Manchester Guardian*, 22 September 1920.
129. Mark Sturgis's diary, 22 September 1920; PRO, 30/59/2; quoted in D.G. Boyce, *Englishmen and Irish Troubles*, 1972, p. 52.
130. *Women's International League Monthly News Sheet*, November 1920, p. 1.
131. *Ibid.*, p. 3.
132. *Ibid.*, December 1920. See also February 1921 issue.
133. Helena Swanwick, *I Have Been Young*, 1935, p. 336. See also *The American Commission on Conditions in Ireland: Interim Report*, 1921.
134. *Hansard*, 20 October 1920, col. 925.
135. *Ibid.*, col. 938.
136. *Ibid.*, col. 944.
137. *Ibid.*, col. 953.
138. Henry W. Nevinson, *Fire of Life*, 1935, p. 362.
139. Quoted in D.G. Boyce, *Englishmen and Irish Troubles*, 1972, p. 65. On the deportation of Mrs Bryce, see *Times*, 1 November 1920; *Annual Register*, 1920, p. 125.
140. *Daily News*, 29 October 1920. See also *Daily Telegraph*, 29 October 1920; Michael G.P. Maguire, 'A symbol of Irish defiance', *Irish Post*, 3 November 1979.
141 Henry W. Nevinson, *Fire of Life*, as above, p. 363.
142. *Times*, 23 November 1920.
143. Tom Barry, *Guerilla Days in Ireland*, 1981, p. 23.
144. On these events, see the Home Office Directorate of Intelligence's 'Reports of Revolutionary Organisations in theUnited Kingdom', in the Cabinet Papers, Cab 24/115, CP 2187, 28 November 1920; Cab 24/118, 3 January 1921; Cab 24/120, CP 2603, 17 February 1921; Cab 24/120, CP 2631, dated 24 February 1921; Cab 24/120, CP 2698, 11 March 1921. See also Dorothy Macardle, *The Irish Republic*, as above, pp. 371-2, 407; *Annual Register*, 1920, pp. 135-6. An autobiographical account by a Liverpool IRA man is James Brady, *Ireland's Secret Service in England*, 1928; but articles in *An Phoblacht*, 3 March 1928, suggest that he exaggerated his role.

Chapter 11: Partition and Truce

1. Quoted in Peadar Livingstone, *The Fermanagh Story*, 1969, p. 300.
2. Quoted in Michael Farrell, *Arming the Protestants*, 1983, p. 37.
3. General Sir Nevil Macready, *Annals of an Active Life*, vol. 2, 1924, p. 488.
4. *Daily News*, 15 September 1920.
5. Quoted in Michael Farrell, *Arming the Protestants*, as above, p. p. 42-3.
6. See Rev. John Redmond, *Church: State: Industry 1827-1929 in East Belfast*, 1960, pp. 25-7.

7. *Fermanagh Herald*, 27 November 1920.
8. *Manchester Guardian*, 1 March 1921.
9. Government of Ireland Act, 1920, 1(1).
10. *Ibid.*, 2.
11. *Hansard*, 11 November 1920, col. 1433.
12. *Ibid.*, col. 1434.
13. *Ibid.*, col. 1435.
14. *Ibid.*, col. 1437.
15. *Ibid.*, col. 1442.
16. *Ibid.*, col. 1445ff.
17. *Ibid.*, col. 1452.
18. *Ibid.*, col. 1455.
19. Cecil John Charles Street, *Ireland in 1921*, 1922, pp. 14-15.
20. Winston S. Churchill, *The World Crisis: The Aftermath*, first pub. 1929, 1941 edition, p. 286.
21. Thomas Jones, *Whitehall Diary*, vol. III, Ireland, 1971, p. 23.
22. *Ibid.*, pp. 31-2.
23. Quoted in introduction by Thomas P. O'Neill to Frank Gallagher, *The Anglo-Irish Treaty*, 1965, p. 23.
24. Letter dated 10 December 1920, quoted in General Sir Nevil Macready, *Annals of an Active Life*, vol. 2, 1924, p. 520.
25. Thomas Jones, *Whitehall Diary*, vol. III, as above, p. 47.
26. General Sir Nevil Macready, *Annals*, vol. 2, as above, p. 537.
27. Quoted in Tom Barry, *Guerilla Days in Ireland*, 1981, p. 61.
28. Labour Party, *Report of the Labour Commission to Ireland*, 1921, p. 35.
29. Labour Party, Annual Conference Report June 1918, p. 69; quoted in Geoffrey Bell, *The British Working Class Movement and the Irish National Question, 1916-1921*, PhD thesis, Dept of Politics, University of Leeds, 1992.
30. Labour Party, Annual Conference Report, 1920, p. 161; quoted in Geoffrey Bell, thesis, as above.
31. *Catholic Herald*, 3 July 1920, p. 6.
32. *Hansard*, 11 November 1920, cols. 1417-18.
33. General Sir Nevil Macready, *Annals*, vol. 2, as above, p. 523.
34. Quoted in Frank Gallagher [pseudonym David Hogan], *The Four Glorious Years*, 1953, pp. 270-1.
35. Kathleen Clarke, *Revolutionary Woman*, 1991, pp. 185-6.
36. Thomas Jones, *Whitehall Diary*, vol. III, as above, p. 52.
37. Quoted by Captain Wedgwood Benn MP, *Hansard*, 21 February 1921, col. 617.
38. *Times*, 19 February 1921; see also *Irish News*, 18 February 1921.
39. *Times*, 21 February 1921.
40. *Hansard*, 21 February 1921, col. 613.
41. *Hansard*, House of Lords, 22 February 1922, col. 89.
42. Brig.-General F.P. Crozier, *Impressions and Recollections*, 1930, p. 242.
43. *Ibid.*, p. 264.
44. Ernie O'Malley, *On Another Man's Wound*, 1979, p. 312.
45. Tom Barry, *Guerilla Days in Ireland*, as above, p. 116.
46. *Daily News*, 5 April 1921. See also *Irish Bulletin*, 7 April 1921; Frank Gallagher, *The Four Glorious Years*, as above, p. 102; D.G. Boyce, *Englishmen and Irish Troubles*, 1972, pp. 87-8; C.J.C. Street, *Ireland in 1921*, as above, appendix, note A.
47. Kathleen McKenna, 'The Irish Bulletin', *Capuchin Annual*, 1970, p. 524.
48. *Ibid.*, p. 525.
49. *Irish News*, 4 April 1921.
50. *Irish Bulletin*, 6 April 1921.
51. *Manchester Guardian*, 19 April 1921.

52. Thomas Jones, *Whitehall Diary*, vol. III, as above, p. 54.
53. *Ibid.*, p. 55.
54. *Ibid.*
55. Mark Sturgis's diary, quoted in Charles Townshend, *The British Campaign in Ireland 1919-1921*, 1975, p. 179.
56. Thomas Jones, *Whitehall Diary*, vol. III, as above, p. 60.
57. *Ibid.*.
58. Quoted in Randolph S. Churchill, *Lord Derby: 'King of Lancashire'*, 1959, p. 410.
59. *Ibid.*
60. *Ibid.*, p. 411.
61. *Ibid.*, pp. 420-1.
62. Quoted in Thomas Jones, *Whitehall Diary*, vol. III, as above, p. 68.
63. Quoted in John Bowman, *De Valera and the Ulster Question 1917- 1973*, 1982, p. 47.
64. Quoted in introduction by Thomas P. O'Neill to Frank Gallagher, *The Anglo-Irish Treaty*, 1965, p. 33.
65. *Ibid.*, pp. 33-4.
66. Maire Comerford, *The First Dáil*, 1969, p. 90.
67. Dáil Éireann, 11 March 1921, quoted in Maire Comerford, *The First Dáil*, as above, p. 91.
68. Quoted in Maire Comerford, *The First Dáil*, as above, p. 93.
69. *Irish News*, 3 May 1921.
70. *Irish News*, 28 March 1921.
71. *Irish News*, 5 April 1921.
72. *Irish News*, 9 April 1921.
73. *Irish News*, 19 April 1921.
74. *Ibid.*
75. *Irish News*, 4 May 1921.
76. *Irish News*, 7 May 1921.
77. *Irish News*, 26 April 1921.
78. *Ibid.*
79. *Irish News*, 16 May 1921.
80. *Irish News*, 18 May 1921.
81. *Ibid.*
82. *Irish News*, 19 May 1921.
83. *Daily News*, 19 May 1921. On the conduct of the election campaign, also see the *Irish Bulletin*, 24 and 26 May 1921.
84. *Manchester Guardian*, 25 May 1921.
85. *Ibid.*
86. *Irish News*, 25 May 1921.
87. *Irish News*, 28 May 1921.
88. See the *Irish News*, 11, 13, 14, 15, 18 June 1921; and Fr John Hassan [pseudonym G.B. Kenna], *Facts and Figures of the Belfast Pogrom 1920-22*, 1922.
89. C.J.C. Street, *Ireland in 1921*, as above, p. 26.
90. Memo dated 23 May 1921, in Cabinet Papers, 24 May 1921; quoted in Charles Townshend, *The British Campaign*, as above, p. 182.
91. Maj.-Gen. Sir C.E. Callwell, *Field-Marshal Sir Henry Wilson: His life and diaries*, vol. 2, London 1927, p. 292.
92. General Sir Nevil Macready, *Annals*, vol. 2, as above, p. 563.
93. *Ibid.*, p. 565.
94. *Ibid.*
95. Thomas Jones, *Whitehall Diary*, vol. III, as above, p. 76.
96. *Ibid.*, p. 77.
97. Quoted in Charles Townshend, *The British Campaign*, as above, p. 190.
98. Tom Barry, *Guerilla Days in Ireland*, as above, p. 190.

99. Quoted in Dorothy Macardle, *The Irish Republic*, first pub. 1937, 1968 edition, p. 426.
100. *Ibid.*
101. See W.H. Hancock, *Smuts*, vol. 2, 1968, pp. 49-61; Thomas Jones, *Whitehall Diary*, vol. III, as above, pp. 74-9, 247-8.
102. Reproduced in Patrick Buckland, *Irish Unionism 1885-1923*, 1973, pp. 455-6.
103. Thomas Jones, *Whitehall Diary*, vol. III, as above, p. 79.
104. *Ibid.*, p. 80.
105. C.J.C. Street, *Ireland in 1921*, as above, p. 82.
106. *Irish News*, 4 July 1921.
107. General Sir Nevil Macready, *Annals*, vol. 2, as above, pp. 572-3.
108. *Prison Letters of Countess Markievicz*, first pub. 1934, reissued 1986, p. 300.
109. *Irish News*, 11 July 1921.
110. *Irish News*, 12 July 1921.

Chapter 12: Postscript

1. The text of the treaty is included in, among others, *eds*. Arthur Mitchell and Pádraig Ó Snodaigh, *Irish Political Documents 1916-1949*, Dublin 1985, pp. 116-121.
2. Peadar Livingstone, *The Fermanagh Story*, Enniskillen 1969, p. 318; a useful summary of the Boundary Commission story is in 'The Sealing of Partition' by Brendan Ó Cathaoir, *Irish Times*, 4 December 1975. The commission's report was published in *ed* Geoffrey Hand, *The Report of the Irish Boundary Commission*, 1969.
3. On the consolidation of the Northern Ireland state, see Michael Farrell, *Northern Ireland: The Orange State*, 1980; and Michael Farrell, *Arming the Protestants*, 1983; 'The real case against partition', *Capuchin Annual*, 1943; Frank Gallagher, *The Indivisible Island*, 1957.
4. *Report of a Commission of Inquiry... into the Purpose and Effect of the Civil Authorities (Special Powers) Acts (Northern Ireland), 1922 and 1933*, National Council for Civil Liberties, London 1936, pp. 39-40.
5. *Capuchin Annual*, 1943, p. 315.

Bibliography

This bibliography includes details of author, title and date of publication. It does not follow the convention of supplying place and publisher, since neither are necessary for locating books in libraries or bookshops. The bibliography contains books and articles cited in the references: newspapers, Cabinet minutes, etc. referred to in footnotes are not.

AE, *A Plea for Justice*, undated.
American Commission on Conditions in Ireland: Interim Report, 1921.
An Englishman [Douglas Goldring], *Explorations and Reflections*, 1917.
Andrew, Christopher, *Secret Service*, 1986.
Armstrong, D.L., 'Social and economic conditions in the Belfast linen industry, 1850-1900', *Irish Historical Studies*, vol. VII, no. 28, September 1951.
Atmaprana, Pravrajika, *Sister Nivedita*, 2nd ed., 1967.
Bardon, Jonathan, *Belfast: An Illustrated History*, 1982.
Barry, Tom, *Guerilla Days in Ireland*, 1981.
Beaslai, Piaras, 'How the fight began!', in *Dublin's Fighting Story*, c. 1948.
Beckett, Ian F.W., ed. *The Army and the Curragh Mutiny*, 1986.
Beckett, J.C., *Confrontations: Studies in Irish History*, 1972.
Beckett, J.C., *The Making of Modern Ireland 1603-1923*, 1981.
Bell, Geoffrey, *The British Working Class Movement and the Irish National Question, 1916-1921*, PhD thesis, Dept of Politics, University of Leeds, 1992.
Bell, Geoffrey, 'The TUC and Ireland', *Socialist Outlook*, no. 4, November/December 1987.
Bell, Geoffrey, *This We Will Maintain: Ulster Unionism and the Protestant Working Class, 1868-1972*, unpublished thesis.
Bell, Geoffrey, *Troublesome Business*, 1982.
Berresford Ellis, Peter, *A History of the Irish Working Class*, 1972.
Berresford Ellis, Peter, *The Rising of the Moon*, 1987.
Besant, Annie, *An Autobiography*, 1893.
Besant, Annie, *Coercion in Ireland*, 1882.
Blake, Robert, *The Unknown Prime Minister*, 1955.
Blunt, Wilfred Scawen, *The Land War in Ireland*, 1912.
Blunt, Wilfred Scawen, *My Diaries 1888-1914*, 1932.
Bourke, Austin, *The Visitation of God: The Potato and the Great Famine*, 1993.
Bowman, John, *De Valera and the Ulster Question 1917-1973*, 1982.
Boyce, D.G., 'British opinion, Ireland and the war, 1916-1918', *Historical Journal*, vol. 17, 1974.
Boyce, D.G., *Englishmen and Irish Troubles*, 1972.
Boyce, D.G., 'How to settle the Irish question', in ed. A.J.P. Taylor, *Lloyd George: Twelve Essays*, 1971.
Boyd, Andrew, *Holy War in Belfast,* 1987.
Bradley, Ian, 'The Highland Land War of the 1880s', *History Today*, December 1987.
Brady, James, *Ireland's Secret Service in England*, 1928.
Breen, Dan, *My Fight for Irish Freedom*, 1924.
Buckland, Patrick, *Irish Unionism*, vol. 1, 1972.

Buckland, Patrick, *Irish Unionism*, vol. 2, 1973.
Buckland, Patrick, *Irish Unionism 1885-1923*, 1973
Buckland, Patrick, *James Craig*, 1980.
Budge, Ian and O'Leary, Cornelius, *Belfast: Approach to Crisis*, 1973.
Bullitt-Grabisch, Agatha M., 'Roger Casement and the "German Plot"', in William
      G. Fitz-Gerald, *The Voice of Ireland*, 1923.
Butt, Isaac, *Irish Federalism*, 1874.
Cahill, Liam, *Forgotten Revolution*, 1990.
Callwell, Maj.-Gen. Sir C.E., *Field-Marshal Sir Henry Wilson: His life and diaries*,
      vol. 2, 1927.
Campbell, Stephen J., *The Great Irish Famine*, 1994.
Campbell, T.J., *Fifty Years of Ulster 1890-1940*, 1941.
Churchill, Randolph S., *Lord Derby: 'King of Lancashire'*, 1959.
Churchill, Winston S., *The World Crisis: The Aftermath*, first pub. 1929, 1941 edition.
Clarke, Kathleen, *Revolutionary Woman*, 1991.
Clarke, Thomas J, *Glimpses of an Irish Felon's Prison Life*, 2nd edition, 1970.
Clarkson, J.D., *Labour and Nationalism in Ireland*, 1925.
Collins, Michael, *The Path to Freedom*, 1968.
Colum, Mary, *Life and the Dream*, revised edition, 1966.
Colum, Padraic, *Arthur Griffith*, 1949.
Colvin, Ian, *The Life of Lord Carson*, 1934.
Comerford, Maire, *The First Dail*, 1969.
Connolly, James, *Collected Works*, 1988.
Connolly, James, *Labour in Irish History*, 1967 edition.
Connolly, James, *Labour, Nationality and Religion*, 1910, reprinted 1954.
Connolly, Nora, *The Unbroken Tradition*, 1918.
Coogan, Tim Pat, *Michael Collins*, 1990.
Cook, Chris and Keith, Brendan, *British Historical Facts 1830-
1900*, 1975.
Corfe, Tom, *The Phoenix Park Murders*, 1986.
Corrigan, D.J., *On Famine and Fever as Cause and Effect in Ireland*, 1846.
Côté, Jane McL., *Fanny and Anna Parnell*, 1991.
Cousins, James and Margaret, *We Two Together*, 1950.
Coxhead, Elizabeth, *Daughters of Erin*, 1979.
Crawford, Margaret, ed., *Famine: The Irish Experience*, 1989.
Cronin, Seán, *Irish Nationalism*, 1980.
Cronin, Seán, *Irish Revolutionaries*, 1971.
Cronin, Seán, *The McGarrity Papers*, 1972.
Crozier, Brig.-General F.P., *Impressions and Recollections*, 1930.
Cullen Owens, Rosemary, *Smashing Times: A History of the Irish Women's Suffrage
      Movement 1889-1922*, 1984.
Curriculum Development Unit, *1913*, 1982.
Curtis, Edmund, *A History of Ireland*, 1961.
Curtis, Edmund and McDowell, R.B. eds., *Irish Historical Documents 1172-1922*,
      1943, 1968.
Curtis, L.P. Jr., *Coercion and Conciliation in Ireland 1880-1892*, 1963.
D'Alton, Rev. E.A., *History of Ireland*, 1910.
Dangerfield, George, *The Damnable Question*, 1977.
Dangerfield, George, *The Strange Death of Liberal England*, 1935.
Davitt, Michael, *The Boer Fight for Freedom*, 1902.

Davitt, Michael, *The Fall of Feudalism in Ireland*, 1904.
De Paor, Liam, *Divided Ulster*, Harmondsworth, 1971.
De Tocqueville, Alexis, 'Journey to Ireland (1835)', in J.P. Mayer, ed., *Journeys to England and Ireland*, 1958.
De Valera, Eamon, *India and Ireland*, 1920.
Denvir, John, *The Irish in Britain*, 1892.
Denvir, John, *The Life Story of an Old Rebel*, 1910, reprinted 1972.
Devon Commission, *Royal Commission on the Occupation of Land in Ireland*, Parliamentary Papers 1845.
Devoy, John, *Recollections of an Irish Rebel*, first published 1929, reissued 1969.
Dillon, Thomas, 'Birth of the new Sinn Fein and the Ard Fheis 1917', *Capuchin Annual*, 1967.
Dublin and the Sinn Fein Rising, 1916.
Dudley Edwards, Ruth, *Patrick Pearse: The triumph of failure*, 1977.
Duffy, Charles Gavan, *Four Years of Irish History*, 1883.
Duffy, Charles Gavan et al., *The Revival of Irish Literature*, 1894.
Earl of Longford and O'Neill, Thomas P., *Eamon de Valera*, 1970.
Earl of Oxford and Asquith, *Memories and Reflections*, vol. 2, 1928.
Eldridge, C.C., *Victorian Imperialism*, 1978.
Elizabeth, Countess of Fingall, *Seventy Years Young*, 1937.
Elliott, Marianne, *Partners in Revolution*, 1969.
Ellmann, Richard, *The Artist as Critic: Critical writings of Oscar Wilde*, 1970.
Ellmann, Richard, *Yeats: The man and the masks*, 1977.
Ervine, St. John, *Craigavon: Ulsterman*, 1949.
Farrell, Brian, *The Founding of Dail Eireann*, 1971.
Farrell, Michael, *Arming the Protestants*, 1983.
Farrell, Michael, *Northern Ireland: The Orange State*, 1980.
Irish Transport and General Workers Union, *Fifty Years of Liberty Hall*, 1959.
Finegan, John, ed., *The Prison Journal of Anne Devlin*, 1968.
Forester, Margery, *The Lost Leader*, 1971.
Foster, R.F., *Lord Randolph Churchill*, 1981.
Fox, R.M., *Green Banners*, 1938.
Fox, R.M., *Rebel Irishwoman*, 1967.
Fryer, Peter, *Staying Power*, 1984.
Furlong, Nicholas, *Fr John Murphy of Boolavogue*, 1991.
Gallagher, Frank, *The Anglo-Irish Treaty*, 1965.
Gallagher, Frank, *Days of Fear*, 1967.
Gallagher, Frank [pseudonym David Hogan], *The Four Glorious Years*, 1953.
Gallagher, Frank, *The Indivisible Island*, 1957.
Garvin, Tom, 'Home rule hiatus spawned drive to independence', *Irish Times*, 10 June 1986.
Gibbon, Peter, *The Origins of Ulster Unionism*, 1975.
Gleichen, Major General Lord Edward, *A Guardsman's Memories*, 1932.
Gonne MacBride, Maud, *A Servant of the Queen*, 1938.
Gough, Hugh and Dickson, David, eds., *Ireland and the French Revolution*, 1990.
Gray, John, *City in Revolt: James Larkin and the Belfast Dock Strike of 1907*, 1985.
Greaves, C. Desmond, *Liam Mellows and the Irish Revolution*, 1971.
Greaves, C. Desmond, *The Irish Transport and General Workers' Union: The formative years*, 1982.
Greaves, C. Desmond, *The Life and Times of James Connolly,* 1976.

Griffith, Kenneth and O'Grady, Timothy E., *Curious Journey*, 1982.
Grousset, Paschal, *Ireland's Disease*, first published 1887, reprinted 1986.
Gwynn, Denis, *The History of Partition*, 1950.
Gwynn, Denis, *The Life of John Redmond*, 1932.
Halligan, Brendan, 'Triumph of the green flag , *Irish Times*, 5 July 1982.
Hammond, J.L., *Gladstone and the Irish Nation*, 1964.
Hampton, Christopher, *A Radical Reader*, 1984.
Hancock, W.II., *Smuts*, vol. 2, 1968.
Hand, Geoffrey, ed., *The Report of the Irish Boundary Commission*, 1969.
Handcock, W.D., *English Historical Documents*, XII (2), 1977.
Hassan, Fr John, [pseudonym G.B. McKenna], *Facts and Figures of the Belfast Pogrom 1920-1922*, 1922.
Haverty, Anne, *Constance Markievicz: An independent life*, 1988.
Henry, R.M., *The Evolution of Sinn Fein*, c. 1920.
Higginbottom, Frederick J., *The Vivid Life*, 1934.
Hobsbawm, Eric and Ranger, Terence, eds., *The Invention of Tradition*, 1983.
Hobson, J.A., *Traffic in Treason*, 1914.
Horgan, J.J, *The Complete Grammar of Anarchy*, 1918.
Hughes, Robert, *The Fatal Shore*, 1987.
Inglis, Brian, *Roger Casement*, 1974.
Jackson, T.A., *Ireland Her Own*, 1976.
Jalland, Patricia, *The Liberals and Ireland: The Ulster question in British politics to 1914*, 1980.
Jeffery, Keith, ed., *The Military Correspondence of Field Marshal Sir Henry Wilson 1918-1922*, 1985.
Jenkins, Roy, *Asquith*, 1986.
Johnson, D.S., 'The Belfast boycott, 1920-1922', in eds. J.M. Goldstrom and L.A. Clarkson, *Irish Population, Economy and Society*, 1981.
Jones, Mary, *These Obstreporous Lassies: A history of the IWWU*, 1988.
Jones, Thomas, *Whitehall Diary*, vol. 3, Ireland 1918-1925, 1971.
Kapp, Yvonne, *Eleanor Marx*, 1979.
Kennedy, David, 'Ulster and the antecedents of home rule, 1850-86', in T.W. Moody and J.C. Beckett, *Ulster Since 1800*, 1954.
Knight, Denis, ed., *Cobbett in Ireland: A warning to England*, 1984.
Labour Party [British], *Report of the Labour Commission to Ireland*, 1921.
Laffan, Michael, *The Partition of Ireland*, 1983.
Lansbury, George, *My Life*, 1928.
Lecky, W.E.H., *A History of Ireland in the Eighteenth Century*, 1892.
Lecky, W.E.H., *Leaders of Public Opinion in Ireland*, 1912.
Lee, J.J., *Ireland 1912-25*, 1989
Lenin, V.I., *Against Imperialist War*, 1974.
Levenson, Samuel, *James Connolly*, 1977.
Livingstone, Peadar, *The Fermanagh Story*, 1969.
Lloyd, A.L., 'On an unpublished Irish ballad', in ed. Maurice Cornforth, *Rebels and Their Causes: Essays in honour of A.L. Morton*, 1978.
Lloyd George, David, *War Memoirs*, vol. 5, 1936.
Lyons, F.S.L., *Charles Stewart Parnell*, 1977.
Lyons, F.S.L., *Ireland Since the Famine*, 1973.
Lytton, Henry, *A Wandering Minstrel*, 1933.
Macardle, Dorothy, *The Irish Republic*, 1968.

MacBride White, Anna and Jeffares, A. Norman, eds., *The Gonne-Yeats Letters 1893-1938*, 1992.
Mac Curtain, Margaret, 'Women, the vote and revolution', in eds. Margaret Mac Curtain and Donncha Ó Corrain, *Women in Irish Society*, 1978.
MacDonnell, Kathleen Keyes, *There is a Bridge at Bandon*, 1972.
Mace, Rodney, *Trafalgar Square*, 1976.
Mackenzie, John M., *Propaganda and Empire*, 1984.
MacKinnon, Janice R. and Stephen R., *Agnes Smedley*, 1988.
MacLean, John, *The Irish Tragedy: Scotland's Disgrace*, 1920, reprinted c. 1974.
MacManus, Seumas, ed., *The Four Winds of Eirinn*, 1918.
Mac Nevin, Thomas, *The History of the Volunteers of 1782*, 1846.
Macready, Sir Nevil, *Annals of an Active Life*, 1924.
Madden, R.R., *The Life and Times of Robert Emmet Esq.*, 1847.
Madden, R.R., *The United Irishmen*, 3rd series, vol. 1, 1846.
Maguire, Conor A., 'The Republican Courts', *Capuchin Annual*, 1969.
Majumdar, Ramesa-Chandra, *History of the Freedom Movement in India*, vol. 2.
Mandle, W.F., 'The I.R.B. and the beginnings of the Gaelic Athletic Association', *Irish Historical Studies*, vol. 20, no. 80, Sept. 1977.
Mansergh, Nicholas, *The Irish Question 1840-1921*, 1975.
Martin, F.X. ed., *The Howth Gun-Running*, 1964.
Martin, F.X. ed., *The Irish Volunteers 1913-1915*, 1963.
Martin, Hugh, *Ireland in Insurrection*, 1921.
Martin, Ralph G., *Lady Randolph Churchill*, 1969.
Marx, Karl and Engels, Frederick, *Ireland and the Irish Question*, 1971.
McCartney, Donal, 'From Parnell to Pearse', in eds. T.W. Moody and F.X. Martin, *The Course of Irish History*, 1967.
McCracken, J.L., *Representative Government in Ireland*, 1958.
McDowell, R.B., *The Irish Convention 1917-1918*, 1970.
McGarry, Patsy, 'The Gaelic Dream of Douglas Hyde', *Magill*, July 1988.
McGlynn, Pat, ed., *Éirí Amach Na Casca*, 1986.
McHugh, Roger, ed., *Dublin 1916*, 1976.
McHugh, Roger, ed., *W.B. Yeats: Letters to Katharine Tynan*, 1953.
McKenna, Kathleen, 'The Irish Bulletin', *Capuchin Annual*, 1970.
McKenzie, F.A., *The Irish Rebellion: What happened and why*, 1916.
McNeill, Mary, *The Life and Times of Mary Ann McCracken*, 1770-1866, 1988.
Melville, Joy, *Mother of Oscar: The life of Jane Francesca Wilde*, 1994.
Mhic Sheáin, Bríghid, *Glimpses of Erin: Alice Milligan: poet, Protestant, patriot*, pamphlet published with *Fortnight* 326.
Mitchell, Arthur, *Labour in Irish Politics 1890-1930*, 1974.
Mitchell, Arthur and Ó Snódaigh, Pádraig, eds., *Irish Political Documents 1916-1949*, 1985.
Moody, T.W., *Davitt and Irish Revolution 1846-82*, 1982.
Moody, T.W., 'Michael Davitt and the British Labour Movement 1882-1906', *Transactions of the Royal Historical Society*, fifth series, vol. 3, 1953.
Moody, T.W. ed., *The Fenian Movement*, 1968.
Moody, T.W. and Vaughan, W.E. eds., *A New History of Ireland*, 1986.
Morris, James, 'High Noon of Empire', in *The British Empire*, vol. 4, 1979.
Morris, James, *Pax Britannica*, 1969.
Mowat, C.L., 'The Irish question in British politics (1916-1922)', in ed. T. Desmond Williams, *The Irish Struggle 1916-1926*, 1966.

Murdoch, John, *For the People's Cause*, 1986.
Murphy, Cliona, *The Women's Suffrage Movement and Irish Society*, 1989.
National Council of Civil Liberties, *Report of a Commission of Inquiry... into the Purpose and Effect of the Civil Authorities (Special Powers) Acts (Northern Ireland), 1922 and 1933*, 1936.
Nevin, Donal, 'The Irish Citizen Army', in ed. Owen Dudley Edwards and Fergus Pyle, *1916: The Easter Rising*, 1968.
Nevinson, Henry W., *Fire of Life*, 1935.
Norman, Diana, *Terrible Beauty: A life of Constance Markievicz*, 1987.
Norway, Mrs Hamilton, *The Sinn Fein Rebellion As I Saw It*, 1916.
O'Brien, R. Barry, ed., *The Autobiography of Wolfe Tone*, 1893.
O'Brien, William, *Evening Memories*, 1920.
O'Brien, William, *Forth the Banners Go*, 1969.
O'Brien, William, *Randolph Churchill*, 1906.
O'Brien, William, *The Irish Revolution* 1923.
O'Brien, William and Ryan, Desmond, eds., *Devoy's Postbag*, 1953, reissued 1979.
Ó Broin, Leon, *Dublin Castle and the 1916 Rising*, 1966.
Ó Broin, Leon, *Revolutionary Underground: The story of the Irish Republican Brotherhood 1858-1924*, 1976.
Ó Broin, Leon, *The Chief Secretary: Augustine Birrell in Ireland*, 1970.
O'Casey, Seán, *The Story of the Irish Citizen Army*, 1980.
Ó Cathaoir, Brendan, 'The Sealing of Partition' *Irish Times*, 4 December 1975.
O'Connor, T.P., *The Cabinet of Irish Literature*, vol. IV, undated.
O'Connor, Ulick, *A Terrible Beauty is Born*, 1981.
O'Connor Lysaght, D.R., *The Making of Northern Ireland*, undated.
O'Connor Lysaght, D.R., *The Story of the Limerick Soviet*, 2nd ed., c. 1984.
O'Donnell, Peadar, *There Will Be Another Day*, 1963.
O'Donoghue, Florence, *No Other Law*, 1954.
O'Donoghue, Florence, 'Re-organisation of the Irish Volunteers 1916-1917', *Capuchin Annual*, 1967.
O'Donoghue, Florence, 'Volunteer "Actions" in 1918', *Capuchin Annual*, 1968.
O'Donovan Rossa, Jeremiah, *Irish Rebels in English Prisons*, 1991.
Ó Duigneain, Prionnsias, *North Leitrim in Land League Times 1880-84*, pamphlet, undated.
Ó Fiaich, Tomás, 'The Irish bishops and the conscription issue 1918', *Capuchin Annual*, 1968.
O Gadhra, Nollaig, 'Public reaction to the 1916 rising', *An Aisling*, 1976.
Ó Gráda, Cormac, *The Great Irish Famine*, 1989.
Ó Háinle, Cathal, *Promhadh Pinn*, 1978.
O'Halpin, Eunan, 'British Intelligence in Ireland, 1914-21', in eds. Christopher Andrew and David Dilks, *The Missing Dimension*, 1984.
O'Halpin, Eunan, *The Decline of the Union*, 1987.
O'Leary, John, *Recollections of Fenians and Fenianism*, 1896, reissued 1969.
O'Leary, John, ed., *The Writings of Fintan Lalor*, 1895.
Ó Luing, Seán, *Fremantle Mission*, 1965.
O Mahony, Seán, *Frongoch*, 1987.
O'Malley, Ernie, *On Another Man's Wound*, 1979.
O'Neill, Thomas P., 'The General Election 1918', *Capuchin Annual* 1968.
Orr, Philip, *The Road to the Somme*, 1987.
Ó Tuathaigh, Gearoid, *Ireland Before the Famine 1798-1848*, 1972.

Pakenham, Thomas, *The Year of Liberty*, 1969.

Pankhurst, Richard K.P., 'Anna Wheeler: A pioneer socialist and feminist', *The Political Quarterly*, April-June 1954, vol. xxv, no. 2.

Pankhurst, Richard K.P., *William Thompson: Britain's Pioneer Socialist, Feminist and Co-operator*, 1954.

Pankhurst, Sylvia, *The Suffragette Movement*, 1931, reissued 1977.

Parnell, Anna, *The Tale of a Great Sham*, 1986.

Patterson, Henry, *Class Conflict and Sectarianism*, 1980.

Pearse, Padraic, *The Murder Machine*, 1912, reissued 1976.

Pearse, Padraic, *Political Writings and Speeches*, 1952.

Petrie, Charles, Bt., *Walter Long and his Times*, 1936.

Petrie, George, ed., *The Petrie Collection of the Ancient Music of Ireland*, 1855.

Porter, Bernard, *The Lion's Share*, 1975.

Postgate, Raymond, *Life of George Lansbury*, 1951.

Prison Letters of Countess Markievicz, first published 1934; reissued 1987.

Quinlivan, Patrick and Rose, Paul, *The Fenians in England 1865-1872*, 1982.

Ranelagh, John, *Ireland: An Illustrated History*, 1981.

Redmond, Rev. John, *Church: State: Industry 1827-1929 in East* 1960.

Remond-Howard, L.G., *Six Days of the Irish Republic*, 1916.

Richards, Shaun, 'Polemics on the Irish Past', *History Workshop*, Spring 1991.

Robbins, Frank, *Under the Starry Plough*, 1977.

Roebuck, Peter, ed., *From Plantation to Partition*, 1981.

Rose, Paul, *The Manchester Martyrs*, 1970.

Roskill, Stephen, *Hankey: Man of Secrets*, 1972.

Russell, Dave, 'Some early Irish movements in South London', *South London Record*.

Ryan, Desmond, *Remembering Sion*, 1934.

Ryan, Mark, *Fenian Memories*, 1946.

Ryan, W.P., *The Irish Labour Movement*, 1919.

Ryan, W.P., *The Irish Literary Revival*, 1894.

Savage, D.C., 'Origins of the Ulster Unionist Party, 1885-6', in *Irish Historical Studies*, vol. XII, no. 47, March 1961.

Saville, John, *Ernest Jones: Chartist*, 1952.

Saville, John, *1848: The British state and the Chartist movement*, 1987.

Scrope, G. Poulett, *How Is Ireland to Be Governed?*, first pub. 1834, 1846.

Second Earl of Birkenhead, *The Life of F.E. Smith, First Earl of Birkenhead*, 1960.

Selected Poems of Byron, 1913 edition, reprinted 1960.

Sheedy, Kieran, *Upon the Mercy of the Government*, 1988.

Sheehy, Jeanne, *The Rediscovery of Ireland's Past*, 1980.

Sheehy Skeffington, Hanna, 'Reminiscences of an Irish Suffragette', in eds. Andree Sheehy Skeffington and Rosemary Owens, *Votes for Women*, 1975.

Sheehy Skeffington, Hanna, 'The Women's Movement – Ireland', *The Irish Review*, July 1912.

Sheehy Skeffington, Francis, *In Dark and Evil Days*, 1916.

Shelley, Percy Bysshe, *An Address to the Irish People*, first pub. 1912, reprinted with *Proposals for an Association*, undated.

Short, K.R.M., *The Dynamite War: Irish-American bombers in Victorian Britain*, 1979.

Sinn Fein Rebellion Handbook, 1917.

Skinnider, Margaret, *Doing My Bit For Ireland*, 1917.

Spater, George, *William Cobbett: The Poor Man's Friend*, vol. 2, 1982.

Spindler, Karl, *Gun Running for Casement in the Easter Rebellion*, 1921.
Stanhope, Earl, *Life of William Pitt*, vol. 3, 1862.
Steps to Partition, Public Records Office of Northern Ireland.
Stevenson, Frances, *Lloyd George*, 1971.
Stewart, A.T.Q., *The Narrow Ground*, 1977.
Stewart, A.T.Q., *Ulster Crisis*, 1969.
Strauss, Emil, *Irish Nationalism and British Democracy*, 1951.
Street, C.J.C., [pseudonym I.O.], *The Administration of Ireland 1920*, 1921.
Street, C.J.C., *Ireland in 1921*, 1922.
Swanwick, Helena, *I Have Been Young*, 1935.
Sweeney, Detective Inspector John, *At Scotland Yard: experiences during twenty-seven years' service*, 1904.
Talbot, Hayden, *Michael Collins' Own Story*, 1923.
Taylor, A.J.P. ed., *Lloyd George: Twelve Essays*, 1974.
Taylor, Rex, *Michael Collins*, 1970.
'The real case against partition', *Capuchin Annual*, 1943.
Third Report of the Royal Commission on the Condition of the Poorer Classes in Ireland, Parliamentary Papers 1836, vol. XXX.
Thompson, Dorothy, *The Chartists*, 1986.
Thompson, E.P., *The Making of the English Working Class*, 1970.
Thompson, William, *An inquiry into the principles of the distribution of wealth most conducive to human happiness*, 1824.
Thompson, William, *Appeal of one-half of the human race, women, against the pretensions of the other half, men, to retain them in political, and thence in civil and domestic, slavery*, 1825, reprinted 1983.
Thornton, A.P., *The Imperial Idea and Its Enemies*, 1959.
Townsend, Molly, *Not by Bullets and Bayonets: Cobbett's Writings on the Irish Question 1795-1835*, 1983.
Townshend, Charles, *The British Campaign in Ireland 1919-1921*, 1975.
Townshend, Charles, *Political Violence in Ireland*, 1983.
Tynan, Katharine, 'The Pursuit of Diarmuid and Grainne', from *Shamrocks*, 1887.
Tynan, Katharine, *Twenty-five Years: Reminiscences*, 1913.
Van Voris, Jacqueline, *Constance de Markievicz*, 1967.
Vaughan, W.E. and Fitzpatrick, A.J., eds., *Irish Historical Statistics: Population 1821-1971*, 1977.
Ward, Alan J., *Ireland and Anglo-American Relations 1899-1921*, 1969.
Ward, Margaret, *Maud Gonne*, 1990.
Ward, Margaret, *Unmanageable Revolutionaries*, 1983.
Watson, G.J., *Irish Identity and the Literary Revival*, 1979.
White, J.R., *Misfit: An autobiography*, 1930.
White, Newman Ivey, *Shelley*, vol. 1, 1947.
Williams QC, Montagu, *Leaves of a Life*, 1890.
Wolfe Tone, Theobald, *Autobiography*, 1893.
Wolfe Tone, William Theobald, ed., *Memoirs of Theobald Wolfe Tone*, 1826.
Woodham-Smith, Cecil, *The Great Hunger*, 1977.
Wyse-Power, J., 'The Political Influence of Women in Modern Ireland', in ed. William G. Fitz-gerald, *The Voice of Ireland*, undated, c. 1920s.
Yeats, W.B., *Autobiographies*, 1926.
Young, Arthur, *A Tour in Ireland*, 2nd ed., 1780.
Young, G.M. and Hancock, W.D., *English Historical Documents* XII (1) 1833-1874, 1956.

Index